Essentials of Management

5 EDITION

Andrew J. DuBrin

Professor of Management
College of Business
Rochester Institute of Technology

 South-Western College Publishing

an International Thomson Publishing company I(T)P®

Cincinnati • Albany • Boston • Detroit • Johannesburg • London • Madrid • Melbourne • Mexico City
New York • Pacific Grove • San Francisco • Scottsdale • Singapore • Tokyo • Toronto

Publisher: Dave Shaut
Executive Editor: John Szilagyi
Developmental Editor: Mary Pommert,
    Custom Editorial Productions
Marketing Manager: Rob Bloom
Media and Technology Editor: Kevin von Gillern
Media Production Editor: Robin K. Browning
Production Editor: Amy S. Gabriel
Manufacturing Coordinator: Dana Began Schwartz

Internal Design: A Small Design Studio/Ann Small
Cover Design: Joe Devine
Cover Illustrator: © 1999 SIS/John S. Dykes
Photo Manager: Cary Benbow
Production House: WordCrafters Editorial
    Services, Inc.
Compositor: MATRIX Publishing Services
Printer: World Color—Taunton, MA

I⊤P   The ITP logo is a registered trademark under license.

Printed in the United States of America
3 4 5 6 7 8 9 10

International Thomson Publishing Europe
Berkshire House
168-173 High Holborn
London, WC1V7AA, United Kingdom

Inernational Thomson Editores
Seneca, 53
Colonia Polanco
11560 México D.F. México

Nelson ITP, Australia
102 Dodds Street
South Melbourne
Victoria 3205 Australia

International Thomson Publishing Asia
60 Alberta Street #15-01
Albert Complex
Singapore 189969

Nelson Canada
1120 Birchmount Road
Scarborough, Ontario
Canada M1K 5G4

International Thomson Publishing Japan
Hirakawa-cho Kyowa Building, 3F
2-2-1 Hirakawa-cho, Chiyoda-ku
Tokyo 102, Japan

International Thomson Publishing Southern Africa
Building 18, Constantia Square
138 Sixteenth Road, P.O. Box 2459
Halfway House, 1685 South Africa

Library of Congress Cataloging-in-Publication Data

DuBrin, Andrew J.
    Essentials of management / Andrew J. DuBrin.—5th ed.
        p.   cm.
    Includes bibliographical references and index.
    ISBN 0-324-00703-5 (pbk.)
    1. Management.   I. Title.
HD31.D793   1999   99-25803
658—dc21   CIP

Essentials of Management is a blend of current and traditional topics organized around the functional, or process, approach to the study of management. Although other approaches have been developed, the functional approach remains a general framework, flexible enough to incorporate many viewpoints about management.

This book is written for newcomers to the field of management and for experienced managers seeking updated information and a review of the fundamentals. The book is also written for the many professionals and technical persons who work closely with managers and who take their turn at performing some management work. An example would be the member of a cross-functional team who is expected to have the perspective of a general manager.

Based on extensive research about curriculum needs, *Essentials of Management* is designed to be used in introductory management courses and supervision courses offered in educational and work settings. Earlier editions of the text were used in the study of management in colleges and universities, as well as in career schools in such diverse programs as hospitality and tourism management. The book can also be used as a basic resource for management courses that rely heavily on lecture notes, handouts, and videos rather than an encyclopedia-like text.

ASSUMPTIONS UNDERLYING THE BOOK

The approach to synthesizing knowledge for this book is based on the following five assumptions.

1. A strong demand exists for practical and valid information about solutions to managerial problems. The information found in this text reflects the author's orientation toward translating research findings, theory, and experience into a form useful to both the student and the practitioner.
2. Managers and professionals need both interpersonal and analytical skills to meet their day-to-day responsibilities. Although this book concentrates on managing people, it also provides ample information about such topics as decision making, job design, organization structure, effective inventory management, and information technology.
3. The study of management should emphasize a diversity of large, medium, and small work settings, as well as profit and not-for-profit organizations. Many students of management, for example, intend to become small-busi-

ness owners. Examples and cases in this book therefore reflect diverse work settings, including retail and service firms.

4. Effective managers and professionals are heavily concerned with productivity, quality, and teamwork. These three factors are therefore noted frequently throughout the text.

5. Introductory management textbooks have become unrealistically comprehensive. Many introductory texts today are over 800 pages long. Such texts overwhelm students who attempt to assimilate this knowledge in a single quarter or semester. Toward this end, I have developed a text that I think represents the basis for a realistically sized introduction to the study of management.

FRAMEWORK OF THE BOOK

The first four chapters present an introduction to management. Chapter 1, "The Manager's Job," explains the nature of managerial work with a particular emphasis on managerial roles and tasks. Chapter 2, "International Management, Cultural Diversity, Technology, and the Internet," describes three major forces affecting the work of managers at all levels. Chapter 3, "Ethics and Social Responsibility," examines the moral aspects of management. Chapter 4, "Managing for Quality and Customer Satisfaction," summarizes information managerial workers need to achieve quality and customer satisfaction.

The next three chapters address the subject of planning. Chapter 5, "Essentials of Planning," presents a general framework for planning—the activity underlying almost any purposeful action taken by a manager. Chapter 6, "Problem Solving and Decision Making," explains the basics of decision making, with an emphasis on creativity and other behavioral aspects. Chapter 7, "Specialized Techniques for Planning and Decision Making," describes several adjuncts to planning and decision making such as break-even analysis, PERT, and production scheduling methods used for both manufacturing and services.

The next three chapters focus on organizing, culture, and staffing. Chapter 8, "Job Design and Work Schedules," explains how jobs are laid out and work schedules arranged to enhance productivity and customer satisfaction. Chapter 9, "Organization Structure, Culture, and Change," explains how work is organized from the standpoint of the organization, how culture profoundly influences an organization, and how to cope with and capitalize on change. Chapter 10, "Staffing and Human Resource Management," explains the methods by which people are brought into the organization, trained, and evaluated.

The following three chapters, on leading, deal directly with the manager's role in influencing group members. Chapter 11, "Leadership," focuses on different approaches to leadership available to a manager and on the personal characteristics associated with leadership effectiveness. Chapter 12, "Motivation," describes what managers can do to increase or sustain employee effort toward achieving work goals. Chapter 13, "Communication," deals with the complex problems of accurately sending and receiving messages. Chapter 14, "Teams, Groups, and Teamwork," explains the nature of teams and how managers can foster group members' working together cooperatively.

The next two chapters, on controlling, each deal with an important part of keeping performance in line with expectations. Chapter 15, "Essentials of Control," presents an overview of measuring and controlling performance. It also describes how managers work with a variety of financial measures to monitor performance. Chapter 16, "Managing Ineffective Performers," describes current approaches to dealing with substandard performers, with an emphasis on elevating performance.

The final chapter in the text, Chapter 17, "Enhancing Personal Productivity and Managing Stress," describes how personal effectiveness can be increased by developing better work habits and time management skills and keeping stress under control. A major theme of the chapter is that good work habits help prevent and manage stress.

PEDAGOGICAL FEATURES

Essentials of Management is designed to aid both students and instructors in explaining their interest in and knowledge of management. The book contains the following features:

- Learning objectives coordinate the contents of each chapter. They preview the major topics to be covered. The same objectives are integrated into the text by indicating which major topics relate to the objectives. The end-of-chapter Summary of Key Points, based on the chapter learning objectives, pulls together the central ideas in each chapter.
- An opening case example illustrates a major topic to be covered in the chapter.
- Manager in Action, Organization in Action, and similar features present a portrait of how specific individuals or organizations practice an aspect of management covered in the chapter.
- Concrete, real-world examples with which the reader can readily identify are found throughout the text. Many of the examples are original, while others are researched from information published in magazines, newspapers, and journals.
- Exhibits, which include figures, tables, and self-assessment quizzes, aid in the comprehension of information in the text.
- Key terms and phrases highlight the management vocabulary introduced in each chapter. Their definitions are also highlighted in notes that appear in the margin.
- Questions at the end of each chapter assist learning by encouraging the reader to review and reflect on the chapter objectives.
- Skill-building exercises, including Internet activities, appear at the end of each chapter.
- Case problems also located at the end of each chapter can be used to synthesize the chapter concepts and simulate the practice of management.

WHAT'S NEW IN THE FIFTH EDITION?

A number of significant changes and additions have been incorporated into this edition. Following is a brief listing of these changes. A more detailed look at some of the exciting new Fifth Edition features follows the list.

- All seventeen chapters have been thoroughly updated.
- Half of the end-of-chapter cases are new.
- Nearly all of the chapter-opening cases are new.
- About 90 percent of the Manager in Action and Organization in Action boxes are new and have been expanded.
- A new Internet skill-building activity can now be found at the end of each chapter.

- Web site addresses mentioned in the chapters are highlighted in a second color for easy reference.
- A new 150-slide, full-color *PowerPoint* package supplements the text.

Visit the Web Site

The Web site address for *Essentials of Management*, Fifth Edition, is http://dubrin. swcollege.com. Instructors and students alike are invited to visit the site.

What's New in the Chapters?

Several of the most important additions, from selected chapters, are highlighted here.

CHAPTER 2 This chapter has been completely reorganized to focus on three major forces in managerial life: the internationalization of the workplace, cultural diversity, and technology (with a look at both the positive and negative consequences for today's manager), with an emphasis on the Internet and E-commerce.

CHAPTER 4 This chapter now includes a discussion of mass customization. The well-established Levi Strauss program, Personal Pairs, is used as the example and is easy for students to relate to. The chapter also includes timely advice from experts for companies considering mass customization. Finally, a discussion of poka-yoke, a Japanese quality control mechanism for preventing mistakes, has been added to the quality improvement section.

CHAPTER 6 This chapter includes a new section on emotional intelligence, the ability to understand and control your own feelings and understand the emotions of others. The discussion focuses on how emotional intelligence influences decision making. The topic of creativity receives more attention in this edition. Students will learn about the conditions necessary for creativity as well as the results that occur in organizations that encourage imaginative and original thinking.

CHAPTER 8 The alternative workplace (30 to 40 million Americans now work at home) is spotlighted in this chapter, with special attention paid to telecommuters. The advantages and disadvantages of telecommuting are discussed, and suggestions for managers of teleworkers are provided. In the section on job enrichment, the results of a 1998 Shell Oil Co. survey showing that workers can be categorized into six groups (fulfillment seekers, high achievers, clock punchers, risk takers, ladder climbers, and paycheck cashers) lead to a discussion on job design and motivation.

CHAPTER 9 Because today's managers must manage change effectively on an almost daily basis, Chapter 9 now focuses on the topic of change. Four aspects of change are covered: change at the individual versus the organizational level, change as a process, why people resist change, and how managers can gain support for change. Reengineering receives only light mention in this edition.

CHAPTER 13 In addition to all the traditional topics of communication, this chapter now touches on the communication problems associated with e-mail. It also covers the topic of metacommunication (communicating about how well you're communicating), as well as the effect of organizational (or office) politics on communications. Both ethical and unethical office politics tactics are discussed.

CHAPTER 14   By popular demand this chapter now includes expanded discussions of both cross-functional teams and top-level management teams. In addition, potential problems with teams (such as slower career advancement), conflict among team members (both cognitive and affective), and five methods of conflict resolution are all addressed. Also new to this chapter is a listing of the seven characteristics of highly effective teams.

What New Topics Have Been Added to the Text?

Dozens of current and cutting-edge topics have been added to the Fifth Edition, including:

- E-commerce and e-tailing
- Twelve of the greatest management decisions ever made
- Emotional intelligence
- Idea quotas
- A corporate tip sheet on sexual harassment
- EVA (economic value added)
- ABC (activity-based costing)
- Mass customization
- Poka-yoke
- Outsourcing
- Chief knowledge officer (CKO)
- Finding a job on the web
- Open-book company
- Servant leader
- Informal leader
- Ethical and unethical office politics
- Rumor theory
- Metacommunication
- Webcasting and push technology
- Dealing with cynics and bullies

Brand New Internet Skill-Building Exercises

In addition to the end-of-chapter management skill-building exercises that you are accustomed to from previous editions, every chapter in the Fifth Edition now contains an Internet-based skill-building exercise designed to connect students to Web sites that will boost their knowledge of management topics and issues. These include:

- Entrepreneurs on the Net (www.cyberstudy101.com, www.twmall.com) (Chapter 1)
- Becoming Multicultural (www.france2.fr) (Chapter 2)
- What's New in Quality Management? (www.ISO.ch, www.ASQ.org) (Chapter 4)
- Business Strategy Research (www.prnewswire.com) (Chapter 5)
- Recruiting on the Net (www.careermosaic.com, www.nationjob.com) (Chapter 10)
- Enhancing Your Nonverbal Communication E-Mail Skills (Chapter 13)
- The Dale Carnegie Approach to Building Teamwork (www.dalecarnegie.com) (Chapter 14)
- Can This Employee Be Salvaged? (www.morebusiness.com) (Chapter 16)

Self-Quizzes

Self-quizzes, a popular end-of-chapter feature of the Fourth Edition, can now be found within the chapters. Not only will students enjoy taking the self-quizzes, but they will learn about their management strengths and weaknesses in the process. Your students will benefit from taking the following:

- The Ethical Reasoning Inventory (Chapter 3)
- How Decisive Are You? (Chapter 6)
- Understanding Your Bureaucratic Orientation (Chapter 9)
- Team Skills Inventory (Chapter 14)
- The Self-Sabotage Questionnaire (Chapter 16)

Brand New Action Inserts

There is now one Manager in Action or Organization in Action insert in every chapter. All of these inserts are new to this edition and focus on managers or companies that highlight points made in the chapters. Take these, for example:

- Durk Jager of Procter & Gamble Takes a Global View (Chapter 2)
- You Can Work and Have a Life at Eddie Bauer (Chapter 3)
- Jill Barad, Chair and CEO of Mattel, Inc. (Chapter 5)
- Jack Welch of GE, the Manager's Manager (Chapter 11)
- Lloyd Ward of Maytag: Team Builder and Super Salesman (Chapter 14)
- Work Habits of the World's Richest Person (Chapter 17)

New End-of-Chapter Cases

Nineteen of the cases in the Fifth Edition are brand new, including the following:

- Managing the Gap (Chapter 1)
- The Great American Sweatshops (Chapter 3)
- The Holiday Turkey Meltdown (Chapter 4)
- Protecting the Computer Athletes (Chapter 8)
- Big Changes at State Bank of India, California (Chapter 11)
- Revenge Has Its Price (Chapter 16)

New PowerPoint Slide Package

Supplementing the Fifth Edition is a brand new, 150 full-color slide package. Many of the slides in this package are reproductions of the exhibits found within the text chapters and are designed for easy lecture use.

INSTRUCTIONAL RESOURCES

Essentials of Management is accompanied by comprehensive instructional support materials.

- *Instructor's Manual with Test Bank and Transparency Masters*. The instructor's manual (ISBN: 0-324-00704-3) provides resources to increase the teaching and learning value of *Essentials of Management*. The *Manual* contains "Chapter Outline and Lecture Notes," of particular value to instructors whose time budget does not allow for extensive class preparation.

    For each text chapter, the *Manual* provides a statement of purpose and scope, outline and lecture notes, lecture topics, comments on the end-of-chapter questions and activities, responses to case questions, an experiential activity, and an examination. The examination contains twenty-five multiple-choice questions, twenty-five true/false questions, and three essay questions.

The *Manual* contains two comprehensive cases that will be useful for instructors who wish to integrate the topics covered within the course. In addition, instructions are provided for the use of Computer-Aided Scenario Analysis (CASA). CASA is a user-friendly technique that can be used with any word-processing software. It allows the student to insert a new scenario into the case and then to re-answer the questions based on the new scenario. CASA helps to develop creative thinking and an awareness of contingencies or situational factors in making managerial decisions.

A set of transparency masters that duplicates key figures in the text is included in the manual.

- *Computerized Test Package.* The examinations presented in the *Manual* are also available on disk with the test generator program, Thomson Learning Testing Tools™ (ISBN: 0-324-00708-6). This versatile software package allows instructors to create new questions and edit and delete existing questions from the test bank.
- *Study Guide.* The *Study Guide* (ISBN: 0-324-00706-X) that accompanies the Fifth Edition of *Essentials of Management* will be a real asset for your students. For each text chapter, the *Study Guide* includes an overview; the objectives and key terms; an expanded study outline; and review questions—matching, multiple-choice, true/false, and fill-in. Each chapter also contains an application exercise that requires use of the concepts presented in the text chapter.
- *PowerPoint Slides.* A set of 150 professionally prepared *PowerPoint* slides (ISBN: 0-324-00705-1) accompanies the text for the first time. This slide package is designed for easy classroom use and includes reproductions of many of the exhibits found in the text.

A NOTE TO THE STUDENT . . .

The information in the general preface is important for students as well as instructors. Here, I offer additional comments that will enable you to increase the personal payoffs from studying management. My message can be organized around several key points.

- *Management is not simply common sense.* The number one trap for students in studying management is to assume that the material is easy to master because many of the terms and ideas are familiar. For example, just because you have heard the word *teamwork* many times, it does not automatically follow that you are familiar with specific field-tested ideas for enhancing teamwork.
- *Managerial skills are vital.* The information in the course for which you are studying this text is vital in today's world. People with formal managerial job titles such as supervisor, team leader, department head, or vice president are obviously expected to possess managerial skills. But many other people in jobs without managerial titles are also supposed to have managerial skills. Among them are administrative assistant, customer-service representative, and inventory-control specialist.
- *The combination of managerial, interpersonal, and technical skills leads to outstanding career success.* A recurring myth is that it is better to study "technical" or "hard" subjects than management because the pay is better. In reality, the people in business making the big money are those who combine technical

skills with managerial and interpersonal skills. Executives and business owners, for example, can earn incomes rivaled only by leading professional athletes and show-business personalities.

- *Studying management, however, has its biggest payoff in the long run.* Entry-level
management positions are in short supply. Management is a basic life process.
To run a major corporation, manage a restaurant or a hair salon, organize a
company picnic, plan a wedding, or run a good household, management
skills are an asset. We all have some knowledge of management, but formally
studying management can multiply one's effectiveness.

Take advantage of the many study aids in this text and the *Study Guide*. You
will enhance your learning of management by concentrating on such learning assists as the chapter objectives, summaries, discussion questions, self-quizzes, skill-
development exercises, and glossary. Carefully studying a glossary is an effective
way of building a vocabulary in a new field. Studying the glossary will also serve
as a reminder of important topics. Activities such as the cases, discussion questions, and skill-development exercises facilitate learning by creating the opportunity to think through the information. Thinking through information, in turn,
leads to better comprehension and long-term retention of information. The *Study
Guide* will provide excellent review and preparation for examinations.

ACKNOWLEDGMENTS

Any project as complex as this text requires a team of dedicated and talented
people to see that it gets completed effectively. Many reviewers made valuable
comments during the development of this new edition as well as the previous
four editions of the text. I appreciate the helpful suggestions of the following colleagues:

Thelma Anderson
Montana State University – Northern

Tom Birkenhead
Lane Community College

Brenda Britt
Fayetteville Technical Community College

Michael Cardinale
Palomar College

Gary Clark
North Harris College

Jose L. Curzet
Florida National College

Rex Cutshall
Vincennes University

Robert Desman
Kennesaw State College

Kenneth Dreifus
Pace University

Ben Dunn
York Technical College

Thomas Fiock
Southern Illinois University at Carbondale

Dan Geeding
Xavier University

Philip C. Grant
Hussen College

Randall Greenwell
John Wood Community College

David R. Grimmett
Austin Peay State University

Robert Halliman
Austin Peay State University

Paul Hegele
Elgin Community College

Thomas Heslin
Indiana University

Peter Hess
Western New England College

Nathan Himelstein
Essex County College

Judith A. Horrath
Lehigh Corbon Community College

B. R. Kirkland
Tarleton State University

Patricia Manninen
North Shore Community College

Noel Matthews
Front Range Community College

Christopher J. Morris
Adirondack Community College

Ilona Motsiff
Trinity College of Vermont

David W. Murphy
University of Kentucky

Ronald W. Olive
New Hampshire Technical College

J. E. Pearson
Dabney S. Lancaster Community College

Joseph Platts
Miami-Dade Community College

Thomas Quirk
Webster University

Jane Rada
Western Wisconsin Technical College

James Riley
Oklahoma Junior College

William Searle
Asnuntuck Community Technical College

William Shepard
New Hampshire Technical College

Lynn Suksdorf
Salt Lake Community College

Gary Tilley
Surry Community College

Bernard Weinrich
St. Louis Community College

Blaine Weller
Baker College

Alex Wittig
North Metro Technical College

Thanks also to the members of the South-Western Marketing and Management Team who worked with me on this edition: executive editor for management John Szilagyi, developmental editor Mary Pommert, production editor Amy Gabriel, designer Joe Devine, and photo editor Cary Benbow. The contribution of Ann Mohan at WordCrafters is also noted. Writing without loved ones would be a lonely task. My thanks therefore go to my family, Drew, Douglas, Gizella, Melanie, Rosie, and Clare. In addition, my thanks go to Polly, the woman in my life.

Andrew J. DuBrin

ABOUT THE AUTHOR

Andrew J. DuBrin is a Professor of Management in the College of Business at the Rochester Institute of Technology, where he teaches courses and conducts research in management, organizational behavior, leadership, and career management. He has also served as department chairman and team leader in previous years. He received his Ph.D. in Industrial Psychology from Michigan State University. DuBrin has business experience in human resource management and consults with organizations and individuals. His specialties include career management leadership, and management development. DuBrin is an established author of both textbooks and trade books, and he also contributes to professional journals, magazines, newspapers, and online shows. He has written textbooks on management, leadership, organizational behavior, and human relations. His trade books cover many current issues, including charisma, team play, office politics, overcoming career self-sabotage, and preventing workplace problems.

brief contents

Contents

PART 4 Leading

PART 5   Controlling

PART 6   Managing for Personal Effectiveness

Chapter One

Dineh Mohajer is young, sharp, and a millionaire whose business and managerial success started unexpectedly. One day while still a pre-medical student, she painted her nails blue and went shoe shopping. Dozens of shoppers approached Mohajer and insisted on knowing where she bought that polish. She explained that she had mixed the polish herself in her kitchen. A shoe store sales associate told Dineh that the polish perfectly complemented the store's spring line of shoes.

At that moment Dineh and her sister, Pooneh, decided to put together a business plan over lunch and start selling the polish under the name Hard Candy. Dineh's boyfriend, Benjamin Einstein, was also brought in as a cofounder. Shortly thereafter, while Dineh was pitching the nail polish to an upscale specialty store, a teenager bought the entire stock of samples. Later *Seventeen* and *Elle* featured the pastel-colored polish. Next, Nordstrom, Bloomingdale's, and Saks Fifth Avenue called in orders. By the time Dineh was 25, Hard Candy had $20 million in annual sales.

Runaway success put heavy pressure on Dineh. Establishing reliable suppliers, distribution networks, accounting systems, and a corporate structure was an overwhelming task, while managing high-speed growth at the same time. Hard Candy caught on so fast that customers were ordering more than the company could possibly make. Nine months after officially beginning the business, Dineh was physically and emotionally exhausted.

OBJECTIVES

After studying this chapter and doing the exercises, you should be able to:

1 Explain the term *manager*, and identify different types of managers.

2 Describe the process of management, including the functions of management.

3 Describe the various managerial roles, along with the roles currently emphasized.

4 Identify the basic managerial skills and understand how they can be developed.

5 Identify the major developments in management thought, along with several best management practices.

The Manager's Job

2

"I didn't know anything about the business," Dineh explains. "I didn't have any computers, except for this Macintosh with Quickbooks on it. I was over-whelmed and burned out." Dineh's mother then lent a hand and set up a Visa machine to make phone orders possible. She helped in finding a reliable manu-facturer and in handling invoices. Mom and Dad also invested in the business, making it possible to for Hard Candy to move into a commercial office in 1995. Despite the help from her parents, Dineh was still overwhelmed and near-paralyzed with fatigue. At that point, she decided it was time to turn to professional management for help. Assisted by a consulting firm, Dineh hired William Botts, a former cosmetics-industry executive who understood her vision for Hard Candy.

Botts whipped Hard Candy into shape by applying a broad range of man-agement skills. It was his expertise that has allowed Hard Candy to function like a true multimillion-dollar business. Pooneh, who is an attorney, handled con-tracts, administration, and financial management. Dineh and her boyfriend now focus more on the creative end of the business. She feels constant pressure to keep coming up with hot new colors like Trailer Trash, a metallic silver. Dineh's market is mostly 12- to 25-year-old women, and because of her age, she fits right in. Yet she recently added Candy Man, a nail polish for men, to her line, and the company now sells other cosmetics as well. Hard Candy also released a white nail polish, Love, to benefit AIDS research.

Hard Candy is now a well-managed creative company with exciting plans for the future.[1]

Whether or not you intend to become a business owner, the case history just presented sets the stage for the serious study of management. To effectively manage an enterprise, you need a mix of skills including creative thinking, work-ing with employees and customers, and organizing activities. An effective man-ager combines business skills, such as knowledge about marketing and finances, with people skills to achieve important results. Management is the force that makes things happen. It pulls together resources to get important objectives ac-complished. A manager's job is therefore inherently exciting.

The alternative to placing effective managers in charge of an operation is chaos. Dineh Mohajer was feeling overwhelmed because the success of Hard Candy was spinning the company out of control. Poor management (and lead-ership) is one of the major reasons so many businesses of various sizes fail. These firms lack people who can tie together loose ends and get important things ac-complished. When business firms fail because of competitive pressures or a dwin-dling economy, it is often the case that astute management could have overcome the problem. For example, when Frontier Communication (a national telecom-munications company) recently needed to upgrade its telephone-equipment ser-vice, the decision was made to double the number of supervisors. Adding su-pervisors gave the large number of new field technicians the technical and emotional support they needed to learn their jobs. Customer complaints decreased substantially after more supervisors applied their management skills.

WHO IS A MANAGER?

Explain what the term *man-ager* means, and identify different types of managers.

A **manager** is a person responsible for the work performance of group mem-bers. (Because organizations have become more democratic, the term *group mem-ber* or *team member* is now frequently used as a substitute for *subordinate*.) A man-ager has the formal authority to commit organizational resources, even if the approval of others is required. For instance, the manager of an H & R Block income-tax service outlet has the authority to order the repainting of the reception area. The income-tax specialists reporting to that manager, however, do not have the authority to have the area repainted.

The concepts of manager and managing are intertwined. From the viewpoint of Peter Drucker, a noted management authority, management is the specific practice that converts a mob into an effective, goal-directed, and productive group.[2] The term **management** in this book refers to the process of using organizational resources to achieve organizational objectives through the functions of planning, organizing and staffing, leading, and controlling. These functions represent the broad framework for this book and will be described later. In addition to being a process, the term *management* is also used as a label for a specific discipline, for the people who manage, and for a career choice.

manager
A person responsible for the work performance of group members.

management
The process of using organizational resources to achieve organizational objectives through planning, organizing and staffing, leading, and controlling.

Levels of Management

Another way of understanding the nature of a manager's job is to examine the three levels of management shown in Exhibit 1-1. The pyramid in this figure indicates that there are progressively fewer employees at each higher managerial level. The largest number of people is at the bottom organizational level. (Note that the term *organizational level* is sometimes more precise than the term *managerial level*, particularly at the bottom organizational level, which has no managers.)

TOP-LEVEL MANAGERS

Most people who enter the field of management aspire to become **top-level managers**—managers at the top one or two levels in an organization. Top-level managers are empowered to make major decisions affecting the present and future of the firm. Only a top-level manager, for example, would have the authority to purchase another company, initiate a new product line, or hire hundreds of employees. Top-level managers are the people who give the organization its general direction; they decide where it is going and how it will get there. The terms *executive* and *top-level manager* can be used interchangeably.

top-level managers
Managers at the top one or two levels in the organization.

EXHIBIT 1-1

Managerial Levels and Sample Job Titles
Many job titles can be found at each level of management.

Note: some individual contributors, such as financial analysts and administrative assistants, report directly to top-level managers or middle managers.

4

middle-level managers
Managers who are neither executives nor first-level supervisors, but who serve as a link between the two groups.

MIDDLE-LEVEL MANAGERS   **Middle-level managers** are managers who are neither executives nor first-level supervisors, but who serve as a link between the two groups. Middle-level managers conduct most of the coordination activities within the firm, and they disseminate information to upper and lower levels. The jobs of middle-level managers vary substantially in terms of responsibility and income. A branch manager in a large firm might be responsible for over 100 workers. In contrast, a general supervisor in a small manufacturing firm might have 20 people reporting to him or her. Other important tasks for many middle-level managers include helping the company undertake profitable new ventures and finding creative ways to reach goals. Quite often the middle-level manager conducts research on the Internet to gather ideas for new ventures.

first-level managers
Managers who supervise operatives (also known as first-line managers or supervisors).

FIRST-LEVEL MANAGERS   Managers who supervise operatives are referred to as **first-level managers**, first-line managers, or supervisors. Historically, first-level managers were promoted from production or clerical positions into supervisory positions. Rarely did they have formal education beyond high school. A dramatic shift has taken place in recent years, however. Many of today's first-level managers are career school graduates who are familiar with modern management techniques. The current emphasis on productivity and quality has elevated the status of many supervisors.

To understand the work performed by first-level managers, reflect back on your first job. Like most employees in entry-level positions, you probably reported to a first-level manager. Such a manager might be supervisor of newspaper carriers, dining room manager, service station manager, maintenance supervisor, or department manager in a retail store. Supervisors help shape the attitudes of new employees toward the firm. Newcomers who like and respect their first-level manager tend to stay with the firm longer. Conversely, new workers who dislike and disrespect their first supervisor tend to leave the firm early.

TYPES OF MANAGERS

The functions performed by managers can also be understood by describing different types of management jobs. The management jobs discussed here are functional and general managers, administrators, entrepreneurs and small-business owners, and team leaders. (The distinction between line and staff managers will be described in Chapter 9 about organization structure.)

Functional and General Managers

Another way of classifying managers is to distinguish between those who manage people who do one type of specialized work and those who manage people who engage in different specialties. *Functional managers* supervise the work of employees engaged in specialized activities, such as accounting, engineering, quality control, food preparation, marketing, sales, and telephone installation. A functional manager is a manager of specialists and of their support team, such as office assistants.

General managers are responsible for the work of several different groups that perform a variety of functions. The job title "plant general manager" offers insight into the meaning of general management. Reporting to the plant general manager are a number of departments engaged in both specialized and generalized work, such as plant manufacturing, plant engineering, labor relations, quality control, safety, and information systems. Company presidents are general managers. Branch managers also are general managers if employees from different disciplines report to them.

Six key tasks form the foundation of every general manager's job. These tasks are:[3]

1. Shaping the work environment—setting up performance standards
2. Crafting a strategic vision—describing where the organization is headed
3. Allocating resources—deciding who gets how much money, people, material, and access to the manager
4. Developing managers—helping prepare people for their first and more advanced managerial jobs
5. Building the organization—helping solve important problems so the organization can move forward
6. Overseeing operations—running the business, spotting problems, and helping solve them

The six tasks of a general manager highlight many of the topics contained in the study of management. These tasks will therefore be reintroduced at various places in this book.

Administrators

An *administrator* is typically a manager who works in a public (government) or nonprofit organization rather than in a business firm. Among these managerial positions are hospital administrator and housing administrator. Managers in all types of educational institutions are referred to as administrators. The fact that individual contributors in nonprofit organizations are sometimes referred to as administrators often causes confusion. An employee is not an administrator in the managerial sense unless he or she supervises others.

Entrepreneurs and Small-Business Owners

Millions of students and employees dream of turning an exciting idea into a successful business. Many people think, "If Michael Dell started Dell computers from his dormitory room and he is the wealthiest man in Texas today, why can't I do something similar?" Success stories such as Dell's kindle the entrepreneurial spirit. An **entrepreneur** is a person who founds and operates an innovative business. John Clow, a director of business education programs, refers to entrepreneurs as "the creative forces within the economy, offering new ideas and bringing improvement in the human condition."[4] After the entrepreneur develops the business into something bigger than he or she can handle alone or with the help of a few people, that person becomes a general manager. Remember how Hard Candy grew too big for Dineh Mohajer, her boyfriend (even though he is an Einstein!), and her sister?

Similar to an entrepreneur, the owner and operator of a small business becomes a manager when the firm grows to include several employees. **Small-business owners** typically invest considerable emotional and physical energy into their firms. Note that entrepreneurs are (or start as) small-business owners, but that the reverse is not necessarily true. You need an innovative idea to be

entrepreneur
A person who founds and operates an innovative business.

small-business owner
An individual who owns and operates a small business.

6

an entrepreneur. Simply running a franchise that sells submarine sandwiches does not make a person an entrepreneur.

Team Leaders

A major development in types of managerial positions during the last decade is the emergence of the **team leader.** A manager in such a position coordinates the work of a small group of people, while acting as a facilitator or catalyst. Team leaders are found at several organizational levels, and are sometimes referred to as project managers, program managers, process managers, and task-force leaders. Note that the term *team* could also refer to an executive team, yet a top executive almost never carries the title *team leader.* You will be reading about team leaders throughout this text.

The accompanying Manager in Action describes the activities of an effective executive. After reading about him, decide which type of manager described so far best fits his activities.

Describe the process of management, including the functions of management.

THE PROCESS OF MANAGEMENT

A helpful approach to understanding what managers do is to regard their work as a process. A process is a series of actions that achieves something—making a profit or providing a service, for example. To achieve an objective, the manager uses resources and carries out four major managerial functions. These functions are planning, organizing and staffing, leading, and controlling. Exhibit 1-2 illustrates the process of management.

Resources Used by Managers

Managers use resources to accomplish their purposes, just as a carpenter uses resources to build a porch. A manager's resources can be divided into four types: human, financial, physical, and informational.

Human resources are the people needed to get the job done. Managers' goals influence which employees they choose. John Blystone has the goal of delivering automotive supplies and tools to auto and truck manufacturers. Among the human resources he chooses are manufacturing technicians, sales representatives, information technology specialists, and a network of dealers.

Financial resources are the money the manager and the organization use to reach organizational goals. The financial resources of a business organization are profits and investments from stockholders. A business must occasionally borrow cash to meet payroll or to pay for supplies. The financial resources of community agencies come from tax revenues, charitable contributions, and government grants.

Physical resources are a firm's tangible goods and real estate, including raw materials, office space, production facilities, office equipment, and vehicles. Vendors supply many of the physical resources needed to achieve organizational goals.

Information resources are the data that the manager and the organization use to get the job done. For example, to supply leads to the firm's sales representatives, the sales manager of an office-supply company reads local business newspapers to learn about new firms in town. These newspapers are information resources. Michael Dell of Dell Computer surfs the Internet regularly to learn about developments in the computer industry, thus using the Net as an information resource.

Manager *in Action*

John Blystone of SPX Tackles Inefficiency

General Electric is one of the world's leading companies for developing management talent. One of GE's many successful graduates is John Blystone, who has played a major role in turning around SPX, based in Muskegon, Michigan. The company manufactures auto parts such as filters, tools needed to service engines, and sophisticated diagnostic tools for measuring emissions. Blystone joined the company in 1997 as the company's highest-ranking executive. His three job titles are chairman, president, and CEO (chief executive officer).

When Blystone joined SPX revenues were flat, the stock price was moving downward, and the company was operating inefficiently. Relying on a thorough understanding of effective management practices learned during 14 years at GE, Blystone was intent on overhauling SPX. As his initial step, he decided to follow the guiding principle of Jack Welch (the famous GE chairman): "Reality means seeing the way it is, not the way we want it to be."

As Blystone analyzed SPX, he found nothing fundamentally wrong with its products. The bulk of the inefficiency, Blystone thought, stemmed from its being run as a loose collection of companies, with the mindset of a holding company. (A holding company owns other companies but does not operate them.) Considerable overlap was found among the various divisions in products and distribution. In many instances, the divisions competed against each other.

Blystone smoothed out the organization, combining certain divisions and selling others. He also introduced EVA to all operations as a measure of financial performance. EVA stands for economic value added; it is derived from subtracting the cost of capital (such as interest) from after-tax operating profit. For example, if you can earn 8 percent by investing capital in bonds, or you are borrowing capital at 8 percent, a net operating profit of 9 percent is not impressive. EVA is useful in assessing how good a company is at creating shareholder wealth. The company moved from a negative $51 million the year before Blystone came on board to a negative $20 million one year later. During the same time period, the stock quadrupled in value. Stock analysts have observed that SPX is the best company in the automotive field for taking care of shareholders' interests.

Blystone has been able to recruit talented people to the company by linking compensation to EVA for most of his employees. In one year, several SPX managers earned as much as 200 percent of their base pay as an EVA bonus. Blystone has been able to upgrade the company culture by adopting a series of leadership principles. "At GE it wasn't simply a matter of getting the job done," he says. "It was just as important *how* you got the job done." Company values are spelled out carefully for employees in many places, including the annual report, e-mail, and the factory walls. The core values include comfort with change, obsession with winning, and commitment to cultural diversity.

Blystone also has his management team thinking big. SPX is part of an alliance of companies seeking to develop a radical departure for the automobile industry—an open standard for auto maintenance. This means that repair shops will be able to purchase compatible equipment that links the service process together, from work order to diagnosis to parts inventory billing. According to Blystone, "We're trying to get out ahead of what's happening."

Source: Adapted from Justin Martin, "Another GE Veteran Rides to the Rescue," *Fortune*, December 29, 1997, p. 282; www.SBX.com.

EXHIBIT 1-2

The Process of Management
The manager uses resources and carries out functions to achieve goals.

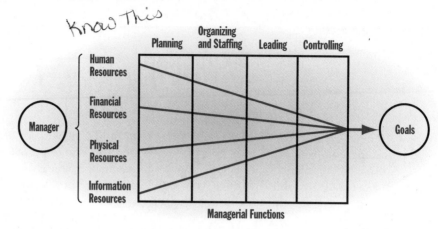

Source: Ricky W. Griffin, *Management*, 4e, Copyright © 1993 by Houghton Mifflin Co., p. 6. Used with permission.

The Four Managerial Functions

Exhibit 1-2 showed the four major resources in the context of the management process. To accomplish goals, the manager performs four managerial functions. These functions are planning, organizing and staffing, leading, and controlling.

PLANNING   Planning involves setting goals and figuring out ways of reaching them. Planning is considered the central function of management, and it pervades everything a manager does. In planning, a manager looks to the future, saying, "Here is what we want to achieve, and here is how we are going to do it." Decision making is usually a component of planning, because choices have to be made in the process of finalizing plans. Planning multiples in importance because it contributes heavily to performing the other management functions. For example, managers must make plans to do an effective job of staffing the organization. Planning is also part of marketing. Dineh Mohajer made plans to expand her product line beyond nail polish. The next time you visit a cosmetics department, check to see how well her plans are progressing.

ORGANIZING AND STAFFING   Organizing is the process of making sure the necessary human and physical resources are available to carry out a plan and achieve organizational goals. Organizing also involves assigning activities, dividing work into specific jobs and tasks, and specifying who has the authority to accomplish certain tasks. Another major aspect of organizing is grouping activities into departments or some other logical subdivision. Staffing involves making sure there are the necessary human resources to achieve organizational goals. Hiring people for jobs is a typical staffing activity. Staffing is such a major activity that it is sometimes classified as a function separate from organizing.

LEADING   Leading is influencing others to achieve organizational objectives. As a consequence, it involves energizing, directing, activating, and persuading others. Leadership involves dozens of interpersonal processes: motivating, communicating, coaching, and showing group members how they can reach their goals. Leadership is such a key component of managerial work that management is sometimes seen as accomplishing results through people. The leadership aspect of management focuses on inspiring people and bringing about change, whereas the other three functions focus more on maintaining a stable system. John Blystone brought about major changes at SPX in order to improve the company's efficiency.

CONTROLLING   Controlling is ensuring that performance conforms to plans. It is comparing actual performance to a predetermined standard. If there is a significant difference between actual and desired performance, the manager must take corrective action. He or she might, for example, increase advertising to boost lower-than-anticipated sales.

A secondary aspect of controlling is determining whether the original plan needs revision, given the realities of the day. The controlling function sometimes causes a manager to return to the planning function temporarily to fine-tune the original plan. In the early 1990s, for example, paper mills decreased their capacity based on predictions of the paperless office. The paperless office has not yet materialized, despite the explosion of information technology. By the mid-1990s, paper mills could not meet the demand for paper. Company executives then had to plan how to upgrade paper-making capacity quickly. By the end of the decade, demand and supply for paper had achieved a balance.

The Functions Emphasized at Different Levels of Management

One important way in which the jobs of managers differ is in the relative amounts of time spent on planning, organizing and staffing, leading, and controlling. Executives ordinarily spend much more time on strategic (high-level and long-range) planning than do middle- or first-level managers.[5] Lower-level managers are more involved with day-by-day and other short-range planning.

One notable difference in time allocation is that, compared to middle managers and executives, first-level managers and team leaders spend more time in face-to-face leadership of employees, as Exhibit 1-3 shows. Exhibit 1-4 reveals that executives spend most of their time monitoring the business environment. Such monitoring is a form of controlling. By analyzing what is going on in the outside world, the manager can help the firm compete effectively.

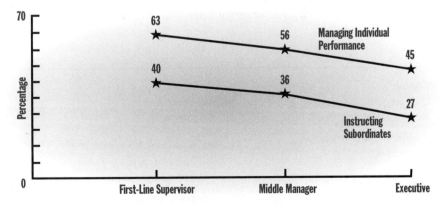

*Numbers refer to the percentage of managers who said the task was of "the utmost" or "considerable" importance.

Source: Allen I. Kraut et al., "The Role of Manager: What's Really Important in Different Management Jobs," *The Academy of Management Executive,* November 1989, p. 287.

EXHIBIT 1-3

Time Spent on Supervising Individuals at the Three Levels of Management* First-level supervisors place the most importance on dealing directly with group members.

10

Time Spent on Monitoring the Business Environment* Executives place the most importance on monitoring the environment.

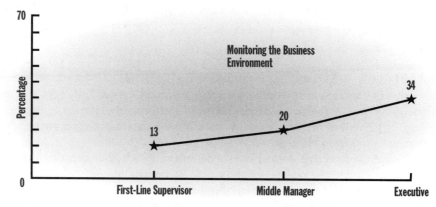

*Numbers refer to the percentage who said the task was of "the utmost" or "considerable" importance.

Source: Kraut et al., "The Role of the Manager," p. 288.

THE SEVENTEEN MANAGERIAL ROLES

Describe the various managerial roles, along with the roles currently emphasized.

role
An expected set of activities or behaviors stemming from a job.

To further understand the manager's job, it is worthwhile to examine the various roles managers play. A **role,** in the business context, is an expected set of activities or behaviors stemming from a job. Henry Mintzberg conducted several landmark studies of managerial roles.[6] Other researchers extended his findings.[7] In the sections that follow, the roles delineated by these researchers appear under the major managerial functions they pertain to most closely. (Roles and functions are closely related. They are both activities carried out by people.) The description of the 17 roles should help you appreciate the richness and complexity of managerial work. These roles are described next and listed in Exhibit 1-5.

Planning

Two managerial roles—strategic planner and operational planner—relate to the planning function.

1. *Strategic Planner.* Top-level managers engage in strategic planning, usually assisted by input from others throughout the organization. Specific activities in this role include (a) setting a direction for the organization, (b) helping the firm deal with the external environment, and (c) helping develop corporate policies.

The Seventeen Managerial Roles

Planning
  1. Strategic planner
  2. Operational planner

Organizing and Staffing
  3. Organizer
  4. Liaison
  5. Staffing coordinator
  6. Resource allocator
  7. Task delegator

Leading
  8. Figurehead

  9. Spokesperson
  10. Negotiator
  11. Coach
  12. Team builder
  13. Team player
  14. Technical problem solver
  15. Entrepreneur

Controlling
  16. Monitor
  17. Disturbance handler

2. *Operational Planner.* Operational plans relate to the day-to-day operation of a company or unit. Two such activities are (a) formulating operating budgets and (b) developing work schedules for the unit supervised. Middle-level managers are heavily involved in operational planning; first-level managers are involved to a lesser extent.

Organizing and Staffing

Five roles that relate to the organizing and staffing function are organizer, liaison, staffing coordinator, resource allocator, and task delegator.

3. *Organizer.* As a pure organizer, the manager emerges in activities such as (a) designing the jobs of group members; (b) clarifying group members' assignments; (c) explaining organizational policies, rules, and procedures; and (d) establishing policies, rules, and procedures to coordinate the flow of work and information within the unit.

4. *Liaison.* The purpose of the liaison role is to develop and maintain a network of work-related contacts with people. To achieve this end, the manager (a) cultivates relationships with clients or customers; (b) maintains relationships with suppliers, customers, and other persons or groups important to the unit or organization; (c) joins boards, organizations, or public-service clubs that might provide useful, work-related contacts; and (d) cultivates and maintains a personal network of in-house contacts through visits, telephone calls, e-mail, and participation in company-sponsored events.

5. *Staffing Coordinator.* In the staffing role, the manager tries to make sure that competent people fill positions. Specific activities include (a) recruiting and hiring staff; (b) explaining to group members how their work performance will be evaluated; (c) formally evaluating group members' overall job performance; (d) compensating group members within the limits of organizational policy; (e) ensuring that group members are properly trained; (f) promoting group members or recommending them for promotion; and (g) terminating or demoting group members.

6. *Resource Allocator.* An important part of a manager's job is to divide resources in the manner that best helps the organization. Specific activities to this end include (a) authorizing the use of physical resources (facilities, furnishings, and equipment); (b) authorizing the expenditure of financial resources; and (c) discontinuing the use of unnecessary, inappropriate, or ineffective equipment or services.

7. *Task Delegator.* A standard part of any manager's job is assigning tasks to group members. Among these task-delegation activities are (a) assigning projects or tasks to group members; (b) clarifying priorities and performance standards for task completion; and (c) ensuring that group members are properly committed to effective task performance. (The role of task delegator could be considered a part of the role of organizer.)

Leading

Eight roles have been identified that relate to the leadership function. These roles are figurehead, spokesperson, negotiator, coach, team builder, team player, technical problem solver, and entrepreneur.

8. *Figurehead.* Figurehead managers, particularly high-ranking ones, spend some of their time engaging in ceremonial activities or acting as a figurehead.

Such activities are (a) entertaining clients or customers as an official representative of the organization, (b) being available to outsiders as a representative of the organization, (c) serving as an official representative of the organization at gatherings outside the organization, and (d) escorting official visitors.

9. *Spokesperson.* When a manager acts as a spokesperson, the emphasis is on answering letters or inquiries and formally reporting to individuals and groups outside the manager's organizational unit. As a spokesperson, the manager keeps five groups of people informed about the unit's activities, plans, and capabilities. These groups are (a) upper-level management, (b) clients and customers, (c) other important outsiders (such as labor unions), (d) professional colleagues, and (e) the general public. Usually, top-level managers take responsibility for keeping outside groups informed.

10. *Negotiator.* Part of almost any manager's job is trying to make deals with others for needed resources. Three specific negotiating activities are (a) bargaining with supervisors for funds, facilities, equipment, or other forms of support, (b) bargaining with other units in the organization for the use of staff, facilities, and other forms of support; and (c) bargaining with suppliers and vendors about services, schedules, and delivery times.

11. *Coach.* An effective manager takes time to coach group members. Specific behaviors in this role include (a) informally recognizing employee achievements; (b) giving encouragement and reassurance, thereby showing active concern about the professional growth of group members; (c) giving feedback about ineffective performance; and (d) giving group members advice on steps to improve their performance.

12. *Team Builder.* A key aspect of a manager's role is to build an effective team. Activities contributing to this role include (a) ensuring that group members are recognized for their accomplishments (by issuing letters of appreciation, for example); (b) initiating activities that contribute to group morale, such as giving parties and sponsoring sports teams; and (c) holding periodic staff meetings to encourage group members to talk about their accomplishments, problems, and concerns.

13. *Team Player.* Three behaviors of the team player are (a) displaying appropriate personal conduct, (b) cooperating with other units in the organization, and (c) displaying loyalty to superiors by fully supporting their plans and decisions.

14. *Technical Problem Solver.* It is particularly important for first- and middle-level managers to help group members solve technical problems. Two such specific activities related to problem solving are (a) serving as a technical expert or advisor and (b) performing individual contributor tasks, such as making sales calls or repairing machinery on a regular basis. The managers most in demand today are those who combine a technical specialty with knowledge of other areas.

15. *Entrepreneur.* Managers who work in large organizations have some responsibility for suggesting innovative ideas or furthering the business aspects of the firm. Three entrepreneurial role activities are (a) reading trade publications and professional journals and searching the Internet to keep up to date; (b) talking with customers or others in the organization to keep abreast of changing needs and requirements; and (c) getting involved in activities outside the unit that could result in performance improvements within the manager's unit. These activities might include visiting other firms, attend-

ing professional meetings or trade shows, and participating in educational programs.

Controlling

One role, that of monitor, fits the controlling function precisely, because the term *monitoring* is often used as a synonym for *controlling*. The role of disturbance handler is categorized under controlling because it involves changing an unacceptable condition to an acceptable stable condition.

16. *Monitor.* The activities of a monitor are (a) developing systems that measure or monitor the unit's overall performance, (b) using management information systems to measure productivity and cost, (c) talking with group members about progress on assigned tasks, and (d) overseeing the use of equipment and facilities (for example, telephones and office space) to ensure that they are properly used and maintained.

17. *Disturbance Handler.* Four typical activities of a disturbance handler are (a) participating in grievance resolution within the unit (working out a problem with a labor union, for example); (b) resolving complaints from customers, other units, and superiors; (c) resolving conflicts among group members; and (d) resolving problems about work flow and information exchange with other units. Disturbance handling might also be considered a leadership role.

Managerial Roles Currently Emphasized

Managerial work has shifted substantially away from the controller and director role to that of coach, facilitator, and supporter. As reflected in the position of team leader, many managers today deemphasize formal authority and rank. Instead, they work as partners with team members to jointly achieve results. Managers today emphasize horizontal relationships and deemphasize vertical (top-down) relationships. Exhibit 1-6 presents a stereotype of the difference between the role of the modern and the traditional manager. We encourage you not to think that traditional (old) managers are evil, while new managers are good.

Old Manager	New Manager
Thinks of self as manager or boss	Thinks of self as sponsor, team leader, or internal consultant
Follows the chain or command	Deals with anyone necessary to get the job done
Works within a set organizational structure	Changes organizational structures in response to market change
Makes most decisions alone	Invites others to join in decision making
Hoards information	Shares information
Tries to master one major discipline, such as marketing or finance	Tries to master a broad array of managerial disciplines
Demands long hours	Demands results

Source: Adapted from Brian Dumaine, "The New Non-Managers," *Fortune*, February 22, 1991, p. 81; Joe McGavin, "You're a Good Manager If You . . ." *Manager's Edge*, September 1998, p. 7.

EXHIBIT 1-6

Traditional versus Modern Managerial Roles
"Old" managers and "new" managers see things differently.

14

The Influence of Management Level on Managerial Roles

A manager's level of responsibility influences which roles he or she is likely to engage in most frequently. Exhibit 1-3 and 1-4 showed this by indicating how managers' levels of responsibility influence which functions they emphasize. (Recall that roles are really subsets of functions.)

Information about the influence of level on roles comes from research conducted with 228 managers in a variety of private-sector service firms (such as banks and insurance companies) and manufacturing firms. The roles studied were basically those described in this chapter. One clear-cut finding was that, at the higher levels of management, four roles were the most important: liaison, spokesperson, figurehead, and strategic planner. Another finding was that the role of leader is very important at the first level of management.[8]

Identify the basic managerial skills and understand how they can be developed.

FIVE KEY MANAGERIAL SKILLS

To be effective, managers need to possess technical, interpersonal, conceptual, diagnostic, and political skills. The sections that follow will first define these skills and then comment on how they are developed. Whatever the level of management, a manager needs a combination of all five skills.

Technical Skill

Technical skill involves an understanding of and proficiency in a specific activity that involves methods, processes, procedures, or techniques. Technical skills include the ability to prepare a budget, lay out a production schedule, program a computer, or demonstrate a piece of electronic equipment. A well-developed technical skill can facilitate the rise into management. For example, Bill Gates of Microsoft Corp. launched his career by being a competent programmer.

Interpersonal Skill

Interpersonal (or human relations) skill is a manager's ability to work effectively as a team member and to build cooperative effort in the unit. Interpersonal skills are more important than technical skills in getting to the top. Communication skills are an important component of interpersonal skills. They form the basis for sending and receiving messages on the job.

An important subset of interpersonal skills for managers is **multiculturalism**, or the ability to work effectively and conduct business with people from different cultures. Closely related is the importance of bilingualism for managers as well as other workers. Being able to converse in a second language has become an important asset in today's global and multicultural work environment.

multiculturalism
The ability to work effectively and conduct business with people from different cultures.

Conceptual Skill

Conceptual skill is the ability to see the organization as a total entity. It includes recognizing how the various units of the organization depend on one another and how changes in any one part affect all the others. It also includes visualizing the relationship of the individual business to the industry; the community; and the political, social, and economic forces of the nation as a whole. For top-level management, conceptual skill is a priority because executive managers have the most contact with the outside world.

Conceptual skill has increased in importance for managers because many of them have to rethink substantially how work is performed. One such mind-bender is that many organizations are shifting away from departments and toward processes. Instead of a group of specialists performing work under the direction of an authoritative manager, people work together in teams as generalists.

Drucker emphasizes that the only comparative advantage of the developed countries is in the number of knowledge workers (people who work primarily with concepts). Educated workers in underdeveloped countries are just as smart as those in developed countries, but their numbers are smaller. According to Drucker and many other authorities, the need for knowledge workers and conceptual knowledge will continue to grow.[9]

Diagnostic Skill

Managers are frequently called on to investigate a problem and then to decide on and implement a remedy. Diagnostic skill often requires other skills, because managers need to use technical, human, conceptual, or political skills to solve the problems they diagnose. Much of the potential excitement in a manger's job centers on getting to the root of problems and recommending solutions.

Political Skill

An important part of being effective is being able to get your share of power and prevent others from taking power away from you. Political skill is the ability to acquire the power necessary to reach objectives. Other political skills include establishing the right connections and impressing the right people.

Political skill should be regarded as a supplement to job competence and the other basic skills. Managers who overemphasize political skill at the expense of doing work of substance focus too much on pleasing company insiders and advancing their own careers. Too much time invested in office politics takes time away from dealing with customer problems and improving productivity.

DEVELOPMENT OF MANAGERIAL SKILLS

This text is based on the assumption that managerial skills can be learned. Education for management begins in school and continues in the form of training and development programs throughout a career. Examples of such a program are a seminar about how to be an effective leader and a workshop about using the Internet to expand business.

Developing most managerial skills is more complex than developing structured skills such as computing a return on investment ratio or retrieving e-mail messages. Nevertheless, you can develop managerial skills by studying this text and doing the exercises, which follows a general learning model:

1. *Conceptual knowledge and behavioral guidelines.* Each chapter in this text presents useful information about the practice of management, including step-by-step procedures for a method of group decision making called the nominal group technique.
2. *Conceptual information demonstrated by examples.* Brief descriptions of managers and professionals in action, including small-business owners, are presented throughout the text.
3. *Skill-development exercises.* The text provides an opportunity for practice and personalization through cases and self-assessment exercises. Self-quizzes are included because they are an effective method of helping you personalize the information.

4. *Feedback on skill utilization, or performance, from others.* Feedback exercises appear at several places in the text. Implementing some of these managerial skills outside of the classroom will provide additional opportunities for feedback.

Experience is obviously important in developing management skills. Yet experience is likely to be more valuable if it is enhanced with education. Take an analogy to soccer. A person learning soccer might read and watch on video the proper way to kick a soccer ball. With this education behind her she now kicks the ball with the side of her foot instead of toe first. She becomes a competent kicker by combining education and experience. People often make such statements as "You can't learn to be a manager (or leader) from a book." However, you can learn managerial concepts from a book, or lecture, and then apply them. People who move vertically in their careers usually have both education and experience in management techniques.

Identify the major developments in management thought, along with several best management practices.

MAJOR DEVELOPMENTS IN MANAGEMENT THOUGHT

Management is such a complex subject that it can be approached from different perspectives or major developments in thought. Although these developments, or schools of thought, are different, they do not compete with each other as statements of truth about management. Instead, they complement and support each other. Well-trained managers select the management ideas that seem to fit the problem at hand. Correspondingly, this text borrows ideas from the major developments in management thought.

The classical, behavioral, and management-science schools are the major developments in management thought. They are supplemented by the contingency and systems approaches, both of which attempt to integrate these three major developments.

The Classical School

classical school of management
The original formal approach to studying management. This school of thought searches for solid principles and concepts that can be used to manage people and work productively.

The **classical school of management** is the original formal approach to studying management. Its followers search for solid principles and concepts that can be used to manage work and people productively. The core of management knowledge is based on the classical school. One of its key contributions has been to study management from the framework of planning, organizing, directing, and controlling. The term *leading* is now often used to replace *directing*, which sounds harsher.

The major strength of the classical school is that it provides a systematic way of managing people and work that has proved useful over time. Its major limitation is that it sometimes ignores differences among people and situations. For example, some of the classical principles for designing an organization are not well suited to fast-changing situations.

The Behavioral School

behavioral school of management
The approach to studying management that emphasizes improving management through understanding the psychological makeup of people.

Concerns that the classical school did not pay enough attention to the human element led to the **behavioral school of management**. Its primary emphasis is on improving management through understanding the psychological makeup of people. The behavioral school has had a profound influence on management, and much of this book is based on behavioral theory. Typical behavioral school topics include leadership, motivation, communication, group decision making, and conflict. Through its insistence that effective leadership depends on understanding the situation, the behavioral school initiated the contingency approach to management.

Much of the behavioral school is rooted in the work of psychologists who applied their insights and research findings to the workplace. Pioneering management thinkers such as Abraham Maslow, Douglas McGregor, and Frederick Herzberg are (or were) psychologists.

The primary strength of the behavioral school is that it encourages managers to take into account the human element. Many valuable methods of motivating employees are based on behavioral research. The primary weakness of the behavioral approach is that it sometimes leads to an oversimplified view of managing people. Managers sometimes adopt one simple behavioral theory and ignore other relevant information. For example, several psychological theories of motivation pay too little attention to the importance of money in peoples' thinking.

Impressive support for the behavioral approach to management comes from an analysis of the relationship between profits and good people management. Jeffrey Pfeffer conducted research on this topic in such companies as Men's Wearhouse, Service-Master, Volkswagen, United Airlines, and banks in the United States and Germany. He found that the lasting source of competitive advantage derived from how well companies managed people. Among the many studies demonstrating this point was one based on an index of how well people were managed in 702 firms. When the human resource system index improved by one major unit on the scale, shareholder wealth increased by $41,000 per employee.[10]

The Management-Science School

The **management-science school** provides managers with a scientific basis for solving problems and making decisions. It uses a wide array of mathematical and statistical techniques. To many people, the use of computers in management is synonymous with management science. Many quantitative techniques for quality improvement stem from the management-science school. Chapter 7, "Specialized Techniques for Planning and Decision Making," describes several important applications of management science.

The primary strength of management science is that it enables managers to solve problems that are so complex they cannot be solved by common sense alone. For example, management-science techniques are used to make forecasts that take into account hundreds of factors simultaneously. A weakness of management science is that the answers it produces are often less precise than they appear. Although management science uses precise methods, much of the data are based on human estimates, which can be unreliable.

management-science school
The school of management thought that concentrates on providing management with a scientific basis for solving problems and making decisions.

The Systems Approach

The **systems approach** to management is more a perspective for viewing problems than a school of thought. It is based on the concept that an organization is a system, or an entity of interrelated parts. If you adjust one part of the system, other parts will be affected automatically. For example, suppose you offer low compensation to job candidates. According to the systems approach, your action will influence product quality. The "low-quality" employees who are willing to accept low wages will produce low-quality goods. Exhibit 1-2, which showed the process of management, reflected a systems viewpoint.

Another aspect of systems theory is to regard the organization as an open system, one that interacts with the environment. As illustrated in Exhibit 1-7, the organization transforms inputs into outputs and supplies them to the outside world. If these outputs are perceived as valuable, the organization will survive and pros-

systems approach
A perspective on management problems based on the concept that the organization is a system, or an entity of interrelated parts.

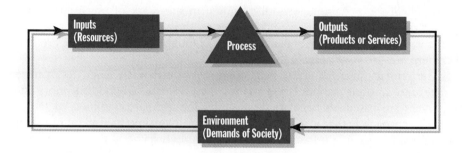

18

EXHIBIT 1-7

A Systems View of Organization
A systems perspective keeps the manager focused on the external environment.

per. The feedback loop indicates that acceptance of the outputs by society gives the organization new inputs for revitalization and expansion. Managers can benefit from this diagram by recognizing that whatever work they undertake should contribute something of value to external people (such as customers and clients).

Two other important concepts for managers from systems theory are entropy and synergy. **Entropy** is the tendency of a system to run down and die if it does not receive fresh inputs from its environment. As indicated in Exhibit 1-7, the organization must continually receive input from the outside world to make sure it stays in tune with, or ahead of, the environment. **Synergy** means that the whole is greater than the sum of the parts. When the various parts of an organization work together, they can produce much more than working independently. For example, a few years ago, product developers at Cadillac thought about building a luxury sports utility vehicle called the Escalade. The developers consulted immediately with manufacturing, engineering, purchasing, and dealers to discuss the feasibility of their idea. Working together, the units of the organization produced a successful product launch in a tightly competitive market.

The Contingency Approach

The **contingency approach to management** emphasizes that there is no one best way to manage people or work. A method that leads to high productivity or morale in one situation may not achieve the same results in another. The contingency approach is derived from the leadership aspects of the behavioral school. Specifically, psychologists developed detailed explanations of which style of leadership would work best in which situation. An example would be for the manager to give more leeway to competent group members. Common sense also contributes heavily to the contingency approach. Experienced managers know that not all people and situations respond identically to identical situations. The contingency approach is emphasized throughout this book.

The strength of the contingency approach is that it encourages managers to examine individual and situational differences before deciding on a course of action. Its major problem is that it is often used as an excuse for not acquiring formal knowledge about management. If management depends on the situation, why study management theory? The answer is because a formal study of management helps a manager decide which factors are relevant in particular situations.

Best Management Practices

Be careful not to dismiss the schools of management thought with historical information that is no longer relevant. Practicing managers can use all five major developments in management thought. An astute manager selects information

entropy
A concept of the systems approach to management that states that an organization will die without continuous input from the outside environment.

synergy
A concept of the systems approach to management that states that the whole organization working together will produce more than the parts working independently.

contingency approach to management
A perspective on management that emphasizes that there is no one best way to manage people or work. It encourages managers to study individual and situational differences before deciding on a course of action.

EXHIBIT
1-8

Eight Key Managerial Practices of Successful Organizations

1. **Employment security.** Workers are not in constant threat of being downsized or fired for flimsy reasons.

2. **High standards in selecting personnel.** The company attracts a large number of applicants and strives to find highly qualified candidates for all positions.

3. **Extensive use of self-managed teams and decentralized decision making.** Workers are organized into teams with the authority to make decisions. Managers throughout the company can make many decisions independently.

4. **Comparatively high compensation based on performance.** Paying employees better than the competition leads to success, as does paying employees based on their own performance or that of the department or company.

5. **Extensive employee training.** The most successful companies invest in training as a matter of faith, because they believe that a well-trained workforce contributes to profits in the long run.

6. **Reduction of status differences between higher management and other employees.** Successful firms take steps to de-emphasize status differences among individuals and groups that make some people feel less valued. Examples include calling everyone an "associate" and decreasing differences in compensation among levels of workers.

7. **Information sharing among managers and other workers.** Sharing information about such matters as financial performance and company plans helps build trust among employees. Having ready access to useful information also helps many workers perform their job better.

8. **Promotion from within.** Loyalty is enhanced when employees believe that they have a shot at being promoted to good jobs within the company.

Source: Gathered from information in Jeffrey Pfeffer, *The Human Equation* (Boston: Harvard Business School Press, 1998), pp. 64–98; Pfeffer, "Producing Sustainable Competitive Advantage through the Effective Management of People," *Academy of Management Executive*, February 1995, pp. 64–65.

from the various schools of thought to achieve good results in a given situation. Visualize John Blystone making SPX more efficient and effective. He relied on the classical school of management by changing the organizational structure. Blystone also drew from the behavioral school by discovering a creative way of motivating talented people.

To give you a preliminary idea of what outstanding managers are doing these days to manage people and organize work, see Exhibit 1-8. All of these practices will be covered at various points in the text.

SUMMARY OF KEY POINTS

To facilitate your study and review of this and the remaining chapters, the summaries are organized around the learning objectives.

 Explain what the term *manager* means, and identify different types of managers.

A manager is a person responsible for work performance of other people. Management is the process of using organizational resources to achieve specific objectives through the functions of planning, organizing and staffing, leading, and controlling. Organizational levels consist of top-level managers, middle-level managers, first-level managers, and individual contributors. Categories of managers include functional managers (who deal with specialties within the firm) and general managers, administrators (typically managers in non-profit firms), entrepreneurs (those who start innovative businesses), small-business owners, and team leaders.

 Describe the process of management, including the functions of management.

To accomplish organizational goals, managers use resources and carry out the basic management functions. Resources are divided into four categories: human, financial, physical, and informational. Top-level managers emphasize high-level planning, whereas first-level managers concentrate on person-to-person leadership. Executives place more emphasis on monitoring the environment than do managers in the other two levels.

Describe the various managerial roles, along with those currently emphasized.

The work of a manager can be divided into 17 roles that relate to the four major functions. Planning roles include strategic planner and operational planner. Organizing and staffing calls for the organizer, liaison, staffing-coordinator, resource-allocator, and task-delegator roles. Leading roles include figurehead, spokesperson, negotiator, coach, team builder, team player, technical problem solver, and entrepreneur. Controlling involves the monitor and disturbance-handling roles. Managerial work has shifted substantially away from the controller and director role to that of coach, facilitator, and supporter. Top-level managers occupy more external roles than do lower-ranking managers.

Identify the basic managerial skills and understand how they can be developed.

Managers need interpersonal, conceptual, diagnostic, and political skills to accomplish their jobs. An effective way of developing managerial skills is to follow a general learning model. The model involves conceptual knowledge, behavioral guidelines, following examples, skill-development exercises, and feedback. Manage-ment skills are also acquired through a combination of education and experience.

Identify the major developments in management thought, along with several best management practices.

The three major developments in management thought are the classical, behavioral, and management-science schools. Each complements and supports the others. They are supplemented by the systems and contingency approaches to management, which attempt to integrate the three schools. The best practices of managers today include elements of the five major developments in management thought.

KEY TERMS AND PHRASES

Manager, *3*

Management, *3*

Top-level managers, *3*

Middle-level managers, *4*

First-level managers, *4*

Entrepreneur, *5*

Small-business owner, *5*

Team leader, *6*

Role, *10*

Multiculturalism, *14*

Classical school of management, *16*

Behavioral school of management, *16*

Management-science school, *17*

Systems approach, *17*

Entropy, *18*

Synergy, *18*

Contingency approach to management, *18*

QUESTIONS

Here, as in other chapters, the questions and cases can be analyzed by groups or individuals. We strongly recommend small-group discussion to enhance learning.

1. Define the term *manager* in your own terms.
2. In what way does this chapter contradict the spirit of the popular cartoon strip *Dilbert*?
3. Many people in good-paying technical jobs actively seek to become managers. What do you suspect are their reasons?

4. Why might the role of the "new" manager require a higher level of interpersonal skill than that required by the "old" manager?
5. Why do large companies want many of their employees to "think like entrepreneurs"?
6. Why should executives place more emphasis on monitoring the external environment than do first-level managers?
7. How do students use the four management functions to accomplish their goal of graduating?

SKILL-BUILDING EXERCISE 1-A: Identifying Managerial Roles

Interview a manager at any level in any organization, including a retail store or restaurant. Determine which of the 17 managerial roles the manager you interview thinks apply to his or her job. Find out which one or two roles the manager thinks are the most important. Be ready to discuss your findings in class.

SKILL-BUILDING EXERCISE 1-B: Managerial Skills for Conducting a Project

Form a group of about six students. Your task is to plan a substantial project such as developing a business that can be conducted over the Internet, or creating a fund-raising campaign. Include both general and specific tasks that will have to be accomplished to achieve your goals. As you formulate your plans, identify the managerial skills you will need to get the work accomplished. For each skill you mention, provide a specific example of why the skill is necessary. For instance, in developing an Internet business you will need the technical competence to work your way through the system. You will also need interpersonal skills to attract the right employees and motivate them.

INTERNET SKILL-BUILDING EXERCISE: Entrepreneurs on the Net

Use your favorite search engines to identify an entrepreneurial business on the Net. After you locate a business that interests you, explain why you would classify the enterprise as an entrepreneurship rather than merely a small business. To give you a few ideas, check out cyberstudy101.com or twmall.com.

CASE PROBLEM 1-A: Managing The Gap

The Gap Inc. has earned the reputation as the most popular and profitable specialty clothing chain in America today. Sales at The Gap and its affiliates, GapKids, Banana Republic, and Old Navy, are currently running at close to $5 billion annually. Earnings were $700 million in a recent year. The company currently has about 2,400 stores in five countries. The two top executives at The Gap are president Mickey S. Drexler and the founder, chairman Donald G. Fisher.

The formula behind The Gap's extraordinary success is "good style, good quality, good value." Store sites are carefully selected by Fisher, and each Gap store is clean and well lit. Gap stores make it possible for consumers to shop easily and quickly. The atmosphere at the stores leads employees to fuss over details such as cleaning floors and, at GapKids, rounding the corners of the fixtures to prevent puncture wounds. The company boasts a high-tech distribution system that keeps the Gap outlets stocked with fresh merchandise.

Fisher, regarded as low-key and conservative in personal style, enjoys working on the details of site selection, store construction, and clothing manufacturing. Drexler, in contrast, makes most of the major merchandising decisions.

Several years ago Drexler simplified the way The Gap did business. He replaced executives who relied too heavily on complicated quantitative research. He preferred executives who relied quickly on intuition in selecting merchandise and deciding when to pull slow sellers from the shelves.

Both Drexler and Fisher have pushed heavily for quality. The company has placed its own quality inspectors in many of the manufacturing sites around the world that make clothing for the Gap label. The company designs its own clothing, chooses its own materials, and monitors manufacturing carefully.

At one time Drexler supervised every major design decision, and he still keeps close tabs on design. He characteristically roams around the stores, dropping in unexpectedly on employees to praise or criticize projects in design, advertising, and merchandising. For reasons such as these, Drexler has been described as a hands-on president.

Drexler devotes considerable time and energy to fixing problems. When Drexler was hired in 1983, The Gap's merchandise wasn't compelling, the stores were drab, and the competition was also selling private labels. Drexler swung into action. He dumped all the private labels except the Gap line. He hired new designers, upgraded the quality of the clothes, and overhauled the appearance of the stores. A retail analyst said, "You really have to give Mickey credit for reinventing the whole company. It was one of the great turnarounds in retail history." Drexler's strategy was to give the store's everyday products a brand image.

Despite impressive successes between 1983 and 1991, new problems arose that required fixing. The competition jumped on The Gap's bandwagon and started selling basics. In 1992, The Gap's stock price dropped by one-half. From that point through 1995, growth was flat. Even Drexler was concerned that the chain was losing its spark, so a new fix was in order. Drexler gambled with a new approach to discount marketing.

The gamble took the form of Old Navy, a trendy discount store with stylish, yet low-priced clothing. Old Navy stores have exposed pipes and raw concrete floors. Some of the clothing is showcased in old grocery-store refrigerator cases that once displayed frozen foods and similar items. T-shirts are shrink-wrapped like packages of ground beef or sausages. Old Navy was an instant success, due in part to a trend whereby it is chic to buy good merchandise at a discount.

Drexler had more fixing to do because Gap stores were still staggering. In a field visit to one Gap outlet, he was dissatisfied with the merchandising and the condition of the store. Drexler intensely disliked an advertising campaign that reminded him of heroin chic. In his perception the campaign said, "If you're a Gap customer, don't come into The Gap." Drexler ended the campaign. He also spent over two months going through every item in the clothing line that did not fit his idea of the pure Gap style.

To further strengthen The Gap, Drexler decided to make it more like Coca-Cola and McDonald's in terms of omnipresence and large market share. The Gap went on another expansion surge that included Banana Republic, Old Navy, and GapKids. An upstart is Gap-to-Go, with a menu of 21 basic Gap items that can be ordered by fax and delivered to the home or office by the end of the day. Gap Online was another piece of the turnaround.

The changes Drexler has implemented all support the grand strategy of making The Gap the Gillette and Coca-Cola of the apparel business. His vision is Gap stores modeled after busy supermarkets with deep inventory and long checkout lines.

Discussion Questions

1. Identify the managerial skills of Drexler and Fisher as revealed in the preceding case.
2. Which approaches to management thought are illustrated in the management techniques of the two Gap executives?
3. Which management functions can be identified in the preceding case?
4. What managerial skills does Drexler emphasize?

Source: Russell Mitchell, "The Gap," *Business Week,* March 9, 1992, pp. 58–64; Nina Munk, "Gap Gets It," *Fortune,* August 3, 1998, pp. 68–82.

CASE PROBLEM 1 - B: The Family Copy and Print Shop

After four years of night courses, Kathy Lundquist received an associate's degree in business administration. Shortly thereafter, top management at the bank where she worked promoted her to head teller. Lundquist expressed her appreciation for the promotion and inquired about prospects for future advancement. She was told that, due to the closing of so many branches in the bank, future promotions would be scarce.

Six months after her appointment to head teller, Kathy's uncle on her father's side died. Two weeks after the funeral, Kathy's aunt, Lisa Lundquist, invited Kathy for dinner to discuss some urgent family business. "Now that your uncle has died, I want to phase out of the copy and print shop that he and I have owned for 15 years. You can start right away as the manager, and I'll help you run the business. Within one year, I'll retire, and retain a 25 percent interest in the business. With luck, you should be earning much more than you are at the bank."

After discussing details of the deal for several weeks, Kathy decided to accept the position as manager of Lundquist Copy and Print. Aunt Lisa had painted a rosy picture of the business. After one month with the business, Kathy uncovered several disturbing problems. "What do you expect me to do about the following problems I've uncovered?" she asked her aunt. In checklist fashion, Kathy reviewed her findings:

"1. A new Sir Speedy (a national chain specializing in photocopying, printing, and desktop publishing) opened two blocks away. It looks like 20 percent of our customers have jumped ship to Sir Speedy.

"2. My analysis is that our business has not earned a profit in six months, after you take into account a decent salary for the owners.

"3. Many of our customers are more than 90 days overdue on their accounts, suggesting that we will never be paid.

"4. We have nobody on the staff who knows anything about desktop publishing, making it difficult for us to modernize the business."

Lisa Lundquist smiled, and said, "Kathy, I offered you this job because you have the background and the smarts to fix little problems like that. Just think of how much money you will make, and all the fun you will have if you take care of those problems."

Discussion Questions

1. What managerial functions and roles must Kathy Lundquist emphasize to fix the problems she uncovered?
2. How realistic is it for Kathy to solve the problems she has identified?
3. If you were Kathy, would you quit? Or would you stay to work on the problems?

ENDNOTES

1. Lisa Davis, "Working Women 500: No. 399, Dineh Mohajer," *Working Woman*, May 1998, p. 46; Gayle Sato Stodder, "Painting the Town," *Entrepreneur*, February 1997, pp. 132–137.

2. Peter F. Drucker, *The Frontiers of Management* (New York: Truman Talley Books, Dutton, 1986), p. 1.

3. Andrall E. Pearson, "Six Basics for General Managers," *Harvard Business Review*, July–August 1989, pp. 94–101.

4. "Entrepreneurship in the 90s," *Keying In*, March 1998, p. 1.

5. Allen I. Kraut et al., "The Role of the Manager: What's Really Important in Different Management Jobs," *The Academy of Management Executive*, November, 1989, pp. 286–293.

6. This research is reported in Henry Mintzberg, *The Nature of Managerial Work* (New York: Harper & Row, 1973).

7. J. Kenneth Graham, Jr. and William L. Mihal, *The CMI Managerial Job Analysis Inventory* (Rochester, NY: Rochester Institute of Technology, 1987); Jeffrey S. Shippman, Erich Prien, and Gary L. Hughes, "The Content of Management Work: Formation of Task and Job Skill Composite Classifications," *Journal of Business and Psychology*, Spring 1991, pp. 325–354; Joe McGavin, "You're a Good Manager if You . . ." *Manager's Edge*, September 1998, p. 7.

8. Cynthia M. Pavett and Alan W. Lau, "Managerial Work: The Influence of Hierarchical Level and Functional Specialty," *Academy of Management Journal*, March 1983, pp. 170–177.

9. Peter F. Drucker, "The Future That Has Already Happened," *Harvard Business Review*, September–October 1997, p. 22.

10. Jeffrey Pfeffer, *The Human Equation: Building Profits by Putting People First* (Boston: Harvard Business School Press, 1998), p. 35.

OBJECTIVES

After studying this chapter and doing the exercises, you should be able to:

1. Appreciate the importance of multinational corporations and emerging markets in international business.
2. Recognize the importance of sensitivity to cultural differences in international enterprise.
3. Identify major challenges facing the global managerial worker.
4. Explain various methods of entry into world markets.
5. Pinpoint success factors in the global marketplace.
6. Explain the importance of valuing demographic and cultural diversity in the workplace.
7. Present an overview of how information technology influences a manager's job.
8. Explain how the Internet influences the manager's job.

Several years ago the deepening economic crisis in Indonesia and other Asian countries was threatening the lifelong dreams of M. Sinivasan. The chief executive began 35 years ago as a fabric maker with a single loom. Step by step, Sinivasan has built his Texmaco Group into an industrial force that manufactures a wide range of products from machine tools to auto parts. Annual sales for the group are around $2 billion. The company's first truck, the 7.5 ton Perkasa, was introduced in late summer 1998. "The best time to hit is when the morale of our competitors is weak," said the company's operations director, H. N. Subba Rao.

Despite the brave talk, the truck operations faced a survival threat that year. Car sales in Indonesia plummeted 75 percent to a mere 100,000 units. Just keeping plants running is a challenge because auto makers are unable to obtain financing to import key parts. Texmaco faces a bigger hurdle than many other Asian companies. It must soon repay or refinance $200 million in offshore loans. Its main competitor, Mitsubishi Motors Corp., has a year's worth of unsold inventory. Industry and government officials in Indonesia thought 1998 would be the year its auto industry would become a formidable competitor. Instead, it has become a nightmare that won't go away.[1]

The Texmaco incident illustrates the complexity of managing in a global business environment. External forces

International Management, Cultural Diversity, Technology, and the Internet

such as a sudden recession in your country and others can disrupt plans and prof-its. In this chapter we describe major aspects of the international environment facing managers. We then look at two other major forces in the environment af-fecting managers and organizations—cultural diversity, which is a major aspect of conducting business both internationally and nationally, and information tech-nology and the Internet. Globalization, cultural diversity, and information tech-nology are such major forces in the workplace that they receive some attention throughout our study of management.

INTERNATIONAL MANAGEMENT

Appreciate the importance of multinational corporations and emerging markets in international business.

An important environmental influence on the manager's job is the internation-alization of business and management. Approximately 10 to 15 percent of all jobs in the United States and Canada are dependent upon trade with other countries. In general, as business has become more global, the manager must adapt to the challenges of working with organizations and people from other countries. Even keeping time-zone differences clearly in mind challenges many people. Here we present information about some of the key sets of knowledge necessary for be-coming an international managerial worker.

The Multinational Corporation

multinational corporation (MNC)
A firm with units in two or more countries in addi-tion to its own.

The heart of international trade is the **multinational corporation (MNC)**, a firm with units in two or more countries in addition to its own. Today's MNC has headquarters in one country and subsidiaries in others. However, it is more than a collection of subsidiaries that carry out decisions made at headquarters. A multinational corporation develops new products in several countries and pro-motes key executives regardless of nationality. A multinational corporation some-times hires people from its country of origin (expatriates) for key positions in overseas facilities. At other times, the MNC will hire citizens of the country in which the division is located (host-country nationals) for key positions. The ac-companying Manager in Action illustrates the scope of a multinational corpora-tion, and it highlights the executive who directs the enterprise.

The continued growth of the multinational corporation has been facilitated in recent years by two agreements—the North American Free Trade Agreement and the General Agreement on Tariffs and Trade—as well as by the formation of the European Union.

The North American Free Trade Agreement (NAFTA) establishes liberal trading relationships among the United States, Canada, and Mexico. The agree-ment creates a giant trading zone extending from the Arctic Ocean to the Gulf of Mexico. Many companies have benefited from NAFTA because they now have better access to the two other countries. During the first three years that NAFTA was operating, Eastman Kodak Company increased its exports to Mexico by 114 percent, and its exports to Canada by 12.5 percent.

Many labor union representatives argue that NAFTA has created a job loss for American workers.[2] By 1998 Mexico exported $19.2 billion in autos and auto parts, up from only $7.2 billion five years previously. The Mexican auto indus-try employs 360,000 workers, and exports close to 1 million vehicles, almost all to the United States. Much of the surge in the Mexican auto industry can be attributed to the substantial drop in tariffs among North American trading partners.

Manager in Action

Durk Jager of Procter & Gamble Takes a Global View

Durk Jager, a Procter & Gamble Co. veteran, became the company's chief in January 1999. He is regarded as a candid and somewhat blunt strategist with a global perspective developed in nearly 20 years working in the European and Far Eastern markets for his company. All five of the company's global regions report directly to Jager. (The regions are Europe, the Middle East, Africa, Asia, and Latin America.)

A retired vice-president describes Jager as a driven man who is not hesitant to publicly criticize or praise people who work for him. "With Durk you know where you stand. He is very straightforward—very focused, very smart. He has a tremendous command of facts and knowledge of the business." Despite his directness, Jager is regarded as a consensus builder. Before he makes a decision, he gets input from the mangers of the five global regions.

The appointment of Jager, who speaks seven languages, signals that the global era for Procter & Gamble has fully arrived. In 1997, net worldwide sales totaled $35.7 billion, about evenly divided between North America and the rest of the world. Of 106,000 worldwide P&G employees, 61 percent or 65,000 work outside of North America.

Wall Street analysts believe that Jager will keep a sharp eye on the global bottom line. Said one analyst, "He's a tough cookie—a no-nonsense tough guy. As tough as they come." Jager's toughness and determination also show up in managerial activities off the job. Susan Doward, campaign director for the Fine Arts Fund, says that when Jager throws himself into a project, there's no halfway.

Jager joined Procter & Gamble in 1970 in the Netherlands. He then held posts in Australia and Japan, and in 1988 he was appointed group vice-president of the Far East and Asia Pacific divisions. He joined the board of directors in 1989, and moved to Cincinnati (world headquarters for P&G) in 1990. In 1991 he became executive vice-president of U.S. business. In July 1995 he was promoted to president and chief operating officer.

Source: John Eckberg, "Globalist to Take P&G Helm: Jager Called 'Very Direct,' " *The Cincinnati Enquirer*, September 10, 1998, pp. A1, A4; Ronald Henkoff, "P&G: New and Improved!" *Fortune*, October 14, 1996, p. 152.

The European Union (EU) is a 19-nation alliance that virtually turns member countries into a single marketplace for ideas, goods, services, and investment strategies. The EU trades with member nations, the United States and Canada, and other countries throughout the world. In addition, Japanese firms are now investing rapidly in Europe. The EU represents a $6.4 trillion economy, second largest in the world.

A major forward thrust to the European Union is the European monetary union in which 11 countries will trade in their national money for a new currency called the Euro. Companies as well as individuals can then all trade in the same currency, which ends such problems as worrying about how much one's currency is worth in another country. Already bank accounts, credit cards, and prices are measured in Euros. National currencies are scheduled to be replaced by Euros in 2002. The monetary union reflected by the Euro is seen by some as the catalyst for Europe's economic revival.[3]

The General Agreement on Tariffs and Trade (GATT) liberalizes trade among many nations throughout the world. Although the GATT has been replaced by the World Trade Organization (WTO), the term "GATT" is still in current use. The idea is to lower trade barriers, thereby facilitating international trade. The GATT cut tariffs and other barriers on 8,000 categories of manufactured goods. The WTO now has about 130 member countries which account for about 95 percent of world trade. Based on lower trade barriers, consumers do not pay artificially high prices for imported goods.

A concern about facilitating trade is that global trade liberalization leads to continuous job cuts and downward pressures on wages in industrialized nations.[4] This occurs because companies from low-wage countries can export more readily into high-wage countries. The counter-argument is that free trade, in the long run, creates more job opportunities by making it possible to export more freely.

A side issue related to multinational corporations and free trade is what constitutes a foreign versus a domestic product. More specifically, an emotional issue is the meaning of the label "Made in USA." The Federal Trade Commission has a requirement that forbids companies from using the label if a product exceeds more than a small amount of foreign content. Yet the Commission had proposed guidelines that would have allowed merchandise with as little as 75 percent U.S. parts or content to read "Made in USA." Labor unions and some lawmakers have opposed the changed guidelines, because they believe the changes would encourage American corporations to send jobs overseas. By 1999, it appeared that the FTC was moving toward a requirement of at least 90 percent American parts and labor for a product to be labeled "Made in USA." What do you think is a fair definition of "Made in USA"?

Sensitivity to Cultural Differences

Recognize the importance of sensitivity to cultural differences in international enterprise.

cultural sensitivity
Awareness of local and national customs and their importance in effective interpersonal relationships.

multicultural worker
An individual who is aware of and values other cultures.

The guiding principle for people involved in international enterprise is sensitivity to cultural differences. **Cultural sensitivity** is awareness of local and national customs and their importance in effective interpersonal relationships. Ignoring the customs of other people creates a communications block that can impede business and create ill will. For example, Americans tend to be impatient to close a deal while businesspeople in many other cultures prefer to build a relationship slowly before consummating an agreement. Exhibit 2-1 presents a sampling of cultural differences that can affect business.

Cultural sensitivity is also important because it helps a person become a **multicultural worker**. Such an individual is convinced that all cultures are equally good, and enjoys learning about other cultures. Multicultural workers are usually people who have been exposed to more than one culture in childhood. Being multicultural leads to being accepted by a person from another culture. According to Gunnar Beeth, a *multilingual* salesperson can explain the advantages of a product in other languages, but it takes a multicultural salesperson to motivate foreigners to buy.[5]

Candidates for foreign assignments generally receive training in the language and customs of the country they will work in. Intercultural training exercises include playing the roles of businesspeople from a different culture. The aircraft-engine unit of General Electric Co. is one of many companies preparing people for the international work environment. Groups of middle-level engineers and managers receive cross-cultural training, including training in foreign-language skills. Although not all of these managers are scheduled to live abroad, the training is designed to help them work effectively with people from another culture.

29

Cultural Mistakes to Avoid in Selected Regions and Countries

EUROPE

Great Britain
- Asking personal questions. The British protect their privacy.
- Thinking that a businessperson from England is unenthusiastic when he or she says, "Not bad at all." English people understate positive emotion.
- Gossiping about royalty.

France
- Expecting to complete work during the French two-hour lunch.
- Attempting to conduct significant business during August—les vacances (vacation time).
- Greeting a French person for the first time and not using a title such as "sir" or "madam" (or monsieur, madame, or mademoiselle).

Italy
- Eating too much pasta, as it is not the main course.
- Handing out business cards freely. Italians use them infrequently.

Spain
- Expecting punctuality. Your appointments will usually arrive 20 to 30 minutes late.
- Making the American sign for "okay" with your thumb and forefinger. In Spain (and many other countries) this is vulgar.

Scandinavia (Denmark, Sweden, Norway)
- Being overly rank conscious. Scandinavians pay relatively little attention to a person's place in the hierarchy.

ASIA

All Asian countries
- Pressuring an Asian job applicant or employee to brag about his or her accomplishments. Asians feel self-conscious when boasting about individual accomplishments, and prefer to let the record speak for itself. In addition, they prefer to talk about group rather than individual accomplishment.

Japan
- Shaking hands or hugging Japanese (as well as other Asians) in public. Japanese consider the practices to be offensive.
- Not interpreting "We'll consider it" as a no when spoken by a Japanese businessperson. Japanese negotiators mean no when they say, "We'll consider it."
- Not giving small gifts to Japanese when conducting business. Japanese are offended by not receiving these gifts.

China
- Using black borders on stationery and business cards. Black is associated with death.
- Giving small gifts to Chinese when conducting business. Chinese are offended by these gifts.

Korea
- Saying "no." Koreans feel it is important to have visitors leave with good feelings.

India
- Telling Indians you prefer not to eat with your hands. If the Indians are not using cutlery when eating, they expect you to do likewise.

MEXICO AND LATIN AMERICA

Mexico
- Flying into a Mexican city in the morning and expecting to close a deal by lunch. Mexicans build business relationships slowly.

Brazil
- Attempting to impress Brazilians by speaking a few words of Spanish. Portuguese is the official language of Brazil.

Most Latin American countries
- Wearing elegant and expensive jewelry during a business meeting. Most Latin Americans think people should appear more conservative during a business meeting.

Note: A cultural mistake for Americans to avoid when conducting business in most countries outside the United States and Canada is to insist on getting down to new business quickly. North Americans in small towns also like to build a relationship before getting down to business.

The importance of such training was revealed by a study that found that 30 percent of placements in foreign countries were unsuccessful. These mistakes were due primarily to the employees' failures to adjust properly to a new culture.[6] (See Exhibit 2-1.)

Another approach to developing cross-cultural sensitivity is to recognize cross-cultural differences in managerial styles. These differences are cultural stereotypes applicable to many managers from the same country. As in all aspects of human behavior, considerable individual differences can be observed among managers from the same culture. National stereotypes of management styles, as revealed by the research of Geert Hofstede and his collaborators, are as follows:[7]

Germany: German managers are expected to be primarily technical experts, or *meisters*, who assign tasks and help solve difficult problems.

Japan: Japanese managers rely on group consensus before making a decision, and the group controls individual behavior to a large extent. Japanese managers are perceived as more formal and businesslike, and less talkative and emotional, than their American counterparts.

France: French managers, particularly in major corporations, are part of an elite class, and they behave in a superior, authoritarian manner.

Holland: Dutch managers emphasize equality and consensus and do not expect to impress group members with their status. Dutch managers give group members ample opportunity to participate in problem solving.

The Overseas Chinese: Many managers from China work in Pacific Rim countries such as Taiwan, Hong Kong, Singapore, Malaysia, and the Philippines. In companies managed by Chinese, major decisions are made by one dominant person, quite often of advanced years. The Chinese manager maintains a low profile.

Challenges Facing the Global Managerial Worker

Identify major challenges facing the global managerial worker.

Managerial workers on assignment in other countries, as well as domestic managers working on international dealings, face a variety of challenges. Rising to these challenges can be the difference between success and failure. Among the heaviest challenges are economic crises, balance of trade problems, collecting money, the liability of being a foreigner, human rights violations, culture shock, and differences in negotiating style.

ECONOMIC CRISES IN OTHER COUNTRIES   A major threat to the international manager is dealing with economic crises that originate in other countries yet have a negative impact on his or her country. The best-publicized of these crises is the Asian crisis, which is predicted to last several years into the new century. Many observers trace the origins of this crisis to Thailand devaluing its currency in July 1997. At the same time, stock prices and the real estate market plunged and the banking system was severely weakened. Currency markets also plunged in other Southeast Asian countries including Japan, South Korea, and the Philippines.

Japan's crisis has received the most publicity because it is the world's second largest economy, trailing only the United States. A major cause of Japan's recession has been a mountain of bad debt, and losses in real estate values. Nonperforming bank loans were the most striking feature of the bad debt. According to rating firms, Japanese banks at one point had $770 billion in debts that would be difficult to collect. Total problem loans were estimated to be $1 trillion. (A trillion is 1,000 billion.) Debt exceeded the value of stocks by an average of 4 to 1, forcing many companies into bankruptcy. With bad financial news circulating so freely, Japanese consumers cut back on spending. Furthermore, distrust of banks grew, prompting many Japanese to hoard money rather than deposit it in banks. Property values, in general, fell 10 percent to 20 percent from their pre-crisis levels. Public (government) debt reached $11 trillion.[8]

Of concern to managers involved in both domestic and international trade, the Asian crisis spread rapidly to Russia and Latin America. As a result the world economy was threatened with recession. (Exhibit 2-2 portrays the magnitude of the economic crisis.) For example, it became much more difficult to export to Asian countries whose economies were suffering. At first the United States and Europe escaped the financial crisis. Many American businesses were threatened as Brazil soon faced a recession. One reason is that 2,000 American businesses operate in Brazil.

By Fall 1998, the worldwide recession had made its first dents on the U.S. economy. The unemployment rate rose a tenth of a point, and the increase in new jobs slowed down. Many layoffs in U.S. companies were attributed to a sharp decline in exports to financially troubled countries who could no longer afford them. As a result, many American companies were forced to cut jobs and production.[9]

Closely tied in with an economic crisis is the challenge to international business created by inflation and currency devaluation. If the currency of a country suddenly gains in value, it may be difficult to export products made in that country. For example, the U.S. dollar rose 50 percent against the Japanese yen and 20 percent against the German mark during the 1997–98 period. At the same time the Canadian dollar fell to an all-time low against the U.S. dollar. Products and services become more expensive in importing countries where the currency has declined in value. On the positive side, the country, such as Japan, whose currency has fallen in value may soon find it easier to sell its exports. The impact of the Asian, Russian, and Latin American crises will be softened if more Americans and Europeans purchase their exports, which have become cheaper.

BALANCE OF TRADE PROBLEMS   A concern at the broadest level to an international manager is a country's **balance of trade**, the difference between exports and imports in both goods and services. Many people believe that it is to a

EXHIBIT 2-2

Countries in Recession		Countries Vulnerable to Recession	
New Zealand	−0.5	Iran	+0.0
Russia	−6.0	Kuwait	+1.3
Japan	−2.5	Saudi Arabia	+0.4
South Korea	−7.0	Turkey	+3.7
Philippines	−0.6	South Africa	+0.8
Indonesia	−15.0	Nigeria	+2.0
Malaysia	−6.4	Brazil	+1.5
Thailand	−8.0	Peru	+3.0
Ukraine	−0.1	Colombia	+2.7
Romania	−4.0		
Venezuela	−2.5		

Source: Based on information from the International Monetary Fund, as reported in "U.S., Europe Carrying the Load; Clinton Urges More Global Aid," Associated Press story, October 3, 1998.

Global Recession
The Southeast Asian crisis that began more than a year ago has spread to Russia and is now threatening Latin America. A look at the projected annual change in the inflation-adjusted gross domestic product for 1998 of some of the countries in recession or vulnerable to recession. Plus and minus signs indicate direction of change. The countries listed in each category are placed in roughly the order from east to west position on the globe.

balance of trade
A measure of the dollar volume of a country's exports relative to its imports over a specified time period.

country's advantage to export more than it imports. Yet in 1998, the current-account deficit, which includes trade in merchandise, services, and investments, reached $167 billion. The trade deficit is a direct result of the slump in export sales triggered by the economic crises described above. An individual manager might want to contribute to the national economy by exporting more than importing. In an effort to accomplish this, the manager might have to find ways to cut costs on products or services offered for export. An alternative would be to design products or services so attractive they would sell well despite their relative high price in foreign markets. Examples include American movies and Harley-Davidson motorcycles.

COLLECTING MONEY   A more specific financial problem facing the international manager can be collecting money from overseas customers. The most common way to get paid is through a letter of credit, a document issued by a bank. It guarantees a company will get paid as soon as it can provide documents showing that the goods or services were delivered as promised. Even with a letter of credit there can be serious delays in getting paid. Eastern Europe, China, and Russia are areas where getting money out of a country can be difficult.

Sometimes a country will forbid money being exported, so the seller has to spend the money in the foreign country. A company sending machine parts to one country might have to use its proceeds to purchase that country's product, and then resell the product in another country. For example, a company might purchase furniture in the overseas country with the proceeds from selling its own product, and then sell the furniture back home or in another country. Another reason it can be difficult to receive payments in these countries is that some companies are controlled by criminals. They accept shipment of the goods, but then refuse to pay and threaten anyone who attempts to collect payment.

LIABILITY OF BEING A FOREIGNER   When doing business abroad, a company faces costs arising from such factors as an unfamiliar environment, and from cultural, political, and economic differences. It is also difficult to coordinate activities across geographic boundaries. A study of Western and Japanese banks suggested that an effective way of overcoming the problem of being foreign is simply to use a firm's best businesses and managerial practices abroad.[10]

HUMAN RIGHTS VIOLATIONS   International managers can face ethical problems because their customers and suppliers might reside in countries where human rights are violated. Should a U.S. rug distributor purchase carpets from a supplier that employs 10-year-old children who work 11 hours a day for the equivalent of four American dollars? Should a U.S. shoe manufacturer buy components from a country that uses political prisoners as free labor? Ethical issues require careful thought, especially because they are often not clear-cut. To a child in an underdeveloped country, receiving $4 per day can mean the difference between malnutrition and adequate food.

The subject of human rights violations is complicated and touchy. According to Amnesty International, the United States sets high standards when it comes to human rights in other countries. Yet these standards are frequently violated within its own borders. A book-length report released by the organization cited many abuses in the United States, including forcing prisoners to wear shock-emitting stun belts, and police who beat suspects without cause and bind their wrists and ankles together. Also, the United States did not sign the United Nations Convention on the Rights of the Child, which seeks to promote human rights for children. In addition, Amnesty International regards capital punishment as a human rights violation because it is "racist, arbitrary, and unfair."[11]

CULTURE SHOCK   A problem faced by many managers and professionals on overseas assignments is **culture shock**. The condition refers to a group of physical and psychological symptoms that can develop when a person is abruptly placed in a foreign culture. Among them are excessive hand washing and concern for sanitation, fear of physical contact with others, fear of being mugged, and strong feelings of homesickness.[12] Culture shock contributes to the relatively high rate of expatriates (employees sent to another country) who return home early because they are dissatisfied with their assignments. Somewhere between 16 percent and 50 percent of these international workers return early. Based on research into successful and unsuccessful expatriate assignments, two researchers found that certain human resource practices could help make overseas assignments more pleasing. These same practices, outlined next, also help reduce culture shock for the expatriates and their families:

culture shock
Physical and psychological symptoms that can develop when a person is placed in a foreign culture.

- Give families realistic information about their assignments and language training.
- Arrange company-sponsored social functions for employees and families that give them an opportunity to interact with nationals from the host company.
- Provide family members back home with e-mail or other information technology advances such as teleconferencing.
- Provide job search assistance for spouses who want to work overseas.
- Assist with obtaining work permits or visas for spouses.
- Offer continuing education benefits packages that will finance either local or correspondence courses.[13]

DIFFERENCES IN NEGOTIATING STYLE   A recurring challenge in other countries, as indicated in Exhibit 2-1, is that the international managerial worker may have to use a different negotiation style. A do-or-die attitude is often self-defeating. American negotiators, for example, often find that they must be more patient, use a team approach, and avoid being too informal. Patience is a major factor in negotiating outside the United States. Asian negotiators are willing to spend many days negotiating a deal. Much of their negotiating activity seems to be ceremonial (including elaborate dining) and unrelated to the task. Americans can be frustrated by this agonizing process.

Although members of another culture spend a long time working a deal, they may still take a tough stance. A key example is that foreign firms seeking access to the Chinese market of 1.2 billion people face extraordinary demands by Chinese state planners. These planners demand that the foreign country hand over valuable technology and job-generating investments, especially in strategically-important area such as autos, aerospace, and electronics. Companies who refuse these demands lose out to competitors.[14]

METHODS OF ENTRY INTO WORLD MARKETS

Firms enter the global market in several different ways, and new approaches continue to evolve. A striking example is that at one time a small firm would have to rely on an importer-exporter or distributor to enter the world market. Now

Explain various methods of entry into world markets.

even some home-based businesses sell throughout the world by establishing a Web site. Eight methods of entry into world markets are described next.

1. *Exporting.* Goods produced in one country are then sold for direct use or resale to one or more companies in foreign countries. Many small firms specialize in helping companies gain entry to foreign markets through exporting. An overseas distributor can be quite helpful, but one must be chosen carefully. Current research suggests than an in-person visit to a prospective overseas distributor eliminates many problems.[15]

2. *Licensing.* Companies operating in foreign countries are authorized to produce and market products or services with specific territories on a fee basis. A franchise arrangement, such as a U.S. citizen operating a Subway store in Madrid, would fit this category.

3. *Local warehousing and selling.* Goods that are produced in one country are shipped directly to storage and marketing facilities of the parent company or subsidiary in one or more foreign countries. Many products, including radios and pocket calculators, are manufactured by Asian companies and shipped directly to American companies, such as Tandy Corporation, for distribution in the United States.

4. *Local assembly and packaging.* In this arrangement, components rather than finished products are shipped to company-owned facilities in other countries. There assembly is completed and the goods are marketed. Trade regulations sometimes require that a large product, such as a mainframe computer, be assembled locally rather than shipped from the exporting country as a finished product.

   An example of local assembly and packaging by U.S. companies is the use of maquiladoras. A **maquiladora**, a manufacturing plant in Mexico close to the U.S. border, is a plant established specifically to assemble American products. The U.S. owners of maquiladoras pay no import tax on components. When maquiladora products are exported to the United States, they are taxed only on the value added in Mexico.

   The maquiladora industry was established for two main purposes. First, it gave U.S. businesses the opportunity to use high-quality, inexpensive labor. (The average pay of a maquiladora worker is $2.50 per hour.) Second, it gave many economically disadvantaged northern Mexicans an opportunity for a relatively high-paying job and good working conditions. General Motors is one American company that is making extensive use of maquiladoras. The explosive growth of the Mexican auto industry mentioned in the discussion of NAFTA has been facilitated by maquiladoras.

5. *Joint venture (or strategic alliance).* Instead of merging formally with a firm of mutual interest, a company in one country pools resources with one or more foreign companies. Jointly they produce, warehouse, transport, and market products. Profits or losses from these operations are shared in some predetermined proportion. The advanced camera system that combines film and digital photography is a joint venture among five of the world's leading photo companies.

6. *Direct foreign investment.* The most advanced stage of multinational business activity takes place when a company in one country produces and markets products through wholly owned facilities in foreign countries. Toyota Motor Co. and Ford Motor Co. are two well-known multinational corporations that conduct business in this manner. Direct foreign investments are greatly

maquiladora
A manufacturing plant close to the U.S. border that is established specifically to assemble American products.

facilitated by forming **transnational teams**, work groups composed of multinational members whose activities span multiple countries. The group is composed of workers representing each company in the venture, whose intent is to help the companies pursue a global business strategy.[16] An example of a transnational team is representatives of the European and North American divisions of Chrysler working together to build and sell the Dodge Caravan. Teamwork is important because the Caravan components are built in several countries, and the vehicle has some export sales.

Research with 25 Dutch companies suggests a factor contributing to whether a company expands internationally through a foreign investment rather than an acquisition. Companies that already operate in diverse markets are more likely to start a new venture in another country rather than acquire another company.[17]

7. *Global merger.* An increasingly frequent method of gaining entry to foreign markets, or increasing business activity in these markets, is to merge with a foreign company. You can find an example of a global merger almost weekly by reading the business section of the newspaper. An example of a highly successful global merger is San Francisco-based Barclays Global Investors (BGI). A merger of four multinational corporations in 1996 made BGI one of the world's largest institutional investment managers with clients in more than 20 countries. Half of all mergers fail, and the failure rate for global mergers is even higher because of cultural differences. A senior executive at BGI comments about mergers:

> If you're going to do it, you have to invest very heavily in mitigating all the forces that work against it. Essentially, mergers have very tribal characteristics to them. You're asking different tribes to come together as a nation, and you'd better find out why it's in their mutual interest to do so. Otherwise, they'll use the opportunity of the merger to express their differences.[18]

8. *Global startup.* A **global startup** is a small firm that comes into existence by serving an international market. By so doing, the firm circumvents the methods described above. Logitech, Inc., the leading manufacturer of the computer mouse, is one of the most successful global startups. The company was founded in 1982 by a Swiss and two Italians who wanted to have an international company from the start. Logitech began with headquarters, manufacturing, and engineering in California and Switzerland and then established facilities in Taiwan and Ireland. Founders of global startups have one key characteristic in common: some international experience before going global.[19]

Selling through the Internet facilitates creating a global startup, particularly in the European market. Given that English is the universal language of business, it is possible to sell to European customers with Web sites in English. However, adding several other language options to the Web site could facilitate sales. European usage of the Internet, including PCs installed in the home, is increasing rapidly. Television hookups to the Net are also increasing rapidly, facilitating the sale of consumer products such as jewelry, clothing, and sporting goods. Europeans may soon have available cellular telephones with small screens for Web access. Online business (or E-commerce) in Europe is expected to increase soon to $65 billion annually.[20]

Of the methods of entry into the global marketplace, exporting offers the least protection for the company doing business in another country. Each suc-

transnational teams
A work group composed of multinational members whose activities span multiple countries.

global startup
A small firm that comes into existence by serving an international market.

cessive step through global mergers offers more protection against political and economic risks. One major risk is that the firm in the other country may drop its affiliation with the multinational firm and sell the product on its own. The affiliate thus becomes a competitor. To avoid this risk, direct foreign investment is recommended as the best way to protect the company's competitive advantage. The advantage is protected because the manager of a foreign subsidiary can control its operation.

Global start-ups offer similar protection to direct foreign investment. A problem, however, is that because the cost of attempting to sell through a Web site is small, both domestic and foreign competitors might readily copy your idea. Note that selling through the Web can be expensive if you hook up with a major portal such as Yahoo or Excite. You would then have to pay a commission and other fees to sell your product or service.

Success Factors in the Global Marketplace

Pinpoint success factors in the global marketplace.

Success in international business stems from the same factors that lead to success at home. The ultimate reason for the success of any product or service is that it satisfies customer needs. Additional strategies and tactics, however, are required for success in the global marketplace. It is important to recognize this, because internationalization of business is not always successful. Most of these strategies and tactics are a logical extension of topics discussed previously in this chapter.

THINK GLOBALLY, ACT LOCALLY   A competitive enterprise combines global scale and world-class technology with deep roots in local markets. Local representatives of the firm behave as though their primary mission is to serve the local customer.

DIVERSIFY INTO SIMILAR PRODUCT MARKETS   Diversification into product markets similar to markets currently served may result in several competitive advantages. First, managers understand their customer. Second, the structural characteristics of the new industry are likely to be familiar, which facilitates responding to competitive challenges. Third, some of the firm's current skills may be transferred to the new product or market. A fast-food chain might diversify into a fast-food item that is popular in another culture.[21] For instance, Burger King might sell tacos in its restaurants in Mexico.

BE FAMILIAR WITH LOCAL BUSINESS CONCEPTS, LAWS, AND CUSTOMS   Success in foreign markets is contingent upon close familiarity with the local scene. U.S. companies that have established maquiladoras have discovered the importance of this principle. For example, a unique aspect of Mexican law comes into play when an officially recognized labor union declares a strike. All employees, including managers, must leave the building, and red and black flags are hung at entrances to the plant. Furthermore, employees receive full pay for all the time they are out on a legal strike.

RECRUIT TALENTED NATIONALS   A major success factor in building a business in another country is to hire talented citizens of that country to fill important positions. To recruit the right local people for overseas operations, it is important to establish good contacts in the target country. Greg Green, the human resources director for Sunglass Hut International offers three words of advice: network, network, network. One way to network would be to make a list of other companies from your country that are already established in your destination country.[22]

Western firms have the best chance of penetrating the perplexing Japanese market if they hire top Japanese talent. After the host-company nationals are hired, they must be taught the culture of the parent company. By teaching the overseas managers the values and traditions of the firm, those managers can better achieve corporate objectives.

At times the prevailing management style in the host country may not fit the parent company culture. Teaching the culture then becomes even more important. An example follows:

> Chicago-based Tellabs Inc., a manufacturer of telecommunications products, opened a branch in Munich, Germany. Tellabs had an informal and flexible culture in which all employees had access to senior management. The German culture was much more informal. Laura Bozich, the regional director for Central Europe, was sent to Munich to explain the corporate culture to the newly hired manager.[23]

RESEARCH AND ASSESS POTENTIAL MARKETS Another basic success strategy in international markets is to acquire valid information on the firm's target market. Trade statistics are usually a good starting point. If the company manufactures long-lasting light bulbs, it must find out where such bulbs sell the best. Basic trade data are often available at foreign embassies, banks with international operations, and departments of commerce.

HIRE OR DEVELOP MULTICULTURAL WORKERS A contributing factor to success in global markets is to hire multicultural workers. Multiculturalism enhances acceptance of your firm by overseas personnel and customers. Included in multiculturalism is the ability to speak the language of the target (or host) country. Even though English is the official language of business and technology, overseas employees should develop the right foreign language skill. Being able to listen to and understand foreign customers speaking in their native language about their requirements may reveal nuances that would be missed by having them speak in English. Showing that one has made an effort to learn the native language can earn big dividends with employees, customers, prospective customers, bankers, and government officials. To be impressive, however, it is important to go beyond the most basic skill level.

UNDERSTAND YOUR COMPETITORS, POTENTIAL PARTNERS, AND THE DIVERSE MEMBERS OF THE MANAGEMENT TEAM The most comprehensive strategy for success in international business is to thoroughly analyze and understand the people upon whom your success depends. Understanding your competitors includes such information as their managerial values and strategy, and predicting the types of products and services they will offer in the future. Understanding partners in an overseas alliance includes figuring out what they expect to gain from the relationship. Understanding the diverse members of your management team refers to factors such as knowing their culture and work experiences.[24]

MANAGING DEMOGRAPHIC AND CULTURAL DIVERSITY

Explain the importance of valuing demographic and cultural diversity in the workplace.

demographic diversity
Mix of group characteristics in an organization's workforce, including sex, race, and religion.

Cultural diversity
Mix of cultures and subcultures in an organization's workforce, such as the Hispanic culture, Deaf culture, or gay culture.

The globalization of business means that the managerial worker must be able to deal effectively with people from other countries. At the same time it is important to deal effectively with different cultural groups within one's own country and company. Both the international and domestic work force are demographically and culturally diverse. **Demographic diversity** refers to the mix of group characteristics of the organization's work force. Demographic characteristics include such factors as age, sex, race, religion, physical status, and sexual orientation. **Cultural diversity** refers to the mix of cultures and subcultures to which the organization's work force belongs. Among these cultures are the Hispanic culture, the deaf culture, the gay culture, the Jewish culture, the Native-American culture, and the Inuit (Eskimo) culture.

It is possible for people with the same demographic characteristics not to share the same cultural characteristics. A deaf person who went to school with hearing people, whose parents are hearing, and most of whose friends can hear, may be deaf from a demographic standpoint, yet the person does not identify with the deaf culture. In this text, the term diversity is used to reflect both demographic and cultural diversity. Here we look at the advantages diversity brings to an organization, and what firms are doing to foster and appreciate diversity.

The Competitive Advantage of Diversity

Encouraging demographic and cultural diversity within an organization is a moral responsibility of managers. Also, diversity often brings a competitive advantage to a firm. The accompanying Organization in Action illustrates how valuing diversity improves the business results of a large automobile dealership.

A key advantage of a diverse work force is that it *improves productivity and profits*. A survey revealed that companies with a diverse work force tend to be innovative and creative. Diverse teams also proved to be more productive.[25] A representative work force facilitates reaching a multicultural market. For example, Avon Corporation faced low profitability in its inner-city markets. The company then gave African-American and Hispanic managers considerable authority over these markets. Soon the inner-city markets became highly profitable for Avon.

Companies with a favorable record in managing diversity are at a distinct advantage in *recruiting and retaining talented people*. The shortage of qualified workers in Silicon Valley has intensified company efforts to treat people with different backgrounds with fairness and respect. As a result, these information technology companies have attracted workers from around the world and the United States. (We cannot, however, rule out the recruiting attractiveness of the high wages paid by these companies.)

A diverse work force leads to better rapport with culturally diverse customers, often leading to more sales. Norman Lockwood explains: "In a board meeting in China, Americans are greeted by hosts who are frequently a homogeneous group, both in race and gender. However, if all the Americans are white males, a certain wariness can creep into the proceedings. If there are nonwhite Americans among the visitors, there is a slightly more cordial atmosphere."[26]

Diversity within a firm can *improve customer service*. Managing diversity is even more important in a service organization. Promoting respect among em-

38

Organization *in Action*

Diversity Pays Off in Big Sales for Toyota Dealership

at Longo Toyota in El Monte, California, the 60-person sales staff speaks a total of 20 different languages. Longo has catered to its increasingly diverse customer base and become one of the country's highest sales volume dealerships. Providing bilingual service is commonplace in many parts of North America. What makes this dealership unique is that it assembled such a diverse sales staff without a formal affirmative action program.

By hiring and recruiting the best available talent, the staff at Longo has evolved naturally into an extremely diverse and effective sales group. Human resources manager Ken Rankin has played an integral role in creating the diverse environment. When asked how the human resources department is attempting to maintain diversity, he said, "We'll continue to go after different markets from a business and marketing standpoint. We will also continue to hire those people who are the most qualified for the position and can best satisfy our customers' needs, be they bilingual or otherwise."

The dealership retains an incredibly high 90 percent of its diverse sales staff. Rankin explains that the salespeople have a tremendous opportunity to have good and consistent income because the dealership has such a huge customer base. He says, "We also work very hard to be responsive to the employee, and we have stuck to our goal of promoting from within."

The promote-from-within policy has contributed to more than two-thirds of the managers being minorities. Rankin explains that his policy has helped with recruitment and retention of a diverse sales staff. "The policy only benefits us," he notes. "When you enter an organization, you try to anticipate what it's going to be like. When you walk in here, it becomes readily apparent that we recruit from within, and we don't restrict anything to any specific group or class. That really helps."

Asked about whether cultural diversity can lead to problems of people not working well together, Rankin said, "Minor issues do pop up from time to time, but it only happens at the individual level. Somebody might say an off-color joke or something that offends somebody else, but we have not had any larger, across-the-board problems with groups not being able to work together."

Rankin believes that if you do not recruit for diversity, you are missing a lot of talent. He says, "When you try to solve problems at any organization, you look for diverse perspectives, and that's certainly a great strength of ours. Also, I think our customers feel comfortable because it's obvious we encourage diversity. As opposed to walking into an environment where everyone is of the same culture and the customer may feel awkward, our diversity helps the customer relax."

"In fact, I can't think of any negative effects of diversity," concludes Rankin. "Diversity is an absolute strength of ours, especially from a business perspective."

Source: Excerpted from "Diversity Pays Off in Big Sales for Toyota Dealership" by Kevin Wallsten, copyright September 1998. Used with permission of ACC Communications Inc./*Workforce*, Costa Mesa, CA. All rights reserved.

ployees as a corporate value encourages employees to respect diverse work mates as well as the diverse customers with whom they interact. If employees regularly work with people from different countries, they are less likely to be patronizing toward customers from other countries and regions. Have you ever noticed that some people shout when they communicate with a person with a strong foreign accent? Organizational diversity tends to reduce such inappropriate behavior.

An amusing advantage of a diverse work force is that it *reduces possible cultural bloopers*. One example is that you can readily get the input from the right person to help with translations and product names aimed at other countries. A U.S. telecommunications system labeled Chat Box didn't change its name when it marketed the system in France. Unfortunately for the company, "chat" is the French word for "cat," so many potential customers were confused about the purpose of the system.

Organizational Practices to Improve the Management of Diversity

The combined forces of the spirit of the times and the advantages of valuing diversity have led organizations to take initiatives to manage diversity well. Exhibit 2-3 provides details about five business firms with the best record of hiring, promoting, and retaining people of color, as determined by a *Fortune* magazine analysis. ("People of color" is but one dimension of diversity.) Three representative organizational practices that enhance diversity management are corporate policies about diversity, the establishment of employee network groups, and valuing differences programs.

CORPORATE POLICIES FAVORING DIVERSITY   Many companies formulate policies that encourage and foster diversity. A typical policy is "We are committed to recruiting, selecting, training, and promoting individuals based

EXHIBIT 23

Five Major Companies with Excellent Performance in Managing Diversity

Company	% Minority Officials and Managers	Comment on Diversity Practices
Pacific Enterprises	34	Employees nominate themselves for the company's fast-track management training program
Advantica	29.9	The parent company of Denny's bounced back from discrimination charges and now has diverse groups of suppliers and franchisees. All charitable giving goes to groups that benefit primarily minorities.
BankAmerica	25.9	Management makes the company a comfortable place for everyone to work, and the best people—black, white, Hispanic, or native American—rise to the top.
Fannie Mae	22.8	In breaking down barriers to home ownership for blacks and Hispanics, Fannie Mae has found a new growth business. About 18% of the single-family homes it financed were bought by minorities.
Marriott International	18.5	A year ago only one franchise was owned by a person of color. Now 29 are: 20 by Asians, 5 by blacks, 4 by Hispanics. As many as 30 languages are spoken at some Marriotts.

Source: Based on information in "The Diversity Elite," *Fortune*, August 3, 1998, p. 114.

solely on their capabilities and efforts. To accomplish this goal, we value all differences among our workforce." A study conducted by *Working Woman* and the YWCA indicated that such policies do lead to effective management of diversity. Survey participants included top managers and business owners, middle managers and first-level managers, and nonsupervisory professionals. The respondents indicated that a commitment to diversity was most likely to succeed if the company established a corporate diversity policy. In companies that had been successful in achieving diversity, 47 percent had a stated policy, versus 28 percent that did not have one.[27]

EMPLOYEE NETWORK GROUPS   A company approach to recognizing cultural differences is to permit and encourage employees to form **employee network groups.** The network group is composed of employees throughout the company who affiliate on the basis of group characteristics such as race, ethnicity, sex, sexual orientation, or physical ability status. Group members typically have similar interests, and look to the groups as a way of sharing information about succeeding in the organization. Although some human resource specialists are concerned that network groups can lead to divisiveness, others believe they play a positive role. At 3M Corporation employee network groups serve as advisors to business units. For example, the company's network group for employees with disabilities is often consulted by 3M product development groups. Company network groups also help their organizations recruit through such means as providing links to minority group members in the community.[28]

employee network groups
Employees within a company who affiliate on the basis of race, ethnicity, sex, sexual orientation, or physical ability to discuss ways to succeed in the organization.

VALUING DIVERSITY TRAINING PROGRAMS   To help employees relate comfortably to people of different cultures and appreciate diversity, many companies conduct **valuing diversity programs.** These programs provide an opportunity for employees to develop the skills necessary to deal effectively with each other and with customers in a diverse environment. Quite often the program is aimed at minimizing open expressions of racism and sexism. All forms of valuing differences training center around increasing people's awareness of and empathy for people who are different in some noticeable way from themselves.

valuing diversity programs
Company training programs designed to develop skills employees need in a diverse work environment.

Training programs in valuing differences focus on the ways that men and women, or people of different races, reflect different values, attitudes, and cultural backgrounds. These sessions can vary from several hours to several days. Sometimes the program is confrontational, sometimes not. As described by R. Roosevelt Thomas, Jr., the objectives of the valuing differences training program include one or more of the following:[29]

- Fostering awareness and acceptance of individual differences
- Helping participants understand their own feelings and attitudes about people who are "different"
- Exploring how differences might be tapped as assets in the workplace
- Exploring work relations between people who are different from each other

An essential part of relating more effectively to diverse groups is to empathize with their point of view. To help training participants empathize, representatives of various groups explain their feelings related to workplace issues. During one of these training sessions a Chinese woman said she wished people would not act so shocked when she is assertive about her demands. She claimed that many people she meets at work expect her to fit the stereotype of the polite, compliant Chinese woman.

INFORMATION TECHNOLOGY AND THE MANAGER'S JOB

Present an overview of how information technology influences a manager's job.

So far we have described how the globalization of business and cultural diversity have a major impact on managers and organizations. An equally pervasive force is information technology (IT). In this section we describe a few ways in which information technology influences managerial work. In the next section we focus on the impact of the Internet on the manager's job.

Information technology is integrated into the everyday work of first-level, and middle-level managers. A more surprising fact is that top-level executives now use office technology themselves. A recent survey of 821 CEOs found that 83 percent are using a PC on their desk for actual work. Over 80 percent send and answer e-mail messages themselves. About 70 percent use their computer for spreadsheets, and 56 percent are familiar with databases. About 74 percent devote around two hours per week to the Internet, and about 60 percent use a corporate intranet (an organization's internal computer network). Younger CEOs tend to make more extensive use of information technology tools.[30]

The Positive Consequences of Information Technology

The information technology revolution would not have lasted so long if it were not helping managers, other workers, and organizations perform better. A description of the positive consequences of IT follows, with an emphasis on managerial work.

IMPROVED PRODUCTIVITY AND TEAMWORK   A major justification for installing information technology is that it improves productivity. Measuring the productivity improvements stemming from computers in the service sector has proved to be more difficult than measuring improvements in manufacturing.[31] Yet managers, such as Susan Cramm at Taco Bell, are often convinced that information technology improves productivity in their organization. When Cramm joined the company she emphasized using computers for three purposes: controlling costs, helping employees do their jobs better, and giving local managers the information they need to perform more effectively.[32]

Small business owners have increased their productivity in many ways by exploiting information technology. An advanced application of IT is using online services to find sources of investment capital. The business owner posts a message, and then potential investors can respond. Finding investors on line can be quicker than an extensive letter-writing and telephone-calling campaign.

Information technology can enhance teamwork because team members can maintain frequent contact with each other through e-mail and pagers. Even if the group does not have the time to hold an in-person meeting, team members can give electronic feedback to each other's ideas. Furthermore, with extensive use of IT, teammates do not even have to work in the same physical location.

EXHIBIT
24

Top-Selling Software for
PCs

43

According to PC Data, Inc., the top-selling software in August 1998 were as follows:

1. Print Artist Platinum (Cendant Software)
2. Printmaster Premier (Learning Company)
3. Quicken Deluxe (Intuit)
4. Home Office (GT Interactive)

5. Quicken (Intuit)
6. Microsoft Works (Microsoft)
7. Microsoft Publisher (Microsoft)
8. Microsoft Home Essentials (Microsoft)
9. Microsoft Money (Microsoft)
10. Printmaster Platinum 7.0 (Learning Company)

Source: www.pcdata.com/Main.asp (accessed October 12, 1998).

Managers use a variety of software to enhance productivity. Exhibit 2-4 lists top-selling PC software for enhancing productivity used by managers and professionals.

GAINING COMPETITIVE ADVANTAGE Effective use of information technology can give a firm a competitive advantage. Judicious use of *infotech* enables companies to conduct business in ways that would be impossible without such technology. How one company in the energy field gained control of another illustrates this point. Jack L. Messman, the CEO of Union Pacific Resources Group Inc., launched a hostile takeover of Pennzoil Co. Before taking action he compiled every piece of available data on Penzoil's fields throughout the world. Using computer programs that help locate hidden oil and natural gas, he concluded that Penzoil had more reserves than it realized. As a result he made a more aggressive takeover offer. "Technology is what's driving this business today," says Messman, a former computer company executive turned oilman.[33]

Today, not using modern information technology makes a company noncompetitive. Imagine how embarrassing it would be for a company to have neither a Web site nor e-mail for interacting with customers and suppliers.

IMPROVED CUSTOMEOR-SERVICE AND SUPPLIER RELATIONSHIPS Advances in information technology, including networking, can lead to improved customer service and smoother working relationships with suppliers. Customer service is improved when service representatives have immediate access to information that can resolve a customer problem. USAA, a large financial services firm, is a model for the industry in terms of prompt service. The company sells insurance directly to the public, without the use of external sales representatives or insurance agents. Policyholders can call an 800 number to receive immediate answers to complex questions such as how much rates will increase if a 16-year-old family member becomes a licensed driver.

Supplier relationships can be more productive when suppliers and purchasers are part of the same network. Large retailers such as Wal Mart authorize some of their suppliers to ship and stock goods based on electronic messages sent from point of purchase to the suppliers' computers. When inventory gets low on a fast-moving item, supplies are replenished automatically without a retail store official having to make a phone call or send a letter.

A current development to improve customer services is the **extranet,** a secure section of a Web site that only visitors with a password can enter. Many financial services firms use an extranet to allow customers to manage accounts and trade stocks on line. The extranet is also used to share inventory or customer information with suppliers, send information to vendors, and sell products and services.

extranet
A Web site that requires a password to enter.

44

virtual office
An arrangement whereby employees work together as if they were part of a single office despite being physically separated.

ENHANCED COMMUNICATION AND COORDINATION   Nowhere is the impact of information technology on the manager's job more visible than in communication and coordination. By relying on information technology, managers can be in frequent contact with office members without being physically present. They can also be part of the **virtual office**, in which employees work together as if they were part of a single office despite being physically separated. The most familiar tools of the virtual office are fax machines, modems, pagers, and cellular telephones.

The technology supporting the virtual office continues to evolve. For example, HotOffice Technologies Inc. provides a virtual office that functions like a Web site. The manager rents a private work space through an Internet provider that serves as a single location for group members to meet, post documents, and share ideas in real time. In essence, the group members in various locations sit at their computers and interact with each other. A tangible benefit of building virtual groups is the reduction in travel time and costs involved in working with people in far-flung locations. Placing most of the work on line makes it possible, with a small investment, to manage, discuss, and work on tasks with people who are physically separate.[34]

A similar idea to the virtual office is the cybermeeting, a gathering of participants in scattered locations using videoconferencing equipment or e-mail. A videoconference enables people to see and hear each other through real-time video. Cybermeetings can accommodate from 4 to 200 people. Large firms often have their own videoconferencing centers, whereas smaller firms typically rent a center as needed.

Frequent contact with company employees, customers, and suppliers enhances coordination. The alternative is for the manager to communicate primarily when back at the office. A high-tech manager is never away from the office—even if he or she would like to be!

QUICK ACCESS TO VAST INFORMATION   Information technology gives managers quick access to vast amounts of information. A careful library researcher could always access vast amounts of business-related information. Advances in information technology, however, allow for fingertip access if the manager has the right computer skills. For example, a sales manager might want a targeted list of prospects for her company's new pool tables. She uses an electronic directory to locate sporting-goods stores in her region, ranking them by revenue and zip code to streamline her sales strategy.

information super-highway
The combination of computer, Internet, telecommunications, and video technologies for the purpose of disseminating and acquiring information.

company intranet
A Web site designed only for company employees, often containing proprietary information.

In general, the manager obtains quick access to vast—and relevant—information by learning how to navigate the information superhighway. The **information superhighway** is the combination of computer, Internet, telecommunication, and video technologies for the purpose of disseminating and acquiring information. Managers also use the info superhighway to let others know of their products, services, and job openings. Furthermore, a manager might use an online service to list an unusual requirement such as requiring a part for an obsolete machine.

A major contributor to accessing information quickly is the **company intranet**, a Web site for company use only. A striking example is that Ford Motor Company estimates it will save billions of dollars over a few years by using an intranet. Ford's intranet connects over 120,000 workstations around the world to thousands of Web sites. The Web sites contain proprietary information like market research, analyses of components, and rankings of the most effective suppliers.

All vehicle teams have their own Web sites, enabling team members to post questions and progress reports, point out bottlenecks, and resolve quality problems. Sharing all this information has helped Ford reduce the cycle time on new models from 36 months down to 24 months. Using the intranet, the manager can achieve better results such as cost savings and quicker model introductions.[35]

ENHANCED ANALYSIS OF DATA AND DECISION MAKING Closely related to gathering a wider array of information, IT allows for better analysis of data and decision making. Managers at business firms of all sizes are now analyzing data better to improve efficiency. A before-and-after example follows:

> Years ago, Pink Jeep Tours, a Sedona, Arizona, company that offers guided Jeep tours through nearby red-rock formations, booked tours by entering basic customer information into a DOS-based program and then scheduling and organizing tour lengths and party sizes on magnetic boards. Unfortunately, if someone brushed up against the boards, magnets would come tumbling off, tour guides wouldn't have a clue as to which parties were scheduled when, and chaos would ensue. Then the company installed a Windows-based reservations system that electronically schedules each day's tours.[36]

Another way in which information technology helps managers make better decisions is through computer-assisted decision making. A variety of software has been designed for such purposes. The most directly relevant for most managers is **decision-making software**. It is any computer program that helps a decision maker work through problem-solving and decision-making steps. Such software usually asks the user questions about values, priorities, and the importance attached to factors such as price and quality.

The decision-making process used in these programs is referred to as "intuitive" because the programs rely more on human judgment than on quantitative analysis. The intent of the programs is to improve the quality of decisions rather than to just make computations or generate data. A decision-making program might help a traffic manager decide whether to make a large shipment by truck, railroad, or airplane.

decision-making software
Any computer program that helps a decision maker work through problem-solving and decision-making steps.

FACILITATION OF EMPOWERMENT AND FLATTER ORGANIZATIONS
The widespread use of information technology gives more workers access to information they need for decision making. As a result, more workers can be empowered to make decisions. Fewer layers of management are required because so many middle managers are no longer needed to act as information conduits. Instead, workers at lower levels access information directly through computer networks. Information technology therefore provides line employees with the documents they need to perform their jobs more effectively and make decisions on their own.

The Negative Consequences of Information Technology

Information technology's contribution to organizational health has been extraordinary. Nevertheless, the same exciting technology produces some unintended negative consequences. Awareness of these potential problems can help managers

computer goof-offs
People who spend so much time attempting new computer routines and accessing information of questionable value that they neglect key aspects of the job.

prevent them from occurring. One subtle problem is that managers and other employees become **computer goof-offs**. They spend so much time attempting new computer routines and accessing information of questionable value that they neglect key aspects of their job. Many managers, for example, would prefer to surf the Internet for low-value information than to confront an employee about a discipline problem.

Surfing the Net needlessly on company time often centers around accessing a sports site, such as www.ESPN.com, or pornography. A study by Elron Software (www.elronsoftware.com) found that 62 percent of firms with Internet access saw some traffic on pornographic Web sites. In addition to draining productivity, displaying pornography on company computer monitors could lead to sexual harassment charges. Elron offers software that can block out sites, as well as track where employees are spending their time online.[37]

Computer goofing off in extreme form leads to an *online addiction*, in which the person spends so much time surfing the Internet on and off the job that productivity and interpersonal relationships suffer. For the addicted, the Internet becomes the most important satisfaction in life. A number of students suffer from online addiction, often not attending class because they have stayed up all night surfing the Internet. Some psychologists specialize in treating online addiction, and many support groups are available.

techno-obsessives
Individuals obsessed with technological devices.

Closely related to online addicts are **techno-obsessives**, people who cannot detach from technology and keep information technology devices poised for immediate use in the office and elsewhere. These are the people who keep on hand devices such as cellular telephones, palm-size computers, and laptop computers. A study showed that 29 percent of e-mail users feel anxious about important messages that may be waiting for them.[38]

As you will read in Chapter 6, information technology has contributed heavily to repetitive stress disorders in the workplace. In addition to well-designed workplaces, a new technology is improving that may decrease repetitive motion disorders. Voice recognition systems enable computer users to dictate commands into word processors, thereby cutting back on keyboarding. The software is cumbersome at present because it has to be adapted to an individual user's speech patterns, including pronunciation and accents. Dictation software now allows for continuous speech, rather than pauses between words as in the past. Two such programs are Dragon NaturallySpeaking and IBM Viavoice. But watch out for the "Wreck a nice beach" problem. (Repeat "Wreck a nice beach" a few times until you get the joke.)

A problem of considerable magnitude is that customer service sometimes deteriorates because of information technology. Many banks, for example, force customers with a service problem to call an 800 number rather than allowing them to deal with a branch representative. A voice-response system instructs the customer to punch in lengthy account numbers and make choices from a complicated menu. The process is time-consuming and impersonal, and difficult for customers unfamiliar with information technology. A related problem is that highly automated customer-service operations may appear unfriendly and detached.

Information technology has resulted in *wired managerial workers*. As a result of being electronically connected to the office at all times, many managers and professionals complain that their employers expect them to be always available for consultation. Many managers, for example, are expected to bring pagers and cellular telephones on vacation so they can respond to inquiries from the office.

THE INTERNET AND THE MANAGER'S JOB

Explain how the Internet influences the manager's job.

As implied from the previous discussion, the Internet has a profound impact on how business is conducted. As a consequence, managerial work is also influenced by the Internet. The effects are more direct with respect to the technical problem solver role of a manager who might be contributing ideas about such work as marketing, purchasing, and information systems. Even when managers are not directly involved in such specialized activities, they are still concerned with making decisions about the Internet.

A survey by Price Waterhouse LLP found that many CEOs are using the Internet to gain an edge over the competition. These business leaders are making Internet technology part of their corporate strategy. Fifty-six percent use the Internet to communicate with customers, and 43 percent market their products on line. Peter Solomon, the chairman of an investment bank, observes that the Internet is a revolutionary business tool—a sentiment echoed by thousands of other businesspersons and infotech specialists.[39] Here we describe briefly four of the ways in which the Internet has a combined influence on business and managers.

E - Commerce

The biggest impact of the Internet on business is that much commerce is now transacted on the Internet. Business firms purchase from each other over the Internet, and consumers buy products directly in a similar manner. Eighty percent of business conducted on the Net today is between firms rather than by individuals. E-commerce in the United States alone is predicted to reach $349 billion by 2002.[40] Manufacturers of computers and other high-tech hardware have been pioneers in selling over the Net. Almost one-half of durable goods manufacturers have followed their path. Wholesalers of office supplies, electronic goods, and scientific instruments also make extensive use of E-commerce. Many small-business owners welcome conducting business over the Internet because they can compete better with larger firms than if they sold through direct sales workers or distributors. A Web site can make any size enterprise appear big.

Sales of domestic products and services including books, airline tickets, sporting event and concert tickets, food, wine, and houses are surging on the Internet. Exhibit 2-5 presents an advertisement from a well-known consumer-products company, and points to some of the enhancements offered by E-commerce.

Managerial work is affected by E-commerce in two major ways. First, the manager must be familiar with E-commerce to help in suggesting strategies for marketing over the Internet and resolving problems. Second, managers who formerly worked directly with salespeople (such as coaching and motivating) may have many fewer subordinates. One **Web master** might replace 50 face-to-face salespeople. The manager would therefore have fewer people to supervise, and would spend more time developing business strategy and perhaps interacting with a few major customers.

Web master
An individual responsible for the creation and maintenance of a company's Web site.

Efficiencies in Industrial Purchasing

An important consequence of E-commerce is that it sometimes enables companies to purchase more efficiently than they could by speaking to sales representatives or purchasing through catalogs or over the telephone. A growing number of compa-

EXHIBIT
25

48

*An Example of
Consumer-oriented E-com-
merce.*

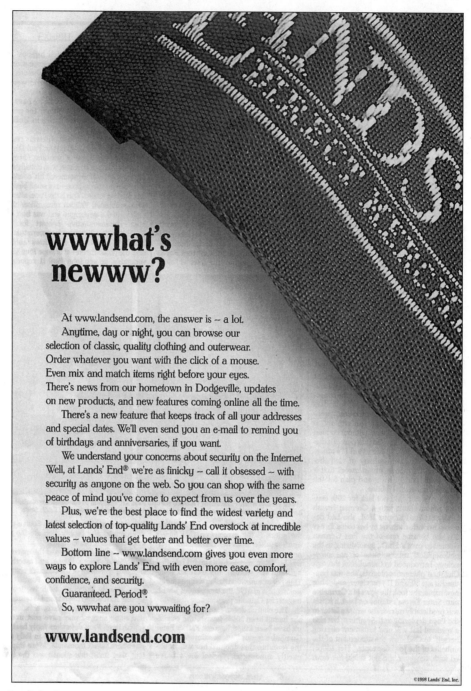

wwwhat's newww?

At www.landsend.com, the answer is -- a lot.

Anytime, day or night, you can browse our selection of classic, quality clothing and outerwear. Order whatever you want with the click of a mouse. Even mix and match items right before your eyes. There's news from our hometown in Dodgeville, updates on new products, and new features coming online all the time.

There's a new feature that keeps track of all your addresses and special dates. We'll even send you an e-mail to remind you of birthdays and anniversaries, if you want.

We understand your concerns about security on the Internet. Well, at Lands' End® we're as finicky -- call it obsessed -- with security as anyone on the web. So you can shop with the same peace of mind you've come to expect from us over the years.

Plus, we're the best place to find the widest variety and latest selection of top-quality Lands' End overstock at incredible values -- values that get better and better over time.

Bottom line -- www.landsend.com gives you even more ways to explore Lands' End with even more ease, comfort, confidence, and security.

Guaranteed. Period®.

So, wwwhat are you wwwaiting for?

www.landsend.com

©1998 Lands' End, Inc.

Source: Reprinted with permission of Lands' End, Inc.

nies encourage both customers and suppliers to conduct business with them over the Internet. An example is Anson Machine & Manufacturing in Louisville, Kentucky. It sells millions of dollars worth of parts to General Electric Co.'s aircraft-engine unit over the Internet. Several years ago GE purchasing managers invited an Anson manager to use a new bulletin board system to bid on the business. Now several other GE units purchase from him, using the same system.[41]

Companies find that the transaction costs are smaller, and time is saved, by purchasing over the Net. As a result, product prices tend to be lower than purchasing through sales representatives or catalogs. The purchaser can also ask many questions on line about products and services. A good starting point for any company wanting to purchase over the Internet would be to visit www.yahoo.com/business. The manager or professional can quickly locate companies that offer the product or service he or she needs, and then make inquiries.

Purchasing over the Net is also a time saver because the purchasing agents spend less time talking to and being entertained by sales representatives. Be aware, however, that E-commerce has not completely eliminated the human touch in business. Many big deals are still made over lunch and on the golf course, and executives tend to purchase from people they like.

Internet-Based Pressures Toward Cost Control

The changing flow of information created by the Internet has tipped the balance of power from sellers to buyers. In the past, sellers had almost all the information about profit margins and manufacturer's true costs. Industrial buyers and individual consumers can now use the Web to uncover information about costs that puts them on the same level as professionals.[42] Many prospective car purchasers today walk into dealer's offices with copies of factory invoices showing the true dealer cost of a given car model. The dealer can no longer claim, "We are giving you this car at $50 over dealer cost," unless it is true.

Given that the buyer knows so much about costs, the seller must offer products with lower profit margins than in the past. The manager is therefore responsible for controlling costs in any sensible way possible including reducing turnover, minimizing expenditures, and using the Internet for purchasing! To reduce costs, one manager decided to discontinue the practice of allowing company employees to accumulate frequent flyer miles when they traveled on company business. Instead, the company would keep the miles, thus getting some company airplanes trips for free.

Living with Increased Visibility

An unanticipated consequence of the Internet is that companies must adjust to a different kind of visibility than in the past. People who like or dislike the organization can disseminate this information over the Internet. Fan sites and anti-fan sites appear more frequently on the Internet. At one point, for example, over 200 Web sites could be found that expressed disapproval of Bill Gates and Microsoft. Often these negative comments can be dismissed as the work of jealous people or kooks, but the exposure can badly hurt the corporate image. Another problem is that disgruntled employees might disseminate over the Internet nasty comments about the organization.

The managerial action required in relation to increased visibility is to work extra hard to create fans, and deal openly with the issues that make people dislike you. Suppose a company subcontracts the manufacture of a clothing line to a company that hires prison labor at very low wages under punitive working conditions. The company might set higher standards for subcontractors to minimize negative publicity over the Net.[43]

SUMMARY OF KEY POINTS

 Appreciate the importance of multinational corporations and international markets.

Multinational corporations (MNCs) are at the heart of international business. The continued growth of the MNC has been facilitated by the North American Free Trade Agreement, the General Agreement on Tariffs and Trade, and the European Union.

 Recognize the importance of sensitivity to cultural differences in the international enterprise.

The guiding principle for people involved in international enterprise is sensitivity to cultural differences. Candidates for foreign assignments generally receive training in the language and customs of the country in which they will work. Another approach to developing cross-cultural sensitivity is to recognize national differences in managerial styles.

 Identify major challenges facing the global managerial worker.

Challenges facing global managerial workers include economic crises in other countries (such as the Asian crisis), balance of trade problems, collecting money, the liability of being a foreigner, human rights violations, culture shock, and differences in negotiating style.

 Explain various methods of entry into world markets.

Firms enter global markets via the following methods: exporting, licensing, local warehousing and selling, local assembly and packing, joint ventures, direct foreign investment, global merger, and global startup.

 Pinpoint success factors in the global marketplace.

Success factors for the global marketplace include (a) think globally, act locally, (b) diversify into similar product markets, (c) be familiar with local business concepts, laws, and customs, (d) recruit talented nationals, (e) research and assess potential markets, (f) hire or develop multicultural workers, and (g) understand your competitors, potential partners, and the diverse members of the management team.

 Explain the importance of valuing demographic and cultural diversity in the workplace.

It is as important to deal effectively with different cultural groups within one's own country as it is to deal effectively with people from other countries. Diversity often brings a competitive advantage to the firm, including the following: improved productivity and profits; recruiting and retaining talented people; improved customer service; and the reduction of possible cultural bloopers. Organizational practices favoring diversity include (a) corporate policies favoring diversity, (b) employee network groups, and (c) valuing diversity training programs.

 Present an overview of how information technology influences a manager's job.

Positive consequences of IT on the manager's job include improved productivity and teamwork, gaining competitive advantage, improved customer service and supplier relationships, enhanced communication and coordination, quick access to vast information, enhanced analysis of data and decision making, and facilitation of empowerment and flatter organizations. Negative consequences of information technology include computer goofing off, online addiction, techno-obsessive behavior, repetitive motion disorders, rude customer service, and wired managerial workers.

 Explain how the Internet influences the manager's job.

Many CEOs are using the Internet to gain an edge over the competition. Managerial work in general is affected by four key factors related to the Internet : conducting business through E-commerce; efficiencies in industrial purchasing; pressures toward cost control; and living with increased visibility.

KEY TERMS AND PHRASES

QUESTIONS

1. Why do so many firms go through the trouble of expanding into overseas markets?
2. Assume that an American manager is sent abroad to manage in a division in another country. Explain whether that manager should change styles to fit the preferred management style in the other country.
3. If you were a top-level manager or business owner, how would the Asian crisis that started in the late 1990s affect your opinion about trading with Asian countries?
4. What steps can you take, starting this week, to ready yourself to become a multicultural worker?
5. Suppose an African-American couple opens a restaurant that serves African cuisine, hoping to appeal mostly to people of African descent. The restaurant is a big success, yet the couple finds that about 40 percent of its clientele are Caucasians. Should the restaurant owners then hire several Caucasians so the employee mix will match the customer mix?
6. What do you regard as the most important use a manager can make of information technology?
7. Describe at least one way in which information technology influences the way a manager manages people.

SKILL-BUILDING EXERCISE 2-A: Going International

The class organizes into groups of about five members who assume the roles of the members of the management team of a company that produces videos of rap music and country music. Annual sales volume in North America is now about $4 million. The company president says she wants to expand overseas and puts the team in charge of the project. Sketch out your plans for going international. Identify the strengths and weaknesses of your plans. The various teams will then compare plans, including specific tactics.

INTERNET SKILL-BUILDING EXERCISE: Becoming Multicultural

A useful way of developing skills in a second language, and learning more about another culture, is to create a "bookmark" or "favorite" written in your target language. In this way, each time you go on the Internet on your own computer, your cover page will contain fresh information in the language you want to develop. To get started, use a search engine like Yahoo or Excite that offers choices in several languages. Enter a key word like "newspaper" or "current events" in the search probe. Once you find a suitable choice, enter the edit function for "Favorites" or "Bookmarks" and insert that newspaper as your cover page. For example, imagine that French were your choice. The Yahoo France search engine might have brought you to www.france2.fr. This Web site keeps you abreast of French and international news, sports, and cultural events—written in French. Now every time you access the Internet, you can spend five minutes becoming multicultural. You can save a lot of travel costs and time using the Internet to help you become multicultural.

CASE PROBLEM 2-A: The Tale of a Cultural Translator

Gunnar Beeth works in seven languages throughout Europe, from his own executive search firm, IMA-CONSULT S.A. in Brussels, Belgium. He observes that joint ventures between Western and Japanese companies usually run into a series of small conflicts that escalate over the years. The small conflicts often become big emotional battles, due mainly to cultural differences. Beeth tells the tale of how one company he worked for as a director of international operations attempted to avoid a culture clash primarily through the activities of one employee:

George Schreiber was an installation engineer responsible for starting up our equipment. The company needed to send a person to train the new Japanese employees in the unique technology. Schreiber accepted a two-year contract for a temporary transfer to Japan. Before departing he was first sent to an intensive course in Japanese. Schreiber did not belong to the management group in the American company but had a solid understanding of the technical products, their installation, and use. On this basis he was highly qualified for training the Japanese engineers.

Schreiber quickly became well accepted by the Japanese employees. The Japanese managers perceived that the nonassertive Schreiber was no threat to their man-

52

agement careers, despite representing the U.S. owner. So they did not hesitate to ask his advice on a large number of matters, some outside his expertise but within his sharply developed common sense. The engineers throughout the company appreciated Schreiber's frequent help with a multitude of problems they encountered in the beginning. Soon the engineers began consulting Schreiber on almost any problem they faced. The support workers in the office were eager to help this nice American bachelor improve his wretched spoken Japanese.

The joint venture became profitable ahead of schedule, and was thriving and growing. Scheiber's first two-year contract came to an end. By that time he had learned Japanese customs. His spoken Japanese improved to a satisfactory level. He drank green tea at all hours, ate rice at all meals, and liked to sleep on Japanese tatami mats instead of a bed. He had become "tatamized."

Schreiber was offered a second two-year contract, which he accepted immediately. Other contracts followed for the joint venture. The venture soon had more than 100 Japanese employees, and the Japanese engineers soon surpassed Schreiber in the intricacies of the new equipment, which changed rapidly. As a consequence, Schreiber had nothing left to teach them in technical matters. Instead of returning to the American company, or finding new employment, Schreiber became a *cultural translator*.

When a message arrived from the American headquarters and the capable Japanese joint-venture president felt offended, he stormed into Schreiber's small office and threw the message in front of him, fuming. George read the message and explained calmly that the American had not really meant it in the way such a message would be understood in Japan.

For communication from Japan to the United States, the written English of one of the Japanese secretaries was quite adequate. But at times something far more important than good Japanese was needed. At one time the American auditors demanded an explanation for two expense items. One issue was why the Japanese company spent $46,534 on 874 December holiday presents. Another was why the Japanese affiliate continued to keep a chemist on the payroll whose specialty had become obsolete a year earlier.

When the Western managers came traveling to Japan, Schreiber accompanied them to ensure that they didn't do or say anything too stupid, from the Japanese viewpoint. Whenever they did, he corrected them at once: "What you really mean is. . . ." And he did the same thing from the opposite direction. He prevented many conflicts from arising, and he smoothed over small conflicts before they became big, emotional, and costly.

Discussion Questions

1. How justifiable is it to keep a full-time employee on the payroll as a "cultural translator"?
2. Placing yourself in George Schreiber's role, how would you explain to the auditor, the money spent on the holiday gifts and the salary paid to the obsolete engineer?
3. What alternatives can you recommend to renewing Schreiber's contract for a third term?

Source: Adapted from Gunnar Beeth, "Multicultural Managers Wanted," *Management Review*, May 1997, p. 17.

CASE PROBLEM 2-B: The Great International Computer Worker Debate

Steve D. Schultz, a computer programmer, is skeptical whether there is really a labor shortage in Silicon Valley. The 48-year-old information technology worker spent five years designing software for a drug manufacturer. Then his employer suddenly brought in a junior programmer from Taiwan at half the $160,000 Schultz earned as a contract employee.

When Schultz's contract was up for renewal, the drugmaker declined to offer him a new contract. Schultz searched for four months for a new position but could not find employment, even by taking a giant pay cut. Finally, his employer called him back as a temporary worker to train his replacement. "The computer industry isn't begging for workers," claims Schultz. "It's looking for 20-year-olds who will put in 80-hour weeks or people from overseas who will be captive at one company."

For several years computer industry officials have warned that labor shortages in skilled workers could slow down the industry. Representatives from Microsoft Corp., Intel Corp., and other leading high-tech firms have pleaded with Congress to double the 65,000 visas for skilled foreign workers. The influx of foreign information technology specialists would help fill the 350,000 vacant positions. According to Harris N. Miller, president of the Information Technology Association, a trade group, high-tech firms are lacking the talent to develop new products and grow their businesses.

Yet some industry analysts think Schultz might be revealing an important truth. They reason that employment has jumped only for the highest-skilled computer scientists, not programmers or systems analysts. Many of the analyst and programmer positions go to immigrants on high-skills visas. An economist, Robert L. Lerman, notes that "There's no evidence that the computer industry has worse labor shortages than other high-skilled industries." He also notes that the information technology industry may feel the pinch more sharply because it relies more heavily on temporary employees than do other industries. Microsoft, for example, hires 5,000 contract workers to supplement its 17,000 permanent U.S. employees.

Some critics argue that age discrimination contributes to the shortage of information technology specialists, particularly programmers. The demanding work pace is difficult to maintain when workers form a committed relationship or when they have children. Employers also prefer to hire recent graduates who know the latest computer languages. The director of recruiting at Microsoft has commented that recent graduates have good training and are open to new technologies.

According to the high-skills visa program, American employers are required to pay foreigners the going U.S. wage for the same work. Yet a U.S. Department of Labor audit found that three-fourths of employers could not produce evidence that visa workers are paid as well as their American counterparts. Pritchard of Microsoft pointed out that since his company pays to relocate workers, they are actually paid more than Americans.

During a meeting of Silicon Valley managers, the director of recruiting at one of the lesser known information technology companies addressed the group about the problem of hiring so many programmers and systems analysts from other countries. He also discussed the problem of alleged age discrimination. His major recommendations were as follows:

- Hire information technology workers from other countries based on the proportion of the world population represented by that country. For example, given that India rep-

resents about one-sixth the world population, about one-sixth of our computer specialists should be from India.
- Implement a quota system for information technology workers age 40-and-over, whereby one-fifth of our positions should be filled by people in the 40-and-over age bracket.
- Place restrictions on our working hours, whereby information technology workers should be encouraged to work no more than 55 hours per week.

One of the managers present at the meeting commented, "Imposing these restrictions on ourselves would be more severe than any restriction the government could dream up. Why put ourselves in a position that could make recruiting computer specialists even more difficult than it is now?"

Another manager retorted, "Our speaker raises some good points. If we don't take a better planned approach to hiring overseas workers for our information technology positions, restrictive government legislation might be coming down the road."

Discussion Questions

1. What policy changes might companies make to lessen their shortage of high-level computer workers?
2. Is it justifiable for U.S. companies to pay computer programmers and systems analysts from other countries less than they do Americans, when the foreign workers are working in the United States?
3. What is your evaluation of the recommendations given by the manager at the meeting of representatives from Silicon Valley companies?

Source: Some of the facts in this case are from Aaron Bernstein and Steve Hamm, "Is There Really a Techie Shortage? Yes—But It's Not as Dire as the Computer Industry Says," *Business Week,* June 29, 1998, pp. 93, 94.

ENDNOTES

1. Based on information in Michael Shari and Emily Thornton, "Carmakers are Hitting the Wall," *Business Week*, May 11, 1998, p. 44; www.Texmaco.com.
2. Geri Smith and Elisabeth Malkin, "Why Mexico Scares the UAW," *Business Week*, August 3, 1998, p. 37
3. Thane Peterson, "The Euro," *Business Week*, April 27, 1998, pp. 90–94.
4. Adam Pilarski, "Globalization—Working Harder for Less," *Business Forum*, Winter/Spring 1996, pp. 36–37.
5. Gunnar Beeth, "Multicultural Managers Wanted," *Management Review*, May 1997, p. 17.
6. Marvina Shilling, "Avoid Expatriate Culture Shock," *HRMagazine*, July 1993, p. 58.
7. Geert Hofstede, "Cultural Constraints in Management Theories," *The Academy of Management Executive*, February 1993, pp.
81–94; David C. Thomas and Elizabeth C. Ravlin, "Responses of Employees to Cultural Adaptation by a Foreign Manager," *Journal of Applied Psychology*, February 1995, p. 138.
8. Brian Bremner, "Japan's Real Crisis," *Business Week*, May 18, 1998; p. 138; Bruce Nussbaum, "Time to Act," *Business Week*, September 14, 1998, p. 34.
9. "U.S., Europe Carrying the Load," Associated Press story, October 3, 1998.
10. Srilata Zaheer, "Overcoming the Liability of Foreignesss," *Academy of Management Journal*, April 1995, pp. 341–363.
11. "Group Lists U.S. Rights Abuses," Associated Press story, October 6, 1998.
12. Harry C. Triandis, *Culture and Social Behavior* (New York: McGraw-Hill, 1994), p. 263.
13. Margaret A. Shaffer and David A. Harrison, "Expatriates' Psych-

ological Withdrawal from International Assignments: Work, Non-work, and Family Influences," *Personnel Psychology*, Spring 1998, p. 114.

14. Paul Blustein, "China Plays Rough: 'Invest and Transfer Technology, or No Market Access,'" *The Washington Post*, October 25, 1997, p. C1.

15. Eugene H. Fram and Riad A. Ajami, "International Distributors and the Role of US Top Management: A Requirement for Export Competitiveness?" *Journal of Business and Industrial Marketing*, 9:4, pp. 33–44.

16. Charles C. Snow, Sue Canney Davison, Scott A. Snell, and Donald C. Hambrick, "Use Transnational Teams to Globalize Your Company," *Organizational Dynamics*, Spring 1996, p. 52.

17. Harry G. Barkema and Freek Vermeulen, "International Expansion through Start-Up or Acquisition: A Learning Perpsective," *Academy of Management Journal*, February 1998, pp. 7–26.

18. Charlene Marmer Solomon, "Corporate Pioneers Navigate Global Mergers," *Global Workforce* (Supplement to *Workforce*), September 1998, p. 14.

19. Benjamin M. Oviatt and Patricia Phillips McDougall, "Global Start-Ups: Entrepreneurs on a Wordwide Stage," *The Academy of Management Executive*, May 1995, p. 30.

20. Stephen Baker, "Finally, Europeans Are Storming the Net," *Business Week*, May 11, 1998, pp. 48–49.

21. Michael A. Hitt and R. Duane Ireland, "Building Competitive Strength in International Markets," *Long Range Planning*, February 1987, pp. 115–122.

22. Valerie Frazee, "Handling Recruiting as a Business Traveler," *Global Workforce* (Supplement to *Workforce*), July 1998, p. 22.

23. Charlene Marmer Solomon, "Learning to Manage Host-country Nationals," *Personnel Journal*, March 1995, p. 61.

24. Michael A. Hitt, Beverly B. Tyler, Camilla Hardee, and Daewoo Park, "Understanding Strategic Intent in the Global Marketplace," *The Academy of Management Executive*, May 1995, p. 18.

25. Sherri Eng, "Diversity Good for Business," Knight Ridder News story, December 8, 1997.

26. Norman Lockman, "Corporations Turning to the Diversity 'Tool'," *Wilmington News Journal* syndicated column, February 24, 1998.

27. Harris Collingwood, "Who Handles a Diverse Work Force Best?" *Working Woman*, February 1996, p. 25.

28. Patricia Digh, "Well-Managed Employee Networks Add Business Value," *HRMagazine*, August 1997, pp. 67–72.

29. R. Roosevelt Thomas, Jr., *Beyond Race and Gender: Unleashing the Power of Your Total Work Force by Managing Diversity* (New York: AMACOM, 1991), p. 25.

30. Survey by *Chief Executive Magazine* and Anderson Consulting reported in Milldlred L. Culp, "Survey Shows CEOs Are Techno Savy," Passage Media, October 11, 1998.

31. "Do Computers Slow Us Down?" *Fortune*, March 30, 1998, pp. 34–35.

32. Bronwyn Fryer, "Managing Technology When You're Not a Techie," *Working Woman*, October 1995, p. 24.

33. Gary McWilliams, "Technology Is What's Driving This Business," *Business Week*, November 3, 1997, p. 146.

34. Heather Page, "Remote Control," *Entrepreneur*, October 1998, p. 146.

35. Mary J. Cronin, "Ford's Intranet Success," *Fortune*, March 30, 1998, p. 158.

36. Heather Page, "Wired for Success," *Entrepreneur*, May 1997, p. 132.

37. "Ask Success," *Success*, August 1998, p. 26.

38. Yankelovich Partners survey reported in Mildred Culp, "Are You 'Techno-obsessive?' Step Back," Passage Media, August 23, 1998.

39. Anthony Effinger, "CEOs are Joining the Wired World," Bloomberg News story, February 23, 1998.

40. Peter Coy, "You Ain't Seen Nothin' Yet," *Business Week*, June 22, 1998, p. 130.

41. "E-Sourcing: 'A Cheaper Way of Doing Business'," *Business Week*, August 5, 1998, pp. 82–83.

42. "Net Profits: Making the Internet Work for You and Your Business," *Fortune Technology Buyer's Guide*, July 27, 1998, p. 241.

43. Esther Dyson, "Mirror, Mirror, on the Wall," *Harvard Business Review*, September–October 1997, pp. 24–25.

Chapter Three

The new corporate wallet card is no longer an identification tag or a mission statement. It's an invitation to turn in coworkers for ethics abuses such as theft, harassment, or accepting kickbacks. Bausch & Lomb Inc., a major manufacturer of vision-care products, began issuing the wallet cards a couple of years ago. Printed on each card is a toll-free, 24-hour, seven-day-a-week hotline run by Pinkerton Services Group, a division of the nationwide security company. Employees who are uncomfortable talking to management are urged to call, even to report petty workplace conflicts.

In starting the ethics hotline, Bausch & Lomb (B&L) joins a legion of other corporations across the United States. Pinkerton has signed 800 clients, mostly large companies, since introducing the hotline five years ago. Ethically challenged companies are embracing the trend. Increasingly the ethics job is being outsourced. W. Michael Hoffman, an ethics specialist, said hotlines used to be viewed as "1-800-RATFINK." Now, though, dial-in programs run by independent companies are gaining credibility because many employees feel safer having their complaints heard by a neutral third party.

Here's how the program works: An employee calls the number and gets a Pinkerton counselor who has been trained to elicit information from the caller. If the caller wants to remain anonymous, the Pinkerton employee assigns a code number to the case,

OBJECTIVES

After studying this chapter and doing the exercises, you should be able to:

1 Identify the philosophical principles behind business ethics.

2 Explain how values relate to ethics.

3 Identify factors contributing to lax ethics, and common ethical temptations and violations.

4 Apply a guide to ethical decision making.

5 Describe the stakeholder viewpoint of social responsibility, and corporate social performance.

6 Present an overview of social-responsibility initiatives.

7 Summarize the benefits of ethical and socially responsible behavior, and how managers can create an environment that fosters such behavior.

Ethics and Social Responsibility

takes a report, and prioritizes the call. An "A" complaint, such as a worker storing weapons in a desk, would merit immediate attention. A less serious complaint, such as on-the-job favoritism, would be referred to B&L's human resources department. All complaints are turned over to the client company for investigation. Clay Osborne, B&L's director of diversity and work environment, said, "It's just a tool we can use to reinforce that we are creating a culture where misconduct is not tolerated by anyone."[1]

The hotline for reporting possible legal and ethical violations illustrates the importance many business firms today place on keeping ethical problems under control. Many of the firms using the hotline have faced serious ethical violations in the past. These firms use the Pinkerton service to help prevent further problems. The purpose of this chapter is to explain the importance of ethics and social responsibility. To accomplish this purpose we present various aspects of ethics and social responsibility. We also present guidelines to help managerial workers to make ethical decisions and to conduct socially responsible acts.

BUSINESS ETHICS

Understanding and practicing good business ethics is an important part of a manager's job. One of many reasons ethics are important is that customers and suppliers prefer to deal with ethical companies. **Ethics** is the study of moral obligation, or separating right from wrong. Although many unethical acts are illegal, others are legal. An example of an illegal unethical act is giving a government official a kickback for placing a contract with a specific firm. An example of a legal, yet unethical, practice is hiring an employee away from a competitor, "picking her brains" for competitive ideas, and then eliminating her job.

A useful perspective in understanding business ethics emphasizes **moral intensity**, or the magnitude of an unethical act.[2] When an unethical act is not of large consequence, a person might behave unethically without much thought. However, if the act is of large consequence, the person might refrain from unethical or illegal behavior. For example, a manager might make a photocopy of an entire book or copy someone else's software (both unethical and illegal acts). The same manager, however, might hesitate to dump toxins into a river.

Business ethics will be mentioned at various places in this text. Here we approach the subject from several perspectives: philosophical principles, values, contributing factors to ethical problems, common ethical problems, and a guide to ethical decision making. To better relate the study of ethics to yourself, take the self-quiz presented in Exhibit 3-1.

Philosophical Principles Underlying Business Ethics

A standard way of understanding ethical decision making is to know the philosophical basis for making these decisions. When attempting to decide what is right and wrong, managerial workers can focus on (1) consequence; (2) duties, obligations, and principles; or (3) integrity.[3]

FOCUS ON CONSEQUENCES   When attempting to decide what is right or wrong, people can sometimes focus on the consequences of their decision or action. According to this criterion, if no one gets hurt, the decision is ethical.

---

ethics
The study of moral obligation, or separating right from wrong.

moral intensity
The magnitude of an unethical act.

① Identify the philosophical principles behind business ethics.

The Ethical Reasoning Inventory

Describe how much you agree with each of the following statements, using the following scale: disagree strongly (DS); disagree (D); neutral (N); agree (A); agree strongly (AS). Circle the answer that best fits your level of agreement.

	DS	D	N	A	AS
1. When applying for a job, I would cover up the fact that I had been fired from my most recent job.	5	4	3	2	1
2. Cheating just a few dollars in one's favor on an expense account is OK if the person needed the money.	5	4	3	2	1
3. Employees should inform on each other for wrongdoing	1	2	3	4	5
4. It is acceptable to give approximate figures for expense account items when one does not have all the receipts.	5	4	3	2	1
5. I see no problem with conducting a little personal business on company time.	5	4	3	2	1
6. I would fix up a purchasing agent with a date just to close a sale.	5	4	3	2	1
7. To make a sale, I would stretch the truth about a delivery date.	5	4	3	2	1
8. I would flirt with my boss just to get a bigger salary increase.	5	4	3	2	1
9. If I received $100 for doing some odd jobs, I would report it on my income tax returns.	1	2	3	4	5
10. I see no harm in taking home a few office supplies.	5	4	3	2	1
11. It is acceptable to read the e-mail and fax messages of coworkers even when not invited to do so.	5	4	3	2	1
12. It is unacceptable to call in sick to take a day off, even if only done once or twice a year.	1	2	3	4	5
13. I would accept a permanent, full-time job even if I knew I wanted the job for only six months.	5	4	3	2	1
14. I would check company policy before accepting an expensive gift from a supplier.	1	2	3	4	5
15. To be successful in business, a person usually has to ignore ethics.	5	4	3	2	1
16. If I were physically attracted toward a job candidate, I would hire him or her over another candidate.	5	4	3	2	1
17. I tell the truth all the time on the job.	1	2	3	4	5
18. Software should never be copied, except as authorized by the publisher.	1	2	3	4	5
19. I would authorize accepting an office machine on a 30-day trial period, even if I knew I had no intention of making a purchase.	5	4	3	2	1
20. I would never accept credit for a coworker's ideas.	1	2	3	4	5

Scoring and interpretation: Add the numbers you have circled to obtain your score.

90–100 You are a strongly ethical person who may take a little ribbing from coworkers for being too straight-laced.

60–89 You show an average degree of ethical awareness, and therefore should become more sensitive to ethical issues.

41–59 Your ethics are underdeveloped, but you have at least some awareness of ethical issues. You need to raise your level of awareness about ethical issues.

20–40 Your ethical values are far below contemporary standards in business. Begin a serious study of business ethics.

Focusing on consequences is often referred to as *utilitarianism*. The decision maker is concerned with the utility of the decision. What really counts is the net balance of good consequences over bad. An automotive body shop manager, for example, might decide that using low-quality replacement fenders is ethically wrong because the fender will rust quickly. To focus on consequences, the decision maker would have to be aware of all the good and bad consequences of a given decision. The body-shop manager would have to estimate such factors as how angry customers would be whose cars were repaired with inferior parts, and how much negative publicity would result.

FOCUS ON DUTIES, OBLIGATIONS, AND PRINCIPLES

Another approach to making an ethical decision is to examine one's duties in making the decision. The theories underlying this approach are referred to as *deontological*, from the Greek word *deon*, or duty. The deontological approach is based on universal principles such as honesty, fairness, justice, and respect for persons and property.

Rights, such as the rights for privacy and safety, are also important. From a deontological perspective, the principles are more important than the consequences. If a given decision violates one of these universal principles, it is automatically unethical even if nobody gets hurt. An ethical body-shop manager might think "It just isn't right to use replacement fenders that are not authorized by the automobile manufacturer. Whether or not these parts rust quickly is a secondary consideration."

FOCUS ON INTEGRITY (VIRTUE ETHICS)

The third criterion for determining the ethics of behavior focuses on the character of the person involved in the decision or action. If the person in question has good character, and genuine motivation and intentions, he or she is behaving ethically. The ingredients making up character will often include the two other ethical criteria. One might judge a person to have good character if she or he follows the right principles and respects the rights of others.

The decision maker's environment, or community, helps define what integrity means. You might have more lenient ethical standards for a person selling you a speculative investment than you would for a bank vice-president who accepted your cash deposit.

The virtue ethics of managers and professionals who belong to professional societies can be judged readily. Business-related professions having codes of ethics include accountants, purchasing managers, and certified financial planners. To the extent that the person abides by the tenets of the stated code, he or she is behaving ethically. An example of such a tenet would be for a financial planner to be explicit about any commissions gained from a client accepting the advice.

When faced with a complex ethical decision, a manager would be best advised to incorporate all three philosophical approaches. The manager might think through the consequences of a decision, along with an analysis of duties, obligations, principles, and intentions. A case in point took place several years ago. A deranged person, labeled the Unabomber, had threatened to set off an explosion in the Los Angeles airport, LAX. He then said he was not serious. Many managers had to decide whether to send subordinates on business trips that went through LAX. Should business be conducted as usual despite the remote possibility of harm? To reach a decision, managers had to think through all three philosophical principles related to ethics.

Values and Ethics

Values are closely related to ethics. Values can be considered clear statements of what is critically important. Ethics become the vehicle for converting values into actions, or doing the right thing. For example, a *clean environment* is a value, whereas *not littering* is practicing ethics.[4] Many firms contend that they "put people before profits" (a value). If this were true, a manager would avoid actions such as delaying payments to a vendor just to hold on to money longer, or firing a group member for having negotiated a deal that lost money.

A person's values also influence which kind of behaviors he or she believes are ethical. An executive who strongly values profits might not find it unethical to raise prices more than are needed to cover additional costs. Another executive who strongly values family life might suggest that the company invest money in an on-premises child-care center.

Values are also important because the right values can lead to a competitive advantage. According to business writer Perry Pascarella, winning executives see values as a competitive tool that enables their organizations to respond quickly and appropriately. These executives invest time in nurturing values they think will help the organization, including honesty, integrity, teamwork, and risk taking. Another key value is satisfying the customer.[5] A contributing factor to the success of Land's End (remember the ad in Chapter 2) is that associates are taught to try extra hard to please customers.

The concept of **ethically centered management** helps put some teeth into an abstract discussion of how values relate to ethics. Ethically centered management emphasizes that the high quality of an end product takes precedence over its scheduled completion. At the same time, it sets high quality standards for dealing with employees and managing production. Robert Elliott Allinson believes that many work-related catastrophes can be attributed to a management team that is not ethically centered. One such example was the failure of the Hubbell telescope to function properly in outer space because of a flaw in a mirror. (The problem was later corrected.)

According to Allinson, management acted irresponsibly by not emphasizing the importance of quality control and clearly designating officials to be in charge of quality. Also, top management at NASA disowned responsibility for finding out and ensuring that the end product was problem-free and of highest quality.[6]

Contributing Factors to Ethical Problems

Individuals, organizations, and society itself must share some of the blame for the prevalence of unethical behavior in the workplace. Major contributors to unethical behavior are an individual's greed and gluttony, or the desire to maximize self-gain at the expense of others.

Another major contributor to unethical behavior is an organizational atmosphere that condones such behavior. According to one study, even employees with high ethical standards may stray in a climate that rewards unethical behavior. A firm's official code of ethics may not coincide with its actual climate. It is the firm's top executives who set the company's moral tone.[7]

A more recent study on unethical employees found similar results. One-third of employees admitted to having stolen from their employer. The most frequent forms of theft were misuse of the employee-discount privilege and theft of company mer-

Explain how values relate to ethics.

ethically centered management
An approach to management that emphasizes that the high quality of an end product takes precedence over its scheduled completion.

Identify factors contributing to lax ethics, and common ethical temptations and violations.

chandise or property. The researchers concluded that a perceived management climate more lenient than the norm for management is accompanied by employee attitudes that are more protheft. The opposite was also true: a management climate strongly opposed to theft leads to stronger antitheft attitudes by employees.[8]

A third case of unethical behavior is **moral laxity**, a slippage in moral behavior because other issues seem more important at the time. The implication is that the businessperson who behaves unethically has not carefully planned the immoral behavior but lets it occur by not exercising good judgment. Many workplace deaths fit into this category. Over 300 people were killed and about 900 injured when a shopping mall collapsed in Seoul, South Korea. Officials blamed the disaster on shoddy construction and negligence by executives of the shopping complex. Police said that the executives knew the floor was crumbling hours before the disaster. Nevertheless, they decided not to close and left the premises without warning anyone.[9]

Unethical behavior is often triggered by pressure from higher management to achieve goals. One study found that 56 percent of all workers feel some pressure to act unethically or illegally. Forty-eight percent of workers surveyed admitted they had engaged in one or more unethical or illegal actions during the year. Among the most common ethical violations were (a) cutting corners on quality, (b) covering up incidents that would make them look bad, (c) deceiving customers, (d) lying to a supervisor or group member, and (e) taking credit for a coworker's idea.[10] A contributing factor to these five types of unethical behavior is that the person has an incentive for being unethical. For example, if a worker cuts corners on quality, thereby saving the company money (at least in the short run), he or she might be rewarded for good performance. An experiment with business students showed that people are willing to misrepresent the truth if given an incentive.[11]

A new explanation for the cause of unethical behavior emphasizes the strength of relationships among people as a major factor.[12] Assume that two people have close ties to each other, such as having worked together for a long time, or knowing each other both on and off the job. As a consequence, they are likely to behave ethically toward each other on the job. In contrast, if a weak relationship exists between the two people, either party is more likely to engage in an unethical relationship. The owner of an auto service center is more likely to behave unethically toward a stranger passing through town than a long-term customer. The opportunity for unethical behavior between strangers is often minimized because individuals typically do not trust strangers with sensitive information or valuables.

Ethical Temptations and Violations

Certain ethical mistakes, including illegal actions, recur in the workplace. Familiarizing oneself with these behaviors can be helpful in managing the ethical behavior of others as well as monitoring one's own behavior. A list of commonly found ethical temptations and violations, including criminal acts, follows:[13]

1. *Stealing from employers and customers.* Employee theft costs U.S. and Canadian companies about $50 billion annually. Retail employees often steal goods from their employers, and financial service employees often steal money. Examples of theft from customers includes airport baggage handlers who steal from passenger suitcases, and bank employees, stockbrokers, and attorneys who siphon money from customer accounts.

moral laxity
A slippage in moral behavior because other issues seem more important at the time.

60

2. *Illegally copying software.* A rampant problem in the workplace is making unauthorized copies of software for either company or personal use. Similarly, many employees make illegal copies of videos, books, and magazine articles instead of purchasing these products.

3. *Treating people unfairly.* Being fair to people means equity, reciprocity, and impartiality. Fairness revolves around the issue of giving people equal rewards for accomplishing the same amount of work. The goal of human resource legislation is to make decisions about people based on their qualifications and performance—not on the basis of demographic factors like sex, race, or age. A fair working environment is where performance is the only factor that counts (equity). Employer-employee expectations must be understood and met (reciprocity). Prejudice and bias must be eliminated (impartiality).

4. *Sexual harassment.* Sexual harassment involves making compliance with sexual favors a condition of employment, or creating a hostile, intimidating environment related to sexual topics. Harassment violates the law and is also an ethical issue because it is morally wrong and unfair. A study of about 750 women who worked for either a private firm or a university revealed that 65 percent had been sexually harassed at least once during the last 24 months. Furthermore, sexual harassment led to problems of psychological well-being such as dissatisfaction with work. After being harassed, women also tended to be absent and tardy more frequently.[14] Sexual harassment is such a widespread problem that most employers take steps to prevent the problem. Exhibit 3-2 describes actions employers can take to protect themselves against harassment charges.

5. *Conflict of interest.* Part of being ethical is making business judgments only on the basis of the merits in a situation. Imagine that you are a supervisor

---

The U.S. Supreme Court has given companies guidelines on how to protect themselves against sexual-harassment charges. Most of these suggestions reflect actions that many companies are already taking to prevent and control sexual harassment.

- Develop a zero-tolerance policy on harassment, and communicate it to employees.
- Ensure that victims can report abuses without fear of retaliation.
- Take reasonable care to prevent and promptly report any sexually harassing behavior.
- When defending against a charge of sexual harassment, show that an employee failed to use internal procedures for reporting abusive behavior.
- Publicize antiharassment policies aggressively and regularly—in handbooks, on posters, in training sessions, and in reminders in paychecks.
- Give supervisors and employees real-life examples of what could constitute offensive conduct.
- Ensure that workers do not face reprisals if they report offending behavior. Designate several managers to take these complaints so that employees do not have to report the problem to their supervisor, who may be the abuser.
- Train managers at all levels in sexual harassment issues.
- Provide guidelines to senior managers explaining how to conduct investigations that recognize the rights of all parties involved.
- Punishment against harassers should be swift and sure.

Source: Based on information in Susan B. Garland, "Finally, A Corporate Tip Sheet On Sexual Harassment," *Business Week*, July 13, 1998, p. 39; Jonathan A. Segal, "Prevent Now or Pay Later," *HRMagazine*, October 1998, pp. 145–149.

EXHIBIT 3-2

A Corporate Tip Sheet on Sexual Harassment

conflict of interest
A situation that occurs when one's judgment or objectivity is compromised.

who is romantically involved with a worker within the group. When it came time to assigning raises, it would be difficult for you to be objective. A **conflict of interest** occurs when your judgment or objectivity is compromised.

6. *Divulging confidential information.* An ethical person can be trusted by others not to divulge confidential information unless the welfare of others is at stake. The challenge of dealing with confidential information arises in many areas of business, including information about performance-appraisal results, compensation, personal problems of employees, disease status of employees, and coworker bankruptcies.

7. *Misuse of corporate resources.* A corporate resource is anything the company owns, including its name and reputation. Assume that a man named Jason Hedgeworth worked for Microsoft Corporation. It would be unethical for him to establish a software consulting company and put on his letterhead "Jason Hedgeworth, software designer, Microsoft Corporation." Using corporate resources can fall into the gray area, such as whether to borrow a laptop computer to prepare income taxes for a fee.

8. *Greed, gluttony, and avarice.* An ethical temptation, particularly among top-level executives, is to misuse corporate resources in an extravagant, greedy manner. The temptation is greater for top executives because they have more control over resources. Examples of the greedy use of corporate resources include using the corporate jet for personal vacations for oneself, friends, and family members; and paying for personal items with an expense account. A case in point is Lars Bildman, the former chief executive of Astra-USA, a drug company. He bilked the company out of $1 million, including having his house renovated by contractors who were doing work for his company. Bildman instructed the contractors to bury the costs of renovating his home in their bill for legitimate work for Astra.[15]

Apply a guide to ethical decision making.

A Guide to Ethical Decision Making

A practical way of improving ethical decision making is to run contemplated decisions through an ethics test when any doubt exists. The ethics test presented next was used at the Center for Business Ethics at Bentley College as part of corporate training programs. Decision makers are taught to ask themselves:[16]

1. *Is it right?* This question is based on the deontological theory of ethics that there are certain universally accepted guiding principles of rightness and wrongness, such as "thou shall not steal."

2. *Is it fair?* This question is based on the deontological theory of justice, implying that certain actions are inherently just or unjust. For example, it is unjust to fire a high-performing employee to make room for a less competent person who is a personal friend.

3. *Who gets hurt?* This question is based on the utilitarian notion of attempting to do the greatest good for the greatest number of people.

4. *Would you be comfortable if the details of your decision were reported on the front page of your local newspaper or through your company's e-mail system?* This question is based on the universalist principle of disclosure.

5. *Would you tell your child (or young relative) to do it?* This question is based on the deontological principle of reversibility, referring to reversing who carries out the decision.

6. *How does it smell?* This question is based on a person's intuition and com-

mon sense. For example, underpaying many accounts payable by a few dollars to save money would "smell" bad to a sensible person.

A decision that was obviously ethical, such as donating some managerial time for charitable organizations, would not need to be run through the six-question test. Neither would a blatantly illegal act, such as not paying employees for work performed. But the test is useful for decisions that are neither obviously ethical nor obviously unethical. Among such gray areas would be charging clients based on their ability to pay and developing a clone of a successful competitive product.

Another type of decision that often requires an ethical test is choosing between two rights (rather than right versus wrong).[17] Suppose a blind worker in the group has personal problems so great that her job performance suffers. She is offered counseling but does not follow through seriously. Other members of the team complain about the blind worker's performance because she is interfering with the group achieving its goals. If the manager dismisses the blind worker, she might suffer severe financial consequences. (She is the only wage earner in her family.) However, if she is retained the group will suffer consequences of its own. The manager must now choose between two rights, or the lesser of two evils.

SOCIAL RESPONSIBILITY

Many people believe that firms have an obligation to be concerned about outside groups affected by an organization. **Social responsibility** is the idea that firms have obligations to society beyond their economic obligations to owners or stockholders and also beyond those prescribed by law or contract. Both ethics and social responsibility relate to the goodness or morality of organizations. However, business ethics is a narrower concept that applies to the morality of an individual's decisions and behaviors. Social responsibility is a broader concept that relates to an organization's impact on society, beyond doing what is ethical.[18] To behave in a socially responsible way, managers must be aware of how their actions influence the environment.

An important perspective is that many socially responsible actions are the by-products of sensible business decisions. For instance, it is both socially responsible and profitable for a company to improve the language and math skills of entry-level workers. Literate and numerate entry-level workers for some jobs may be in short supply, and employees who cannot follow written instructions or do basic math may be unproductive.

An expanded view of social responsibility regards organizations as having a **corporate social consciousness.** The term refers to a set of consciously held shared values that motivate and guide individuals to act in a responsible way. As part of being responsible, the interests of the corporation are balanced against its accountability for the effect of its actions upon society, the environment, and other interested parties.[19] A company with a strong corporate social consciousness would be profitable, pay high wages, attract high-quality job candidates, and be admired by the general public and the government. Companies who fit this description include Southwest Airlines, Hewlett Packard, and Harley-Davidson. All of them are included in the popular listing called the "100 Best Companies to Work for in America."[20]

This section will examine three aspects of social responsibility: the two viewpoints of social responsibility; corporate social performance; and a sampling of specific social responsibility initiatives.

Describe the stakeholder viewpoint of social responsibility, and corporate social performance.

social responsibility
The idea that firms have obligations to society beyond their obligations to owners or stockholders and also beyond those prescribed by law or contract.

corporate social consciousness
A set of consciously held shared values that guide decision making.

Stockholder Versus Stakeholder Viewpoints

stockholder viewpoint
The traditional perspective on social responsibility that a business organization is responsible only to its owners and stockholders.

64

stakeholder viewpoint
The viewpoint on social responsibility contending that firms must hold themselves responsible for the quality of life of the many groups affected by the firm's actions.

The **stockholder viewpoint** of social responsibility is the traditional perspective. It holds that business firms are responsible only to their owners and stockholders. The job of managers is therefore to satisfy the financial interests of the stockholders. By so doing, says the stockholder view, the interests of society will be served in the long run. Socially irresponsible acts ultimately result in poor sales. According to the stockholder viewpoint, corporate social responsibility is therefore a by-product of profit seeking.

The **stakeholder viewpoint** of social responsibility contends that firms must hold themselves responsible for the quality of life of the many groups affected by the firm's actions. These interested parties, or stakeholders, include those groups composing the firm's general environment. Two categories of stakeholders exist. Internal stakeholders include owners, employees, and stockholders; external stakeholders include customers, labor unions, consumer groups, and financial institutions. Exhibit 3-3 depicts the stakeholder viewpoint of social responsibility.

Many organizations regard their various stakeholders as partners in achieving success, rather than as adversaries. The organizations and the stakeholders work together for their mutual success. For example, Ford Motor Company owns 49 percent of the Hertz rental car company, which is also a major Ford customer. An example of a company partnership with a labor union is the establishment of joint committees on safety and other issues of concern to employees.[21]

Part of understanding the stakeholder viewpoint is to recognize that not all stakeholders are the same. Instead, they can be differentiated along three dimensions. Some stakeholders are more powerful than others, such as the United Auto Workers (UAW) union being more powerful than a small group of protesters. Some stakeholders are more legitimate than others, such as the UAW, which is

EXHIBIT 3-3

The Stakeholder Viewpoint of Social Responsibility
An organization has to satisfy the interests of many groups.

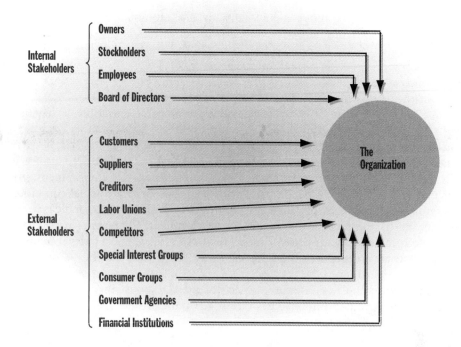

Internal Stakeholders
- Owners
- Stockholders
- Employees
- Board of Directors

External Stakeholders
- Customers
- Suppliers
- Creditors
- Labor Unions
- Competitors
- Special Interest Groups
- Consumer Groups
- Government Agencies
- Financial Institutions

The Organization

a well-established and legal entity. Some stakeholders are more urgent than others because they require immediate attention. A group of protesters chaining themselves to a company fence because they accused the company of polluting the ground, would require immediate attention.[22]

Corporate Social Performance

Corporate social performance is the extent to which a firm responds to the demands of its stakeholders for behaving in a socially responsible manner. After stakeholders have been satisfied with the reporting of financial information, they may turn their attention to the behavior of the corporation as a good citizen in the community. One way of measuring social performance is to analyze the company's annual report in search of relevant statistical information.

Two accounting professors interested in social responsibility scanned the annual reports of the top 100 corporations on the *Fortune* 500 list. The corporations were involved in a variety of industries including chemicals, health, petroleum, manufacturing, foods, electronics, aerospace, and information technology.[23] The analysis most closely tied to social performance was the disclosure of environmental measures, with the following rates of activity being reported:

- Pollution measures, 74%
- Contributions to crime prevention, 0%
- Contribution to the homeless, 10%
- Contributions to AIDS treatment and substance abuse programs, 10%
- Contributions to the arts, 17%
- Contributions to education, 44%

The authors were encouraged that the rate of disclosure in this and other categories had improved over the past. Another approach to measuring corporate social performance is to observe how a company responds to social issues by examining programs in more detail. The next section describes corporate activity in relation to a variety of social issues.

Social Responsibility Initiatives

Creating opportunities for a diverse work force, as described in Chapter 2, is an important social responsibility initiative. Here we describe positive corporate responses to other important social issues. A firm that takes initiatives in these areas can be considered socially responsible. The six social responsibility initiatives described here are: environmental management, work/life programs, social leaves of absence, community redevelopment projects, acceptance of whistle blowers, and compassionate downsizing.

ENVIRONMENTAL MANAGEMENT
Many companies take the initiative to preserve the natural environment in a way that pleases environmental groups. As a result, the company works in partnership with a group intent on such purposes as preserving forests or a species of fish or animal. An example is that Southern California Edison developed a guidebook to train company employees to recognize sensitive habitats and endangered species. The guidebook became so popular with environmental groups that it was published through an alliance with the Audubon Society. Another example is that Ciba-Geigy, the chemical company, initiated worldwide dialogue with a large number of environmental organiza-

corporate social performance
The extent to which a firm responds to the demands of its stakeholders for behaving in a socially responsible manner.

Present an overview of social-responsibility initiatives.

tions. One result of these dialogues is that Ciba is involved with a coalition of 111 business firms and associations that developed solutions to many of the problems of hazardous waste site cleanup.[24]

Another key aspect of environmental management is to prevent pollution rather than control wastes after they have surfaced. For example, a company might eliminate the use of mercury in electrical switches and instead substitute a metal such as copper that is less toxic to the environment.[25] The concern is that when the switch is discarded, the highly poisonous mercury could eventually work its way into the ground.

WORK/LIFE PROGRAMS   A major social responsibility initiative is for organizations to establish programs that facilitate employees balancing the demands of work and personal life. Typically these programs are termed work/life or work/family programs. The intent is to help employees lead a more balanced life, and be more satisfied and productive on the job. A *Business Week* survey found that family-friendly companies enjoy a big return on their investment from their work/family programs. Absenteeism falls, turnover decreases, and productivity and profits rise.[26] For more details about work/life programs see Exhibit 3-4 and the accompanying Organization in Action.

SOCIAL LEAVES OF ABSENCE   Some companies offer employees paid leaves of absence, of anywhere from several weeks to six months, to help them prevent burnout. A **social leave of absence**, however, gives select employees time away from the job to perform a significant public service. For example, American Express Travel-Related Services allows employees with 10 or more years of service to take up to six months to contribute to the community. Obtaining a leave of absence is competitive. Candidates for the leave fill out an application that describes the employee's plans and qualifications for performing the community work. As with other firms offering social leaves, the community work must be integrated into the department's work plans.

social leave of absence
An employee benefit that gives select employees time away from the job to perform a significant public service.

A Variety of Work/Life Programs

- Childcare resource and referral
- Part-time options
- Flexible work schedules
- Compressed workweek
- Telecommuting
- Job sharing among two or more employees
- Eldercare resource and referrals
- Eldercare case management and assessment
- Subsidy for emergency care for dependents
- "Family sick days" that permit employees to stay home and care for sick children or relatives
- Arrangements for school counselors to meet with parents on site during regular working hours
- Electric breast pumps for mothers of young children who want to return to work and continue breastfeeding

- Maintenance worker on company payroll whom employees can hire for household tasks, by paying only for supplies
- Laundry service, including ironing, on company premises
- Concierge service in which company employee runs a variety of errands for employees
- Postal service
- Automatic teller machines
- On-site fitness centers including massages

Source: Michelle Neely Martinez, "An Inside Look at Making the Grade," *HRMagazine*, March 1998, p. 61; Jim Harris, *Getting Employees to Fall in Love with Your Company* (New York: AMACOM, 1996); William M. Mercer's *Work/Life Diversity Initiatives Benchmarking Survey*, 1996 (Louisville Galleria, Louisville KY 40202); "Work/Life Benefits Are Valuable, But Value Isn't Measured," *Workforce*, January 1998, pp. 27–29.

Organization *in Action*

You Can Work and Have a Life at Eddie Bauer

Eddie Bauer Inc., the casual lifestyle retailer based in Redmond, Washington, has a corporate culture that emphasizes employees achieving a balance between home and work. The company has approximately 12,000 employees and 450 stores throughout the United States, Canada, Japan, and Germany. Eddie Bauer also operates a global mail-order catalog business.

The company uses its work/life programs to help associates lead more productive and balanced lives. The human resources group at Eddie Bauer has carefully assembled a benefits package that covers both the routine and nonroutine challenges of work and home. The investment is cost effective because many of the programs result in lowered health-care costs. However, the programs also help associates be more focused and productive at work, knowing that resources are available to help deal with personal-life needs.

Many of the company's benefits are simple programs—relatively easy to execute—that recognize that people sometimes need a break. One such program is Balance Day—an essentially free day intended for associates to schedule a "call in well" absence. All employees are entitled to one Balance Day annually, in addition to normal time off, accrued vacation, three personal holidays, national holidays, and sick leave. Eddie Bauer associates welcome the bonus day, using it to run errands, attend to children, or pursue hobbies.

Sue Storgaard, director of work/life services, says, "We value the commitment our associates make to Eddie Bauer, and conversely, we realize that they have another life outside of work that's important to them. Through carefully researched programs, we're offering our associates—whether they're single, married, parents, or nonparents—an environment that reduces their stress at work and gives them more flexibility in their personal lives."

Eddie Bauer's human resource staff started to develop the specialized work/life benefits plan by asking themselves, "What do our employees really want, and can we afford to give it to them?" The company offers the usual array of benefits and services common to many companies, including various group insurance and savings programs. Extras related to balancing work and personal life include subsidies for liberal paid parental leave, and alternative transportation options such as preferred parking for carpools and a 40 percent subsidy for vanpools. And under its Customized Work Environment program, the company offers such options as job sharing (two people share a job, usually equally), a compressed workweek, and telecommuting. In the last several years, Eddie Bauer has introduced 20 new programs, from on-site mammography (x-rays to detect breast cancer) to emergency child-care services.

The ultimate goal of all these programs is to make Eddie Bauer a highly desirable place to work. A series of discussions with corporate and retail-store associates provided a road map for company executives. Clearly evident was the need to address dual-parenting roles, the increase in working mothers, and the maturation of the baby-boomer market. In addition to their jobs, Eddie Bauer Associates were juggling numerous personal responsibilities. A key program resulting from these interviews was a Child and Eldercare Consulting and Referral service provided by an outside firm, Working Solutions.

Eddie Bauer recognized the development of an eldercare program as meeting an imminent need. Under the eldercare resource and referral program, the company assists associates in a variety of ways. Included are assistance in

(continued)

68

dealing with housing concerns to issues for caregivers (those who provide for other people). About 170 associates used the program in a recent year. Associates can also access books, articles, and videos on subjects related to taking care of elders.

New programs continue to be added to the Eddie Bauer package. Among them are Home and Healthy Postpartum Visits, adoption assistance, and a plan that allows associates to enjoy group buying power through

arrangements for mortgage loan discounts. Under the Visits program, a registered pediatric nurse is sent to the home of the new parent, whether the parent be an Eddie Bauer female associate or the wife (or partner) of a male associate, within 24 to 72 hours of hospital discharge.

Source: Excerpted from "At Eddie Bauer You Can Work and Have a Life" by Leslie Faught, copyright April 1997. Used with permission of ACC Communications Inc./*Workforce*, Costa Mesa, CA. All rights reserved.

The social good performed by the person on leave often takes the form of lending business expertise to a nonprofit agency. An example would be a corporate controller developing a financial plan for a youth agency. At other times the social leave is to perform work indirectly related to one's professional expertise, such as a human resources professional volunteering as a high-school drug counselor for six months.[27]

COMMUNITY REDEVELOPMENT PROJECTS   A large-scale social responsibility initiative is for business firms to invest resources in helping rebuild distressed communities. Investment could mean constructing offices or factories in an impoverished section of town, or offering job training for residents from these areas. The Prudential Insurance Company helps rebuild inner cities by investing money in ventures such as grocery stores, housing, and entertainment. The New Jersey Performing Arts Center is one of their investment projects.

Peter Goldberg, president of the Prudential Foundation, explains the rationale for community redevelopment projects: "The future well-being of this company, this industry, and of corporate America is very much intertwined with the health and well-being of American society."[28]

A variation on community redevelopment funds is for investors to create jobs in relatively poor neighborhoods within large cities. The New York City Investment Fund headed by financier Henry R. Kravis is the lead organization in this endeavor. The Fund consists of a group of investors who help create jobs and support African-American businesses. Over 60 New York-based companies have invested about $1 million each, and also have contributed executive talent to the project. A specific example is that money from the fund has been invested in Sylvia's Restaurant, a popular soul food dining place in the Harlem section of New York. The project in which funds are invested must meet tough criteria: create jobs, earn satisfactory financial returns, and nurture important industries and African-American-owned businesses.[29] Enough information has not been collected to evaluate the success of this project, but it represents a hard-hitting social initiative.

whistle blower
An employee who discloses organizational wrongdoing to parties who can take action.

ACCEPTANCE OF WHISTLE BLOWERS   A **whistle blower** is an employee who discloses organizational wrongdoing to parties who can take action. Whistle blowers are often ostracized and humiliated by the companies they hope to improve, by such means as no further promotions or poor performance evaluations. More than half the time, the pleas of whistle blowers are ignored. A representative example of whistle blowing and its negative consequences for the individual took place at the Department of Energy radioactive materials clean-up program. Stephen Buckely, who now delivers pizzas, said he was fired from his position as an environmental protection specialist because he objected to wasteful and expensive procedures. He objected to a department policy that extensive 300-page environmental impact studies be routinely conducted even though, in his opinion, less expensive procedures would work. Buckely said he was fired because top management at the Energy Department was upset. He is not alone. An independent government agency that investigates and prosecutes illegal workplace practices received 814 complaints of reprisals against whistle blowers in one year.[30]

Only an organization with a strong social conscience would embrace employees who inform the public about its misdeeds. Yet some companies are becoming more tolerant of employees who help keep the firm socially responsible by exposing actions that could harm society.

COMPASSIONATE DOWNSIZING   To remain competitive and provide shareholders with a suitable return on investment, about 80 percent of large organizations have undergone **downsizing.** Downsizing is the slimming down of operations to focus resources and boost profits or decrease expenses. Downsizing is also referred to as *rightsizing*, because the intent is to ensure that the organization is the right size to achieve maximum efficiency. Downsizings are incessant, even during generally prosperous times. So long as the company itself faces a downturn in earnings, it is likely to lay off large numbers of workers. For example, before the general business downturn took place in 1998, defense contractor Raytheon Co. slashed 16 percent of its work force, or 14,000 jobs. Merrill Lynch, the world's biggest security firm, laid off 2,000 employees at the same time.

Among the dozens of negative human consequences of downsizing are work overload for the remaining workers, job insecurity, excessive stress, and financial problems for laid-off workers who cannot find new employment at the same income level. Less obvious problems include the possibility of a dramatic increase in family conflict, including spouse and child battering by laid-off workers. Suicide rates among the fired workers also increase. Customers often suffer because customer service may deteriorate as a result of fewer customer-service personnel.

As a starting point in downsizing compassionately, a company might ponder if downsizing is worthwhile from a financial perspective. The consensus of many studies is that downsizing leads to improved financial performance in only about 50 percent of the cases. Based upon his review of dozens of studies, Jeffrey Pfeffer concludes:

> The evidence indicates that downsizing is guaranteed to accomplish only one thing—it makes organizations smaller. But downsizing is not a sure way of increasing the stock price on a medium- to long-term horizon, nor does it necessarily provide higher profits or create organization efficiency or productivity.[31]

At times companies find that downsizing is necessary for survival, such as the layoffs at Apple Computer Co. in the late 1990s, just before its turnaround was spearheaded by the successful personal computer, the iMac. Compassionate downsizing would include actions such as:

- The redeployment of as many workers as possible by placing them in full-time or temporary jobs throughout the organization, where their skills and personality fit.

downsizing
The slimming down of operations to focus resources and boost profits or decrease expenses.

- Providing outplacement services to laid-off employees, thereby giving them professional assistance in finding a new position or redirecting their careers. (The vast majority of employers do provide outplacement services to laid-off workers.)
- Providing financial and emotional support to the downsized worker. Included here is treating employees with respect and dignity rather than escorting them out the door immediately after the downsizing announcement. Many companies already provide severance pay and extended health benefits to the laid-off workers. Financial assistance with retraining is also helpful.
- Giving hope to the more qualified employees who were laid off by reassuring them they will be on the top of the list if a job recall does take place in the future.

BENEFITS DERIVED FROM ETHICS AND SOCIAL RESPONSIBILITY

Summarize the benefits of ethical and socially responsible behavior, and how managers can create an environment that fosters such behavior.

Highly ethical behavior and socially responsible acts are not always free. Investing in work/life programs, granting social leaves of absence, and telling customers the absolute truth about potential product problems may not have an immediate return on investment. Nevertheless, recent evidence suggests that high ethics and social responsibility are related to good financial performance. Here we look at evidence and opinions about the advantages of ethics and social responsibility.

A study was conducted about the impact of discovered unethical behavior on the performance of a company's stock. The researchers found that unethical behavior that is discovered and publicized has a negative impact on the stock price for an appreciable period of time. Unethical behavior, therefore, decreases a firm's wealth.[32] An example of this type of unethical behavior would be a tobacco company charged with hiding evidence about the health risks of smoking cigarettes. As a result many shareholders sell their shares, and other investors lose interest in buying stock in the company.

Another perspective on the relationship between profits and social responsibility is that it works two ways. More profitable firms can better afford to invest in social responsibility initiatives, and these initiatives in turn lead to more profits. Sandra A. Waddock and Samuel B. Graves conducted a large-scale study that supports the two-way conclusion. The researchers analyzed the relationship between corporate social performance and corporate financial performance for 469 firms, spanning 13 industries, for a two-year period. Many different measures of social and financial performance were used.

It was found that levels of corporate social performance were influenced by prior financial success. This suggests that financial success creates enough money left over to invest in corporate social performance. The study also found that good corporate social performance contributes to improved financial performance as measured by return on assets and return on sales. Waddock and Graves concluded that the relationship between social and financial performance may be a *virtuous circle*, meaning that corporate social performance and corporate financial performance feed and reinforce each other.[33]

Being ethical also helps avoid the costs of paying huge fines for being unethical. So many firms have been fined for unethical and illegal activities, it is almost unfair to select one as an example. However, the $180 million in fines Texaco Corporation paid for discriminating against black people illustrates the gravity of the problem.

A big payoff from socially responsible acts is that they often attract and retain socially responsible employees and customers. To accommodate the interests of socially responsible business people, a trade group has been formed called Businesses for Social Responsibility (BSR). Its charter is to make social, environmental, and worker-friendly practices a key part of business and government policy making. A spokesperson for BSR points to a compelling benefit derived from social responsibility:

> This way of doing business is inevitable. The growth in green marketing and socially screened investing shows that consumers and investors are becoming increasingly sensitive to both the quality of products they purchase and the business practices of the company they buy from.[34] ("Green marketing refers to selling environmentally sound products.)

CREATING AN ETHICAL AND SOCIALLY RESPONSIBLE WORKPLACE

Establishing an ethical and socially responsible workplace is not simply a matter of luck and common sense. Top managers, assisted by other managers and professionals, can develop strategies and programs to enhance ethical and socially responsible attitudes. We turn now to a description of several of these initiatives.[35]

FORMAL MECHANISMS FOR MONITORING ETHICS
Forty-five percent of companies with 500 or more employees have ethics programs of various types, including the ethics hotline described in the opening case to this chapter. Large organizations frequently set up ethics committees to help ensure ethical and socially responsible behavior. Committee members include a top-management representative plus other managers throughout the organization. An ethics and social responsibility specialist from the human resources department might also join the group. The committee helps establish policies about ethics and social responsibility, and might conduct an ethical audit of the firm's activities. In addition, committee members might review complaints about ethical violations. Many of the ethical violations involve charges of sexual harassment by managers.

A hard-hitting formal mechanism is the appointment of an ethics officer, an action taken by many large firms. Sometimes the ethics officer is the general counsel, and at other times he or she is a full-time specialist. A representative job title for this position is "corporate vice-president, ethics and business conduct." The ethics officer is supposed to provide leadership and guidance about fair business conduct and socially responsible acts.

WRITTEN ORGANIZATIONAL CODES OF CONDUCT
Many organizations use written ethical codes of conduct to serve as guidelines for ethical and socially responsible behavior. Such guidelines have increased in importance because workers placed in self-managing teams have less supervision than previously. Some aspects of these codes are general, such as requiring people to conduct themselves with integrity and candor. Here is a statement of this type from the Johnson & Johnson (medical and health supplies) code of ethics:

> We believe our first responsibility is to the doctors, nurses, and patients,
> to mothers and fathers and all others who use our products and services.
> In meeting these needs everything we do must be of high quality.

Other aspects of the codes might be specific, such as indicating the maximum gift that can be accepted from a vendor. In many organizations, known code violators are disciplined.

WIDESPREAD COMMUNICATION ABOUT ETHICS AND SOCIAL RE-SPONSIBILITY   Extensive communication about the topic reinforces ethical and socially responsible behavior. Top management can speak widely about the competitive advantage of being ethical and socially responsible. Another effective method is to discuss ethical and social responsibility issues in small groups. In this way the issues stay fresh in the minds of workers. A few minutes of a team meeting might be invested in a topic such as "What can we do to help the homeless people who live in the streets surrounding our office?"

Lockheed Martin has an ethics communication program labeled "Top-Down Cascade Training." The chairman of the board trains the managers directly reporting to him, who in turn train their staff. Eventually, all 200,000 employees hear the same core message about ethics delivered at annual training sessions.

LEADERSHIP BY EXAMPLE   A high-powered approach to enhancing ethics and social responsibility is for members of top management to behave in such a manner themselves. If people throughout the firm believe that behaving ethically is "in" and behaving unethically is "out," ethical behavior will prevail. Visualize a scenario in which a group of key people in an investment banking firm vote themselves a $3 million year-end bonus. Yet to save money, entry-level clerical workers earning $8.00 an hour are denied raises. Many employees might feel that top management has a low sense of ethics, and therefore that being ethical and socially responsible is not important.

ENCOURAGE CONFRONTATION ABOUT ETHICAL DEVIATIONS   Unethical behavior may be minimized if every employee confronts anyone seen behaving unethically. For example, if you spotted someone making an unauthorized copy of software, you would ask the software pirate, "How would you like it if you owned a business and people stole from *your* company?" The same approach encourages workers to ask about the ethical implications of decisions made by others in the firm.

TRAINING PROGRAMS IN ETHICS AND SOCIAL RESPONSIBILITY   Many companies now train managerial workers about ethics. Forms of training include messages about ethics from executives, classes on ethics at colleges, and exercises in ethics. These training programs reinforce the idea that ethically and socially responsible behavior is both morally right and good for business. Much of the content of this chapter reflects the type of information communicated in such programs. In addition, Skill-Building Exercise 3-A represents the type of activity included in ethical training programs such as those given at CitiCorp.

SUMMARY OF KEY POINTS

 Identify the philosophical principles behind business ethics.

When deciding on what is right and wrong, people can focus on consequences; duties, obligations, and principles; or integrity. Focusing on consequences is called utilitarianism, because the decision maker is concerned with

the utility of the decision. Examining one's duties in making a decision is the deontological approach, and is based on universal principles such as honesty and fairness. According to the integrity (or virtue) approach, if the decision maker has good character, and genuine motivation and intentions, he or she is behaving ethically.

Explain how values relate to ethics.
Ethics becomes the vehicle for converting values into action, or doing the right thing. A firm's moral standards and values also influence which kind of behaviors managers believe are ethical. According to ethically centered management, the high quality of an end product takes precedence over meeting a delivery schedule. Catastrophes can result when management is not ethically centered.

 Identify factors contributing to lax ethics, and common ethical temptations and violations.
Major contributors to unethical behavior are greed and gluttony, and an organizational atmosphere that condones unethical behavior. Other contributors are moral laxity (other issues seem more important at the time), and pressure from higher management to achieve goals. Incentives for being unethical, such as being rewarded for cutting back on quality, can contribute to low ethics, as can weak relationships among people.

Recurring ethical temptations and violations, including criminal acts, include the following: stealing from employers and customers, illegally copying software, treating people unfairly, sexual harassment, conflict of interest, divulging confidential information, and misusing corporate resources. Greed, gluttony, and avarice among top executives is a separate category of ethical problems.

 Apply a guide to ethical decision making.
When faced with an ethical dilemma, ask yourself: Is it right? Is it fair? Who gets hurt? Would you be comfortable with the deed exposed? Would you tell your child to do it? How does it smell?

 Describe the stakeholder viewpoint of social responsibility, and corporate social performance.
Social responsibility refers to a firm's obligations to society. Corporate consciousness expands this view by referring to values that guide and motivate individuals to act responsibly. The stakeholder viewpoint of social responsibility contends that firms must hold themselves accountable for the quality of life of the many groups affected by the firm's actions. Corporate social performance is the extent to which a firm responds to the demands of its stakeholders for behaving in a socially responsible way.

 Present an overview of social responsibility initiatives.
Creating opportunities for a diverse work force is a major social responsibility initiative. Also important are environmental management, work/life programs, social leaves of absence, community redevelopment projects, acceptance of whistle blowers, and compassionate downsizing.

 Summarize the benefits of ethical and socially responsible behavior, and how managers can create an environment that fosters such behavior.
High ethics and social responsibility are related to good financial performance, according to research evidence and opinion. Also, more profitable firms can invest in good corporate social performance. Being ethical helps avoid big fines for being unethical, and ethical organizations attract more employees. Initiatives for creating an ethical and socially responsible workplace include (a) formal mechanisms for monitoring ethics, (b) written codes of conduct, (c) communicating about the topic, (d) leadership by example, (e) confrontation about ethical deviations, and (f) training programs.

KEY TERMS AND PHRASES

Ethics, 56
Moral intensity, 56
Ethically centered management, 59
Moral laxity, 60
Conflict of interest, 62

Social responsibility, 63
Corporate social consciousness, 63
Stockholder viewpoint, 64
Stakeholder viewpoint, 64
Corporate social performance, 65

Social leave of absence, 66
Whistle blower, 68
Downsizing, 69

QUESTIONS

1. Why should managers study ethics and social responsibility?
2. Give examples of rights that you think every employee is entitled to.
3. Why is ethically centered management supposedly helpful in preventing industrial disasters?
4. Describe a specific way in which stakeholders can damage a company.

5. What do you think of the ethics of *cookies* (software devices that can furnish a lot of information about the preferences of people who visit a particular Web site)?

6. Come up with an example of "choosing between two rights" either through your own imagination or experience or talking to an experienced manager.

7. What is the potential danger to an individual's career of making extensive use of work/life benefits?

SKILL-BUILDING EXERCISE 3-A : Ethical Decision Making

Working in small groups, take the following two ethical dilemmas through the six steps for screening contemplated decisions. You might also want to use various ethical principles in helping you reach a decision.

SCENARIO 1: TO RECYCLE OR NOT

Your group is the top-management team at a large insurance company. Despite information technology making paper less necessary, your firm still generates tones of paper each month. Customer payments alone account for truckloads of envelopes each year. The paper recyclers in your area contend that they can hardly find a market any longer for used paper, so they will be charging you just to accept your paper for recycling. Your group is wondering whether to continue to recycle paper.

SCENARIO 2: JOB APPLICANTS WITH A PAST

A state (or provincial) government official approaches your bank asking you to hire three people soon to be released from prison. All were found guilty of fraudulently altering computer records for personal gain in a bank. The official says these people have paid their debt to society and that they need jobs. Your company has three openings for computer specialists. All three people obviously have good computer skills. Your group is wondering whether to hire them.

INTERNET SKILL-BUILDING EXERCISE : What Ever Happened to "It Doesn't Matter"?

After you have commented on and analyzed Case Problem 3-A about KTNT Communications, use the Internet to find out the fate of the company. Did they receive a certificate to operate? Are they still in business? Try several of your favorite search engines. As a starting point, use the search phrases "KTNT Communications" and long-distance telephone carriers. The amount of digging you will have to do to uncover this story will give you valuable experience in conducting research on the Net.

CASE PROBLEM 3-A : Cashing In on Phone Caller Indifference

KTNT Communications, a Texas phone company started in 1995, had achieved $1 million in annual revenue several years later. KTNT has decided to use two different names for the long-distance phone service it plans to operate in Florida: "I Don't Care" and "It Doesn't Matter." If a Floridian uses either of these terms when asked to choose a long-distance carrier, the caller would be automatically switched to the long-distance provider "I Don't Care" or "It Doesn't Matter." Even if the caller uses an equivalent phrase such as "Honey, I don't care," during an operator-assisted phone call, he or she would be connected to KTNT Communications.

The plan by KTNT was deferred at the Florida Public Service Commission (PSC) a year ago when the Texas phone company requested to use the names and offer long-distance service in the state. KTNT then withdrew its request. The company has reapplied to use its unusual names for long-distance service. Many Florida state officials regard the names as being a deceptive business practice. The Florida Public Service Commission has recommended approving KTNT's request to use the names, despite objections from the Attorney General and the Office of Public Counsel.

The company's main business is to provide long-distance service to people at pay phones or other places when they need to use an operator. When someone at a pay phone asks the operator to make a toll call, and the operator asks which long-distance company the caller prefers, and the caller says "I don't care" or 'It doesn't matter," the caller would most likely wind up using KTNT.

"The names in question and KTNT's use of them are controversial, but the record does not indicate they are necessarily deceptive in practice," the PSC staff wrote in its recommendation. "We're dead set against it," said Charlie Beck of the Office of Public Counsel. "It's wrong, deceptive, and unfair to customers."

A PSC spokesperson, Kevin Bloom, says the agency's staff may believe it has no choice. He says, "My take on it is that legal staff and communications staff believe that they have no option but to recommend to grant a certificate to this company under these names. It appears that the staff assigned to this believe the company met all legal requirements for obtaining a long-distance certificate."

A defender of KTNT pointed out, "So what if they get a little extra business? KTNT has reasonably competitive rates,

and the call will get through. Nobody is getting hurt." According to *Living Cheap News*, however, KTNT charges twice as much as the big carriers.

Discussion Questions

1. Use the guide to ethical decision making to evaluate the business practice KTNT plans to use in Florida.
2. What is your evaluation of the position that "Nobody is getting hurt" by labeling the long-distance services "I Don't Care" and "It Doesn't Matter"?
3. If you were responsible for preparing advertising for KTNT long-distance services, what advertising theme would you propose?

Source: "Phone Company Tries to Cash In on Apathy," Knight Ridder news story, August 30, 1998; "Name that Company," Rochester, New York *Democrat and Chronicle*, April 28, 1998, p. 3C.

CASE PROBLEM 3-B: The Great American Sweatshops

Based on a tipoff in August 1995, U.S. federal agents raided an El Monte, California, garment manufacturer. Evidence was found that the company held 75 Thai immigrants behind barbed wire and paid them $1.00 per hour. The names of several large retailers were found on the boxes in the grimy, poorly lit shop. Among the names were Sears, Montgomery Ward, and Dayton Hudson. Company representatives agreed to meet with Labor Secretary Robert B. Reich to discuss ways to combat the use of sweatshops.

The representative explained that they had no idea of the deplorable conditions at the El Monte manufacturer. Furthermore, they promised to adopt a statement of principles requesting that their suppliers adhere to federal labor laws.

The Department of Labor estimates that 20,000 small U.S. garment makers supply the one-half of the country's clothing that is not imported. Many of these firms require their employees to work under cramped, poorly ventilated, and unsafe conditions. A Labor Department spot check of 69 garment-making firms in Southern California uncovered health and safety violations in all but seven of them. The workers are mostly female immigrants from Latin America and Asia who earn an average of $7.34 an hour. Wages are just over the federal poverty level. However, they are comparable to pay for many jobs in the service industry, and well above the minimum wage.

Labor Secretary Reich wants the retail industry to play a major role in enforcing restrictions against sweatshops. He urges retailers to use their enormous purchasing power to ensure that subcontractors comply with labor laws. Part of the plan is for large retailers to hire inspectors to visit shops randomly and without warning. Most retailers say such demands

are unfair and that they would create a hardship and inflate the price of clothing. Sears alone has 10,000 direct suppliers. The suppliers in turn subcontract work to smaller firms. It is also difficult for civilian inspectors to detect violations of the complex wage and hour laws.

Robert L. Mettler, the president of apparel at Sears, wants fellow retailers to find ways to combat the problem of suppliers who are sweatshops or who subcontract to sweatshops. The executive vice-president of a giant retailer on the verge of insolvency looks at the problem from a different perspective: "We simply cannot afford to hire inspectors. We won't knowingly do business with a supplier that hires slave labor. Yet if you close down all these alleged sweatshops, a lot of families will go hungry. A $7.00 per hour steady job is decent extra money for a low-income family. A lot of people are lined up looking for these jobs.

"Yet with the pressure the Department of Labor is putting on us, we'll have to think of some official position on the issue."

David R. Henderson, a research fellow with the Hoover Institute, observes that a low-paying job in Honduras or in Los Angeles's garment district may seem horrible to many people. Yet for many adults and children, it represents their best option. He believes that you don't make somebody better off by taking away the best of her bad options. An apparel worker in Honduras told a reporter: "This is an enormous advance, and I give thanks to the *maquila* (factory) for it. My monthly income is seven times what I make in the countryside."

Some Honduran girls allegedly make about 31 cents an hour at 70-hour-per-week jobs. Assuming a 50-week year, the girl can earn over $1,000 per year. Yet the per capita income in Honduras is about $700 per person. The clothing made in these Honduran factories is often done on a subcontract basis for an American firm. Or sometimes the Honduran subcontractor makes components of clothing, such as coat liners, that are later assembled into final garments in an American shop.

Discussion Questions

1. Explain whether retailers have a social responsibility to inspect vendors for possible violation of wage and safety laws.

2. What advice can you offer the large retailer who claims his company cannot afford inspectors?

3. What is your position about a $7.00-per-hour job being a good opportunity for many workers?

Source: Facts in this case are based on Susan Chandler, "Look Who's Sweating Now," *Business Week*, October 16, 1995, pp. 96–98; David R. Henderson, "The Case for Sweatshops," *Fortune*, October 28, 1996, pp. 48, 52.

ENDNOTES

1. J. Leslie Sopko, "B&L Plugs Into Ethics Hotline," Rochester, New York *Democrat & Chronicle*, December 17, 1997, pp. 1A, 12A. Adapted with permission.

2. Thomas M. Jones, "Ethical Decision Making by Individuals in Organizations," *Academy of Management Review*, April 1991, p. 391.

3. Linda K. Treviño and Katherine A. Nelson, *Managing Business Ethics: Straight Talk about How to Do it Right* (New York: Wiley, 1965), pp. 66–70; Larue Tone Hosmer, "Trust: The Connecting Link Between Organizational Theory and Philosophical Ethics," *Academy of Management Review*, April 1995, pp. 396–397.

4. H. D. Karp quoted in "Ethics is 'Doing the Right Thing,' So How Do You Know What's Right?" *Marriott Executive Memo*, 8(1), 1996, p. 4.

5. Perry Pascarella, "Winners Supply New Leaders," *Management Review*, November 1997, p. 52.

6. Robert Elliott Allinson, "A Call for Ethically Centered Management," *The Academy of Management Executive*, February 1995, pp. 73–74.

7. "Lax Moral Climate Breeds White-Collar Crime Wave," *Personnel*, January 1988, p. 7.

8. John Kamp and Paul Brooks, "Perceived Organizational Climate and Employee Counterproductivity," *Journal of Business and Psychology*, Summer 1991, p. 455.

9. "24 Extracted from Mall Ruins After 4 Days," Associated Press, July 2, 1995.

10. Samuel Greengard, "50% Of Your Employees Are Lying, Cheating, and Stealing," *Workforce*, October 1997, p. 46.

11. Ann E. Tenbrunsel, "Misrepresentation and Expectations of Misrepresentation in an Ethical Dilemma: The Role of Incentives and Temptation," *The Academy of Management Journal*, June 1998, pp. 330–339.

12. Daniel J. Brass, Kenneth D. Butterfield, and Bruce C. Skaggs, "Relationships and Unethical Behavior: A Social Network Perspective," *The Academy of Management Review*, January 1998, pp. 14–31.

13. The first seven items on the list are from Treviño and Nelson, pp. 47–57; Samuel Greengard, "Theft Control Starts with HR Strategies," *Personnel Journal*, April 1993, pp. 81–91.

14. Kimberly T. Schneider, Suzanne Swan, and Louise F. Fitzgerald, "Job-Related and Psychological Effects of Sexual Harassment in the Workplace: Empirical Evidence from Two Organizations," *Journal of Applied Psychology*, June 1997, pp. 401–415.

15. Mark Maremount, "Sex, Lies, and Home Improvements," *Business Week*, March 31, 1997. P. 40.

16. James L. Bowditch and Anthony F. Buono, *A Primer on Organizational Behavior*, 4th ed. (New York: Wiley, 1997), p. 4.

17. Joseph L. Badaracco, Jr., *Defining Moments: When Managers Must Choose Between Right and Right* (Boston: Harvard Business School Press, 1997).

18. Gregory M. Bounds, Gregory H. Dobbins, and Oscar S. Fowler, *Management: A Total Quality Perspective* (Cincinnati: South-Western College Publishing, 1995), p. 150.

19. Keith A. Lavine and Elna S. Moore, "Corporate Consciousness: Defining the Paradigm," *Journal of Business and Psychology*, Summer 1996, p. 401–413.

20. Robert Levering and Milton Moskowitz, "The 100 Best Companies to Work for In America," *Fortune*, January 12, 1998, pp. 84–95.

21. Jeffrey S. Harrison and Caron H. St. John, "Managing and Partnering with External Stakeholders," *Academy of Management Executive*, May 1996, pp. 46–60.

22. Ronald K. Mitchell, Bradly R. Agle, and Donna J. Wood, "Toward A Theory of Stakeholder Identification and Salience: Defining the Principle of Who and What Really Counts," *Academy of Management Review*, October 1997, p. 869.

23. Jane Park and Adnan Abdeen, "Are Corporations Improving Efforts at Social Responsibility?" *Business Forum*, Summer/Fall 1994, pp. 26–30.

24. Gail Dutton, "Green Partnerships," *Management Review*, January 1996, pp. 24–26.

25. Michael A. Berry and Dennis A. Rondinelli, "Proactive Corporate Environmental Management: A New Industrial Revolution," *Academy of Management Executive*, May 1998, pp. 42–43.

26. Keith H. Hammonds, "Balancing Work and Family," *Business Week*, September 16, 1996, pp. 74–80.

27. "Time for a Sabbatical?" *HRfocus*, July 1995, p. 10.

28. Samuel Greengard and Charlene Marmer Solomon, "The Fire This Time," *Personnel Journal*, February 1994, p. 60.

29. Leah Nathans Spiro, "Henry Kravis . . . Do-Gooder?" *Business Week*, March 2, 1998, pp. 86–88.

30. "Whistleblower Numbers Grow," Scripps Howard News Service, August 3, 1998.

31. Jefferey Pfeffer, *The Human Equation: Building Profits by Putting People First* (Boston: Harvard Business School Press, 1998), p. 174.

32. Research reported in *Positive Leadership*, sample issue, October 1998, p. 5.

33. Sandra A. Waddock and Samuel B. Graves, "The Corporate Social Performance–Financial Performance Link," *Strategic Management Journal*, Spring 1997, pp. 303–319.

34. Larry Reynolds, "A New Social Agenda for the New Age," *Management Review*, January 1993, p. 40.

35. John Davidson, "The Business of Ethics," *Working Woman*, February 1998, pp. 68–70; Susan J. Harrington, "What Corporate America is Teaching about Ethics," *The Academy of Management Executive*, February 1991, p. 21; Linda Klebe Treviño and Bart Victor, "Peer Reporting of Unethical Behavior: A Social Context Perspective," *Academy of Management Journal*, March 1991, p. 74.

Chapter Four

Ila Smith, customer-service representative, and Jean Clement, customer-service supervisor, are experts at assisting customers of Plasti-Kote Co., Inc., in Medina, Ohio. These workers go the extra mile to solve customer problems that their company, an ISO-9001-certified manufacturer of spray paint and small-job brushing paints, didn't even create.

Most of Plasti-Kote's direct customers are distributors who buy the paint, then sell it to retailers. When a distributor experiences a delivery problem or an incorrect shipment, Jean and Ila go to work. For example, distributors occasionally telephone to complain that they received the wrong paint color. "Even if I'm absolutely certain the customer ordered the wrong item in the first place, I never tell them they made the error," says Jean. "I simply apologize and say, 'I must have heard you wrong.'" Once you realize it's simply the way to do business, and that it's not a reflection on you personally, you can assume responsibility and handle the problem in a calm and friendly way."

"Sometimes we get calls from people who need a color we don't make," says Jean. "If it's a car color, we tell the person to try his or her dealer. As a last resort, we'll even send someone to a competitor if we know that's the only way the customer will find the needed color."

Before taking that drastic step, Jean and Ila look for creative ways to satisfy the customer. One customer wanted a certain

OBJECTIVES

After studying this chapter and doing the exercises, you should be able to:

 Fully understand the meaning of quality.

 Describe the principles and practices of quality management related to attitudes and people.

 Describe principles and practices of quality management related to work processes and technology.

 Summarize principles and techniques of customer satisfaction for managers as well as customer-service workers.

 Explain how mass customization contributes to customer satisfaction.

 Explain various specialized techniques for quality improvement.

Managing for Quality and Customer Satisfaction

paint color as a brush paint, and it's available from Plasti-Kote only as an aerosol. They suggested that the customer spray the paint into the plastic lid of the aerosol can, then use a brush to apply it. "Most people never even think of doing this," says Ila, "so the customer was pleased with such a simple solution."[1]

The story about the two customer-service representatives at a paint company illustrates two important points about quality management. First, it is important that companies meet quality standards, such as the ISO-9000 standards, that are discussed later in the chapter. Second, customer satisfaction requires careful thought. The purpose of this chapter is to help the reader achieve an understanding of major aspects of managing for quality and customer satisfaction. Toward this end, we discuss the meaning of quality and key principles of quality management and customer satisfaction including mass customization. We also describe several widely used techniques for improving quality, such as cause-and-effect analysis, and poka-yoke. In addition, we mention how the historically important Deming principles continue to contribute to quality.

THE MEANING OF QUALITY

Fully understand the meaning of quality.

quality
The totality of features and characteristics of a product or service that bears on its ability to satisfy given needs.

Although the term *quality* has an important meaning to every reader, it lacks a universally acceptable definition. The definition developed by the American Society for Quality Control is informative and useful: **Quality** is the totality of features and characteristics of a product or service that bears on its ability to satisfy given needs. Because need satisfaction is an individual matter, what constitutes quality for a specific product or service will vary among people. Quality has been defined in the following major ways:

- Conformance to expectations
- Conformance to requirements
- Loss avoidance
- Meeting and/or exceeding customers' expectations
- Excellence and value[2]

In general, if a product or service does what it is supposed to do, it is said to be of high quality. If the product or service fails in its mission, it is said to be of low quality. The requirements can be objective or subjective. A high-quality automobile might contain certain parts that deviate less than 0.0005 inches from standard. With such a small deviation, the parts meet objective requirements. The same automobile might also generate a high-quality image, thus meeting a subjective requirement of quality.

Given the many nuances to the meaning of quality, be cautious when instructing others to achieve high-quality results. Make sure that you and the other person have a similar perception. For example, can a high-quality pair of jeans cost $35, or must the price be $95 to achieve quality?

total quality management (TQM)
A management system for improving performance throughout a firm by maximizing customer satisfaction and making continuous improvements.

PRINCIPLES AND PRACTICES OF QUALITY MANAGEMENT

A major strategy for achieving high quality is **total quality management (TQM)**, a management system for improving performance throughout a firm by maximizing customer satisfaction, making continuous improvements, and relying heavily on employee involvement. Many managers and scholars have dropped the word "total," and refer to the system simply as quality management.

Whichever term you use, quality is still important. As John M. Ivancevich explains:

> There are some cynics who propose that "quality" is a management fad that has run its course. These cynics have used the negative word "fad." The facts of organizational life clearly illustrate that quality is not a fad or a technique that will be here today and gone tomorrow. Quality is about people, value, caring, passion, effectiveness, and doing what is right. What quality is about will be with us for many decades.[3]

To develop a thorough understanding of the scope and intent of quality management, think through the following definition:

> A system of management that involves all people in an organization delivering products or services that meet or exceed customer requirements. It is a preventive, proactive approach to doing business. As such it reflects strategic leadership, common sense, data-driven approaches to problem solving and decision making, employee involvement, and sound management practice. Its basic philosophy is the customer is the driver of the business, suppliers are joint partners, and leaders exist to ensure that the entire organization and all its people are positioned and empowered to meet competitive demand.[4]

If the definition just presented seems like a short course rather than a definition, your perception is accurate. Proponents of total quality management tend to consider a wide range of good management practices as part of TQM. To achieve better focus, this section approaches quality management by dividing its principles and practices into two categories: those that apply to attitudes and managing people and those that primarily relate to work processes and technology. All aspects of quality management are geared toward satisfying internal and external customers. A separate section will focus on the vital topic of total customer satisfaction.

Dealing with Attitudes and People

A system of total quality management directs the effort of an entire firm toward higher customer satisfaction, continuous improvement, and employee involvement. Many quality-management principles are, therefore, expressed in terms of changing individuals' attitudes and the organization culture. It has been suggested that total quality management is 90 percent attitude, specifically the attitude of listening to customers.[5] Such a profound attitude change results in a culture change.

Describe the principles and practices of total quality management related to attitudes and people.

START WITH A VISION AND VALUES   A helpful way to launch a quality-management program is to establish a lofty image of the future, called a vision. (Chapter 5 about planning will provide more information about vision.) The purpose of vision in this case is to point employees toward high-quality achievements and excite them about quality. The Green Giant division of The Pillsbury Co. has a vision of being the world's leading provider of tasty and nutritious vegetables. No wonder the Green Giant is so jolly! If a vision of this nature is repeated enough, it can help keep workers at all levels focused on quality.

Values enter the picture because they are the beliefs that support the vision. Relevant values for quality management would be to place great importance on quality and take good care of customers. A Green Giant worker harboring such values would discard any vegetable he or she spotted that looked damaged or spoiled.

OBTAIN TOP-LEVEL COMMITMENT   To achieve quality management, executive-level managers must give top priority to quality, not simply lip service. They must allocate resources to prevent, as well as to repair, quality problems. Quality must be included in the organizational strategy because the strategy supports the vision. Top management must have the desire to transform the company into the best in the business. Quality management is looked upon as a long-range strategy, rather than a tool for obtaining quick improvements.[6]

Part of top-level commitment is that every organizational unit must be responsible for quality. Workers throughout the firm must perceive the quest for quality as a top-management directive. High-level managers must, therefore, make frequent references to quality and reward quality performance. Executives must also show that they really believe in quality by such measures as accepting a late penalty rather than shipping a defective product.

MAINTAIN CUSTOMER SENSITIVITY THROUGHOUT THE ORGANIZATION   The essence of quality is to satisfy the needs of internal and external customers. An *internal customer* is someone in the firm who uses the output of another or interacts with someone else for work purposes. If you prepare monthly statistics for the head of another department, that manager is your customer. An *external customer* is a person outside the firm who pays for its goods or services. A person who obtains a home mortgage is thus a bank customer. Workers throughout the firm must get the message that the true purpose of their jobs is to satisfy customer requirements. Every action they take should be linked to customer satisfaction. A telemarketer might say, for example, "Is putting my caller on hold and playing music over the phone in the best interests of the customer?"

COMMUNICATE WIDELY ABOUT QUALITY   Top management in companies that won Baldrige quality awards systematically communicated the quality message throughout the firm. Federal Express, Cadillac, and IBM Rochester use their internal television networks to broadcast quality issues to employees. Most high-quality companies regularly send messages about quality over e-mail. In addition to print and electronic messages, top-level managers conduct face-to-face meetings with employees to share quality victories and future quality objectives. Motorola, management conducts quarterly town meetings at company sites. These meetings are supplemented by rap sessions between high-level managers and employee groups, with quality topics often discussed.

MAKE CONTINUOUS IMPROVEMENT A WAY OF LIFE   Just as the team must focus on continuous improvement, so must the individual employee. An employee who is committed to the TQM culture searches daily for ways of improving his or her work process and output. This approach embodies the spirit of *kaizen*, a philosophy of continuing gradual improvement in one's personal and work life. The kaizen philosophy is important because quality improvement is usually a gradual process.

Paine & Associates, a public relations firm in Costa Mesa, California, applied kaizen with excellent results. David Paine, the founder and president, was using brainstorming to develop ideas for media campaigns. The results were satisfactory but short of exceptional. Paine turned to kaizen. With a series of minor changes, including inviting more people to the brainstorming sessions and using simple creativity tools such as flash cards, creative output improved substantially. Within three years, Paine's agency was rated one of the country's ten most creative by an industry journal. Kaizen was also applied to other aspects of the business. "We've seen tremendous success in every facet of our business," said Paine.[7]

EMPOWER AND INVOLVE EMPLOYEES   To achieve total quality management, managers must empower employees to fix and prevent problems. Equally important, workers have to accept the authority and become involved in the improvement process. Empowerment is valuable because it may release creative energy. For example, at Advance Circuits of Hopkins, Minnesota, an empowered team eliminated pinhole-sized defects in circuit-board film. Team members discovered that by using a smaller darkroom they could eliminate many airborne particles that caused the defects.[8]

LISTEN TO EMPLOYEES   A successful quality-improvement effort creates an atmosphere in which the manager listens to employees. Management by walking around is therefore standard practice in a quality-management organization. Managers should listen for suggestions about even minor aspects of quality. Weyerhauser Mortgage of Woodland Hills, California, was experiencing delays in receiving reimbursement checks from FHA-insured home loans. Team members contended that company mistakes in completing forms were the culprit—not the government. The company listened and eliminated the mistakes. The checks now arrive in one-sixth the time, resulting in substantial savings.[9]

EMPHASIZE THE HUMAN SIDE OF QUALITY   Statistical and decision-making techniques contribute heavily to quality improvement. Yet the real thrust of quality management is for all employees to have positive attitudes toward quality. They must pay attention to detail, take pride in their work, and believe that high quality improves profits. Not paying enough attention to the human side of quality cost Chrysler Corporation a temporary drop in customer satisfaction ratings several years ago. Part of the problem was that large doses of overtime resulted in stressed workers who could not perform up to the high quality standards typical of Chrysler vehicles.[10]

REWARD HIGH-QUALITY PERFORMANCE   The best quality results are likely to be achieved when employees receive financial as well as nonfinancial rewards for achieving quality. Several key figures of the quality movement in the United States have downplayed the importance of financial incentives in achieving quality. Often these experts point to the outstanding quality of Japanese manufactured goods. Nevertheless, the Japanese approach to quality improvement has always emphasized financial bonuses for good performance. PQ Corp., a chemical manufacturer in Pennsylvania, implemented a program of giving financial rewards for achieving high quality. Company management observed that the rewards had a positive impact on maintaining continuous improvements.[11] In their quest for high quality, many other companies are replacing cash awards with such rewards as plaques, banquets, and certificates for quality achievement.[12]

Whether the rewards are cash or noncash, the principle remains the same. Some workers may be motivated by the joy of doing quality work, yet most workers would also like other rewards in addition.

The accompanying Organization in Action illustrates one company's effort to convert to a quality-management organization. Note that its quest for excellence is both comprehensive and ongoing.

82

3

Describe principles and practices of quality management related to work processes and technology.

Dealing with Work Processes and Technology

Quality management began in manufacturing. As a result, many quality management ideas are aimed at improving work processes and making effective use of technology. Many of the quality techniques developed for manufacturing are also applied to service firms such as banks, retailers, and hospitals. The later discussion of customer satisfaction can be regarded as an approach to improving the quality of service. Quality in the service section is particularly important because 85 percent of the U.S. work force is involved in service activities, rather than manufacturing.

The paragraphs that follow describe major principles of quality management dealing with work processes and technology. More of these ideas will be presented later, in the section about specialized techniques for quality improvement. Before proceeding, let's clarify the widely used term, **process**. A process is a set of activities designed to achieve a goal, such as the process of refinishing a table. The accompanying Manager in Action explains a work process in more depth.

process
A set of activities designed to achieve a goal.

IMPLEMENT A FORMAL QUALITY PROGRAM TO SUPPORT THE QUALITY PROCESS

Sponsoring a quality program helps establish a quality culture and supports the process of quality management. Motorola has developed "six sigma," which is both a program and an incredibly tight goal. The name refers to a quality standard in which 3.4 errors occur in one million opportunities. Six-sigma quality means work that is 99.999997 percent error free. For example, this standard allows only one input error in an 800-page document. Larry Bossidy, the chief of AlliedSignal, says that six sigma and total quality are still important to his firm. He also adds,

> We've had, I think, a good TQ program—but if I go around and see TQ posters on the wall and people hugging each other, I know they've missed the point. Because it's not about that. It's about substance—trying to have people learn new tools, work in teams, be more competitive. To be successful, TQ has to be kept evergreen. You've got to establish goals for what it's supposed to achieve. If you do that, it's got a long life. If you don't, it's over.[13]

ENGAGE IN BENCHMARKING

A basic total quality principle is to compare the firm's performance to an industry standard or world-class performance. **Benchmarking** is comparing a firm's quality performance to that achieved by competing firms, or some aspect of performance from a firm in another field. The firm in the other field might have achieved outstanding success in some aspect of the business that is relevant even if different. Benchmarking surged in popularity when it became widely known that Xerox Corp. compared its shipping capabilities to those of mail-order merchant L. L. Bean. Bean is noted for

benchmarking
The process of comparing a firm's quality performance to that achieved by a competing firm.

Organization *in Action*

Mercury Aircraft Flies the Quality Route

When Mercury Aircraft Inc. first embarked on a total quality journey it realized that the road to continuous improvement was never-ending. Today, five years after completing the Energizing Quality program conducted by a local technical institute, the company has maintained its forward momentum in its quest for excellence. Mercury is continuing to reap the rewards of its quality training.

Located in the wine country of Hammondsport, New York, Mercury Aircraft is one of the industry's largest contract manufacturers of precision sheet metal parts and subassemblies. "If it can be made from metal," says vice-president Pete Hannan, "Mercury can manufacture it."

Mercury has always been a quality-driven company, but five years ago management realized that it needed to take steps to ensure its continued success. With the goal of improving productivity, especially in terms of reducing unit costs and accelerating cycle time, Mercury wanted a custom training program for its 700 employees.

Over the next six months, senior managers and other personnel participated in a series of training sessions to spearhead the quality initiative. Topics included a total quality overview, organizational assessment, leadership training, quality planning, development of in-house experts, program implementation, and monitoring of results.

In the months after the training, Hannan noticed significant improvements in productivity. Most notably, Mercury was able to cut its lead time—from prototype development to product shipment—by as much as one half. Because Mercury produces customized products, each new order begins as a prototype. The faster the prototype can become a reality, the better for the customer and for Mercury's bottom line.

Faster cycle time improved the rate of on-time deliveries and increased manufacturing capacity. By improving quality, reducing costs, and delivering in a competitive time frame, Mercury boosted its competitive edge, Hannon reports. The training in quality also enabled Mercury to enhance its work processes, as evidenced by the number of teams, both relatively permanent and special purpose, that had been formed.

According to Hannan, Mercury employees are working smarter because they operate as a team and develop new ways to cut time and conserve materials in the manufacturing process. An employee opinion survey encourages the free expression of ideas and helps ensure open dialogue with management.

After taking part in Energizing Quality, Mercury employees understood that it is often the end user who drives fundamental changes and improvements in their products. Mercury routinely monitors customer satisfaction with customer audits as well as visits to their customers' headquarters. The customer–supplier relationship is interactive and includes room for praise. Mercury employees at every level of support and service—including those on the production line—have been recognized at customer special events.

For Mercury, new-business teams are one key to its success. By setting up enhanced communication channels, these teams ensure that every sales opportunity is addressed. Mercury created a Federal Systems Division to serve the needs of the government. As a result, the company has built a working partnership with new customers 3,000 miles away on the West Coast. It also enables the company to enlarge its global market share in Europe, especially in the United Kingdom.

Over the past five years, continuous improvement has become part of the corporate

(continued)

culture at Mercury. It is now ingrained in the company as a way of doing business, Hannan says. Senior managers have become quality drivers for the company, whereas other employees have taken on the function of in-house trainers and facilitators.

Hannon adds that an effective follow-up program that includes regular monitoring and measuring of results is critical in keeping the quality initiative alive and well.

Source: Adapted from "Quality Is Still Soaring at Mercury Aircraft," *Priority Report* (Rochester Institute of Technology), May 1997, p. 4.

filling orders quickly and accurately, and for avoiding an oversupply of some types of merchandise and shortages of others. Many companies now use the software program *Business Process Benchmarking* to learn from the successes of Xerox.

Several telemarketing firms have recently achieved good success by benchmarking the multilingual services offered by the customer-service departments of public utilities. Specifically, the telemarketers make their pitch in the mother tongue of the person from whom they want an order. The telemarketer knows in advance which language prevails in a particular neighborhood.

SELECT HIGH-QUALITY SUPPLIERS AND TRAIN THEM PROPERLY

A company needs high-quality components and materials to produce high-quality products. Careful selection of suppliers (or vendors) is, therefore, a major aspect of ensuring reliable and defect-free production. Once the right suppliers are selected, they must be clearly informed about the company's quality requirements. Sharp Electronics Corp. exemplifies this approach. The company teaches many of its suppliers how to produce high-quality components.

Manager *in Action*

Jim Riley Explains a Work Process

James F. Riley, Jr., is senior vice-president of the Juran Institute Inc., a firm that offers training and consulting about total quality management. When asked to give an example of a work process, he replied: "Take product development. New products begin in the research department with a concept. This progresses to the engineering department for the development of a prototype, which they make ready for manufacturing. The manufacturing function designs a way to produce the product affordably, quickly, and within production schedules. The product then must become ready to enter the marketplace, which involves the marketing, sales, and delivery functions.

"To achieve quality, you have to improve work performance at each stage of this process so that you can make a product that's free of defects, meets customer needs, and is manufactured in the least possible time, at the least possible cost. By necessity, TQM emphasizes teamwork for these reasons: Processes cut through an organization; and no one function, employee, or manager owns the entire process."

Source: Reprinted with permission from "Just Exactly What Is Total Quality Management?" *Personnel Journal* (February 1993), p. 32.

ENSURE THE EXCELLENCE OF INCOMING RAW MATERIALS AND SUP-PLIES   To achieve quality management, a work group must accept only high-quality raw materials and supplies. The premise is that a high-quality product cannot be made with low-quality materials. Many companies have vendor certification programs to ensure excellent supplies and materials.

DECREASE CYCLE TIME   An important goal of quality management is a short **cycle time**, the interval between the ordering and delivery of a product or service. Receiving goods promptly contributes to a customer's perception of quality. In addition, working toward shorter and shorter cycle times also can expose areas of weakness that adversely affect quality. A small firm that produced videotapes for product demonstrations set out to reduce its cycle time. In the process, managers discovered a bottleneck: a cumbersome procedure for estimating production costs.

cycle time
The interval between the ordering and delivery of a product or service.

PAY PAINSTAKING ATTENTION TO DETAIL   The quality of goods and services is greatly enhanced if everybody pays careful attention to detail. Paying attention to detail enables a worker to satisfy a major tenet of total quality management: Do work right the first time. The importance of attention to detail highlights the role personality factors play in contributing to quality. Workers who rank high on the personality trait of conscientiousness are much more likely to avoid mistakes. A conscientious data-entry clerk is much less likely to make an error such as making a deposit to a wrong account number or spelling a customer's name incorrectly. At one securities firm a client named Frank L. Forrest sent a $15,000 check for deposit to his bond account. The data-entry specialist deposited the check in the account of Frank T. Forrest. "T. Forrest" never reported the error, but "L. Forrest" demanded to know what happened to his $15,000 deposit. Errors like these take time to rectify and can result in a loss of customer goodwill.

INSTITUTE STRINGENT WORK STANDARDS FOR EVERY INDIVIDUAL
Recall the earlier discussion of how Motorola Inc. instituted a six-sigma work standard. For a quality management program to take hold, individuals have to fully accept such standards. Another stringent performance standard used in some TQM programs is **zero defects**, the absence of any detectable quality flaws in a product or service. Quality consultant Philip B. Crosby claimed that if people are truly committed to error-free work, they will accomplish it.[14] The importance of error-free work is a function of the product delivered or service provided. In recent years two incidents have been publicized of surgeons amputating the wrong leg of a patient. This is much more critical than a sack of potatoes being three ounces short of the five pounds promised.

zero defects
The absence of any detectable quality flaws in a product or service.

Another viewpoint is that error-free work is virtually unattainable. A human problem associated with virtually unattainable goals such as zero defects is that it results in needless frustration and stress for employees. It might be possible to achieve zero defects in producing a physical product such as brake linings. But picture yourself as a tax accountant who is told that not even one mistake in preparing a season's worth of tax forms will be tolerated.

CALCULATE THE RETURN ON QUALITY   For some aspects of goods and services, achieving the highest quality is a poor investment. The guiding principle is that a quality improvement is a poor investment if the customer does not care about the improvement or it leads to customer neglect. A vacuum-equipment unit of Varin Associates Inc. became obsessed with meeting schedules in their quest for total quality. In their race to meet deadlines, however, the staff did not return customer telephone calls, and the operation lost money. At Johnson & Johnson, quality-improvement teams for several product lines criss-crossed the country to conduct benchmarking. Unfortunately, costs skyrocketed beyond the value of the information obtained from benchmarking.[15]

Today, many corporate managers are carefully calculating whether quality management is a good investment. Properly implemented, the answer is quite frequently yes.

TRAIN INDIVIDUALS IN QUALITY   As part of quality management, almost every employee receives quality-related training. Each individual must learn the basic concepts of TQM, including problem-solving, decision-making, and interpersonal skills. Manufacturing operatives learn about statistical techniques useful for quality control, such as sampling and measuring variation.

Problems Associated with Quality Management Systems

Any mention of the limitations of total quality management systems and programs does not mean that quality is unimportant. Instead, the argument is that there are less time-consuming and cumbersome ways of achieving quality than through quality management. A problem in measuring the contribution of total quality systems and programs is that total quality management has lost its focus. As mentioned previously, TQM advocates appear to include virtually every useful management technique under the quality framework.

Many companies have found that some quality standards are arbitrary and not cost-effective. United Parcel Service, for example, has backed off on rapid delivery at any cost. Gradually, company officials discovered that many customers enjoyed interacting with the neatly groomed UPS drivers and did not want them rushing off to the next delivery. Drivers now have more time to converse with customers, which has improved customer relations and improved sales.[16]

Despite how impressive some quality techniques may appear, they do not always produce outstanding quality performance. A case in point is the quality improvement efforts of Motorola. The company is so widely regarded as a quality leader that they offer consulting services to other companies. In recent years, however, Motorola has experienced serious quality problems. In March 1998, unreliable network equipment contributed to the loss of a $500-million contract with a digital service carrier. Motorola also faced quality problems with its digital cellular phones. The company had to issue a software upgrade to digital phones in South America because the handsets turned off when they received unfamiliar signals from network equipment.[17]

According to a study conducted with 584 companies in four countries, many total quality programs fail because they attempt too much. The programs attempt to make hundreds of changes instead of focusing on a small number of decisive changes. A consultant noted that many companies are not seeing significant positive results from quality-improvement programs because they isolate these programs from day-to-day operations. Instead, companies should regard total quality management as a way of meeting business objectives.[18]

Oren Harari has analyzed a number of shortcomings of quality-management programs. Two of his criticisms are shared by many others. One concern is that quality management develops its own cumbersome bureaucracy in the form of reams of paper, hundreds of electronic messages, numerous committee meetings, and endless surveys. Add to the list dozens of techniques that must be followed carefully, and a growing staff of people to supervise quality. Another concern is that quality management drains entrepreneurship and innovation from corporate culture. Harari writes that "Obsessing internally until one achieves a zero-defects, do-it-right-the-first-time routine is a dangerous luxury that often slows down new breakthrough developments in products and services."[19]

Quality management programs work best when managers follow the principles and practices described so far. Although commitment of top-level managers is essential, they cannot become so obsessed with quality management that they neglect other aspects of management.

PRINCIPLES AND TECHNIQUES OF CUSTOMER SATISFACTION

Satisfying customer needs is the major strategy of quality management. Achieving customer satisfaction is also part of the strategy of many successful firms that do not have a total quality program. The ultimate goal in achieving customer satisfaction is to achieve **zero defections**—that is, to keep every customer the company can profitably serve. Notice that *zero defections* is a takeoff on the term *zero defects*, but it does not mean the same thing. Zero defections is an important goal to work toward because customer retention has a major impact on profits. Companies can almost double profits by retaining only 5 percent more of their customers.[20] A related consideration is that most customer dissatisfaction stems from the areas of service and the business relationship. Nevertheless, most of the quality-improvement staffing resources and energy are directed toward the product.[21]

This section describes key principles and techniques for building constructive customer relationships and achieving high levels of customer satisfaction (or total customer satisfaction). The examples focus on external customers in a retail setting, yet many of them apply also to industrial customers or selling business to business. The principles and techniques for achieving customer satisfaction can be categorized according to whether they require managerial input or whether frontline customer-service workers alone can implement them. Another approach to customer satisfaction is through mass customization.

Summarize principles and techniques of customer satisfaction for managers as well as customer-service workers.

zero defections
Keeping every customer a company can profitably serve.

Principles and Techniques for Managers

A major justification for satisfying customers is to obtain their loyalty.[22] Managers must assume responsibility for implementing many of these principles, techniques, and methods that lead toward high customer satisfaction:

1. *Concentrate your efforts on creating value for customers.* By creating value for customers, or giving them products or services that are useful to them, they will become loyal. USAA, the financial services giant, loses less than 1 percent of its customers per year in an industry with considerable customer turnover. (Many of USAA's lost customers are those who die, or no longer need a product such as automobile insurance.) The vast majority of USAA customers believe that they are receiving an excellent return for their pre-

miums or investment dollars. Customer retention and outstanding service are both part of the company strategy.

2. *Establish customer-satisfaction goals.* Managers must decide how much help to give to customers. They need to raise questions such as: Will employees attempt to satisfy every customer within 10 minutes of his or her request? Is the company striving to provide the finest customer service in its field? Is our goal zero customer defections to competitors? The answers will dictate how much effort and the type of effort the manager and the team members must put into pleasing customers.

3. *Give decision-making authority to customer-service workers.* Customer service is enhanced when frontline workers are empowered to deal with customer problems without seeking several levels of approval. Such authority includes the ability to grant refunds, exchanges, concessions, and preferred delivery dates. At the Hampton Inn hotels, all customer-contact workers are empowered to give a voucher for an overnight stay to a customer who expresses dissatisfaction with service. The empowerment is part of its 100% Satisfaction Guarantee program, shown in Exhibit 4-1.

4. *Thoroughly screen applicants for customer-service positions.* According to one study, an average of 68 percent of customers who switch to a competitor do so because they perceive indifference on the part of a customer-service employee. (The fact that a competitor's products or services were perceived as better accounts for only 14 percent of customer defections.[23]) Customer-service employees should therefore be of high caliber. Companies noted for their good service seek candidates who have good communication skills, project a professional image, display empathy, and appear happy. Screening for conscientiousness and extroversion is also important. Attracting good customer-service and customer-contact workers will often lead to imaginative solutions to customer problems.

5. *Hire full-time, permanent store associates.* To reduce costs, a growing number of retailers hire many part-time or temporary store associates. These workers frequently lack the commitment and product knowledge of full-time, permanent store (or sales) associates. David Fagiano, past president of the American Management Association, believes this practice is wrong. He says that to handle difficult customer transactions requires a representative who is highly skilled in the job functions. Also, the representative must be motivated to provide superior service. Such service requires a degree of company loyalty not typically found in a temporary worker.[24]

6. *Establish a favorable work climate for customer service.* An indirect but effective approach to achieving customer perceptions of high-quality service is to provide an atmosphere that supports customer service. A study conducted in 134 branches of a large bank supported the link between establishing a climate for service and customer perceptions of good service. For example, when employees perceive that they are rewarded for delivering quality service, their organization's service climate will be stronger. Also, if employees believe that customer service is important to management the climate for service will be enhanced.[25] The performance evaluation system at Saturn car dealerships gives considerable weight to customer service. As a result, the climate for customer service is enhanced.

Another important way to establish a climate favorable to customer service is to train customer-contact workers in areas such as problem solving, listening, communication, and stress management. Training in product knowl-

EXHIBIT
4-1

The 100% Satisfaction Guarantee Policy at Hampton Inn

89

Source: Courtesy the Hampton Inn Inc.

edge is also essential because many instances of customer dissatisfaction stem from a sales associate's insufficient knowledge of the merchandise.

7. *Solicit customer feedback regularly.* Business firms that listen to their customers can make adjustments to improve service quality from the customer's viewpoint that will often enhance customer retention.[26] Many top-level managers regularly visit company facilities that serve customers, such as stores, restaurants, and hotels. An advanced system of obtaining customer feedback is to not rely strictly on what the customers say. Instead, observe customers' actions to obtain insights into their preferences for present and future products. For example, market research indicated that consumers wanted low-

fat, nutritious fast foods such as McDonald's McLean, KFC's skinless fried chicken, and Pizza Hut's low-cal pizza. Yet all products failed to meet expectations. In reality, when it comes to diet, there is a big disparity between what people intend to eat (healthy foods) and what they actually eat (fat, tasty foods). One way of learning what consumers really do is to observe them directly or through video cameras.[27] A caution is that the use of video cameras for this purpose is considered unethical by many people.

8. *Communicate the fact that everyone contributes to the customer's perception of service.* Customers evaluate the quality of service on the basis of their total perception of how they are treated by all people with whom they interact. For example, shabby treatment by a parking lot attendant can detract from high-quality service received within the store.

9. *Find ways to buy from your customer.* A powerful tactic for building customer relationships is to buy as many products or services as possible from the customer. Assume that a construction company purchases an enormous amount of bricks, cinder blocks, and cement from a builder's supply company. When the supply company decides to build a new office, the contract might go to the construction company in question. Reciprocity is one of the oldest principles in business.

    The tactic of buying from customers generally applies best to industrial customers. A retail store manager, however, might be able to buy from customers who are themselves store owners or store managers. An example is that a good customer of a clothing store might be a car dealer. When it came time to purchase a vehicle, the clothing store owner might first visit the car dealer who is his or her customer. An effective procedure is to ask customers for a full listing of the products and services their firms offer. Key managers in the company should have access to this list so they might find a way to make a purchase.

10. *Develop efficient systems of order fulfillment.* A potential barrier to excellent customer service is a mediocre order-fulfillment process. No matter how courteous and friendly the sales representative, a customer will be upset when orders are filled slowly or inaccurately. Many firms use the Internet to fill orders, which can enhance customer service if the system is user friendly and does not crash frequently in the middle of an order. Two Web sites with efficient Internet order-fulfillment systems for books and music products are amazon.com and barnesandnoble.com. Many other retailers have modeled their order-fulfillment systems after amazon.com.

Principles and Techniques for Customer-Service Workers

Customer-contact workers, especially sales associates, play a major role in moving an organization toward total customer satisfaction. The list that follows describes a number of techniques that customer-service workers can use:

1. *Contribute to establishing customer bonds.* A major way of satisfying customers and retaining them is to establish an emotional bond between the customer and a producer or supplier. As a result of the emotional bond the customer will buy repeatedly or exclusively from the supplier, and recommend that supplier to others. Furthermore, the person who forms an emotional bond with the product, service, or provider will resist sales appeals from competitors.[28]

Bonding takes place to the extent that the customer-contact workers provide outstanding service, and that the customer trusts the supplier or producer. A formidable challenge for any company that manufactures and sells printers for computers is to break the bond that many consumers have formed with Hewlett-Packard (HP) printers. Part of the bond stems from the trust many people have in the quality of HP printers. Building a warm personal relationship with the customer also helps because people tend to purchase from salespersons they like unless there is a dramatic difference in price for a competitive product or service. The other techniques described here, as well as in the previous section, contribute to bonding.

2. *Understand customer needs.* The most basic principle of selling is to identify and satisfy customer needs. One challenge in applying the principle is that many customers may not be able to express their needs clearly. To help identify customer needs, you may have to probe for information. For example, an associate in a camera and video store might ask, "What uses do you have in mind for your video camera?" Knowing this information will help the associate identify the camcorder that will satisfy the customer's needs.

3. *Put customer needs first.* After customer needs have been identified, the focus must be on satisfying them rather than oneself or the firm. Assume the customer says, "The only convenient time for me to receive delivery this week would be Thursday or Friday afternoon." The sales associate should not respond, "On Thursdays and Fridays our truckers prefer to make morning deliveries." Instead, the associate should respond, "I'll do whatever is possible to accommodate your request."

4. *Respond positively to moments of truth.* An effective customer-contact worker performs well during situations in which a customer comes in contact with the company and forms an impression of its service. Such situations are referred to as **moments of truth**. If the customer experiences satisfaction or delight during a moment of truth, the customer is likely to return. A person who is frustrated during a moment of truth will often not be a repeat customer.

5. *Show care and concern, and be helpful with complaints.* During contacts with customers, show concern for their welfare. Ask questions such as "How have you enjoyed the digital television system you bought here several months ago?" or "How are things going for you at school?" After asking the question, project a genuine interest in the answer.

   Another key aspect of showing care and concern is to be helpful rather than defensive when a customer complains. Listen carefully and concentrate on being helpful. The upset customer cares primarily about having the problem resolved and does not care whether you are at fault. Use a statement such as "I understand this mistake is a major inconvenience. I'll do what I can right now to solve the problem." Remember also that complaints that are taken care of quickly and satisfactorily will often create a more positive impression than mistake-free service.

6. *Communicate a positive attitude.* A positive attitude is conveyed by such attributes as pleasing appearance, friendly gestures, a warm voice tone, and good telephone communication skills. When a customer seems apologetic about making a demand, a possible response might be: "No need to apologize. My job is to please you. Without you, we wouldn't be in business."

7. *Smile at every customer.* Smiling is a natural relationship builder and can help build bonds with customers. Sales associates should smile several times during each customer contact, even if the customer is angry with the product or service.

moment of truth
A situation in which a customer comes in contact with the company and forms an impression of its service.

Few retail or industrial firms can achieve all of the above principles and techniques for total customer satisfaction. Furthermore, according to one market research firm, you can please only about 80 percent of your customers no matter what you do. Few firms can avoid customers who either are chronic complainers or have unrealistic expectations.[29] Nevertheless, as with total quality management, principles of customer satisfaction represent ideals to strive toward.

Mass Customization for Customer Satisfaction

Explain how mass customization contributes to customer satisfaction.

mass customization

A manufacturing system that allows hundreds of variations of a single product in order to respond to the unique preferences of individual customers.

An important new trend in customer satisfaction is to give customers the opportunity to have a personal variation of a mass-produced product. Examples include ordering a new car with a custom-designed package of accessories. Dell Computer Corp., with its build-to-order method of selling, offers personal variations of a mass-produced product. **Mass customization** is a hybrid technique whereby a production line spins out hundreds of variations on a single product. Achieving mass customization requires a highly flexible manufacturing system that can handle a variety of options. The idea is to retain most of the benefits of mass production while at the same time responding to the unique preferences of individual customers.

A well-established example of mass customization is Personal Pairs, a Levi Strauss program that enables women to order jeans to their exact measurements. The customer pays a little more for the privilege and has to wait a few days for the jeans. The difference between Personal Pairs and having jeans custom made is that Levi Strauss mass produces all but the finishing touches and sizing on the jeans. A more recent example of mass customization is Custom Foot, a shoe retailer that makes shoes to meet individual tastes and size requirements, yet still mass produces shoes in Italian factories. The prices are higher than many premium brands of shoes sold off the shelf, but less than the price of completely customized shoes. Custom Foot outlets keeps only display models in inventory, and the customer's foot size is measured precisely by an electronic scanner. However, the company does set liberal limits by offering 670 sizes.[30]

Mass customization is a juggling act between attempting to please every customer and still manufacturing efficiently. Researcher Eric Torbenson has gathered advice from mass customization experts for companies that want to move toward mass customization:[31]

1. *Evaluate the products in customers' terms.* Successful mass customizers measure success in terms of how well a product serves customers. By adapting to unique customer needs, sales are likely to increase. For example, some people are eager to buy multivitamins tailored to their needs.

2. *Offer customers the appropriate number of choices.* It is important not to overempower customers (to let them order anything they want) because the cost can be prohibitive. The manufacturer must find a product range that satisfies customers and still lets a company make money. For example, a 7' 6" person can usually not be fitted for a shoe at Custom Foot through its ordinary system. Instead, he or she would have to order a completely custom-made pair of shoes.

3. *Create a modular production system.* Most successful mass customizers build their products in discrete modules. With each step in production organized into a separate module, the steps can be rearranged like Lego bricks. Dell Computer Corp. has set the standard for such production of computers whereby every computer purchaser can choose a unique combination of features.

4. *Provide fingertip access to all information.* For mass customization to succeed, all workers in the company should be able to access relevant information about customer orders and the individual steps of production. For example, ChemStation International Inc. custom mixes industrial soaps. Engineers and field representatives have dial-up access to the database containing formulas for all ChemStation customers. When dealing with a new or prospective customer, the engineers or reps can call up similar customer requirements on their laptops. In this way ChemStation has a head start on creating new customized formulas.

5. *Collect information about customer preferences directly.* When customers place their customized orders, there is an opportunity to study customer preferences directly. Production can be made even more efficient when patterns emerge of what customers want and don't want. Saturn Corp. allows customers to special order a variety of accessories. This is one reason Saturn doesn't accumulate inventories of orange-colored cars without tape cassette and CD players!

6. *Make it difficult for customers to go elsewhere.* Mass customization can create a customer relationship that is habit-forming to consumers because they get exactly what they want. Paris Miki, based in Japan, differentiates itself from other eyeware manufacturers through an interactive software program that allows customization of its rimless glasses. Precise measurements are taken of the customer's face, including nose length. Customers can even choose styles from such image words as intelligent, sexy, distinctive, or professional. The selection is so precise, customers are unlikely to want to shop elsewhere.

Mass customization improves customer service because many customers get the exact features they want. Nevertheless, some consumers believe that the highest level of customer service is to be able to take a product off the shelf and bring it home immediately. Also, with mass-produced products you can see the final version at the time of purchase.

SPECIALIZED TECHNIQUES FOR QUALITY MANAGEMENT

So far this chapter has described techniques and attitudes that contribute to enhanced quality. Technical methods form another important part of assuring quality. These specialized techniques originated in manufacturing but are also used to improve the quality of services. Among the techniques are quality control, statistical process control, graph techniques, robust design, and poka-yoke.

Explain various specialized techniques for quality improvement.

Quality Control

Long before total quality management, manufacturers attempted to ensure product quality. A standard technique to ensure quality is **quality control**—determining the extent to which goods or services match a specified quality standard. There are two primary ways to control quality. One way is to inspect all units of output (100-percent inspection). Another is to inspect samples of the total output, such as checking every 200th can of tuna fish produced. Similarly, a random sample can be used instead of inspecting predetermined units of the product.

quality control
Any method of determining the extent to which goods or services match some specified quality standard.

THE 100-PERCENT INSPECTION Under the *100-percent inspection technique*, all units are inspected. Those that do not meet quality standards are rejected. A 100-percent inspection is impossible when the process of inspection ruins the product. After a can of tuna is inspected, for instance, it cannot be sold. In contrast, visually inspecting a hair dryer does no harm to the unit.

A 100-percent inspection technique is necessary when the cost of poor quality is enormous. The cost could be measured in terms of money, human lives, or human suffering. Suffering or loss of life would result if there were defects in products such as contact lenses, automobile brakes, airplane controls, and heart pacemakers. The cost of lawsuits would be significant also.

Inspecting every unit is quite expensive when humans perform the inspection. To decrease inspection costs, robots are now used for some forms of inspection. An even more recent development in quality control is machine-vision systems. Such systems have a sensing device that can, for example, check the size of holes in parts going along a conveyor belt. The system can reject parts with holes too big or too small.

Even a 100-percent inspection technique will not catch every defective product. The inspection device—whether human or electronic—is not perfect. The person or machine may have quality problems too.

INSPECTION BY SAMPLING When a sample is used for quality control, managers must decide how many units to inspect and what to inspect. One strategy is *acceptance inspection*, or checking completed products. The completed products may be finished goods for sale to consumers or they may be intermediate goods that will be used in further production.

Another strategy is *in-process inspection*, in which products are checked during production. If flaws are detected, changes can be made before the product is assembled. Tearing down finished products is expensive and may result in considerable scrap. It is much better to find pieces of fish tail in a batch of tuna meat before it is canned than afterward.

Sampling is used to evaluate the quality of services as well as goods. The next time you order by phone or call a help desk you might hear the message "This call may be monitored to help provide you better service." The statement is made to avoid violating laws concerning invasion of privacy. Supervisors or specialists review the sample tapes to assess the quality of service being provided by the service representatives.

Another strategy for quality control combines acceptance and in-process inspection. Goods and services of the highest quality generally receive both types of inspection. Waterman Ideal, a manufacturer of pens and pencils, uses both types of inspection to ensure the quality of their writing instruments. Because of this, all Waterman Ideal products are guaranteed for three years from the date of purchase.

In a sampling procedure, a small number of items (the *sample*) are drawn from the *lot*, or the total number of units. Characteristics of the lot are inferred from those of the sample. Assume that a lot of 10,000 plastic containers of tennis balls are being manufactured. A quality control inspector selects 20 of these containers at random. If one of these containers lacks the required air pressure, the inspector can assume that 5 percent of the lot is defective. In other words, approximately 500 cans in the lot have unacceptably low pressure.

In practice, sampling is much more complicated than the example just given. The inspector would have to pick a representative sample and specify the probability of making errors in prediction. Using a sampling technique is less expensive and time-consuming than inspecting every unit. The technique also has disadvantages. In any sampling technique, some defective parts will go undetected, so there is the risk that consumers will purchase low-quality products. There is, therefore, increased probability that customer goodwill may decline. Any method of quality control requires managers to determine an acceptable number of defects or poor-quality products.

Statistical Process Control

Early attempts to improve the quality of products focused primarily on the inspection of outgoing products. In effect, producers tried to inspect quality into their products. The production process itself and work in process went unmonitored. As thinking about quality became more advanced, many firms shifted the focus of their quality-improvement efforts to in-process inspection.

Process management is the monitoring, controlling, and improving of a production process for the purpose of improving the quality of the output of the process. W. Edwards Deming developed a refinement of in-process inspection, referred to as **statistical process control**. This method uses graphical displays for analyzing deviations in production processes during manufacturing rather than after the completion of a part or product. Similar to other methods of quality control, the goal of statistical process control is to reduce variation in the finished product.

In many cases, variation is inherent in the process; it cannot be predicted or easily eliminated. The causes of such variation are called common causes, and only improved process technology can eliminate them. In other cases, variation is due to assignable (identifiable) causes, such as worn tools or worker error. Assignable causes can be corrected, so even a superior production process needs a method for controlling quality. A process whose output variance is due only to common causes is said to be in a state of *statistical control*. When assignable causes are present, the process is *out of control* and needs to be corrected.

Statistical process control gauges the effectiveness of the manufacturing process by carefully monitoring changes in whatever is being produced. Potential problems are detected before they result in poor-quality products. Experts can diagnose the reasons for the deviation and modify the process as necessary. Part of the continuing success of Harley-Davidson Motor Co. Inc. has been attributed to the application of statistical process control. Reducing output variation is so important that the U.S. Air Force specifies that suppliers must use statistical process control in the manufacture of parts and armaments.

statistical process control
A technique for spotting defects during production that utilizes graphical displays for analyzing deviations.

95

Graph Techniques

PARETO DIAGRAM   To gain continuous improvement in quality, problems must be identified and corrected. One problem-identification technique involves using a **Pareto diagram**, a bar graph that ranks types of output variations by frequency of occurrence. Managers and workers use Pareto diagrams to identify the most important problems or causes of problems that affect output quality. Identification of the "vital few" allows management or quality circle teams to focus on the major cause or causes of a quality problem.

An example might be an investigation of laser printer failures. As Exhibit 4-2 shows, the causes of a problem are plotted on the *x*-axis (horizontal). The cumulative effects are plotted on the *y*-axis (vertical). In a Pareto diagram, the bars are arranged in descending order of height—that is, frequency of occurrence—from left to right across the *x*-axis. Thus, the most important causes are at the left of the chart. Priorities are then established for taking action on the few causes that account for most of the effect. According to the Pareto principle, generally 20 percent or fewer of the causes contribute to 80 percent or more of the effects.

Pareto diagram
A bar graph that ranks types of output variations by frequency of occurrence.

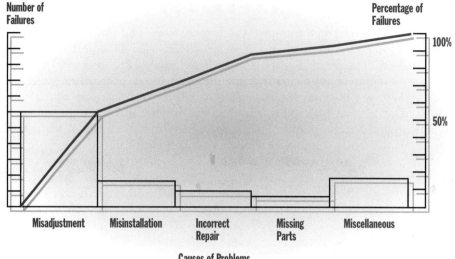

EXHIBIT 42

A Pareto Analysis of Laser Printer Failure

CAUSE-AND-EFFECT ANALYSIS   This is another graphical technique for analyzing the factors that contribute to a quality problem. The diagram used in cause-and-effect analysis is known as an *Ishikawa diagram* (after its originator, Karou Ishikawa) or a *fishbone diagram* (because of its shape). According to **cause-and-effect analysis**, any work process can be divided into major categories or causes, as Exhibit 4-3 illustrates. The main line of the chart represents the process, and the first branches are the immediate causes of the problem shown. Four causes often used are people, machines and equipment, methods, and materials.

Cause-and-effect diagrams are often developed through brainstorming, and the general causes are usually subdivided further into specific contributors to the causes. For example, the people category might be divided into employee selection, education, training, motivation, and job satisfaction. Digging further, a quality defect might be traced to low job satisfaction of employees who are disgruntled about physical working conditions. The job of the quality-improvement team is to investigate the possibility.

Once the team identifies the quality problem and its causes, they can develop possible solutions. Each suggested solution is analyzed in terms of costs, time,

cause-and-effect analysis
A graphical technique for analyzing the factors that contribute to a problem. It relies on a Ishikawa, or fishbone, diagram.

EXHIBIT 43

A Basic Cause-and-Effect Diagram

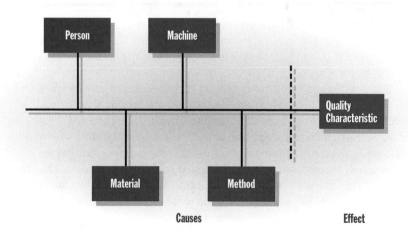

barriers to implementation, effects on workers and managers, and expected results. After a solution is chosen, an implementation plan must be determined.

Robust Design (The Taguchi Method)

The specialized techniques described so far deal with quality control. Quality improvement also involves the prevention of quality problems. One of the most widely used principles of quality-problem solving is that of robust design, developed by Genichi Taguchi as part of a method that bears his name. **Robust design** means that engineers must design the part or process so well that it can withstand fluctuations on the production line without a loss of quality. A major goal of robust design is to prevent products from failing while they are being used by customers. For example, if an automobile tire is not designed properly, it might pass 100-percent inspection but still develop a slow leak after 30,000 miles.

The principle of robust design is said to surpass in-process inspection methods that concentrate on keeping the production lines stable through constant monitoring. It is vastly superior to traditional acceptance inspection quality control, which relies on inspection, rejection, and rework.

The *Taguchi method* is based on the concept that in any process there are a number of factors that can be combined in an almost infinite number of ways. Finding the best way to run the process by experimenting with all the possible combinations could take years. Robust design provides statistical methods to define a specific sample that reveals the trends toward the best conditions for the process. As a result, engineers can specify an optimal process by running just a small number of experiments.

A major thrust of robust design is to consistently meet quality targets rather than tolerate acceptable deviations. A case several years ago involving Ford Motor Co. and Mazda Motor Corp. illustrates this difference. Ford, which owns about 25 percent of Mazda, requested that Mazda manufacture some of the transmissions for a car sold in the United States. Both companies were supposed to build the transmissions with identical specifications. Ford used the zero defects standard of quality, while Mazda adhered to robust design.

After the cars had been in the hands of consumers for a while, the Ford transmissions had generated more warranty claims and more complaints about noise. Ford engineers disassembled and carefully measured samples of transmissions made by itself and Mazda. Ford parts met specifications—in other words, there were no detectable defects. The Mazda gearboxes, however, showed no variability at all from targets. Many of the Ford-built transmissions were close to the outer limit of specified tolerances. Minor variations in one part were creating a domino effect on other parts. Because of these slight variations, parts interacted with each other. The effect was more friction than the parts could endure. The key point of this example is the critical difference in managers' approaches to quality control. Mazda managers assumed that robustness began with meeting targets consistently. Ford managers, in contrast, assumed that staying within tolerance would prevent quality problems.

The principle of robust design sends four important messages to the manager:

- Work hard to achieve designs that can be produced consistently, and demand consistency from the factory. Domino-effect problems tend to occur from scattered deviations within specifications, not from consistent deviation outside specification.

- Where deviation from a target is consistent—such as an ink-jet cartridge that is always too light—adjustment is possible.

robust design
The concept of designing a part or process so well that it can withstand fluctuations on the production line without a loss of quality.

- You gain virtually nothing in shipping a product that barely satisfies the manufacturing standard over a product that just fails. A problem is that many of the products that barely meet the standard will be perceived as unsatisfactory by customers. The cost of returns and rework is intolerably high. It is preferable to get on target rather than focusing on meeting specifications.[32]

Poka-Yoke

If you are familiar with *idiot proofing,* you already understand the Japanese method for preventing problems called *poka-yoke* (pronounced poh-kay yoh-kay). A **poka-yoke** device is any mechanism that either prevents a mistake or makes the mistake obvious at a glance. Part of the underlying philosophy is that you have to prevent people from making errors so an object can be manufactured or used correctly. If you have ever loaded film into a 35mm camera you may have noticed that you cannot insert the film upside down. The reason is that the film canister only fits in one direction. Although this poka-yoke device may sound trivial, it has helped stabilize sales of 35mm cameras. Loading film is a major problem for the casual photographer who uses 35mm cameras. Being able to insert the film canister upside down would make matters worse.

A foundation principle of poka-yoke is to incorporate the function of a checklist into an operation so the operator does not neglect something important. Assume that an operator needs to insert a total of seven rivets into a subassembly. You would then modify the container so it releases seven rivets at a time. If a rivet is left over, the operator knows that the operation is not complete. Shigeo Shingo, a developer of the method, recommends four principles for implementing poka-yoke:

1. *Control upstream, as close to the source of the potential defect as possible.* As with the film canister, you might purposely make a part asymmetrical so it can only fit if placed in one position. You may have noticed that you cannot insert a $3^1/_2''$ floppy disk upside down into a computer drive unless you tap it in with a hammer.
2. *Establish controls in relation to the severity of the problem.* A simple beep or flashing light may be sufficient to check an error that is easily corrected by the operator, such as putting a protective coating on a part. It is even better to construct a control that prevents further progress until the error is corrected. A dramatic example would be stopping a motorcycle assembly line until the brake linings were all installed properly.
3. *Think smart and small.* Search for the simplest, most efficient, and most economical control technique. The holder that dispensed only seven rivets at a time exemplifies simplicity. Thinking smart may also involve simplifying operations to decrease the cost of inspection. Having the minimum number of moving parts in a machine fits the requirement of simplifying operations.
4. *Avoid delaying improvement by overanalyzing.* Poka-yoke ideas can often be introduced simply and inexpensively. Keep these ideas in place until a more robust design can be developed in the future.[33]

Many excellent applications of mistake-proofing can be found in everyday products, as collected by researcher John R. Grout.[34] Each one of the devices in the list below reflects the kind of poka-yoke thinking that can prevent customer dissatisfaction, product damage, injuries, and lawsuits against a company.

poka-yoke
A quality control device initiated to prevent human errors in the manufacturing process and to assure proper use of the product on the part of the consumer.

- File cabinets can fall over if too many drawers are pulled out at the same time. For many file cabinets, opening one door locks the others, making it unlikely that the cabinet will tip.
- The fueling area of many passenger vehicles has two mistake-proofing devices: (1) The filling pipe prevents a larger, leaded-fuel nozzle from being inserted, and (2) the gas cap tether does not allow the motorist to drive off without the cap.
- In most passenger vehicles with an automatic transmission the keys cannot be removed until the vehicle is in park, thus preventing a vehicle being left in neutral and rolling away from where it was parked.
- New lawnmowers are required to have a safety bar on the handle that must be pulled back in order to start the engine and keep it running. If the safety bar is released the mower blade stops in three seconds, thus minimizing the risk of a runaway mower injuring the operator or another person. This device is an adaptation of the "dead-person" switch from locomotives.
- Circuit breakers (the forerunners to fuses) prevent electrical overloads and the fires that may result. When the electrical load becomes excessive, the circuit is broken.

ISO 9000 QUALITY STANDARDS

Another approach to achieving high quality is to adhere to an internationally recognized standard. **ISO 9000** is a series of management and quality-assurance standards developed for firms competing in international markets. The standards were originally developed by the International Standards Organization for manufacturing firms, but are now also used by service firms. Although referred to as ISO 9000, the set of standards is divided into five subsets:

ISO 9000
A series of management and quality-assurance standards developed for firms competing in international markets.

ISO 9000   The general guidelines for use of the set of standards

ISO 9001   A model for assuring quality in design, development, production, installation, and service of the product

ISO 9002   A complementary model for production and installation

ISO 9003   Specifications for final inspection and testing

ISO 9004   Principal concepts and a guide for overall quality management

To obtain ISO accreditation, the organization must follow 20 steps covering tasks such as identifying business processes and writing a quality manual. Writing procedures and work instructions are also required.

Another development in these international standards is QS-9000, the common supplier quality standard for DaimlerChrysler AG, Ford Motor Company, and General Motors Corporation. QS-9000 is based on ISO 9001 but contains additional requirements that are of particular interest to the automotive industry. QS-9000 applies to suppliers of production materials, production and service parts, heat treating, painting and plating, and other finishing services. Suppliers of these kinds of parts and services who want to do business with the Big Three auto makers have to be certified in QS-9000.[35]

The Deming Principles

Much of the quality movement, including specialized techniques for quality improvement, has been influenced by W. Edwards Deming. He formulated 14 steps that managers should take to lead firms toward a quality goal. Exhibit 4-4 lists

Deming's 14 Steps to Quality

100

1. Continually improve products and services to enhance the firm's competitive position.
2. Adopt the new philosophy of quality without delay.
3. Do not rely on mass inspections to detect defects. Instead, use statistical controls to ensure that quality is built into the product.
4. Do not select suppliers based on price alone. Reduce the number of suppliers and establish long-term, trusting, single-source partnerships in which both buyer and seller can pursue quality improvements.
5. Identify problems—whether caused by faulty systems or by operatives—and correct them.
6. Use modern methods of on-the-job training.
7. Improve and modernize methods of supervision.
8. Drive out fear from the workplace so that everyone can work productively.

9. Open up communications and break down barriers among departments.
10. Eliminate numerical goals, slogans, and posters as a way to motivate workers without giving them the methods to achieve these goals.
11. Eliminate work standards that assign numerical quotas.
12. Remove barriers that deprive employees of pride in their work.
13. Establish a dynamic program of education and training.
14. Create an executive structure that will emphasize the above 13 points every day.

Sources: Laura B. Forker, "Quality: American, Japanese, and Soviet Perspectives," *Academy of Management Executive*, November 1991, p. 65; Andrea Gabor, *The Man Who Discovered Quality: How W. Edwards Deming Brought the Quality Revolution to America—The Stories of Ford, Xerox, and GM* (New York: Times Books, 1990).

the steps. Some top-level managers post these steps in their offices to remind them of the importance of managing for quality.

Many of the ideas of this chapter stem from and support Deming's steps. However, many managers would rightfully resist doing away with mass inspections and numerical quotas. Would you take medicine to cure a serious illness if you knew the medicine was inspected by sampling alone? If you were running a business, would you do away with numerical production and sales quotas?

SUMMARY OF KEY POINTS

 Fully understand the meaning of quality.
Quality is the totality of features and characteristics of a product or service that bears on its ability to satisfy given needs. If a product or service does what it is supposed to do, it is said to be of high quality.

 Describe the principles and practices of quality management related to attitudes and people.
Nine quality management principles relate primarily to attitudes and people: (1) start with a vision and values, (2) obtain top-level commitment, (3) maintain customer sensitivity throughout the organization, (4) communicate widely about quality, (5) make continuous improvement a way of life, (6) empower and involve employees, (7) listen to employees, (8) emphasize the human side of quality, and (9) reward high-quality performance.

 Describe principles and practices of quality management related to work processes and technology.
Nine quality management principles relate primarily to work processes and technology: (1) implement a formal quality program to support the quality process, (2) engage in benchmarking, (3) select high-quality suppliers and train them properly, (4) ensure the excellence of incoming raw materials and supplies, (5) decrease cycle time, (6) pay painstaking attention to detail, (7) institute stringent work standards for every individual, (8) calculate the return on quality, and (9) train individuals in quality.

 Summarize principles and techniques of customer satisfaction for managers as well as customer-service workers.
The ultimate goal in terms of customer satisfaction is zero defects—keeping every customer a company

can profitably serve. The customer-satisfaction principles calling for managerial action include: (1) concentrate your efforts on creating value for customers, (2) establish customer satisfaction goals, (3) give decision-making authority to customer-service workers, (4) thoroughly screen applicants for customer-service positions, (5) hire full-time, permanent store associates, (6) establish a favorable work climate for customer service, (7) solicit customer feedback regularly, (8) communicate the fact that everyone contributes to the customer's perception of service, (9) find ways to buy from your customer, and (10) develop efficient systems of order fulfillment.

Customer-contact workers can use a variety of techniques to move an organization toward total customer satisfaction: (1) contribute to establishing customer bonds, (2) understand customer needs, (3) put customer needs first, (4) respond positively to moments of truth, (5) show care and concern, and be helpful with complaints, (6) communicate a positive attitude, and (7) smile at every customer.

 Explain how mass customization contributes to customer satisfaction.

Mass customization contributes to customer satisfaction by giving customers the opportunity to purchase a personal variation of a mass-produced product, such as your own combination of features on a personal computer. Achieving mass customization requires a highly flexible manufacturing system that can handle a variety of options. Suggestions for mass customization include: (1) evaluate the products in customers' terms, (2) offer customers the appropriate number of choices, (3) create a modular production system, (4) provide fingertip access to all information, (5) collect information about customer preferences directly, and (6) make it difficult for customers to go elsewhere.

 Explain various specialized techniques for quality improvement.

Quality control involves determining the extent to which goods or services match some specified quality standard. A 100-percent inspection involves checking every unit. Inspection by sampling achieves quality control by checking samples from a lot. Acceptance inspection is the checking of completed products. Another strategy is in-process inspection, in which products are checked during production. A third strategy combines acceptance and in-process techniques.

A refinement of in-process inspection is statistical process control, a technique for detecting potential problems before they result in poor-quality products. One tool used to identify quality problems is a Pareto diagram, a bar graph that ranks causes of process variation by frequency of occurrence. Cause-and-effect analysis is another graphical technique for analyzing the contributing factors to a problem. The result is referred to as an Ishikawa diagram, or fishbone diagram. Cause-and-effect analysis divides work processes into major areas such as person, machine, method, and material. The causes can then be further subdivided.

A widely used principle of quality assurance is robust design, the concept of designing a part or process so well that it can withstand fluctuations on the production line without a loss of quality. One major goal of robust design is to prevent products from failing while they are being used by customers. To achieve this, robust design tries to consistently hit quality targets, rather than just tolerate acceptable deviations. Another way of achieving high quality is to adhere to the ISO 9000 standards. Following these standards helps firms compete in international markets.

Poka-yoke is a method for preventing problems by preventing mistakes or making the mistake obvious at a glance. The method is based on the belief that you have to prevent people from making errors so an object can be manufactured or used correctly. A foundation principle of poka-yoke is to incorporate the function of a checklist into an operation so the operator does not neglect something important.

W. Edwards Deming formulated 14 steps to help managers improve quality. These principles have been incorporated by many managers into managing for quality.

KEY TERMS AND PHRASES

QUESTIONS

1. Why would a well-managed firm need a program of quality management?
2. A business strategy of Gillette and Schick is to produce high-quality disposable razors. In what way might these companies be defining quality?
3. In what way does employee empowerment contribute to achieving quality?
4. Identify two principles or techniques of customer service

described in this chapter that you think are often neglected by customer-service workers.
5. What is the difference between a suit that is mass customized versus buying a suit that is made to order?
6. What type of mistake-proofing device could be incorporated into an ordinary fax machine?
7. One of the Deming principles is about driving fear out of the workplace. What kind of fear might exist in the workplace?

SKILL-BUILDING EXERCISE 4-A: Evaluating Customer Service

Teams of three or four students arrange to meet outside of class to visit a retail establishment such as a franchise restaurant, a sports bar, or a retail outlet. During the visit, students should make mental and physical notes of the quality of customer service as related to ideas in this chapter. To pro-

vide structure to the assignment, students might make up a checklist of customer-satisfaction principles listed in this chapter. Students report their findings back to the class, including recommendations to managers of the establishments visited.

INTERNET SKILL-BUILDING EXERCISE: What's New in Quality Management?

To help keep you abreast of developments in the technical side of quality management visit the following two Web sites: www.ISO.ch and www.ASQ.org. The ISO site presents in-depth information about international standards for quality. The ASQ site is prepared by the American Society for Quality

Control, a highly-reliable and original source of information about quality management. As you visit the sites, look especially for information that expands upon what has been presented in this chapter.

CASE PROBLEM 4-A: The Holiday Turkey Meltdown

Management consultant Meredith Belbin was conducting quality seminars in England. He asked participants at each seminar to describe a "quality calamity," a situation in which a quality flaw cost the company a substantial amount of money. Participants were instructed to analyze, to the best of their ability, why and how the problem took place. Belbin collected details on 121 of these episodes. Many were dramatic, yet they were kept hidden from the public to avoid loss of consumer confidence and future business. Here is a representative quality calamity reported in the seminar:

Top management at a well-established appliance manufacturer rushed a new split-level oven to market to meet a difficult sales target. Market research indicated there was a strong demand for the oven so the company was even more eager to get to the market first. To save time in the product development cycle, the company decided to skip extensive

testing of the completed product. A marketing executive made the observation, "There's got to be a limit to how much you inspect a product before it goes out the door. Too much testing has two costs. First, is paying for all the inspection, including such costs as the salary and benefits for quality inspectors. Second, is the opportunity costs. While you hold a product up in the shop inspecting for every conceivable disaster, you lose money by not having a new product in the hands of distributors. After all, we're selling home appliances, not Rolls Royces."

Management's judgment seemed vindicated because the oven sold well and reorders from stores suggested the product was a solid success. Despite the initial market acceptance, the oven had a problem. The insulation surrounding the oven was inadequate, causing heat to escape progressively into the controls above. Nevertheless, the heat buildup caused no problem with typical cooking tasks, such as baking a cake or cooking lasagna.

A longer period of continuous heating revealed the fatal flaw. A large turkey cooking for about four hours was more than the oven could handle. Before the turkey was cooked, the accumulation of heat would melt the oven's controls. Shocked and irate customers called the retail outlets by the hundreds the first day the stores were open after Christmas Day. By the time this problem was discovered, the ovens had been distributed and were in use throughout Great Britain.

The company salvaged the situation the best it could through a recall program. Customers were offered a credit toward another stove model made by the company. A few customers were so angry, the credit would not satisfy them. A woman from Sheffield, England wrote the company a letter explaining that she intended to sue them. Among her comments were, "You have caused me the greatest humiliation of my life. Imagine having six people for Christmas dinner.

Instead of serving my guests a delightful turkey dinner, I served them poison smoke from melted plastic."

Although the other models were less fancy, their controls did not melt in the process of cooking a turkey. The company incurred a financial loss on the first run of split-level ovens. Later they reintroduced the same model with improved insulation.

Discussion Questions

1. How can the company in question prevent another calamity of this type happening in the future?
2. Which principles of quality, including specialized quality techniques, were not observed in this case?
3. What is your evaluation of the comments made by the marketing executive about the company making household appliances, not Rolls Royces?

Source: Expanded from Meredith Belbin, *The Coming Shape of Organization* (Oxford, England: Butterworth-Heineman, 1996).

CASE PROBLEM 4 - B : The Troublesome Demo Mode

Early in the basketball season, Billy Appletree, an ardent UCLA Bruins fan, decided that he and his family had suffered enough. After all, their 13″ television set was 12 years old. Billy, a credit manager at a furniture company, conferred with his wife, Maria, a dietitian, and their 11-year-old daughter, Jennifer. All agreed that a big-screen television would contribute greatly to family entertainment.

Friday night the Appletree family shopped for a television set at Consumer Electronics. Maria spotted a 32″ TV set that seemed ideal. A store associate confirmed her judgment by explaining that the set had the highest quality in its class. The cost, including a three-year complete service warranty, was $1,157.

The television set was delivered Monday evening as scheduled. For several days the Appletree family enjoyed watching programs on their big-screen set. Friday evening, however, the family was mystified by an image that appeared on the screen. Shortly after Jennifer punched the menu button, an advertisement appeared on the screen touting the features of the set.

Billy laughed and explained that the demonstration mode was somehow triggered. He said that the solution would be to punch the right buttons. Maria and he punched every button on the television receiver and the TV remote, but the demonstration mode remained. Billy then pulled the plug and reinserted it, but the demonstration mode reappeared. The family scanned the owner's manual but found no information relating to the problem.

Billy telephoned the dealer. He got through to the service department after being placed on hold for six minutes. The service representative said that he knew nothing about the problem, but that Billy should speak to the sales department. After Billy explained his problem to the sales associate, he was told to speak to the service department.

Billy called back the service department and explained the problem again. A customer-service specialist said that the store relied on an outside TV and appliance repair firm to handle such problems. The specialist said she would telephone the repair firm on Monday, and the firm would contact the Appletree family. By Tuesday morning, there was still no word from the repair firm.

Exasperated, Billy scanned a customer-information booklet that came with the television set. He found a list of 10 authorized service centers throughout the U.S. and Canada that repaired his brand of television. Billy telephoned a service center in California to take advantage of the time-zone difference.

A woman with a cheerful voice answered the phone and listened to Billy's problems. With a sympathetic laugh, she said, "We get lots of calls like this. No problem. Just push the volume-up and volume-down buttons at the same time. The demo mode will disappear. The mode was activated when somebody pressed the menu-up and menu-down buttons at the same time. Anybody in your family have arthritis?" Billy raced into the living room and triumphantly restored the TV set to normal functioning.

A representative from the local television service store telephoned on Friday. She said, "This is Modern TV and Appliance. Do you still need service on your set?" With anger in her voice, Maria explained how the problem was finally resolved.

Later that night, as the family gathered to watch the Bruins, Billy said, "I guess we all love our new large-screen TV, but I wouldn't go back to Consumer Electronics even to buy a videotape."

Discussion Questions

1. Trace the quality and customer-service mistakes made in this case by all parties involved.
2. How can the demonstration mode problem be fixed so it will not occur again with other customers?
3. What work process and methodology problems relating to quality are revealed in this case?

ENDNOTES

1. Adapted and excerpted from "These Service Pros Go the Extra Mile to Solve Customer Problems," *The Customer Service Professional*, September 1997, p. 2.
2. Carol A. Reeves and David A. Bednar, "Defining Quality: Alternatives and Implications," *The Academy of Management Review*, July 1994, pp. 419–421.
3. John M. Ivancevich, "Quality Is Here to Stay Because It Makes a Difference," *Back to Basics*, April 1997, p. 1.
4. Carla C. Carter, *Human Resource Management and the Total Quality Imperative* (New York: AMACOM, 1993), p. 1.
5. George Labovitz, Y. S. Chang, and Victor Rosansky, *Making Quality Work: A Leadership Guide for the Results-Driven Manager* (New York: Harper Collins, 1993).
6. Thomas Y. Choi and Orlando C. Behling, "Top Managers and TQM Success: One More Look after All These Years," *The Academy of Management Executive*, February 1997, p. 38.
7. Mark Henricks, "Step by Step," *Entrepreneur*, March 1996, p. 70.
8. Del Jones, "1992 Quality Cup Finalists," *USA Today*, April 10, 1992, p. 2B.
9. Jones, "1992 Quality Cup Finalists," p. 2B.
10. David Woodruff, "An Embarassment of Glitches Galvanizes Chrysler," *Business Week*, April 17, 1995, p. 76.
11. Jeanne C. Poole, William F. Rathgeber III, and Stanley W. Silverman, "Paying for Performance in a TQM Environment," *HRMagazine*, October 1993, p. 68.
12. Kathryn Troy, "Recognize Quality Achievement with Noncash Awards," *Personnel Journal*, October 1993, pp. 111–117.
13. "Larry Bossidy Won't Stop Pushing," *Fortune*, January 13, 1997, p. 136.
14. Philip P. Crosby, *Quality is Still Free: Making Quality Certain in Uncertain Times* (New York: McGraw-Hill, 1996).
15. David Greising, "Quality: How to Make It Pay," *Business Week*, August 8, 1994, p. 55.
16. David Greising, "How Companies Are Rethinking Quality," *Business Week*, August 8, 1994, p. 57.
17. Roger O. Crockett, "Wireless Goes Haywire at Motorola," *Business Week*, March 9, 1998, p. 32; Crockett, "Motorola Girds for a Shakeup, *Business Week*, April 13, 1998, p. 33.
18. Gilbert Fuchsberg, "Quality Programs Show Shoddy Results," *The Wall Street Journal*, May 14, 1992, p. B1.
19. Oren Harari, "Ten Reasons TQM Doesn't Work," *Management Review*, January 1997, pp. 40, 43.
20. Frederick F. Reichheld and W. Earl Sasser, Jr., "Zero Defections: Quality Comes to Services," *Harvard Business Review*, September–October 1990, p. 106; Reicheld, "Learning from Customer Defections," *Harvard Business Review*, March–April 1996, pp. 56–69.
21. Forler Massnick, "Customer Service Can Kill You," *Management Review*, March 1997, p. 33.
22. William B. Martin, *Quality Customer Service: A Positive Guide to Superior Service*, rev. ed. (Los Altos, CA: Crisp Publications, 1989); Massnick, "Customer Service Can Kill You," pp. 33–35; Jeff W. Johnson, "Linking Employee Perceptions of Service Climate to Customer Satisfaction," *Personnel Psychology*, Winter 1996, pp. 831–851; Michael Warshaw, "Captivate Every Customer," *Success*, July–August 1997, pp. 48–49.
23. Research cited in Stephen J. Wall, *The New Strategists* (New York: The Free Press, 1996).
24. David Fagiano, "Service in a Temporary World," *Management Review*, February 1994, p. 4.
25. Benjamin Schneider, Susan S. White, and Michelle C. Paul, "Linking Service Climate and Perceptions of Service Quality: Test of a Causal Model," *Journal of Applied Psychology*, April 1998, pp. 150–163.
26. Schneider, White, and Paul, "Linking Service Climate," p. 160.
27. Justin Martin, "Ignore Your Customer," *Fortune*, May 1, 1995, p. 126.
28. Howard E. Butz, Jr., and Leonard D. Goodstein, "Measuring Customer Value: Gaining the Strategic Advantage," *Organizational Dynamics*, Winter 1996, p. 63.
29. "Good Service Is Good Enough," *Working Smart*, July 1993, p. 1.
30. Justin Martin, "Give 'Em *Exactly* What They Want," *Fortune*, November 10, 1997, pp. 283–284.
31. www.cio.com/archive/enterprise/021598_mass_content.html. Accessed October 23, 1998.
32. Genichi Taguchi and Don Clausing, "Robust Quality," *Harvard Business Review*, January–February 1990, p. 67.
33. Connie Dyer, "On-Line Quality: Shigeo Shingo's Shop Floor," *Harvard Business Review*, January–February 1990, p. 73.
34. John R. Grout, "Everyday Examples of Mistake-Proofing," www.campbell.berry.edu/faculty/jgrout/everyday.html. Accessed June 17, 1998.
35. www.asq.org/standcert/9000.html. Accessed October 23, 1998.

Chapter Five

Taiwan-born Marty and Helen Shih, brother and sister, began their business careers in the United States by selling flowers from a small stand in downtown Los Angeles. Since then, they have built a business empire serving the huge multicultural Asian-American market. The market consists of close to 10 million members and 500,000 Asian-owned companies. The Shihs zeroed in on this elusive market by building relationships with customers one at a time.

In the early days, every time a customer purchased flowers, the Shihs would ask for the customer's name, address, and phone number, and the occasion for which flowers were being bought. They would note whether the flowers were bought for friends, sweethearts, spouses, or parents. Before special occasions, such as Valentine's Day or anniversaries, the Shihs would telephone or send post cards to remind customers of the date.

As the years passed, wherever the Shihs went, they worked to broaden their customer database by copying down the names and phone numbers of people with Asian names. From this painstaking effort was born the Asian American Association of El Monte, California. Today the Association comprises 13 companies and has branches across the United States. The Association channels the vast purchasing power of new Asian immigrants to American business and provides many numerous products and services to the Asian community. By 2000, the Internet would bring them most of their business (www.aan.com).

Essentials of Planning

105

OBJECTIVES

After studying this chapter and doing the exercises, you should be able to:

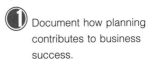 **1** Document how planning contributes to business success.

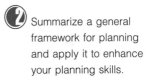 **2** Summarize a general framework for planning and apply it to enhance your planning skills.

 **3** Describe the nature of business strategy.

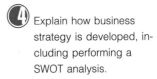 **4** Explain how business strategy is developed, including performing a SWOT analysis.

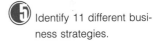 **5** Identify 11 different business strategies.

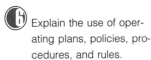 **6** Explain the use of operating plans, policies, procedures, and rules.

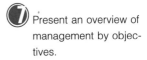 **7** Present an overview of management by objectives.

Marty Shih describes another part of the plan he used to tap into the Asian market: "New immigrants would come to our stand for flowers because they could talk to us in Chinese and because we could do things like decorate the ribbons with Chinese words."[1]

The case history just presented about the two small merchants who built an empire illustrates how planning (in this case building customer databases by hand) contributes to success. The Shih success story also exemplifies a *focus strategy*, one of the many business strategies, or master plans, that you will read about in this chapter. By virtue of planning, including developing strategy, we manage the future instead of being guided by fate.

The purpose of this chapter is to describe the planning function in such a way that you can use what you learn to plan more effectively as a manager or individual contributor. First the chapter will look at the value of planning and a framework for its application. You will also learn about high-level, or strategic planning, including how strategy is developed and the types of strategy that result from strategic planning. We will then describe operating plans, policies, procedures, and rules, and a widely used method for getting large numbers of people involved in implementing plans: management by objectives.

Document how planning contributes to business success.

THE CONTRIBUTION OF PLANNING

Planning is important because it contributes heavily to success and gives you some control over the future. According to one analysis, the value of planning is in the process itself. By planning, you set aside your daily tasks and deadlines so you can enlarge your mental focus and see the bigger picture.[2] More specifically, planning often leads to improvement in productivity, quality, and financial results.

Extensive research evidence supports the value of planning, as revealed by an analysis of 26 studies. Companies that engaged in strategic (high-level and long-range) planning achieved better financial results. They also did a better job of fitting into their environment, such as an automotive company adapting to changing preferences for vehicles. Planning was also found to contribute to corporate growth.[3]

Despite the many advantages of planning, it can interfere with the spontaneity necessary for success. Astute businesspeople often seize opportunities as they occur, even if they are not part of any plan. For example, a report cited the contribution of red wine to lowering cholesterol among French people. Several wineries in the United States seized this marketing opportunity by rapidly increasing the production of red wine. Another problem is that planning can create blinders designed to focus direction and block out peripheral vision. As management theorist Henry Mintzberg says, "Setting oneself on a predetermined course in uncharted waters is the perfect way to sail straight into an iceberg."[4]

An effective antidote to the disadvantages of planning is to allow some slack in your plan for capitalizing on the unexpected. For example, in planning a job search, leave room to explore opportunities you did not envision in your plan.

Summarize a general framework for planning and apply it to enhance your planning skills.

A GENERAL FRAMEWORK FOR PLANNING

Planning is a complex and comprehensive process involving a series of overlapping and interrelated elements or stages. There are at least three types of planning: strategic, tactical, and operational. **Strategic planning** is establishing master plans that shape the destiny of the firm. When Wal-Mart decided to expand beyond the United States and Canada into Europe and Asia, that represented strategic planning. (Strategic planning and business strategies will be described later in the chapter.) A second type of planning is needed to support strategic planning, such as how to select expansion sites in Europe and Asia. **Tactical planning** translates strategic plans into specific goals and plans that are most relevant to a particular organizational unit.

A third type of planning is aimed more at day-to-day operations or the nuts and bolts of doing business. **Operational planning** identifies the specific procedures and actions required at lower levels in the organization. If your local Wal-Mart wanted to add produce, such as vegetables, to its merchandise, operational plans would have to be drawn. In practice, the distinction between tactical planning and operational planning is not clear cut. However, both tactical plans and operational plans must support the strategic plan such as the globalization of Wal-Mart.

The framework presented in Exhibit 5-1 summarizes the elements of planning. With slight modification the model could be applied to strategic, tactical, and operational planning. A planner must define the present situation, establish goals and objectives, forecast aids and barriers to goals and objectives, develop action plans to reach goals and objectives, develop budgets, implement the plans, and control the plans.

This chapter will examine each element separately. In practice, however, several of these stages often overlap. For example, a manager might be implementing and controlling the same plan simultaneously.

strategic planning
A firm's overall master plan that shapes its destiny.

tactical planning
Planning that translates a firm's strategic plans into specific goals by organizational unit.

operational planning
Planning that requires specific procedures and actions at lower levels in an organization.

107

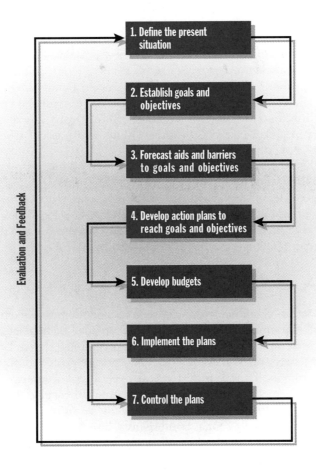

EXHIBIT 5-1

A Framework for Planning Planning at its best is a systematic process.

The planning steps are not always followed in the order presented in Exhibit 5-1. Planners frequently start in the middle of the process, proceed forward, and then return to an earlier step. This change of sequence frequently happens because the planner discovers new information or because objectives change. Also, many managers set goals before first examining their current position.

To illustrate the general framework for planning we turn to Wal-Mart, whose plan is to globally dominate the retail industry. President and CEO David Glass said, "Our priorities are that we want to dominate North America first, then South America and then Asia and then Europe."[5] The plan for global domination would proceed approximately as described next, without presenting confidential company information.

Define the Present Situation

Knowing where you are is critical to establishing goals for change. Wal-Mart top management knows it is already the world's largest retailer, being three times as large as Sears, its closest competitor. The plan toward global domination is well under way. By 1999 Wal-Mart was already serving 90 million customers per week outside the United States through 2,400 discount stores, 450 wholesale Sam's Clubs, and 600 other stores. David Glass and other managers investigate whether the company has sufficient funds to keep on expanding overseas. The answer is affirmative: Continue with plans for global domination.

Defining the present situation includes measuring success and examining internal capabilities and external threats. Wal-Mart management must therefore engage in two more activities to complete this first step. *Success* in this situation would mean that new stores overseas would soon contribute a positive cash flow to the company. *Internal capabilities* refer to the strengths and weaknesses of the firm, or organizational unit, engaging in planning. The capabilities of Wal-Mart are extensive. Among them are a world-recognized brand name, thousands of experienced and competent managers and specialists, exceptional financial health, and a reputation for low prices. In addition, the company has achieved considerable success in global markets. And the "Made in America" label is appealing to consumers around the world.

External threats and opportunities include several tough competitors such as France's Carrefour and the Netherlands SHV Makro, economic crises, and sudden currency fluctuations in other countries. Another potential threat is that some communities do not want to be dominated by Wal-Mart. Predicting which products will sell well in different cultures could lead to inventory problems. Finding local talent with retailing knowledge could also be a problem.

Establish Goals and Objectives

The second step in planning is to establish goals and identify objectives that contribute to the attainment of goals. (Goals are broader than objectives, whereas objectives function as smaller goals that support the bigger goals.) Being a carefully planned enterprise, Wal-Mart already has precise goals and objectives. Total global domination itself can be regarded as an overall goal or strategic goal. Specific goals for the intermediate future include opening 80 retail outlets outside the United States in countries where Wal-Mart already has stores. Among these countries are Argentina, Brazil, China, South Korea, and Mexico. Another goal is for one-third of Wal-Mart sales and earnings to come from the international division by 2003. Objectives to support these goals would include establishing target dates for opening stores in the various countries, stocking the shelves and warehouses, and advertising in the target countries.

Forecast Aids and Barriers to Goals and Objectives

As an extension of defining the present situation, the manager or other planner attempts to predict which internal and external factors will foster or hinder attainment of the desired ends. David Glass and other Wal-Mart managers and professionals rely on past experience and intuition about the feasibility of further penetration into the global market. Market research also is used to assess demand for giant, one-stop retailers in the various countries. The Wal-Mart team concludes that its many present successes in the international market make further expansion a likely success.

Despite the optimistic forecast, Wal-Mart faces some barriers. One is economic instability, such as the Asian crisis of 1998. Sudden changes in currency valuation, such as the rapidly changing value of the Mexican peso in recent years, can create pricing problems. Another barrier to success is making accurate predictions about seasonal demands when getting started in a foreign country. An example is that when the company opened its first superstore in Brazil in November 1995, managers there were overwhelmed when sales were quadruple those in the United States. In general, it is difficult to predict accurately the type of Wal-Mart that best fits each location. One tricky factor is predicting the best ratio of locally made goods to those imported from the United States.

Develop Action Plans to Reach Goals and Objectives

Goals and objectives are only wishful thinking until action plans are drawn. An **action plan** is the specific steps necessary to achieve a goal or objective. The Wal-Mart planners have to figure out specifically how they are going to acquire or rent the real estate necessary to build their stores, wholesale clubs, and supercenters. Teams have to be assembled to research specific countries and cities such as a suburb of Sydney, Australia. Action plans also have to be drawn for meeting with local government officials and citizens' groups to obtain necessary approvals for launching a Wal-Mart. Many local groups have opposed a Wal-Mart presence in their town. Two of hundreds of possible action plans would be:

- Consult with construction companies in Caracas, Venezuela, to determine if they can accomplish the work needed to be done, when we need it done, and at the price we are willing to pay.
- Hire a local translator to ensure none of our signs translated from English into the native language will in any way be considered an insult, a vulgar term, or a cultural blooper of any type.

Develop Budgets

Planning usually results in action plans that require money to implement. For example, Wal-Mart spends about $13 million to open each store in another country. Money must be budgeted for advertising after the store opens, and for real

action plan
The specific steps necessary to achieve a goal or objective.

109

estate taxes. A formal budget would indicate how much money a manager can afford to spend on each action plan. A company like Wal-Mart has deeper pockets than most firms, with 1998 profits of about $4 billion from $135 billion in sales. Nevertheless, all expenditures are accounted for by a budget. Some action plans require almost no cash outlay, such as speaking to customers in retail outlets overseas about their preferences. The purpose of these talks would be to assess how well Wal-Mart is doing in serving the needs of customers in a given country. The feedback can be useful in planning expansion in the same country.

Implement the Plans

If the plans developed in the previous five steps are to benefit the firm, they must be put to use. A frequent criticism of planners is that they develop elaborate plans and then abandon them in favor of conducting business as usual. In contrast, David Glass and the other members of the Wal-Mart executive team are particularly strong at implementation. They move ahead relentlessly, learning from their mistakes such as having too many or too few American-made goods in a foreign location.

Control the Plans

Planning does not end with implementation, because plans may not always proceed as conceived. The purpose of the control process is to measure progress toward goal attainment and to take corrective action if too much deviation is detected. The deviation from expected performance can be negative or positive. Site purchase and construction expenditures could run over budget or under budget. After a given store opens, sales could be higher or lower than anticipated. Higher sales than anticipated could mean inventory shortages (such as getting caught short on Hispanic Barbie Dolls), which might hurt goodwill in launching a new store.

In Exhibit 5-1, note the phrase "Evaluation and Feedback" on the left. The phrase indicates that the control process allows for the fine tuning of plans after their implementation. One common example of the need for fine tuning is a budget that has been set too high or too low in the first attempt at implementing a plan. A manager controls by making the right adjustment.

Make Contingency Plans

contingency plan
An alternative plan to be used if the original plan cannot be implemented or a crisis develops.

Many planners develop a set of backup plans to be used in case things do not proceed as hoped. A **contingency plan** is an alternative plan to be used if the original plan cannot be implemented or a crisis develops. (The familiar expression "Let's try plan B" gets at the essence of contingency planning.) A hurricane or typhoon could wreck a local economy as Wal-Mart is about to enter that country. Or a sudden outburst from local merchants could create an unfavorable climate for the giant retailer. If Wal-Mart discovers that the timing is poor to enter a given country, the executive team might be able to attain the expansion goal by shifting focus to another country. If plans for a store in Caracas must be changed suddenly, Wal-Mart might decide instead to quickly plan an opening in Quito, Ecuador.

Contingency plans are often developed from objectives in earlier steps in planning. The plans are triggered into action when the planner detects, however early in the planning process, deviations from objectives. Construction projects, such as building a retail supercenter, are particularly prone to deviations from completion dates because so many different contractors and subcontractors are involved.

STRATEGIC PLANNING AND BUSINESS STRATEGIES

The framework for planning can be used to develop and implement strategic plans, as well as tactical and operational plans. The output of one aspect of strategic planning by Wal–Mart was globalization, or the penetration of international markets. The emphasis of strategic planning in the current era is to help the firm move into emerging markets, or invent the future of the firm.

Strategic planning should result in managerial workers throughout the organization thinking strategically. This would include wondering about how the firm adapts to its environment and how it will cope with its future. A strategically minded worker at any level would think, "How does what I am doing right now support corporate strategy?" The help-desk worker at Hewlett-Packard might say to himself, "Each time I help a customer solve a problem I am contributing to the strategy of having the highest quality products in all the markets we serve." To sensitize you to the realities of business strategies, the accompanying Manager in Action illustrates the type of strategic thinking behind the Barbie doll. A caution here is that some strategy experts would not agree that the thinking displayed by the manager, Jill Barad, is revolutionary enough to qualify as strategy.

Business strategy is a complex subject that can be viewed from a variety of perspectives. Here we look at business strategy from three major perspectives: its nature, how it is developed, and a sampling of the various types of strategy in use.

The Nature of Business Strategy

What constitutes business strategy has been described in dozens of ways. A **strategy** is the organization's plan, or comprehensive program, for achieving its vision, mission, and goals in its environment. A recent explanation of business strategy developed by Michael Porter, a leading authority, provides useful guidelines for managers who need to develop strategy. According to Porter, true business strategy has four components as outlined in Exhibit 5-2 and described next.[6]

STRATEGY INVOLVES MORE THAN OPERATIONAL EFFECTIVENESS
A starting point in understanding the nature of business strategy is to understand that it involves more than operational effectiveness or being efficient. In recent years many firms in the private and public sector have become more efficient through such means as downsizing, performing work more efficiently, and outsourcing (paying outsiders to perform some activities). Although the improvement in operations have often been dramatic, these changes rarely lead to sustainable improvements in profitability. As many top-level executives have said, "You can't cost-cut your way to growth." Strategy essentially involves performing activities differently, such as 1–800–MATTRESS, the company that pioneered selling mattresses over the phone. Being able to purchase a mattress over the phone is a convenience that adds value to the purchase of a mattress.

STRATEGY RESTS ON UNIQUE ACTIVITIES   Competitive strategy means deliberately choosing a different set of activities to deliver a unique value. An often cited example is Southwest Airlines Company. Their uniqueness is to offer

Describe the nature of business strategy.

strategy
The organization's plan, or comprehensive program, for achieving its vision, mission, and goals.

Manager *in Action*

Jill Barad, Chair and CEO of Mattel Inc.

In 1981, Jill E. Barad joined toy-maker giant Mattell as a product manager to begin her rapid rise in the corporation. In 1997, she was appointed CEO, and later chair of the board of directors. Barad is also on the board of directors of Microsoft Corp. and Pixar Inc. As one of only two women top-level executives of *Fortune* 500 companies, she has become a key role model for a generation of young women managers and professionals. She recently received an award from Girls Inc., formerly Girls Clubs of America.

Barad is striking in appearance and projects charisma through her energetic, engaging personality. Her flamboyance and outspokenness have created a few enemies, particularly earlier in her career. She can be warm and loving toward work associates, and she can also be abrasive and sarcastic. Barad makes no apologies for being the driving force behind the Barbie doll. "At Mattel I worked on a brand that changed my life, and her name was Barbie. When Barbie is in a little girl's hands, she is a vehicle for dreaming, for imagining what girls can be."

Marketing strategy has been Barad's major contribution to Mattel, particularly in regard to the Barbie doll. Worldwide sales of Barbie dolls now approach $2 billion annually, and account for one-third of Mattel's revenue. Barbie (and give "Ken" a little credit also) is one of the most recognizable brands in the world. The average American girl owns nine Barbie dolls.

The Barbie doll is no longer exclusively the demure, thin-waisted doll so many women's groups have opposed because it sets up an unrealistic image for girls. Feminists have long considered Barbie sexist and demeaning. Barad helped create hundreds of different versions of the doll, including Astronaut Barbie and Carnival Cruise Barbie.

Furthermore, Barbie is being resized to a figure that is more representative of the majority of girls and women.

As the Barbie doll approaches saturation in the United States, Barad hopes to penetrate further foreign markets. A new line of dolls is being introduced, tailored to regional cultures. Her plans are to double international sales to $3.4 billion within five years. If the globalization strategy does not work well, Barad will find a contingency plan. She notes, "When it comes to strategic underpinnings and what is broken and what needs to be fixed, those are the challenges that I love. I've been looking for the holes."

Another Barad strategy that has paid handsome financial results was an expanded agreement with Walt Disney Co. for the right to license toys based on its films. She also forged a similar deal with Nickelodeon before the cable network became a smash success.

From her early days at Mattel, her sharp tongue and combative nature helped Barad succeed. A former boss says, "It [Mattel] is a shark pond. You throw people in and see if they can swim fast enough to stay alive. For Jill, it was a fit." After two years of ordinary assignments, including a rubber worm that slithered down walls, Barad was assigned to the Barbie team. Barad built Barbie into a mega-hit by focusing on a segmentation strategy. The idea was to elevate sales by selling dolls for numerous "play patterns," such as shopping, dating, engaging in sports, or going to the beach. Barad did not invent the strategy, but she executed it extraordinarily well.

Despite the success of the Barbie doll, Barad keeps focused on the competition. Rival toy companies Hasbro and Galoob won the exclusive rights to create toys for the *Star Wars* movies. A recent product enhancement is to blend traditional toys with computers and the Internet. Many of the new toys are stuffed with microprocessors. The most electronically advanced is a Barbie digital camera that enables girls to photograph themselves, then transfer their images to appear on the screen with Barbie.

To further prepare for the competitive thrust, Barad has chosen a strategy of cost cutting and acquisitions. In 1998 she announced the elimination of 2,700 jobs. Acquisitions included the purchase of Tyco,

the maker of Tickle Me Elmo, and Barbie CD-ROM software.

Barad's knack for fine-tuning marketing strategy has helped her career and her company. Yet her intense, in-your-face attitude, high energy, and relentless ambition are also major contributors to her success.

Sources: Based on Kathleen Morris, *Business Week*, May 25, 1998, pp. 112–119; "The Top 20 Best-Paid Women in Corporate America," *Working Woman*, February 1998, pp. 28–29.

short-haul, low-cost, direct service between mid-size cities and secondary airports in large cities. Southwest's frequent departures and low fares attract price conscious customers who would otherwise travel by car or bus. Southwest customers are willing to forego the frill of in-flight meals to save money and have a wide choice of flight departures. All Southwest activities are geared toward delivering low-cost, convenient service on its routes. By doing away with added features such as meals and interline transfer of baggage, the airline can achieve gate turnarounds in about 15 minutes. Planes can then be airborne more of the time, allowing for more frequent flights. By using automated ticketing, passengers can bypass travel agents, which saves Southwest money on commissions.

EXHIBIT 5-2

The Nature of Strategy

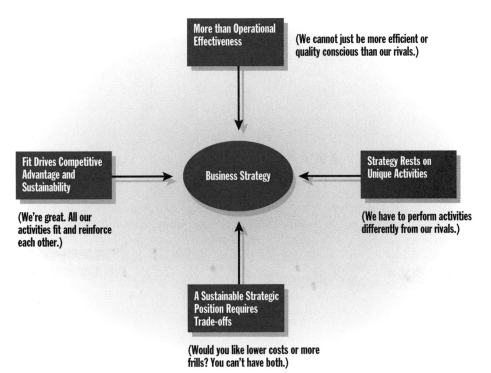

More than Operational Effectiveness
(We cannot just be more efficient or quality conscious than our rivals.)

Fit Drives Competitive Advantage and Sustainability
(We're great. All our activities fit and reinforce each other.)

Business Strategy

Strategy Rests on Unique Activities
(We have to perform activities differently from our rivals.)

A Sustainable Strategic Position Requires Trade-offs
(Would you like lower costs or more frills? You can't have both.)

Source: Figure compiled from information throughout Michael E. Porter, "What Is Strategy?" *Harvard Business Review*, November–December 1996, pp. 61–78.

Another unique activity is flying only 737 aircraft, which boosts the efficiency of maintenance.

A SUSTAINABLE STRATEGIC POSITION REQUIRES TRADE-OFFS

After a firm finds a strategic position (or place in the market), it can best sustain it by making trade-offs with other positions. Trade-offs are necessary when activities are incompatible. A good example is shopping through the Internet. If you want the convenience of shopping anytime and from your home or office, you sacrifice interacting with a sales associate who can answer your questions. Another trade-off with E-commerce (and shopping by phone) is that defective merchandise has to be repacked and shipped back to the manufacturer. Repacking and reshipping is more inconvenient for many people than, for example, driving back to the merchant with a computer that doesn't work.

A confusing application of the trade-off strategy is the sports utility vehicle (SUV). If you want a rough riding, moderate cost vehicle, with off-the-road capabilities, you purchase the basic SUV in the manufacturer's line. However, if you want an SUV with off-the-road capabilities, a smooth ride, and a luxury interior and exterior, you must pay the equivalent price of a luxury sedan. You can own an SUV with the comforts of a luxury sedan, but not at the price of an ordinary SUV—that's your trade-off.

FIT DRIVES BOTH COMPETITIVE ADVANTAGE AND SUSTAINABILITY

Strategy includes efficiently combining activities related to making a product or service. The chain of company activities fit and support each other to form an effective system. Bic Corporation is an example of the *fit* aspect of strategy. The company sells a narrow line of standard, low-priced ballpoint pens to the major customer markets (retail, commercial, promotional) through practically every available channel. Bic targets the common need for a low-price, acceptable pen throughout the markets it serves. The company gains the benefit of consistency across nearly all activities, meaning that they do not have to have different equipment or staff to conduct their business with different customer groups. Bic achieves fit by a product design that emphasizes ease of manufacturing, manufacturing plants designed for low-cost, large-scale purchasing to minimize material costs, and in-house parts production whenever cost effective.

The Development of Business Strategy

Explain how business strategy is developed, including performing a SWOT analysis.

vision
An idealized picture of the future of an organization.

mission
The firm's purpose and where it fits into the world.

Business strategy develops from planning. Strategic planning encompasses those activities that lead to the statement of goals and objectives and the choice of strategies to achieve them. The final outcomes of strategic planning are statements of vision, mission, strategy, and policy. A **vision** is an idealized picture of the future of the organization. The **mission** identifies the firm's purpose and where it fits into the world. Specifying a mission answers the question, "What business are we really in?" A mission is more grounded in present-day realities than is a vision, but some companies use the terms interchangeably. A firm's mission may not be apparent to the casual observer. For example, Packard Bell is a leading manufacturer of personal computers the United States and Canada, selling almost entirely in retail stores. Yet, according to one business analyst, "Packard Bell is not a PC company, it's a consumer-electronics company."[7] Exhibit 5-3 presents a few examples of company visions and mission statements.

EXHIBIT
5-3

> **Chrysler Corporation:** "Chrysler Corporation is committed to providing our customers with the world's highest level of satisfaction with our products and service."
>
> **McCormick & Company Inc.:** "The primary mission of McCormick & Company Inc. is to expand its worldwide leadership position in the spice, seasoning, and flavoring market."
>
> **CNN:** The vision of Ted Turner, its founder, is to "create the first truly global information company, the global network of record, seen in every nation on the planet, broadcast in most major languages."
>
> **Bombardier:** "Bombardier's mission is to be the leader in all the markets in which it operates. This objective will be achieved through excellence in design, manufacturing, and marketing in the fields of transportation equipment, aerospace, recreational products, financial services, and services related to its products and core competencies." (Did you know that this global giant based in Montreal, Quebec, was the first manufacturer of the snowmobile—the Skidoo?)
>
> **Fico's Automotive Repair & Refinish Collision:** "We intend to be the premier body shop for high-quality auto or small-truck restoration, refinishing, or body repair. We will be highly respected by auto buffs and insurance companies." (Fico's mission statement illustrates that even small enterprises can have a mission or vision.)

Planning alone does not create strategy. Corporate values also influence strategy because well-managed organizations tend to develop strategy to fit what the people in power think is important. If the company highly values innovation, it will not adopt a strategy of being successful by imitating (or benchmarking) other successful products. Piaget, for example, has remained successful for over 200 years by staying with its own high-quality watches, and not imitating other trends in the watch industry.

Under ideal circumstances a firm arrives at strategy after completing strategic planning. In practice, many firms choose a strategy prior to strategic planning. Once the firm has the strategy, a plan is developed to implement it. A chief executive might say, "Let's compete by becoming the most recognizable company in our field." The executive team would then develop specific plans to implement that strategy, rather than strategic planning leading to the conclusion that brand recognition would be an effective strategy. For many medium- and small-size organizations it is strategy first, followed by planning.

Three major approaches to developing strategy are gathering multiple inputs, analyzing the realities of the business situation, and doing a SWOT analysis. All three of these approaches are consistent with, and extensions of, the basic planning model presented in Exhibit 5-1.

GATHERING MULTIPLE INPUTS TO FORMULATE STRATEGY   Strategic managers and leaders are often thought of as mystics who work independently and conjure up great schemes for the future. In reality, many strategic leaders arrive at their ideas for the organization's future by consulting with a wide range of parties at interest. Strategy theorist Gary Hamel advises executives to make the strategy-creation process more democratic. He reasons that imagination is scarcer than resources. As a consequence, "we have to involve hundreds, if not thousands, of new voices in the strategy process if we want to increase the odds of seeing the future."[8]

A positive example of using multiple input to formulate strategy is J. S. Smucker Co., the manufacturer of high-quality jams and jellies. President Richard

K. Smucker enlisted a team of 140 employees (7 percent of the work force) who devoted nearly half of their time to a major strategy exercise for more than six months. Instead of having only the 12 top-level company executives working on the strategy, the 140 team members were used as ambassadors to solicit input from 2,000 employees. Strategy formulation was necessary because the company was in a bind as it struggled to grow in a mature market. Smucker now has a dozen new product initiatives that are predicted to double its revenues over the next five years. One of these initiatives is an alliance with Brach & Brock Confections Inc. to produce Smucker's jellybeans, the first of several co-branded products. The idea stemmed from a team of workers who would ordinarily not participate in strategy formulation.[9]

A caution about the Smucker example is that some strategy theorists would dismiss the example as incrementalism rather than true strategic leadership such as moving the company into a new business or reinventing the future. Yet from a practical standpoint, pointing a company in a direction that will double its revenues despite competing in a mature business is effective strategic management.

ANALYZING THE REALITIES OF THE BUSINESS SITUATION

To develop effective strategy, the strategist must make valid assumptions about the environment. When the assumptions are incorrect, the strategy might backfire. Let's get preposterous for a moment. Assume that Wal-Mart regards E-commerce as the wave of the future, and therefore halts its plans to achieve globalization by opening retail outlets throughout the world. Instead, Wal-Mart develops Web sites so people from all over the world can purchase everything from dish detergent to soccer balls over the Web. Worldwide sales do increase, but by such a small amount that profits are barely effected. The wrong assumption is that potential Wal-Mart customers throughout the world own computers, are on line, and have credit cards. The globalization strategy fails because assumptions about the potential customer base were flawed.

Greyhound Lines, Inc., is an example of a company that almost went bankrupt by making false assumptions about its customer base. To boost sales, the company attempted to apply an airline reservation system and promotional efforts to the bus business. However, bus travelers are so different demographically from airplane travelers that the system failed miserably. For example, over 80 percent of people who made reservations through a toll-free reservations system were no-shows.[10] Intercity bus travelers much prefer to just show up at the ticket office about one hour before departure time.

Accurately analyzing the environment in terms of understanding customers, potential customers, production capability, and the relevant technology is a time-consuming and comprehensive activity. Yet for strategy to work well, the manager has to understand both the external environment and the capabilities of the firm, as already implied from the basic planning model. Exhibit 5-4 presents a series of questions the strategist is supposed to answer to accurately size up the environment. Finding valid answers to these questions will often require considerable interviewing, including interviewing groups of consumers, and information gathering.

CONDUCTING A SWOT ANALYSIS

Quite often strategic planning takes the form of a **SWOT analysis**, a method of considering the strengths, weaknesses, opportunities, and threats in a given situation. Elements of a SWOT analysis are

SWOT analysis
A method of considering the strengths, weaknesses, opportunities, and threats in a given situation.

A Strategic Inventory

The purpose of the *Strategic Inventory* is to help a manager relate ideas about strategy to his or her own organization. By finding answers to these questions, the manager is likely to do a better job of sizing up the competition, the customers, and the technology necessary to compete effectively. The manager will often need the assistance of others in finding answers to these challenging questions.

Defining the Boundaries of the Competitive Environment

- What are the boundaries of our industry? What market do we serve? What products or services do we provide?
- Who are our customers? Who has chosen not to buy from us? What is the difference between these two groups?
- Who are our competitors? Which firms do not compete with us? What makes one firm a competitor and not the other?

Defining the Key Assumptions Made about the Environment, Customers, Competition, and the Capabilities of the Firm

- Who is our customer? What product or service features are important to that customer? How does the customer perceive us? What kind of relationship do we have with the customer?
- Who are our competitors? What are their strengths and weaknesses? How do they perceive us? What can we learn from our customers?
- Who are our potential competitors? New entrants? What changes in the environment or their behavior would make them competitors?
- What is the industry's value chain (points along the way in which value is added)? Where is value added? What is the industry's cost structure? How does our firm compare? How about the cost structure of our competitors?
- What technologies are important in our industry? Product technologies? Delivery and service technologies? How does our firm compare? How about our competitors?
- What are the key factors of production? Who are the suppliers? Do we rely on just a few suppliers and sources? How critical are these relationships to our success? How solid are these relationships?
- What are the bases for competition in our industry? What are the key success factors? How do we measure up on these success factors? How do our competitors measure up?
- What trends and factors in the external environment are important in our industry? How are they likely to change? What is likely to be the time period for the changes?
- Are we able, in assessing our knowledge and assumptions, to clearly separate fact from assumption?
- Which of the above assumptions are the most important in terms of the impact on our business?

Examining the Process for Reviewing and Validating Our Key Assumptions and Premises

- Do we have a process already established? Have responsibilities been assigned? Are periodic reviews planned and scheduled?

Source: Adapted and abridged from Joseph C. Picken and Gregory G. Dess, "Right Strategy—Wrong Problem," *Organizational Dynamics*, Summer 1998, p. 47.

117

included in the general planning model, and in using the strategic inventory to size up the environment. Given that SWOT has a straightforward appeal, it has become a popular framework for strategic planning. The framework, or technique, is useful in identifying a niche the company has not already exploited. To illustrate the use of the model, we return to Piaget, one of the world's finest watch makers. The price range of Piaget watches is between $7,000 and $20,000. (No, the last figure is not a typographical error.) Assume that top executives at Piaget are thinking about finding another niche by manufacturing luxury pens in the $200 to $500 range. Some of their thinking in regard to a SWOT analysis might proceed as follows:

Strengths. *What are good points about a particular alternative. Use your judgment and intuition; ask knowledgeable people.* Selling luxury pens appears to be a reasonable fit with the watch line because a luxury pen is often worn as jewelry. People who just want a writing instrument could settle for a Bic or competitive brand. The profit margins on luxury pens are quite good, and they are not likely to be deep discounted in department stores or discount stores. We can also maintain low inventories until we assess the true demand. As our sales representatives and distributors receive orders, we can manufacture the pens quickly.

Weaknesses. *Consider the risks of pursuing a particular course of action, such as getting into a business you do not understand.* There are only a handful of luxury pen manufacturers, so it could be that this is a tough market to crack. (We will need to do some market research here.) Another risk is that we will cheapen the Piaget name. The average price of a Piaget product is now about $11,000. With a brand of luxury pens, a person could take home a Piaget brand product for about $400. This could result in a scaling down of our image. Another problem is that we are not presently linked to all the distribution channels that sell luxury pens, such as office supply stores. We might have to rely on new distributors to get us into that channel.

Opportunities. *Think of the opportunities that welcome you if you choose a promising strategic alternative. Use your imagination and visualize the opportunities.* The opportunities could be quite good in terms of snob appeal. Maybe there are large numbers of consumers who would welcome the opportunity to carry a Piaget anything in their shirt pocket, handbag, or attaché case. Many of the people who become Piaget luxury pen customers might want to take a step up to become a Piaget watch owner.

Threats. *There's a downside to every alternative, so think ahead to allow for contingency planning. Ask people who have tried in the past what you are attempting now. But don't be dissuaded by the naysayers, heel draggers, and pessimists. Just take action.* Several manufacturers of high-end products in jewelry, clothing, and automobiles have cheapened their image and lost market share when they spread their brand name too thin. Following this approach, we could wind up having Piaget pens, wallets, and handbags. At that point the high prestige of the Piaget brand would be at risk.

As a result of this SWOT analysis, Piaget is sticking to its knitting (or watch making) and continuing to make world-class watches. Do you think they are making the right decision? Or do you think the brand equity (value of the brand name) warrants putting the Piaget label on another product?

A Variety of Business Strategies

The nature of strategy and how it is developed may appear complex. Yet strategy statements themselves, as expressed by managers and planners, are usually straightforward, and expressed in a few words, such as "We will be cost leaders." A variety of business strategies have already been mentioned in this and previous chapters. To help you appreciate what strategy means in practice, let us look at a sampling of current business strategies. Keep in mind that business people are likely to have a less precise and less scientific meaning of strategy than do strategy researchers.

COST LEADERSHIP   The cost leader provides a product or service at a low price in order to gain market share. Wal-Mart and Kmart are masters at cost leadership because their massive buying power enables them to receive huge price concessions from suppliers. A cost leadership strategy can create ethical problems because of what suppliers must do to cut costs. A striking example is the presence of sweatshops in the Chinatown section of New York City. These firms make garments for clothing manufacturers whose customers include Wal-Mart and Kmart. The workers are illegal immigrants from the Fujian province of China, who are often paid about $1 per hour, and function like slave labor. They live in cramped and unhygienic living quarters provided by the employer.[11]

IMITATION   If you cannot be imaginative, why not imitate the best? Benchmarking has given a new impetus to the imitation strategy. (Note that Michael Porter does not think imitation is a true strategy.) The entire industry of PC clones is based on an imitation strategy. Amazon.com Inc. was the first organization to sell virtually any book title in print over the Internet. As such, the company competed directly with bookstores with physical locations. Giant bookseller Barnes & Noble quickly imitated this successful approach to book sales (along with a few other products) to form the Web shopfront www.barnesandnoble.com.

PRODUCT DIFFERENTIATION   A differentiation strategy attempts to offer a product or service that is perceived by the customer as different from available alternatives. Executives at Sears believe strongly that their own brands like Craftsman, Kenmore, and DieHard attract customer loyalty and give them a competitive advantage. Marketer John Costello says that brands are a company's most valuable assets: "Competitors can copy your features, but they can't steal your brand."[12]

FORMING STRATEGIC ALLIANCES   An increasingly popular business strategy is to form alliances, or share resources, with other companies to exploit a market opportunity. A strategic alliance is also known as a virtual corporation. A ground-breaking strategic alliance in the service industry is the cooperative working relationship between KLM Royal Dutch Airlines and Northwest Airlines Inc. The two carriers have melded their operations to fly into each other's markets. By marketing their services jointly, they are gaining market share at a lower cost than previously.

REDEFINING THE INDUSTRY   To be a true leader, an organization must change the nature of the industry or change the rules of the game. Dell Computer exemplifies redefining an industry by finding ways to eliminate distributors in selling computers. Selling first by telephone, and then via the Internet, the company is credited with helping to define Internet commerce. The company sold about $1 billion of equipment on its Web site alone in 1998. A money manager said about Dell's accomplishments: "Think about it. Going directly to customers. Eliminating the middleman. Selling over the Internet. Wouldn't a Chrysler like to do that? Wouldn't everybody want to do business like that?"[13]

HIGH SPEED   Satisfy customer needs more quickly and you will make more money. High-speed managers focus on speed in all of their business activities, including speed in product development, sales response, and customer service. Knowing that "time is money," they choose to use time as a competitive resource. It is important to get products to market quickly because the competition might get there first. Part of Domino's Pizza's original success was based on getting pizzas delivered more quickly than competitors. The strategy had to be modified slightly when too many deliverers sacrificed auto safety to enhance delivery speed. Dell Computer relies on high speed as part of its strategy. A custom order placed at 9 A.M. on Wednesday can be on a delivery truck by 9 P.M. on Thursday.

GLOBAL DIVERSIFICATION   A widely practiced business strategy is to diversify globally in order to expand business. Global diversification has already been described here in relation to Wal-Mart. The information about international business in Chapter 2 also describes global diversification. Global diversification gives a business firm a much larger potential customer base. Without global diversification, many American companies would be much less profitable. You may recall that an astonishing 80 percent of the sales of Coca-Cola are *outside* the United States. Goodyear Tire & Rubber now ranks third among the world's tire manufacturers, and would like to regain the first position it held years ago. A key component of their growth plan rests on an aggressive international expansion strategy. The company already achieves $3 billion in sales from China, India, the Philippines, Poland, and South America—and top management wants more overseas sales.[14]

DIVERSIFICATION OF GOODS AND SERVICES   "Don't put all your eggs in one basket" is a standard business strategy. One of the many reasons that diversification is an effective strategy is that it serves as a hedge in case the market for one group of products or services softens. In recent years sales of traditional Nike products such as basketball shoes have softened. Nike has responded by investing considerable resources into promoting its soccer products around the world. For example, Nike paid $200 million to sponsor Brazil's national team. The Nike strategy of product diversification is simultaneously a strategy of global diversification.

STICKING TO CORE COMPETENCIES   It may be valuable to not put all your eggs in one basket, but also guard against spreading yourself too thin. Many firms of all sizes believe they will prosper if they confine their efforts to business activities they perform best—their core competencies. When Thomas C. McDermott was president of Gould Pumps, he said his company was going to expand overseas by strategic acquisitions. Nevertheless, he insisted on companies that are either in or related to the pump business. He said, "We're going to stick to our knitting." Many companies that diversified in the past have sold their acquisitions so they can concentrate on their core businesses. Xerox Corp., for example, sold off all the financial services businesses it once regarded as a major diversification strategy. The reason was that Xerox wanted to concentrate on imaging, so it could truly achieve its mission of being "The Document Company."

FOCUS   In a focus strategy, the organization concentrates on a specific regional market or buyer group. To gain market share, the company will use either a differentiation or a cost leadership approach in a targeted market. The formation of the Asian American Association by the Shis, described at the beginning of this chapter, illustrates a focus strategy, with Asian Americans being the target group.

PUTTING "WOW" BACK IN THE BUSINESS   Business sage Tom Peters contends that a key success strategy is for managers to provide products or services that they find exciting. He says that if you can't remember the last time your business really turned you on, you are in big trouble. The underlying psychology is that if the manager is not passionate about the company's products or services, it will be difficult to convince others. In turn, this will lead customers toward other firms offering more exciting products and services. Oldsmobile and Buick lost some market share in the 1980s and 1990s because these models did not excite a large enough number of consumers—especially younger ones. (What is your opinion?)

The various business strategies just described are not mutually exclusive. A firm might implement one or more of these strategies simultaneously. For example, a firm might get to market rapidly with a differentiated product in a global environment while forming a strategic alliance! Whichever combination of strategies is chosen, current thinking is that the firm should adopt an ambitious strategy that stretches its capability.

OPERATING PLANS, POLICIES, PROCEDURES, AND RULES

Strategic plans are formulated at the top of the organization. Four of the vehicles through which strategic plans are converted into action are operating plans, policies, procedures, and rules.

Explain the use of operating plans, policies, procedures, and rules.

Operating Plans

Operating plans are the means through which strategic plans alter the destiny of the firm. Operating plans involve organizational efficiency (doing things right), whereas strategic plans involve effectiveness (doing the right things). Both strategic and operational plans involve such things as exploring alternatives and evaluating the effectiveness of the plan. In a well-planned organization, all managers are responsible for making operating plans that mesh with the strategic plans of the business. Operational plans (a term used synonymously with *operating plans*) provide the details of how strategic plans will be accomplished. In many firms, suggestions to be incorporated into operating plans stem from employees at lower levels. As David Glass of Wal-Mart said over a decade ago, "Most of the good ideas come from the bottom up. We keep changing a thousand little things."[15]

Operating plans focus more on the firm than on the external environment. To illustrate, the strategic plan of a local government might be to encourage the private sector to take over government functions. One operating unit within the local government might then formulate a plan for subcontracting refuse removal to private contractors and phasing out positions for civil-service sanitation workers.

Operating plans tend to be drawn for a shorter period than strategic plans. The plan for increasing the private sector's involvement in activities conducted by the local government might be a ten-year plan. In contrast, the phasing out of government sanitation workers might take two years.

operating plans
The means through which strategic plans alter the destiny of the firm.

121

Policies

policies
General guidelines to follow in making decisions and taking action.

Policies are general guidelines to follow in making decisions and taking action; as such, they are plans. Many policies are written; some are unwritten, or implied. Policies are designed to be consistent with strategic plans and yet allow room for interpretation by the individual manager. One important managerial role is interpreting policies for employees. Here is an example of a policy and an analysis of how it might require interpretations.

> Policy: When hiring employees from the outside, consider only those candidates who are technically competent or show promise of becoming technically competent and who show good personal character and motivation.

A manager attempting to implement this policy with respect to a given job candidate would have to ask the following questions:

- What do we mean by "technical competence"?
- How do I measure technical competence?
- What do we mean by "show promise of becoming technically competent"?
- How do I rate the promise of technical competence?
- What do we mean by "good personal character and motivation"?
- How do I assess good personal character and motivation?

Policies are developed to support strategic plans in every area of the firm. Many firms have strict policies against employees accepting gifts and favors from vendors or potential vendors. For example, many schools endorse the Code of Ethics and Principles advocated by the National Association of Educational Buyers. One of the specific policies states that buyers should "decline personal gifts or gratuities which might in any way influence the purchase of materials."

Procedures

procedures
A customary method for handling an activity. It guides action rather than thinking.

Procedures are considered plans because they establish a customary method of handling future activities. They guide *action* rather than *thinking*, in that they state the specific manner in which a certain activity must be accomplished. Procedures exist at every level in the organization, but they tend to be more complex and specific at lower levels. For instance, strict procedures may apply to the handling of checks by salesclerks. The procedures for check handling by managers may be much less strict.

Rules

rule
A specific course of action or conduct that must be followed. It is the simplest type of plan.

A **rule** is a specific course of action or conduct that must be followed; it is the simplest type of plan. Ideally, each rule fits a strategic plan. In practice, however, many rules are not related to organizational strategy. When rules are violated, corrective action should be taken. Two examples of rules follow:

- Any employee engaged in an accident while in a company vehicle must report that accident immediately to his or her supervisor.
- No employee is authorized to use company photocopying machines for personal use, even if he or she reimburses the company for the cost of the copies.

The next section describes a program that thousands of organizations use to apply the principles and techniques of planning and goal setting.

MANAGEMENT BY OBJECTIVES: A SYSTEM OF PLANNING AND REVIEW

Management by objectives (MBO) is a systematic application of goal setting and planning to help individuals and firms be more productive. An MBO program typically involves people setting many objectives for themselves. However, management frequently imposes key organizational objectives upon people. An MBO program usually involves sequential steps, which are cited in the following list. (Note that these steps are related to those in the basic planning model shown in Exhibit 5-1.)

1. *Establishing organizational goals.* Top-level managers set organizational goals to begin the entire MBO process. Quite often these goals are strategic. A group of hospital administrators, for example, might decide upon the strategic goal of improving health care to poor people in the community. After these broad goals are established, managers determine what the organizational units must accomplish to meet these goals.

2. *Establishing unit objectives.* Unit heads then establish objectives for their units. A cascading of objectives takes place as the process moves down the line. Objectives set at lower levels of the firm must be designed to meet the general goals established by top management. Lower-level managers and operatives provide input because a general goal usually leaves considerable latitude for setting individual objectives to meet that goal. The head of inpatient admissions might decide that working more closely with the county welfare department must be accomplished if the health-care goal cited earlier in this list is to be met. Exhibit 5-5 suggests ways to set effective goals.

3. *Reviewing group members' proposals.* At this point, group members make proposals about how they will contribute to unit objectives. For example, the assistant to the manager of inpatient admissions might agree to set up a task force

Present an overview of management by objectives.

management by objectives (MBO)
A systematic application of goal setting and planning to help individuals and firms be more productive.

123

Effective goals and objectives have certain characteristics in common. Effective goals and objectives

Are clear, concise, and unambiguous. An example of such an objective is "Reduce damaged boxes of photocopying paper from April 27 to April 30 of this year."

Are accurate in terms of the true end state or condition sought. An accurate objective might state, "The factory will be as neat and organized as the front office after the cleanup is completed."

Are achievable by competent workers. Goals and objectives should not be so high or rigid that the majority of competent team members become frustrated and stressed by attempting to achieve them.

Include three difficulty levels: routine, challenging, and innovative. Most objectives deal with routine aspects of a job, but they should also challenge workers to loftier goals.

Are achieved through team-member participation. Subordinates should participate actively in setting objectives.

Relate to small chunks of accomplishment. Many objectives should concern small, achievable activities, such as uncluttering a work area. Accomplishing small objectives is the building block for achieving larger goals.

Specify what is going to be accomplished, who is going to accomplish it, when it is going to be accomplished, and how it is going to be accomplished. Answering the "what, who, when, and how" questions reduces the chance for misinterpretation.

EXHIBIT 5-5

Guide to Establishing Goals and Objectives

to work with the welfare department. Each team member is also given the opportunity to set objectives in addition to those that meet the strategic goals.

4. *Negotiating or agreeing.* Managers and team members confer together at this stage to either agree on the objectives set by the team members or negotiate further. In the hospital example, one department head might state that he or she wants to reserve ten beds on the ward for the exclusive use of indigent people. The supervisor might welcome the suggestion but point out that only five beds could be spared for such a purpose. They might settle for setting aside seven beds for the needy poor.

5. *Creating action plans to achieve objectives.* After the manager and team members agree upon objectives, action plans must be defined. Sometimes the action plan is self-evident. For example, if your objective as a sales manager is to hire three new telemarketers this year, you would begin by consulting with the human resources department.

6. *Reviewing performance.* Performance reviews are conducted at agreed-upon intervals (a semiannual or annual review is typical). Persons receive good performance reviews to the extent that they attain most of their major objectives. When objectives are not attained, the manager and the team member mutually analyze what went wrong. Equally important, they discuss corrective actions. New objectives are then set for the next review period. A new objective for one hospital manager, for example, is to establish a task force to investigate the feasibility of establishing satellite health-care facilities in poor sections of town. Because establishing new objectives is part of an MBO program, management by objectives is a process that can continue for the life of an organization.

Hewlett-Packard is one of many companies that implement management by objectives to improve organizational performance. Its Web site, www.hp.com, explains its general approach to MBO: "Individuals at each level contribute to company goals by developing objectives which are integrated with their manager's and those of other parts of HP. Flexibility—and innovation in recognizing alternative approaches to meeting objectives—provide effective means of meeting customer needs."

SUMMARY OF KEY POINTS

 Document how planning contributes to business success.
One value of planning is the process of self-examination itself. Extensive research shows that planning contributes to financial success and corporate growth.

 Summarize a general framework for planning and apply it to enhance your planning skills.
A generalized planning model can be used for strategic planning, tactical planning, and operational planning. The model consists of seven related and sometimes overlapping elements: defining the present situation; establishing goals and objectives; forecasting aids and barriers to goals and objectives; developing action plans; developing budgets; implementing the plan; and controlling the plan. Contingency plans should also be developed.

 Describe the nature of business strategy.
A current explanation of business strategy emphasizes four characteristics. First, strategy involves more than operational effectiveness. Second, strategy rests on unique activities. Third, a sustainable strategic position requires trade-offs. Fourth, fit among organizational activities drives both competitive advantage and sustainability.

Explain how business strategy is developed, including performing a SWOT analysis.

Business strategy usually develops from planning, and is also influenced by values. Gathering multiple inputs is important in developing strategy. Analyzing the realities of the business situation is important because the strategist could be making false assumptions about customers, production capability, and the relevant technology. Strategy is often developed by using a SWOT analysis, which considers the strengths, weaknesses, opportunities, and threats in a given situation.

 Identify 11 different business strategies.

Strategy development leads to many different strategies, including the following: cost leadership; imitation; product differentiation; forming strategic alliances; redefining the industry; high speed; global diversification; diversification of goods and services; sticking to core competencies; focus; and putting "wow" back in the business. These strategies are not mutually exclusive and several are often used in combination.

 Explain the use of operating plans, policies, procedures, and rules.

Operating plans provide the details of how strategic plans will be accomplished or implemented. They deal with a shorter time span than do strategic plans. Policies are plans set in the form of general statements that guide thinking and action in decision making. Procedures are plans that establish a customary method of handling future activities. A rule sets a specific course of action or conduct and is the simplest type of plan.

 Present an overview of management by objectives.

Management by objectives (MBO) is the most widely used formal system of goal setting, planning, and review. In general, it has six elements: establishing organizational goals, establishing unit objectives, obtaining proposals from group members about their objectives, negotiating or agreeing to proposals, developing action plans, and reviewing performance. After objectives are set, the manager must give feedback to team members on their progress toward reaching the objectives.

125

KEY TERMS AND PHRASES

QUESTIONS

1. In what way does planning control the future?
2. How can you use the information in this chapter to help you achieve your career and personal goals?
3. Why do managers whose work involves strategic planning typically receive much higher compensation than those involved with operational planning?
4. What is your analysis of the assumptions regarding differences between intercity bus travelers and airline travelers?
5. Which several business strategies are likely to be the most relevant for a group of individuals who open a restaurant?
6. Identify two business strategies that you think The Gap or Old Navy use successfully.
7. Give an example of how a rule could fit the corporate strategy of "high speed."

SKILL-BUILDING ACTIVITY 5-A: Conducting a SWOT Analysis

In this chapter you have read the basics of conducting a SWOT analysis. Now gather in small groups to conduct one. Develop a scenario for a SWOT analysis, such as the group starting a chain of coffee shops, pet-care service centers, or treatment centers for online addictions. Or, conduct a SWOT analysis for reorganizing a company from being mostly hierarchical to one that is mostly team based. Since you will probably have mostly hypothetical data to work with, you will have to rely heavily on your imagination. Group leaders might share the results of the SWOT analysis with the rest of the class.

INTERNET SKILL-BUILDING ACTIVITY: Business Strategy Research

The purpose of this assignment is to find three examples of business strategy by searching the Internet. A good starting point is to visit www.prnewswire.com. After copying down several strategic statements (or transferring them to a floppy disk or your hard drive) compare them to the section of this chapter called "A Variety of Business Strategies." Attempt to match the company statement about its strategy to a type of strategy listed in the chapter. If you cannot find the information you need in the publicity releases found in www.prnewswire.com, research companies you are curious about by inserting their name in a search engine. The following address will get you to most companies: www.*company name*.com, such as www.apple.com.

CASE PROBLEM 5-A: Simplicity at Unisys

Lawrence A. Weinbach is the chairman and president of Unisys, one of the world's largest computer companies. Before that he was the chief executive for Anderson Worldwide, the giant accounting and consulting firm. When he took over the Unisys job in the fall of 1997, the company faced substantial problems. Weinbach noticed that no one in the halls of company headquarters in Blue Bell, Pennsylvania, smiled. And when he visited big customers he was asked whether Unisys was going to survive. After one year of Weinbach's leadership, Unisys's debt load had been slashed, the company was profitable, and the stock price had doubled. Now Weinbach is attempting to boost the company's service business (such as helping other companies manage their networks). At the same time, he has to deal with the expected decline in the company's mainframe business.

Should you visit Weinbach at company headquarters in Blue Bell, you will find his office decorated with wooden, three-legged stools. You will also notice that he wears a lapel pin shaped like a three-legged stool. Many Unisys employees are curious about all these stools in their CEO's office.

As Weinbach explains it, the three-legged stools are all about vision. Weinbach believes that vision has always been important to effective leadership, but that vision can get overblown. He observes, "At a lot of companies, their vision statement is a dozen sentences hanging up on the wall, and nobody can remember it or tell you what it is. I've learned that it's best to keep things simple."

Simplicity is where the stools come in. "Here at Unisys, we wear our vision statement on our lapels," Weinbach explains. "Our vision statement is embodied by three words: customers, employees, and reputation. A stool needs all three legs to remain stable; take one leg away, and it falls over. Likewise, as a company Unisys needs to focus on its customers, its employees, and its reputation. If we're taking care of these three things, we'll be successful."

That simple vision helps employees stay focused and helps Weinbach deliver a crisp, consistent message, regardless of audience. "When I talk to the board, when I talk to employees, when I talk to investors, when I talk to customers, I talk about those three things," he says. "I say the same things over and over, and people begin to realize it's important. It's amazing how many employees can tell you those three words. In just a few months we've embedded this concept into the organization—not because it's profound, but because it's simple.

"My wife thinks it's a little hokey," Weinbach laughs, pointing to his lapel pin. "But it works. And when people ask me about it, it gives me a chance to tell our story. They often ask for a pin for themselves—and I'm glad to share mine with them. In fact, I've given away so many that I now keep a supply on hand."

Weinbach and other members of the Unisys executive team support the vision with several specific plans, focusing on services, product, and talent. The three-part plan is as follows:

Services: Unisys intends to focus on key markets where the company has expertise, including financial services, publishing, and transportation. The goal is to increase the operating income from services to about 65 percent of corporate revenues in a few years from about 39 percent now.

Products: The company plans to continue to upgrade the present line of mainframe computers. At present, hardware sales, mostly from mainframes, account for 33 percent of total revenue. At the same time Unisys will develop a line of servers that will run Microsoft's Windows NT software.

Talent: After years of downsizing, the company is attempting to boost morale and upgrade the work force. Unisys University is being established to upgrade the service expertise within the company. Also, the company reinstated matching employee contributions to the 401(k) retirement program.

Discussion Questions

1. What is your opinion of the "three-legged stool" as a vision for a large, high-technology firm like Unisys?
2. What evidence would you need to be convinced that the Unisys vision works, as claimed by Larry Weinbach?

3. What would you add to the Unisys plans to help ensure the company's success?

Sources: Based on Peter Haapaniemi, "The Power of Simplicity," *Unisys Exec*, September 1998, p. 11; Amy Barrett, "Unisys Aims for the Top of the Tree," *Business Week*, November 9, 1998, pp. 138–140; www.unisys.com.

CASE PROBLEM 5-B: How Do You Put "Wow" in a Shoe-Repair Shop?

Derek Johnson owns and operates three shoe-repair shops in suburban Atlanta, Georgia. In addition to repairing and restoring shoes, Johnson's shops also repair and renovate leather handbags and leather jackets. Johnson has been moderately satisfied with the success of his business. He squeezes out an acceptable living from the salary he draws from the business. Johnson is thinking of opening a fourth store, provided that he can find a good location at an affordable price.

Johnson thought to himself, however, that before planning for expansion he should first improve his existing business. He is concerned that profits are too thin to fund an expansion that might not be immediately profitable. In search of good business ideas, Johnson enrolled in a seminar given by business consultant Tom Peters. The subject of the seminar was achieving long-term competitiveness, with a special emphasis on small- and medium-size businesses. Johnson was concerned that he might be the owner of the smallest business of anybody in the seminar.

The seminar room was packed, and Johnson was greeted warmly by the other serious-minded participants. The people in attendance included business owners, corporate managers, consultants, and business professors. By the end of the day, ideas were swimming around in Johnson's head. To focus his thinking, he circled several key ideas in his seminar notebook:

- Get to know at least one person who revels in telling you that you are full of hooey. A person of this type would

not be afraid to challenge your thinking. Johnson thought that his girlfriend Shawna could fit this requirement.
- Hire rebels who will challenge your preconceptions of how your business should be run. Johnson reasoned that he can barely meet his payroll right now, so he might rely on people in his network to perform this function for free.
- Come up with a good next act. For Johnson's stores, this might mean offering a new service he is not offering now. He had tentatively thought of promoting an attaché-case repair and restoration service. Yet he was concerned about the cost of promotion.
- Put "wow" back in your business. Somehow your business should be different and interesting. The owner should be getting an emotional charge when he or she walks through the store, franchise, or factory. Johnson thought to himself, "Somedays I'm not as charged up as I should be. Maybe I should find a way to put more "wow" back in Derek's Shoe Repair."

Discussion Questions

1. What action steps, if any, should Johnson take to improve his business based on the first three points circled in his notebook?
2. What do you recommend that Johnson do to put more "wow" back in Derek's Shoe Repair?

Source: Some of the facts in this case are based on Robert McGarvey, "The Big Thrill: Top Management Guru Says Put the Wow Back In Your Business," *Entrepreneur*, July 1995, p. 86–91.

ENDNOTES

1. Based on information in Carol Mauro-Noon, "American Dream: How They Rose from Street Peddlers to Millionaires," *Success*, March 1997, pp. 37–42; www.aan.com.
2. "The Real Value of Planning," *Working Smart*, January 1995, p. 1.
3. C. Chet Miller and Laura B. Cardinal, "Strategic Planning and Firm Performance: A Synthesis of More than Two Decades of Research," *The Academy of Management Journal*, December 1994, pp. 1649–1665.
4. Henry Mintzberg, "The Strategy Concept II: Another Look at Why Organizations Need Strategies," *California Management Review*, January 1987, p. 26.
5. Quoted in Lorrie Grant, "Wal-Mart Yearns for Global Market Domination," Gannett News Service, November 8, 1998. Most of the facts about Wal-Mart in the planning example are from this source along with "Wal-Mart Spoken Here," *Business Week*, June 23, 1997, pp. 138–145.
6. Michael E. Porter, "What Is Strategy?" *Harvard Business Review*, November–December 1996, pp. 61–78.

7. Larry Armstrong, "More Red Meat, Please," *Business Week*, January 16, 1995, p. 35.

8. John A. Byrne, "Three of the Busiest New Strategists," *Business Week*, August 26, 1996, p. 50.

9. John A. Byrne, "Strategic Planning: After a Decade of Gritty Downsizing, Big Thinkers Are Back in Corporate Vogue," *Business Week*, August 26, 1996, p. 52.

10. Joseph C. Picken and Gregory G. Dess, "Right Strategy—Wrong Problem," *Organizational Dynamics*, Summer 1998, p. 35.

11. Edward Barnes, "Slaves of New York," *Time*, November 2, 1998, pp. 72–75.

12. Quoted in Patricia Sellers, "Sears: The Turnaround Is Ending; The Revolution Has Begun," *Fortune*, April 28, 1997, p. 108.

13. Quoted in Andy Serwer, "Michael Dell Rocks," *Fortune*, May 11, 1998, p. 60.

14. Alex Taylor III, "Goodyear Wants to Be No. 1 Again," *Fortune*, April 27, 1998, p. 132.

15. "Make that Sale, Mr. Sam," *Time*, May 18, 1987, p. 55.

The Ritz Carlton chain, with Horst Schulze as president, had received an award as the best hotel in the world. Yet complaints by guests were not eliminated. At one hotel, guests complained for three years that room service was late. To solve the problem, Schulze dispatched a team composed of a room-service order taker, a waiter, and a cook. Everything seemed fine except that the service elevator took a long time. Neither the engineering department nor an elevator company specialist could find a technical problem with the elevator.

Next, team members took turns riding the elevators at all hours for a week. Finally, one of them observed that everytime the elevator made its trip from the first floor to the twenty-fourth, it stopped four or five times. At each stop, housemen (who assisted the maids) got on the elevator to go to different floors. The housemen were stealing towels from other floors to bring them to housekeepers on their own floors who were short of towels. Foraging for towels was slowing down the elevators.

The Ritz Carlton didn't really have a room-service problem; it had a towel shortage. After the hotel bought more towels, room-service complaints dropped 50 percent.[1]

OBJECTIVES

After studying this chapter and doing the exercises, you should be able to:

1. Differentiate between nonprogrammed and programmed decisions.

2. Explain the steps involved in making a nonprogrammed decision.

3. Understand the major factors influencing decision making in organizations.

4. Understand the nature of creativity and how it contributes to managerial work.

5. Describe organizational programs for improving creativity.

6. Implement several suggestions for becoming a more creative problem solver.

7. Appreciate the value and potential limitations of group decision making.

Problem Solving and Decision Making

problem
A discrepancy between ideal and actual conditions.

decision
A choice among alternatives.

As illustrated by the Ritz Carlton incident, solving difficult problems is a key part of a manager's job. Often the solution requires perceptive investigation. This chapter explores how managerial workers solve problems and make decisions individually and in groups. A **problem** is a discrepancy between ideal and actual conditions. The ideal situation in the hotel example would be no complaints, while the actual situation was the presence of complaints about slow room service. A **decision** is choosing among alternatives, such as buying more towels rather than adding more elevators!

Problem solving and decision making are important components of planning, and they are also required to carry out the other management functions. For example, while managers are controlling, they must make a series of decisions about how to solve the problem of getting performance back to standard. Understanding decision making is also important because decision making contributes to job satisfaction. Jobs allowing for more decision-making authority are generally more satisfying.

Another important perspective on decision making is that it lies at the heart of management. A distinguishing characteristic of a manager's job is the authority to make decisions. The accompanying Manager in Action lists some of the most important decisions ever made by managers in business.

Differentiate between nonprogrammed and programmed decisions.

nonprogrammed decision
A decision that is difficult because of its complexity and the fact that the person faces it infrequently.

programmed decision
A decision that is repetitive, or routine, and made according to a specific procedure.

NONPROGRAMMED VERSUS PROGRAMMED DECISIONS

Some decisions that managerial workers face are difficult because they occur infrequently. These unique decisions are **nonprogrammed decisions** (or nonroutine decisions). In contrast, a **programmed decision** is repetitive, or routine, and made according to a specific procedure.

When a problem has not taken the same form in the past or is extremely complex or significant, it calls for a nonprogrammed decision. A complex problem is one that contains many elements. Significant problems affect an important aspect of an organization. The room-service problem at a Ritz Carlton hotel was complex because there were several potential causes. It was significant because it affected customer satisfaction. Virtually all strategic decisions are nonprogrammed.

A well-planned and highly structured organization reduces the number of nonprogrammed decisions. It does so by formulating hundreds of policies to help managers know what to do when faced with a given problem. In contrast, many small firms do not offer much guidance about decision making. An exception is that many small-business owners make most of the nonprogrammed decisions themselves.

Handling a nonprogrammed problem properly requires original thinking. The skill required for decision making varies inversely with the extent to which it is programmed. Highly routine decisions require minimum decision-making skill; highly nonroutine decisions require maximum skill.

Managers and nonmanagers also make many small, uncomplicated decisions involving alternatives that are specified in advance. Procedures specify how to handle these routine, programmed decisions. Here is an example: A person who earns $24,000 per year applies to rent a two-bedroom apartment. The manager makes the decision to refuse the application because there is a rule that families with annual incomes of $28,000 or less may not rent in the building.

Under ideal circumstances, top-level management concerns itself almost exclusively with nonroutine decisions and lower-level management handles all rou-

Manager *in Action*

Eleven of the Greatest Management Decisions Ever Made

many people consider good decision making to be the essence of management. So a business writer for *Management Review* asked experts for their nominations of the 75 greatest decisions ever made. All these decisions were successful and had a major impact. Here we list 12 of these decisions related directly to business rather than to government or religion. For example, we excluded Queen Isabella's decision to sponsor Christopher Columbus's voyage to the new world in 1492. Each decision's rank among 75 is listed in brackets.

1. **Walt Disney** listened to his wife and named his cartoon mouse Mickey instead of Mortimer. Entertainment was never the same after Mickey and Minnie debuted in "Steamboat Willie" in 1928 (1).
2. **Frank McNamara**, in 1950, found himself in a restaurant without money, prompting him to come up with the idea of the Diners Club Card. This first credit card changed the nature of buying and selling throughout the world (5).
3. **Thomas Watson, Jr.**, of IBM, decided in 1962 to develop the System/360 computer, at a cost of $5 billion. Although IBM's market research suggested it would sell only two units worldwide, the result was the first mainframe computer (7).
4. **Robert Woodruff** was president of Coca-Cola during World War II when he committed to selling bottles of Coke to members of the armed services for a nickel a bottle, starting around 1941. The decision led to enormous customer loyalty, including the fact that returning soldiers influenced family members and friends to buy Coca-Cola (12).
5. **Jean Nidetch**, in 1961, was put on a diet in an obesity clinic in New York City.

She invited six dieting friends to meet in her Queens apartment every week. The decision created Weight Watchers and the weight-loss industry (20).

6. **Bill Gates**, in 1981, decided to license MS/DOS to IBM, while IBM did not require control of the license for all non-IBM PCs. The decision laid the foundation for Microsoft's huge success and a downturn in IBM's prestige and prominence (21).
7. A **Hewlett-Packard** engineer discovered in 1979 that heating metal in a specific way caused it to splatter. The management decision to exploit this discovery launched the ink-jet printer business, and laid the groundwork for more than $6 billion in revenue for HP (25).
8. **Sears, Roebuck and Co.**, in 1905, decided to open its Chicago mail-order plant. The Sears catalogue made goods available to an entirely new customer base, and also provided a model for mass production (40).
9. **Ray Kroc** liked the McDonald brothers' stand that sold hamburgers, french fries, and milk shakes so much that he decided to open his own franchised restaurant in 1955 and form McDonald's Corp. Kroc soon created a giant global company and a vast market for fast food (58).
10. **Procter & Gamble**, in 1931, introduced its brand management system, which showcased brands and provided a blueprint that management has followed ever since (62).
11. **Michael Dell** made the decision in 1986 to sell PCs direct and build them to order. Others in the industry are now trying to imitate Dell Computer's strategy (73).

Source: Based on information in Stuart Crainer, "The 75 Greatest Management Decisions Ever Made," *Management Review*, November 1998, pp. 16–24.

tine ones. In reality, executives do make many small, programmed decisions in addition to nonprogrammed ones. Some top executives sign expense-account vouchers and answer routine correspondence, for example. Middle managers and first-level managers generally make both routine and nonroutine decisions, with first-level managers making a higher proportion of routine decisions. A well-managed organization encourages all managers to delegate as many nonprogrammed decisions as possible.

STEPS IN PROBLEM SOLVING AND DECISION MAKING

Explain the steps involved in making a nonpro-grammed decision.

132

Problem solving and decision making can be regarded as an orderly process, similar to the planning model described in Chapter 5. Yet not every effective solution or decision is the product of an orderly process. The key principle is that managers find better solutions to complex problems—and therefore make better major, or nonprogrammed, decisions—when they follow an orderly process. Drawing a consistent distinction between problem solving and decision making is difficult because they are part of the same process. The basic purpose of making a decision is to solve a problem, but you must analyze the problem prior to making the decision. A broader and grander purpose of decision making is to move the organization forward, to seize opportunities, and to avoid problems.

As shown in Exhibit 6-1, and described next, problem solving and decision making can be divided into steps.

EXHIBIT 6-1

Steps in Problem Solving and Decision Making
Managers who are thorough in their decision making will often proceed through the steps shown here.

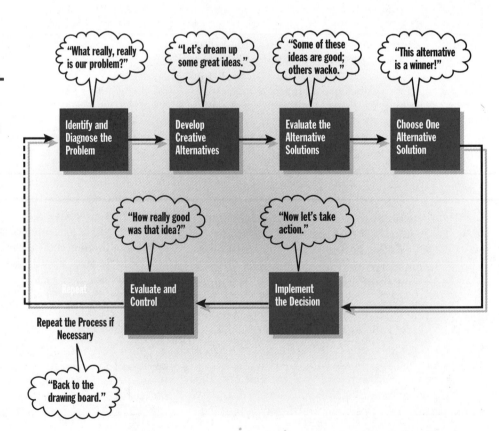

Identify and Diagnose the Problem

Problem solving and decision making begin with the awareness that a problem exists. In other words, the first step in problem solving and decision making is identifying a gap between desired and actual conditions. At times, a problem is imposed on a manager, such as when customer complaints increase. At other times, he or she has to search actively for a worthwhile problem or opportunity. For example, a sales manager actively pursued a problem by conducting an audit to find out why former customers stopped buying from the company.

INDICATORS OF PROBLEMS   Identifying problems requires considerable skill. Managers may become aware of a problem by noticing one of four typical indicators.[2]

1. *Deviation from past performance.* If performance figures are down, a problem almost surely exists. Common problem indicators are declining sales, increased employee turnover, higher scrap rates, increased customer complaints, and an increased number of bad checks cashed.
2. *Deviations from the plan.* When the results you hoped to attain with a plan are not forthcoming, you have a problem. This type of problem identification requires you to see a deviation from anticipated *future* performance. The possibility exists that the established plan was unduly optimistic.
3. *Criticism from outsiders.* Managers sometimes become aware of problems by hearing complaints from individuals and groups who are not employees of the firm. These sources of criticism include customers, government regulators, and stockholders.
4. *Competitive threats.* The presence of competition can create problems for an organization. Compaq Computer, for example, has slashed its prices in recent years to compete with lower-priced brands.

DIAGNOSIS   A thorough diagnosis of the problem is important because the real problem may be different from the one that a first look suggests. The ability to think critically helps a person get at the real problem. To diagnose a problem properly, you must clarify its true nature. The Ritz Carlton team invested considerable time and energy into uncovering why room service was slow at one of the hotels.

An important part of the decision process for making the right diagnosis is how you frame the decision. According to J. Edward Russo, framing puts you on the right track by defining what must be decided, and separating out what is important. A classic example of the right frame is the development of the Gillette Sensor for Women razor. Gillette management asked Jill Shurtleff, an industrial designer on their staff, to investigate the women's shaving market. The designer put herself on the right track by rejecting the frame that had previously been used in developing shavers for women—start with a man's razor and then modify it for women. Instead, Shurtleff focused on how women shave and developed a razor that became the greatest success ever in its product category.[3]

Develop Creative Alternative Solutions

The second step in decision making is to generate alternative solutions. This is the intellectually freewheeling aspect of decision making. All kinds of possibilities are explored in this step, even if they seem unrealistic. Often the difference between good and mediocre decision makers is that the former do not accept the first alternative they think of. Instead, they keep digging until they find the best solution.

Evaluate Alternative Solutions

The next step involves comparing the relative value of the alternatives. The problem solver examines the pros and cons of each one and considers the feasibility of each. Some alternatives may appear attractive, but implementing them would be impossible or counterproductive. Adding a service elevator to speed up room service is an extreme example of this idea.

Comparing relative value often means performing a cost and savings analysis of each alternative. Alternatives that cost much more than they save are infeasible. The possible outcome of an alternative should be part of the analysis. If an unsatisfactory outcome is almost a certainty, the alternative should be rejected. For example, if a firm is faced with low profits, one alternative would be to cut pay by 20 percent. The outcome of this alternative would be to lower morale drastically and create high turnover, so a firm should not implement that alternative. High employee turnover is so expensive that it would override the cost savings.

One approach to examining the pros and cons of each alternative is to list them on a worksheet. This approach assumes that virtually all alternatives have both positive and negative consequences.

Choose One Alternative Solution

The process of weighing each alternative must stop at some point. You cannot solve a problem unless you choose one of the alternatives—that is, make a decision. Several factors influence the choice. A major factor is the goal the decision should achieve. The alternative chosen should be the one that appears to come closest to achieving it.

Despite a careful evaluation of alternatives, ambiguity remains in most decisions. The decisions faced by managers are often complex, and the factors involved in them are often unclear. Even when quantitative evidence strongly supports a particular alternative, the decision maker may be uncertain. Human resource decisions are often the most ambiguous because making precise predictions about human behavior is so difficult. Deciding which person to hire from a list of several strong candidates is always a challenge.

Implement the Decision

Converting the decision into action is the next major step. Until a decision is implemented, it is not really a decision at all. Many strategic decisions represent wasted effort because nobody is held responsible for implementing them. Much of a manager's job involves helping subordinates implement decisions.

A fruitful way of evaluating the merit of a decision is to observe its implementation. A decision is seldom a good one if people resist its implementation or if it is too cumbersome to implement. Suppose a firm tries to boost productivity by decreasing the time allotted for lunch or coffee breaks. If employees resist the decision by eating while working and then taking the allotted lunch break, productivity will decrease. Implementation problems indicate that the decision to boost productivity by decreasing break time would be a poor one.

Evaluate and Control

The final step in the decision-making framework is to investigate how effectively the chosen alternative solved the problem. Controlling means ensuring that the results the decision obtained are the ones set forth during the problem identification step.

After gathering feedback, characterize the quality of the decision as optimum, satisficing, or suboptimum. Optimum decisions lead to favorable outcomes. **Satisficing decisions** provide a minimum standard of satisfaction. Such decisions are adequate, acceptable, or passable. Many decision makers stop their search for alternatives when they find a satisficing one. Accepting the first reasonable alternative may only postpone the need to implement a decision that really solves the problem. For example, slashing the price of a personal computer to match the competition's price can be regarded as the result of a satisficing decision. A longer-range decision might call for a firm to demonstrate to potential buyers that the difference in quality is worth the higher price.

Suboptimum decisions lead to negative outcomes. Their consequences are disruptive to the employees and to the firm. When you obtain suboptimum results, you must repeat the problem-solving and decision-making process.

Evaluating and controlling your decisions will help you improve your decision-making skills. You can learn important lessons by comparing what actually happened with what you thought would happen. You can learn what you could have improved or done differently and use this information the next time you face a similar decision.

CRITICISM OF THE RATIONAL DECISION-MAKING MODEL So far, this chapter has presented the classical model of problem solving and decision making. The model regards the activities as an orderly and rational process. In reality, decision making is seldom logical and systematic. Michael Dell, for example, did not require a study to decide that selling computers by telephone had substantial consumer appeal. Instead, he used his marketing and business intuition to arrive at that conclusion.

Awareness that decision making is not always so orderly stems from the research of psychologist and economist Herbert A. Simon. He proposed that bounds (or limits) to rationality are present in decision making. These bounds are the limitations of the human organism, particularly related to the processing and recall of information.[4] **Bounded rationality** means that people's limited mental abilities, combined with external influences over which they have little or no control, prevent them from making entirely rational decisions. Satisficing decisions result from bounded rationality.

You should strive to follow the orderly steps of problem solving and decision making. However, there is usually more than one problem in need of attention, and you may not have the time to carefully evaluate each alternative. The next section will discuss the factors that influence the decision-making process and how they affect the quality of decisions.

satisficing decision
A decision that meets the minimum standards of satisfaction.

bounded rationality
The observation that people's limited mental abilities, combined with external influences over which they have little or no control, prevent them from making entirely rational decisions.

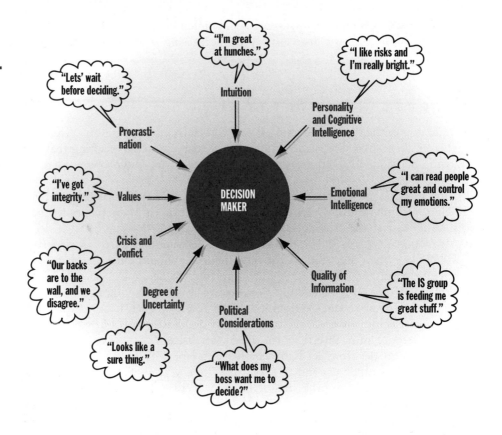

*Factors Influencing
Decision Making*

136

INFLUENCES ON DECISION MAKING

Understand the major factors influencing decision making in organizations.

Although most people can follow the decision-making steps described, not everybody can arrive at the same quality of decision. Decision-making ability varies from person to person, and other forces can hamper anyone from finding optimum solution. Exhibit 6-2 shows the factors that influence decision making.

I n t u i t i o n

intuition
An experience-based way of knowing or reasoning in which weighing and balancing evidence are done unconsciously and automatically.

Intuition is another personal characteristic that influences decision making. Effective decision makers do not rely on analytical and methodological techniques alone. They also use their hunches and intuition. **Intuition** is an experience-based way of knowing or reasoning in which weighing and balancing evidence are done unconsciously and automatically. Intuition is also a way of arriving at a conclusion without using the step-by-step logical process. (Yet the intuitive person might be racing through the steps in his or her mind without realizing it.) The fact that experience contributes to intuition means that decision makers can become more intuitive by solving many difficult problems.

Intuition, of course, can be wrong. One reason is that intuitions are stored information packaged in a new way. If the information being packaged is faulty, then so will be the intuition.[5] A company CEO decided to relocate headquarters from its current metropolitan setting to a rural area 40 miles away. His intuition told him that employees would much prefer rural tranquillity to urban congestion. The CEO's intuition was wrong. Many key employees quit rather than sacrifice the conveniences and excitement of working in the metropolitan area. As a check on your intuition, from time to time attempt to trace the reasons behind your decision. The CEO in question might have asked, "Now what *evidence* do I have that our best associates want to work in a rural location?"

The distinction between analytical and intuitive thinking is often traced to which half of the brain is dominant. The left half of the brain controls analytical thinking; the right half controls creative and intuitive thinking. Effective problem solvers achieve a balance between analytical and intuitive, or left-brain and right-brain thinking. Rather than operating independently of each other, the analytical and intuitive approaches should be complementary components of decision making.

Personality and Cognitive Intelligence

The personality and cognitive intelligence of the decision maker influence his or her ability to find effective solutions. The term *cognitive intelligence* refers to the traditional type of intelligence involved in solving difficult problems and doing well in school. Today psychologists recognize other types of intelligence also, such as being imaginative and adapting well to your environment, or having practical intelligence.

A particularly relevant personality dimension is a person's propensity for taking risks. A cautious, conservative person typically opts for a low-risk solution. If a person is extremely cautious, he or she may avoid making major decisions for fear of being wrong. Organizational pressures can also influence a person's propensity for risk taking. A study was conducted of the risk-taking attitudes of commercial loan officers in Norwest banks. A key finding was that company pressures for profitability appeared to influence the risk ratings borrowers received. Newer borrowers were more likely to receive overly favorable risk ratings by the loan officers. Also, larger loans tended to receive overly favorable assessments.[6]

In addition to being related to risk taking, cautiousness and conservatism are related to **decisiveness**, the extent to which a person makes up his or her mind promptly and prudently. Good decision makers, by definition, are decisive. Take the quiz presented in Exhibit 6-3 to examine your degree of decisiveness.

Perfectionism has a notable impact on decision making. People who seek the perfect solution to a problem are usually indecisive because they are hesitant to accept the fact that a particular alternative is good enough. Self-efficacy, the feeling of being an effective and competent person on a specific task, also has an influence. Researchers note, for example, that having the right amount of gall contributes to innovative thinking.[7]

Rigid people have difficulty identifying problems and gathering alternative solutions. People who are mentally flexible perform well in these areas. Optimism versus pessimism is another relevant personality dimension. Optimists are more likely to find solutions than pessimists are. Pessimists are more likely to give up searching, because they perceive situations as being hopeless.

Cognitive (or traditional) intelligence has a profound influence on decision-making effectiveness. In general, intelligent and well-educated people are more likely to identify problems and make sound decisions than are those who have less intelligence and education. A notable exception applies, however. Some intelligent, well-educated people have such a fondness for collecting facts and analyzing them that they suffer from "analysis paralysis." One plant manager put it

decisiveness
The extent to which a person makes up his or her mind promptly and prudently.

137

EXHIBIT
63

How Decisive Are You?

Answer the following questions by placing a check in the appropriate space: N = never; R = rarely; Oc = occasionally; Of = often.

	N	R	Oc	Of
1. Do you let the opinions of others influence your decisions?	—	—	—	—
2. Do you procrastinate when it's time to make a decision?	—	—	—	—
3. Do you let others make your decisions for you?	—	—	—	—
4. Have you missed out on an opportunity because you couldn't make a decision?	—	—	—	—
5. After reaching a decision do you have second thoughts?	—	—	—	—
6. Did you hesitate while answering these questions?	—	—	—	—

Scoring and interpretation: Score one point for each "often" response, two points for each "occasionally," three points for each "rarely," and four points for each "never."

19–24   You are very decisive and probably have no problem assuming responsibility for the choices you make.

13–18   Decision making is difficult for you. You need to work at being more decisive.

12 or   You are going to have a big problem unless you learn to overcome below your timidity. When a decision has to be made, face up to it and do it!

Source: Adapted from Roger Fritz, "A Systematic Approach to Problem Solving and Decision Making," *Supervisory Management*, March 1993, p. 4. Reprinted with permission of the American Management Association.

this way: "I'll never hire a genius again. They dazzle you with facts, figures, and computer graphics. But when they get through with their analysis, they still haven't solved the problem." A manager has to make it clear to team members that decision making is more important than data collection. One way for the manager to get this message across is to act as a good model.[8]

Emotional Intelligence

How effective you are in managing your feelings and reading other people can affect the quality of your decision making. For example, if you cannot control your anger you are likely to make decisions that are motivated by retaliation, hostility, and revenge. An example would be shouting and swearing at your team leader because of a work assignment you received. **Emotional intelligence** refers to qualities such as understanding one's own feelings, empathy for others, and the regulation of emotion to enhance living. This type of intelligence generally has to do with the ability to connect with people and understand their emotions. If you cannot read the emotions of others you are liable to make some bad decisions involving people, such as pushing your boss too hard to grant a request. Emotional intelligence contains five key factors, all of which can influence the quality of our decisions:[9]

emotional intelligence
The ability to connect with people and understand their emotions.

1. *Self-awareness:* The ability to understand your moods, emotions, and needs, as well as their impact on others. Self-awareness also includes using intuition to make decisions you can live with happily. (A manager with good self-awareness knows whether he is pushing group members too hard.)

2. *Self-regulation:* The ability to control impulsiveness, calming down anxiety, and reacting with appropriate anger to situations. (A manager with high self-regulation would not suddenly decide to drop a project because the work was frustrating.)

3. *Motivation:* A passion to work for reasons in addition to money or status. Also, drive, persistence, and optimism when faced with setbacks. (A manager with this type of motivation would make the decision to keep trying when faced with a serious obstacle such as a drastic budget cut.)

4. *Empathy:* The ability to understand and respond to the unspoken feelings of others. Also, the skill to respond to people according to their emotional reactions. (A manager with empathy would take into account the most likely reaction of group members before making a decision affecting them. Remember the manager who relocated the company to a rural area and lost some key personnel because of his decision?)

5. *Social Skill:* Competency in managing relationships and building networks of support, and having positive relationships with people. (A manager with social skill would decide to use a method of persuasion that is likely to work with a particular group.)

Quality and Accessibility of Information

Reaching an effective decision usually requires high-quality, valid information. A major justification for information systems is to supply managers with high-quality information. Accessibility may be even more important than quality in determining which information is used or not used. Sometimes it takes so much time and effort to search for quality information that the manager relies on lower-quality information that is close at hand. One manager was researching the potential market for transformers in Ireland. After three hours of making telephone calls and digging through search engines without finding the information he needed, the manager finally relied on ten-year-old information his predecessor had used.

Closely related to quality and accessibility of information is the tendency to be influenced by the first information we receive when attempting to solve a problem or make a decision. **Anchoring** occurs during decision making when the mind gives too much weight to the first information it receives. Initial impressions, estimates, or data hold back, or anchor, later thoughts and judgments.[10] The manager who used the old information about the market for transformers in Ireland might be overly influenced by that information. Having been received first, the anchored information becomes the standard against which to judge other information. When an assistant brings in more current information about the Irish market for transformers that indicates a smaller market, the manager might think, "This information with the lower estimate is less important than the information I already have." Anchoring can therefore lead to wasting useful information that is received after the first information.

anchoring
In the decision-making process, placing too much value on the first information received and ignoring later information.

Political Considerations

Under ideal circumstances, organizational decisions are made on the basis of the objective merits of competing alternatives. In reality, many decisions are based on political considerations, such as favoritism, alliances, or the desire of the decision maker to stay in favor with people who wield power.

139

Political factors sometimes influence which data are given serious consideration in evaluating alternatives. The decision maker may select data that support the position of an influential person whom he or she is trying to please. For instance, one financial analyst was asked to investigate the cost-effectiveness of the firm owning a corporate jet. She knew the president wanted the status of having a private jet, so she gave considerable weight to the "facts" supplied by a manufacturer of corporate jets. This allowed her to justify the expense of purchasing the plane.

A study of the effectiveness of strategic decisions compared those that were made rationally versus those made mostly on the basis of politics. *Politics* as measured in this study referred to factors such as people being more concerned about their own goals than those of the organization, and the use of power and influence with group members. The study found that managers who collected information and used analytical techniques made more effective decisions than those who did not. It was also found that managers who used power or pushed hidden agendas (both political tactics) were less effective than those who did not.[11] So in this study, political factors hampered good decision making.

A person with professional integrity arrives at what he or she thinks is the best decision and then makes a diligent attempt to convince management of the objective merits of that solution.

Degree of Uncertainty

The more certain a decision maker is of the outcome of a decision, the more calmly and confidently the person will make the decision. Degree of certainty is divided into three categories: certainty, risk, and uncertainty. A condition of certainty exists when the facts are well known and the outcome can be predicted accurately. A retail store manager might predict with certainty that more hours of operation will lead to more sales. It might be uncertain, however, whether the increased sales would cover the increased expenses.

A condition of risk exists when a decision must be made based on incomplete, but accurate, factual information. Managers frequently use quantitative techniques to make decisions under conditions of risk. Suppose a promoter schedules a tour for a popular singing group. Some statistical information about costs and past ticket sales would be available. The promoter can, to an extent, calculate the risk by studying factual information from the past.

Effective managers often accept a condition of risk. A calculated risk is where the potential return is well worth the cost that will be incurred if the effort fails. Ronald L. Zarella, a General Motors marketing executive, was willing to take the risk several years ago of launching the Catera, a sporty new Cadillac designed to appeal to a hipper consumer group. The Catera has been a success, thereby vindicating Zarella's risk-taking behavior.

Crisis and Conflict

In a crisis, many decision makers panic. They become less rational and more emotional than they would in a calm environment. Decision makers who are adversely affected by crisis perceive it to be a stressful event. As a consequence, they concentrate poorly, use poor judgment, and think impulsively. Under crisis, some managers do not bother dealing with differences of opinion because they are under so much pressure. A smaller number of managers perceive a crisis as an exciting challenge that energizes them toward their best level of problem solving and decision making. Larry Weinbach, the Unisys executive described in Chapter 5, is such a manager. He welcomed the opportunity to bring a failing organization back to health.

Conflict is related to crisis because both can be an emotional experience. When conflict is not overwhelming, and is directed at real issues, not personalities, it can be an asset to decision making. By virtue of opposing sides expressing different points of view, problems can be solved more thoroughly, which leads to better decisions. One study analyzed strategic decision making by top-management teams in both the food-processing and furniture-making industries. The researchers found that the quality of a decision appears to improve with the introduction of conflict. However, the conflict often had the negative side effect of creating antagonistic relationships among some members of the management team.[12]

Values of the Decision Maker

Values influence decision making at every step. Ultimately, all decisions are based on values. A manager who places a high value on the personal welfare of employees tries to avoid alternatives that create hardship for workers and implements decision in ways that lessen turmoil. Another value that significantly influences decision making is the pursuit of excellence. A manager who embraces the pursuit of excellence will search for the high-quality alternative solution.

Attempting to preserve the status quo is a value held by many managers, as well as others. Clinging to the status quo is perceived as a hidden trap in decision making that can prevent optimum decision making. People tend to cling to the status quo because by not taking action they can prevent making a bad decision.[13] If you value the status quo too highly, you may fail to make a decision that could bring about major improvements. At one company, the vice-president of human resources received numerous inquires about when the firm would begin offering benefits for domestic partners (of the opposite or same sex). The vice-president reasoned that since the vast majority of employees rated the benefit package highly, a change was not needed. A few employees took their complaints about "biased benefits" to the CEO. The vice-president of human resources was then chastised by the CEO for not suggesting an initiative that would keep the company in the forefront of human resources management. As you can see, preserving the status quo can sometimes lead to procrastination.

Procrastination

Many people are poor decision makers because they **procrastinate**, or delay taking action without a valid reason. Procrastination results in indecisiveness and inaction and is a major cause of self-defeating behavior. Procrastination is a deeply ingrained behavior pattern. Yet recent research suggests it can be overcome by learning how to become self-disciplined.[14] Part of the process involves setting goals for overcoming procrastination and conquering the problem in small steps. For example, a person might first practice making a deadline for a decision over a minor activity such as ordering a box of copier paper. We will return to the problem of procrastination in Chapter 17.

procrastinate
To delay in taking action without a valid reason.

CREATIVITY IN MANAGERIAL WORK

Understand the nature of creativity and how it contributes to managerial work.

creativity
The process of developing novel ideas that can be put into action.

Creativity is an essential part of problem solving and decision making. To be creative is to see new relationships and produce imaginative solutions. **Creativity** can be defined simply as the process of developing novel ideas that can be put into action. By emphasizing the application of ideas, creativity is closely linked to innovation. To be innovative, a person must produce a new product, service, process, or procedure.

Without some creativity a manager cannot solve complex problems or contribute to any types of organizational breakthroughs. A new perspective on creativity helps illustrate the point that it is not a rarified talent of the privileged few. Psychology professor Ellen Langer believes that learning to be *mindful* is more important than attempting to be creative. Mindfulness is paying attention to what you are doing and what's going on around you, instead of mindlessly cruising through life on automatic.[15] A mindful person can recognize an opportunity or see a problem that needs to be fixed. The accompanying Small-Business in Action illustrates how being mindful of an everyday event can result in a career breakthrough.

Our discussion of managerial creativity focuses on the creative personality, the necessary conditions for creativity, the creative organization, creativity programs, and suggestions for becoming more creative.

Creative Aspects of a Manager's Job

A manager's workday is a collection of miscellaneous activities, from holding scheduled meetings and doing analytical work on a computer to engaging in impromptu conversations. Managers jump from task to task and from person to person. To fashion order from this potential chaos requires creative problem solving. Managers can display creativity in the way they arrange and rearrange, juggle schedules, collect and disseminate information and ideas, make assignments, and lead people.

An important point about creativity in managerial work is that many successful new business ideas are straightforward and uncomplicated. Examples include potato chips in a can (Pringles), selling autos over the Internet, and a gloved sweatshirt. Can you think of another simple, breakthrough idea in business?

The Creative Personality

Creative people are more emotionally open and flexible than their less-creative counterparts. People who rarely exhibit creative behavior tend to be closed-minded and rigid. They suffer from "hardening of the categories"; they cannot overcome the traditional way of looking at things. In business jargon, creative people can *think outside the box*, or get beyond the usual constraints when solving problems.

Yet another way of characterizing creative thinkers is that they *break the rules*. An unusual example took place in relation to paying life insurance benefits. The rules say that the company pays benefits *after* a person dies. Yet Living Benefits, Inc., a New Mexico company, developed the idea of *viatical settlements*, the purchase life insurance policies from terminally ill people. The policies are purchased at a discount, and the company collects the face amount of the policy when the person dies. The longer the person lives, the poorer the investment. Assume that

Small Business *in Action*

Hitting It Big with a Gloved Sweatshirt

Chuck Mellon remembers being tossed to the ground and tearing his sweatshirt one day four years ago as he tried to turn his motorbike on an icy mountain trail. Later, as he put the sweatshirt back on, his thumb poked a hole in the sleeve, accidentally pulling the cuff down over his hand. That's when the idea struck him for a new type of sweatshirt—one with sleeves that extend over most of the hand and have thumbholes but are fingerless so they can be rolled back into a normal cuff.

The gloved-sweatshirt concept has been catching on ever since Mellon and his younger brother Bob started Handcuffs Sweatshirts. The Mellons report that sales for the new-style sweatshirt have quadrupled in each of the company's first four years, and gross earnings have climbed from about $100,000 three years ago to around $10 million today. They recently landed their biggest client yet—JCPenney Co. Inc., which placed an $8.5 million order.

The specially designed shirts have been catching on with hunters, fishers, and Harley-Davidson riders, who like the shirts because they don't take away their sense of touch. Parents like them for children because they keep their hands warm but can't be lost like gloves.

Finding success in the garment industry has been a journey of trial and error for the Mellons. The brothers had spent most of their lives in blue-collar fields and lacked retail trade experience. Chuck, 40, is a former electrician. Bob, 38, installed pool tiles. Both were relying on these incomes before Penny's became their main customer.

In spring 1997, they received their biggest break when a business contact put them in touch with a buyer at Penney's, and they were invited to the company's headquarters outside of Dallas. A buyer for the Penney catalogue had enough faith in the idea to place an immediate order for 20,000 shirts, and put a two-page spread in the winter catalogue. The sweatshirts were a bestseller. The order was filled three days after the catalogue was mailed, and the company ordered 15,000 more.

The brothers are grateful, though not surprised by their success. Both believed from the beginning that the idea would catch on.

Source: "Ripped Shirt Results in Big Business for Brothers," The Associated Press, November 16, 1998. Adapted with permission.

---

a man with lung cancer is slowly dying. He holds a $300,000 life insurance policy and needs cash now to pay living expenses. A company such as Living Benefits buys the rights to his policy for $200,000. When the man dies, the company collects the $300,000 from the life insurance company. Even if you think viatical settlements are ghoulish, they do illustrate breaking the rules.

Creative people are also described as those who can make a paradigm shift. A **paradigm** consists of the perspectives and ways of doing things that are typical of a given context. For example, top management at Toys 'Я' Us was able to shift away from the paradigm that only Japanese-made toys can be sold in Japan.

Closely related to making paradigm shifts is the ability to think laterally. **Lateral thinking** spreads out to find many different solutions to a problem.

paradigm
The perspectives and ways of doing things that are typical of a given context.

lateral thinking
A thinking process that spreads out to find many different alternative solutions to a problem.

vertical thinking
An analytical, logical process that results in few answers.

Vertical thinking, in contrast, is an analytical, logical process that results in few answers. A problem requiring lateral thinking would be to specify a variety of ways in which a small-business owner could increase income. A vertical thinking problem would be to calculate how much more money the small-business owner needs each month to earn a 10 percent profit.

Lateral thinking is thus divergent, while vertical thinking is convergent. Creative people are able to think divergently. They can expand the number of alternatives to a problem, thus moving away from a single solution. Yet the creative thinker also knows when it is time to think convergently. For example, the divergent thinker might generate 25 ways to reduce costs. Yet at some point he or she will have to converge toward choosing the best of several cost-cutting procedures. Two lateral thinking problems are presented next. Compare your solutions to the ones given at the end of the chapter.[16]

A truck approached a low overpass on the highway. It was just about the same height as the arch, and managed to get itself in, but not out. Halfway through, the truck became wedged in. It could not move forward or back out without severely damaging its roof. No one could figure a way to get it out, until a small girl suggested a solution. What was it?

Kurt and Jessica were co-owners of a building, with both their names on the mortgage. The two people ended their business relationship, and decided to split their assets. Kurt wanted ownership of the building, and Jessica agreed. However, Kurt had to pay Jessica $25,000 for her share of the building. To come up with the $25,000 he needed a second mortgage. Five consecutive banks told Kurt the same story, "We cannot lend you a second mortgage so long as Jessica's name is on the first mortgage." Kurt replied, "Please help me. Jessica's name stays on the mortgage until I give her the $25,000." After weeks of mulling over the problem, Kurt finally solved his Catch-22 problem. What did he do?

Conditions Necessary for Creativity

Well-known creativity researcher Teresa M. Amabile has summarized 22 years of research about the conditions necessary for creativity in organizations. Creativity takes place when three components join together: expertise, creative-thinking skills, and motivation.[17] Expertise refers to the necessary knowledge to put facts together. The more facts floating around in your head, the more likely you are to combine them in some useful way. The brothers who developed the gloved sweatshirt had some knowledge about how certain people need to keep their hands warm yet still have their fingers free. They also needed to know about retailing, along with many other factors.

Creative-thinking refers to how flexibly and imaginatively individuals approach problems. If you know how to keep digging for alternatives, and to avoid getting stuck in the status quo, your chances of being creative multiply. Persevering, or sticking with a problem to a conclusion, is essential for finding creative solutions. A few rest breaks to gain a fresh perspective may be helpful, but the creative person keeps coming back until a solution emerges. Quite often an executive will keep sketching different organization charts on paper or on the computer before the right one surfaces that will help the firm run smoothly.

The right type of motivation is the third essential ingredient for creative thought. A fascination with, or passion for, the task is more important than searching for external rewards. People will be the most creative when they are motivated primarily by the satisfaction and challenge of the work itself. Remember Dineh Mohajer, the creative force behind Hard Candy who you read about in Chapter 1? She became successful as a byproduct of being passionate about making her own nail polish. Her intent was not to find a hobby that could lead to fame and fortune.

In addition to the internal conditions that foster creativity, two factors outside the person have a significant effect. An environmental need must stimulate the setting of a goal. This is another way of saying, "Necessity is the mother of invention." For example, an inventory control manager might be told, "We've got too much inventory in the warehouse. Reduce it by 75 percent, but do not lose money for us." No standard solution is available. The manager sets the goal of reducing the inventory, including working with the marketing department to accomplish the feat.

Another condition that fosters creativity is enough conflict and tension to put people on edge. Creativity expert Mike Vance says, "Almost any company can benefit from irritants on the staff. Don't put too much emphasis on harmony—that can undermine the commitment to creativity."[18] In the inventory reduction problem, an irritant might challenge people by declaring that selling the old inventory through the same channels won't work. A new channel of distribution must therefore be sought. Being challenged in this way can foster creative thinking.

The Creative Organization

Another perspective on the conditions necessary for creativity is to recognize that certain managerial and organizational practices foster creativity. The most important characteristic of the creative organization is an atmosphere that encourages creative expression. A manager who encourages imaginative and original thinking, and does not punish people for making honest mistakes, is likely to receive creative ideas from group members. At the same time, supervision that is supportive of employees encourages creative expression. Among the specifics of being supportive are showing concern for employees' feelings and needs, and encouraging them to voice their concerns. It is also important for the supervisor to provide feedback that is informational rather than harsh, and to help employees with personal development.[19]

Six categories of activities summarize much of what is known about what managers can do to establish a creative atmosphere, as described next. Much of this information stems from Amabile's research, yet her findings have been supported by others as well.[20]

1. *Challenge.* Giving employees the right type and amount of challenge is part of providing a creative atmosphere. Employees should be neither bored with the simplicity of the task, nor overwhelmed by its difficulty. A good creativity-inducer for a new sales representative might be for the manager to say, "How would you like to go through our ex-customer file, and attempt to bring back 5 percent of them? It would have a great impact on profits."
2. *Freedom.* To be creative, employees should have the freedom to choose how to accomplish a goal, but not which goal to accomplish. For example, creativity would be encouraged if a manager said to a group member, "I would like to improve our Internet service, and you figure out how." A creative result would be less likely if the manager said, "I would like you to improve our service, and you decide which service to improve and how to do it."

3. *Resources.* Managers need to allot time and money carefully to enhance creativity. Tight deadlines can get the creative juices flowing, but people still need enough time to let creative ideas swirl around in their heads for a while. Employees also need large enough budgets to purchase the equipment and information necessary to get the job done. At one company, top management asked employees to be more creative and at the same time canceled subscriptions to trade magazines and limited book purchases. The result was that many readily accessible sources of good ideas dried up.

4. *Supervisory Encouragement.* For people to sustain creative effort, they need to feel that their work matters to the employer. Just as the elementary school teacher says to the 8-year old, "I love your drawing. Keep up the good work," the manager might say, "I love your idea for reducing shipping costs. Keep up the good work."

5. *Organizational Support.* The organization as well as the manager must support creativity. Support can take such forms as giving recognition and financial rewards for successful new ideas. 3M has long been recognized as an organization that supports creativity. One of the leading companywide programs lets workers invest 15 percent of their time on their own projects. Such projects do not have to fit into the strategic business plan. One of the most successful projects to come from the program is Post-it Notes, a top-selling product in the United States.

6. *Encouraging Risk Taking.* Employees are sometimes hesitant to make creative suggestions for fear of being zapped if their new idea fails when implemented. In contrast, if risk taking is encouraged by informing employees that it is okay to fail, more people will be willing to take chances. Neville Isdell, president of Coca-Cola Co.'s Greater Europe Group illustrates this point as follows: "We celebrated the 10th anniversary of the launch of the New Coke. We celebrated the failure because it led to fundamental learning and showed that it's okay to fail."[21]

Organizational Programs for Improving Creativity

Describe organizational programs for improving creativity.

Another aspect of the creative organization is formal programs or mechanisms for creativity improvement. Four such mechanisms are creativity training, brainstorming, idea quotas, and suggestion programs.

CREATIVITY TRAINING   About 30 percent of medium- and large-sized American firms provide some sort of creativity training. An outstanding example is the Center for Creativity and Innovation at DuPont. A typical event at the center is a seminar on creative thinking techniques. A representative training exercise used in many firms is the **pet-peeve technique**. The group thinks up as many complaints as possible about every facet of the department. The group is encouraged to take the views of external and internal customers, competitors, and suppliers. The group is also encouraged to throw in some imaginary complaints. "No holds barred" is the rule. A complaint might be "We set up a work schedule to suit our own convenience, not that of the customer." In addition, participants can solicit feedback on themselves from coworkers or from the people they serve. Diplomacy is required for giving constructive feedback, and the technique works best in an atmosphere of trust.

pet-peeve technique
A creativity-training (or problem-solving) exercise in which the group thinks up as many complaints as possible about every facet of the department.

As with many creativity-training exercises, the pet-peeve technique loosens people up and provides information for improving operations. Participants can laugh at their own weaknesses in a friendly setting. Laughter is important because humor facilitates creativity. The pet-peeve technique can also be used outside the training program, as a method for improving productivity, quality, and service.

BRAINSTORMING   The best-known method of improving creativity is **brainstorming**. This technique is a method of problem solving carried out by a group. Group members spontaneously generate numerous solutions to a problem, without being discouraged or controlled. Brainstorming produces many ideas; it is not a technique for working out details. People typically use brainstorming when looking for tentative solutions to nontechnical problems. In recent years, however, many information systems specialists have used brainstorming to improve computer programs and systems. By brainstorming, people improve their ability to think creatively. To achieve the potential advantages of brainstorming, the session must be conducted properly. Exhibit 6-4 presents the rules for conducting a brainstorming session.

Some types of business problems are well suited to brainstorming. These include coming up with a name for a new sports car, developing an idea for a corporate logo, identifying ways to attract new customers, and making concrete suggestions for cost cutting.

Brainstorming can also be conducted through e-mail, generally referred to as electronic brainstorming. In brainstorming by e-mail, group members simultaneously enter their suggestions into a computer. The ideas are distributed to the screens of other group members. Or ideas can be sent back at different times to a facilitator who passes the contributions along to other members. In either approach, although group members do not talk to each other, they are still able to build on each other's ideas and combine ideas. Electronic brainstorming researcher

brainstorming
A group method of solving problems, gathering information, and stimulating creative thinking. The basic technique is to generate numerous ideas through unrestrained and spontaneous participation by group members.

147

EXHIBIT
6-4

Rules for Conducting a Brainstorming Session

RULE 1	Enroll five to eight participants. If you have too few people, you lose the flood of ideas; if you have too many, members feel that their ideas are not important, and there can be too much chatter.
RULE 2	Give everybody the opportunity to generate alternative solutions to the problem. Have them call out these alternatives spontaneously. One useful modification of this procedure is for people to express their ideas one after another, to decrease possible confusion.
RULE 3	Do not allow criticism or value judgments during the brainstorming session. Make all suggestions welcome. Above all, members should not laugh derisively or make sarcastic comments about other people's ideas.
RULE 4	Encourage freewheeling. Welcome bizarre ideas. It is easier to tone down an idea than it is to think one up.
RULE 5	Strive for quantity rather than quality. The probability of discovering really good ideas increases in proportion to the number of ideas generated.
RULE 6	Encourage members to piggyback, or build, on the ideas of others.
RULE 7	Record each idea or tape-record the session. Written notes should not identify the author of an idea because participants may worry about saying something foolish.
RULE 8	After the brainstorming session, edit and refine the list of ideas and choose one or two for implementation.

Keng L. Siau suggests that brainstorming via e-mail can increase both the quantity and quality of ideas. When participants do not face each other directly, they can concentrate more on the creativity task at hand, and less on the interpersonal aspects of interaction.[22]

IDEA QUOTAS   An increasingly popular technique for encouraging creative input from employees is to set quotas for employee suggestions. Being creative therefore becomes a concrete work goal. Dana Corp., for example, sets a quota of two ideas per employee per month. All employees are involved, including the CEO and entry-level workers in manufacturing. Dana management favors ideas that help streamline problem areas. Employees are asked to make suggestions about quality, customer service, production control, office efficiency, and security. Monthly raffles are held to reward ideas with cash. Noncash rewards are also given. Employees receive a leather jacket for having submitted 100 ideas. Another part of the program is a sincere effort by management to implement 80 percent of the ideas.

Since Dana introduced the idea-quota system in one division seven years ago, the number of employee ideas from that division's 3,600 employees increased from 9,000 to 64,000. Division profitability has increased by 40 percent, and morale is an all-time high.[23] We can assume that at least some of the increase in profitability and morale is attributed to the idea quotas.

SUGGESTION PROGRAMS   To encourage creative thinking, companies throughout the world use **suggestion programs**. They are a formal method for collecting and analyzing employee suggestions about processes, policies, products, and services. Suggestion programs have been around for many years. Unlike idea quotas, suggestion programs rely on voluntary submissions. Typically, the employee who makes a suggestion that is implemented receives a percentage of the savings resulting from it. Useful suggestions save money, earn money, or increase safety or quality. Pollution Prevention Pays is the name of a topic-specific suggestion system at 3M. Since its inception 25 years ago, some 4,200 projects have saved the company $750 million and kept 65,000 tons of pollution from entering the environment.[24] A more typical suggestion program is the one at American Airlines in which a group of mechanics received a $37,500 award for developing a tamper-proof security door.

Committees evaluate submissions and make awards in suggestion programs. These programs foster creativity by offering financial rewards and by conferring prestige on employees whose ideas are implemented. In addition, suggestion programs help get employees involved in the success of their organization.

Suggestion programs are sometimes criticized because they collect loads of trivial suggestions and pay small awards just to humor employees. One employee, for example, was paid $50 for suggesting that the firm dust light bulbs more frequently to increase illumination.

Self-Help Techniques for Improving Creativity

In addition to participating in organizational programs for creativity improvement, you can help yourself become more creative. Becoming a more creative problem solver and decision maker requires that you increase the flexibility of your thinking. Reading about creativity improvement or attending one or two

suggestion program
A formal method for collecting and analyzing employees' suggestions about processes, policies, products, and services.

brainstorming sessions is insufficient. You must also practice the methods described in the following sections. As with any serious effort at self-improvement, you must exercise the self-discipline to implement these suggestions regularly. Creative people must also be self-disciplined to carefully concentrate on going beyond the obvious in solving problems.

TEN SPECIFIC CREATIVITY-BUILDING SUGGESTIONS   To develop habits of creative thinking, you must regularly practice the suggestions described in the list that follows.[25]

Implement several suggestions for becoming a more creative problem solver.

149

1. Keep track of your original ideas by maintaining an idea notebook. Few people have such uncluttered minds that they can recall all their past flashes of insight when they need them.

2. Stay current in your field. Having current facts at hand gives you the raw material to link information creatively. (In practice, creativity usually takes the form of associating ideas that are unassociated, such as associating the idea of selling movie tickets with the idea of selling through vending machines.)

3. Listen to other people as another medium for gathering creative ideas you can use. Creative people rarely believe they have all the answers. The CEO of the company that includes Chili's restaurants introduced the fajita because he listened to the menu suggestion of a busperson.

4. Learn to think in the five senses, or in various combinations thereof, because it enhances your perceptiveness of what might work. The concept is particularly applicable if you are developing a product or service that would be experienced in many ways, such as a restaurant, nightclub, or clothing. Suppose you were trying to think of a creative idea for an office party. Using the five-senses approach you would imagine what the setting would look like, how it would sound, what the food would taste like, how the decorations would feel, and the aroma of the party.

5. Improve your sense of humor, including your ability to laugh at your own mistakes. Humor helps reduce stress and tensions, and you will be more creative when you are relaxed.

6. Adopt a risk-taking attitude when you try to find creative solutions. You will inevitably fail a few times.

7. Develop a creative mental set; allow the foolish side of you to emerge. Creativity requires a degree of intellectual playfulness and immaturity. Many creative people are accomplished practical jokers.

8. Identify the times when you are most creative and attempt to accomplish most of your creative work during that period. Most people are at their peak of creative productivity after ample rest, so try to work on your most vexing problems at the start of the workday. Schedule routine decision making and paperwork for times when your energy level is lower than average.

9. Be curious about your environment. The person who routinely questions how things work (or why they do not work) is most likely to have an idea for improvement.

10. When faced with a creativity block, step back from the problem and engage in a less mentally demanding task for a brief pause, or even a day. Sometimes by doing something quite different, your perspective will become clearer and a creative alternative will flash into your head when you return to your problem. Although creative problem solvers are persistent, they will sometimes put a problem away for awhile so they can come back stronger.

PLAY THE ROLES OF EXPLORER, ARTIST, JUDGE, AND LAWYER

One method for improving creativity incorporates many of the suggestions discussed so far. It requires you to adopt four roles in your thinking. First, you must be an explorer. Speak to people in different fields to get ideas you can use. Second, be an artist by stretching your imagination. Strive to spend about 5 percent of your day asking "what if?" questions. For example, an executive in a swimsuit company might ask, "What if the surgeon general decides that since sunbathing causes skin cancer, we have to put warning labels on bathing suits?" Third, know when to be a judge. After developing some wild ideas, evaluate them. Fourth, achieve results with your creative thinking by playing the role of a lawyer. Negotiate and find ways to implement your ideas within your field or place of work. You may spend months or years getting your best ideas implemented.[26]

Despite all the positive things that have been said about creativity, when an organization does not want to disturb the status quo, being creative can work to a person's disadvantage. Also, creativity for its own sake can result in discarding traditional, but useful, ideas.

GROUP PROBLEM SOLVING AND DECISION MAKING

Appreciate the value and potential limitations of group decision making.

group decision
The process of several people contributing to a final decision.

We have described how individuals go about solving problems and making decisions. However, most major, nonroutine decisions in organizations are made by groups. **Group decisions** result when several people contribute to a final decision. Since so much emphasis has been placed on teams in organizations and participative decision making, an increasing number of decisions are made by groups rather than individuals. Group decision making is often used in complex and important situations such as:

- Developing a new product, such as a car, or a service such as selling equipment replacement parts over the Internet
- Deciding which employees should be placed on a downsizing list
- Deciding whether to operate a company cafeteria with company personnel or to outsource the activity to a company that specializes in running company cafeterias

The group problem-solving and decision-making process is similar to the individual model in one important respect. Groups often work on problems by following the decision-making steps shown in Exhibit 6-1. Many groups, however, tend to ignore formal sequencing.

We will examine the advantages and disadvantages of group decision making, describe when it is useful, and present a general problem-solving method for groups.

Advantages and Disadvantages of Group Decision Making

Group decision making offers several advantages over the same activity carried out individually. First, the quality of the decision might be higher because of the combined wisdom of group members. A second benefit is a byproduct of the first. Group members evaluate each other's thinking, so major errors are likely to be avoided. The marketing vice-president of a company that sells small appliances such as microwave ovens, toasters, and coffee pots decided the company should sell direct through E-commerce. Before asking others to begin implementing the decision, the executive brought the matter up for group discussion. A sales manager in the group pointed out that direct selling would enrage their dealers, thus doing damage to the vast majority of their sales. The marketing vice-president then decided she would back off on direct marketing until a new product was developed that would not be sold through dealers.

Third, group decision making is helpful in gaining acceptance and commitment. People who participate in making a decision will often be more committed to the implementation than if they were not consulted. Fourth, groups can help people overcome blocks in their thinking, leading to more creative solutions to problems.

Group decision making also has some notable disadvantages. The group approach consumes considerable time and may result in compromises that do not really solve the problem. An intelligent individual might have the best solution to the problem, and time could be saved by relying on his or her judgment.

The explosion of the space shuttle Challenger presents a serious example of the disadvantages of group decision making. According to several analyses of this incident, NASA managers were so committed to reaching space program objectives that they ignored safety warnings from people both inside and outside the agency. An internal NASA brief reported that astronauts and engineers were concerned about agency management's groupthink mentality. (This term will be explained later.) Furthermore, the brief characterized NASA managers as having the tendency not to reverse decisions or heed the advice of people outside management. (The analysis of the style was made several years before the Challenger explosion.)[27]

Seriously flawed group decisions have occurred so frequently in government and business that they have been extensively analyzed and researched. Well-publicized flawed group decisions include the arms-for-hostage deal (an illegal arms sale to Iran to fund Contras in Nicaragua) and the decision by Chrysler Corporation executives to sell, as new cars, autos they had personally sampled. The illusion of newness was created by cleaning up the cars and turning back the odometers. Another example of a seriously flawed decision took place at several different telephone companies. The long-distance service of many individuals was switched to another company without the individuals' consent, a practice known as *slamming*. Several of these companies received heavy fines because of their illegal and unethical decisions.

Flawed decisions of the type just described have generally been attributed to **groupthink**, a psychological drive for consensus at any cost. Groupthink makes group members lose their ability to evaluate bad ideas critically. Glen Whyte believes that many instances of groupthink are caused by decision makers who see themselves as choosing between inevitable losses. The group believes that a sure loss will occur unless action is taken. Caught up in the turmoil of trying to make the best of a bad situation, the group takes a bigger risk than any individual member would.

The arms-for-hostages decision was perceived by those who made it as a choice between losses. The continued captivity of American citizens held hostage by terrorist groups was a certain loss. Making an arms deal with Iran created some hope of averting that loss, although the deal would most likely fail and create more humiliation.[28]

Groupthink can often be avoided if the team leader encourages group members to express doubts and criticisms of proposed solutions. It is helpful to show

groupthink
A psychological drive for consensus at any cost.

by example that you are willing to accept criticism. It is also important for someone to play the role of the devil's advocate. This person challenges the thinking of others by asking such questions as, "Why do you think so many consumers are so stupid that they won't recognize they have been switched to another long-distance phone company without their consent?"

When to Use Group Decision Making

Because group decision making takes more time and people than individual decision making, it should not be used indiscriminately. Group decision making should be reserved for nonroutine decisions of reasonable importance. Too many managers use the group method for solving such minor questions as "What should be on the menu at the company picnic?"

Aside from being used to enhance the quality of decisions, group decision making is often used to gain acceptance for a decision. If people contribute to a decision, they are more likely to be committed to its implementation.

A General Method of Group Problem Solving

When workers at any level gather to solve a problem, they typically hold a discussion rather than rely on a formal decision-making technique. These general meetings are likely to produce the best results when they follow the decision-making steps. Exhibit 6-5 recommends step for conducting group decision making. These steps are quite similar to the decision-making steps presented in Exhibit 6-1.

In addition, a problem-solving group should also follow suggestions for conducting an effective meeting. Five of these suggestions particularly related to problem solving are:

1. *Have a specific agenda and adhere to it.* Meetings are more productive when an agenda is planned and followed carefully. People should see the agenda in advance so they can prepare for the session.
2. *Rely on qualified members.* Groups often arrive at poor solutions because the contributors do not have the necessary knowledge and interest. An uninformed person is typically a poor decision maker. Also, a person who attends a meeting reluctantly will sometimes agree to any decision just to bring the meeting to a close.
3. *Have the leader share decision-making authority.* A key attribute of an effective problem-solving meeting is a leader who shares authority. Unless authority is shared, the members are likely to believe that the hidden agenda of the meeting is to seek approval for the meeting leader's decision.
4. *Provide summaries for each major point.* Decision-making quality improves when members clearly understand the arguments that have been advanced for and against each alternative. Summarizing major points can help. Summaries also keep the meeting focused on major issues, because minor issues are excluded from the summary.
5. *Build consensus so the decision is more likely to be implemented.* When group decision making is really team decision making, obtaining general agreement is particularly important. The emphasis on a *team* rather than merely on a *group* means that there is particular emphasis on members working together

EXHIBIT
6.5

*Steps for Effective Group
Decision Making*

1. **Identify the problem.** Describe specifically what the problem is and how it manifests itself.
2. **Clarify the problem.** If group members do not perceive the problem in the same way, they will offer divergent solutions. Make sure everyone shares the same definition of the problem.
3. **Analyze the cause.** To convert "what is" into "what we want," the group must understand the causes of the specific problem and find ways to overcome them.
4. **Search for alternative solutions.** Remember that multiple alternative solutions can be found to most problems.
5. **Select alternatives.** Identify the criteria that solutions must meet, and then discuss the pros and cons of the proposed alternatives. No solution should be laughed at or scorned.
6. **Plan for implementation.** Decide what actions are necessary to carry out the chosen solution.
7. **Clarify the contract.** The contract is a restatement of what group members have agreed to do, and it includes deadlines for accomplishment.
8. **Develop an action plan.** Specify who does what and when to carry out the contract.
9. **Provide evaluation and accountability.** After the plan is implemented, reconvene to discuss its progress and hold people accountable for results that have not been achieved.

Source: Derived from Andrew E. Schwartz and Joy Levin, "Better Group Decision Making," *Supervisory Management* (June 1990):4.

smoothly and depending on each other. Consensus is most likely to happen when key points are discussed thoroughly and each member's input is asked for in reference to the point. It also helps to take at least a small part of each member's idea and incorporate it into the final decision. At one company, the group decided not to have a wellness center on company premises. A member from the human resources department was quite disturbed about the decision, and the team needed her concurrence. So the team leader incorporated her suggestion about having a jogging track in the woods near the office, thereby incorporating some of her thinking. The human resources member then supported the group decision.

A Specific Method of Group Problem Solving: The Nominal-Group Technique

A manager who must make a decision about an important issue sometimes needs to know what alternatives are available and how people would react to them. An approach called the **nominal-group technique (NGT)** has been developed to fit this situation. NGT is a group decision-making technique that follows a highly structured format. The term *nominal* means that, for much of the activity, the participants are a group in name only; they do not interact.

A problem that is an appropriate candidate for NGT is the decision about which plants of a multiplant firm should be closed because of declining demand for a product. A decision of this type is highly sensitive and will elicit many different opinions. Suppose Sherry McDivott, the company president, faces the

nominal-group technique (NGT)
A group decision-making technique that follows a highly structured format.

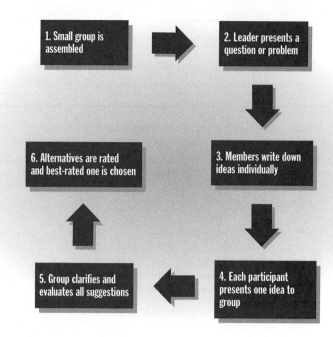

The Nominal-Group Technique
Observe that when the group reaches Step 6, the job is completed except for implementation. An important purpose of the NGT is to find a high-quality solution to a problem that will result in an effective decision.

plant-closing problem. A six-step decision process follows. It uses the nominal-group technique, as summarized in Exhibit 6-6.[29]

1. Group members (called the target group) are selected and assembled. McDivott includes her five top managers, each representing a key function of the business, and informs them in advance of the topic.
2. The group leader presents a specific question. McDivott tells the group, "Our board of directors says we have to consolidate our operations. Our output isn't high enough to justify keeping five plants open. Whatever we do, we must cut operating expenses by about 20 percent.

    "Your assignment is to develop criteria for choosing which plant to close. However, if the group can think of another way of cutting operating costs by 20 percent, I'll give it some consideration. I also need to know how you feel about the alternative you choose and how our employees might feel."
3. Individual members write down their ideas independently, without speaking to other members. Using notepads, the five managers write down their ideas about reducing operating costs by 20 percent.
4. Each participant, in turn, presents one idea to the group. The group does not discuss the ideas. The administrative assistant summarizes each idea by writing it on a flip chart. Here are some of the group's ideas:

    Alternative A. Close the plant with the most obsolete equipment and facilities. We all know that the Harrisburg plant is running with equipment built about 100 years ago. Close the plant in 60 days. Give employees six months of severance pay and assist them to find new jobs. Transfer the most outstanding staff to our other plants.

    Alternative B. Close the plant with the least flexible, most unproductive work force. A lot of employees are likely to complain about this type of closing. But the rest of the work force will get the message that we value productive employees.

Alternative C. Forget about closing a plant. Instead, take our least productive plant and transfer all its manufacturing to our other four plants. Then, work like fury to get subcontracting business for the emptied-out plants. I think our employees and stockholders will be pleased if we take such a brave stance.

Alternative D. We need a careful financial analysis of which plant is producing the lowest return on investment of capital, all factors considered. We simply close that plant. Employees will accept this decision because they all know that business is based on financial considerations.

Alternative E. Closing one plant would be too much of a hardship on one group of people. Let's share the hardship evenly. Cut everybody's pay by 25 percent, eliminate dividends to stockholders, do not replace anybody who quits or retires for the next year, and ask all our suppliers to give us a 15 percent discount. These measures would be the starting point. We could then appoint a committee to look for other savings. If everybody pulls together, morale will be saved.

5. After each group member has presented his or her idea, the group clarifies and evaluates the suggestions. The length of the discussion for each of the ideas varies substantially. For example, the discussion about cutting salaries 25 percent and eliminating dividends lasts only 3 minutes.

6. The meeting ends with a silent, independent rating of the alternatives. The final group decision is the pooled outcome of the individual votes. The target groups is instructed to rate each alternative on a 1-to-10 scale, with 10 being the most favorable rating. The ratings that follow are the pooled ratings (the sum of the individual ratings) received for each alternative. (50 represents the maximum score):

Alternative A, close obsolete plant: 35
Alternative B, close plant with unproductive work force: 41
Alternative C, make one plant a subcontractor: 19
Alternative D, close plant with poorest return on investment: 26
Alternative E, cut everybody's pay by 25 percent: 4

McDivott agrees with the group's preference for closing the plant with the least productive, most inflexible work force. Ultimately, the board accepts Alternative B. The best employees in the factory chosen for closing are offered an opportunity to relocate to another company plant.

NGT is effective because it follows the logic of the problem-solving and decision-making method and allows for group participation. It also provides a discipline and rigor that are often missing in brainstorming.

SUMMARY OF KEY POINTS

 Differentiate between nonprogrammed and programmed decisions.

Unique decisions are nonprogrammed decisions, whereas programmed decisions are repetitive or routine, and made according to a specific procedure.

 Explain the steps involved in making a nonprogrammed decision.

The recommended steps for solving problems and making nonprogrammed decisions call for a problem solver to identify and diagnose the problem, develop creative alternative solutions, evaluate the alternatives, choose an alternative, implement the decision, evaluate and control, and repeat the process if necessary.

Understand the major factors influencing decision making in organizations.

People vary in their decision-making ability, and the situation can influence the quality of decisions. Factors that influence the quality of decisions are intuition, personality and cognitive intelligence, emotional intelligence, quality and accessibility of information, political considerations, degree of uncertainty, crisis and conflict, values of the decision maker, and procrastination.

Understand the nature of creativity and how it contributes to managerial work.

Creativity is the process of developing novel ideas that can be put into action. Many aspects of managerial work, including problem solving and establishing effective work groups, require creativity. Creative people are generally more open and flexible than their less creative counterparts. They are also better able to make paradigm shifts, think laterally, and break the rules.

Creativity takes place when three components join together: expertise, creative-thinking skills, and internal motivation. Perseverance in digging for a solution is also important, and so is an environmental need that stimulates the setting of a goal. Conflict and tension can also prompt people toward creativity. Certain managerial and organizational practices foster creativity. Above all, the atmosphere must encourage creative expression, including supportive supervision. To establish a creative atmosphere, managers can (a) provide the right amount of job challenge, (b) give freedom on how to reach goals, (c) provide the right resources, (d) encourage employees, (e) support creativity by such means as rewards, and (f) encourage risk taking.

Describe organizational programs for improving creativity.

One organizational program for improving creativity is to conduct creativity training, such as a session that uses the pet-peeve technique. Brainstorming is the best-known method of improving creativity. The method can also be conducted by e-mail, known as electronic brainstorming. Giving employees idea quotas often enhances creativity, as do suggestion programs.

Implement several suggestions for becoming a more creative problem solver.

Self-discipline is required to improve creative thinking ability. Creativity-building techniques include staying current in your field, thinking in five senses, improving your sense of humor, and taking risks. A broad approach for improving creativity is to assume the roles of an explorer, artist, judge, and lawyer. Each role relates to a different aspect of creative thinking.

Appreciate the value and potential limitations of group decision making.

Group decision making often results in high-quality solutions, because many people contribute. It also helps people feel more committed to the decision. However, the group approach consumes considerable time, may result in compromise solutions that do not really solve the problem, and may encourage groupthink. Groupthink occurs when consensus becomes so important that group members lose their ability to evaluate ideas. It is likely to occur when decision makers have to choose between inevitable losses.

General problem-solving groups are likely to produce the best results when the decision-making steps are followed closely. Other steps for conducting an effective meeting include (1) adhering to an agenda, (2) relying on qualified members, (3) sharing decision-making authority, and (4) providing summaries of major points.

The nominal-group technique (NGT) is recommended for a situation in which a manager needs to know what alternatives are available and how people will react to them. Using the technique, a small group of people contribute written thoughts about the problem. Other members respond to their ideas later. Members rate each other's ideas numerically, and the final group decision is the value of the pooled individual votes.

KEY TERMS AND PHRASES

QUESTIONS

1. Describe a problem the construction manager for a new office building might face, and point out the actual and ideal conditions in relation to this problem.
2. In what way does the use of empowered teams influence the proportion of nonprogrammed decisions made by lower-ranking workers?
3. In what way do the steps for problem solving and decision making resemble any aspects of the scientific method familiar to you?
4. Which one of the factors influencing decision making would likely give you the most trouble? What can you do to get this factor more in your favor?
5. Give a specific example of how having good emotional intelligence could help you make better decisions.
6. What is a potential disadvantage of giving employees prizes, such as a leather jacket, for submitting 100 ideas in the idea-quota program?
7. How might individual creativity contribute to the effectiveness of group problem solving?

SKILL-BUILDING EXERCISE 6-A: The Forced-Association Technique

A widely used method for releasing creativity is to make forced associations between the properties of two objects to solve a problem. Apply the method by working in small groups. One group member selects a word at random from a dictionary, textbook, or newspaper. Next, the group lists all the properties and attributes of this word. Assume you randomly chose the word *rock*. Among its attributes are "durable," "low-priced," "abundant in supply," "decorative," and "expensive to ship."

You then force-fit these properties to the problem you are facing. Your team might be attempting to improve the quality of an office desk chair. Reviewing the properties of the rock might give you the idea to make the seat covering more durable because this is a quality hot point.

Think of a problem of your own, or perhaps the instructor will assign you one. Another possibility is to use as your problem the question of how to expand the market for snow tires. The groups might work for about 15 minutes. To make the technique proceed smoothly, keep up the random search until you hit a noun or adjective. Prepositions usually do not work well in the forced-association technique. Group leaders share their findings with the rest of the class.

INTERNET SKILL-BUILDING EXERCISE: Learning about Creativity Training

Use the Internet to learn more about what companies are doing to enhance employee creativity. Be specific when you make an entry in your search engine to avoid being deluged with a choice of Web sites far removed from your topic. A sample phrase to enter into your search engine would be "creativ-ity training programs for business." When you have located one or two sites that give some details about a training program, compare the information you've found to the information in this chapter about creativity training. Note similarities and differences, and be prepared to discuss your findings in class.

CASE PROBLEM 6-A: Penn Ball Gets Creative: Arf, Arf, Arf!

Sales of tennis balls by Penn Racquet Sports have plateaued in recent years. Sales peaked at close to $100 million in 1991, then declined steadily until 1994 to about $75 million annually. From 1994 forward, sales have remained about the same. Penn, the number one manufacturer of tennis balls in the United States, has been suffering from a close to ten-year decline in recreational tennis. In addition to a decline in sales, the retail price of tennis balls has been about the same for 15 years, not adjusted for inflation.

Executives and other problem solvers at Penn explored various options for finding more customers. One approach the company has taken to improve sales and make the Penn ball more appealing to customers is to invest in a Research and Development Group. The group seeks ways to improve the ball, such as looking for the best possible felt for the cover. In addition to improving the product, alternatives considered for boosting sales were going global, selling direct through a toll-free number, and selling on the Internet. Direct selling by phone (1-800-BUY-PENN), and a Web site for selling Penn products (www.BuyPenn.com), were implemented. However, more resources were invested in increasing sales by appealing to another species. Penn has begun marketing its familiar fuzzy, yellow balls to dog owners. The dog ball, however, is white.

R. P. Fetchem's is a traditional tennis ball that has been dressed up as a "natural felt fetch toy" for dogs. (Customers can also purchase them for cats and toddlers.) Penn president Gregg R. Weida, who owns a schnauzer named Jake, explains that "Ten times more people own pets than play tennis." Penn hopes to boost sales of tennis balls by 5 to 10 percent through its tennis balls for dogs. For the benefit of the four-legged end user, the balls are dye-free. They carry the Ralston Purina Co. logo, under a licensing agreement with the dog-food manufacturer.

A major change is the price of the new line of tennis balls: $4 to $5 for a container of two Fetchem's versus around $2.50 for a container of three conventional tennis balls. PetsMart Inc. plans to test the new line of balls by ordering 400 cases for its 413 stores. "The fact that it's got the Ralston name and the natural felt are pluses," says Greg Forquer, the vice-president for merchandising at PetsMart.

Penn is a small division of GenCorp Inc., a multidivision company specializing in chemicals and defense products. Making a move into dog toys is an attempt to combat the problem of declining interest in tennis in North America. Recreational play is down almost 20 percent over the last decade, and ball sales have dropped 29 percent since 1991. Yet there is still a remaining base of over 5 million players. Brad Patterson, executive director of the Tennis Industry Association says, "Twenty years ago there was no inline skating, no Blockbuster Video, no home computers. It's harder to grab mind share."

The dog-toy solution has been floating around Penn for years. Laura Kurzu, who directs the Penn account at an advertising agency, has connections at Ralston Purina. She was

convinced that the two should enter into a licensing deal, but says she was at first laughed at from both sides. Yet Penn sees a growth opportunity in marketing to dog owners. (Until dogs earn income and are issued credit cards, you cannot really market to them.) Pet-pampering is a booming business. Human beings will pay $5.95 per box for doggie pasta, $59.95 for a pet canopy bed, and $500 for a heated dog house.

Of more direct relevance to Penn, pet owners buy toys. In a recent year they spent close to $42 million on dog toys sold in pet stores. Given that many dog toys sell for as much as $25, paying $5 for a package of two tennis balls is a small expense. Jim Sweeney, a regional manager in Chicago for Pet Supplies Plus, predicts that Penn could sell 1,000 cans (really plastic containers) of Fetchum's per month.

Penn faces competitive threats with its new venture. Melia Luxury Pet Products makes six flavors of dog tennis balls including "zesty orange," and sales have reached several hundred thousand dollars per year. A representative of a pet industry trade association said about recreational products for dogs, "Everyone and their brother wants to get in."

Discussion Questions

1. What alternatives to increasing the sales of tennis balls for people would you recommend to Penn management?
2. What recommendations can you give Penn for increasing the market for Fetchum's?
3. Serious tennis players use a can of balls no more than twice. How can Penn encourage dog owners to purchase Fetchum's as frequently?
4. To what extent has Penn solved the problem of declining sales of tennis balls?

Source: Based on facts in Dennis Berman, "Now Tennis Balls Are Chasing the Dogs," *Business Week*, July 13, 1998, p. 138; www.pennracquet.com.

CASE PROBLEM 6-B: Where to Put My Next Mail Boxes Etc.?

Mail Boxes Etc. is a nationwide franchise offering a variety of services to individuals and small businesses. Your local Mail Boxes Etc. can wrap and ship packages, make photocopies, and collect your mail. Some Mail Boxes Etc. locations offer concierge services such as picking up flowers, arranging limousines, and collecting dry cleaning. Concierge services are offered primarily at Mail Boxes Etc. sites in office buildings.

Many Mail Boxes Etc. franchisees own multiple locations of these profitable, efficient units. One such multiple franchise owner is Audrey Ritt, a Michigan resident. She was recently contemplating opening another franchise. She knew that any location she chose would have to meet with the approval of the franchisor. Ritt also knew that the market for the types of services Mail Boxes Etc. offers has become highly competitive.

Ritt believes strongly that the amount of consumer traffic surrounding a Mail Boxes Etc. store is more important than the size of the unit. She believes that a cubbyhole in Chicago's O'Hare Airport would beat a spacious location in an infrequently visited mall. She therefore is giving careful thought to suggesting a new location for her next Mail Boxes Etc.

Discussion Questions

1. What problem-solving process should Ritt use to choose her next location?
2. Working in a group, or by yourself, take a stand and recommend a new Mail Boxes Etc. location for Ritt.

Source: As reported in Carol Steinberg, "Break All the Rules," *Success*, October 1995, p. 83.

ANSWERS TO THE LATERAL THINKING PROBLEMS

For the first problem, the girl suggested that the driver let some air out of the truck's tires. He let out enough air to lower the truck by the small amount required to let it pass under the bridge. This problem requires lateral thinking because presumably other alternative solutions might be found.

For the second problem, Kurt finally overcame his traditional mental set of going to a *bank* for a second mortgage. Instead, he called a financial services firm with a loan company. He had his second mortgage in ten days, gave Jessica her $25,000, and the two business partners departed on good terms.

ENDNOTES

1. Duncan Maxwell Anderson (ed.), "Hidden Forces," *Success*, April 1995, p. 12.
2. John M. Ivancevich, James H. Donnellly, Jr., and James L. Gibson, *Managing for Performance: An Introduction to the Process of Managing*, Revised Edition (Burr Ridge, IL: Irwin, 1983), pp. 83–84.
3. Russo is quoted in "Our Decision Can't Be 100% Right, but Our Decision Process Can," *Marriott Executive Memo*, Number 2, 1996, p. 2.
4. Herbert A. Simon, "Rational Choice and the Structure of the Environment," *Psychological Review*, 63, 1956, pp. 129–138; Jon W. Payne, James R. Bettman, and Eric J. Johnson, *The Adaptive Decision Maker* (New York: Cambridge University Press, 1993).
5. Roger Frantz, "Intuition at Work," *Innovative Leader*, April 1997, p. 4.
6. Gerry McNamara and Philip Bromiley, "Decision Making In an Organizational Setting: Cognitive and Organizational Influences on Risk Assessment in Commercial Lending," *Academy of Management Journal*, October 1997, pp. 1063–1088.
7. Michael A. West and James L. Farr (eds.), *Innovation and Creativity at Work: Psychological and Organizational Strategies* (New York: Wiley, 1990).
8. Richard Sharwood Gates, "The Gordian Knot: A Parable for Decision Makers," *Management Review*, December 1990, p. 47.
9. Marian M. Jones, "Unconventional Wisdom," *Psychology Today*, September–October 1997, pp. 34–36; Daniel Goleman, "What Makes a Leader?" *Harvard Business Review*, November–December 1998, pp. 92–102.
10. John S. Hammond, Ralph L. Keeney, and Howard Raiffa, "The Hidden Traps in Decision Making," *Harvard Business Review*, September–October 1998, p. 48.
11. James W. Dean, Jr., and Mark P. Sharfman, "Does Decision Process Matter? A Study of Strategic Decision-Making Effectiveness," *Academy of Management Journal*, April 1996, pp. 368–396.
12. Allen C. Amason, "Distinguishing the Effects of Functional and Dysfunctional Conflict on Strategic Decision Making: Resolving a Paradox for Top Management Teams," *Academy of Management Journal*, February 1996, pp. 123–148.
13. Hammond, Keeney, and Raiffa, "The Hidden Traps," p. 50.
14. Andrew J. DuBrin, *Getting It Done: The Transforming Power of Self-Discipline* (Princeton, NJ: Peterson's/Pacesetter Books, 1995), pp. 49–71.

15. Research cited in Nancy Ross-Flanigan, "Pro-Creative: Free the Original Thinker Inside Yourself and Life Will Be More Fulfilling, Experts Say," Knight-Ridder New Service, May 8, 1995.
16. Paul Sloane, *Lateral Thinking Puzzlers* (New York: Sterling Publishing, 1992).
17. Teresa M. Amabile, "How to Kill Creativity," *Harvard Business Review*, September–October 1998, pp. 78–79.
18. Quoted in Robert McGarvey, Turn It On: Creativity Is Crucial to Your Business' Success," *Entrepreneur*, November 1996, p. 156.
19. Greg R. Oldham and Anne Cummings, "Employee Creativity: Personal and Contextual Factors at Work," *Academy of Management Journal*, June 1996, p. 611.
20. Amabile, "How to Kill Creativity," pp. 81–84; Oldham and Cummings, "Employee Creativity," pp. 607–634; Thomas D. Kuczmarski, "Creating an Innovative Mind-set," *Management Review*, November 1996, pp. 47–51.
21. Gail Dutton, "Enhancing Creativity," *Management Review*, November 1996, p. 45.
22. Keng L. Siau, "Electronic Brainstorming," *Innovative Leader*, April 1997, p. 3.
23. Southwood J. Morcott, writing in G. William Dauphinais and Colin Price (eds.), *Straight from the CEO: The World's Top Business Leaders Reveal Ideas that Every Manager Can Use* (New York: Simon & Schuster, 1998).
24. Dutton, "Enhancing Creativity," p. 46.
25. Eugene Raudsepp, "Exercises for Creative Growth," *Success*, February 1981, pp. 46–47; Mike Vance and Diane Deacon, *Think Out of the Box* (Franklin Lakes, NJ: Career Press, 1995); "Test: Can You Laugh at His Advice?" (Interview with John Cleese), *Fortune*, July 6, 1998, pp. 203–204.
26. "Be a Creative Problem Solver," *Executive Strategies*, June 6, 1989, pp. 1–2.
27. Kenneth A. Kovach and Barry Render, "NASA Managers and Challenger: A Profile of Possible Explanation," *Personnel*, April 1987, p. 40.
28. Glen Whyte, "Decision Failures: Why They Occur and How to Prevent Them," *Academy of Management Executive*, August 1991, p. 25.
29. Andrew H. Van de Ven and Andrew L. Delbercq, "The Effectiveness of Nominal, Delphi, and Interacting Group Decision-Making Processes," *Academy of Management Journal*, December 1972, p. 606.

Vermont Crafters Inc., owned and operated by Russ Cortland and Maggie Cortland, has been in business since 1991. The small maker of handcrafted dining room and kitchen tables and chairs employs two full-time furniture makers. The work force also includes several part-time employees who are hired as needed. Vermont Crafters' gross sales have been around $350,000 for the last several years. About one-half the sales are made directly to individuals, and the other half to furniture distributors.

Vermont Crafters was launched when the couple extended their furniture-making hobby into selling custom-made dining room sets to a few friends. As word about their fine designs and high quality spread, the couple found they could no longer meet demand by making furniture only at night and on weekends. So they both quit their corporate jobs to manufacture and sell Vermont Crafters furniture full time. They began advertising through display ads in home decoration magazines and local newspapers. Although the couple was eking out a living, they believed that the sales potential of Vermont Crafters was hardly being tapped.

While shoveling snow together one Sunday afternoon, Russ said to Maggie, "What would you think of our marketing our furniture on the Internet? You know, go modern with E-commerce." Maggie responded, "Could be a golden opportunity, but let me check with my friend Kathy Ramon, the marketing instructor."

After studying this chapter and doing the exercises, you should be able to:

 Explain the use of forecasting techniques in planning.

 Describe how to use Gantt charts, milestone charts, and PERT planning techniques.

 Describe how to use break-even analysis and decision trees for problem solving and decision making.

 Describe how to manage inventory by using materials requirement planning (MRP), the economic order quantity (EOQ), and the just-in-time (JIT) system.

161

Specialized Techniques for Planning and Decision Making

One week later the couple had dinner with Ramon. She told them, "Sure, you could become the Internet giant of handcrafted furniture in two years. Or you could experience a serious profit drain that would put you out of business a couple of thousand dollars at a time. *E-tailing* (retailing over the Internet) is a tricky business. Let me read you some information from Kenneth Cassar, an analyst from the research firm, Jupiter Communications. He notes that Internet retailing should reach $41 billion by 2002, with 61 million people making purchases. But Cassar also said that e-tailers of all categories face one common problem—a lack of profits.

"I agree with Cassar that site development is expensive. Sales and marketing is expensive. You need to create a strong awareness of your brand on line. Before you two jump into e-tailing, let's figure out what the true costs are. You will also need to make an accurate forecast of how much furniture you will have to sell to cover your costs. I think you should go modern, but not at the expense of going bankrupt."[1]

The story about Vermont furniture makers illustrates an important point about managing a business. You sometimes need to use specialized planning and decision-making techniques to help put you on the right track. In this case the couple, assisted by a marketing instructor, was looking to figure out how much sales volume they would need to cover their expenses from venturing into e-tailing. At the same time, they would need to make accurate forecasts about the increase in sales they could anticipate by selling over the Internet.

To make planning and decision making more accurate, a variety of techniques based on the scientific method, mathematics, and statistics have been developed. This chapter will provide sufficient information for you to acquire basic skills in several widely used techniques for planning and decision making. You can find more details about these techniques in courses and books about production and operations management and accounting. All these quantitative tools are useful, but they do not supplant human judgment and intuition. For example, a decision-making technique might tell a manager that it will take four months to complete a project. She might say, "Could be, but if I put my very best people on the project, we can beat that estimate."

As you read and work through the various techniques, recognize that software is available to carry them out. A sampling of appropriate software is presented in Exhibit 7-1. Before using a computer to run a technique, however, it is best to understand the technique and try it out manually or with a calculator. Such firsthand knowledge can prevent accepting computer-generated information that is way off track. Similarly, many people use spell checkers without a good grasp of word usage. The results can be misleading and humorous, such as "Each of our employees is assigned to a *manger*." Another such error is "The company picnic will proceed as scheduled *weather* or not we have good *whether*."

FORECASTING METHODS

Explain the use of forecasting techniques in planning.

All planning involves making forecasts, or predicting future events. Forecasting is important because if a manager fails to spot trends and react to them before the competition does, the competition can gain an invaluable edge. As noted in an executive newsletter: "The handwriting is on the wall. The way your business reacts to newly emerging trends is perhaps the best barometer of your future success."[2] The forecasts used in strategic planning are especially difficult to make because they involve long-range trends. Unknown factors might crop up between the time the forecast is made and the time about which predictions are

EXHIBIT 7-1

Technique or Method	Representative Software
Forecasting Techniques	DecisionPro 3.0 (Vanguard Software); IMA FORECAST (PowerFlex Software Systems, Inc.) Spreadsheet programs can also be used to make forecasts.
Gantt Charts and Milestone Charts	Milestones, Etc. is a project management, planning, scheduling, and Gantt charting program. (KIDASA Software, Inc.)
PERT Diagrams	PERT Chart EXPERT; Project 98 (Both distributed by Microsoft Project).
Break-Even Analysis	Alpha Plus, Inc. (Security Development Corporation)
Decision Trees	DecisionPro 3.0 (Vanguard Software Corporation)
Materials Requirement Planning (MRP)	Solomon IV® includes a module for materials requirement planning. (Solomon Software)
Economic Order Quantity	Software would be superfluous. Use pocket calculator.
Just-in-Time (JIT) Inventory Management	AGAMA Integrated Manufacturing Software (Manufacturing Information Systems, Inc.)
All Techniques Combined	Enterprise software controls an entire company's operations, linking them together. The software automates finance, manufacturing, and human resources, incorporating stand-alone software such as that designed for PERT and break-even analysis. Enterprise software also helps make decisions based on market research. Specific types of enterprise software have many different names. (Two key suppliers are SAP and PeopleSoft.)

Software for Specialized Planning and Decision-Making Techniques
Managers and professionals generally rely on computers to make use of specialized planning and decision-making techniques. Examples of applicable software are presented at the left, and should be referred to for on-the-job application of these techniques.

163

made. The accompanying Organization in Action illustrates how inaccurate forecasts can lower organizational performance. This section will describe approaches to and types of forecasting.

Qualitative and Quantitative Approaches

Forecasts can be based on both qualitative and quantitative information. Most of the forecasting done for strategic planning relies on a combination of both. *Qualitative* methods of forecasting consist mainly of subjective hunches. For example, an experienced executive might predict that the high cost of housing will create a demand for small, less expensive homes, even though this trend cannot be quantified. One qualitative method is a **judgmental forecast,** a prediction based on a collection of subjective opinions. It relies on analysis of subjective inputs from a variety of sources, including consumer surveys, sales representatives, managers, and panels of experts. For instance, a group of potential home buyers might be asked how they would react to the possibility of purchasing a compact, less expensive home.

Quantitative forecasting methods involve either the extension of historical data or the development of models to identify the cause of a particular outcome. A widely used historical approach is **time-series analysis.** This technique is simply an analysis of a sequence of observations that have taken place at regular in-

judgmental forecast
A qualitative forecasting method based on a collection of subjective opinions.

time-series analysis
An analysis of a sequence of observations that have taken place at regular intervals over a period of time (hourly, weekly, monthly, and so forth).

Organization *in Action*

Tinted Forecasts at Sunglass Hut

Jack B. Chadsey, CEO of Sunglass Hut International, likes to talk about the glory days when the retailer fought its way to the top: "We came through like Pac-Man and took away share from the department and optical stores." The number of stores kept growing, reaching 2,000 in 1998. Nevertheless, the fortunes of the company have changed in recent years. The company has been struggling to make a profit in the last two years, as growth has slowed down.

Chadsey attributes some of the blame to sunglass manufacturers, and some to cool weather. He also believes that the lack of exciting new products to sell has hurt sales. Suppliers take a different view of Sunglass's financial troubles. They believe that overly optimistic forecasts by Sunglass managers created many of the problems. During the summer season of 1996, the company misjudged consumer tastes, had difficulty consolidating its warehouses, and struggled with a key acquisition. "They assumed there was an almost infinite demand for product because the retail outlets were so hot early on," says R. Fulton McDonald, president of retail consultant International Business Development.

Sunglass Hut first became a public company in 1993, and expanded rapidly with its initial public offering. New stores were opened in malls, airports, and department stores (like a store within a store). Soon Sunglass Hut bought its biggest competitor, Sunsations. Sales and the company stock price continued to climb. By 1995, problems began to surface. A research analyst sent a report to his investor clients warning that Sunglass Hut's operating cash flow (a measure of financial health) had fallen badly and inventories were climbing.

Despite the signs of bad news, Chadsey remained confident. Retailers and investors were anticipating a surge in sales in 1996, assisted by trendy new designs such as a metal "wrap" look by Oakely Inc. A cooler than usual summer lowered demand, and the consumers who did shop were less than de-

lighted. The new designs were perceived as not much different than those of the previous season.

Some internal problems such as software failures in developing a consolidated shipping system added to Sunglass Hut's troubles. Other inventory management problems were also detected. The CEO of sunglass maker Oakely said there was a two- to three-month period in which Sunglass Hut didn't have a good handle on what inventory they had. Inventories swelled to a hazardous level.

Chadsey says he warned investors that sales growth would one day cool down, but he was tight lipped about the extent of the company's troubles. In January 1997, four individuals filed a class action lawsuit against the company. The plaintiffs allege that Sunglass Hut misled the public with false claims of financial success that caused the stock price to rise to an undeserved level. The price of the stock plunged when the problems of declining sales, shrinking product offerings, and failing expansion plans became known to the public. An attorney for one of the plaintiffs says Sunglass Hut "led the market to believe that there would be substantial continuing growth for the company, which we believe was misleading." Chadsey denies these allegations.

Unable to keep inventory under control, Sunglass Hut halted nearly all orders from key suppliers at one point, and sought to return glasses. In retaliation for the returns, some suppliers canceled rebate and discount programs causing Sunglass Hut's merchandising costs to rise. In late 1998, management decided to close 225 underperforming stores to reduce expenses. Several of these outlets are Watch Station stores. Sunglass Hut management could no longer wait for demand for sunglasses to meet their rosy forecasts.

Sources: Gail DeGeorge, "Sunglass Hut Is Feeling the Glare," *Business Week*, June 9, 1997, pp. 89–91; www.mediacentral.com/Magazines/CatalogAge/Weekly/1997013002.htm/, accessed November 25, 1998; "Sunglass Hut Eliminating 225 Stores," Rochester, New York, *Democrat and Chronicle*, November 20, 1998, p. 12D.

tervals over a period of time (hourly, weekly, monthly, and so forth). The underlying assumption of this approach is that the future will be much like the past. Exhibit 7-2 shows a basic example of a time-series analysis chart. This information might be used to make forecasts about when people would be willing to take vacations. Such forecasts would be important for the resort and travel industry.

Many firms use quantitative and qualitative approaches to forecasting. Forecasting begins with a quantitative prediction, which provides basic data about a future trend. An example of a quantitative prediction is the forecast of a surge in demand for handheld personal digital assistants (PDAs). (The PDA is a palm-size computer that can also record voice memos, function as a date book and calculator, and retrieve e-mail.) Next, the qualitative forecast is added to the quantitative forecast, somewhat as a validity check. For example, a quantitative forecast might predict that, if the current growth trend continues, every household in North America will contain two handheld personal digital assistants by 2004.

The quantitative forecast is then adjusted according to the subjective data supplied by the qualitative forecast. In this case, it could be reasoned that the growth trend was extrapolated too aggressively. In many instances, a quantitative forecast will serve as a validity check on qualitative forecasts because numerical data is more accurate than intuition. It is possible that Sunglass Hut relied too heavily on qualitative forecasts.

Three errors or traps are particularly prevalent when making forecasts or estimates.[3] One is the *overconfidence trap*, whereby people overestimate the accuracy of their forecasts. A CEO might be so confident of the growth of her business that she moves the company into expensive new headquarters. Based on her confidence, she does not prepare contingency plans in case the estimated growth does not take place. A second problem is the *prudence trap*, in which people make cautious forecasts "just to be on the safe side." Being safe can mean taking extra measures just not to be caught short, such as a restaurant owner buying ten extra boxes of strawberries "just to be safe." If the strawberry desserts go unsold the owner is stuck unless he can make strawberry pudding for tomorrow's menu.

A third problem is the *recallability trap* whereby our forecasts are influenced by extremely positive or negative incidents we recall. If a manager vividly recalls success stories from global expansion to Singapore, he might overestimate the chances of succeeding in that country.

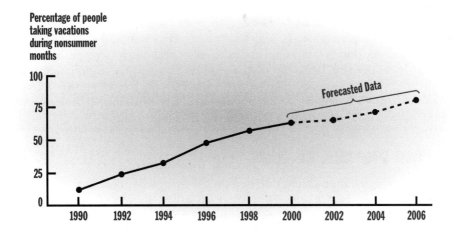

EXHIBIT 7-2

Time Series Analysis Chart
A time-series analysis uses the past to make predictions.

Being aware of these traps can help you take a more disciplined approach to forecasting. For example, to reduce the effect of the overconfidence trap, start by considering the extremes—the possible highs and lows. Try to imagine a scenario in which your forecast could be way too high or way too low and make appropriate adjustments if necessary. For a reality check, discuss your forecasts with other knowledgeable people. To become a good forecaster, you need to make a large number of predictions and then look for feedback on the accuracy of these predictions.

Types of Forecasts

Three types of forecasts are used most widely: economic, sales, and technological. Each of these forecasts can be made by using both qualitative and quantitative methods.

ECONOMIC FORECASTING   No single factor is more important in managerial planning than predicting the level of future business activity. Strategic planners in large organizations rely often on economic forecasts made by specialists they hire. Planners in smaller firms are more likely to rely on government forecasts. However, forecasts about the general economy do not necessarily correspond to business activity related to a particular product or service.

A major factor in the accuracy of forecasts is time span: Short-range predictions are more accurate than long-range predictions. Strategic planning is long-range planning, and many strategic plans have to be revised frequently to accommodate changes in business activity. For example, a sudden recession may abort plans for diversification into new products and services.

SALES FORECASTING   The sales forecast is usually the primary planning document for a business. Even if the general economy is robust, an organization needs a promising sales forecast before it can be aggressive about capitalizing on new opportunities. Strategic planners themselves may not be involved in making sales forecasts, but to develop master plans they rely on forecasts that the marketing unit makes. For instance, the major tobacco companies have embarked on strategic plans to diversify into a number of nontobacco businesses, such as soft drinks. An important factor in the decision to implement this strategic plan was a forecast of decreased demand for tobacco products in the domestic market. The cause for decreased demand will be health concerns of the public.

TECHHNOLOGICAL FORECASTING   A technological forecast predicts what types of technological changes will take place. Technological forecasts allow a firm to adapt to new technologies and thus stay competitive. For example, forecasts made in the late 1990s about the explosive growth of E-commerce have enabled many firms to ready themselves technologically for the future. Even if a lot of the activity is not yet profitable, the majority of industrial and consumer companies are now prepared to buy and sell over the Internet.

GANTT CHARTS AND MILESTONE CHARTS

②

Describe how to use Gantt charts, milestone charts, and PERT planning techniques.

Two basic tools for monitoring the progress of scheduled projects are Gantt charts and milestone charts. Closely related to each other, they both help a manager keep track of whether activities are completed on time.

Gantt Charts

A **Gantt chart** graphically depicts the planned and actual progress of work over the period of time encompassed by a project. Gantt charts are especially useful for scheduling one-time projects such as constructing buildings, making films, and launching satellites. Charts of this type are also called time-and-activity charts, because time and activity are the two key variables they consider. Time is plotted on the horizontal axis; activities are listed on the vertical axis.

Despite its simplicity, the Gantt chart is a valuable and widely used control technique. It is also the foundation of more sophisticated types of time-related charts, such as the PERT chart, which will be described later.

Exhibit 7-3 shows a Gantt chart used to schedule the opening of a nightclub. Gantt charts used for most other purposes would have a similar format. At the planning phase of the project, the manager lays out the schedule by using rectangular boxes. As each activity is completed, the appropriate box is shaded. At any given time, the manager can see which activities have been completed on time. For example, if the club does not have a liquor license by 30 November, the activity would be declared behind schedule.

The Gantt chart presented here is quite basic. On most Gantt charts, the bars are movable strips of plastic. Different colors indicate scheduled and actual progress. Mechanical boards with pegs to indicate scheduled dates and actual progress can also be used. Some managers and specialists are now using computer graphics to prepare their own high-tech Gantt charts.

Because Gantt charts are used to monitor progress, they are also control devices. When the chart shows that the liquor license activity has fallen behind schedule, the manager can investigate the problem and solve it. The Gantt chart gives a convenient overall view of the progress made against the schedule. However, its disadvantage is that it does not furnish enough details about the subactivities that need to be performed to accomplish each general item.

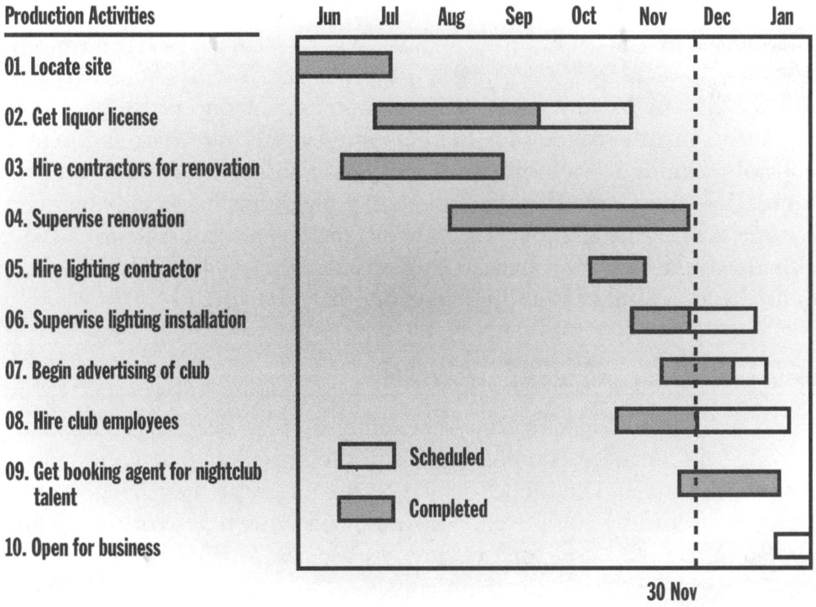

Gantt chart
A chart that depicts the planned and actual progress of work during the life of a project.

167

EXHIBIT 7-3

A Gantt Chart Used for Opening a Nightclub
A Gantt chart helps keep track of progress on a project.

EXHIBIT 7-4

A Milestone Chart Used for Opening a Nightclub A milestone chart goes into detail about the steps in a project.

Production Activities	Jun	Jul	Aug	Sep	Oct	Nov	Dec	Jan
01. Locate site	1 2 3							
02. Get liquor license		4	4	5 6	7	8 9		10
03. Hire contractors for renovation			11	12 13				
04. Supervise renovation		14	15	16 17	18	19		
05. Hire lighting contractor					20 21			
06. Supervise lighting installation					22	23 24		
07. Begin advertising of club						25 26		
08. Hire club employees					27	28 29	30	
09. Get booking agent for nightclub talent						31	32	
10. Open for business								33

Milestones to be Accomplished

•
•
•

27. Speak to friends and acquaintances about job openings
28. Put ad in local newspapers
29. Conduct interviews with applicants and check references of best candidates
30. Make job offers to best candidates
•
•
•
33. Have grand-opening celebration 5 January

168

Milestone Charts

milestone chart
An extension of the Gantt chart that provides a listing of the subactivities that must be completed to accomplish the major activities listed on the vertical axis.

A **milestone chart** is an extension of the Gantt chart. It provides a listing of the subactivities that must be completed to accomplish the major activities listed on the vertical axis. A milestone is the completion of one phase of an activity. The inclusion of milestones adds to the value of a Gantt chart as a scheduling and control technique. Each milestone serves as another checkpoint on progress. In Exhibit 7-4, the Gantt chart for opening a nightclub has been expanded into a milestone chart. The numbers in each rectangle represent milestones. A complete chart would list each of the 33 milestones. In Exhibit 7-4 only the milestones for hiring employees and the opening date are listed.

PROGRAM EVALUATION AND REVIEW TECHNIQUE

program evaluation and review technique (PERT)
A network model used to track the planning activities required to complete a large-scale, nonrepetitive project. It depicts all of the interrelated events that must take place.

Gantt and milestone charts are basic scheduling tools, exceeded in simplicity only by a "to do" list. A more complicated method of scheduling activities and events uses a network model. The model depicts all the interrelated events that must take place for a project to be completed. The most widely used network-modeling tool is the **program evaluation and review technique (PERT).** It is used to track the planning activities required to complete a large-scale, nonrepetitive project.

A scheduling technique such as PERT is useful when certain tasks have to be completed before others if the total project is to be completed on time. In the nightclub example, the site of the club must be specified and a lease drawn up before the owner can apply for a liquor license. (The liquor commission will grant a license only after approving a specific location.) The PERT diagram indicates such a necessary sequence of events.

PERT is used most often in engineering and construction projects. It has also been applied to such business problems as marketing campaigns, company relocations, and convention planning.

Key PERT Concepts

Two concepts lie at the core of PERT: event and activity. An **event** is a point of decision or the accomplishment of a task. Events are also called milestones. The events involved in the merger of two companies would include sending out announcements to shareholders, changing the company name, and letting customers know of the merger.

An **activity** is the physical and mental effort required to complete an event. One activity in the merger example is working with a public-relations firm to arrive at a suitable name for the new company. Activities that have to be accomplished in the nightclub example include supervising contractors and interviewing job applicants.

Steps Involved in Preparing a PERT Network

The events and activities included in a PERT network are laid out graphically, as shown in Exhibit 7-5. Preparing a PERT network consists of four steps:

1. Prepare a list of all the activities necessary to complete the project. In the nightclub example, these would include locating the site, getting the liquor license, and so forth. Many more activities and subactivities could be added to this example.
2. Design the actual PERT network, relating all the activities to each other in the proper sequence. Anticipating all the activities in a major project requires considerable skill and judgment. In addition, activities must be sequenced—the planner must decide which activity must precede another. In the nightclub example, the owner would want to hire employees before booking talent.
3. Estimate the time required to complete each activity. This must be done carefully because the major output of the PERT method is a statement of the total time required by the project. Because the time estimate is critical, several people should be asked to make three different estimates: optimistic time, pessimistic time, and probable time.

    Optimistic time (O) is the shortest time an activity will take if everything goes well. In the construction industry, the optimistic time is rarely achieved.

    Pessimistic time (P) is the amount of time an activity will take if everything goes wrong (as it sometimes does with complicated projects such as installing a new subway system).

    Most probable time (M) is the most realistic estimate of how much time an activity will take. The probable time for an activity can be an estimate of the

event
In the PERT method, a point of decision or the accomplishment of a task.

activity
In the PERT method, the physical and mental effort required to complete an event.

169

EXHIBIT 7.5

A PERT Network for Opening a Nightclub
Each numeral in the diagram equals the expected time for an activity, such as 5 weeks to locate site (between circles A and B) and 13 weeks to supervise lighting installation (between circles E and F). The critical path is the estimated time for all the activities shown above the thick arrows (13 + 30 + 6 + 13 + 8 + 14 + 8 + 1 = 93).

Information for Preparing the PERT Diagram

Event	Activity	Estimated Time in Weeks	Preceding Event
A	Locate site	5	None
B	Get liquor license	30	A
C	Hire renovation contractors	13	A
D	Supervise renovation	30	C
E	Hire lighting contractor	6	D
F	Supervise lighting installation	13	E
G	Begin advertising club	8	B, F
H	Hire club employees	14	G
I	Get booking agent	8	G, H
J	Open club for business	1	I

➡ = Critical Path (thick arrow)

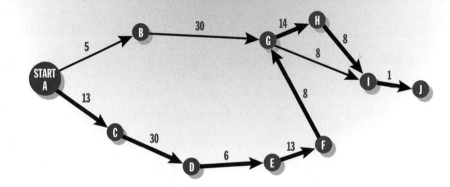

170

time taken for similar activities on other projects. For instance, the time needed to build a cockpit for one aircraft might be based on the average time it took to build cockpits for comparable aircraft in the past.

After the planner has collected all the estimates, he or she uses a formula to calculate the **expected time.** The expected time is the time that will be used on the PERT diagram as the needed period for the completion of an activity. As the following formula shows, expected time is an "average" in which most probable time is given more weight than optimistic time and pessimistic time.

expected time
The time that will be used on the PERT diagram as the needed period for the completion of an activity.

$$\text{Expected time} = \frac{O + 4M + P}{6}$$

optimistic + 4(most prob) + pessimistic over 6 (handwritten)

(The denominator is 6 because *O* counts for 1, *M* for 4, and *P* for 1.)

Suppose the time estimates for choosing a site location for the nightclub are as follows: optimistic time (*O*) is 2 weeks; most probable time (*M*) is 5 weeks; and pessimistic time (*P*) is 8 weeks. Therefore,

$$\text{Expected time} = \frac{2 + (4 \times 5) + 8}{6} = \frac{30}{6} = 5 \text{ weeks}$$

critical path
The path through the PERT network that includes the most time-consuming sequence of events and activities.

4. Calculate the **critical path,** the path through the PERT network that includes the most time–consuming sequence of events and activities. The length of the entire project is determined by the path with the longest elapsed time. The logic behind the critical path is this: A given project cannot be consid-

ered completed until its lengthiest component is completed. For example, if it takes one year to get the liquor permit, the nightclub project cannot be completed in less than one year, even if all other events are completed earlier than scheduled.

Exhibit 7-5 shows a critical path that requires a total elapsed time of 93 weeks. This total is calculated by adding the numerals that appear beside each thick line segment. Each numeral represents the number of weeks scheduled to complete the activities between each lettered label. Notice that activity completion must occur in the sequence of steps indicated by the direction of the arrows. In this case, if 93 weeks appeared to be an excessive length of time, the nightclub owners would have to search for ways to shorten the process. For example, the owner might be spending too much time supervising the renovation.

When it comes to implementing the activities listed on the PERT diagram, control measures play a crucial role. The project manager must ensure that all critical events are completed on time. If activities in the critical path take too long to complete, the project will not be completed on time. If necessary, the manager must take corrective action to move the activity along. Such action might include hiring additional help, dismissing substandard help, or purchasing more productive equipment.

In practice, PERT networks often specify hundreds of events and activities. Each small event can have its own PERT diagram. Many computer programs are available to help perform the mechanics of computing paths. Furthermore, software has been developed to help planners use advanced scheduling techniques that are based on PERT. Despite increasingly sophisticated approaches to scheduling, however, computerized versions of PERT diagrams remain standard tools in high-tech organizations.

BREAK-EVEN ANALYSIS

"What do we have to do to break even?" This question is asked frequently in business. Managers often find the answer through **break-even analysis,** a method of determining the relationship between total costs and total revenues at various levels of production or sales activity. Managers use break-even analysis because—before adding new products, equipment, or personnel—they want to be sure that the changes will pay off. Break-even analysis tells managers the point at which it is profitable to go ahead with a new venture.

Exhibit 7-6 illustrates a typical break-even chart. It deals with a proposal to add a new product to an existing line. The point at which the Total Costs line and the Revenue line intersect is the break-even point. Sales shown to the right of the break-even point represent profit. Sales to the left of this point represent a loss.

Describe how to use break-even analysis and decision trees for problem solving and decision making.

break-even analysis
A method of determining the relationship between total costs and total revenues at various levels of production or sales activity.

Break-Even Formula

The break-even point (*BE*) is the situation in which total revenues equal fixed costs plus variable costs. It can be calculated with several algebraic formulas. One standard formula is:

$$BE = \frac{TFC}{P - AVC}$$

171

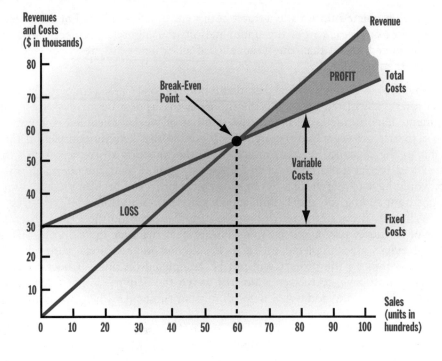

EXHIBIT 7-6

Break-Even Chart for Adding a New Product to an Existing Line
A break-even chart indicates at what point a venture becomes profitable.

where

$\quad\quad\quad P$ = selling price per unit

$\quad AVC$ = average variable cost per unit, the cost that varies with the amount produced

$\quad TFC$ = total fixed cost, the cost that remains constant no matter how many units are produced

Another version of the preceding formula uses variable cost instead of average variable cost, and fixed cost instead of total fixed cost. Professor Ron Olive, however, believes that using AVC and TFC is more accurate from the standpoint of economics.[4]

The chart in Exhibit 7-6 is based on the plans of Vermont Crafters to sell furniture over the Internet. For simplicity, we provide data only for the dining room sets. The average selling price (P) is $1,000 per unit; the average variable cost (AVC) is $500 per unit, including Internet commission fees for sales made through major Web sites (portals). The total fixed costs are $300,000.

$$BE = \frac{\$300,000}{\$1,000 - \$500} = \frac{\$300,000}{\$500} = 600 \text{ units}$$

Under the conditions assumed and for the period of time in which these costs and revenue figures are valid, a sales volume of 600 dining room sets would be required for Vermont Crafters to break even. Anything volume above that would produce a profit and anything below that would result in a loss. (We are referring to Internet sales only. Sales through their customary channels would have to be figured separately.) If the sales forecast for dining room sets sold through E-commerce is above 600 units, it would be a good decision to sell on the Net. If the sales forecast is less than 600 units, Vermont Crafters should not attempt E-commerce for now. However, if the husband-and-wife team are willing to absorb losses now to build for the long range, they might start E-commerce anyway. Break-even analysis would tell the couple how much money they are likely to lose.

Advantages and Limitations of Break-Even Analysis

Break-even analysis helps managers keep their thinking focused on the volume of activity that will be necessary to justify a new expense. The technique is also useful because it can be applied to a number of operations problems. Break-even analysis can help a manager decide whether to drop an existing product from the line, to replace equipment, or to buy rather than make a part.

Break-even analysis has some drawbacks. First, it is only as valid as the estimates of costs and revenues that managers use to create it. Second, the analysis is static in that it assumes there will be no changes in other variables. The dynamic nature of business makes this a questionable assumption. The third limitation of break-even analysis is potentially more serious. Exhibit 7-6 indicates that variable costs and sales increase together in a direct relationship. In reality, unit costs may decrease with increased volume. It is also possible that costs may increase with volume: Suppose that increased production leads to higher turnover because employees prefer not to work overtime.

Break-even analysis relates to decisions about whether to proceed or not to proceed. The next section will examine a more complicated decision-making technique that relates to the desirability of several alternative solutions.

DECISION TREES

Another useful planning tool is called a **decision tree,** a graphic illustration of the alternative solutions available to solve a problem. Decision trees are designed to estimate the outcome of a series of decisions. As the sequences of the major decision are drawn, the resulting diagram resembles a tree with branches.

To illustrate the essentials of using a decision tree for making financial decisions, return to the nightclub owner who used the Gantt and milestone charts. One major decision facing the owner is whether to open a nightclub only or to open a nightclub and dinner restaurant. According to data from a restaurant industry association, the probability of having a good first year in 0.6 and the probability of having a poor one is 0.4.

Discussion with an accountant indicates that the payout, or net cash flow, from a good season with the nightclub only would be $100,000. The payout from a poor first year with the same alternative would be a loss of $10,000. Both these figures are conditional values because they depend on business conditions. The owner and accountant predict that a good first year with the alternative of a nightclub and dinner restaurant would be $150,000. A poor first year would result in a loss of $30,000.

Using this information, the manager computes the expected values and adds them for the two alternatives. An **expected value** is the average value incurred if a particular decision is made a large number of times. Sometimes you would

decision tree
A graphic illustration of the alternative solutions available to solve a problem.

expected value
The average return on a particular decision being made a large number of times.

earn more, and sometimes less, with the expected value being your average return.

Expected value: nightclub only = 0.6 × $100,000 = $60,000
0.4 × −10,000 = −4,000
$56,000

Expected value: nightclub and
dinner restaurant = 0.6 × $150,000 = $90,000
0.4 × −30,000 = −12,000
$78,000

As Exhibit 7-7 graphically portrays, the decision tree suggests that the nightclub-restaurant will probably turn a first-year profit of $78,000. The nightclub-only alternative is likely to show a profit of $56,000. Over one year, running a nightclub and dinner restaurant would be $22,000 more profitable.

The advantage of a decision tree is that it can be used to help make sequences of decisions. After having one year of experience in running a nightclub and dinner restaurant, the owner may think of expanding. One logical possibility for expansion would be to open the restaurant for lunch as well as dinner. The owner would add a new branch to the decision tree to compare the conditional values for the nightclub and dinner restaurant with those of the nightclub and dinner-lunch restaurant.

The new branch of the decision tree might take the form shown in Exhibit 7-8, which focuses on the decision of whether to add luncheon service. The nightclub owner would now have more accurate information about the conditional values for a nightclub and dinner restaurant—the choice the owner made when opening the establishment. With one year of success with the nightclub and dinner restaurant, the probability of having a second good season might be raised to 0.8. With each successive year, the owner would have increasingly accurate information about the conditional values.

EXHIBIT 7-7

First-Year Decision Tree for Nightclub Owner

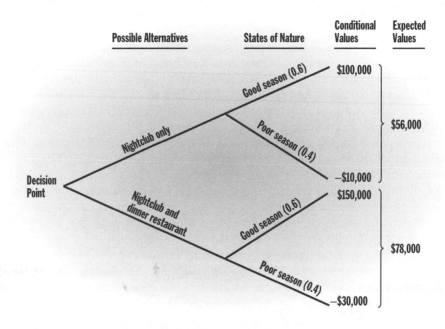

| Possible Alternatives | States of Nature | Conditional Values | Expected Values |

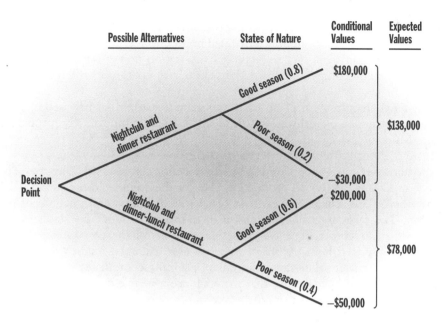

EXHIBIT
7-8

Second-Year Decision Tree for Nightclub Owner

175

Following is an explanation of how the expected values are calculated for the new branch of the decision tree in question, shown in Exhibit 7-8.

Expected value: nightclub and = 0.8 × $180,000 = $144,000
    dinner restaurant   0.2 × −30,000 = −6,000
                                                  $138,000

Expected value: nightclub and
    dinner-lunch restaurant = 0.6 × $200,000 = $120,000
                              0.4 × −50,000 = −20,000
                                                $100,000

INVENTORY CONTROL TECHNIQUES

A problem faced by managers of manufacturing and sales organizations is how much inventory to keep on hand. If an organization maintains a large inventory, goods can be made quickly, customers can make immediate purchases, or orders can be shipped rapidly. However, stocking goods is expensive. The goods themselves are costly, and money tied up in inventory cannot be invested elsewhere. You will recall that Sunglass Hut experienced financial problems because the company carried too much inventory in stores and warehouses. This section will describe three decision-making techniques used to manage inventory and control production: materials-requirement planning (MRP), the economic-order quantity (EOQ), and the just-in-time (JIT) system.

Describe how to manage inventory by using materials-requirement planning (MRP), the economic-order quantity (EOQ), and the just-in-time (JIT) system.

M a t e r i a l s - R e q u i r e m e n t   P l a n n i n g

Manufacturing a finished product is complicated. It involves various production functions, including scheduling, purchasing, and inventory control. Many firms use a master plan to coordinate these production functions. **Materials-requirement planning (MRP)** is a computerized manufacturing and inventory-control system designed to ensure that materials handling and inventory control are

materials-requirement planning (MRP)
A computerized manufacturing and inventory-control system designed to ensure that materials handling and inventory control are efficient.

efficient. The system is designed to manage inventories that come from components or raw materials to support scheduled production of finished goods. A manufacturer of dishwashers such as Maytag Corporation uses MRP because a dishwasher has many components, including electric motors, rubber belts, and sheet metal.

Materials-requirement planning is important because the parts used in building a product such as dishwashers are needed at exact times in the production cycle. MRP helps smooth the parts-ordering cycle and provides immediate information about the inventory levels of critical parts.

Materials-requirement planning has three major components. The *master production schedule* is the overall production plan for the completed products, such as dishwashers. This schedule is expressed in terms of timing and quantity of production. The *inventory record file* consists of information about the status of each item held in inventory. The *bill of materials* is a list of the components needed for each completed item. A bill of materials, for example, might list the many parts of a dishwasher. Materials-requirement planning coordinates all this data and provides information to ensure that materials are available when needed.

Materials requirement planning makes an important contribution by reducing inventory levels and direct labor costs. For this system to work effectively accurate information is necessary, along with good cooperation among the individuals and groups involved.

Economic-Order Quantity

economic-order quantity (EOQ)
The inventory level that minimizes both administrative costs and carrying costs.

The **economic-order quantity (EOQ)** is the inventory level that minimizes both administrative costs and carrying costs. The EOQ represents the reorder quantity of the least cost. Carrying costs include the cost of loans, the interest foregone because money is tied up in inventory, and the cost of handling the inventory. EOQ is expressed mathematically as

$$EOQ = \sqrt{\frac{2DQ}{C}}$$

where

D = annual demand in units for the product
O = fixed cost of placing and receiving an order
C = annual carrying cost per unit (taxes, insurance, and other expenses)

Assume that the annual demand for Funtime Products swimming pools is 100 units and that it costs \$1,000 to order each unit. Furthermore, suppose the carrying cost per unit is \$200. The equation to calculate the most economic number of pools to keep in inventory is:

$$EOQ = \sqrt{\frac{2 \times 100 \times \$1{,}000}{\$200}}$$

$$= \sqrt{\frac{\$200{,}000}{\$200}}$$

$$= \sqrt{1{,}000}$$

$$= 32 \text{ pools (rounded figure)}$$

Therefore, the president of Funtime concludes that the most economical number of pools to keep in inventory during the selling season is 32. (The assumption is that Funtime has a large storage area.) If the figures entered into the EOQ formula are accurate, EOQ calculations can vastly improve inventory management.

Just-in-Time System

An important thrust in manufacturing is to keep just enough parts and components on hand to fill current orders. The **just-in-time (JIT) system** is an inventory control method designed to minimize inventory and move it into the plant exactly when needed. The key principle of the system is to eliminate excess inventory by producing or purchasing parts, subassemblies, and final products only when—and in the exact amounts—needed. JIT helps a manufacturing division stay "lean." Imagine Vermont Crafters having raw wood delivered to its door within an hour or so after an order is received over the Internet. Just-in-time is generally used in a repetitive, single-product, manufacturing environment. However, the system is now also used to improve operations in sales and service organizations.

just-in-time (JIT) system
A system to minimize inventory and move it into the plant exactly when needed.

PHILOSOPHIES   Three basic philosophies underlie the specific manufacturing techniques of JIT.[5] *First, setup time for assembly and cost must be reduced.* The goal of JIT is to make setup time and cost so low that small batch sizes are economical, even to the point of manufacturing just one finished product. *Second, safety stock is undesirable.* Stock held in reserve is expensive and hides problems, such as inefficient production methods. "Just in time" should replace "just in case." *Third, productivity and quality are inseparable.* JIT is only possible when high-quality components are delivered and produced. The goal of the JIT system is 100 percent good items at each manufacturing step.

PROCEDURES AND TECHNIQUES   Just-in-time inventory control is part of a system of manufacturing control. Therefore, it involves many different techniques and procedures. Seven of the major techniques and procedures are described in the list that follows.[6] Knowing them provides insight into the system of manufacturing used by many successful Japanese companies.

1. *Kanbans.* The JIT system of inventory control relies on *kanbans*, or cards, to communicate production requirements from the final point of assembly to the manufacturing operations that precede it. When an order is received for a product, a kanban is issued that directs employees to finish the product. The finishing department selects components and assembles the product. The kanban is then passed back to earlier stations. This kanban tells workers to resupply the components. Kanban communication continues all the way back to the material suppliers. In many JIT systems, suppliers locate their companies so they can be close to major customers. Proximity allows suppliers to make shipments promptly. At each stage, parts and other materials are delivered just in time for use.
2. *Demand-driven pull system.* The just-in-time techniques requires producing exactly what is needed to match the demand created by customer orders. Demand drives final assembly schedules, and assembly drives subassembly timetables. The result is a pull system—that is, customer demand pulls along activities to meet that demand.
3. *Short production lead times.* A JIT system minimizes the time between the arrival of raw material or components in the plant and the shipment of a finished product to a customer.

4. *High inventory turnover (with the goal of zero inventory and stockless production).* The levels of finished goods, work in process, and raw materials are purposely reduced. Raw material in a warehouse is regarded as waste, and so is idle work in process. (A person who applied JIT to the household would regard backup supplies of ketchup or motor oil as shameful!)

5. *Designated areas for receiving materials.* Certain areas on the shop floor or in the receiving and shipping department are designated for receiving specific items from suppliers. At a Toyota plant in Japan, the receiving area is about half the size of a football field. The designated spaces for specific items are marked with yellow paint.

6. *Designated containers.* Specifying where to store items allows for easy access to parts, and it eliminates counting. For example, at Toyota the bed of a truck has metal frame mounts for exactly eight engines. A truckload of engines means eight engines—no more, no less. No one has to count them.

7. *Neatness.* A JIT plant that follows Japanese tradition is immaculate. All unnecessary materials, tools, rags, and files are discarded. The factory floor is as neat and clean as the showroom.

ADVANTAGES AND DISADVANTAGES OF THE JIT INVENTORY SYSTEM

Manufacturing companies have realized several benefits from adopting JIT. Just-in-time controls can lead to organizational commitment to quality in design, materials, parts, employee-management and supplier-user relations, and finished goods. With minimum levels of inventory on hand, finished products are more visible and defects are more readily detected. Quality problems can therefore be attacked before they escalate to an insurmountable degree. Low levels of inventory also shorten cycle times.

Being able to support a customer's JIT system can provide a competitive advantage. A case in point is Wausau Paper Mills Co., which has recently achieved outstanding success based on its speed of product delivery. Wausau uses an inventory and production system called time-based competition. The system depends on having large supplies of product on hand so that an order can be delivered quickly. Wausau then holds inventory for customers until it is needed, thus supporting their customers' question for just-in-time deliveries. In some cases, the company reduced delivery time from four weeks to overnight.[7]

Despite the advantages just-in-time management can offer large manufacturers, it has some striking disadvantages. Above all, a just-in-time system must be placed in a supportive or compatible environment. JIT is applicable only to highly repetitive manufacturing operations such as car or residential furnace manufacturing. Small companies with short runs of a variety of products often may suffer financial losses from just-in-time practices. One problem they have is that suppliers are often unwilling to promptly ship small batches to meet the weekly needs of a small customer.[8]

Product demand must be predictable for JIT to work well. If customer demand creates a surge of orders, a tight inventory policy will not be able to handle this windfall. The savings from just-in-time management can be deceptive. Several manufacturers who used JIT discovered that their suppliers were simply building up inventories in their own plants and adding that cost to their prices.[9] Just-in-time inventory practices also leave a company vulnerable to work stoppages, such as a strike. With a large inventory of finished products or parts, the company can continue to meet customer demand while the work stoppage is being settled.

Just-in-time inventory control also presents ethical problems. The big company saves money by forcing the supplier to maintain expensive inventories, so it (the big company) can be served promptly. Another ethical concern about JIT occurs when a manufacturer ceases dealing with a supplier. The supplier will usually have to close the facility it built just to be in proximity to the manufacturer.

SUMMARY OF KEY POINTS

 Explain the use of forecasting techniques in planning.

All planning includes making forecasts, both qualitative and quantitative. A judgmental forecast makes predictions on subjective opinions. Time-series analysis is a widely used method of making quantitative forecasts. Three widely used forecasts are economic, sales, and technological.

 Describe how to use Gantt charts, milestone charts, and PERT planning techniques.

Gantt and milestone charts are simple methods of monitoring schedules, and are particularly useful for one-time projects. Gantt charts graphically depict the planned and actual progress of work over the period of time encompassed by a project. A milestone chart lists the subactivities that must be completed to accomplish the major activities.

Managers use PERT networks to track complicated projects when sequences of events must be planned carefully. In a PERT network, an event is a point of decision or accomplishment. An activity is the physical and mental effort required to complete an event. To complete a PERT diagram, a manager must sequence all the events and estimate the time required for each activity. The expected time for each activity takes into account optimistic, pessimistic, and probable estimates of time. The critical path is the most time-consuming sequence of activities and events that must be followed to implement the project. The duration of the project is determined by the longest critical path.

 Describe how to use break-even analysis and decision trees for problem solving and decision making.

Managers use break-even analysis to estimate the point at which it is profitable to go ahead with a new venture. It is a method of determining the relationship between total costs and total revenues at various levels of sales activity or operation. Break-even analysis determines the ratio of total fixed costs to the difference between the selling price and the average variable cost for each

unit. The results of break-even analysis are often depicted on a graph. Break-even analysis is based on an assumption of static costs.

A decision tree provides a quantitative estimate of the best alternative. It is a tool for estimating the outcome of a series of decisions. When the sequences of the major decisions are drawn, they resemble a tree with branches.

 Describe how to manage inventory by using materials-requirement planning (MRP), the economic-order quantity (EOQ), and the just-in-time (JIT) system.

Materials-requirement planning (MRP) is a computerized manufacturing and inventory-control system designed to make materials handling and inventory control efficient. The economic-order quantity (EOQ) is a decision-support technique widely used to manage inventory. The EOQ is the inventory level that minimizes both ordering and carrying costs. The EOQ technique helps managers in a manufacturing or sales organization decide how much inventory to keep on hand.

Just-in-time (JIT) inventory management minimizes stock on hand. Instead, stock is moved into the plant exactly when needed. Although not specifically a decision-making technique, JIT helps shape decisions about inventory. The key principle underlying JIT systems is the elimination of excess inventory by producing or purchasing items only when and in the exact amounts they are needed.

Just-in-time processes involve (1) *kanbans*, or cards for communicating production requirements to the previous operation, (2) a customer demand-driven system, (3) short production lead times, (4) high inventory turnover, (5) designated areas for receiving materials, (6) designated containers, and (7) neatness throughout the factory.

JIT inventory management is best suited for repetitive manufacturing processes. One drawback of JIT is that it places heavy pressures on suppliers to build up their inventories to satisfy sudden demands of their customers who use the system.

KEY TERMS AND PHRASES

Judgmental forecast, *163*

Time-series analysis, *163*

Gantt chart, *167*

Milestone chart, *168*

Program evaluation and review
  technique (PERT), *168*

Event, *169*

Activity, *169*

Expected time, *170*

Critical path, *170*

Break-even analysis, *171*

Decision tree, *173*

Expected value, *173*

Materials-requirement planning
  (MRP), *175*

Economic-order quantity (EOQ), *176*

Just-in-time (JIT) system, *177*

QUESTIONS

1. How could the information presented in this chapter help you become a better manager?
2. What is the difference between a milestone chart and a "to do" list?
3. Describe two possible job applications for a PERT network.
4. How could you use break-even analysis to estimate if attaining your diploma or degree is cost effective?
5. What similarity do you see between the purposes of break-even analysis and a decision tree?
6. One of the key figures of the Apple Computer Corp. turnaround in 1998 was the inventory manager. (His nickname is "Atilla the Hun of Inventory.") How can an inventory-control manager help a company increase profits?
7. A criticism of the just-in-time system is that it simply transfers inventory problems from the manufacturer to the supplier. What does this criticism mean, and how valid is it?

SKILL-BUILDING EXERCISE 7-A: Developing a PERT Network

Use the following information about a quality improvement project to construct a PERT diagram. Be sure to indicate the critical path with a dark arrow. Work individually or in small groups.

Event	Description	Time Required (units)	Preceding Event
A	Complete quality audit	6	none
B	Benchmark	15	A
C	Collect internal information	6	A
D	Identify performance problems	3	B, C
E	Identify improvement practices	7	D
F	Elicit employee participation	20	A
G	Implement quality program	6	E, F
H	Measure results	8	G

Source: Reprinted with permission from Raymond L. Hilgert and Edwin C. Leonard, Jr., *Supervision: Concepts and Practices of Management*, 6th ed. (Cincinnati: South-Western College Publishing, 1995), p. 191.

SKILL-BUILDING EXERICSE 7-B: Break-Even Analysis

On recent vacation trips to Juarez, Mexico, you noticed small stores and street vendors selling original art. The prices ranged from $2 to $20 US. A flash of inspiration hit you. Why not sell Mexican art back home to Americans, using a van as your store? Every three months you would drive the 350 miles to Mexico and load up on art. You anticipate receiving generous large-quantity discounts.

You would park your van on busy streets and nearby parks, wherever you could obtain a permit. Typically you would display the art outside the van, but on a rainy day people could step inside. Your intention is to operate your traveling art sale about 12 hours per week. If you could make enough money from your business, you could attend classes full-time during the day. You intend to sell the original painting at an average of $12 a unit.

Based on preliminary analysis, you have discovered that your primary fixed costs per month would be: $450 for payments on a van, $75 for gas and maintenance, $50 for insurance, and $45 for a street vendor's permit. You will also be driving down to Mexico every three months at $300 per trip, resulting in a $100 per month travel cost. Your variable costs would be an average of $3 per painting and 25¢ for wrapping each painting in brown paper.

1. How many paintings will you have to sell each month before you start to make a profit?
2. If the average cost of your paintings rises to $5, how many pieces of art will you have to sell each month if you hold your price to $12 per unit?

INTERNET SKILL-BUILDING EXERCISE: Inventory Management Techniques

Use the Internet to find additional information on what a specific company, or companies in general, are doing to match inventory with demand. To find the information you are seeking, insert into several search engines specific phrases such as, "Inventory management techniques used by retailers," or "Inventory management techniques used in manufacturing." Try these search engines: Lycos, Webcrawler, www.metacrawler.com, and www.megacrawler.com. Part of the excitement, and frustration, of searching the Internet is that you never know when you will find the information you are seeking. Finding information on the Internet is a skill, not a scientific procedure.

CASE PROBLEM 7-A: Inventory Build-Up at Motorola

In February 1995, Motorola Inc. concluded that its earnings estimates for the previous year presented an overly optimistic picture of its financial position. Motorola had reported record fourth-quarter earnings of $515 million on sales of $6.45 billion. The high earnings estimates stemmed from overenthusiastic ordering of cellular telephones by retail distributors. The spurt in sales during the holiday season may have come at the expense of its sales for the first half of the next year (1995). New orders for cellular phones declined during that period.

According to industry sources, several distributors, including U S West and BellSouth, overordered by a wide margin. Part of the problem was that distributors were reacting defensively. During the previous two holiday seasons, Motorola could not meet consumer demands for handsets, forcing the Bells and other distributors to turn away business. Hoping not to repeat the mistake, the Bell cellular units placed orders early and often. The distributors failed to warn Motorola to cut back on production until it was too late.

The distributors were shocked when the phone orders

kept pouring in. Working under a total quality system, Motorola had eliminated practically all bottlenecks and was therefore able to meet holiday demand. An electronics company analyst contends that Motorola did not properly monitor incoming orders. The analyst adds, "Motorola should have known that orders were going beyond demand."

Motorola Inc. is not faced with serious financial problems because of the overshipments, but top management prefers that dealers do not face inventory problems. A problem for some stockholders, however, is that the stock went down 10 percent because of the inventory accumulation.

Discussion Questions

1. How much responsibility should Motorola take for the problem of excess inventory?
2. What forecasting method can Motorola use to prevent inflated orders from happening again?
3. What advice on inventory management can you give the Motorola dealers?

CASE PROBLEM 7-B: Selling Snow Boards Just in Time

Sharon Prell is the general manager of three Sports Vancouver stores located in shopping malls around Vancouver, British Columbia. About 75 percent of their business stems from the sales of equipment and clothing for ice hockey, figure skating, and snow skiing. The other 25 percent of their business is derived mostly from swimming gear, and golf and tennis equipment.

Prell believes strongly than an important success factor in her business is maintaining the right inventory levels. She notes that she wants her stores to be stocked fully enough so as to excite and entice consumers. Yet she has data to prove that inventory piling up on the showroom floor or in the back room is costly.

Prell says, "If a customer asks for an item in his or her

size or color that is not available in one store, we can often get that item in a hurry from one of our other stores. You might say I'm kind of a just-in-time inventory nut."

Two months after making that statement, the Sports Vancouver stores experienced a glorious winter season. Skates, skis, hockey sticks, pucks, and related clothing were being rung up at the cash registers at a heart-warming clip. Sales of snow boards, however, boomed. Fifteen days before Christmas, the stores had sold out every snow board in stock. Frantic pleas to the snow board manufacturers brought in only an extra 25 snow boards. All were sold out in two more days. Prell then asked two competitors to lend them their inventory of snow boards. The competition, however, wanted to hold on to their dwindling stocks to satisfy their own customers.

The ski-department manager kept a log of all the demand for snow boards that Sports Vancouver could not sat-

isfy. By January 5, the figure was 250 boards. In discussing the problem with Prell, the ski-department manager said, "Sharon, I think our just-in-time policy was implemented just in time to choke off what could have been a record season."

Prell responded, "I catch your dig, but this problem warrants further study. Losing money on unsold inventory is the problem on the other side of the ditch."

Discussion Questions

1. How might Prell prevent the snow board-shortage problem (or a similar problem) in the future?
2. How might Prell make more effective use of just-in-time inventory management?
3. How applicable would the economic-order quantity be to the snow board problem?

ENDNOTES

1. Case researched by Francesca Palladino, Rochester Institute of Technology, November 1998. The e-tailing facts are from Frank Bilovsky, "Internet Sales Take Off," Rochester, New York, *Democrat and Chronicle*, November 22, 1998, pp. 1E–2E.
2. Daniel Levinas, "How to Stop the Competition from Eating Your Lunch!" *Executive Focus*, May 1998, p. 15.
3. John S. Hammond, Ralph L. Keeney, and Howard Raiffa, "The Hidden Traps in Decision Making," *Harvard Business Review*, September–October 1998, pp. 55–58.
4. Personal communication from Ron Olive, New Hampshire Technical College, May 17, 1992.
5. Ramon L. Aldag and Timothy M. Stearns, *Management*, 2nd ed. (Cincinnati: South-Western College Publishing, 1991), pp. 645–646.
6. Lance Heiko, "Some Relationships Between Japanese Culture and Just-in-Time," *The Academy of Management Executive*, November 1989, pp. 319–321.
7. Kathleen Madigan, "Masters of the Game," *Business Week*, October 12, 1992, pp. 117–118.
8. Barbara Marsh, "Allen-Edmonds Shoe Tries 'Just-in-Time' Production," *The Wall Street Journal*, March 4, 1993.
9. Doron P. Levin, "Is Auto Plant of the Future Almost Here?" *The New York Times*, June 14, 1993, p. D8.

Chapter Eight

OBJECTIVES

After studying this chapter and doing the exercises, you should be able to:

1 Identify the major dimensions and different types of job design.

2 Describe job enrichment, including the job characteristics model.

3 Describe job involvement, enlargement, and rotation.

4 Recognize how work teams are related to job design.

5 Illustrate how ergonomic factors can be part of job design.

6 Summarize the various modified work schedules.

Continental Insurance Company wanted to increase productivity and breathe new life into a large insurance policy processing operation located in Glens Falls, New York. The location was seen as the firm's most troublesome in terms of staffing. Furthermore, the unit generated no revenue, just expense. Management wanted to develop ways to get the work done, serve customers better, and also give employees more control over the work and how it gets accomplished.

To help accomplish these goals, the vice-president for employee relations at the time, Anne M. Pauker, introduced Total Flex, a program that authorized employees to decide how and when they wanted to work. Top management did not specify core hours during which employees had to be present. However, employees had to keep in mind the hours that coverage was essential. Management then introduced Option 30 in order to meet demand for extended business hours, Saturdays included. The program did not include adding to staff or running up overtime expenses. Option 30 enabled employees to volunteer for a reduced, nontraditional work-hour schedule.

Eighty percent of employees in the Glens Falls location participated in alternative work arrangements, including Option 30. According to Pauker, "The productivity of this office was more than triple any other office in the company mainly because employee morale was uplifted thanks to management's new open-mindedness."

Job Design and Work Schedules

The key appeared to be allowing employees to decide how and when they worked. The Glens Falls operation became Continental's most desirable operation.[1]

Not every company can achieve the same dramatic turnaround in productivity and satisfaction in an organizational unit as did Continental Insurance Company. Nevertheless, the principle is noteworthy: Modifying job design and work schedules can be an important contributor to the success of an operation. Employers use a variety of job designs and work schedules to increase productivity and job satisfaction. Modifying job design and giving workers more control over schedules are the two major topics of this chapter.

To accomplish large tasks, such as building ships or operating a hotel, you must divide work among individuals and groups. There are two primary ways of subdividing the overall tasks of an enterprise. One way is to design specific jobs for individuals and groups to accomplish. The shipbuilding company must design jobs for welders, metal workers, engineers, purchasing agents, and contract administrators. In addition, many workers may be assigned to teams that assume considerable responsibility for productivity and quality. The other primary way of subdividing work is to assign tasks to different units within the organization—units such as departments and divisions.

This chapter will explain basic concepts relating to job design, such as making jobs more challenging and giving employees more control over their working hours and place of work. The next chapter will describe how work is divided throughout an organization.

184

BASIC CONCEPTS OF JOB DESIGN

Identify the major dimensions and different types of job design.

job design
The process of laying out job responsibilities and duties and describing how they are to be performed.

Understanding how tasks are subdivided begins with **job design.** It is the process of laying out job responsibilities and duties and describing how they are to be performed. The purpose of job design is to achieve an organization's goals. Each position in the organization is supposed to serve an important purpose. Job design is also important because of its potential for motivating workers. This section will describe several major aspects of job design: different types of job design; job specialization; and job enrichment, including the job characteristics model.

Four Different Types of Job Design

Michael Campion and his associates have conducted extensive research into job design. Based on their results, they have identified four approaches to job design: motivational, mechanistic, biological, and perceptual/motor.[2]

1. *The motivational approach.* A motivational approach to job design makes the job so challenging and the worker so responsible that the worker is motivated just by performing the job. Job enrichment and the job characteristics model, described later, are examples of this approach.
2. *The mechanistic approach.* The mechanistic approach to job design emphasizes total efficiency in performing a job. It assumes that work should be broken down into highly specialized and simplified tasks that involve frequent repetition of assignments. The mechanistic approach is described in the section "Job Specialization." The mechanistic approach to job design has its roots in scientific management and the work of Frederick W. Taylor (see Chapter 1).
3. *The biological approach.* The biological approach to job design is based on ergonomics. Its goal is to reduce the physical demands of work and the discomforts and injuries caused by these demands. The biological approach fo-

cuses on minimizing physical strain on the workers. It does so by reducing strength and endurance requirements and making improvements to upsetting noise and climate conditions. The biological approach results in less discomfort, fatigue, and illness for workers. The ergonomic workstation shown later in this chapter is based primarily on the biological approach to job design.

4. *The perceptual/motor approach.* The perceptual/motor approach concentrates on mental capabilities and limitations. The perceptual/motor approach aims to ensure that the attention and concentration required by a job are within the capability of the least competent worker. For example, the instruction manual for a piece of equipment should not exceed the information-processing abilities of its least intelligent user. The perceptual/motor approach aims to reduce mental stress, fatigue, training time, and chances for error.

Exhibit 8-1 summarizes research about the four types of job design. This table merits careful attention because it provides an overview of job design and lists the benefits and costs of each approach.

Approach	Characteristics	Benefits	Costs
MOTIVATIONAL	*i* Variety *i* Autonomy *i* Significance *i* Skill usage *i* Participation *i* Recognition *i* Growth *i* Achievement *i* Feedback	*i* Satisfaction *i* Motivation *i* Involvement *i* Performance *d* Absenteeism	*i* Training *i* Staffing difficulty *i* Errors *i* Mental fatigue *i* Stress *i* Mental abilities *i* Compensation
MECHANISTIC	*i* Specialization *i* Simplification *i* Repetition *i* Automation *d* Spare time	*d* Training *d* Staffing difficulty *d* Errors *d* Mental fatigue *d* Mental abilities *d* Compensation	*d* Satisfaction *d* Motivation *i* Absenteeism
BIOLOGICAL	*d* Strength requirements *d* Endurance requirements *i* Seating comfort *i* Postural comfort *d* Environmental stressors	*d* Physical abilities *d* Physical fatigue *d* Aches & pains *d* Medical incidents	*i* Financial costs *i* Inactivity
PERCEPTUAL/ MOTOR	*i* Lighting quality *i* Display and control quality *d* Information processing requirements *i* User-friendly equipment	*d* Errors *d* Accidents *d* Mental fatigue *d* Stress *d* Training *d* Staffing difficulty *d* Compensation *d* Mental abilities	*i* Boredom *d* Satisfaction

i = increased
d = decreased

EXHIBIT 8-1

185

The Four Types of Job Design

Source: Adapted with permission from Michael A. Campion and Michael J. Stevens, "Neglected Aspects in Job Design: How People Design Jobs, Task-Job Predictability, and Influence of Training," *Journal of Business and Psychology,* Winter 1991, p. 175.

EXHIBIT
8·2

Job Description for Branch Manager, Insurance

Manages the branch office, including such functions as underwriting, claims processing, loss prevention, marketing, and auditing, and resolves related technical questions and issues. Hires new insurance agents, develops new business, and updates the regional manager regarding the profit-and-loss operating results of the branch office, insurance trends, matters having impact on the branch office function, and competitor methods. Makes extensive use of information technology to carry out all of these activities, including spreadsheet analyses and giving direction to establishing customer databases.

job description
A written statement of the key features of a job, along with the activities required to perform it effectively.

In practice, managers may blend these four approaches to job design to create a productive and satisfying job. For example, the job of information systems specialist might be primarily designed along motivational lines. Yet it might also take into account the perceptual/motor demands of working with a computer frequently.

Before choosing a job design, managers and human resource professionals develop a job description. The **job description** is a written statement of the key features of a job, along with the activities required to perform it effectively. Sometimes a description must be modified to fit basic principles of job design. For example, the job description of a customer-service representative might call for an excessive amount of listening to complaints, thus creating too much stress. Exhibit 8-2 presents a job description of a middle-level manager.

Job Specialization

A major consideration in job design is how specialized the job holder must be. **Job specialization** is the degree to which a job holder performs only a limited number of tasks. The mechanistic approach favors job specialization. Specialists are supposed to be able to handle a narrow range of tasks very well. High occupational level specialists include the stock analyst who researches companies in one or two industries and the surgeon who concentrates on liver transplants. Specialists at the first occupational level are usually referred to as *operatives*. An assembly-line worker who fastens two wires to one terminal is an operative.

job specialization
The degree to which a job holder performs only a limited number of tasks.

A generalized job requires the handling of many different tasks. The motivational approach to job design favors generalized jobs. An extreme example of a top-level generalist is the owner of a small business who performs such varied tasks as making the product, selling it, negotiating with banks for loans, and hiring new employees. An extreme example of a generalist at the first (or entry) occupational level is the maintenance worker who packs boxes, sweeps, shovels snow in winter, mows the lawn, and cleans the lavatories.

ADVANTAGES AND DISADVANTAGES OF JOB SPECIALIZATION   The most important advantage of job specialization is that it allows for the development of expertise at all occupational levels. When employees perform the same task repeatedly, they become highly knowledgeable. Many employees derive status and self-esteem from being experts at some task.

Specialized jobs at lower occupational levels require less training time and less learning ability. This can prove to be a key advantage when the available labor force lacks special skills. For example, McDonald's could never have grown so large if each restaurant needed to be staffed by expert chefs. Instead, newcomers to the work force can quickly learn such specialized skills as preparing hamburgers and french fries. These newcomers can be paid entry-level wages—an advantage from a management perspective only!

Job specialization also has disadvantages. Coordinating the work force can be difficult when several employees do small parts of one job. Somebody has to be responsible for pulling together the small pieces of the total task. Some employees prefer narrowly specialized jobs but the majority prefer broad tasks that give them a feeling of control over what they are doing. Although many technical and professional workers join the work force as specialists, they often become bored by performing a narrow range of tasks.

AUTOMATION AND JOB SPECIALIZATION   Ever since the Industrial Revolution, automation has been used to replace some aspects of human endeavor in the office and the factory. Automation typically involves a machine performing a specialized task previously performed by people. Automation is widely used in factories, offices, and stores. Two automation devices in the store are optical scanners and the automatic recording of remaining inventory when a customer checks out. The computerization of the workplace represents automation in hundreds of ways, such as personal computers decreasing the need for clerical support in organizations. Today, only high-level managers have personal secretaries. Others rely on their computers to perform many chores. The fax machine has automated the delivery of many types of messages once sent by mail or messenger service. Similar to many machines, the fax machine is quite specialized. It doesn't respond to the request, "On your way back, pick up some bagels and donuts."

Job Enrichment and the Job Characteristics Model

Job enrichment is an approach to making jobs involve more challenge and responsibility, so they will be more appealing to most employees. At its best, job enrichment gives workers a sense of ownership, responsibility, and accountability for their work. Because job enrichment leads to a more exciting job, it often increases employee job satisfaction and motivation. People are usually willing to work harder at tasks they find enjoyable and rewarding, just as they will put effort into a favorite hobby. The general approach to enriching a job is to build into it more planning and decision making, controlling, and responsibility. Most managers have enriched jobs; most data entry specialists do not.

CHARACTERISTICS OF AN ENRICHED JOB   According to industrial psychologist Frederick Herzberg, the way to design an enriched job is to include as many of the characteristics in the following list as possible.[3] (Exhibit 8-3 summarizes the characteristics and consequences of enriched jobs.) It is important that these characteristics are perceived to exist by the person holding the job. Research indicates that supervisors and group members frequently have different perceptions of job characteristics. For example, supervisors are more likely to think that a job has a big impact on the organization.[4] A worker who is responsible for placing used soft-drink cans in a recycling bin might not think his job is significant. Yet the supervisor might perceive the individual to be contributing to the social responsibility goal of creating a cleaner, less congested environment.

1. *Direct feedback.* Employees should receive immediate evaluation of their work. This feedback can be built into the job (such as the feedback that closing a sale gives a sales representative) or provided by the supervisor.

2

Describe job enrichment, including the job characteristics model.

job enrichment
An approach to making jobs involve more challenge and responsibility, so they will be more appealing to most employees.

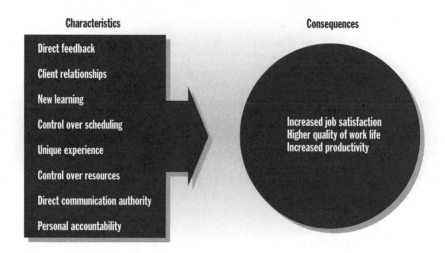

EXHIBIT 8-3

Characteristics and Consequences of an Enriched Job
Enriched jobs have eight distinguishing characteristics. If the job characteristics listed in the box are incorporated into a job, you can often expect the consequences listed in the circle. We are assuming, however, that the job holder welcomes challenge and excitement.

Characteristics

Direct feedback

Client relationships

New learning

Control over scheduling

Unique experience

Control over resources

Direct communication authority

Personal accountability

Consequences

Increased job satisfaction
Higher quality of work life
Increased productivity

2. *Client relationships.* A job is automatically enriched when an employee has a client or customer to serve, whether that client is inside or outside the firm. Serving a client is more satisfying to most people than performing work solely for a manager.

3. *New learning.* An enriched job allows its holder to acquire new knowledge. The learning can stem from job experiences themselves or from training programs associated with the job.

4. *Control over scheduling.* The ability to schedule one's own work contributes to job enrichment. Scheduling includes the authority to decide when to tackle which assignment and having some say in setting working hours.

5. *Unique experience.* An enriched job has some unique qualities or features. A public-relations assistant, for example, has the opportunity to interact with visiting celebrities.

6. *Control over resources.* Another contributor to enrichment is having some control over resources, such as money, material, or people.

7. *Direct communication authority.* An enriched job provides workers the opportunity to communicate directly with other people who use their output. A software specialist with an enriched job, for example, handles complaints about the software he or she developed. The advantages of this dimension of an enriched job are similar to those derived from maintaining client relationships.

8. *Personal accountability.* In an enriched job, workers are responsible for their results. They accept credit for a job done well and blame for a job done poorly.

A highly enriched job has all eight of the preceding characteristics and gives the job holder an opportunity to satisfy high-level psychological needs, such as self-fulfillment. Sometimes the jobs of managers are too enriched; they have too much responsibility and too many risks. A job with some of these characteristics would be moderately enriched. An impoverished job has none.

Information technology workers are another occupational group that may suffer from overenriched jobs. Working with computers and software at an advanced level may represent healthy job enrichment for many workers—working directly with information technology gives a person direct feedback, new learning, and personal accountability. However, many other computer workers are stressed by the complexity of information technology, the amount of continuous learning involved, and frequent hardware and software breakdowns beyond the control of the worker. According to Clare-Marie Karat, a psychologist at

IBM who studies how humans interface with computers, the problem is simple: The engineers and computer scientists who design software and hardware lack sufficient knowledge about the needs and frustrations of computer users. Among the major frustrations of users are difficult-to-interpret error messages, and the difficulty in getting problems resolved when calling a help desk.[5] (To a computer whiz, these problems are exciting challenges that are enriching.)

THE JOB CHARACTERISTICS MODEL OF JOB ENRICHMENT   The concept of job enrichment has been expanded to create the **job characteristics model,** a method of job enrichment that focuses on the task and interpersonal dimensions of a job.[6] As Exhibit 8-4 shows, five measurable characteristics of jobs improve employee motivation, satisfaction, and performance. These characteristics are:

1. *Skill variety*, the degree to which there are many skills to perform.
2. *Task identity*, the degree to which one worker is able to do a complete job, from beginning to end, with a tangible and visible outcome.
3. *Task significance*, the degree to which work has a heavy impact on others in the immediate organization or the external environment.
4. *Autonomy*, the degree to which a job offers freedom, independence, and discretion in scheduling and in determining procedures involved in its implementation.
5. *Feedback*, the degree to which a job provides direct information about performance.

As Exhibit 8-4 reports, these core job characteristics relate to critical psychological states or key mental attitudes. Skill variety, task identity, and task significance lead to a feeling that the work is meaningful. The task dimension of autonomy leads quite logically to a feeling that one is responsible for work outcomes. And the feedback dimension leads to knowledge of results. According to

job characteristics model
A method of job enrichment that focuses on the task and interpersonal dimensions of a job.

189

The Job Characteristics Model of Job Enrichment Job enrichment can be made more precise and scientific by following the model presented here.

Core Job Characteristics	Critical Psychological States	Outcomes
Skill variety / Task identity / Task significance	Experienced meaningfulness of work	High internal work motivation
Autonomy	Experienced responsibility for work outcomes	High general job satisfaction / High "growth" satisfaction
Feedback from job	Gained knowledge of actual results of work activities	Low turnover and absenteeism / High-quality work performance
Strength of employee growth need		

the model, a redesigned job must lead to these three psychological states for workers to achieve the outcomes of internal motivation, job satisfaction, low turnover and absenteeism, and high-quality performance.

The notation in Exhibit 8-4, *strength of employee growth need*, provides guidelines for managers. It signifies that the link between the job characteristics and outcomes will be stronger for workers who want to grow and develop.

GUIDELINES FOR IMPLEMENTING A JOB ENRICHMENT PROGRAM

Before implementing a program of job enrichment, a manager must first ask if the workers need or want more responsibility, variety, and growth. Some employees already have jobs that are enriched enough. Many employees do not want an enriched job because they prefer to avoid the challenge and stress of responsibility. Brainstorming is useful in pinpointing changes that will enrich jobs for those who want enrichment.[7] The brainstorming group would be composed of job incumbents, supervisors, and perhaps an industrial engineer. The workers' participation in planning changes can be useful. Workers may suggest, for example, how to increase client contact.

Fresh insights into the type of workers likely to benefit from job enrichment (or any other motivational approach to job design) stem from a survey of 1,123 American workers sponsored by Shell Oil Co. The results showed that workers generally fit into one of six categories:[8]

1. *Fulfillment seekers.* The majority of fulfillment seekers believe a good job is one that "allows me to use my talents and make a difference," rather than one that provides a good income and benefits. Most fulfillment seekers believe they have a career as opposed to a job, and the majority say they are team players rather than leaders.
2. *High achievers.* The high achievers carefully plan their careers, have the highest level of education, and are the highest income group. Most are leaders who take initiative, and a majority hold managerial positions.
3. *Clock punchers.* These workers are the least satisfied of any group surveyed, with nearly all of them saying they have a job rather than a career. An overwhelming majority said they wound up in their job by chance, and nearly three quarters said they would make different career choices given another chance. Clock punchers have the lowest educational level and income of the six groups in the study.
4. *Risk takers.* Members of this group are the most willing to take risks to pursue large financial rewards. Risk takers are young people who enjoy moving from one employer to another in search of the best job, and are strongly motivated by money.
5. *Ladder climbers.* These are company people who appreciate the stability of staying with one firm a long time. Most prefer a stable income over the possibilities of great financial success, and consider themselves to be leaders rather than team players.
6. *Paycheck cashers.* The majority of paycheck cashers prefer jobs that provide good income and benefits over those that allow them to use their talents and make a difference. Members of this group are young. Although a majority say they will takes risks to achieve big financial success, an even larger number also want job security with one employer. Most paycheck cashers have limited education and prefer working in a large company or agency.

The groups most likely to want and enjoy enriched jobs are the fulfillment seekers, high achievers, risk takers, and perhaps ladder climbers. The less enriched jobs are best assigned to clock punchers and paycheck cashers. Which one of the six types do you think best characterizes you now, or will in the future?

JOB INVOLVEMENT, ENLARGEMENT, AND ROTATION

Job enrichment, including the job characteristics model, is a comprehensive program. Managers can also improve the motivational aspects of job design through less complicated procedures: job involvement, job enlargement, and job rotation. All three processes are built into the more comprehensive job enrichment.

   Job involvement is the degree to which individuals are identified psychologically with their work. It also refers to the importance of work to a person's total self-image. If an insurance claims examiner regards his job as a major part of his identity, he experiences high job involvement. For example, at a social gathering the claims examiner would inform people shortly after meeting them, "I'm a claims examiner with Nationwide Insurance." The employee-involvement groups in quality management are based on job involvement. By making decisions about quality improvement, the team members ideally identify psychologically with their work. Exhibit 8-5 gives you an opportunity to think about job involvement as it applies to you.

Describe job involvement, enlargement, and rotation.

job involvement
The degree to which individuals are identified psychologically with their work.

191

EXHIBIT 8-5

How Involved Are You?

Indicate the strength of your agreement with the following statements by circling the number that appears below the appropriate heading: DS = disagree strongly; D = disagree; N = neutral; A = agree; AS = agree strongly. Respond in relation to a present job, the job you hope to have, or schoolwork.

	DS	D	N	A	AS
1. The major satisfaction in my life comes from my work.	1	2	3	4	5
2. Work is just a means to an end.	5	4	3	2	1
3. The most important things that happen to me involve my work.	1	2	3	4	5
4. I often concentrate so hard on my work that I'm unaware of what is going on around me.	1	2	3	4	5
5. If I inherited enough money, I would spend the rest of my life on vacation.	5	4	3	2	1
6. I'm a perfectionist about my work.	1	2	3	4	5
7. I am very much involved personally in my work.	1	2	3	4	5
8. Most things in life are more important than work.	5	4	3	2	1
9. Working full-time is boring.	5	4	3	2	1
10. My work is intensely exciting.	1	2	3	4	5

Score _____

Scoring and interpretation: Total the numbers circled, and then use the following guide to interpretation.

45–50 Your attitudes suggest intense job involvement. Such attitudes should contribute highly to productivity, quality, and satisfaction.

28–44 Your attitudes suggest a moderate degree of job involvement. To sustain a high level of productivity and quality, you would need to work toward becoming more involved in your work.

10–27 Your attitudes suggest a low degree of job involvement. It would be difficult to sustain a successful, professional career with such low involvement.

Source: Six of the above statements are quoted or adapted from Myron Gable and Frank Dangello, "Job Involvement, Machiavellianism, and Job Performance," *Journal of Business and Psychology*, Winter 1994, p. 163.

Manager *in Action*

Job Rotation at Eli Lilly

A study was conducted in the financial component (department) of Eli Lilly and Co., the pharmaceutical maker, to investigate the impact of job rotation on a person's overall training and career development. (The financial department, or component, includes such areas as treasury, accounting, and payroll.) Eli Lilly has used job rotation more than most companies, regarding it as a key part of the company's culture of professional development. Eli Lilly's reputation for job rotation has helped recruit valuable employees to the company.

The study consisted of executive interviews, an analysis of training needs, and a survey of the costs and benefits of job rotation. Employee work histories were also analyzed as part of the study. Employees in the financial component rotated an average of one nonfinancial assignment during their careers, usually lasting 1.5 years. (An example of a nonfinancial assignment would be for an accountant to work as a market analyst for two years.) The financial group has a planning committee consisting of executives who meet monthly to coordinate job rotations for the component. Job rotation assignments are based on the available openings, the development needs and interests of employees, and the staffing requirements of the business.

One part of the study found that interest in job rotation was much greater among managers with less than ten years of experience. Approximately 75 percent of these early-career managers wanted job rotation. Also, about 66 percent of early-career professionals (such as financial analysts and accountants with less than five years at Lilly) also sought rotation to help with their development. Managers with more than ten years of experience rotated less often, usually waiting six years or more to change jobs. About 60 percent of clerical support workers, secretaries included, expressed an interest in experiencing job rotation. Executives had the least interest in job rotation. Some of these executives were satisfied with their present assignment, and others said they had already had enough job rotation in their careers.

The interviews revealed that early in their careers employees think rotation will help them more in developing their careers. From the company standpoint, rotation has a bigger payoff with employees early in their careers because these people will have more years ahead of them to demonstrate their increased skills and knowledge.

Another key finding is that higher-performing employees tend to take on more job rotations. Part of the reason is that higher-level managers use job rotation to reward high-performing employees. Employees recognize that upper-level management regards job rotation as valuable, so they are eager to get on this list of promotable employees. Employees who experience job rotation tend to be promoted faster than those who rotate less. Many employees therefore perceive job rotation as one step closer to promotion. Job rotation was also favored because it had an even bigger impact on getting a salary increase than getting promoted.

Employees who rotated jobs believed that rotation helped them the most with business skills. These skills include knowledge of the financial component and other departments the employees support, and how the company operates. Rotation was seen to help less with acquiring technical skills (such as accounting and finance) or interpersonal skills.

The study suggested that job rotation has many career benefits such as career satisfaction and involvement in one's career. Yet job rotation did have the drawback of increasing the workload for many employees. Productivity loss was also a problem as employees

Sources: Lisa Cheraskin and Michael A. Campion, "Study Clarifies Job-rotation Benefits," *Personnel Journal*, November 1996, pp. 31–38; Susan Stites-Doe, "The New Story About Job Rotation," *Academy of Management Executive*, February 1996, pp. 86–87.

learned their new jobs. Nevertheless, Eli Lilly and Co. is pleased with how well job rotation benefits the employees and the company.

Job enlargement refers to increasing the number and variety of tasks within a job. Because the tasks are approximately at the same level of responsibility, job enlargement is also referred to as *horizontal job loading*. In contrast, job enrichment is referred to as *vertical job loading*, because the job holder takes on higher-level job responsibility. The claims examiner would experience job enlargement if he were given additional responsibilities such as examining claims for boats and motorcycles as well as automobiles.

As responsibilities expand in job enlargement, the job holder usually has to juggle multiple priorities. Two, three, four, or even more demands might be facing the worker. One approach to handling multiple priorities is to rank them in order of importance, and then tackle the most important one first. A problem here is that the lowest-priority tasks might be neglected. A more recommended approach is to finish the top-priority task, and then move immediately to all other tasks. After the lesser tasks are completed, you are ready to tackle a top-priority item again. Yet if the manager or team leader insists that a specific task must be done immediately, it is good office politics to work on that task. Some catch-up time at night or on weekends might then be invested in work so you do not fall behind on other projects.

Job rotation is a temporary switching of job assignments. In this way employees develop new skills and learn about how other aspects of the unit or organization work. However, the potential advantages of job rotation are lost if a person is rotated from one dull job to another. A motivational form of job rotation would be for our claims examiner to investigate auto and small-truck claims one month, and large trucks the next. Job rotation helps workers prevent the feeling of going stale or being in a rut. The importance of job rotation for career development is illustrated in the accompanying Management in Action.

Another approach to job rotation is sharing employees with another organization that has a different seasonal demand for workers. An example is that AT&T in Maine has a sharing arrangement with L.L. Bean, the mail-order company whose peak business is during the holiday season. AT&T outdoor workers, such as line repair technicians, spend part of the winter picking and packing and answering telephones at L.L. Bean. During the slower-selling summer season, some L.L. Bean employees hold down outdoor positions for AT&T.[9]

job enlargement
Increasing the number and variety of tasks within a job.

job rotation
A temporary switching of job assignments.

WORK TEAMS AND JOB DESIGN

An extension of enriching individual jobs has been enriching the job of group members by forming a work team. Teams have already been mentioned at several places in the text. Given their importance in the modern workplace, they will also receive separate mention in Chapter 14. A **work team** is a group of employees responsible for an entire work process or segment that delivers a product or service to an internal or external customer. Terms for the same type of group include *self-managing work team*, *semi-autonomous group*, and *production work team*.

Recognize how work teams are related to job design.

work team
A group of employees responsible for an entire work process or segment that delivers a product or service to an internal or external customer.

Working in a team is enriching because it broadens the responsibility of team members. The managerial activities performed by team members have been divided into three levels of responsibility (or complexity):[10]

Level 1 begins with quality responsibilities, followed by continuous improvement in work methods, managing suppliers, external customer contact, and hiring team members.

Level 2 begins with forming teams of people from different functions, followed by vacation scheduling, choosing team leaders, equipment purchase, and facility design.

Level 3 begins with budgeting, followed by product modification and development, team member performance appraisal, handling the disciplinary process, and making compensation decisions.

A majority of U.S. corporations use some form of team structure[11] in their organizations and often these team structures are the type of self-managing team in question here. In general, teams have resulted in productivity gains and have become a permanent part of organizational life. A team is only a form of job design where careful attention is paid to having individuals perform work differently than if they were working alone. A "team" of bookkeepers working independently does not make for job enrichment. Yet a group of bookkeepers working together in unison to develop a better system for recording business expenses does constitute a team, and results in jobs with more challenge.

Illustrate how ergonomic factors can be part of job design.

cumulative trauma disorders
Injuries caused by repetitive motions over prolonged periods of time.

ERGONOMICS AND JOB DESIGN

As mentioned in the biological approach to job design, a job should be laid out to decrease the chances that it will physically harm the incumbent. A basic example is that jackhammer operators are required to wear sound dampeners and kidney belts to minimize trauma. A major hazard in the modern workplace is **cumulative trauma disorders,** injuries caused by repetitive motions over prolonged periods of time. These disorders now account for almost half the occupational injuries and illnesses in the United States.

Any occupation involving excessive repetitive motions, including bricklayer and meat cutter, can lead to cumulative trauma disorder. The surge in the number of cumulative trauma disorders stems from the use of computers and other high-tech equipment such as price scanners. Extensive keyboarding places severe strain on hand and wrist muscles, often leading to *carpal tunnel syndrome.* This syndrome occurs when frequent bending of the wrist causes swelling in a tunnel of bones and ligaments in the wrist. The nerve that gives feeling to the hand is pinched, resulting in tingling and numbness in the fingers.

The symptoms of carpal tunnel syndrome are severe. Many workers suffering from the syndrome are unable to differentiate hot and cold by touch and lose finger strength. They often appear clumsy because they have difficulty with everyday tasks such as tying their shoes or picking up small objects. Treatment of carpal tunnel syndrome may involve surgery to release pressure on the median nerve. Another approach is anti-inflammatory drugs to reduce tendon swelling.

To help prevent and decrease the incidence of cumulative trauma disorders, many companies are selecting equipment designed for that purpose. Exhibit 8-6 depicts a workstation based on ergonomic principles developed to engineer a

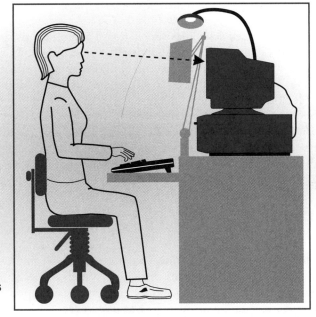

- Screen is below eye level.

- Elbows are on same level with the homekey row, keeping wrists and lower arms parallel to the floor.

- Back and thighs are supported.

- Upper legs are parallel to the floor.

- Feet are placed flat on the floor.

- Task lamp supplements adequate room lighting.

EXHIBIT 86

An Ergonomically Designed Workstation

195

good fit between person and machine. In addition, the following steps should be taken to prevent cumulative trauma disorders:[12]

- Analyze each job with an eye toward possible hazards on that job, including equipment that is difficult to operate.
- Install equipment that minimizes awkward hand and body movements. Try ergonomically designed keyboards to see if they make a difference.
- Encourage workers to take frequent breaks, and rotate jobs so that repetitive hand and body movements are reduced.
- Use voice recognition systems as a substitute for keyboarding where feasible, especially for repetitive functions. (However, guard against creating vocal chord strain from talking into the computer for too long periods of time!)
- Make less use of the mouse by using more key commands. Overuse of the mouse can cause repetitive motion injury. To avoid this, find ways to use the left hand more, such as for tapping function keys.

Workers must also recognize that if they spend many nonworking hours using a keyboard, they increase the probability of developing carpal tunnel syndrome.

MODIFIED WORK SCHEDULES AND JOB DESIGN

One of the key characteristics of job enrichment is to give workers authority in scheduling their own work. Closely related is the widespread practice of giving workers some choice in deviating from the traditional five-day, 40-hour work week. A **modified work schedule** is any formal departure from the traditional hours of work, excluding shift work and staggered work hours. Yet shift work presents enough unique managerial challenges that it will be described here. Modified work schedules include flexible working hours, a compressed work

Summarize the various modified work schedules.

modified work schedule
Any formal departure from the traditional hours of work, excluding shift work and staggered work hours.

week, job sharing, an alternative workplace (such as working at home), and part-time work.

Modified work schedules serve several important organizational purposes in addition to being part of job design. They are intended to increase job satisfaction and motivation and to recruit workers who prefer to avoid a traditional schedule. Many single parents need flexible working hours to cope with child care. Flexible working hours are popular with many employees. Working at home is popular with a subset of the work force. Yet, as companies continue to remain thinly staffed, employees have shown less willingness to volunteer for job sharing and part-time work. A prevailing attitude is to cling to a full-time job. Many workers also feel that not being seen around the office regularly might hurt their chances for promotion.

Flexible Working Hours

For many office employees, the standard eight-hour day with fixed starting and stopping times is a thing of the past. Instead, these employees exert some control over their work schedules through a system of **flexible working hours.**

flexible working hours
A system of working hours wherein employees must work certain core hours but can choose their arrival and departure times.

Employees with flexible working hours are required to work certain core hours, such as 10:00 A.M. to 3:30 P.M. However, they are able to choose which hours they work from 7:00 A.M. to 10:00 A.M. and from 3:30 P.M. to 6:30 P.M. Exhibit 8-7 presents a basic model of flexible working hours. Time-recording devices are frequently used to monitor whether employees have put in the required work for the week.

Flexible working hours are far more likely to be an option for employees on the nonexempt payroll. Such workers must receive additional pay for work beyond 40 hours per week and premium pay for Saturdays and Sundays. Managers, professional-level workers, and salespeople generally have some flexibility in choosing their work hours. In addition, managers and professionals in corporations work an average of 55 hours per week, including work taken home. Being concerned about fitting into a 40-hour-per-week flextime schedule would therefore not be relevant.

Employees are often more satisfied but not necessarily more productive under flexible working hours. A pioneering study conducted in two government agencies was able to pinpoint the conditions under which flexible working hours do contribute to productivity. Researchers found that when busy workers had to share physical resources, flexible working hours did contribute to productiv-

EXHBIT 8-7

A Typical Flexible-Working-Hours Schedule Flexible working hours have a fixed core time in the middle.

Flexible Arrival Time	Fixed Core Time (designated lunch break)		Flexible Departure Time
7:00 AM	10:00 AM	3:30 PM	6:30 PM

Sample schedules: Early Schedule, 7:00–3:30
Standard Schedule, 9:00–5:30
Late Schedule, 10:00–6:30

ity. Specifically, computer programmers who shared a mainframe computer became more productive under flexible working hours. Data entry operators who did not share resources were as productive in flexible-hours jobs as they were with fixed hours.[13]

Many employees are hesitant to use flexible working hours (as well as other work/life programs) for fear of being perceived as not strongly committed to the organization. A survey of *Fortune* 500 companies conducted by the Conference Board indicated that the flextime option is available at most companies, yet few employees choose the option. The reason is that too many managers question an employee's motives or commitment if he or she requests flexible working hours.[14] A major problem for the career-oriented employee who chooses flextime is that meetings might be held at times beyond the employee's schedule quitting time. Suppose you have agreed to work from 7 A.M. until 4 P.M. on Thursday. The team leader schedules an important meeting at 4:30 for Thursday. You now face a conflict between taking care of personal obligations and appearing to be a dedicated worker.

Flextime often comes about after an employee requests the opportunity to participate in a program. Finding answers to the following questions can help the manager evaluate a flextime request:[15] (The same questions also apply generally to other types of modified work schedules.)

1. *Does the nature of the job allow for a flexible schedule?* Employees who must turn around work quickly or respond to crises might not be good candidates for flexible working hours. Negative indicators for flextime also include other employees being inconvenienced by the altered schedule, and a job that requires frequent interaction with others.

2. *Will this individual work well independently?* Some employees thrive on working solo, such as being in the office at 6 A.M. or 7 P.M. Others lose momentum when working alone. Does the employee have a high level of initiative and self-motivation?

3. *Are you comfortable managing a flex-worker?* A manager who feels the need to frequently monitor the work of employees will become anxious when the employees are working by themselves during noncore hours.

4. *Can you arrange tasks so the employee will have enough to do when you or other workers are not present?* Some employees can find ways to make a contribution in the office alone, while others must be fed work in small doses.

The modern worker who is a member of a self-managing team should be able to rise to the challenge of handling a flexible work schedule responsibly. Yet an effective manager must stay alert to possible differences in employee behavior.

Compressed Work Week

A **compressed work week** is a full-time work schedule that allows 40 hours of work in less than five days. The usual arrangement is 4–40 (working four 10-hour days). Many employees enjoy the 4–40 schedule because it enables them to have three consecutive days off from work. Employees often invest this time in leisure activities or part-time jobs. A 4–40 schedule usually allows most employees to take off Saturdays and Sundays. Important exceptions include police workers, hospital employees, and computer operators.

A compressed work week currently gaining favor is the 9–80. The numerals signify 9-hour days and 80 hours worked every two weeks. Employees on 9–80

compressed work week
A full-time work schedule that allows 40 hours of work in less than five days.

work nine-hour days from Monday through Thursday, and an eight-hour day on Friday. The following Friday is a day off.

Compressed work weeks are well like by employees whose lifestyle fits such a schedule. However, the 4-40 week has many built-in problems. Many workers are fatigued during the last two hours and suffer from losses in concentration. From a personal standpoint, working for 10 consecutive hours can be inconvenient.

Even in situations where employees are strongly in favor of the compressed work week, employers may discover significant problems. An engineering service group conducted a four-month experiment with a 4-40 schedule. In evaluating the schedule, the white-collar employees cited such advantages as the ability to conduct personal business more efficiently, the ability to avoid difficult morning commutes, and improved productivity due to work continuity. Management stopped the program, however, when it appeared that customer service had not really improved.[16]

The Alternative Workplace and Telecommuting

alternative work place
A combination of nontraditional work practices, settings, and locations that supplements the traditional office.

A major deviation from the traditional work schedule is the **alternative workplace,** a combination of nontraditional work practices, settings, and locations that supplements the traditional office. A recent estimate is that some 30 to 40 million people in the United States work at home as corporate employees or for self-employment.[17] In addition to working at home, the alternative workplace can include working from a small satellite office, sharing an office or cubicle, or being assigned a laptop computer and a cellular phone as a substitute for a private work space. Here we concentrate on working at home because it represents the most substantial change in a work schedule.

telecommuting
An arrangement with one's employer to use a computer to perform work at home or in a satellite office.

Telecommuting is an arrangement in which employees use computers to perform their regular work responsibilities at home or in a satellite office. Employees who telecommute usually use computers tied to the company's main office. People who work at home are referred to as *teleworkers*. The vast majority of people who work at home are either assigned a computer by the company or own their own computer and related equipment. Yet a person might do piecework at home, such as making garments or furniture, without using a computer.

In addition to using computers to communicate with their employer's office, telecommuters attend meetings on company premises and stay in contact by telephone and teleconferences. Some telecommuting programs are huge. The Mobility Initiative at IBM, for example, has resulted in 12,500 sales representatives giving up their dedicated work spaces. The sales representative's residence, along with an automobile trunk, becomes his or her office. IBM estimates it is saving $100 million annually on the cost of offices in its North America sales and distribution unit alone. Many small businesses have informal telecommuting programs. An extreme case is ZenaComp of Livonia, Michigan, whose vice-president of sales and marketing, Bonnie Cywinski, works from her home in Buffalo, New York (300 miles away).

ADVANTAGES OF TELECOMMUTING Telecommuting can work well with self-reliant and self-starting employees who have relevant work experience. Work-at-home employees usually volunteer for such an arrangement. As a result, they are likely to find telecommuting to be satisfying. Employees derive many benefits from working at home, including easier management of personal life; lowered costs for commuting, work clothing, and lunch; much less time spent commuting; and fewer distractions. Telecommuting offers these advantages to the employer:[18]

1. *Increased productivity*. Surveys have shown consistently that telecommuting programs increase productivity, usually by at least 25 percent. A survey of employees in the Mobility Initiative program at IBM revealed that 87 percent believe their personal productivity had increased significantly. The productivity for work-at-home employees at Georgia Power increased 10 percent, in part because some of the time spent working was not spent commuting.

2. *Low overhead*. Because the employees are providing some of their own office space, the company can operate with much less office space. Since 1991, AT&T has improved cash flow by $500 million by eliminating offices people no longer need, consolidating others, and reducing related overhead costs. A vice-president of marketing research operations noted that, because of its work-at-home program, the company was able to greatly expand its client load without acquiring additional space. During a five-year period of IBM's Mobility Initiative program, real estate savings alone were $1 billion. (IBM would probably have to sell $10 billion in equipment to earn the same amount of profit.)

3. *Access to a wider range of employee talent*. Companies with regular work-at-home programs are almost always deluged with résumés from eager job applicants. The talent bank includes parents (mostly mothers) with young children, employees who find commuting unpleasant, and others who live far away from their firms.

DISADVANTAGES OF TELECOMMUTING   Work-at-home programs must be used selectively because they pose disadvantages for both employee and employer. The careers of telecommuters may suffer because they are not visible to management. Many telecommuters complain of the isolation from coworkers.

Also, telecommuters can be exploited if they feel compelled to work on company problems late into the night and on weekends. The many potential distractions at home make it difficult for some telecommuters to concentrate on work. Finally, telecommuters are sometimes part-time employees who receive limited benefits and are paid only for what they produce. As one telecommuter, a data entry specialist, said, "If I let up for an afternoon, I earn hardly anything."

Business writer Jenny C. McCune notes that working at home can reinforce negative tendencies: It will facilitate a workaholic to work harder and longer, and it will give a procrastinator ample opportunity to delay work.[19] Some telecommuters with eating disorders have reported that the ready access to food at home is difficult to resist.

Telecommuting programs can be disadvantageous to the employer because building loyalty and teamwork is difficult when so many workers are away from the office. Telecommuters who are not performing measured work are difficult to supervise—working at home gives an employee much more latitude in attending to personal matters during work time. Another problem is that the organization may miss out on some of the creativity that stems from the exchange of ideas in the traditional office.

SUGGESTIONS FOR MANAGERS OF TELEWORKERS To maximize the advantages and minimize the disadvantages of telecommuting, managers should follow a few key suggestions:[20]

1. Choose the right type of work for working at home. If a job requires frequent monitoring, such as reviewing progress on a complex report, it is not well suited for telecommuting. Jobs requiring the use of complicated, large-scale equipment, such as medical laboratory work or manufacturing, cannot be done off premises. Work that requires clients or customers to visit the employee is best done on company premises. In general, positions with measurable work output are best suited for working at home.

2. Teleworkers should be chosen with care. Working at home is best suited for self-disciplined, well-motivated, and deadline-conscious workers. Make sure the telecommuter has a suitable home environment for telecommuting. The designated work area should be as separate from the household as possible and relatively free from distractions. Merrill Lynch insists that its teleworkers first participate in a training program about working at home. The program includes information about work habits and setting up an effective office at home.

3. Agree early on the number of days or months for telecommuting. The optimum number of days depends somewhat on the position and the worker. For corporate telecommuters, about two days per week of working at home is typical.

4. Clearly define productivity goals and deadlines. The more measurable the work output, such as lines of computer code or insurance claims forms processed, the better suited it is for telecommuting. Collect weekly data that relate to the results being achieved, such as orders filled or cases settled.

5. Keep in contact through a variety of means, including e-mail, telephone, phone meetings, and conference calls. Agree on working hours during which the teleworker can be reached. Remember, the manager is not disturbing the worker at home by telephoning that person during regularly scheduled working hours. Also, agree on how frequently the worker will be checking e-mail.

6. Make periodic visits to the workers at home, but give them appropriate lead time. During the visit look to see if equipment is being used in a way that is ergonomically sound. Field visits, so long as they are not perceived as spying, communicate the fact that teleworkers are an important part of the team.

SHARING OFFICE SPACE AND HOTELING Another major aspect of the alternative workplace is for workers to share offices or cubicles, or have use of a shared office (similar to a hotel) only when on premises. Shared office space means simply that more than one employee is assigned to the same office or cubicle because their work schedules allow for such an arrangement. Among the factors allowing for sharing office space are complementary travel schedules, working different shifts, and working from home on different schedules. AT&T discovered that for some groups of employees, as many as six people could use the same desk and equipment formerly assigned to one. The company now has 14,000 employees in shared-desk arrangements. The savings on real estate costs can be enormous from sharing office space.

In *hoteling*, the company provides work spaces equipped and supported with typical office services. The worker who travels frequently might even be assigned a locker for personal storage. A computer system routes phone calls and e-mail as necessary. However, the office space, similar to a hotel (or rented temporary office space) is reserved by the hour, day, or week instead of being permanently assigned.[21]

From the perspective of top management, requiring workers to share office space or have no permanent office space is an excellent method of cost control. From the perspective of many employees, not having a permanent office or cubicle is an indignity and an inconvenience. As many workers lament, "I have no home." Years ago ambitious workers aspired toward having a corner office. Now they aspire toward having any office.

Job Sharing

About one-third of large companies that offer modified work schedules allow more than one employee to share the same job.[22] **Job sharing** is a work arrangement in which two people who work part-time share one job. The sharers divide up the job according to their needs. Each may work selected days of the work week. Or, one person might work mornings and the other work afternoons. The job sharers might be two friends, a husband and wife, or two employees who did not know each other before sharing a job. If the job is complex, the sharers have to spend work time discussing it.

Job sharing is not an option valued by large numbers of employees. It has its greatest appeal to workers whose family commitments do not allow for full-time work. A typical job-sharing situation involves two friends who want a responsible position but can only work part time. A successful example of job sharing takes place at KLIF-AM radio in Dallas, Texas, where two women who are friends have set sales records while sharing a sales position at the station. Job sharing offers the employer an advantage in that two people working half time usually produce more than one person working full time. This is particularly noticeable in creative work. Also, if one employee is sick, the other is still available to handle the job for half the day.

Part-Time and Temporary Work

Part-time work is a modified work schedule offered by about two-thirds of employers today.[23] The category of part-time workers includes employees who work reduced weekly, annual, or seasonal hours and those who have project-based, occasional work. For example, a marketing brand manager might work full days on Mondays, Wednesdays, and Fridays. Many people, such as students and semiretired people, choose part-time work because it fits their lifestyles. Also, many people work part time because they cannot find full-time employment.

Temporary employment is at an all-time high, with some employers even hiring part-time managers, engineers, lawyers, and other high-level workers. Collectively, part-time and temporary employees constitute one-fourth to one-third of the work force. Because they are hired according to, or contingent upon, an employer's need, they are referred to as **contingent workers.** Some contingent workers receive modest benefits. Another contingent worker is the independent contractor, who is paid for services rendered but does not receive benefits. A familiar example is a plumber hired by a homeowner to make a repair. The plumber sets the wage, and receives no benefits.

job sharing
A work arrangement in which two people who work part time share one job.

201

contingent workers
Part-time or temporary employees who are not members of the employer's permanent work force.

Many employees enjoy part-time work because they are willing to trade off the low pay for personal convenience. Employers are eager to hire contingent workers to avoid the expense of hiring full-time workers. Paying limited or no benefits to part-time workers can save employers as much as 35 percent of the cost of full-time compensation. Also, contingent workers can be readily laid off if business conditions warrant. Some seasonally oriented businesses, such as gift-catalog sales firms, hire mostly part-time workers. The disadvantage to the employer is that part-time employment works best for entry-level workers. Building a stable, professional staff composed of part-time employees is difficult in most industries. A long-standing exception is colleges and technical schools, which rely heavily on a stable and professional group of part-time faculty.

The wide-scale use of contingent workers has been criticized, as represented by the comments of famous economist Lester C. Thurow: "With contingent workers, companies get lower labor costs and greater deployment flexibility. Contingent workers get lower wages, fewer fringes (benefits) and paid holidays, and much greater economic risks and uncertainty."[24]

To optimize the contribution of part-time or temporary workers, they should be assigned projects rather than performing a series of unrelated tasks. Completing an entire project helps define the contribution of the part-time or temporary worker and also contributes to job enrichment. The manager should be clear about what is expected and should set a specific direction. A representative project would be for a contingent worker to update the addresses and telephone numbers on a customer database.

Shift Work

To accommodate the needs of employers rather than employees, many workers are assigned to shift work. The purpose of shift work is to provide coverage during nonstandard hours. The most common shift schedules are days (7 A.M. to 3 P.M.), evenings (3 P.M. to 11 P.M.), and nights (11 P.M. to 7 A.M.). Shift work is used in manufacturing to meet high demand for products without having to expand facilities. It is more economical to run a factory 16 or 24 hours per day than to run two or three factories eight hours per day. Service industries make even more extensive use of shift work to meet the demands of customers around the clock, such as in a hotel. Shift work is also necessary in public-service operations such as police work, fire fighting, and health care.

Shift work is more than a deviation from a traditional work schedule. It is a lifestyle that affects productivity, health, family, and social life. Shift work unfortunately disrupts the natural rhythm of the body and creates job problems. Three times the average incidence of drug and alcohol abuse fosters an increased risk of errors and accidents. Many industrial catastrophes, such as ship wrecks, oil spills, and chemical leaks have taken place during the night ("graveyard") shift. Shift workers also experience difficulty in integrating their schedules with the social needs of friends and families.

With proper training, employees can adjust better to shift work. A shift-work consultant, for example, recommends: "Create healthy sleep environments by keeping rooms cool and eliminating daylight with dark shades and curtains or even styrofoam cutouts or black plastic taped to the window frame."[25]

SUMMARY OF KEY POINTS

 Identify the major dimensions and different types of job design.

Job design involves establishing job responsibilities and duties and the manner in which they are to be performed. Four approaches to job design are (1) the motivational approach, (2) the mechanistic approach (which emphasizes efficiency), (3) the biological approach (which emphasizes safety), and (4) the perceptual/motor approach. Each of these approaches has benefits and costs.

Job specialization is the degree to which a job holder performs only a limited number of tasks. Specialists are found at different occupational levels. Job specialization enhances work force expertise at all levels and can reduce training time at the operative level. Specialization, however, can lead to problems. Coordinating the work of specialists can be difficult, and some employees may become bored. Automation, including robotics, contributes to job specialization. Robots perform many specialized tasks, including those that would be unsafe for humans. The computerization of the workplace represents automation in hundreds of ways, such as personal computers decreasing the need for clerical support.

 Describe job enrichment, including the job characteristics model.

Job enrichment is a method of making jobs involve more challenges and responsibility so they will be more appealing to most employees. It is important that the characteristics of an enriched job are perceived to exist by the person holding the job. An enriched job provides direct feedback, client relationships, new learning, scheduling by the employee, unique experience, control over resources, direct communication authority, and personal accountability.

Job enrichment has been expanded to create the job characteristics model, which focuses on the task and interpersonal dimensions of a job. Five characteristics of jobs improve employee motivation, satisfaction, and performance: skill variety, task identity, task significance, autonomy, and feedback. These characteristics relate to critical psychological states which, in turn, lead to outcomes such as internal motivation, satisfaction, low absenteeisms, and high quality.

Finding out which employees want an enriched job is an important part of implementing job enrichment. The groups of employees most likely to want and enjoy enriched jobs can be classified as fulfillment seekers, high achievers, risk takers, and perhaps ladder climbers.

 Describe job involvement, enlargement, and rotation.

Job involvement reflects psychological involvement with one's work and how much work is part of the self-image. Job enlargement is about increasing the number and variety of jobs tasks. Job rotation is switching assignments and can contribute heavily to career development.

 Recognize how work teams are related to job design.

Work teams are groups of employees responsible for an entire work process or segment. Work-team members are multiskilled generalists who plan, control, and improve their own work processes, and sometimes even make compensation decisions.

 Illustrate how ergonomic factors can be part of job design.

Cumulative trauma disorders are injuries caused by repetitive motions over prolonged periods of time. Workstations can be designed to minimize these problems by such measures as supporting the back and thighs, and placing the feet flat on the floor.

 Summarize the various modified work schedules.

Work scheduling is another part of job design. A modified work schedule departs from the traditional hours of work. Modified work scheduling options include flexible working hours, a compressed work week, the alternative workplace and telecommuting, job sharing, and part-time and temporary work. Shift work deviates from a regular day schedule and can lead to health problems, accidents, and family problems.

KEY TERMS AND PHRASES

Job design, *184*

Job description, *186*

Job specialization, *186*

Job enrichment, *187*

Job characteristics model, *189*

Job involvement, *191*

Job enlargement, *193*

Job rotation, *193*

Work team, *193*

Cumulative trauma disorders, *194*

Modified work schedule, *195*

Flexible working hours, *196*

Compressed work week, *197*

Alternative workplace, *198*

Telecommuting, *198*

Job sharing, *201*

Contingent workers, *201*

QUESTIONS

1. In about 35 words write the job description for (a) a restaurant manager, or (b) the top executive at IBM, or (c) the instructor for this course.
2. A study showed that high-level mental ability is generally required to perform well in jobs designed by the motivational approach. Why might this be true?
3. How would a manager go about *enlarging* but not *enriching* a job?
4. What are the benefits of frequent job rotation for a person who would like to become a high-level manager?
5. How well suited would a work schedule of three $13\frac{1}{3}$-hour days per week be for an employee whose job demanded considerable creativity?
6. Now that you have studied the information about ergonomics, what do you think you should do differently with respect to working at the computer?
7. From the standpoint of moving up in the company hierarchy, what might be a limitation of being a telecommuter for several years?

SKILL-BUILDING EXERCISE 8-A: The Ideal Home-Based Office

Gather into teams of about five people to design an ideal office at home for a professional worker. Take about 20 minutes to develop suggestions for the following aspects of a home office: (1) hardware and software, (2) equipment other than computers, (3) furniture, (4) ergonomics design, (5) office layout, and (6) location within the house or apartment. Consider both productivity and job satisfaction when designing your office. After the designs are complete, the team leaders can present them to the rest of the class.

INTERNET SKILL-BUILDING EXERCISE: Learning More About Telecommuting

Telecommuting, working at home, or the alternative workplace. Whatever you want to call it, telecommuting has become a permanent part of the workplace. A few worthwhile Web sites about working at home are listed next. Visit the sites with an eye toward supplementing the information about telecommuting presented in this chapter.

- Arizona Department of Administration/The Telecommuting Zone: www.state.az.us/tpo/telecommuting/
- AT&T Telework Guide: www.att.com/telework/
- Cyberworkers.com: www.cyberworkers.com
- TAC—The International Telework Association: www.telecommute.org
- Telecommute America: www.att.com/Telecommute_America/

CASE PROBLEM 8-A: Protecting the Computer Athletes

Pacifica Distributors supplies hundreds of grocery stores, drugstores, small retail stores, and hospitals with pharmaceutical and health products produced by companies that do not sell directly to large retailers like Krogers, Eckerd Drugs, and Kmart. Approximately 75 distribution specialists spend their entire workweek stationed at computers. Although they interact with some customers by telephone, almost their complete day is spent at the keyboard. Many of the distribution specialists complain of pains in the hand, ocular fatigue, and headaches. During the last several years, at least three specialists have undergone surgery for carpal tunnel syndrome.

Problems of this type concern Jill Bertrand, the Pacifica vice-president of human resources. Based on her concern, she studied a report prepared by Dr. Emil Pasacarelli, professor of clinical medicine at Columbia University College of Physicians and Surgeons. His report notes that people prone to computer injuries should regard themselves as computer athletes—training and cross-training to stay ahead of possible injuries. Pasacarelli wants workers to consider the following accommodations to make their workspace more ergonomically correct:

- Desks should ideally be between 23 and 28.5 inches from the floor, depending on the person's height.

- Ensure adequate knee clearance to accommodate full range of movement at the workstation.
- Use vertical CPU stands and monitor arms to provide extra workspace.
- Include an adjustable back rest and seat for good lumbar (lower-back) support from the chair.
- Chairs with five legs have more stability, and wheels allow for movement and adjustment.
- Reclining seatbacks and adjustable seat pans control the pressure on the back and thighs.
- Use a footrest for support when seat heights are adjusted for fixed-height workstations. They are also helpful for people who have short legs since they relieve pressure on the thighs.
- The top of the monitor screen should be slightly below eye level when sitting straight in a chair. The center of the screen should be about 20 degrees below eye level.
- Source documents should be at the same height and plane as the screen to avoid unnecessary neck and back movements.
- Filter screens on monitors can reduce glare
- Monitor stands allow proper height adjustments of video displays and control glare.
- A detachable keyboard can be positioned for optimum ergonomically correct typing.
- Like desks, keyboards should be on work surfaces that stand between 23 and 28.5 inches from the floor, depending on the person's height. The top surface of the front-row keys should be no higher than 2 to 2.5 inches above the work surface.
- Keyboards should be level with thumb joints. Elbows should be positioned at a 90-degree angle and forearms kept parallel to the floor.
- Wrist rests or supports can help keep wrists in straight positions while allowing freedom of movement.
- Combinations of indirect and task light, plus natural light,

are best. Indirect light alone can reduce eyestrain and fatigue.
- For close work, use task lighting that shines sideways onto the paper and doesn't create glare on the computer screen.
- Task lighting should illuminate source documents on a copy holder under a wide variety of general lighting conditions.
- Grids refract the light pattern of fluorescent lights and reduce glare, which can provide added comfort.

Bertrand scheduled a meeting with Gerry McKinsey, the CEO of Pacifica. She carefully reviewed the findings with him in person, after having sent the report for his review before the meeting. McKinsey said, "I think that a few of the ideas have merit, but I'm not in a big rush to have us implement all of those ideas. It would be very expensive to overhaul all our computer workstations. And no matter what we did, somebody would complain about headaches and wrist aches. You find these complaints in almost every workplace. We can't eliminate every small discomfort. We're a business enterprise, not an ergonomics laboratory."

With a concerned expression, Bertrand said, "Gerry, you might be taking these ergonomics problems too lightly. Many of the suggestions could be implemented quite inexpensively."

McKinsey said, "Maybe we'll take up this problem in a staff meeting in the next few months or so. Send me an e-mail as a reminder."

Discussion Questions

1. What is your evaluation of the practicality of the ergonomic suggestions contained in the report?
2. What impact would these suggestions have on your use of the computer?
3. How might Bertrand more effectively sell the merits of this report to McKinsey?

Source: The Pascarelli report is from "Athletic Accommodations," *Management Review*, February 1996, p. 27.

CASE PROBLEM 8-B: The Airport Security Guard Blues

Patti Freeman, supervisor of airport security at an international airport, met with her boss, Jack Indino, to discuss the job performance of her staff.

"Jack," said Patti, "we're developing a group performance problem with my security staff. I want to lay out the problem with you and then suggest a solution."

"Go ahead," said Indino. "What's one more problem in the life of an airport operations manager?"

"As I see it," said Freeman, "our security guards are bored stiff. Each one of them has told me so either directly

or indirectly. The general complaint is that they get bored—after a while, each face is the same, and every attaché case or handbag looks the same.

"I think the job boredom is also creating performance problems. Some of the guards have become so lethargic that they don't pay serious attention to any potential security violation. Thank goodness no terrorist or hijacker has gotten through."

"What are you proposing to do about this problem?" asked Indino.

"My tentative solution is to enrich the jobs of the guards in some way. We could work out some way to give them more responsibility and challenge. Perhaps we can allow them to interview passengers to get their thoughts about airline safety."

"I don't see that as a solution," said Indino. "FAA regulations require that the guards be on duty all the time, checking passengers. The guards may be bored, but if the airport wants to stay in business, we need security guards doing exactly what they are doing. If our present crew of guards find their jobs boring, we may have to replace them with people who can concentrate on their jobs for a full shift."

"I'll get back to you again about this problem," said Freeman. "I understand your viewpoint, but I've got to find some way to get the security guards more wrapped up in their jobs."

Discussion Questions

1. How effective might job enrichment be for purposes of curing the inattention problem that Freeman observes?
2. What is your evaluation of the tactic of replacing the security guards with others who might be more attentive?
3. What is your evaluation of Freeman's contention that boredom might be adversely affecting the security guards' job performance?

ENDNOTES

1. Genevieve Capowski, "The Joy of Flex," *Management Review*, March 1996, pp. 14–15; "Workplace Flexibility Works Better with Management Flexibility," *Marriott Executive Memo*, Number 8, 1996, p. 4.
2. Michael A. Campion and Michael J. Stevens, "Neglected Aspects in Job Design: How People Design Jobs, Task-Job Predictability, and Influence of Training," *Journal of Business and Psychology,"* Winter 1991, pp. 169–192.
3. Frederick Herzberg, "The Wise Old Turk," *Harvard Business Review*, September–October 1974, pp. 70–80.
4. Marc C. Marchese and Robert P. Delprino, "Do Supervisors and Subordinates See Eye-to-Eye on Job Enrichment?" *Journal of Business and Psychology*, Winter 1998, pp. 179–192.
5. Stephen H. Wildstrom, "A Computer User's Manifesto," *Business Week*, September 28, 1998, p. 18; Wildstrom, "They're Mad as Hell Out There," *Business Week*, October 19, 1998, p. 32.
6. John Richard Hackman and Greg R. Oldham, *Work Redesign* (Reading, MA: Addison-Wesley, 1980), p. 77.
7. J. Barton Cunningham and Ted Eberle, "A Guide to Job Enrichment and Redesign," *Personnel*, February 1990, p. 59.
8. Sixtus Oeschsle, "Who We Are at Work: Six Types of Employee Attitudes," Supplement to the November 1998 *Workforce*, p. 10.
9. "Sharing Employees," *The Pryor Report*, September 1996, p. 9.
10. Richard S. Wellins, William C. Byham, and Jeanne M. Wilson, *Empowered Teams: Creating Self-Directed Work Groups That Improve Quality, Productivity, and Participation* (San Francisco: Jossey-Bass, 1991), pp. 24–28.
11. Anthony M. Towsend, Samuel M. DeMarie, and Anthony R. Hendrickson, "Virtual Teams: Technology and the Workplace of the Future," *Academy of Management Executive*, August 1998, p. 18.
12. "Preventing Carpal Tunnel Syndrome," *HRfocus*, August 1995, p. 4; Neil Gross and Paul C. Judge, "Let's Talk," *Business Week*, February 23, 1998, pp. 61–72.
13. David A. Ralston, William P. Anthony, and David J. Gustafson, "Employees May Love Flextime, But What Does It Do to the Organization's Productivity?" *Journal of Applied Psychology*, May 1985, pp. 272–279.
14. Survey reported in "Flextime Is Not Good If Nobody Uses It," *Positive Leadership*, Sample issue, October 1998, p. 5.
15. The first three points are from "A Time for Change? Maybe Not— Flextime Isn't for Everyone," *Working Smart*, September 1996, pp. 1–2.
16. Spyros Economides, D. N. Beck, and Allen J. Shus, "Longer Days and Shorter Weeks Improve Productivity," *Personnel Administrator*, May 1989, pp. 112–114.
17. Mahlon Apgar, IV, "The Alternative Workplace: Changing Where and How People Work," *Harvard Business Review*, May–June 1998, p. 121.
18. Apgar, "The Alternative Workplace," p. 121; Jenny C. McCune, "Telecommuting Revisited," *Management Review*, February 1998, p. 12; Brian Steinberg, "Separated at Work," *Entrepreneur*, March 1998, p. 135.
19. McCune, "Telecommuting Revisited," p. 13.
20. "Managing Telecommuters: Taking the Mystery Out of Tracking Work from Afar," *Executive Strategies*, March 1998, p. 6; "Tips for Managing Telecommuters," *Human Resources Forum*, January 1995, p. 2.
21. Apgar, "The Alternative Workplace," pp. 124–125.
22. Survey reported in Diana Kunde, "Job Sharing: Best of Both Worlds," *Dallas Morning News* syndicated story, October 6, 1997.
23. Survey reported in Kunde, "Job Sharing," October 6, 1997.
24. Doris A. Van Horn-Christopher, "Will Employee Meltdown Mean a 'Contingent' Work Force?" *Business Forum*, Summer/Fall 1996, p. 11.
25. Ellen Hale, "Lack of Sleep Is Now Grounds for Filing Suit—Or Being Sued," Gannett News Service, August 15, 1993.

Chapter Nine

OBJECTIVES

After studying this chapter and doing the exercises, you should be able to:

1. Describe the bureaucratic form of organization and discuss its advantages and disadvantages.

2. Explain the major ways in which organizations are divided into departments.

3. Describe three modifications of the bureaucratic structure: the matrix structure; flat structures, downsizing, and outsourcing; and organization by process.

4. Specify how delegation, empowerment, and decentralization spread authority in an organization.

5. Identify major aspects of organizational culture, including its management and control.

6. Describe key aspects of managing change including gaining support for change.

The merger between Chrysler Corp. and Daimler-Benz AG was just a couple of days away from being official, and the two parties could not even agree on what the new corporate stationery should look like. But the man at the center of the merger was unruffled by this historic development in the automotive industry. "It's fun," said Chrysler president Thomas Stallkamp. "Sometimes it's hilarious, sometimes you want to cry. Problems happen, but life goes on." Although two other senior executives put the deal together, Stallkamp was the catalyst for making sure the merged company, DaimlerChrysler, started smoothly.

The 52-year-old former purchasing chief relished the role. Whether he's making one-day round trips to Stuttgart, Germany, for executive meetings or answering questions from workers at an engine plant in Detroit, he keeps an even keel. Tom Stallkamp is a self-described "ordinary guy" in an extraordinary situation. He is under intense scrutiny on both sides of the Atlantic as he balances the interests and cultures of two of the world's largest automakers.

Before becoming president of Chrysler in 1997, Stallkamp had spent 17 years in the department of procurement and supply. While head of procurement, he revolutionized the way Chrysler bought its parts and worked with suppliers. He allowed suppliers to keep half the money they saved Chrysler and gave them unprecedented input into new vehicle designs. Stallkamp is also credited with helping other

Organization Structure, Culture, and Change

executives mediate their disputes. Few other auto executives understand the dynamics of culture like Stallkamp, who holds an MBA in organizational behavior (the study of human behavior in the workplace).

Stallkamp recognizes that melding the divergent styles of Chrysler and Daimler is a delicate process. "To be fair, we moved faster and they're much more analytical," he said. "That is one of the big issues. How fast do we do this? This is a big deal, and we don't want to screw it up by crashing some premature integration." Just before the merger took place, Stallkamp was going to release a partial organization chart. He decided, however, to wait until he could thoroughly study the complex situation of putting together two giant companies.[1]

The efforts by the automotive executive to achieve a smooth blending of two companies takes place frequently in today's world of ever-changing organizations. The same anecdote also illustrates that managers sometimes focus on the organization as a whole, rather than on specific individuals. In Chapter 8, we described how the tasks of an organization are divided into jobs for individuals and groups. Work is also subdivided through an **organization structure**—the arrangement of people and tasks to accomplish organizational goals. The structure specifies who reports to whom and who does what. An organization structure is similar to the framework of a building or the skeleton of the body.

The purpose of this chapter is to explain three related aspects of total organizations or large subunits: how organizations subdivide work among their units, the culture (or general atmosphere) of organizations, and how to manage change.

organization structure
The arrangement of people and tasks to accomplish organizational goals.

Describe the bureaucratic form of organization and discuss its advantages and disadvantages.

BUREAUCRACY AS A FORM OF ORGANIZATION

A **bureaucracy** is a rational, systematic, and precise form of organization in which rules, regulations, and techniques of control are precisely defined. It is helpful to think of bureaucracy as the traditional form of organization. Other structures are usually variations of, or supplements to, bureaucracy. Do not confuse the word bureaucracy with bigness. Although most big organizations are bureaucratic, small firms can also follow the bureaucratic model. An example might be a small, carefully organized bank.

bureaucracy
A rational, systematic, and precise form of organization in which rules, regulations, and techniques of control are precisely defined.

Principles of Organization in a Bureaucracy

The entire traditional, or classical, school of management contributes to our understanding of bureaucracy. Yet the essence of bureaucracy can be understood by identifying its major characteristics and principles as listed next:

1. *Hierarchy of authority.* The dominant characteristic of a bureaucracy is that each lower organizational unit is controlled and supervised by a higher one. The person granted the most formal authority (the right to act) is placed at the top of the hierarchy. Exhibit 9-1 presents a bureaucracy as pyramid-shaped. The number of employees increases substantially as you move down to each successive level. Most of the formal authority is concentrated at the top. Observe that the amount of formal authority decreases as you move to lower levels.

2. *Unity of command.* A classic management principle, **unity of command,** states that each subordinate receives assigned duties from one superior only and is accountable to that superior. In the modern organization many people serve on projects and teams in addition to reporting to their regular boss, thus violating the unity of command.

unity of command
The classical management principle stating that each subordinate receives assigned duties from one superior only and is accountable to that superior.

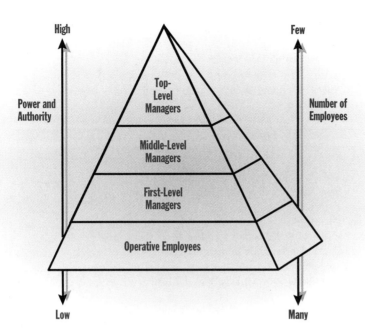

High

Power and
Authority

Top-
Level
Managers

Middle-Level
Managers

First-Level
Managers

Operative Employees

Low

Few

Number of
Employees

Many

EXHIBIT
9-1

*The Bureaucratic Form of
Organization*
*In the bureaucratic organiza-
tion structure people at the
top of the organization have
the most formal authority,
yet there are many more employees at lower levels in the
organization.*

209

3. *Task specialization.* In a bureaucracy, division of labor is based on task specialization (described in Chapter 8). To achieve task specialization, organizations have separate departments, such as manufacturing, customer service,
and information systems. Employees assigned to these organizational units
have specialized knowledge and skills that contribute to the overall effectiveness of the firm.

4. *Duties and rights of employees.* Bureaucracies are characterized by rules that define the rights and duties of employees. In a highly bureaucratic organization, each employee has a precise job description, and policy and procedure
manuals are current and accessible.

5. *Definition of managerial responsibility.* In a bureaucracy, the responsibility and
authority of each manager is defined clearly in writing. When responsibility
is defined in writing, managers know what is expected of them and what
limits are set to their authority. This approach minimizes overlapping of authority and accompanying confusion.

6. *Line and staff functions.* A bureaucracy identifies the various organizational units
as being line or staff. Line functions are those involved with the primary purpose of an organization or its primary outputs. In a bank, people who supervise work related to borrowing and lending money are line managers.
Staff functions assist the line functions. Staff managers are responsible for important functions such as human resources (or personnel) and purchasing.
Although staff functions do not deal with the primary purposes of the firm,
they are essential for achieving the organization's mission.

Advantages and Disadvantages of Bureaucracy

Bureaucracy has made modern civilization possible. Without large, complex organizations to coordinate the efforts of thousands of people, we would not have
airplanes, automobiles, skyscrapers, universities, vaccines, or space satellites.

EXHIBIT 9.2

Understanding Your Bureaucratic Orientation

Answer each question "mostly agree" (MA) or "mostly disagree" (MD). Assume the mental set of attempting to learn something about yourself rather than impressing a prospective employer.

	MA	MD
1. I value stability in my job.	___	___
2. I like a predictable organization.	___	___
3. I enjoy working without the benefit of a carefully specified job description.	___	___
4. I would enjoy working for an organization in which promotions were generally determined by seniority.	___	___
5. Rules, policies, and procedures generally frustrate me.	___	___
6. I would enjoy working for a company that employed 95,000 people worldwide.	___	___
7. Being self-employed would involve more risk than I'm willing to take.	___	___
8. Before accepting a position, I would like to see an exact job description.	___	___
9. I would prefer a job as a freelance landscape artist to one as a supervisor for the Department of Motor Vehicles.	___	___
10. Seniority should be as important as performance in determining pay increases and promotion.	___	___
11. It would give me a feeling of pride to work for the largest and most successful company in its field.	___	___
12. Given a choice, I would prefer to make $90,000 per year as a vice-president in a small company than $100,000 per year as a middle manager in a large company.	___	___
13. I would feel uncomfortable if I were required to wear an employee badge with a number on it.	___	___
14. Parking spaces in a company lot should be assigned according to job level.	___	___
15. I would generally prefer working as a specialist to performing many different tasks.	___	___
16. Before accepting a job, I would want to make sure that the company had a good program of employee benefits.	___	___
17. A company will not be successful unless it establishes a clear set of rules and regulations.	___	___
18. I would prefer to work in a department with a manager than to work on a team where managerial responsibility is shared.	___	___
19. You should respect people according to their rank.	___	___
20. Rules are meant to be broken.	___	___

Score: _____

Scoring and interpretation. Give yourself one point for each question you answered in the bureaucratic direction, then total your score.

1. Mostly agree
2. Mostly agree
3. Mostly disagree
4. Mostly agree
5. Mostly disagree
6. Mostly agree
7. Mostly agree
8. Mostly agree
9. Mostly disagree
10. Mostly agree
11. Mostly agree
12. Mostly disagree
13. Mostly disagree
14. Mostly agree
15. Mostly disagree
16. Mostly agree
17. Mostly agree
18. Mostly agree
19. Mostly agree
20. Mostly disagree

15–20 You would enjoy working in a bureaucracy.
8–14 You would experience a mixture of satisfactions and dissatisfactions if working in a bureaucracy
0–7 You would most likely be frustrated by working in a bureaucracy, especially a large one.

Source: Adapted and updated from Andrew J. DuBrin, *Human relations: A Job Oriented Approach*, 5th edition (Englewood Cliffs, NJ: Prentice Hall, 1991), pp. 434–435.

Many large bureaucratic organizations are successful and continue to grow at an impressive pace. Among the leading giants are Wal-Mart, Hewlett-Packard, Ford Motor Company, Intel, The Aetna, and Southwest Airlines.

Despite the contributions of bureaucracy, it has several key disadvantages. Above all, a bureaucracy can be rigid in handling people and problems. Its well-intended rules and regulations sometimes create inconvenience and inefficiency. For example, if several layers of approval are required to make a decision, the process takes a long time. Other frequent problems in the bureaucratic form of organization are frustration and low job satisfaction. The sources of these negative feelings include red tape, slow decision making, and an individual's limited influence on how well the organization performs.

An example of bureaucracy at its worst took place at the Ravenwood Hospital in Chicago, Illinois. The emergency room workers refused to treat a 15-year-old boy who lay bleeding to death in a nearby alley. He had been shot while playing basketball within steps of the hospital's entrance. The workers followed literally the hospital's policy of forbidding them from going outside of the emergency room to treat patients. A police officer commandeered a wheelchair and took the wounded boy inside the hospital, but it was too late.[2] (Here one might argue that the emergency room workers were at fault for ignoring common sense. A deeper analysis is that the workers were being passive-aggressive; they showed hostility by doing nothing.)

To relate yourself to the bureaucratic form of organization, take the self-quiz presented in Exhibit 9-2.

DEPARTMENTALIZATION

In bureaucratic and other forms of organization, the work is subdivided into departments, or other units, to prevent total confusion. Can you imagine an organization of 300,000 people, or even 300, in which all employees worked in one large department? The process of subdividing work into departments is called **departmentalization.**

This chapter will use charts to illustrate four frequently used forms of departmentalization: functional, territorial, product-service, and customer. In practice, most organization charts show a combination of the various types. Exhibit 9-3, which represents the major businesses of Eastman Kodak Company, illustrates organization, by customer and territory.

The most appropriate form of departmentalization is the one that provides the best chance of achieving the organization's objectives. The organization's environment is an important factor in this decision. Assume that a company needs to use radically different approaches to serve different customers. It would organize the firm according to the customer served. A typical arrangement of this nature is to have one department serve commercial accounts and another department serve the government.

Explain the major ways in which organizations are divided into departments.

departmentalization
The process of subdividing work into departments.

211

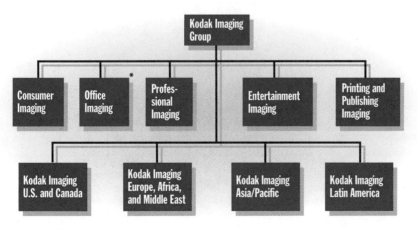

*Now a manufacturing unit for other companies.

EXHIBIT 9-3

Customer and Territorial Departmentalization
The row starting with Consumer Imaging represents organization by customer, whereas the row starting with Kodak Imaging U.S. and Canada represents organization by territory.

Functional Departmentalization

functional departmentalization
An arrangement in which departments are defined by the function each one performs, such as accounting or purchasing.

Functional departmentalization is an arrangement in which departments are defined by the function each one performs, such as accounting or purchasing. Dividing work according to activity is the traditional way of organizing the efforts of people. In a functional organization, each department carries out a specialized activity, such as information processing, purchasing, sales, accounting, or maintenance. Exhibit 9-4 illustrates an organization arranged on purely functional lines.

The advantages and disadvantages of the functional organization, the traditional form of organization, are the same as those of the bureaucracy. Functional departmentalization works particularly well when large batches of work have to be processed on a recurring basis and when the expertise of specialists is required.

Territorial Departmentalization

territorial departmentalization
An arrangement of departments according to the geographic area served.

Territorial departmentalization is an arrangement of departments according to the geographic area served. In this organization structure, all the activities for a firm in a given geographic area report to one manager. Marketing divisions often use territorial departmentalization; the sales force may be divided into the northeastern, southeastern, midwestern, northwestern, and southwestern regions. The bottom row of Exhibit 9-3 shows that territorial departmentalization has divided activities into four major geographic categories.

Given that territorial departmentalization divides an organization into geographic regions, it is generally well suited for international business. Yet a new global business trend is to develop a central structure that serves operations in various geographic locations. A case in point is Ford Motor Company. To economize, Ford has merged its manufacturing, sales, and product-development operations in North America, Europe, Latin America, and Asia.

A key advantage of territorial departmentalization is that it allows decision making at a local level, where the personnel are most familiar with the problems. Territorial departmentalization also has some potential disadvantages. The arrangement can be quite expensive because of duplication of costs and effort. For instance, each region may build service departments (such as for purchasing) that duplicate activities carried out at headquarters. A bigger problem is that top-level management may have difficulty controlling the performance of field units.

Functional Departmentalization
Observe that each box below the level of chief executive officer (CEO) indicates an executive in charge of a specific function or activity, such as being responsible for information systems.

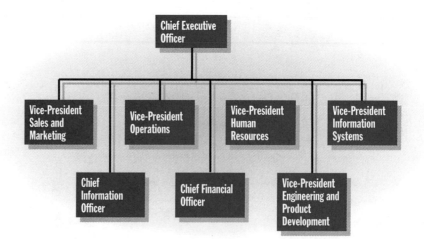

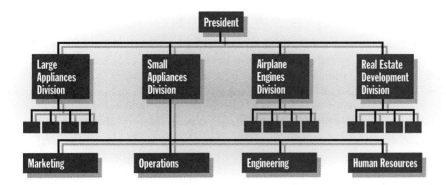

Product–Service Departmentalization
Notice that each division in a product–service form of organization is much like a company of its own. The small appliances division, for example, has key functions of its own: marketing, operations, engineering, and human resources.

Product–Service Departmentalization

Product–service departmentalization is the arrangement of departments according to the products or services they provide. When specific products or services are so important that the units that create and support them almost become independent companies, product departmentalization makes sense.

Exhibit 9-5 presents a version of product–service departmentalization. Notice that the organization depicted offers products and services with unique demands of their own. For example, the manufacture and sale of airplane engines is an entirely different business from the development of real estate.

Organizing by product line is beneficial because employees focus on a product or service, which allows each department the maximum opportunity to grow and prosper. Similar to territorial departmentalization, grouping by product or service helps train general managers, fosters high morale, and allows decisions to be made at the local level.

Departmentalization by product has the same potential problems as territorial departmentalization. It can be expensive, because of duplication of effort, and top-level management may find it difficult to control the separate units.

product–service departmentalization
The arrangement of departments according to the products or services they provide.

213

Customer Departmentalization

Customer departmentalization creates a structure based on customer needs. When the demands of one group of customers are quite different from the demands of another, customer departmentalization is often the result. Many insurance companies, for example, organize their efforts into consumer and commercial departments. Manufacturers of sophisticated equipment typically consist of different groups for processing government and commercial accounts. Customer departmentalization is similar to product departmentalization, and sometimes the distinction between these two forms of organization is blurry. For example, is a bank department that sells home mortgages catering to homeowners, offering a special service, or both?

The middle row in Exhibit 9-3 reflects customer departmentalization. Eastman Kodak manufactures equipment and supplies that differ according to customer group. For example, the company manufactures camera equipment and related film for its Consumer Imaging Group.

customer departmentalization
An organization structure based on customer needs.

MODIFICATIONS OF THE BUREAUCRATIC ORGANIZATION

Describe three modifications of the bureaucratic structure: the matrix structure; flat structures, downsizing, and outsourcing; and organization by process.

To overcome some of the problems of the bureaucratic and functional forms of organization, several other organization structures have been developed. Typically, these nonbureaucratic structures are used to supplement or modify the bureaucratic structure. Virtually all large organizations are a combination of bureaucratic and less bureaucratic forms. This section will describe three popular modifications of bureaucracy: the matrix organization; flat structures, downsizing, and outsourcing; and organization by process. The team structure described in Chapter 8 can also be considered a modification of the bureaucratic design.

The Matrix Organization

project organization
A temporary group of specialists working under one manager to accomplish a fixed objective.

matrix organization
A project structure superimposed on top of a functional structure.

214

Departmentalization tends to be poorly suited to performing special tasks that differ substantially from the normal activities of a firm. One widely used solution to this problem is **project organization,** in which a temporary group of specialists works under one manager to accomplish a fixed objective. The project organization is used most extensively in the military, aerospace, construction, motion-picture, and computer industries. Project management is so widespread that software has been developed to help managers plot out details and make all tasks visible.

The best-known application of project management is the **matrix organization,** a project structure imposed on top of a functional structure. Matrix organizations evolved to capitalize on the advantages of project and matrix structures while minimizing their disadvantages. The project groups act as minicompanies within the firm in which they operate. However, the group usually disbands when its mission is completed. In some instances, the project is so successful that it becomes a new and separate division of the company.

Exhibit 9-6 shows a popular version of the matrix structure. Notice that functional managers exert some functional authority over specialists assigned to the projects. For example, the quality manager would occasionally meet with the quality specialists assigned to the projects to discuss their professional activities. The project managers have line authority over the people assigned to their projects.

A distinguishing feature of the matrix is that the project managers borrow resources from the functional departments. Also, each person working on the project has two superiors: the project manager and the functional manager. For example, observe the quality analyst in the lower right corner of Exhibit 9-5. The analyst reports to the manager of quality three boxes above him or her *and* to the project manager for the personal digital assistant located five boxes to the left.

Users of the matrix structure include banks, insurance companies, aerospace companies, and educational institutions. Colleges often use matrix structures for setting up special-interest programs. Among them are African-American studies, adult education, and industrial training. Each of these programs is headed by a director who uses resources from traditional departments.

Flat Structures, Downsizing, and Outsourcing

Three closely-related approaches to simplifying an organization structure are creating flat structures, downsizing, and outsourcing. A major approach to making an organization less bureaucratic is to reduce its number of layers. Both down-

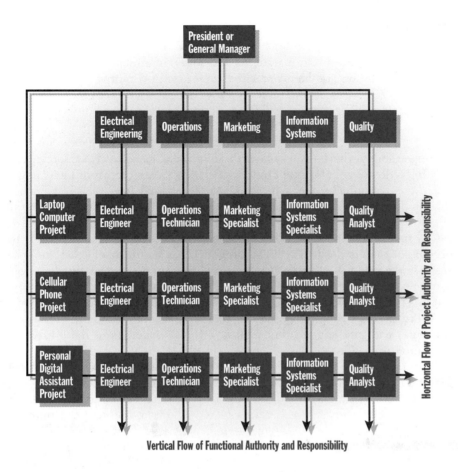

EXHIBIT 9-6

Matrix Organization Structure in an Electronics Company
Personnel assigned to a project all report to two managers: a project head and a functional manager.

215

sizing and outsourcing (contracting work to other firms) typically lead to a flat structure.

FLAT STRUCTURES   Organizations with a bureaucratic structure tend to accumulate many layers of management, and often too many employees in general. At times, too many staff groups are present to assist line groups. Top management may then decide to create a **flat organization structure,** a form of organization with relatively few layers. Most large business corporations have become flatter during the past decade. At one time GM had 22 layers of management, and now about 8 layers are typical within most units of the company. A flat organization structure is less bureaucratic for two reasons. First, few managers are available to review the decisions of other workers. Second, because the chain of command is shorter, people are less concerned about authority decisions. Managers and workers at lower levels can then make decisions more independently.

An important consequence of creating flat structures is that the remaining managers have a larger **span of control**—the number of workers reporting directly to a manager. An exception is when a large number of individual contributors are laid off along with the managers. A large span of control works best when the managers and group members are competent and efficient. When group members are doing relatively similar work, the manager can also supervise more people.

flat organization structure
A form of organization with relatively few layers of management, making it less bureaucratic.

span of control
The number of workers reporting directly to a manager.

DOWNSIZING   In Chapter 3 we analyzed downsizing as related to social responsibility. Downsizing can also be looked at as a way of simplifying an organization to make it less bureaucratic. Under ideal circumstances, downsizing also leads to better profits and higher stock prices. In fact, the motivation behind most downsizings of both assets and workers is to reduce costs, thereby increasing profits. The most striking example is GE. During an 11-year period the company reduced its work force by over 120,000 workers, while profits rose 228 percent and the price of GE stock reached all-time highs.[3] (From the standpoint of social responsibility, the human cost of these financial gains has been substantial.)

Unless downsizing is done carefully it can backfire in terms of increasing efficiency. A nationwide survey of 4,300 workers found that only 57 percent of those in downsizing companies indicated they were generally satisfied with their jobs. In contrast, 72 percent of workers in expanding firms were generally satisfied. A specific complaint about downsizing is that it creates job demands that surviving managers do not have the experience or skill to handle.[4] A more scientific study found that companies that downsized more by reducing headcount than physical assets experienced a decline in their return on assets from 14 percent to 11 percent. In comparison, employers that maintained stable employment levels had only a negligible decline in return on investment. Furthermore, the companies with the largest number of layoffs also experienced the greatest declines in return on assets.[5]

A starting point in effective restructuring is to *eliminate low-value and no-value activities*. This is called *activity-based reduction*—a new term for systematically comparing the costs of a firm's activities to their value to the customer. A starting point in searching for low-value activity is workers monitoring the output of others. *Keeping the future work requirements in mind* is another factor contributing to effective restructuring. The answer to overstaffing is not to let go of people who will be an important part of the firm's future. *Sensible criteria should be used to decide which workers to let go.* In general, the poorest performers should be released first. Offering early retirement and asking for voluntary resignations also leads to less disruption.

An important strategy for getting layoff survivors refocused on their jobs is for *management to share information with employees.* Information sharing helps quell rumors about further reductions in force. *Listening to employees* helps soften the shock of restructuring. Many survivors will need support groups and other sympathetic ears to express sorrow over the job loss suffered by coworkers. A final suggestion here is for management to *be honest with workers.* Managers should inform people ahead of time if layoffs are imminent or even a possibility. Workers should be told why layoffs are likely, who might be affected, and in what way. Employees will want to know how the restructuring will help strengthen the firm and facilitate growth.[6]

outsource
The practice of hiring an individual or another company outside the organization to perform work.

OUTSOURCING   An increasingly common practice among organizations of all types and sizes is to **outsource,** or have work performed for them by other organizations. By outsourcing, a company can reduce its need for employees and physical assets and reduce payroll costs. Many companies outsource work to geographic areas where workers are paid lower wages. Among the many examples of outsourcing would be for a small company to hire another company to manage its payroll and employee benefits, or for a large manufacturing firm to have certain components made by another firm. Even IBM is a contractor for other employers, such as making the hard drives for other computer manufacturers, or manag-

---

WANTED: The Best of the Best

The firm: Aerospace manufacturer Lockheed Martin Corp.'s Ft. Worth, Texas-based Aeronautics Material Management Center (AMMC).

The slice: Twenty-two percent to 28 percent of the company's contracting dollars go to small, disadvantaged, and women-owned businesses. Although actual dollars spent are increasing, fewer subcontractors are winning awards due to downsizing.

The criteria: To be a successful AMMC subcontractor, you must meet the industry's most stringent requirements, including a 98 percent on-time delivery schedule and zero percent production rejection over a 12-month period. For products and services that support the factory, think along the lines of quality and competitive pricing.

The hook: John Morrow, a procurement director for Lockheed's AMMC, describes the corporation as "an expensive operation to do business with." If a subcontractor can offer creative ideas that will save Lockheed time and money, procurement decision makers are sure to take notice. Some examples include warehousing or storing products for Lockheed, or offering one-stop shopping for products and services other than just your core function, thus eliminating Lockheed's need for additional vendors.

The spin: "Don't give up easily and keep knocking on our door," says Morrow. "If there's an opportunity that's compelling, we'll recognize it and allow a subcontractor to bid."

The connection: What makes your product or service superior to the competition's? Determine that, and you're ready to approach one of the company's five nationwide procurement agencies, each of which has a small-business office. Contact Lockheed's Jim Randle at (817) 762-1603 or Jim.W.Randle@lmco.com.

Source: Reprinted from Lockheed Martin Corp. and *Entrepreneur*, August 1998, p. 120. Reprinted with permission.

---

ing their computer systems. The outsourcing movement has been a boon for small- and medium-size firms who perform stable work for larger organizations.

Outsourcing activity in the United States is estimated to be $141 billion annually.[7] Despite this high volume of business, many companies are dissatisfied with the results of outsourcing. A survey of 200 CEOs and other top executives revealed the following satisfaction with five areas of outsourcing: legal, 70 percent; tax, 62 percent; human resources, 43 percent; finance/accounting, 39 percent; and information technology, 33 percent.[8] A possible reason for moderate satisfaction with outsourcing is that large companies establish such demanding standards on their suppliers and subcontractors. Large companies often outsource work to a small, select number of companies. Exhibit 9-7 will give you some insight into the challenge of receiving an outsourcing contract from a large company. Note that not every company doing work for another company is actually a *subcontractor*. To receive a subcontract means you are working on a portion of a large contract received by a bigger company.

Organization by Process Instead of Task

In the bureaucratic form of organization, people in the various organization units are assigned specialized tasks such as purchasing, manufacturing, selling, and shipping. Another approach to organization structure is for a group of people to concern themselves with a process, such as filling an order or developing a new product. Instead of focusing on a specialized task, all team members focus on achieving the purpose of all the activity, such as getting a product in the hands of a customer. In a process organization, employees take collective responsibility for customers.[9]

One approach to switching from a task emphasis to a process emphasis is through **reengineering,** the radical redesign of work to achieve substantial improvements in performance. Reengineering searches for the most efficient way to perform a large task. The emphasis is on uncovering wasted steps, such as people handing off documents to one another to obtain their approval. Exhibit 9-8 presents a process map that traces the path of a task through a company in order to uncover possible inefficiencies.

As a result of reengineering, work is organized horizontally rather than vertically. The people in charge of the process function as team leaders who guide the team toward completion of a core process such as new product development or filling a complicated order. Key performance objectives for the team would include "reduce cycle time," "reduce costs," and "reduce throughput time."

A major challenge in creating a horizontal organization is breaking the functional mind-set. Workers have a natural tendency to think about performing their specialty that interferes with thinking about collaborating with others and having collective responsibility.[10] Nevertheless, many organizations have achieved success with teams that focus on delivering a product to the customer. Digital photography equipment developed by Hewlett-Packard has resulted from horizontally focused teams. A typical team leader statement is, "Our purpose is to deliver a computerized home photography system that will enable our ultimate customers to send superior holiday cards with photos to family and friends."

A major hazard with reengineering to form horizontal structures is that many people will lose their jobs. As a result, the work force is demoralized and suspicious, which results in the same high failure rate of downsizing.[11] If horizontal structures increase productivity without creating layoffs, the result is more likely to be beneficial to the organization.

All organization structures described so far in this chapter are influenced by information technology. Workers from various units throughout an organization

reengineering
The radical redesign of work to achieve substantial improvements in performance.

A Process Map
Observe that the arrows passing through the various departments could suggest that too many people are getting involved in filling the order. Observe also that the bottom portion of the organization chart going from customer request to order fulfillment represents a horizontal organization.

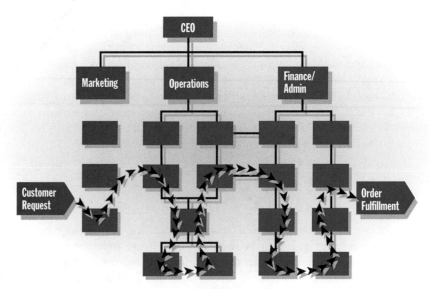

Source: Raymond L. Manganelli and Mark M. Klein, "A Framework for Reengineering," *Management Review*, June 1994, p. 12. Reprinted with permission of the American Management Association.

can solve problems together through information networks without being concerned with "who reports to whom," as indicated by organization charts. Also, entry-level workers can leapfrog layers of management and communicate directly with senior executives through e-mail.

DELEGATION, EMPOWERMENT, AND DECENTRALIZATION

Specify how delegation, empowerment, and decentralization spread authority in an organization.

Collective effort would not be possible, and organizations could not grow and prosper, if a handful of managers did all the work themselves. In recognition of this fact, managers divide up their work. The division can be in one of two directions. Subdividing work in a horizontal direction, through the process of departmentalization, has already been described. The section that follows will discuss subdivision of work in the vertical direction, using the chain of command through delegation and empowerment, and decentralization.

D e l e g a t i o n   o f   R e s p o n s i b i l i t y

Delegation is an old concept that has been revitalized in the modern organization. It refers to assigning formal authority and responsibility for accomplishing a specific task to another person. If managers do not delegate any of their work, they are acting as individual contributors—not true managers. Delegation is closely tied with **empowerment,** the process by which managers share power with group members, thereby enhancing employees' feelings of personal effectiveness. Delegation is a specific way of empowering employees, thereby increasing motivation.

A major goal of delegation is the transfer of responsibility as a means of increasing one's own productivity. At the same time, delegation allows team members to learn how to handle more responsibility and to become more productive. In downsized organizations, delegation is essential because of the increased workload of managers. As managers are required to assume more responsibility, they must find ways to delegate more work. This feat requires imagination, because in a downsized firm support staff has usually been trimmed as well.

A major point about delegation is that, although a manager may hold a group member responsible for a task, the manager has final accountability. (To be accountable is to accept credit or blame for results.) If the group member fails miserably, the manager must accept the final blame. It is the manager who chose the person who failed. As noted in an executive newsletter, "Nothing makes a worse impression than the whining manager who blames a staffer for mishandling a task."[12]

Delegation and empowerment lie at the heart of effective management. Following the eight suggestions presented next improves the manager's chance of increasing productivity by delegating to and empowering individuals and teams.[13] (Note that teams as well as individuals can be the unit of delegation and powersharing, such as asking a team to find a way of filling orders more rapidly.)

1. *Assign duties to the right people.* The chances for effective delegation and empowerment improve when capable, responsible, well-motivated group members receive the delegated tasks. Vital tasks should not be assigned to ineffective performers.
2. *Delegate the whole task.* In the spirit of job enrichment, a manager should delegate an entire task to one subordinate rather than dividing it among several. So doing gives the group member complete responsibility and enhances motivation, and gives the manager more control over results.

delegation
Assigning formal authority and responsibility for accomplishing a specific task to another person.

empowerment
The process by which managers share power with group members, thereby enhancing employees' feelings of personal effectiveness.

219

3. *Give as much instruction as needed.* Some group members will require highly detailed instructions, while others can operate effectively with general instructions. Many delegation and empowerment failures occur because instruction was insufficient. *Dumping* is the negative term given to the process of dropping a task on a group member without instructions.

4. *Retain some important tasks for yourself.* Managers need to retain some high-output or sensitive tasks for themselves. In general, the manager should handle any task that involves the survival of the unit. However, which tasks the manager should retain always depend on the circumstances.

5. *Obtain feedback on the delegated task.* A responsible manager does not delegate a complex assignment to a subordinate, then wait until the assignment is complete before discussing it again. Managers must establish checkpoints and milestones to obtain feedback on progress.

6. *Delegate both pleasant and unpleasant tasks to group members.* When group members are assigned a mixture of pleasant and unpleasant responsibilities, they are more likely to believe they are being treated fairly. Few group members expect the manager to handle all the undesirable jobs. A related approach is to rotate undesirable tasks among group members.

7. *Step back from the details.* Many managers are poor delegators because they get too involved with technical details. If a manager cannot let go of details, he or she will never be effective at delegation or empowerment.

8. *Allow for spending money and using other resources.* To share power is to permit others to spend money. People who have no budget of their own to control do not have much power. Having a budget, for even such small matters as ordering in dinner for an evening meeting, gives team members a feeling of power. Access to other resources, such as use of advanced information technology equipment and office temporaries, is another meaningful sign of empowerment.[14]

Decentralization

decentralization
The extent to which authority is passed down to lower levels in an organization.

centralization
The extent to which authority is retained at the top of the organization.

Decentralization is the extent to which authority is passed down to lower levels in an organization. It comes about as a consequence of managers delegating work to lower levels. **Centralization** is the extent to which authority is retained at the top of the organization. In a completely centralized organization, one chief executive would retain all the formal authority. Complete centralization can exist only in a one-person firm. Decentralization and centralization are, therefore, two ends of a continuum. No firm is completely centralized or decentralized.

The term *decentralization* generally refers to the decentralization of authority. However, the term also refers to decentralization by geography. A multidivision firm departmentalized on the basis of territory has a flat organization structure. A flat organization is often referred to as decentralized, but the reference is to geography, not authority. Unless so noted, this text uses the term *decentralization* in reference to authority.

How much control top management wants to retain is the major factor in deciding on how much to decentralize an organization. Organizations favor decentralization when a large number of decisions must be made at lower organizational levels, often based on responding to customer needs. GE favors decentralization in part because the company is really a collection of different businesses, many with vastly different customer requirements. Division management is much more aware of these needs than are people at company headquarters.

In general, a centralized firm exercises more control over organization units than a decentralized firm. Top management that wants to empower people through such means as teams and horizontal structures must emphasize decentralization.

Another important point is that many firms are centralized and decentralized simultaneously. Certain aspects of their operations are centralized, whereas others are decentralized. Fast-food franchise restaurants such as McDonald's, Long John Silver's, and Wendy's illustrate this trend. Central headquarters exercises tight control over such matters as menu selection, food quality, and advertising. Individual franchise operators, however, make human resource decisions on their own.

ORGANIZATIONAL CULTURE

Identify major aspects of organizational culture, including its management and control.

organizational culture (or corporate culture)
The system of shared values and beliefs that actively influence the behavior of organization members.

Organization structure has sometimes been referred to as the "hard side" of understanding how a firm operates. However, each firm has a "soft side" as well; an understanding of this aspect of an organization contributes to an understanding of how the organization operates. **Organizational culture (or corporate culture)** is the system of shared values and beliefs that actively influence the behavior of organization members. The term *shared* is important because it implies that many people are guided by the same values and that they interpret them in the same way. Values develop over time and reflect a firm's history and traditions. Culture consists of the customs of a firm, such as being helpful and supportive toward new employees and customers.

This section describes significant aspects of organizational culture: its dimensions, consequences, organizational learning, and its management and control. To obtain a quick overview of what a culture can mean to an organization, see the accompanying Management In Action.

Dimensions of Organizational Culture

The dimensions of organizational culture help explain the subtle forces that influence employee actions. Recognize that large units within an organization may have a different culture. For example, the culture of a company's lumber mill may be quite different than the culture of its marketing department. Five dimensions are of major significance in influencing organizational culture.[15]

1. *Values.* Values are the foundation of any organizational culture. The organization's philosophy is expressed through values, and values guide behavior on a day-to-day basis. Representative values of a firm might include concern for employee welfare, a belief that the customer is always right, a commitment to quality, or a desire to please stakeholders.
2. *Relative diversity.* The existence of an organizational culture assumes some degree of homogeneity. Nevertheless, organizations differ in terms of how much deviation can be tolerated. Many firms are highly homogeneous; executives talk in a similar manner and even look alike. Furthermore, people from similar educational backgrounds and fields of specialty are promoted into key jobs. The diversity of a culture also reflects itself in the dress code. Some organizations insist on uniformity of dress, such as wearing a jacket and tie (for men) when interacting with customers or clients. Strongly encouraging all workers to conform to dress-down Fridays is also part of discouraging diversity.

221

Manager *in Action*

The Team Culture at Fuji Town, USA

Greenwood, South Carolina, is home to the U.S. manufacturing arm of Fuji Photo Film Co. Ltd. In Greenwood, Fuji makes videotape, printing-press plates, photographic paper, single-use cameras, and 35 mm color print film. From its secret beginnings in the mid-1980s, Fuji has invested more than $1 billion in factories in Greenwood. Their 500 acres were once home to a cotton plantation and a chicken farm.

At Greenwood, Fuji has an inexpensive and business-friendly climate, factories automated with the latest technology, and a work force that's well-trained and lean. Only three secretaries are found among the 1,200 workers here. "People look at this facility and think we should have 5,000 people working here," says Craig White, a Fuji vice-president. "Fuji is a manufacturing company. Manufacturing is what we do, so most of our resources are employed in that manner. It's a lean organization by design." Fuji's U.S. manufacturing site has helped the company achieve important business goals, including the following:

- Fuji's photographic paper factory added so much industry capacity that industry prices were driven down to commodity levels.
- The single-use camera plant, which pumps out 60,000 of the recyclable QuickSnap cameras a day, has allowed Fuji to build meaningful market share in a fast-growing and highly profitable niche.
- The new film-coating operation has enabled Fuji to maintain low costs for film sold in the U.S. market, helping the company to compete against the number-one filmmaker, Eastman Kodak Company.

At the core of Fuji's successes is an egalitarian team-based culture that allows the company to capitalize on many of the opportunities that come its way. As a manufacturing technician put it, "This is a team plant, and we all take pride in our work."

When Fuji began operations in South Carolina it had the opportunity to build a culture from scratch. Some of the ingredients Fuji used are subtle. All the employees are titled "associates." Executives don't get such perks as reserved parking spaces. On days when meetings keep him out of the office until late morning, Fuji Photo Film president Hirokuni "Harry" Watanabe knows he will face a long stroll from the parking lot to the office. And everyone, from Watanabe and White on down, has to wear a khaki uniform jacket. The jacket was requested and designed by the workers after some of the associates in South Carolina were impressed with the ones worn by their counterparts in Japan. Managers even have to key their own memos and schedule their own meetings.

Whenever Fuji opens a new factory in Greenwood, it sends a contingent of workers to Japan for three months to learn Fuji techniques and the corporate culture. Typically, 20 percent to 25 percent of the work force is sent.

Although the QuickSnap factory is said to employ 100 people, it is so automated that fewer than a dozen people are visible at any one time. Robotic arms install components while the film is loaded and spooled into the camera body inside a mini-darkroom that is right on the assembly line.

Fuji managers, and outside observers such as business professors following the film industry, agree on a key observation. The combination of lean manufacturing and a team culture will help Fuji perform well in the highly competitive film industry.

Source: Adapted and excerpted from William Patalon III, "Fuji's Billion-Dollar Southern Gambit Raises the Stakes for Kodak," Rochester, New York, *Democrat and Chronicle*, November 30, 1997, pp. 1E, 8E. To learn more about Fuji, visit www.fujifilm.com.

3. *Resource allocation and rewards.* The allocation of money and other resources has a critical influence on culture. The investment of resources sends a message to people about what is valued in the firm. If a customer-service department is fully staffed and nicely furnished, employees and customers can assume that customer service is important to the company.

4. *Degree of change.* A fast-paced, dynamic organization has a culture different from that of a slow-paced, stable one. Top-level managers, by the energy or lethargy of their stance, send messages about how much they welcome innovation.

5. *Strength of the culture.* The strength of a culture, or how much influence it exerts, is partially a by-product of the other dimensions. A strong culture guides employees in many everyday actions. It determines, for example, whether an employee will inconvenience himself or herself to satisfy a customer. If the culture is not so strong, employees are more likely to follow their own whims—they may decide to please customers only when convenient.

Members of an organization are often unaware of the dimensions of their culture, despite being influenced by the culture. Sometimes a visitor is best able to observe a dimension of culture and how it controls behavior. A consultant told one CEO that "strong differentiation between executives and other workers" was a notable characteristic of the firm. The CEO denied the characterization until the consultant pointed out that managers at the rank of vice-president and above always kept their jackets on. Also, lower-ranking employees addressed them by their last name. Lower-ranking managers usually removed their jackets, and were addressed by their first name by most workers.

The dimensions presented above represent a formal and systematic way of understanding organizational culture. In practice, people use more glib expressions in describing culture, as illustrated in Exhibit 9-9.

Company employees and industry analysts typically describe an organization's culture in several words. A sampling of these descriptions follow:

Amazon.com   Loose and easy, exemplified by a very liberal dress and appearance code. (Body piercing is welcome.) A customer service director tells the temporary employment agencies, "Send us your freaks."

Exxon/Mobil   Exxon half is reserved, stuffy, buttoned-down, focused on the numbers, controlled, and disciplined. Mobil half is feisty, aggressive, risk taking.

Daimler/Chrysler   Daimler half is analytical, methodical, disciplined, buttoned-down, engineering-driven bureaucracy with conservative styling. Chrysler half is more impulsive and intuitive, focusing on speedy product development and flashy design.

IBM (particularly in marketing and engineering)   Controlling, powerful, smug, and still hierarchical despite mammoth efforts by chairman Louis Gerstner to make IBM more egalitarian and less traditional and conservative. IBM now encourages employees to wear a wide range of clothing to the office.

Microsoft   Adventuresome, creative, worships intelligence, smug, feelings of superiority, and commitment to control its industry. Emphasizes problem-solving ability and creativity much more than rank in decision making.

Southwest Airlines   Preoccupied with customer satisfaction, job satisfaction, and laughter on company time, but intolerant of negative attitudes toward work or customers.

Sources: Several of the above ideas are from "The First Global Car Colossus," *Business Week*, May 18, 1998, p. 42; "amazon.com: The Wild World of E-Commerce," *Business Week*, December 14, 1998, p. 110.

EXHIBIT 9-9

Brief Descriptions of Selected Organizational Cultures

Consequences and Implications of Organizational Culture

Organizational culture has received much attention because it has a pervasive impact on organizational effectiveness. Exhibit 9-10 outlines several key consequences and implications of organizational culture.

A major benefit of the right organization culture is that it can *enhance productivity, quality, and morale.* A culture that emphasizes productivity and quality encourages workers to be more productive and quality conscious. Joseph Clayton, the CEO of Frontier Corp. wanted to improve productivity in an organization that was once a telephone monopoly. To achieve his goal he worked successfully to shift Frontier from its century-old utility mind-set to a quick-footed company in the telecommunications industry. For an increasing number of employees the right organization culture is one that focuses on building relationships rather than emphasizing command and control. Building relationships leads to higher morale.

Developing a *competitive advantage* is a consequence of having a culture that favors high productivity, quality, and morale. A competitive advantage also stems from having a "cool culture" that attracts modern, creative workers. Southwest Airlines, with its emphasis on fun and funky behavior, attracts an enormous number of talented people wanting to join the fun and success.[16] A unique culture is important because it prevents other firms from becoming directly competitive. One of the many factors shaping the success of Microsoft, the software giant, is the extraordinary commitment of its professional and technical staffs. A culture like Microsoft is difficult to imitate because it developed over such a long period of time. The legal battles about Microsoft abusing its power, however, suggest that being too competitive can lead to unethical and illegal business practices.

Corporate culture has an enormous influence on the *compatibility of mergers and acquisitions.* As the DaimlerChrysler story presented at the beginning of this chapter suggests, whether the merger is a success depends on an effective blending of the two corporate cultures. The major reason for failed mergers is incompatibility between the cultures of the merged firms.[17] As explained by executive recruiter Dennis Carey, "The reason most mergers fail has nothing to do with the fact that the strategy didn't make sense, or that the economics didn't make sense. It has everything in almost all cases to do with the integration of people and cultures into a new combined entity."[18]

Another important consequence of corporate culture is that it *directs the activities of an organization's leaders.* Much of an executive's time is spent working with the subtle forces that shape the values of organization members. Of significance, many chief executive officers regard shaping the culture as their most important responsibility. Leaders are also influenced by the existing culture of a firm. It is part of their role to perpetuate a constructive culture.

EXHIBIT 9-10

Consequences and Implications of Organizational Culture Although organizational culture is an abstraction rather than a tangible object, the culture has enormous consequences that influence the success of a firm.

Organizational Culture → Productivity, Quality, and Morale
→ Competitive Advantage
→ Compatibility of Mergers and Acquisitions
→ Direction of Leadership Activity

Organizational Learning and Culture

An important new way of understanding organizations and their cultures is to examine how well they learn. An effective organization engages in continuous learning by proactively adapting to the external environment. In the process, the organization profits from its experiences. Instead of repeating the same old mistakes, the organization *learns*. A **learning organization** is one that is skilled at creating, acquiring, and transferring knowledge. It also modifies its behavior to reflect new knowledge and insights.[19] Although organizational theorists speak of a learning *organization*, it is still the workers who do the learning.

An important indicator of the importance of organization learning is that many large firms have created the position of *chief learning officer* or *chief knowledge officer* (CKO). Behind the rise of these positions is the growing realization that the key to business success is no longer based heavily on physical assets, but on intellectual assets as well. An often-expressed opinion is that intellectual capital (the sum of ideas that give an organization a competitive edge) is the most decisive form of organization wealth. An example of intellectual capital is a pharmaceutical firm's knowledge about which type of consumers are actually using their pills.

Key tasks for most knowledge officers involve collecting knowledge from throughout the company, often using software such as Lotus Notes and an intranet. In addition, the CKO provides external knowledge and research, and makes certain that knowledge is spread as widely as possible throughout the organization. In most organizations there are many people with useful knowledge, such as how to solve a particular problem. Yet other workers who need the information do not know who possesses it.[20] Systematizing such knowledge has been referred to as developing corporate yellow pages.

Going beyond the specialized work of the chief knowledge officer in a learning organization, part of a manager's job is to turn individualized knowledge into shared knowledge. Firms that fail to do this lose the knowledge of workers who leave. Shared knowledge can be retained, such as knowing who the real decision makers are at a particular customer. In a learning organization, considerable learning takes place in teams as the members share expertise. Another key characteristic of a learning organization is that people are taught to realize that whatever they do in their job can have an effect on the organizational system. For example, a manufacturing worker who finds a way to reduce costs can help the sales department win a large order by selling at a lower price.

Organizational learning is related to culture, because the culture must support learning for it to take place. An emphasis on learning gradually becomes part of the organizational culture. The concept of the learning organization has gained considerable momentum in recent years, as organizations have become increasingly dependent on useful knowledge to stay competitive.

learning organization
An organization that is skilled at creating, acquiring, and transferring knowledge.

225

Managing and Controlling the Culture

A major responsibility of top management is to shape, manage, and control the organizational culture. After a new CEO is appointed, the person typically makes a public statement to the effect: "My number-one job is to change the culture." The executive would then have to use his or her best leadership skills to inspire and persuade others toward forming a new culture. Many executives, for example, attempt to move the culture in the direction of higher creativity and risk taking.

Another general way of changing an organization's culture is to undergo organization development, a set of specialized techniques for transforming an organization. Among these techniques would be conducting surveys about the need for change, and then involving many people in making the desirable changes. In addition to working with an organization development consultant to bring about cultural change, a manager might do the following:

- Serve as a role model for the desired attitudes and behaviors. Leaders must behave in ways that are consistent with the values and practices they wish to see imitated throughout the organization. Deere & Co. is going through a major cultural change in which customer needs are satisfied through mass customization. For a strongly traditional company to undergo such change, considerable new training is necessary. Top management at Deere both set up teams for training and participate in the training sessions themselves.[21]

- Educate from the top down. At Axicom Corp., a manufacturer of data products, Charles D. Morgan, the company leader (the company has no executive titles) sat down with his direct reports to begin an education process that eventually cascaded down to the business units and teams. When Axicom eliminated all executive titles, Morgan had to deal with some senior vice-presidents who liked having titles.[22]

- Establish a reward system that reinforces the culture, such as giving huge suggestion awards to promote an innovative culture.

- Select candidates for positions at all levels whose values mesh with the values of the desired culture. At Sony Corporation all new-hires must demonstrate that they care about quality (such as having produced something of quality as a hobby) in order to be hired.

- Sponsoring new training and development programs that support the desired cultural values. Among many examples, top management at Levi Strauss wants to support a culture favoring diversity. Training programs in valuing differences therefore receive high levels of encouragement from Levi Strauss executives.

MANAGING CHANGE

Describe key aspects of managing change including gaining support for change.

"The only constant is change" is a cliché frequently repeated in the workplace. To meet their objectives, managers must manage change effectively on an almost daily basis. Change in the workplace can relate to any factor with an impact on people, including changes in technology, organization structure, competition, human resources, and budgets. The following description of managing change has four components: changes at the individual versus organizational level; a model of the change process; why people resist change; and how to gain support for change. Knowledge of all four components is helpful in managing change that affects oneself or others.

Creating Change at the Individual Versus Organizational Level

Many useful changes in organizations take place at the individual and small group level, rather than at the organizational level. Quite often individual contributors, middle-level managers, team leaders, and individual contributors identify a small need for change and make it happen. One example is the division head at Sears who decided that tools with pink handles were not attractive to the modern woman. As a result the manager discontinued pink handles on tools for women, and sales to women surged.

A study on effective change brought about by individuals was conducted with more than 100 people in a variety of organizations. Each person was identified as a "mover and shaker," someone who brought about constructive change. An example of a constructive change was modifying a software product so as to open new markets. A common characteristic of these people who brought about change was a greater focus on results than on trying not to offend anyone. At the same time they were more concerned about exerting individual initiative than blending into the group.[23]

Change at the organizational level receives much more attention that the small, incremental changes brought about by individuals. Two of these major changes have already been described: the change to quality management (Chapter 4), and changing the organizational culture. Chapter 11 will describe transformational leadership, which is aimed at making far-reaching constructive change. Change at the organizational level can be regarded as change in the fundamental way in which the company operates, such as moving from a government-regulated utility to a competitive organization. A current analysis suggests that for total organizational change to take place, every employee must be able and eager to rise to the challenge of change. Organizational change requires getting individuals at every level involved—such as the thousands of Sears employees helping to bring about the new image (the softer side) of Sears.[24]

The Unfreezing—Changing— Refreezing Model of Change

Psychologist Kurt Lewin developed a three-step analysis of the change process.[25] His unfreezing–changing–refreezing model is widely used by managers to help bring about constructive change. Many other approaches to initiating change stem from this simple model, which is illustrated in Exhibit 9-11. *Unfreezing* involves reducing or eliminating resistance to change. As long as employees oppose a change, it will not be implemented effectively. To accept change, employees must first deal with and resolve their feelings about letting go of the old. Only after people have dealt effectively with endings are they ready to make transitions.

Changing or moving on to a new level usually involves considerable two-way communication, including group discussion. According to Lewin, "Rather than a one-way flow of commands or recommendations, the person implementing the change should make suggestions. The changee should be encouraged to contribute and participate." Refreezing includes pointing out the success of the change and looking for ways to reward people involved in implementing the change.

227

EXHIBIT 9-11

The Change Process
To bring about change, you have to break old habits, create new ones, and solidify the new habits.

Why People Resist Change

Before a company's managers can gain support for change, they must understand why people resist change. People resist change for reasons they think are important, the most common being the fear of an unfavorable outcome, such as less money or personal inconvenience. People also resist change for such varied reasons as not wanting to disrupt social relationships and not wanting to break well-established habits. Change may also be unwelcome because it upsets the balance of an activity,[26] such as the old system of visiting customers in person instead of the new system of strictly electronic communication.

Even when people do not view a change as potentially damaging, they may sometimes cling to a system they dislike rather than change. According to folk wisdom, "People would rather deal with the devil they know." Workers may also resist change because they are aware of weaknesses in the proposed changes that may have been overlooked or disregarded by management.

> A sales manager resisted her company's proposal to shift a key product to dealer distribution. She explained that dealers would give so little attention to the product that sales would plunge. Despite her protests, the firm shifted to dealer distribution. Sales of the product did plunge, and the company returned to selling through sales representatives.

Gaining Support for Change

Gaining support for change, and therefore overcoming resistance, is an important managerial responsibility. Let us look at seven techniques for gaining support for change.

1. *Invest time in planning the change.* A hard-hitting change strategy is to invest time in planning a change before implementation begins. If possible, the people to be involved in the change should help in the planning. A change consultant advises, "One of the biggest mistakes American organizations make is that they do not take the time required to develop a comprehensive change plan and to get buy-in from the people who will be affected by the change."[27]

2. *Allow for discussion and negotiation.* Support for change can be increased by discussing and negotiating the more sensitive aspects of the change. It is important to acknowledge the potential hardships associated with the change, such as longer working hours or higher output to earn the same compensation. The two-way communication incorporated into the discussion helps reduce some employee concerns. Discussion often leads to negotiation, which further involves employees in the change process.

3. *Allow for participation.* The best-documented way of overcoming resistance to change is to allow people to participate in the changes that will affect them. An application of this concept is allowing employees to set their own rules to increase compliance. A powerful participation technique is to encourage people who already favor the change to help in planning and implementation. These active supporters of the change will be even more strongly motivated to enlist the support of others.

4. *Point out the financial benefits.* Given that so many employees are concerned about the financial effects of work changes, it is helpful to discuss these effects openly. If employees will earn more money as a result of the change,

this fact can be used as a selling point. For example, a company owner told his employees, "I know you are inconvenienced and upset because we have cut way back on secretarial support. But some of the savings will be invested in bigger bonuses for you." Much of the grumbling subsided.

5. *Avoid change overload.* Too much change too soon leads to negative stress. So it is helpful to avoid overloading employees with too many sweeping changes in a brief period of time. Too much simultaneous change also causes confusion, and it leads to foot dragging about the workplace innovation. The more far-reaching the innovation, such as restructuring a firm, the greater the reason for not attempting other innovations simultaneously.

6. *Gain political support for change.* Few changes get through organizations without the change agent's forming alliances with people who will support his or her proposals. Often this means selling the proposed changes to members of top-level management before proceeding down the hierarchy. It is much more difficult to create change from the bottom up.

7. *Ask effective questions to involve workers in the change.* An *effective question* aims to move people toward a goal or objective instead of dwelling on what might have gone wrong. The effective question focuses on what is right rather than wrong, thereby offering encouragement. As in active listening, effective questions are open-ended. They also ask *what* or *how* rather than *why*, thereby decreasing defensiveness. (E.g., "How is the software installation coming along?" rather than "Why hasn't the new software been installed?") Effective questions are also you-oriented; they focus on the person who is supposed to implement the change. Two examples of effective questions are:

"How would you describe your progress so far?"

"What kind of support do you need to ensure your success?"[28]

8. *Build strong working relationships.* The better the working relationship with workers, the less the resistance.[29] Among the many factors in a good working relationship are trust and mutual respect. Building strong working relationships is also effective because it helps reduce fear about the changes in process. For example, workers might ordinarily fear that a new system of performance evaluation will result in smaller salary increases. With a good working relationship with management, this fear may be reduced somewhat.

229

SUMMARY OF KEY POINTS

 Describe the bureaucratic form of organization and discuss its advantages and disadvantages.

The most widely used form of organization is the bureaucracy, a multilevel organization in which authority flows downward and rules are regulations are carefully specified. Bureaucracies can be highly efficient organizations that are well suited to handling repetitive, recurring tasks. However, they may be rigid in terms of rule interpretation, and they may result in decision-making delays.

 Explain the major ways in which organizations are divided into departments.

The usual way of subdividing effort in organizations, particularly in bureaucracies, is to create departments. Four common types of departmentalization are functional, territorial, product–service, and customer.

 Describe three modifications of the bureaucratic structure: the matrix structure; flat structures, downsizing, and outsourcing; and organization by process.

The matrix organization consists of a project structure superimposed on a functional structure. Personnel assigned to the projects within the matrix report to a project manager, yet they report to a functional manager also. Flat organizations have fewer layers than traditional hierarchies, and are often the result of downsizings. They are created for such purposes as reducing personnel costs and speeding up decision making. Downsizing can also be looked upon as a way of simplifying an organization to make it less bureaucratic. Unless downsizing is done carefully, it can backfire in terms of increasing efficiency. By outsourcing, a company can reduce its need for employees and physical assets, and reduce payroll costs.

Another approach to organization structure is for a group of people to concern themselves with a process, such as filling an order or development a new product. Team members focus on their purpose rather than their specialty, and take collective responsibility for customers. Switching from a task to a process emphasis can often be done through reengineering.

 Specify how delegation, empowerment, and decentralization spread authority in an organization.

Delegation is assigning formal authority and responsibility for accomplishing a task to another person. Delegation fosters empowerment. The manager remains accountable for the results of subordinates. Effective delegation includes assigning duties to the right people and obtaining feedback on the delegated task. Decentralization stems from delegation. It is the extent to which authority is passed down to lower levels in an organization. Decentralization sometimes refers to geographic dispersion.

 Identify major aspects of organizational culture, including its management and control.

The five key dimensions of organizational culture are values, relative diversity, resource allocation and rewards, degree of change, and the strength of the culture. Culture has important consequences and implications on productivity, quality, and morale. How well an organization learns (or profits from its experiences) is also part of its culture. Top management is responsible for shaping, managing, and controlling culture. Although culture is slow to change, the manager can lead the firm through organization development. The manager can also act as a role model and reward behaviors that fit the desired cultural values.

 Describe key aspects of managing change, including gaining support for change.

Change can take place at the individual and small group levels as well as the organizational level. A model of change suggests that the process has three stages: unfreezing attitudes, followed by attitude change, then refreezing to point to the success of the change. People resist change for reasons they think are important, the most common being the fear of an unfavorable outcome.

Eight techniques for gaining support for change are as follows: invest time in planning the change; allow for discussion and negotiation; allow for participation; point out the financial benefits; avoid change overload; gain political support for change; ask effective questions to involve workers in the change; and build strong working relationships.

KEY TERMS AND PHRASES

Organization structure, *208*

Bureaucracy, *208*

Unity of command, *208*

Departmentalization, *211*

Functional departmentalization, *212*

Territorial departmentalization, *212*

Product–service
  departmentalization, *213*

Customer departmentalization, *213*

Project organization, *214*

Matrix organization, *214*

Flat organization structure, *215*

Span of control, *215*

Outsource, *216*

Reengineering, *218*

Delegation, *219*

Empowerment, *219*

Decentralization, *220*

Centralization, *220*

Organizational culture
  (or corporate culture), *221*

Learning organization, *225*

QUESTIONS

1. Why do some people particularly enjoy working in a bureaucracy?

2. Small and medium-size companies are often eager to hire people with about five years experience working in a large, bureaucratic firm like AT&T. What might be the reason behind the demand for these workers with experience in a bureaucracy?

3. What is the basis for departmentalization in most department stores?

4. Visualize your favorite (or least disliked) worldwide fran-

chise restaurant such as Pizza Hut or Burger King. In what ways is this restaurant centralized? In what ways is it decentralized?

5. What can first- and middle-level managers, as well as team leaders, do about shaping the culture of a firm?

6. In what way might the geographic location for Fuji (a rural southern town) have made it easy for Fuji to establish a team culture in their U.S. manufacturing plants?

7. How can a manager tell whether an employee is resisting change?

SKILL-BUILDING EXERCISE 9-A: Designing a Flat Organization

You and your teammates are assigned the task of creating a flatter structure for the organization depicted in Exhibit 9-12. Draw a new organization chart, with each box carefully labeled. Explain what happens to any managers who might be downsized and why your new structure is an improvement.

EXHIBIT 9-12

Company Organization Chart Before Downsizing

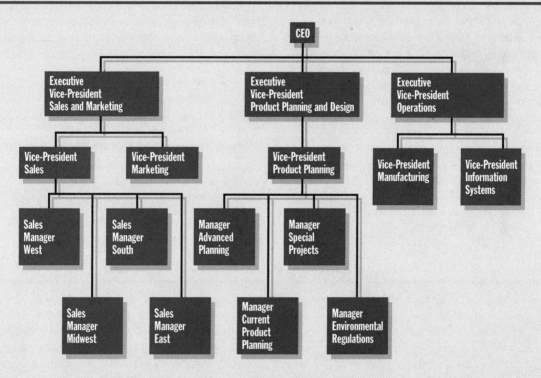

231

INTERNET SKILL-BUILDING EXERCISE: Learning About Outsourcing through the Net

Outsourcing, as described in this chapter, continues to gain momentum in the United States and Canada. A good source for contacts and information on outsourcing is www.hrstore.com/hrstore.html. Place yourself in the role of a manager who wants to learn more about both the advantages and disadvantages of outsourcing as a business strategy. If you do not find enough information at this site, type the following phrase into two different search engines: "outsourcing of work."

CASE PROBLEM 9-A: Pay and Chase at Medicare

Several years ago, Medicare paid a large number of insurance claims that should have been paid by private insurers. (Medicare is the medical care component of Social Security in the United States.) Linda Ruiz was acting director of the Office of Medicare Benefits and Administration at the time. She explained that the government has demanded repayment. Yet because of the agency's record-keeping system, it may be impossible to know how much was recovered. "I know that we had a backlog of $445 million, but what has actually been collected, I don't know," she said. "We put out the demands." (A demand is a request for payment to the private insurance company.)

The collection problem is part of a work process called "Medicare as secondary payer." By law, Medicare has secondary responsibility for medical claims incurred by enrollees who are eligible for Medicare but who also are covered by private medical insurance. Previous to this legislation, Medicare was the primary payer. The purpose of the change was to shift most of the burden to private insurers when senior citizens had dual coverage. Medicare has continued to pay claims as the primary insurer since it cannot accurately determine when an enrollee also has dual coverage.

According to several estimates, Medicare has paid about $1 billion worth of private insurance obligations each year for a decade. The Health Care Financing Administration (HCFA) is the group that runs the Medicare program. After

HCFA discovers it has paid a claim that should have been the primary responsibility of a private insurer, it attempts to collect money from the insurance company. The process is labeled "pay and chase" because the government pays the bill and then chases the insurer for its share.

Part of the problem is that claims are processed for Medicare by private contractors. Under the law Medicare is obliged to hire insurance companies to process the claims. Sometimes an insurance company contracted to process Medicare claims is the insurer that should have paid Medicare the primary portion of the same claims.

Under the present system, there is no way of knowing how much money is legitimately owed the government until a demand for payment is issued to the insurance companies. The insurance companies hired to represent Medicare's interests sometimes neglect to send demands for payments to other insurance companies.

Discussion Questions

1. What disadvantages of bureaucracy are illustrated in this case?
2. What can Medicare do to collect more of its money?
3. How might reengineering help Medicare?

Source: Based on facts reported in Jeff Nesmith, "Medicare May Never Heal Its Wallet-Wound," Cox News Service, August 1, 1993; www.hcfa.gov/stats/.

CASE PROBLEM 9-B: New Rules, New Tools at Micron

Micron Electronics, based in Nampa, Idaho, manufactures PCs. A couple of weeks ago, chief executive Joel Kocher put on a grass skirt and got the production floor shaking. And that's not all that is going on. A new team of leaders at Micron is working to transform the staid corporate culture to something that walks a little on the wild side. The goal stretches beyond simply having more fun at work. The new executive team intends to make Micron more competitive. The plan is to bring the daring, aggressive, less-hierarchical climate common at high-tech business firms in the Silicon Valley to Idaho. "Changing the culture is critical," said Mark Gonzalez, the vice-president of worldwide marketing. "We're not going to be able to adopt a new strategy without changing the culture."

A year ago, Micron employees wouldn't have worn shorts to work. And nobody would have dared to spray-paint the

company's new advertising slogan on the walls. But that's what Rob Wheadon did a few weeks ago. The painting occurred during office hours, after Wheadon and other marketing managers previewed Micron's "New Rules, New Tools" campaign. "We came out pretty jacked about what we'd seen," Wheadon said. "And then I noticed this big, blank wall."

Wheadon and Mike Rosenfelt, Micron's new creative director, kept a low profile after security guards discovered the red and black graffiti inside the company's Meridian offices. "People didn't think it was me," Wheadon said. The prank didn't fit his conservative personality. "I'm the guy wearing a tie on Friday," he said.

It didn't take long before employees in Meridian came back to check out the rumored graffiti. Word spread quickly to the company's Nampa headquarters offices and manufacturing plant. Now Micron's new slogan can be found scrawled on the sides of desks and painted on windows.

Fridays at Micron have been proclaimed "hat day," "Hawaiian day," and "park outside the lines day." Last week, the sales force in Meridian celebrated the end of the fiscal year with party hats and noisemakers. In Nampa, Scan Murphy, manager in the desktop support department, wore a hat made of purple and red balloons while he took customers' calls. "People don't call here because they're happy. This just takes the edge off," Murphy said.

A new stereo system has been installed on the manufacturing floor, and a mixture of rock, country, and mellow music pours in. "I've been watching some of the people out there, and they're kind of shaking their heads to the beat of the music. Working a little faster. Stepping it up," said Steve Laney, vice-president of investor relations.

Top management believes that "stepping it up" is important. The company has received its share of technology awards but it stumbled recently when it lost market share in spite of an expanding market for PCs. As a consequence, about 580 jobs have been eliminated in two restructurings. Employee morale at Micron hit a new low. Company executives admit that some people are embracing the new culture faster than others.

Kocher has also initiated regular meetings with all employees. Workers are also invited to weekly sessions in which customers air their complaints. Gonzalez, the marketing executive, said, "We're trying to be more open. Less hierarchical. Not a command-and-control structure."

Wheadon, the marketing manager who spray-painted the walls, said, "A year ago if you asked me if I were happy, I would have said no. I was told what to do. This is more of a mentoring experience for me and one that will make us a better company."

"I think everyone who is new at Micron is very, very, sensitive—both professionally and personally—about this integration and creation of the new culture based on the best of the old and best of the new," Rosenfelt said. "Most people recognize that this transition, like any, is going to be rocky."

Discussion Questions

1. What is top management at Micron attempting to accomplish by wearing a Hawaiian skirt, allowing spray-painting, and installing a new stereo system in the manufacturing plant?

2. How effective do you think Micron's effort to change the culture will be in the long run?

3. What recommendations can you offer the management group at Micron to improve the chances of changing the corporate culture?

233

Source: Adapted from Michelle Cole, "Micron Electronics Vows to Loosen Up, Live It Up," *Idaho Statesman*, August 9, 1998, p. 6B; www.micronpc.com.

ENDNOTES

1. Bill Vlasic, "His Mission: Make Chrysler, Daimler Mesh," *The Detroit News* syndicated story, November 5, 1998. Reprinted with permission from *The Detroit News*.

2. "When Senselessness Reigns," Rochester, New York, *Democrat and Chronicle*, May 25, 1998, p. 8A.

3. Donald L. Barlett and James B. Steele, "Fantasy Islands: And Other Perfectly Legal Ways that Big Companies Manage to Avoid Billions in Federal Taxes," *Time*, November 16, 1998, p. 88.

4. Gene Koretz, "Morale Got Downsized Too: Can Managers Repair the Damage," *Business Week*, February 20, 1995, p. 26.

5. Wayne F. Cascio, Clifford E. Young, and James R. Morris, "Financial Consequences of Employment-Change Decisions in Major U.S. Corporations," *Academy of Management Journal*, October 1997, pp. 1175–1189.

6. The last suggestion is from Oren Harari, "Layoffs: An Eternal Debate," *Management Review*, October 1993, p. 31.

7. Charlene Marmer Solomon, "Protecting Your Outsourcing Investment," *Workforce*, October 1998, p. 130.

8. "Satisfied with IT Outsourcing?" *HRfocus*, November 1997, p. 7.

9. Ann Majchrzak and Qianwei Wang, "Breaking the Functional Mind-Set in Process Organizations," *Harvard Business Review*, September–October 1996, p. 93.

10. Majchrzak and Wang, "Breaking the Functional Mind-Set," p. 95.

11. Darrell K. Rigby, "What's Today's Special at the Consultant's Café?" *Fortune*, September 7, 1998, p. 163.

12. "The Right Look: How to Get the Most Out of Your Delegating Skills," *Executive Strategies*, January 1993, p. 7.

13. Several items on the list are from "The Power of POWERSHARING, *HR/OD*, July/August 1998, p. 2; Janet Purdy Levaux, "Delegating: Yes, Letting Go Is Hard to Do," *Investor's Business Daily*, January 19, 1995, p. A3.

14. Barbara Ettore, "The Empowerment Gap: Hype vs. Reality," *Management Review*, July/August 1997, p. 13.

15. J. Steven Ott, *The Organizational Culture Perspective* (Chicago: Dorsey Press, 1989), pp. 20–48; Personal communication from Lynn H. Suksdorf, Salt Lake City Community College, October 1998.

16. Anne Bruce, "Southwest: Back to the FUNdamentals," *HRfocus*, March 1997, p. 11.

17. Joanne Cole, "Building Heart and Soul," *HRfocus*, October 1998, p. 9.

18. "Merger May Not Be So Well-oiled," The Associated Press story, December 3, 1998.

19. David A. Garvin, "Building a Learning Organization," *Harvard Business Review*, July–August 1993, p. 80.

20. *Ernst & Young's Business UpShot*, September 1998, Issue 2.8, p. 6.

21. Anita Lienert, "Plowing Ahead in Uncertain Times," *Management Review*, December 1998, p. 19.

22. Charles D. Morgan, "Culture Change/Culture Shock," *Management Review*, November 1998, p. 13.

23. Alan H. Frohman, "Igniting Organizational Change from Below: The Power of Personal Initiative," *Organizational Dynamics*, Winter 1997, pp. 39–53.

24. Richard Pascale, Mark Millemann, and Linda Gioja, "Changing the Way We Change," *Harvard Business Review*, November–December 1997, pp. 126–139.

25. Kurt Lewin, *Field Theory and Social Science* (New York: Harper & Brothers, 1951).

26. Paul Strebel, "Why Do Employees Resist Change?" *Harvard Business Review*, May–June 1996, p. 87.

27. H. James Harrington, *Business Process Improvement: The Breakthrough Strategy for Total Quality, Productivity, and Competitiveness* (New York: McGraw-Hill, 1991).

28. Ed Oakley and Doug Krug, *Enlightened Leadership* (New York: Simon & Schuster, 1993).

29. Rick Maurer, "Transforming Resistance," *HRfocus*, October 1997, p. 10.

Chapter Ten

Nike Corp. was looking for ways to make its employee selection process more efficient. So management turned to Aspen Tree Software to help hire employees for Niketowns—retail stores that showcase Nike products. At a new store in Las Vegas, 6,000 people responded to ads for workers needed to fill 250 positions. Nike used interactive voice technology (IVT) to make the first cut. Applicants respond to eight questions over the telephone. Based on responses to the questions, 3,500 applicants were screened out because they were not available for the required hours, or lacked retail experience. The other 2,500 applicants had a computer-assisted interview at the store (responding to questions displayed on a computer monitor), followed by a personal interview.

"We think it's important to give a personal interview to anyone who comes to the store," says Brian Rogers, Nike's manager of human resources for the retail division. "Applicants are customers as well as potential hires."

The computer interview identified those candidates who had experience in customer service, had a passion for sports, and would make good Nike customer-service representatives. A video showing three scenarios for helping a customer is built into the computer interview, and the applicant is asked to choose the best. As applicants complete the interview, a printer in the next room prints their responses. Areas that need to be probed further are flagged, as

After studying this chapter and doing the exercises, you should be able to:

1 Describe the components of organizational staffing.

2 Be aware of the legal aspects of staffing.

3 Explain the importance of strategic human resource planning.

4 Present an overview of recruitment and selection.

5 Present an overview of employee orientation, training, and development.

6 Explain the basics of a fair and reliable method of evaluating employee performance.

7 Summarize the basics of employee compensation.

235

Staffing and Human Resource Management

are areas that indicate particular strengths. Nike managers also find that the computer interviews help identify applicants who lose their temper in work situations or who demonstrate other undesirable behaviors.

Rogers believes that using computer-assisted interviewing has helped Nike staff key positions rapidly. Also, turnover in the retail division has been reduced by 21 percent in two years. Other management processes in the store, such as coaching, may also have helped reduce turnover. Nike is now exploring the possibility of using computer-assisted interviewing for manufacturing positions.[1]

The success of the job-applicant screening process used at Niketown stores illustrates but one way in which human resource management contributes to company productivity. This final chapter about organizing and staffing deals with the heart of human resource management—staffing the organization. Staffing requires many subactivities, as indicated shortly. The purpose of this chapter is to explain the basics of human resource management as needed by managers to perform their job. Note that human resource management is often referred to as HRM, and human resources, as HR.

THE STAFFING MODEL

Describe the components of organizational staffing.

The model in Exhibit 10-1 indicates that the staffing process flows in a logical sequence. Although not every organization follows the same steps in the same sequence, staffing ordinarily proceeds in the way this section will discuss.

EXHIBIT 10-1

236

The Organization Staffing Model
Under ideal circumstances, organization staffing would proceed through the stages as shown. Terminating (or dehiring) employees might also be considered part of staffing.

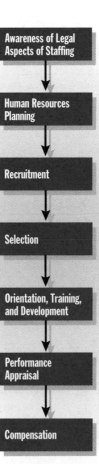

Human resource specialists are engaged in all phases of staffing. Line managers, however, have the ultimate responsibility for staffing their own units. Typically specialists work with managers to help them make better staffing decisions. For example, in addition to your prospective manager or team leader, a human resource specialist may interview you for a job. Most of the techniques described in this chapter have some applicability for organizations of all sizes. However, because large organizations have more resources than small ones, large organizations can engage more fully in most aspects of the staffing model.

LEGAL ASPECTS OF STAFFING

Be aware of the legal aspects of staffing.

Federal, state, provincial, and local laws influence every aspect of organizational staffing. Managers and human resource specialists must keep the major provisions of these laws in mind whenever they make decisions about any phase of employment.

Exhibit 10-2 summarizes major pieces of U.S. federal legislation that influence various aspects of staffing—not just employee selection. Exhibit 10-3 presents highlights of comparable Canadian legislation. Managers need to be aware that such legislation exists, and also be familiar with the general provisions of each law or executive order. When a possible legal issue arises, the manager should review the relevant legislation in depth and confer with a company specialist in employment law.

A key aspect of implementing the spirit and letter of employment discrimination law in the United States has been affirmative action programs. To comply with the Civil Rights Act of 1964, employers with federal contracts or subcontracts must develop such programs to end discrimination. **Affirmative action** consists of complying with antidiscrimination law *and* correcting past discriminatory practices. Under an affirmative action program, employers actively recruit, employ, train, and promote minorities and women who may have been discriminated against by the employer in the past. As a result, they are underrepresented in certain positions. Part of an affirmative action plan might include a career development program for women to help them qualify for management positions.

affirmative action
An employment practice that complies with antidiscrimination law and correcting past discriminatory practices.

237

Recent cross-cultural research about attitudes toward affirmative action indicates that people who perceive themselves to be a disadvantaged minority have the most positive attitudes toward affirmative action. Specifically, French Canadians (who often feel discriminated against) had more positive attitudes toward affirmative action than English-speaking Canadians and Americans. The study was conducted among white, black, and Asian with college students from all three cultural groups. The U.S. group also included Hispanic students.[2]

A national debate continues over whether any person in a competitive situation deserves a preference because of race, ethnicity, or sex. The opposing point of view to affirmative action programs is that race, ethnicity, or sex should *not* be a factor in making employment or business decisions. For example, a job candidate should not be given an edge over other applicants because she is a Hispanic female. What is your opinion on this issue?

A misperception of affirmative action is that it always means preferences or goals. Affirmative action can often be accomplished through recruitment in minority areas or publications geared toward affected minorities. Candidates thus flow naturally to the firm without having to establish a quota such as "hiring only a Hispanic woman for our next opening as a credit analyst."

EXHIBIT 10-2   *Major U.S. Federal Antidiscrimination Legislation and Agreements*

Civil Rights Act of 1964

Title VII of the Civil Rights Act of 1964 prohibits discrimination in all employment decisions on the basis of race, sex, religion, color, or national origin. Sexual harassment is in violation of Title VII.

Equal Employment Opportunity Commission

The Equal Employment Opportunity Commission (EEOC) administers Title VII and investigates complaints about violations. In addition, it has the power to issue guidelines for interpretation of the act. The EEOC's guidelines are not federal law. Instead, they are administrative rules and regulations.

Civil Rights Act of 1991

According to this act, victims of discrimination have rights to compensatory and punitive damages as well as jury trial. In general, in cases of intentional discrimination, the act shifts the burden of proof from employee to employer. Under earlier civil rights legislation, employees could only receive reinstatement, back pay, and attorneys' fees. The act places limits on how much employees can collect in compensatory and punitive damages. The amount depends on the size of the employer, with limits ranging from $50,000 to $300,000.

Age Discrimination in Employment Act, 1967

This act applies to employers with at least 25 employees. As later amended, it prohibits discrimination against people 40 years or older, in any area of employment, because of age. The act ended mandatory retirement for most employees covered by its provisions. Many employees laid off during downsizings have claimed to be victims of age discrimination.

Pregnancy Discrimination Act of 1978

This act broadens the definition of sex discrimination to cover pregnancy, childbirth, and related medical conditions. It also prohibits employers from discrimination against pregnant women in employment benefits if they are capable of performing their job duties. This act applies to employers with more than 21 employees.

Equal Pay Act, 1963

This act prohibits employers from paying unequal wages on the basis of sex. Equal pay must be paid for equal work, regardless of sex. Yet the act still allows employers to pay men and women different wages if the difference is based on ability or seniority.

Americans with Disabilities Act of 1990

The Americans with Disabilities Act (ADA) is designed to protect disabled and chronically ill people from discrimination in employment, public accommodations, transportation, and telecommunications. The act applies to employers with at least 15 employees.

A **disability** is defined as a physical or mental condition that substantially limits an individual's major life activities. Among the physical impairments covered by the ADA are severe vision problems, severe hearing problems, wheelchair confinement, muscular dystrophy, epilepsy, and severe physical disfigurement. Among the mental disabilities included are mental illness, alcoholism, and drug addiction. People who experienced these problems in the past cannot be discriminated against if they can perform the job.

If an employee can perform the essential functions of a job (even with special equipment), he or she should be considered qualified. Employers must accommodate the known disabilities of applicants and employees, unless the accommodations would impose "undue hardship" on the firm.

Family and Medical Leave Act, 1993

The Family and Medical Leave Act applies to employers having 50 or more employees. It requires the employer to provide up to 12 weeks of unpaid, job-protected leave to eligible employees for certain family and medical leave reasons such as caring for a newborn, newly adopted, or seriously ill child. The leave can also be used to take care of an employee's spouse or parent, or to take medical leave for the employee's own illness. The employer must also maintain the employee's health coverage during the leave.

Know This (handwritten annotation)

STRATEGIC HUMAN RESOURCE PLANNING

Explain the importance of strategic human resource planning.

Staffing begins with a prediction about how many and what types of people will be needed to conduct the work of the firm. Such activity is referred to as **strategic human resource planning.** It is the process of anticipating and providing for the movement of people into, within, and out of an organization to support

EXHIBIT 10-3   *Major Canadian Federal and Provincial Employment Antidiscrimination Legislation*

Canadian Federal Equal Pay for Equal Work Legislation

The Canadian federal government has had pay equity (equal pay for equal work) legislation since the 1950s. The legislation prohibits paying different wages to men and women who perform the same or substantially similar work. Examples include janitors and housekeepers, and orderlies and nurses' aides.

Employment-Equity Legislation, 1995 (Ontario, Canada)

Much employment legislation in Canada is at the provincial rather than the national level. In 1995, the New Democratic Party introduced employment-equity legislation. It requires most employers to meet targets for employment of specified groups, including racial minorities, women, aboriginal people, and the handicapped.

Commission on the Rights of People (Québec, Canada)

The Québec Charter of Human Rights and Freedoms was adopted in 1975. The *Commission des droits de la personne* (rights of people) is responsible for seeing that situations jeopardizing human rights and freedoms are corrected. The Charter provides that every person has a right to full and equal recognition and exercise of his or her human rights and freedoms, without distinction, exclusion, or preference based on such factors as: race, color, ethnic or national origin, pregnancy, sexual orientation, age, religion, political convictions, language, social condition, or handicap. Citizens who feel their rights have been violated can file complaints through channels provided by the Québec government.

---

the firm's business strategy. Management attempts, through planning, to have the right number and right kinds of people at the right time.

Business strategy addresses the financial priorities of the organization with respect to identifying what business the firm should be in, product direction, profit targets, and so forth. Human resource planning addresses the question "What skills are needed for the success of this business?" Planning helps identify the gaps between current employee competencies and behavior and the competencies and behavior needed in the organization's future. Strategic human resource planning consists of four basic steps:[3]

1. *Planning for future needs.* A human resource planner estimates how many people, and with what abilities, the firm will need to operate in the foreseeable future.
2. *Planning for future turnover.* A planner predicts how many current employees are likely to remain with the organization. The difference between this number and the number of employees needed leads to the next step.
3. *Planning for recruitment, selection, and layoffs.* The organization must engage in recruitment, employee selection, or layoffs to attain the required number of employees.
4. *Planning for training and development.* An organization always needs experienced and competent workers. This step involves planning and providing for training and development programs that ensure the continued supply of people with the right skills.

Strategic business plans usually involve shifting around or training of people. Human resource planning can therefore be an important element in the success of strategies. Human resource planning can also be a strategic objective in itself. For example, one strategic objective of Pepsi Cola International is the development of talented people. Human resource planning contributes to attaining this objective by suggesting on- and off-the-job experiences to develop talent.

strategic human resource planning
The process of anticipating and providing for the movement of people into, within, and out of an organization to support the firm's business strategy.

239

RECRUITMENT

Present an overview of recruitment and selection.

recruitment
*The process of attracting
job candidates with the
right characteristics and
skills to fill job openings.*

Recruitment is the process of attracting job candidates with the right characteristics and skills to fit job openings. Similar recruitment methods are used for
traditional and contingent workers (see Chapter 8). The preferred recruiting
method is to begin with a large number of possible job candidates and then give
serious consideration to a much smaller number, as does Nikestores. However,
if few candidates are available, the recruiter must be less selective or not fill the
position. In this section we describe the major aspects of recruitment.

Purposes of Recruitment

A major purpose of recruiting and selection is to find employees who fit well
into the culture of the organization. Most job failures are attributed to workers
being a "poor fit" rather than because of poor technical skills or experience. The
poor fit often implies poor relationships with coworkers. A person–organization
fit occurs when the characteristics of the individual complement the organizational culture. The person–organization fit is usually based on a mesh between
the person's values and those of the organization.[4] For example, a person who
values technology and diversity among people—and is qualified—would be a
good candidate to work for Compaq/Digital.

Another important purpose of recruiting is to sell the organization to high-
quality prospective candidates. Recruiters must select candidates who can function in one job today and be retrained and promoted later, as company needs
dictate. Flexible candidates of this type are in demand; therefore, a recruiter may
need to sell the advantages of his or her company to entice them to work there.

Job Descriptions and Job Specifications

A starting point in recruiting is to understand the nature of the job to be filled
and the qualifications sought. Toward this end, the recruiter should be supplied
with job descriptions and job specifications. The job description explains in detail what the job holder is supposed to do. It is therefore a vital document in human resource planning and performance appraisal. An exception is that in some
high-level positions, such as CEO, the person creates part of his or her own job
description. Refer back to Exhibit 8-2 for a sample job description.

job specification
*A statement of the per-
sonal characteristics needed
to perform the job.*

job analysis
*Obtaining information
about a job by describing
its tasks and responsibilities and gathering basic
facts about the job.*

A **job specification** (or person specification) stems directly from the job description. It is a statement of the personal characteristics needed to perform the
job. A job specification usually includes the education, experience, knowledge,
and skills required to perform the job successfully. Both the job description and
the job specification should be based on a careful **job analysis**—obtaining information about a job by describing its tasks and responsibilities. The procedure
requires a systematic investigation of the job through interviews, direct observations, and often completing a form. The data from job analysis become part of
the job description. For example, suppose the job analyst studies the position of
construction supervisor. Assume the analyst observes that the supervisor spends
considerable time settling squabbles about which worker is responsible for certain tasks. Part of the job description would read, "Resolves conflict among trades-
people about overlapping job responsibilities."

Sources of Recruiting

The term *recruitment* connotes newspaper advertisements, online recruiting, and campus recruiters. Yet a frequently stated figure is that 85 percent of jobs are filled by word of mouth. In the last several years, however, recruiting on the Internet has become so widespread that the proportion of jobs filled through personal contacts may have declined. Recruiting sources can be classified into four categories:

1. *Present employees.* A standard recruiting method is to post job openings so that current employees may apply. Another way to recruit current employees is for managers to recommend them for transfer or promotion. A human resources information system is helpful in identifying current employees with the right skills. It minimizes the need to reject unqualified internal applicants.

2. *Referrals by present employees.* If a firm is established, present employees can be the primary recruiters. Satisfied employees may be willing to nominate relatives, friends, acquaintances, and neighbors for job openings.

3. *External sources other than online approaches.* Potential employees outside an organization can be reached in many ways. The best known of these methods is a recruiting advertisement, including both print and radio. Other external sources include: (a) placement offices, (b) private and public employment agencies, (c) labor union hiring halls, (d) walk-ins (people who show up at the firm without invitation), and (e) write-ins (people who write unsolicited job-seeking letters). Labor union officials believe that they simplify the hiring process for employers because only qualified workers are admitted to the union.

   An unconventional external recruiting source that also achieves a social responsibility goal is to recruit from among welfare recipients. Such recruiting is generally aimed at entry-level workers during a tight labor market (labor shortage). The accompanying Manager in Action provides more details about recruiting welfare recipients and those recently on welfare.

4. *Online recruiting.* The Internet has become a major source of recruiting job candidates. One reason is that there are dozens of Web sites free to job candidates, and sometimes to employers. Also, online recruiting services exist for which employers pay a fee just as with an employment agency. An example is Adecco Job Shop. The employer-paid online service screens candidates and claims to provide high-quality job candidates. A recent development of note in online recruiting is job fairs. In an online job fair, a Web site such as Monster Board (www.monster.com) brings together recruiters and job seekers in a particular region or industry.[5] An example would be a fair for the machine-tool industry.

   A factor contributing to the explosive growth of recruiting on the Net is that millions of job seekers every day surf the Net to explore job openings. Exhibit 10-4 provides specific Web sites for recruiting. Online recruiting, however, has not made other recruiting sources obsolete or ineffective. For example, top-level management positions are almost always filled through executive search firms or word of mouth. Finding employees or finding a job is best done through a variety of the methods mentioned here.

Global Recruiting

Global recruiting presents unique challenges. Multinational businesses must have the capability to connect with other parts of the globe to locate talent anywhere in the world. Company recruiters must meet job specifications calling for mul-

241

Manager *in Action*

Marriott Recruits and Trains Welfare Recipients

The U. S. Congress passed the Personal Responsibility and Work Opportunity Reconciliation Act of 1996 with the hope of moving vast numbers of people from welfare to paid work. The act was a monumental overhaul that ended 60 years of federal protection for poor mothers and children. As a result of the act, Congress gave states responsibility for poverty programs and established rigid requirements for performance. Under the reform bill, workfare participants (welfare recipients who also work outside the home) must work a minimum of 20 hours a week (30 hours by 2002). In return, most of those workers in public-sector assignments receive monthly checks from the state, plus food stamps, Medicaid, and other benefits that they received before working.

Many business firms of all sizes have been urged by the government to participate in hiring welfare recipients. Some big businesses have chosen to tap into existing education programs for people on welfare. Other firms such as Intel Corp. and Marriott International, Inc. have developed their own training programs that suit their needs much better. Marriott's Pathways to Independence is one of the best-known corporate welfare-to-work programs. However, the hotel chain had taken the initiative to recruit and train welfare workers for basic hotel and restaurant jobs long before the 1996 act.

"Based on a lot of experience, we found that when you hire people with little or no work experience and put them on the job with minimal training, or just basic orientation, they will be gone in three weeks," says Janet Tully, Marriott's director of community employment training.

To combat this problem, in 1991, Marriott launched Pathways in Atlanta. The six-week training program combines classroom instruction with occupational skills training. "We teach three basic things in training: dependability, accountability, and self-esteem," says Tully.

Guidance and instruction to former welfare recipients does not stop with classes and training, Tully explains. After the instructional program, Marriott guarantees graduates an offer of full-time employment and provides them with a support system of coworkers and supervisors to make sure issues like transportation and day care are solved.

The hotel and restaurant giant could easily afford to pay the entire bill for the training program. Nevertheless, Marriott has teamed up with private industry councils, the Job Corps, the Jewish Vocational Services, and Common Ground community organizations, which reimburse the corporation for about 60 percent of the training costs.

A graduate of the Pathways to Independence program is now a housekeeping supervisor at an urban Marriott Hotel. She observed that "Pathways helped me get on the right track. I had two kids before I was 21. The three of us was [were] sharing a teeny apartment with a girlfriend and her little boy. I had no hopes of ever having my own place for me and my children. After learning what I needed to at Pathways, I was hired as a housekeeper. Two years later I was offered a job as a supervisor. At that moment, I felt my life had turned around."

Sources: Cynthia E. Griffin, "Playing Their Part," *Entrepreneur*, January 1998, p. 118; Eric Schine, "Can Workfare Really Work?" *Business Week*, June 23, 1997, p. 126.

Web Site	Web Address
Adecco Job Shop	www.adecco.com
Best Internet Recruiter	www.bestrecruit.com
Best Jobs in the USA Today	www.bestjobsusa.com
Career Mosaic	www.careermosaic.com
Career Web	www.cweb.com
Christian & Timbers	www.ctnet.com (specializes in high-tech positions)
E-Span Résumé Bank	www.espan.com
Eurojobs	www.eurojobs.com
Fenwick Partners	www.fenwickpartners.com (specializes in high-tech positions)
Hispanstar*	www.hispanstar.com (for employers searching for Hispanic workers, and workers looking to fill such positions)
Job Center	www.jobcenter.com
JobOptions	www.joboptions.com
Job World	www.job.world.com
The Monster Board	www.monsterboard.com; www.monster.com/recruit
Nationjob Network	www.nationjob.com
Online Career Center	www.occ.com
World Hire	www.worldhire.com

243

ticulturalism (being able to conduct business in other cultures) on top of more traditional skills. To fill international positions, the recruiter may have to develop overseas recruiting sources.[6] The recruiter may also require the assistance of a bilingual interviewer to help assess the candidate's ability to conduct business in more than one language.

SELECTION

Selecting the right candidate for a job is part of a process that includes recruitment. Exhibit 10-5 shows the steps in the process. A hiring decision is based on information gathered in two or more of these steps. For instance, a person might receive a job offer if he or she was impressive in the interview, scored well on the tests, and had good references. Another important feature of this selection model is that an applicant can be rejected at any point. An applicant who is abusive to the employment specialist might not be asked to fill out an application form.

Careful screening of job applicants has always been important because competent employees are the lifeblood of any firm. Current judicial rulings have added another reason for employers to evaluate candidates carefully. According to the doctrine of *negligent hiring and retention*, an employer can be liable for the job-related misdeeds of its employees, whether the wrongs affect customers or coworkers.[7] Assume that a supervisor had a pre-employment history of sexual harassment and then sexually harasses another employee during working hours. The employer might be considered negligent for having hired the supervisor. Employers can also be held liable for retaining an employee who commits physically harmful acts.

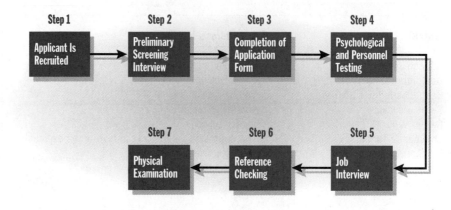

EXHIBIT 10-5

*A Model for Selection
The selection process generally proceeds in the steps as indicated at the right, yet there are many exceptions in terms of which steps are included and in what order. For example, some employers do not use psychological and personnel testing, and others have candidates complete the application form first.*

Preliminary Screening Interview

Selection begins as soon as candidates come to the attention of the recruiter. If candidates come close to fitting the job specifications, a brief screening interview follows, often by telephone. The purpose of the screening interview is to determine if the candidate should be given further consideration. One area of disqualification would be for the candidate to demonstrate such poor oral communication skills over the phone that the person is excluded from consideration for a job requiring considerable customer contact. "Knockout" questions are sometimes used for quickly disqualifying candidates. Assume a person applying for a supervisory position in a nursing home is asked, "How well do you get along with senior citizens?" A candidate who responds, "Very poorly" is immediately disqualified.

Candidates who pass the screening interview are asked to fill out a job application form. Sometimes this process is reversed, and a screening interview is conducted after the candidate successfully completes the application form.

Job Application Forms

Job application forms are a standard part of any selection procedure. They serve two important purposes. First, they furnish basic biographical data about the candidate, including his or her education, work experience, and citizenship. Second, they provide information that could be related to success on the job. A sloppily completed application form *could* indicate that the candidate had poor work habits, whereas a carefully completed form *could* indicate that the candidate has careful work habits.

Job application forms and employment interviewers should not ask direct or indirect questions that could be interpreted as discriminatory. Discussing the following topics in a job interview could be a violation of antidiscrimination laws:[8]

1. Race
2. Religion
3. Gender (male or female)
4. Pregnancy
5. Number of children
6. Ages of children
7. Marital status
8. Child-care plans
9. Height or weight
10. Handicap
11. Age
12. Criminal record
13. Union affiliation
14. Workers' compensation claims on previous job
15. Medical problems (except that information about medical history that can be taken by medical specialist as part of the medical exam).

Questions about any of these topics would be discriminatory if they were not job-related. A *job-related* question or selection device deals with behavior and skills that are required for job success. Asking an applicant for a child-care specialist position if she or he has ever been convicted of child molestation is job-related.

Psychological and Personnel Testing

Hundreds of different tests are used in employment testing. All tests are psychological tests in the sense that measuring human ability is an important part of psychology. This book uses the term *personnel testing* as well as *psychological testing*, because many people think psychological tests deal with personality and personnel tests deal with job skills.

Personnel and psychological testing remains a major approach to employee selection. A recent survey by the American Management Association of 1,085 manufacturing and service employers indicated that nearly two-thirds of the respondents engage in job-skill testing. Also, nearly one-half use one or more methods of psychological measurement to assess individual abilities and behaviors.[9]

TYPES OF PSYCHOLOGICAL AND PERSONNEL TESTS   The five principal types of psychological and personnel tests are achievement, aptitude, personality, integrity, and interest.

1. *Achievement tests* sample and measure an applicant's knowledge and skills. They require applicants to demonstrate their competency on job tasks or related subjects. The most widely used achievement tests relate to computer skills: typing/data entry, word processing software, and spreadsheet/data processing.
2. *Aptitude tests* measure the potential for performing satisfactorily on the job, given sufficient training. Mental-ability tests, the best-known variety of aptitude tests, measure the ability to solve problems and learn new material. Mental-ability tests measure such specific aptitudes as verbal reasoning, numerical reasoning, and spatial relations (the ability to visualize in three dimensions). Many National Football League teams use the Wonderlic Personnel Test, a brief test of mental ability, to help screen draftees. The highest scores on the mental ability test are required for quarterbacks. What do you think is the reason quarterbacks are expected to be the brightest football players?
3. *Personality tests* measure personal traits and characteristics that could be related to job performance. Personality tests have been the subject of considerable controversy for many years. Critics are concerned that these tests invade privacy and are too imprecise to be useful. Nevertheless, personality factors have a profound influence of job performance. Exhibit 10-6 lists the major personality factors related to job performance.

   A recent development in personality testing is to measure the emotional intelligence of job candidates, because dealing effectively with emotions is so important for effective interpersonal relations and selling. For example, a study conducted at American Express found that financial planners who received training in emotional intelligence performed 16 percent better than other planners in the company.[10]
4. *Integrity tests* are designed to measure the extent of a person's integrity as it relates to job behavior. These tests are frequently used in workplaces such as

EXHIBIT
10-6

The Big Five Personality Factors

Many psychologists believe that the basic structure of human personality is represented by what they call the Big Five factors. These factors, which follow, influence job performance. Conscientiousness, for example, is related to the tendency to produce quality work. Furthermore, these factors can be measured by psychological tests.

I.   **Extraversion.** Extraversion (which is the same as extroversion) relates to whether a person is social, gregarious, assertive, talkative, or active.

II. **Emotional stability.** This factor relates to whether a person is anxious, depressed, angry, embarrassed, emotional, or worried.

III. **Agreeableness.** This factor relates to whether a person is courteous, flexible, trusting, good-natured, cooperative, forgiving, soft-hearted, or tolerant.

IV. **Conscientiousness.** This factor relates to whether a person is careful, thorough, responsible, organized, or prepared. This factor also relates to whether a person is hard-working, achievement-oriented, and persevering.

V.   **Openness to experience.** This factor relates to whether a person is imaginative, cultured, curious, original, broad-minded, intelligent, or artistically sensitive.

retail stores, banks, and warehouses, where employees have access to cash or merchandise. A major factor measured by integrity tests is social conscientiousness. People who score high on this personality factor are much more likely to follow organizational rules. Despite controversy over their use, integrity tests are widely used. One justification for their use is that several studies have shown that about one-third of employees admit to engaging in some type of company theft. The theft could be as small as taking home a few office supplies or giving generous discounts to friends.[11]

A study of close to 752 job applicants mostly in the service industry showed a tendency for women to score higher on integrity tests than men. It was also found that older applicants had higher integrity scores than younger applicants.[12] Although the differences were significant, they were not large enough to suggest that employers looking for honest workers hire only older women!

5. *Interest tests* measure preferences for engaging in certain activities, such as mechanical, clerical, literary, or managerial work. They also measure a person's interest in specific occupations, such as accountant, veterinarian, or sales representative. Interest tests are designed to indicate whether a person would enjoy a particular activity or occupation. They do not attempt, however, to measure a person's aptitude for it.

VALIDITY AND EQUAL EMPLOYMENT OPPORTUNITY   The EEOC insists that selection tests be scientifically accurate, job-related, and not discriminatory against any group. These rules also apply to other selection instruments, including application forms and interviews. A specific provision requires a validity study when a selection procedure has an adverse impact on any race, sex, or ethnic group. A *validity study* is a statistical and scientific method of seeing if a selection device does predict job performance. Do high scorers perform well on the job? Do low scores tend to be poor performers?

Thousands of studies have been conducted about the ability of tests to predict job performance. Some studies explore how well groups of tests used in combination predict job performance. These studies are considered the most valuable because, in practice, employment tests are often used in combinations referred to as test batteries. There is considerable disagreement about the contribution of employment tests to the selection process. Nevertheless, it appears that, used as intended, employment testing does improve the accuracy of selection decisions. As a result, productivity improves.

The most consistent finding about the effectiveness of psychological tests in predicting job performance stems from a long series of studies concerning general intelligence and conscientiousness. In general, employees who have good problem-solving ability and are conscientious, are likely to perform well in most jobs.[13] (These findings assume that the employee also has the necessary education and job skills. Yet for basic jobs, the ability to learn and dependability are more important than experience and already existing skills.) General problem-solving ability is measured by mental ability tests, and conscientiousness by a Big Five personality test. A straightforward explanation of these findings is that a bright person will learn quickly, and a conscientious person will try hard to get the job done.

The Job Interview

The interview that follows testing is more thorough and comprehensive than the screening interview. The topics covered in a job interview include education, work experience, special skills and abilities, hobbies, and interests. Interviewers frequently use the candidate's résumé as a source of topics. For example, "I notice you have worked for four employers in three years. Why is that?" Testing results may also provide clues for additional questioning. If a candidate scored very low on a scale measuring conscientiousness, the interviewer might ask about the candidate's punctuality and error rate.

Another effective approach to interviewing is to ask the interviewee open-ended or nondirective questions, such as "What are your best qualities?" Faced with such a wide-open topic, the interviewee is likely to be self-revealing. At any given point, the interviewer can use a probe such as, "You haven't mentioned dependability. Do you have a problem with dependability?"

Validity increases when interviews are carefully structured (tightly organized) and all applicants are asked the same standard questions. Yet unique questions can still be asked of each candidate. Employment interviews are also more valid when the interviewer is trained and experienced. Validity may also increase when several candidates are interviewed for each position, because comparisons can be made among the applicants. In general, the higher the level of the position, the more candidates are interviewed. Southwest Airlines, for example, interviews many more people for a pilot's position than for a baggage handler.

Job interviews have a dual purpose. The interviewer is trying to decide whether the interviewee is appropriate for the organization. At the same time, the interviewee is trying to decide if the job and organization fit him or her. An important approach to helping both the organization and the individual to make the right decision is to offer a **realistic job preview,** a complete disclosure of the potential negative features of a job to a job candidate. For example, an applicant for a help-desk position might be told, "At times customers will scream and swear at you because a computer file has crashed. Around holiday time many frustrated customers go ballistic." Telling job applicants about potential problems leads to fewer negative surprises and less turnover.[14]

Exhibit 10-7 presents guidelines for conducting a job interview. Several of the suggestions reflect a screening approach referred to as behavioral interview-

realistic job preview
A complete disclosure of the potential negative features of a job to a job candidate.

EXHIBIT 10-7   *Guidelines for Conducting an Effective Selection Interview*

1. **Prepare in advance.** Prior to the interview, carefully review the applicant's job application form and résumé. Keep in mind several questions worthy of exploration, such as "I notice you have done no previous selling. Why do you want a sales job now?"
2. **Find a quiet place free from interruptions.** Effective interviewing requires careful concentration. Also, the candidate deserves the courtesy of an uninterrupted interview.
3. **Take notes during the interview.** Take notes on the content of what is said during the interview. Also, record your observations about the person's statements and behavior. For example, "Candidate gets very nervous when we talk about previous work history."
4. **Use a brief warm-up period.** A standard way of relaxing a job candidate is to spend about five minutes talking about neutral topics, such as the weather. This brief period can be extended by asking about basic facts, such as the person's address and education.
5. **Ask open-ended questions.** To encourage the employee to talk, ask questions that call for more than a one- or two-word answer. Sometimes a request for information—a question like "Tell me about your days at business school"—works like an open-ended question.
6. **Follow an interview format.** Effective interviewers carefully follow a predetermined interview format. They ask additional questions that are based on responses to the structured questions.
7. **Give the job candidate encouragement.** The easiest way to keep an interviewee talking is to give that person encouragement. Standard encouragements include "That's very good," "How interesting," "I like your answer," and "Excellent."
8. **Dig for additional details.** When the interviewee brings up a topic worthy of exploration, dig for additional facts. Assume the interviewee says, "I used to work as a private chauffeur, but then I lost my driver's license." Noticing a red flag, the interviewer might respond: "Why did you lose your license?"
9. **Make very limited use of a stress interview.** The purpose of a stress interview is to see how well the interviewee responds to pressure. Among the stress tactics are to insult the interviewee, to ignore him or her, or to stare at the interviewee and say nothing. These tactics create so much ill will that they are hardly worth pursuing. Besides, a job interview is stressful enough.
10. **Spend most of the interview time listening.** An experienced job interviewer spends little time talking. It is the interviewee who should be doing the talking.
11. **Provide the candidate ample information about the organization.** Answer any relevant questions.

ing because the answers to many of the questions reveal behaviors that would be either strengths or weaknesses in a given position. Assume that in response to the open-ended question "What excites you on the job?" the candidate says, "Helping a coworker solve a difficult problem." The behavior indicated could be good teamwork.

Reference Checking and Background Investigation

reference check
An inquiry to a second party about a job candidate's suitability for employment.

A **reference check** is an inquiry to a second party about a job candidate's suitability for employment. The two main topics explored in reference checks are past job performance and the ability to get along with coworkers. Concerns about negligent hiring are causing the comeback of the reference check as an important part of the screening process. Former and prospective employers have a *qualified privilege* to discuss an employee's past performance. As long as the information is given to a person with a legitimate interest in receiving it, discussion of an employee's past misconduct or poor performance is permissible under law.[15]

Despite such rulings, many past employers are hesitant to provide complete references for two key reasons. First, job applicants have legal access to written references unless they specifically waive this right in writing (Privacy Act of 1974). Second, people who provide negative references worry about being sued for libel.

Background investigations are closely related to reference checks, except that they focus on information from sources other than former employers. Areas investigated include driving record, possible criminal charges or convictions, creditworthiness, disputes with the IRS, and coworkers' and neighbors' comments about your reputation. One survey reported that 95 percent of U.S. corporations conduct background investigations of job candidates.[16] A major reason for the widespread use of background investigations is that former employers who are concerned about potential lawsuits release limited information. Background checks are important also because of the potential hazards of negligent hiring.

The Physical Examination and Drug Testing

The physical examination is important for at least two reasons. First, it gives some indication as to the person's physical ability to handle the requirements of a particular job. Second, the physical exam provides a basis for later comparisons. This lessens the threat of an employee claiming that the job caused a particular injury or disease. For example, after one year on the job, an employee might claim that job stress led to heart disease. If the pre-employment physical showed evidence of heart disease before the employee was hired, the employer would have little to fear from the claim.

The physical examination has increased in importance since the passage of the Americans with Disabilities Act. An employer cannot deny a disabled individual a job because of increased insurance costs or the high cost of health benefits. However, the employer can deny employment to a disabled person if having the individual in the workplace poses a threat to his or her safety or the safety of others. If safety is an issue, the applicant might be offered a less hazardous position.

About two-thirds of large companies test all job applicants for use of illegal drugs. (Executives as well as entry-level workers can be drug abusers.) Testing for substance abuse includes blood analysis, urinalysis, analysis of hair samples, observation of eyes, and examination of skin for punctures. Steelcase Inc., the manufacturer of office furniture, is one company that has switched from urinalysis to hair analysis because inspecting a hair sample seems more dignified to most people being tested. Tendencies toward drug abuse are also measured by integrity tests. Positive results trigger testing for physical evidence of drug abuse. Many companies now test job candidates and current employees for abuse of prescription drugs because at least 25 to 30 percent of drug abuse in the workplace now involves prescription drugs.[17]

Some people are concerned that inaccurate drug testing may unfairly deny employment to worthy candidates. A strong argument in favor of drug testing is that employees who are drug abusers may create such problems as lowered productivity, lost time from work, and misappropriation of funds. Accident and absenteeism rates for drug (and alcohol) abusers are substantial, and they also have many more health problems. The cost of all the problems just mentioned is about $100 billion annually. Another concern is that although the rate of drug abuse in the workplace has declined recently, the number of people involved is significant. The overall positive rate on 2.2 million drug tests recently performed by SmithKline Beecham Clinical Laboratories was 5.4 percent.[18]

Cross-Cultural Selection

As with cross-cultural recruitment, most of the selection guidelines and techniques already mentioned can be applied cross-culturally. Many selection devices, such as widely used personnel tests, are published in languages besides English, especially Spanish. Managers and employment interviewers gathering information about job candidates from other countries should familiarize themselves with key facts about the other culture. For example, in France a *grand école* is a high-prestige college of business that qualifies graduates for positions in the best firms. An interviewer unfamiliar with the French culture might miss the significance of an interviewee talking about his diploma from a *grand école*.

An example of adapting selection techniques to cross-cultural requirements took place at a Japanese-American manufacturer of automobile parts. Management practices at the 80 percent Japanese-owned firm emphasized interpersonal skill, team orientation, and high product quality. The U.S.-based company was hiring for assembly jobs Americans who would fit the Japanese organizational culture. Work simulations (or work samples) proved to be the most effective selection device. It was found that applicant characteristics important in a Japanese culture (such as team and quality orientation) could be measured by the simulation. Trained observers rated the candidates on various factors including the following:[19]

- Attention to maintenance and safety
- Team attitude and participation
- Work motivation and involvement
- Quality orientation

After job candidates have been recruited and passed through all the selection screens, such as the physical exam, they are hired. After the hiring decision is made, human resource specialists make sure all the necessary forms, such as those relating to taxes and benefits, are completed. Next comes orientation.

ORIENTATION, TRAINING, AND DEVELOPMENT

Present an overview of employee orientation, training, and development.

Most firms no longer operate under a "sink or swim" philosophy when it comes to employee learning. Instead, employees receive ample opportunity to become oriented to the firm. Later the firm trains and develops them.

Employee Orientation

employee orientation program
A formal activity designed to acquaint new employees with the organization.

A new employee usually begins his or her new job by attending an orientation program. An **employee orientation program** acquaints new employees with the company. Part of the orientation may deal with small but important matters, such as telling the employee how to get a parking sticker. Large firms offer elaborate orientation programs conducted by human resource specialists. The program may include tours of the buildings, talks by department heads, videotape presentations, and generous supplies of printed information.

Employee orientation also includes a manager telling a new employee specifically what his or her job is and what is expected in terms of performance. It is also valuable to hold periodic discussions of this same topic during the employee's time with the firm. In some firms, a *buddy system* is part of the orientation. A buddy, a peer from the new employee's department, shows the new employee around and fills in information gaps.

Walt Disney Corporation exemplifies a company that emphasizes the importance of thoroughly orienting new employees. Managers at Disney believe in making an up-front investment to help new employees become assimilated into the company. Disney provides insight for new cast members (employees) into how the firm operates, and information about the corporate family they are joining. Employees also receive a careful explanation of how their job fits into company strategy.[20] For example, the entry-level worker who parades around as Minnie Mouse supports the corporate strategy of bringing happiness to people.

Another aspect of orientation is informal socialization. In this process, coworkers introduce new employees to aspects of the organizational culture. Coworkers might convey, for example, how well motivated a new employee should be or the competence level of key people in the organization. The disadvantage of informal orientation is that it may furnish the new employee with misinformation.

Training and Development

Training and development deal with systematic approaches to improving employee skills and performance. **Training** is any procedure intended to foster and enhance learning among employees. It is particularly directed at acquiring job skills.

Rapid changes in technology and the globalization of business have spurred the growth of training programs. Today a wide range of employees receive training on the business applications of the Internet and in international business.

Training programs exist to teach hundreds of different skills, such as equipment repair, performance appraisal, and budget preparation. Literacy training has become widespread because such a large proportion of the work force is functionally illiterate. North American Tool & Die had attempted unsuccessfully to obtain ISO 9000 certification. The certification was soon achieved after undertaking basic skills training including literacy. Within six months production efficiency jumped 25 percent.[21]

A substantial amount of skills training in industry is delivered through computers. **Computer-based training** is a learning experience based on the interaction between the trainee and a computer. The computer provides a stimulus or prompt, to which the trainee responds. The computer then analyzes the response and provides feedback to the student. A question in a customer service course might ask if the following is a good response to a customer complaint: "If you don't like my answer, go speak to my boss." A message would then appear suggesting that the trainee take more ownership of the problem. The retail giant Hudson's Bay Co. uses computer-based training for its 65,000 store associates throughout Canada.

Development is a form of personal improvement that usually consists of enhancing knowledge and skills of a complex and unstructured nature. An example of a development program is one that helps managers become better leaders. An important new thrust in management and leadership development is to help the manager/leader become a better lifelong learner. In concrete terms this could mean that the manager learns how to stay abreast of current developments in the outside world that could affect the profitability of the firm. Remember Jill Barad of Mattel Inc., and the Barbie doll? Barad and her staff stay continually alert to changing preferences that could affect the future demand for Barbie. In late 1998, in anticipation of sales for this famous doll cooling down, Mattel purchased educational software maker The Learning Company.

training
Any procedure intended to foster and enhance learning among employees, particularly directed at acquiring job skills.

251

computer-based training
A learning experience based on the interaction between the trainee and a computer.

development
A form of personal improvement that usually consists of enhancing knowledge and skills of a complex and unstructured nature.

Managers play an important role in most types of training and development, particularly with respect to on-the-job training and development. We return to the topic of the manager as teacher in discussions about mentoring in Chapter 11 and coaching in Chapter 16.

Most of this text and its accompanying course could be considered an experience in management training and development. The next paragraphs will describe two vital aspects of training and development for employees and managers: needs assessment and selection of an appropriate program.

NEEDS ASSESSMENT   Before embarking upon a training program, it is important to determine what type of training is needed. This involves such steps as conducting a job analysis and asking the managers themselves, their bosses, and their subordinates about the managers' needs for training. Also, the trainer observes the managers performing their regular duties to identify needs for improvement.

Despite the importance of matching training and development programs to specific needs, there are universal training needs. These include training in communication, motivation, decision making, counseling and coaching, and time management.

SELECTING AN APPROPRIATE TRAINING PROGRAM   After needs are assessed, they must be carefully matched to training and development programs. A program must often be tailored to fit company requirements. The person assigning employees to training and development programs must be familiar with their needs for training and development, know the content of various programs, and enroll employees in programs that will meet their needs. Exhibit 10-8 presents a sample listing of training and development programs.

A current trend is for nonmanagers to participate in training and development usually reserved for managers and future managers. The rationale is that workers assigned to teams manage themselves to some extent. They also deal directly with many managerial activities, such as selection interviewing and budgeting.[22]

In addition to training and development programs, substantial learning takes place outside of the classroom or away from the computer. Many employees learn

EXHIBIT 10-8

A Sample Listing of Training Programs versus Development Programs
Training programs listed in the left column are often included in a program of management development. The programs on the right, however, are rarely considered to be specific skill-based training programs.

Training Programs	Management Development
Understanding financial statements	Effective team leadership
Interviewing job candidates	Mentoring
Listening to employees	Developing a winning corporate culture
Motivating group members	Developing revolutionary strategy
Telemarketing skills	Attaining a competitive advantage
Writing better reports	Developing a learning organization
Getting started in E-commerce	Downsizing with dignity
Fundamentals of e-tailing	Developing cultural sensitivity
Preventing and controlling sexual harassment	Achieving customer delight
Preventing accidents	Open book management
High-power negotiating	Employee retention strategies
ISO 9000 certification	Becoming a charismatic leader

job skills and information by asking each other questions, sharing ideas, and observing each other. Such learning is spontaneous, immediate, and task specific. Much **informal learning** takes place in meetings, on breaks, and in customer interactions. A nationwide survey found that up to 70 percent of employee learning takes place informally.[23] At Siemens, a high-technology company, managers found that software developers acquired considerable job information by congregating in the company cafeteria. Some companies have now installed high round tables around the company so workers can informally exchange ideas in addition to small talk.

informal learning
Any learning that occurs in which the learning process is not determined or designed by the organization.

PERFORMANCE APPRAISAL

Up to this point in the staffing model, employees have been recruited, selected, oriented, and trained. The next step is to evaluate performance. A **performance appraisal** is a formal system for measuring, evaluating, and reviewing performance. Whichever performance appraisal system or technique is chosen, it should meet the same legal standards of fairness as selection devices. One requirement is that categories of evaluation should be job related, such as rating a worker on creativity only if his or her job requires creative thinking.

Explain the basics of a fair and reliable method of evaluating employee performance.

performance appraisal
A formal system for measuring, evaluating, and reviewing performance.

The traditional appraisal involves a manager who evaluates an individual group member. The current emphasis on team structures has changed performance appraisals in two major ways. One is that groups as well as individuals are now evaluated regularly. Another change is the widespread use of multi-rating systems whereby several workers evaluate an individual. The most frequently-used multi-rater system is **360-degree feedback,** in which a person is evaluated by most of the people with whom he or she interacts.

360-degree feedback
A performance appraisal in which a person is evaluated by a sampling of all the people with whom he or she interacts.

An appraisal form for a manager might receive input from the manager's manager, all group members, other managers at his or her level, and even a sampling of customers when feasible. Self-assessment is also included. The manager's manager would then synthesize all the information and discuss it with him or her. Dimensions for rating a manager might include "gives direction," "listens to group members," "coaches effectively," and "helps the group achieve key results." Rating an employee on paper forms often takes about 45 minutes. With a computerized system, the time is usually reduced to about 30 minutes per rater.

253

The rationale for using 360-degree feedback for performance appraisal is that it presents a complete picture of performance. This technique is used as much for management and leadership development as for performance appraisal. An industrial psychologist or human resource specialist counsels the manager based on negative ratings of his or her leadership behavior and attitudes.

Some people object to 360-degree feedback. Key criticisms include the perception by the person being rated that the feedback is inaccurate, and that the raters do not understand the job.[24] Another common concern is that ratings reflect petty office politics; people who like you give you high ratings and people who dislike you use the feedback as an opportunity for revenge. Would you be objective if asked to rate a coworker or manager?

Purposes of Performance Appraisal

Performance appraisals serve a number of important administrative purposes and can also help the manager carry out the leadership function. A major administrative purpose of performance appraisals is to decide who should receive merit increases and the relative size of the increases. The appraisal process also helps identify employees with potential for promotion. High-performing teams can be identified as well. Employee reviews are widely used to provide documentation for discharging, demoting, and downsizing employees who are not meeting performance standards.

Performance appraisals help managers carry out the leadership function in several ways. Productivity can be increased by suggesting areas for needed improvement. Also, the manager can help employees identify their needs for self-improvement and self-development. Appraisal results can be used to motivate employees by providing feedback on performance. Finally, a performance appraisal gives employees a chance to express their ambitions, hopes, and concerns. In the process, career development is enhanced.

Performance appraisals also help managers determine if the previous steps in the staffing model have been effective. For example, if most employees are performing well, recruitment, selection, and training are probably adequate.

Design of the Performance-Appraisal System

A number of different formats and methods of performance appraisal are in current use. They are designed to measure traits, behavior, or results. **Traits** are stable aspects of people, closely related to personality. Job-related traits include enthusiasm, dependability, and honesty. **Behavior,** or activity, is what people do on the job. Job-related behavior includes working hard, keeping the work area clean, maintaining a good appearance, and showing concern for quality and customer service. **Results** are what people accomplish, or the objectives they attain. Under a system of management by objectives, a performance appraisal consists largely of reviewing whether people achieved their objectives.

At first glance, measuring performance on the basis of results seems ideal and fair. Critics of the results method of appraisal, however, contend that personal qualities are important. A performance-appraisal system that measures only results ignores such important traits and behavior as honesty, loyalty, and creativity. Many managers believe that people with good qualities will achieve good results in the long run.

Many performance-appraisal systems attempt to measure both results and behavior or traits. Exhibit 10-9 shows a portion of a peer-rating system that includes both behavior and results. A group of peers indicates whether a particular aspect of job performance or behavior is a strength or a *developmental opportunity*. The initials under "peer evaluations" refer to coworkers doing the evaluation. The person being evaluated then knows who to thank or blame for the feedback. In addition to indicating whether a job factor is a strength or an opportunity, raters can supply comments and developmental suggestions. The results of the peer ratings might then be supplemented by the manager's ratings to achieve a total appraisal.

A major finding of years of research on performance appraisals of various types is that employees are the most satisfied with the system when they participate in the process. Participation can take a number of forms such as jointly setting goals with the manager, submitting a self-appraisal as part of the evaluation, and having the opportunity to fully discuss the results.[25]

traits
Stable aspects of people, closely related to personality.

behavior
In performance appraisal, what people actually do on the job.

254

results
In performance appraisal, what people accomplish, or the objectives they attain.

PERSON EVALUATED: Chris Marina

Skill Categories and Expected Behaviors	Peer Evaluations for Each Category and Behavior					
Customer Care	TR	JP	CK	JT	CJ	ML
Takes ownership for customer problems	O	S	S	S	S	S
Follows through on customer commitments	S	S	S	S	S	S
Technical Knowledge and Skill						
Engages in continuous learning to update technical skills	O	S	S	S	S	O
Corrects problems on the first visit	O	O	S	S	S	S
Work Group Support						
Actively participates in work group meetings	S	S	S	S	O	S
Backs up other work group members by taking calls in other areas	S	O	O	S	S	S
Minimal absence	S	O	S	S	O	S
Finance Management						
Adheres to work group parts expense process	S	S	S	O	S	S
Passes truck audits	S	S	S	O	S	S

Note: S refers to a strength; O refers to a developmental opportunity.

EXHIBIT 10-9

Peer Evaluation of a Customer Service Technician
The person being evaluated here receives input from six different coworkers. Should a person observe that two or more people perceive a developmental opportunity, it could be time for a change in behavior.

COMPENSATION

Compensation, the combination of pay and benefits, is closely related to staffing. A major reason compensation requires so much managerial attention is that it constitutes about two-thirds of the cost of running an enterprise. Here we look at several types of pay and employee benefits. Chapter 12 will describe how compensation is used as a motivational device.

Summarize the basics of employee compensation.

255

Types of Pay

Wages and salary are the most common forms of pay. Wages are payments to employees for their services, computed on an hourly basis or on the amount of work produced. A part-time airline reservations agent might be paid $8.25 per hour, or a garment worker might be paid $2.00 per jogging suit fabricated. Salary is an annual amount of money paid to a worker that does not depend directly on output or hours worked. Nevertheless, future salary is dependent to some extent on how well the worker produced in the previous year. Many workers are eligible for bonuses or incentives to supplement their salary.

Skill-based pay is another way of establishing pay levels. Under a pay-for-knowledge-and-skills system, managers calculate starting pay based on the knowledge and skill level required for a given job. Subsequent increases depend on the worker's mastering additional skills and knowledge specified by the firm. Skill-based pay is gaining acceptance for work teams because members must be multiskilled. Many managers and human resource specialists like skill-based pay because it encourages widespread learning.

An experiment was conducted at the assembly site of a large corporation that manufactured vehicle safety systems. The plant had recently switched from job-based pay (the traditional approach) to skill-based pay. Results at this facility using skill-based pay were compared with those of a comparable facility with job-based pay over a period of 37 months. Skill-based pay contributed important results in terms of plant performance:

- Productivity was higher, as reflected in a 58 percent decrease in labor parts per hour.
- Labor costs per part were 16 percent lower in the plant with skill-based pay.
- Scrap was 82 percent lower than in the comparison plant.[26]

Although these results are impressive because an actual experiment was conducted, it is doubtful that every company will achieve the same exceptional results after switching to skill-based pay. The company in question was highly committed to human resource management by such means as careful skill training and appraisal of learning.

broadbanding
In salary administration, basing pay more on the person than the position, thus reducing the number of pay grades.

Another recent development in salary administration is **broadbanding,** or basing pay more on the person rather than the position. As a result of broadbanding, the company reduces the number of pay grades and replaces them with several pay ranges (or broad bands). For example, a multiskilled employee exceeding goals might receive 115 percent to 135 percent of a target pay range. A new employee or one not achieving goals might receive 80 percent to 95 percent of the target pay range. Broadbanding fits the new, flexible organization because employees are encouraged to move to jobs where they can develop their careers and add value to the firm. The point is that employees take their salaries with them from job to job instead of being paid according to the range for a given job.[27]

Employee Benefits

employee benefit
Any noncash payment given to workers as a condition of their employment.

An **employee benefit** is any noncash payment given to workers as a condition of their employment. Employee benefits cost employers about 35 percent of salaries. Therefore, an employee earning $30,000 per year in salary probably receives a combined salary and benefit package of $40,500.

flexible benefit package
A benefit plan that allows employees to select a group of benefits tailored to their preferences.

A substantial number of firms of various sizes offer a **flexible benefit package.** A benefit plan of this nature allows employees to select a group of benefits tailored to their preferences. Flexible compensation plans generally provide employees with one category of fixed benefits—minimum standards such a medical and disability insurance. The second category is flexible, with a menu of benefits from which each employee is allowed to select up to a certain total cost. An employee who prefers less vacation time, for instance, might choose more life insurance.

Exhibit 10-10 presents a comprehensive list of employee benefits. Organizations vary considerably in the benefits and services they offer employees. No one firm is likely to offer all the benefits listed.

Compensation, including both pay and benefits, plays a major role in attracting and retaining valued employees in general, and particularly during a

Usually Mandatory	
Social security	Group life insurance
Workers' compensation	Disability insurance
Unemployment compensation	Retirement pensions
Family leave	Paid vacations

Optional But Frequently Offered

Group life insurance	Tuition assistance
Retirement pensions	Paid rest or refreshment breaks
Accidental health insurance	Employee assistance program
Paid lunch breaks	Company-subsidized cafeteria
Paid sick leave	Employee training
Health insurance	Personal time off
Relocation allowance, moving costs	Paid maternity leaves
Career development program	Child adoption grants

Optional and Less Frequently Offered

Paid travel time to work	Retirement counseling
Physical fitness and wellness programs	Outplacement counseling
Stress management programs	Child-care centers
Credit unions	Payment of adoption fees
Cash payments for unused vacation time	Paid paternity leave
Discount-purchasing programs	Parental leave
Funeral pay	Vision-care plans
Assistance with adoption fees	Rape counseling
Car-pooling services	Massage therapy
Prepaid legal fees	Consultation and referral service for
Errand running and dog walking	personal problems
Free lease and insurance on	Accelerated death benefits and viatical
luxury vehicle	settlement for terminally-ill employees
On-site diet clinic	(see Chapter 6)
Paid tuition for dependents	

EXHIBIT 10-10

Employee Benefits
Employers are finding that the right package of benefits for an individual worker will increase the chances that he or she will stay with the firm for a relatively long time.

labor shortage. Even when a firm is downsizing, key employees will be recruited and retained by manipulating benefits. Would you be tempted to switch employers if you were given a $5,000 signing bonus and a company-paid vehicle? Sears, Roebuck & Co. in recent years lost a handful of key executives to competitors who offered them much higher compensation. CEO Arthur C. Martinez admitted that because Sears was not doing so well financially he could not offer these valuable executives comparable compensation in the short term.

A major benefit offered professional employees as an inducement to stay is a career development program designed to plot a person's future with the firm and also give career advice. Assisting workers develop their careers fits the new employment relationship, as described by the CEO of Merck & Co., the pharmaceutical firm: "The company is responsible for providing the environment in which people can achieve their full potential, and employees are responsible for developing their skills."[28]

SUMMARY OF KEY POINTS

 Describe the components of organizational staffing.
The staffing model consists of seven phases: awareness of the legal aspects of staffing; strategic human resources planning; recruitment; selection; orientation, training, and development; performance appraisal; and compensation.

 Be aware of the legal aspects of staffing.
Legislation influences all aspects of staffing. Exhibits 10-2 and 10-3 summarize key legislation relating to equal employment opportunity. Managers should be generally familiar with these laws. Affirmative action consists of complying with antidiscrimination law *and* correcting past discriminatory practices.

 Explain the importance of strategic human resource planning.
Strategic human resource planning provides for the movement of people into, within, and out of the organization. At the same time, it relates these activities to business strategy.

 Present an overview of recruitment and selection.
Recruitment is the process of attracting job candidates with the right characteristics and skills to fit job openings and the organizational culture. External and internal sources are used in recruiting. A new approach is recruiting through online computer services.

Selecting the right employees helps build a firm and minimizes the problem of negligent hiring. Selecting the right candidate from among those recruited may involve a preliminary screening interview, completion of an application form, psychological and personnel testing, a job interview, reference checking, and a physical examination. The five types of psychological and personnel tests used most frequently in employee selection are achievement, aptitude, personality, integrity, and interest tests. Most job interviews are semistructured. They

follow a standard format, yet they give the interviewer a chance to ask additional questions. Reference checks play an important role in helping employees prevent the problem of negligent hiring.

 Present an overview of employee orientation, training, and development.
An employee orientation program helps acquaint the newly hired employee with the firm. Training includes any procedure intended to foster and enhance employee skills. Development is a form of personal improvement that generally enhances knowledge and skills of a complex and unstructured nature. A needs assessment should be conducted prior to selecting training and development programs.

 Explain the basics of a fair and reliable method of evaluating employee performance.
A performance appraisal is a standard method of measuring, evaluating, and reviewing performance of individuals as well as teams. A recent appraisal technique, the 360-degree appraisal, involves feedback from many people. Performance appraisals serve important administrative purposes, such as helping managers make decisions about pay increases and promotions. Appraisals also help managers carry out the leadership function. Appraisal systems measure traits, behavior, and results, with some systems taking into account more than one factor.

 Summarize the basics of employee compensation.
Workers are typically paid salaries, bonuses, and sometimes payment for job skills. Broadbanding, which results in fewer pay grades, supports the modern, less hierarchical organization. Employee benefits are a major part of compensation. Flexible benefit packages allow employees to select a group of benefits tailored to their preferences. Compensation is a major factor in recruiting and retaining employees.

KEY TERMS AND PHRASES

QUESTIONS

1. Why should a manager who does not work in the human resources department be familiar with the various aspects of staffing?
2. How does the staffing function contribute to organizational quality and productivity?
3. What have you learned about staffing that you might apply to your own job search?
4. Why do companies continue to invest in training when they reduce expenses in other ways such as through downsizing?
5. Many researchers and union officials think that pay should be based mostly on seniority (time with the company) because performance appraisals are so biased. What is your opinion on this issue?
6. In what way can a manager use benefits as a method of improving retention and reducing turnover?
7. Would you want most of your salary increase to be based on the results of a 360-degree survey? Explain your reasoning.

SKILL-BUILDING EXERCISE 10-A: The Selection Interview

Assume the role of a sales manager or employment interviewer who works for Met Life (Metropolitan Life Insurance Company). After thinking through the job demands of a sales rep for your company, conduct about a 20-minute interview of a classmate who pretends to apply for the sales position. Before conducting the interview, review the guidelines in Exhibit 10-7. Other students on your team might observe the interview and then provide constructive feedback.

INTERNET SKILL-BUILDING EXERCISE: Recruiting on the Net

Place yourself in the role of a manager who is recruiting qualified job applicants to fill one or more of the following positions: (a) sales representative of machine tools, (b) customer service supervisor who speaks English and Spanish, (c) credit analyst, (d) inventory control specialist, (e) Web master. Use the Internet to conduct your search for a pool of candidates. A good starting point might be the following Web sites: (1) www.monster.com/recruit, (2) www.careermosaic.com, (3) www.espan.com, (4) www.worldhire.com, (5) www.nationjob.com. Remember, in this exercise you are looking for job candidates, not a position for yourself. See if you can locate any job applicants without paying an employer fee.

CASE PROBLEM 10-A: The Captive Work Force

Leah Shaffer is the president of Ceramics Limited, a manufacturer of ceramic photo and picture frames decorated with hand painting. The frames are sold through a California distributor to arts and crafts shops and through a New York distributor to retail stores. Although not a runaway success, there is a steady demand for the frames throughout the United States. Shaffer has also been able to obtain some export sales to Canada, England, and Italy. The biggest challenge facing the business these days is finding competent, reliable workers who stay with the company long enough to be productive. Worker turnover has resulted in many orders that cannot be filled, along with high costs of recruiting, selecting, and training employees.

So far Shaffer and her two partners, Harvey Phillips and Sue McDonald, have not solved their work-force problem. One morning Phillips and McDonald found a photocopy of a news-paper article on their desk, with a handwritten note from Shaffer on the top, stating simply, "Harvey and Sue, maybe we should move in this direction. Best, Leah." An abridgment of the article follows:

Like many Americans with in-demand work skills, Lee Gibbs didn't have to go looking for a job—employers sought him out. And he was easy to find. After completing a seven-year drug sentence at a state prison in Lockhart, Texas, Gibbs walked out with more than the traditional $50 and a bus ticket. He had $8,000 in a bank account, expertise in electronic component boards, and a new job starting at more than $30,000 per year.

"They were calling me, offering me jobs even before I got out," said Gibbs, freed from prison over the summer. "With the money I had saved, I was able to get a vehicle, buy clothes for work, pay the first and last month's rent on an apartment, and put down a telephone deposit."

Thirty-year-old Gibbs became marketable through a prison work program run by a Marietta-based company, U.S. Technologies, with subsidiaries that use prison inmates for outsourcing contracts with private companies.

With more Americans than ever behind bars and businesses shopping for workers from a tight labor pool, there is renewed debate over the pros and cons of having "cons" contributing to free-market enterprises. For most of this century, prison work programs have been sharply restricted by concerns about unfair competition and use of inmates as "slave labor." Questions have also arisen about whether criminals deserve to receive training, pay, and job experience.

Yet according to the U.S. Attorney General, the programs can be a force for good. Wages can go to the victims' restitution funds, prison recidivism (return rates) might be reduced, and there could be "another engine" for the national economy.

At the Putnamville (Indiana) Correctional Facilities, 20 inmates earn $7.95 per hour producing Hoosier Hickory Historic Furniture for sale to customers seeking a rustic relic of yesteryear. The hourly wage is not all profit. The workers must pay for room and board, taxes, restitution for victims and outstanding fines. In contrast to the work for Hoosier Hickory, most prison industry programs are barred from selling their products to private buyers. Those that do must follow a strict set of regulations, including a requirement that inmates be paid wages similar to those in private industry.

At the Liberty Correctional Institution in Bristol, Florida, Michael Provence will soon be eligible for parole after serving 25 years for murder in "a drug deal that went bad." After spending years doing menial tasks like making mess-hall tables, he now does computer-assisted drafting and mapping. Facing the outside world isn't as worrisome as it would have been "if I had been isolated from technology the last 25 years," said Provence. He expects to have little problem finding work.

"For a lot of these people, this is the first job they've held," said Ken Smith, chief executive officer of U.S. Technologies. "They learn work habits.

They have to get up, shower and shave and show up for work on time; they have to show initiative, they have to meet goals, they have to stay out of trouble."

In Florida, PRIDE Enterprises, a nonprofit company that started in 1985 training and employing prison inmates to perform useful jobs with a goal of reducing prison recidivism, employs 4,000 inmates in 51 operations. Their jobs range from making eyeglasses to data entry. Pamela Jo Davis, the PRIDE Enterprises president, says studies show that less than 13 percent of the organization's inmate workers landed back in prison, compared to a national rate of about 60 percent.

Inmate work programs are popular with prison officials who see them as a way to reduce idleness that leads to problems. "That's 200 inmates that are not just slogging around on the compound," Russell Smith, assistant superintendent at Liberty Correctional, said of the PRIDE operation there.

About 76,000 of the nation's estimated 1.5 million prisoners work in programs producing goods for private companies. Efforts to expand often run into opposition. "It's hard for me to accept that the government would put the welfare and benefit of convicted felons above the interests of its taxpayers," said Tim Graves. His 100-employee company was forced out of business after 18 years when the government-run Federal Prison Industries took over contracts to produce missile shipping containers.

One day after Phillips and McDonald had read the above report, they joined Shaffer for lunch to discuss the possibilities of Ceramics Limited hiring prison inmates to make some of their frames.

"Wait a minute," warned Phillips, "Before we start looking for prisoners to make our frames, we first have to understand what our distributors and ultimate customers would think. Some of them might be upset."

McDonald added, "At least we won't have to spend money on background checks. We will know in advance that our new workers are convicted felons."

Shaffer replied, "I'm not suggesting that hiring inmates as part of our work force is a perfect solution to our problems. Yet I think we should at least make some preliminary inquiries. Why don't we get in touch with PRIDE Enterprises?"

Discussion Questions

1. If Ceramics Limited does hire prison labor, what selection procedures should they follow?

2. What other recruiting source might Ceramics Limited use to find workers to build their frames?
3. What are the ethical issues with respect to hiring prison labor to work for Ceramics Limited?

Sources: Facts in this case are from Dan Sewell, "Opportunity Knocks for Inmates with Job Skills: Businesses Tap Into Jail Population to Fill Positions in a Tight Labor Market," Associated Press story, October 18, 1998; Charles Hoskinson, "More Prisons Use Inmates to Perform Labor," Associated Press story, December 7, 1998.

CASE PROBLEM 10-B: Sentry Searches for the Right Employees

The Sentry Group, a 60-year-old company, makes safes, security chests, and insulated two-drawer files for homes and small businesses. Sentry employs 700 people, and its annual sales exceed $70 million. The firm is nonunion and family owned. Among its customers are mass-market retailers such as Wal-Mart and Kmart.

As company management recently looked toward an upcoming selling season, it realized that the demand for its products exceeded its capacity to produce. Top management decided to hire 50 production workers to boost output. The beginning pay rate was $7.25 an hour for first-shift jobs, $7.70 for second-shift (3:30 P.M. to midnight), and $7.80 for third-shift (11 P.M. to 7:30 A.M.) jobs. All positions are full time and permanent, but the company agreed to accept applications for short-term assignments.

The company requires a two-year verifiable work history. Experience in production work, however, is not required. Sentry offers a profit-sharing program for employees with annual bonus checks that could be a double-digit percentage of yearly pay.

Bob Legge, vice-president of human resources, says the company is "fairly picky" in its selection process. An important factor in choosing employees is how well the employees fit the corporate culture, which is built on teamwork, quality, and keeping costs low. Legge said the company is interested in people whose attitude is not just "Go to work, do your job, and go home."

Discussion Questions

1. Is Sentry management establishing unrealistic criteria for its new production workers?
2. What is your opinion of the fairness of the pay differential for the three shifts?
3. Which selection methods do you recommend to find employees who fit the Sentry culture and have the right attitude?

Source: Based on facts reported in J. Leslie Sopko, "Sentry Planning for Hire," Rochester, New York, *Democrat and Chronicle*, August 4, 1995, p. 8B.

261

ENDNOTES

1. Adapted and excerpted from Linda Thornburg, "Computer-Assisted Interviewing Shortens Hiring Cycle," *HRMagazine*, February 1998, pp. 72, 75. Reprinted with the permission of *HRMagazine* published by the Society for Human Resource Management, Alexandria, Va.
2. Stéphanie Brutus, Luis Fernando Parra, Madelene Hunter, Brenda Perry, and Francois Ducharme, "Attitudes Toward Affirmative Action in the United States and Canada," *Journal of Business and Psychology*, Summer 1998, pp. 515–533.
3. James A. F. Stoner and R. Edward Freeman, *Management*, 4th ed. (Upper Saddle River, NJ: Prentice Hall, 1989), p. 331.
4. Daniel M. Cable and Timothy A. Judge, "Interviewers' Perceptions of Person-Organization Fit and Organizational Selection Decisions," *Journal of Applied Psychology*, August 1997, p. 546.
5. Mike Frost, "Old-Fashioned Career Fairs Gain Favor Online," *HRMagazine*, April 1998, p. 31.
6. Valerie Frazee, "How to Hire Locally," *Global Workforce*, July 1998, pp. 19–23.
7. Ann Marie Ryan and Maria Lasek, "Negligent Hiring and Defamation: Areas of Liability Related to Pre-Employment Inquiries," *Personnel Psychology*, Spring 1991, pp. 291–308.
8. Philip Ash, "Law and Regulation of Preemployment Inquiries," *Journal of Business and Psychology*, Spring/Summer 1991, pp. 291–308.
9. "Job Skill Testing and Psychological Measurement: 1998 AMA Survey," *Management Review*, June 1998, p. 1.
10. Michelle Neely Martinez, "The Smarts that Count," *HRMagazine*, November 1997, p. 77.
11. Michael R. Cunningham, Dennis T. Wong, and Anita P. Barbee, "Self-Presentation Dynamics on Overt Integrity Tests: Experimental Studies of the Reid Report," *Journal of Applied Psychology*, October 1994, p. 643; Samuel Greengard, "50% of Your Employees Are Lying, Cheating & Stealing," *Workforce*, October 1997, pp. 44–53.
12. Deniz S. Ones and Chocalingam Viswesvaran, "Gender, Age, and Race Differences on Overt Integrity Tests: Results Across Four Large-Scale Job Applicant Data Sets," *Journal of Applied Psychology*, February 1998, pp. 35–42.
13. Orlando Behling, "Employee Selection: Will Intelligence and Conscientiousness Do the Job?" *Academy of Management Executive*, February 1998, pp. 77–86.
14. Robert D. Bretz, Jr., and Timothy A. Judge, "Realistic Job

Previews: A Test of the Adverse Self-Selection Hypothesis," *Journal of Applied Psychology*, April 1998, pp. 330–337.

15. Marlene Brown, "Reference Checking: The Law Is on Your Side," *Human Resource Measurements* (a supplement to the December 1991 *Personnel Journal*, Wonderlic Personnel Test, Inc.).

16. Edward A. Robinson, "Beware—Job Seekers Have No Secrets," *Fortune*, December 28, 1997, p. 285.

17. Jane Easter Bahls, "Drugs in the Workplace," *HRMagazine*, February 1998, pp. 81–87; Joseph G. Rosse, Richard C. Ringer, and Janice L. Miller, "Personality and Drug Testing: An Exploration of the Perceived Fairness of Alternatives to Urinalysis," *Journal of Business and Psychology*, Summer 1996, pp. 459–475.

18. Bahls, "Drugs in the Workplace," pp. 82–83.

19. Kevin G. Love, Ronald C. Bishop, Deanne A. Heinsch, and Matthew S. Montei, "Selection Across Two Cultures: Adapting the Selection of Assemblers to Meet Japanese Performance Standards," *Personnel Psychology*, Winter 1994, pp. 837–846.

20. Alice M. Starcke, "Building a Better Orientation Program," *HRMagazine*, November 1996, p. 108.

21. Frederick Kuri, "Basic-Skills Training Boosts Productivity," *HRMagazine*, September 1996, p. 77.

22. Robert M. Fulmer, "The Evolving Paradigm of Leadership Development," *Organizational Dynamics*, Spring 1997, p. 70.

23. Nancy Day, "Informal Learning Gets Results," *Workforce*, June 1998, p. 31.

24. Richard Lepsinger and Anntoinette D. Lucia, *The Art and Science of 360° Feedback* (San Francisco: Pfeiffer, 1997); Walter W. Tornow and Manuel London, *Maximizing the Value of 360-Degree Feedback* (San Francisco: Jossey-Bass Publishers; and Greensboro, SC: Center for Creative Leadership, 1998).

25. Brian D. Cawley, Lisa M. Keeping, and Paul E. Levy, "Participation in the Performance Appraisal Process and Employee Reactions: A Meta-Analytic Review of Field Investigations," *Journal of Applied Psychology*, August 1998, pp. 615–633.

26. Brian Murray and Barry Gerhart, "An Empirical Analysis of A Skill-Based Program and Plant Performance Outcomes," *Academy of Management Journal*, February 1998, pp. 68–78.

27. Sandra L. O'Neil, "Aligning Pay with Business Strategy," *HRMagazine*, August 1993, pp. 79–86.

28. Aaron Bernstein, "We Want You to Stay. Really," *Business Week*, June 22, 1998, p. 68.

For 15 years Johan Eliasch, a native Swede, has restructured companies in industries as diverse as shipping, oil and gas, consumer products, and media and entertainment. His most recent acquisition is Head Tyrolia Mares (HTM), a Vienna-based sporting goods company he bought for $1 million. "This one I love because it was a turnaround combined with sports," he says. Eliasch combines business with recreation when he can, and uses his athletic prowess to gain publicity for his company. He was recently a forerunner in two major ski races in Austria.

When Eliasch bought HTM from the state-owned tobacco monopoly Austria Tabak, it was sinking under the weight of unprofitable businesses and struggling to regain its formerly dominant position in the ski and tennis markets. The company had a $119 million operating loss on sales of $401 million. Within three years, the company had earned a $21 million surplus on sales of $305 million. Eliasch turned around HTM using a lesson he learned through many years of sports matches: Focus on what you are good at and always keep an eye on the competitor.

First, he dumped what HTM was not good at: sportswear and golf manufacturing, which Head now licenses to other companies, and Tyrolia skis and boots, which were not as successful as the ski bindings. The Mares division, which is number one in scuba diving equipment worldwide, was left alone.

OBJECTIVES

After studying this chapter and doing the exercises, you should be able to:

 Differentiate between leadership and management.

 Describe how leaders are able to influence and empower team members.

 Identify important leadership characteristics and behaviors.

 Describe the leadership continuum, Theory X and Theory Y, Leadership Grid, situational, and entrepreneurial styles of leadership.

263

 Describe transformational and charismatic leadership.

 Explain how to exercise SuperLeadership.

 Explain the leadership role of mentoring.

Leadership

Strengthening HTM's core tennis and ski business required innovation. Soon after Eliasch took over, Head introduced an hourglass-shaped "carving" ski—one that allows skiers to make narrower turns without skidding—that was the first to appeal to average as well as expert skiers. Head also made a big impact in the tennis market by introducing a racquet made of titanium and graphite that is billed as the strongest and lightest available. The racquet, which Head sells with the slogan "The Power of Light" was conceived by Eliasch, who was impressed by titanium's effectiveness in golf balls and Head skis.

In talking about the turnaround, Eliasch says, "You want to beat the competition and excel. It's fun to come up with new products, see that you have an impact out in the market, and also change the course of things. That gives me a buzz. I'm enjoying the ride." But he adds, "Restructuring a company is very time consuming and you really have to roll up your sleeves and sort of dig yourself into the trenches."[1]

The investment banker and CEO just described illustrates one of the most important types of leaders in business, the turnaround specialist or transformational leader. Today, attention focuses on people in the workplace like Eliasch who can inspire and stimulate others to achieve worthwhile goals. The people who can accomplish these important deeds practice **leadership,** the ability to inspire confidence and support among the people who are needed to achieve organizational goals.[2]

leadership
The ability to inspire confidence and support among the people who are needed to achieve organizational goals.

Leadership can be exercised in many settings such as business, government, education, and sports. This chapter focuses on leadership in organizations. Leadership is often thought of as applying to people at the highest levels in organizations, but leadership is important at every level. As explained by author George B. Weathersby: Increasingly the productivity and profitability of every business team, operating department, corporate division, two-person service firm, and franchise operation is the true and lasting foundation of a strong economy in a city, state, nation, and region.[3] Effective leadership contributes to achieving these results. The success of the world's best companies is often attributed primarily to their leadership rather than physical assets. In contrast, ineffective leadership can impair the performance of an organizational unit or an organization.

Another perspective about the importance of leadership is that successful professionals, regardless of their job titles, should have leadership capabilities. In order to cope with frequent change and to solve problems, people are expected to exercise initiative and leadership in taking new approaches to their job. Also, in the modern organization, people slip in and out of leadership roles such as receiving a temporary assignment as a task force leader.[4]

In this chapter we describe the characteristics and behaviors of leaders in organizations, as well as useful leadership theories. You will also have the opportunity to read case histories of two world-class leaders.

THE LINK BETWEEN LEADERSHIP AND MANAGEMENT

Differentiate between leadership and management.

Today's managers must know how to *lead* as well as manage, or their companies will become extinct. (You will recall that leadership—along with planning, organizing, and controlling—is one of the basic functions of management.) Three representative distinctions between leadership and management are as follows:[5]

- Management is more formal and scientific than leadership. It relies on universal skills, such as planning, budgeting, and controlling. Management is a

LEADER	MANAGER
Visionary	Rational
Passionate	Consulting
Creative	Persistent
Flexible	Problem-solving
Inspiring	Tough-minded
Innovative	Analytical
Courageous	Structured
Imaginative	Deliberative
Experimental	Authoritative
Independent	Stabilizing
Shares knowledge	Centralizes knowledge

Sources: Genevieve Capowski, "Anatomy of a Leader: Where Are the Leaders of Tomorrow?" *Management Review*, March 1994, p. 12; David Fagiano, "Managers vs. Leaders: A Corporate Fable," *Management Review*, November 1997, p. 5

EXHIBIT 11-1

Leaders vs. Managers
The difference between leaders and managers is often one of emphasis on certain behaviors. It is important not to regard managers as all being stodgy and unimaginative, whereas leaders are all inspirational and creative.

set of explicit tools and techniques, based on reasoning and testing, that can be used in a variety of situations.

- Leadership, by contrast, involves having a vision of what the organization can become. Leadership requires eliciting cooperation and teamwork from a large network of people and keeping the key people in that network motivated, using every manner of persuasion.
- Management involves getting things done through other people. Leadership places more emphasis on helping others do the things they know need to be done to achieve the common vision.

Exhibit 11-1 presents a stereotype of the difference between leadership and management. Effective leadership and management are both required in the modern workplace. Managers must be leaders, but leaders must also be good managers. Workers need to be inspired and persuaded, but they also need assistance in developing a smoothly functioning workplace.

Exhibit 11-2 presents an overview of the link between leadership and management. It also highlights several of the major topics presented in this chapter.

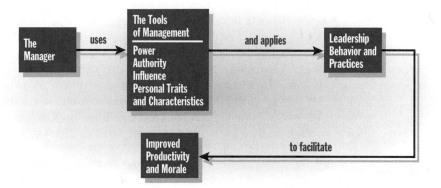

EXHIBIT 11-2

The Links between Management and Leadership
Management and leadership are both applied to improve productivity and morale, as shown in this diagram.

Source: Adapted from John R. Schermerhorn, Jr., *Management for Productivity*, 4th ed. (New York: Wiley, 1993).

The figure illustrates that, to bring about improved productivity and morale, managers do two things. First, they use power, authority, influence, and personal traits and characteristics. Second, they apply leadership behaviors and practices.

THE LEADERSHIP USE OF POWER AND AUTHORITY

Describe how leaders are able to influence and empower team members.

power
The ability or potential to influence decisions and control resources.

authority
The formal right to get people to do things or the formal right to control resources.

Leaders influence people to do things through the use of power and authority. **Power** is the ability or potential to influence decisions and control resources. Powerful people have the potential to exercise influence, and they exercise it frequently. For example, a powerful executive might influence an executive from another company to do business with his or her company. **Authority** is the formal right to get people to do things or the formal right to control resources. Factors within a person, such as talent or charm, help them achieve power. Only the organization, however, can grant authority. To understand how leaders use power and authority, we examine the various types of power, influence tactics, and how leaders share power with team members. Understanding these different approaches to exerting influence can help a manager become a more effective leader.

Types of Power

Leaders use various types of power to influence others. However, the power exercised by team members, or subordinates, acts as a constraint on how much power leaders can exercise. The list that follows describes the types of power exercised by leaders and sometimes by group members.[6]

1. **Legitimate power** is the authentic right of a leader to make certain types of requests. These requests are based on internalized social and cultural values in an organization. It is the easiest type of influence for most subordinates to accept. For example, virtually all employees accept the manager's authority to conduct a performance appraisal. Legitimate power has its limits, however, as described later under "subordinate power."
2. **Reward power** is a leader's control over rewards of value to the group members. Exercising this power includes giving salary increases and recommending employees for promotion.
3. **Coercive power** is a leader's control over punishments. Organizational punishments include assignment to undesirable working hours, demotion, and firing. Effective leaders generally avoid heavy reliance on coercive power, because it creates resentment and sometimes retaliation.
4. **Expert power** derives from a leader's job-related knowledge as perceived by group members. This type of power stems from having specialized skills, knowledge, or talent. Expert power can be exercised even when a person does not occupy a formal leadership position. An advertising copywriter with a proven record of writing winning ad slogans has expert power. A widely used form of expert power is the control of vital information. If a person controls information other people need, power will flow to that person. Having valuable contacts, such as knowing people prepared to invest in startup companies, is a form of controlling vital information.
5. **Referent power** refers to the ability to control based on loyalty to the leader and the group member's desire to please that person. Current research suggests that having referent power contributes to being perceived as charismatic, but expert power also enhances charisma.[7] Some of the loyalty to the

Power Flows Down	Zone of Indifference	Zone of Noncompliance	Power Flows Up
	Orders are acceptable; employees do not exercise subordinate power, but comply with requests and orders.	Orders are unacceptable; employees exercise subordinate power and refuse to comply.	

EXHIBIT 11-3

Subordinate Power and the Zone of Indifference
One source of group member power is refusing to comply with orders they believe are unreasonable. In organizations where hierarchy is deemphasized, group members are likely to have a broader zone of noncompliance.

leader is based on identification with the leader's personal characteristics. Referent power and charisma are both based on the subjective perception of the leader's traits and characteristics.

6. **Subordinate power** is any type of power that employees can exert upward in an organization, based on justice and legal considerations. For example, certain categories of workers cannot be asked to work overtime without compensation. Group members can always exercise expert power, but subordinate power restricts the extent to which power can be used to control them. As Exhibit 11-3 shows, when subordinates perceive an order as being outside the bounds of legitimate authority, they rebel.

Legitimate orders lie within a range of behaviors that the group members regard as acceptable. A legitimate order from above is acceptable to employees and falls within the **zone of indifference.** That zone encompasses those behaviors toward which the employees feel indifferent (do not mind following). If the manager pushes beyond the zone of indifference, the leader loses power. For example, few group members would accept an order to regularly carry out actions that harm the environment, such as dumping toxins.

Through subordinate power, group members control and constrain the power of leaders. Legal rights contribute to subordinate power. For example, an employee has the legal right to refuse sexual advances from the boss.

zone of indifference
The psychological zone that encompasses acceptable behaviors toward which employees feel indifferent (do not mind following).

Influence Tactics

In addition to various types of power, leaders use many other influence tactics to get things done. Seven frequently used influence tactics are as follows.

Leading by example means that the leader influences group members by serving as a positive model of desirable behavior. A manager who leads by example shows consistency between actions and words. For example, suppose a firm has a strict policy on punctuality. The manager explains the policy and is always punctual. The manager's words and actions provide a consistent model.

Assertiveness refers to being forthright in your demands. It involves a manager expressing what he or she wants done and how the manager feels about it. A leader might say, for example, "Your report is late, and that makes me angry. I want you to get it done by noon tomorrow." Assertiveness, as this example shows, also refers to making orders clear.

Rationality means appealing to reason and logic, and it is an important part of persuasion. Strong leaders frequently use this tactic. Rational persuasion has increased in importance because many managers work in situations in which they do not have extensive formal authority, but must rely on persuasion and teamwork. Rationality is also important when a manager must manage across different functions (outside of one's own department).[8] Pointing out the facts of a situation to group members to get them to do something is an example of rationality. For example, a middle-level manager might tell a supervisor, "If our department goes over budget this year, we are likely to be cut further next year." Knowing this, the supervisor will probably become more cost conscious.

Ingratiation refers to getting somebody else to like you, often through the use of political skill. A typical ingratiating tactic would be to act in a friendly manner just before making a demand. Effective managers treat people well consistently to get cooperation when it is needed.

Exchange is a method of influencing others by offering to reciprocate if they meet your demands. Leaders with limited expert, referent, and legitimate power are likely to use exchange and make bargains with subordinates. A manager might say to a group member, "If you can help me out this time, I'll go out of my way to return the favor." Using exchange is like using reward power. The emphasis in exchange, however, is that the manager goes out of his or her way to strike a bargain that pleases the team members.

Coalition formation is a way of gaining both power and influence. A **coalition** is a specific arrangement of parties working together to combine their power, thus exerting influence on another individual or group. Coalitions in business are a numbers game—the more people you can get on your side, the better. For example, a manager might band with several other managers to gain support for a major initiative such as merging with another company.

Joking and kidding are widely used to influence others on the job.[9] Good-natured ribbing is especially effective when a straightforward statement might be interpreted as harsh criticism. In an effort to get an employee to order office supplies over the Internet, one manager said, "We don't want you to suffer from technostress. Yet you're the only supervisor here who still orders office supplies by telephone, paper memos, and carrier pigeon." The supervisor smiled and proceeded to ask for help in learning how to execute orders for office supplies over the Internet.

coalition

A specific arrangement of parties working together to combine their power, thus exerting influence on another individual or group.

WHICH INFLUENCE TACTIC TO CHOOSE   Leaders are unlikely to use all the influence tactics in a given situation. Instead, they tend to choose an influence tactic that fits the demands of the circumstances. Researchers found support for this conclusion in a study of 125 leaders employed by a bank. To determine the influence tactics the leaders used, the researchers asked the leaders' superiors and subordinates to complete a questionnaire. The study found that in crisis situations the leaders used more expert power, legitimate power, referent power, and upward influence than in noncrisis situations. (Upward influence refers to using power to get higher-ranking people to act on one's behalf.) The study also concluded that the leaders were less likely to consult with subordinates in a crisis situation than in a noncrisis situation.[10]

Employee Empowerment and the Exercise of Power

In Chapter 9 empowerment was emphasized as a way of distributing authority in the organization. Empowerment is similarly a way for leaders to share power. When leaders share power, employees experience a greater sense of personal effectiveness and job ownership. Sharing power with group members enables them to feel better about themselves and perform at a higher level. Empowered employees perform better to a large extent because they become better motivated. The extra motivation stems from a feeling of being in charge. An important use of empowerment is to enhance customer service. As employees acquire more authority to take care of customer problems, these problems can be handled promptly—sometimes right on the spot.

A key component of empowerment is the leader's acceptance of the employee as a partner in decision making. Because the team member's experience and information are regarded as equal to those of the leader, he or she shares control. Both the leader and team member must agree on what is to be accomplished. The partnering approach to empowerment builds trust between the employee and the leader.[11]

The accompanying Manager in Action describes a manager who believes strongly in empowerment, yet is also a decisive, independent-thinking manager. The same person illustrates many other aspects of leadership and management presented in this chapter and throughout the text.

CHARACTERISTICS, TRAITS, AND BEHAVIORS OF EFFECTIVE LEADERS

Identify important leadership characteristics and behaviors.

Understanding leadership takes an understanding of leaders. This section will highlight findings about the personal attributes and behaviors of effective managerial leaders. *Effective*, in this context, means that the leader achieves both high productivity and morale, as Exhibit 11-2 illustrated. Be aware that, in this discussion, quality is an aspect of productivity.

Characteristics and Traits of Effective Leaders

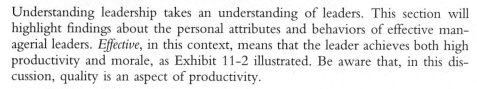

Possessing certain characteristics and traits does not in itself guarantee success. Yet effective leaders differ from others in certain respects. Justification for studying leadership traits is that the traits of leaders are related closely to the degree to which they are perceived to be leaders. For example, managers who are perceived to be good problem solvers are more likely to be accepted as leaders than those who are not.

Hundreds of human qualities can enhance leadership effectiveness in some situations. The list of traits and characteristics that follows is based on several research studies. It presents the factors we believe are the most relevant to the largest number of situations.[12]

1. *Drive and achievement motive, and passion.* Leaders are noted for the effort they invest in achieving work goals and the passion they have for work and work associates. Drive refers to such behaviors as ambition, energy, tenacity, and initiative. Drive also includes **achievement motivation**—finding joy in accomplishment for its own sake. High achievers find satisfaction in competing challenging tasks, attaining high standards, and developing better ways of doing things. Effective leaders are also passionate about their work. Ken Greene, a highly successful franchise operator of Bruegger Bagel Bakery stores, noted, "We love the business and have been very successful." In contrast, Quality Dining, another major Bruegger franchiser, decided to get out of the business said Greene, because "they had a very difficult time getting their arms around the emotions and passion of the business."[13]

2. *Power motive.* Successful leaders have a strong need to control other people and resources. **Power motivation** is a strong desire to control others or get them to do things on your behalf. A leader with a strong power need enjoys exercising power and using influence tactics. Only a manager who uses

achievement motivation
Finding joy in accomplishment for its own sake.

power motivation
A strong desire to control others or get them to do things on your behalf.

269

Manager *in Action*

Jack Welch of GE: The Manager's Manager

General Electric Co. chairman and chief executive Jack Welch is regarded as one of the world's best all-time business leaders, and a manager's manager. No other manager has created more shareholder wealth than Welch. Ever since he became the top executive at GE, Jack Welch has set his sites on turning the industrial conglomerate into the most globally competitive company in the world. By 1999 the company was pushing $100 billion in annual sales, and had 276,000 employees in 100 countries. At that time, GE had a capitalization (value of all the company stock) of over $425 billion, running neck and neck with Microsoft for the highest in the world.

The range of GE products and services include the ubiquitous light bulbs and home appliances, as well as jet engines, power generating systems, and an industrial finance company. Welch regularly warns employees about the dangers of complacency. He says, "We've just got to be faster. We come to work every day on the razor's edge of a competitive battle."

Welch takes great pride in his role in developing a talented group of managers. He claims one of his best contributions as a leader is to help boost the self-confidence of other GE managers, thereby preparing them to take decisive action. Welch's favorite form of communication with employees is a handwritten note, accompanied by a telephone call. Despite this touch of warmth, he is perceived by many as a take-no-prisoners tough guy in his management style.

Welch has a strong passion for winning, and a personality that captivates managers who work with him directly or observe him in training programs. He encourages full candor during the meetings he uses to resolve problems (Work Out sessions). Welch also

has an enormous capacity for understanding thousands of details about the business and people of GE. He pushes for informality throughout the company. Workers at all levels call him Jack. He violates chains of command and encourages his managers to do the same.

Expansion into international markets is a major part of Welch's growth strategy. Overseas sales now approach one-half of the company's revenues. Welch defines success in terms of GE being a dominant power in whatever market it enters. Under his leadership, GE has made 600 acquisitions, and moved from an old-line manufacturing company to one that earns most of its revenue from services. Among these services are lending money, leasing equipment, and running computer networks for other companies.

To increase GE's impact, Welch emphasizes stretch goals, which he defines as attempting to accomplish huge gains yet not knowing how to get there. This forces people to figure out the path to goal accomplishment. Welch sets precise performance targets for his managers and monitors them throughout the year. He believes strongly in the Six Sigma quality standard, despite some bureaucracy created by monitoring the standard.

Welch explains that the way he can contribute best as an executive is to allocate resources, people, and dollars. He reasons that his contribution is to detect opportunities, assign the right people to pursue them, and give them the funds they need to create. "I don't go to a major appliance review and pick out the colors or the crisper trays or all that sort of stuff. That's not my job," says Welch.

Part of Welch's growth strategy is to push GE deeper into services such as management training, servicing jet engines, and helping utilities run power plants. The company is at the forefront of regarding the product they sell as only one component of the business, with helping the customer make best use of the product being another key component. Welch maintains a vigil for new opportunities. A current possibility for expansion is consulting with other companies to show them how to cut costs and boost efficiency, using GE as a model.

Welch and other GE managers pursue every available means to increase profits and shareholder value. Welch has been referred to as Neutron Jack. (A neutron bomb kills people without destroying physical property.) During an 11-year period, GE has eliminated more than 123,000 jobs in the United States, cutting its work force nearly in half. Welch has also closed many factories and sold old-line businesses. Such moves, however, gave GE the cash flow it needed to fuel the growth Welch's competitive spirit demanded.

Under the leadership of Welch, GE managers push for whatever breaks and special favors they can squeeze from state and local government officials. In Louisville, Kentucky, GE plant managers threatened to close a factory unless state and local governments helped subsidize its modernization and 7,000 employees agreed to cost-cutting work rules. Even with $11 million in tax breaks, employment in Louisville continues to fall. Range and dryer production was phased out and moved to Georgia and Mexico, where wages are substantially lower.

Another method GE uses to boost profits is to establish a foreign sales corporation (FSC). The company then shunts its exports through its offshore FSC. No federal income taxes are required on a portion of the export profits. Part of GE's government subsidies have come from its FSC, which has allowed the company to forego payment on more than $500 million in taxes since 1986. During the same period, profits surged 228 percent, while the GE's tax payments to the U.S. Treasury rose 27 percent.

Many GE middle-level managers feel that they are under too much pressure to achieve short-term results, despite Welch's speeches about the importance of the long term. Many first-level managers and production workers, and clerical workers in GE plants and offices, feel that the company pushes them too hard to achieve corporate goals. An especially difficult goal is to be first or second in every market GE serves. Nevertheless, working for GE offers an excellent opportunity to develop as a professional or manager and receive good wages. Welch does not cut himself short on compensation either. He recently cashed in on over $31 million in stock options in one year, on top of $10 million in compensation.

Sources: John A. Byrne, "Jack: A Close-up Look at How America's #1 Manager Runs GE," *Business Week*, June 8, 1998, pp. 90–99; Tim Smart, "Fighting Like Hell to Be No. 1," *Business Week*, July 8, 1996, p. 48; Laura Karmatz and Aisha Labi, "States at War," *Time*, November 9, 1998, p. 46; Donald L. Barlett and James B. Steele, "General Electric: Jack the Nimble Globetrotter," *Time*, November 16, 1998, pp. 88–90; "The Jack and Herb Show," *Fortune*, January 11, 1999, pp. 163–166; www.ge.com.

power constructively could be promoted so rapidly in a modern, well-managed corporation. Bill Gates of Microsoft exemplifies a power-obsessed leader. Although he is already the richest person in the world and his company dominates its field, he attempts aggressively to either take business away from small competitors or buy them out. His obsession with market domination has contributed to his company's facing charges of unfair competition.

3. *Self-confidence.* Self-confidence contributes to effective leadership in several ways. Above all, self-confident leaders project an image that encourages subordinates to have faith in them. Self-confidence also helps leaders make some of the tough business decisions they face regularly.

4. *Trustworthiness and honesty.* Leadership is undermined without a leader being trusted. Trust is regarded as one of the major leadership attributes. Continuing

waves of downsizings, coupled with generous compensation boosts to executives, have eroded employee trust and commitment in many organizations. Effective leaders know they must build strong employee trust to obtain high productivity and commitment. A panel of academics and other experts identified trust as one of the essential attributes of leadership for the present and future. Leaders must be trustworthy, and they must also trust group members.[14] A major strategy for being perceived as trustworthy is to make your behavior consistent with your intentions. Practice what you preach and set the example. Let others know of your intentions and invite feedback on how well you are achieving them.

Closely related to honesty and integrity is being open with employees about the financial operations and other sensitive information about the company. In an **open-book company** every employee is trained, empowered, and motivated to understand and pursue the company's business goals.[15] In this way employees become business partners.

To help you link the abstract concept of trust to day-by-day behavior, take the self-quiz in Exhibit 11-4. You might use the same quiz in relation to any manager you have worked for.

5. *Good intellectual ability, knowledge, and technical competence.* An inescapable conclusion is that effective leaders are good problem solvers and knowledgeable about the business or technology for which they are responsible. A leadership theory based on the problem-solving ability of leaders notes that intelligent and competent leaders make more effective plans, decisions, and action strategies than do leaders with less intelligence and competence.[16] Similarly, an explanation of leadership developed by author Dale Zand indicates that the leader's skills of obtaining, using, and sharing useful knowledge are crucial to success in the Information Age.[17]

A formidable characteristic of an intelligent leader is to ask questions that give others insight into the consequences of their demands or positions. Herman Cain, chairman and CEO of Godfather's Pizza (and vice-president of the National Restaurant Association), attended a town hall meeting given by President Bill Clinton, to discuss covering more workers with health insurance. Cain asked Clinton, "If I'm forced to offer more benefits, what will I tell the people I'll have to fire?"[18]

6. *Sensitivity to people.* Sensitivity to people means taking people's needs and feelings into account when dealing with them. An effective leader tries not to hurt people's feelings or frustrate their needs. A sensitive leader gives encouragement to subordinates who need it and does not belittle or insult poor performers. Insensitivity, in terms of being abrasive and tactless, can sidetrack a manager's career.

7. *Sense of humor.* The effective use of humor is now regarded as an important part of a leader's job. In the workplace, humor relieves tension and boredom and defuses hostility. Because humor helps a leader dissolve tension and defuse conflict, it can help him or her exert power over the group. Claudia Kennedy is a three-star Army general and the Army's senior intelligence official, thereby occupying a key leadership position. During an interview for a magazine article, she mentioned that although she had no regrets, her demanding career had not allowed for having a husband and children. The reporter commented, "You could still get married." Kennedy retorted, "Well certainly—put my phone number in this article."[19]

---

open-book company
A firm in which every employee is trained, empowered, and motivated to understand and pursue the company's business goals.

EXHIBIT
11-4

*Behaviors and Attitudes of
a Trustworthy Leader*

Listed below are behaviors and attitudes of leaders who are generally trusted by their group members and other constituents. After you read each characteristic, check to the right whether this is a behavior or attitude that you appear to have developed already, or does not fit you at present.

	Fits Me	Does Not Fit Me
1. Tells people he or she is going to do something, and then always follows through and gets it done	☐	☐
2. Described by others as being reliable	☐	☐
3. Good at keeping secrets and confidences	☐	☐
4. Tells the truth consistently	☐	☐
5. Minimizes telling people what they want to hear	☐	☐
6. Described by others as "walking the talk"	☐	☐
7. Delivers consistent messages to others in terms of matching words and deeds	☐	☐
8. Does what he or she expects others to do	☐	☐
9. Minimizes hypocrisy by not engaging in activities he or she tells others are wrong	☐	☐
10. Readily accepts feedback on behavior from others	☐	☐
11. Maintains eye contact with people when talking to them	☐	☐
12. Appears relaxed and confident when explaining his or her side of a story	☐	☐
13. Individualizes compliments to others rather than saying something like "You look great" to a large number of people	☐	☐
14. Doesn't expect lavish perks for himself or herself while expecting others to go on an austerity diet	☐	☐
15. Does not tell others a crisis is pending (when it isn't) just to gain their cooperation	☐	☐
16. Collaborates with others to make creative decisions	☐	☐
17. Communicates information to people at all organizational levels	☐	☐
18. Readily shares financial information with others	☐	☐
19. Listens to people and then acts on many of their suggestions	☐	☐
20. Generally engages in predictable behavior	☐	☐

Scoring: These statements are mostly for self-reflection, so no specific scoring key exists. However, the more of the above statements that fit you, the more trustworthy you are—assuming you are answering truthfully. The usefulness of this self-quiz increases if somebody who knows you well answers it for you to supplement your self-perceptions.

8. *Emotional intelligence.* According to the extensive research of Daniel Goleman, most effective leaders are alike in one essential way: They have a high degree of emotional intelligence. Goleman believes that other qualities like good problem-solving ability and technical skills are minimum expectations for demanding leadership positions.[20] You will recall that emotional intelligence involves such capabilities as the ability to work with others and effectively bring about change. Key traits included in emotional intelligence are self-confidence, a sense of humor, a strong drive to achieve, and persuasiveness (all mentioned previously here).

Behaviors and Skills of Effective Leaders

Traits alone are not sufficient to lead effectively. A leader must also behave in certain ways and possess key skills. As Chapter 1 described, managers must have sound conceptual, interpersonal, technical, and political skills. The following actions or behaviors are linked to leadership effectiveness. Recognize, however, that behaviors are related to skills. For example, a leader who gives emotional support to team members is using interpersonal skills. An effective leader:

1. *Is adaptable to the situation.* Adaptability reflects the contingency viewpoint: A strategy is chosen based on the unique circumstances at hand. For instance, if a leader were dealing with psychologically immature subordinates, he or she would have to supervise them closely. Mature and self-reliant subordinates would require less supervision. Also, the adaptive leader selects an organization structure best suited to the situation. The circumstances would determine, for example, if the manager chose a brainstorming group or a committee.

   Another important aspect of adaptability is for a leader to be able to function effectively in different situations. Terry Patterson had been a successful executive in the auto parts industry before she became the CEO of Frederick's of Hollywood, the catalogue retailer of sexy lingerie and other women's clothing. Although the nature of the businesses were radically different, Patterson believed correctly that her overall knowledge of retailing and how to motivate people would be assets at Fredericks.[21]

   The ability to size up people and situations and adapt tactics accordingly is a vital leadership behavior. It stems from an inner quality called insight or intuition—a direct perception of a situation that seems unrelated to any specific reasoning process.

2. *Provides stable performance.* A manager's steadiness under heavy work loads and uncertain conditions helps subordinates cope with the situation. Most people become anxious when the outcome of what they are doing is uncertain. When the leader remains calm, employees are reassured that things will work out satisfactorily. Stability also helps the leader meet the expectation that a manager should be cool under pressure.

   Another asset of being stable is that appearing unstable can prevent a person from obtaining a key position. Steven A. Ballmer, the president of Microsoft (he reports to Bill Gates) was almost rejected for the position based on his explosive personality. Although a brilliant business strategist, he throws temper tantrums on the job and bawls out people violently. The Microsoft board, worried about his fiery temperament, took months to approve his promotion to president.[22]

3. *Demands high standards of performance for group members.* Effective leaders consistently hold group members to high standards of performance, which raises productivity. Setting high expectations for subordinates becomes a self-fulfilling prophecy. People tend to live up to the expectations set for them by their superiors. Setting high expectations might take the form of encouraging team members to establish difficult objectives. Setting high standards of performance is a major component of Jack Welch's managerial approach.

4. *Provides emotional support to group members.* Supportive behavior toward subordinates usually increases leadership effectiveness. A supportive leader is one who gives frequent encouragement and praise. The emotional support gen-

erally improves morale and sometimes improves productivity. Being emotionally supportive comes naturally to the leader who has empathy for people and who is a warm person.

5. *Gives frequent feedback.* Giving group members frequent feedback on their performance is another vital leadership behavior. The manager rarely can influence the behavior of group members without appropriate performance feedback. Feedback helps in two ways. First, it informs employees of how well they are doing, so they can take corrective action if needed. Second, when the feedback is positive, it encourages subordinates to keep up the good work.

6. *Has a strong customer orientation.* Effective leaders are strongly interested in satisfying the needs of customers, clients, or constituents. Their strong customer orientation helps inspire employees toward satisfying customers. Clark Johnson, the CEO of Pier 1 Imports, Inc., is a prime example. His company is a successful retail chain that specializes in imported household goods and gifts. Asked what his job entails, he replied, "I'm the head salesman." Johnson sells his company and his products to customers, and he sells a consistent vision of winning to his employees.[23]

7. *Recovers quickly from setbacks.* Effective managerial leaders are resilient: They bounce back quickly from setbacks such as budget cuts, demotions, and being fired. Leadership resiliency serves as a positive model for employees at all levels when the organization confronts difficult times. During such times effective leaders sprinkle their speech with clichés such as "Tough times don't last, but tough people do," or "When times get tough, the tough get going." Delivered with sincerity, such messages are inspirational to many employees.

8. *Plays the role of servant leader.* Some effective leaders believe that their primary mission is to serve the needs of their constituents. Instead of seeking individual recognition, servant leaders see themselves as working for the group members. The servant leader uses his or her talents to help group members. For example, if the leader happens to be a good planner, he engages in planning because it will help the group achieve its goals.[24] H. Ross Perot, the business executive who ran for president of the United States twice, said he would become a servant leader if elected to office. Many academic administrators see themselves as servant leaders; they take care of administrative work so instructors can devote more time to teaching and scholarship. To be an effective servant leader, a person would need the many leadership traits and behaviors described in this chapter.

LEADERSHIP STYLES

Another important part of the leadership function is **leadership style**. It is the typical pattern of behavior that a leader uses to influence his or her employees to achieve organizational goals. Several different approaches to describing leadership styles have developed over the years. Most of these involve how much authority and control the leader turns over to the group.

First, this section will describe two classical approaches for categorizing leadership styles. We will then discuss the Leadership Grid® styles of leadership, followed by the situational theory of leadership, which emphasizes its contingency nature. We will also describe the entrepreneurial leadership style. Skill-Building Exercise 11-A, at the end of the chapter, gives you a chance to measure certain aspects of your leadership style.

Describe the leadership continuum, Theory X and Theory Y, Leadership Grid, situational, and entrepreneurial styles of leadership.

leadership style
The typical pattern of behavior that a leader uses to influence his or her employees to achieve organizational goals.

The Leadership Continuum

The leadership continuum, or classical approach, classifies leaders according to how much authority they retain for themselves versus how much they turn over to a group. Three key points on the continuum represent autocratic, participative, and free-rein styles of leadership. Exhibit 11-5 illustrates the leadership continuum.

autocratic leader
A task-oriented leader who retains most of the authority for himself or herself and is not generally concerned with group members' attitudes toward decisions.

AUTOCRATIC LEADERSHIP STYLE   **Autocratic leaders** retain most of the authority for themselves. They make decisions in a confident manner and assume that group members will comply. An autocratic leader is not usually concerned with the group members' attitudes toward the decision. Autocratic leaders are considered task-oriented because they place heavy emphasis on getting tasks accomplished. Typical autocratic leaders tell people what to do, assert themselves, and serve as models for group members.

Autocratic leaders are not inevitably mean and insensitive, yet many are difficult people. One of the most demanding, insensitive leaders of a successful enterprise is Robert Crandall, the retired chairman of American Airlines. His uncompromising attitude made him disliked by labor unions, pilots, and nonflight personnel. Crandall cursed incessantly and regularly called weekend meetings with managers. His nicknames included "Darth Vader" and "Fang."[25] (Despite his strategic brilliance Crandall did not practice good human relations.)

participative leader
A leader who shares decision making with group members.

PARTICIPATIVE LEADERSHIP STYLE   A **participative leader** is one who shares decision making with group members. There are three closely related subtypes of participative leaders: consultative, consensus, and democratic. *Consultative leaders* confer with subordinates before making a decision. However, they retain the final authority to make decisions. *Consensus leaders* encourage group discussion about an issue and then make a decision that reflects the general opinion (consensus) of group members. All workers who will be involved in the consequences of a decision have an opportunity to provide input. A decision is not considered final until all parties involved agree with the decision. *Democratic leaders* confer final authority on the group. They function as collectors of opinion and take a vote before making a decision.

Participative leadership takes many forms, including the employee involvement typical of teams in an organization practicing quality management. Royal/Dutch Shell uses participative management in what they term a grass-roots approach to improving company operations. The idea is to empower frontline employees, including service station attendants, to suggest ways of improving Royal/Dutch Shell. Improvements are made in teams composed of workers at several levels. An example of a suggestion was to sell liquified natural gas at service stations in Asia.[26]

EXHIBIT 11-5

The Leadership Continuum

According to the leadership continuum, the autocratic style gives the leader the most authority, whereas the free-rein style gives group members most of the authority.

Amount of Authority Held by the Leader

Autocratic Style	Participative Style	Free-Rein Style
	Consultative Consensus Democratic	

Amount of Authority Held by Group Members

FREE-REIN LEADERSHIP STYLE   The **free-rein leader** turns over virtually all authority and control to the group. Leadership is provided indirectly rather than directly. Group members are presented with a task to perform and are given free rein to figure out the best way to perform it. The leader does not get involved unless requested. Subordinates are allowed all the freedom they want as long as they do not violate company policy. In short, the free-rein leader delegates completely.

free-rein leader
A leader who turns over virtually all authority and control to the group.

Theory X and Theory Y

Autocratic and participative leaders see people differently. This difference in perception is the basis for the Theory X and Theory Y explanation of leadership style, as summarized in Exhibit 11-6. Douglas McGregor developed these distinctions to help managers critically examine their assumptions about workers. Theory X and Theory Y form part of the foundation of the human relations approach to management.

Although Theory X and Theory Y are fading from mention in management books today, the ideas are still relevant. Many leaders and managers stop to examine the assumptions they make about group members in order to manage more effectively. In contrast, leaders and managers who do not assess their assumptions might make errors in attempting to lead others. For example, a manager might wrongly assume that group members are all motivated primarily by money.

Leadership Grid® Leadership Styles

Several approaches to understanding leadership styles focus on two major dimensions of leadership: tasks and relationships. The best known of these approaches is the **Leadership Grid.** It is based on different integrations of the leader's concern for production (tasks) and people (relationships). As Exhibit 11-7 shows, Grid terms are levels of concern on a scale of 1 to 9, with concern for production listed first and concern for people listed second. The Leadership Grid is part of a comprehensive program of leadership training and organizational development.

Leadership Grid
A visual representation of different combinations of a leader's degree of concern for task-related issues.

Theory X and Theory Y

EXHIBIT
11-6

According to Douglas McGregor, leadership approaches are influenced by a leader's assumptions about human nature. Managers make two contrasting assumptions about workers:

Theory X Assumptions. Managers who accept Theory X believe that:

1. The average person dislikes work and will avoid it if possible.
2. Because of this dislike of work, most people must be coerced, controlled, directed, or threatened with punishment to get them to put forth enough effort to achieve organizational objectives.
3. The average employee prefers to be directed, wishes to shirk responsibility, has relatively little ambition, and puts a high value on security.

Theory Y Assumptions. Managers who accept Theory Y believe the statements in the list that follows. Equally impor-

tant, these managers diagnose a situation to learn what type of people they are supervising.

1. The expenditure of physical and mental effort in work is as natural as play or rest for the average human being.
2. People will exercise self-direction and self-control to achieve objectives to which they are committed.
3. Commitment to objectives is related to the rewards associated with their achievement.
4. The average person learns, under proper conditions, not only to accept but to seek responsibility.
5. Many employees have the capacity to exercise a high degree of imagination, ingenuity, and creativity in the solution of organizational problems.
6. Under the present conditions of industrial life, the intellectual potential of the average person is only partially utilized.

Source: Adapted from Douglas McGregor, *The Human Side of Enterprise* (New York: McGraw-Hill, 1960), pp. 33–48.

Concern for production is rated on the Grid's horizontal axis. Concern for production includes results, bottom line, performance, profits, and mission. Concern for people is rated on the vertical axis, and it includes concern for group members and coworkers. Both concerns are leadership attitudes or ways of thinking about leadership. The Grid identifies seven styles, yet a leader's approach could fall into any of 81 positions on the Grid.

EXHIBIT 11-7

The Leadership Grid

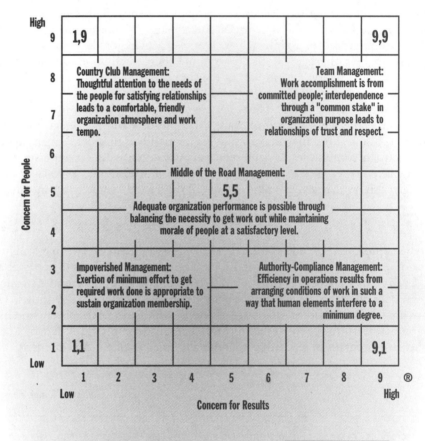

Concern for People

High

9 — **1,9**

8 — **Country Club Management:**
Thoughtful attention to the needs of the people for satisfying relationships leads to a comfortable, friendly organization atmosphere and work tempo.

Team Management:
Work accomplishment is from committed people; interdependence through a "common stake" in organization purpose leads to relationships of trust and respect.

9 — **9,9**

6 —

Middle of the Road Management:

5 — **5,5**

Adequate organization performance is possible through balancing the necessity to get work out while maintaining morale of people at a satisfactory level.

4 —

3 — **Impoverished Management:**
Exertion of minimum effort to get required work done is appropriate to sustain organization membership.

Authority-Compliance Management:
Efficiency in operations results from arranging conditions of work in such a way that human elements interfere to a minimum degree.

2 —

1 — **1,1**   **9,1**

Low

  1   2   3   4   5   6   7   8   9 ®

Low   **High**

Concern for Results

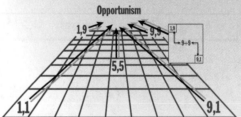

Opportunism

In Opportunistic Management, people adapt and shift to any Grid style needed to gain the maximum advantage. Performance occurs according to a system of selfish gain. Effort is given only for an advantage for personal gain.

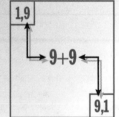

9+9 Paternalism/Maternalism
Reward and approval are bestowed to people in return for loyalty and obedience; failure to comply leads to punishment.

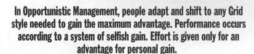

The developers of the Grid argue strongly for the value of team management (9,9). According to their research, the team management approach pays off. It results in improved performance, low absenteeism and turnover, and high morale. Team management relies on trust and respect, which help bring about good results.[27]

The Grid has an important message: When leading others, think first of striving to use the team management style. By so doing you will keep focused on obtaining high productivity, quality, and morale. As a team manager, you will also apply knowledge of human behavior to obtaining results through people.

The Situational Leadership Model

A major perspective on leadership is that effective leaders adapt their style to the requirements of the situation. The characteristics of the group members comprise one key requirement. The **situational leadership model** of Paul Hersey and Kenneth H. Blanchard explains how to match leadership style to the readiness of group members.[28] The situational leadership training program is widely used in business because it offers leaders practical suggestions for dealing with everyday leadership problems.

BASICS OF THE MODEL   Leadership in the situational model is classified according to the relative amount of task and relationship behavior the leader engages in. **Task behavior** is the extent to which the leader spells out the duties and responsibilities of an individual or group. **Relationship behavior** is the extent to which the leader engages in two-way or multi-way communication. It includes such activities as listening, providing encouragement, and coaching. As Exhibit 11-8 shows, the situational model places combinations of task and relationship behaviors into four quadrants. Each quadrant calls for a different leadership style.

The situational leadership model states there is no one best way to influence group members. The most effective leadership style depends on the readiness level of group members. **Readiness** in situational leadership is defined as the extent to which a group member has the ability and willingness or confidence to accomplish a specific task. The concept of readiness is therefore not a characteristic, trait, or motive—it relates to a specific task.

Readiness has two components, ability and willingness. Ability is the knowledge, experience, and skill an individual or group brings to a particular task or activity. Willingness is the extent to which an individual or group has the confidence, commitment, and motivation to accomplish a specific task.

The key point of situational leadership theory is that as a group member's readiness increases, a leader should rely more on relationship behavior and less on task behavior. When a group member becomes very ready, a minimum of task or relationship behavior is required of the leader. Notice that in the readiness condition R4 (as shown in Exhibit 11-8), the group member is able and willing or confident. The manager therefore uses a delegating leadership style (quadrant 4). He or she turns over responsibility for decisions and implementation.

EVALUATION OF THE SITUATIONAL MODEL   The situational model represents a consensus of thinking about leadership behavior in relation to group members: Competent people require less specific direction than do less competent people. The situational model also supports common sense and is therefore

situational leadership model
An explanation of leadership that explains how to match leadership style to the readiness of group members.

task behavior
The extent to which the leader spells out the duties and responsibilities of an individual or group.

relationship behavior
The extent to which the leader engages in two-way or multi-way communication.

readiness
In situational leadership, the extent to which a group member has the ability and willingness or confidence to accomplish a specific task.

279

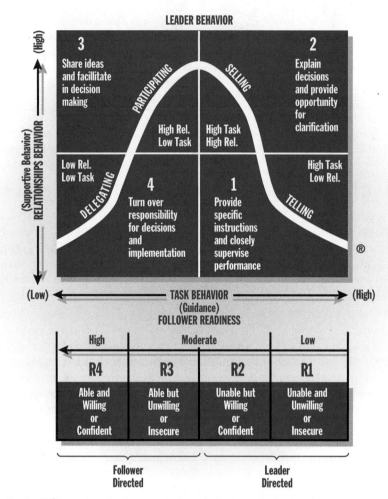

EXHIBIT 11-8

The Situational Model of Leadership

appealing. You can benefit from the model by attempting to diagnose the readiness of group members before choosing the right leadership style.

Nevertheless, the model presents categories and guidelines so precisely that it gives the impression of infallibility. In reality, leadership situations are less clear-cut than the four quadrants suggest. Also, the prescriptions for leadership will work only some of the time. For example, many supervisors use a telling style with unable and unwilling or insecure team members (R1) and still achieve poor results.

The Entrepreneurial Leadership Style

Interest in entrepreneurial leadership continues to grow as start-up companies and other small enterprises become an important source of new employment. Corporate giants like AT&T and GE continue to shrink in terms of number of people employed, often outsourcing both manufacturing and services to smaller companies. Small businesses account for 47 percent of all sales in the United States. John Clow, a director of business education programs, calls entrepreneurs "the creative forces within the economy, offering new ideas and bringing improvement in the human condition."[29]

Managers who initiate one or more innovative business enterprises show some similarity in leadership style. In overview, they tend to be task-oriented and charismatic. Entrepreneurs often possess the following personal characteristics and behaviors:

1. *A strong achievement need.* Entrepreneurs have stronger achievement needs than most managers. Building a business is an excellent vehicle for accomplishment. The high achiever shows three consistent behaviors and attitudes. He or she (a) takes personal responsibility to solve problems, (b) attempts to achieve moderate goals at moderate risks, and (c) prefers situations that provide frequent feedback on results (readily found in starting a new enterprise).[30]

2. *High enthusiasm and creativity.* Related to the achievement need, entrepreneurs are typically enthusiastic and creative. Their enthusiasm in turn makes them persuasive. As a result, entrepreneurs are often perceived as charismatic by their employees and customers. Henry Yeun, a past winner of the National Entrepreneur of the Year Award, says that an entrepreneurial leader is "genetically inclined to be an optimist."[31] Some entrepreneurs are so emotional that they are regarded as eccentric.

3. *Always in a hurry.* Entrepreneurs are always in a hurry. When engaged in one meeting, their minds typically begin to focus on the next meeting. Their flurry of activity rubs off on subordinates and others around them. Entrepreneurs often adopt a simple style of dressing to save time. A male entrepreneur may wear slip-on shoes so he doesn't have to bother with laces in the morning. A female entrepreneur may wear an easy-to-maintain short haircut.

4. *Visionary perspective.* Successful entrepreneurs carefully observe the world around them, in constant search for their next big marketable idea. They see opportunities others fail to observe. One example is Andy Taylor, who founded Enterprise Rent-a-Car. The opportunity he saw was to build a car rental agency that specialized in renting cars to airline travelers and people whose car was being repaired. Enterprise is now a major player in the car rental business.

5. *Uncomfortable with hierarchy and bureaucracy.* Entrepreneurs, by temperament, are not ideally suited to working within the mainstream of a bureaucracy. Many successful entrepreneurs are people who were frustrated by the constraints of a bureaucratic system. Once the typical entrepreneur launches a successful business, he or she would be wise to hire a professional manager to take over the internal workings of the firm. The entrepreneur would then be free to concentrate on making sales, raising capital, and pursuing other external contacts.

6. *A much stronger interest in dealing with customers than employees.* One of the reasons entrepreneurs have difficulty with bureaucracy is that they focus their energies on products, services, and customers. Some entrepreneurs are gracious to customers and moneylenders but brusque with company insiders.

The preceding list implies that it is difficult to find a classic entrepreneur who is also a good organizational manager. Many successful entrepreneurs therefore hire professional managers to help them maintain what they (the entrepreneurs) have built. You will recall that the Dineh Mohajer, the cofounder of Hard Candy, hired a professional manager to help her manage the enterprise she created.

TRANSFORMATIONAL AND CHARISMATIC LEADERSHIP

The major new emphasis in the study of leadership is the **transformational leader**—one who helps organizations and people make positive changes in the way they do things. Transformational leadership is a combination of charisma, inspirational lead-

Describe transformational and charismatic leadership.

281

transformational leader
A leader who helps organizations and people make positive changes in the way they do things.

ership, and intellectual stimulation. It is especially critical to the revitalization of existing business organizations. The transformational leader develops new visions for the organization and mobilizes employees to accept and work toward attaining these visions. Recent research indicates that the transformational style of leader, in contrast to a more traditional leader, actually does improve business-unit performance.[32] This section will describe how transformations take place, the role of charisma, how to become charismatic, and the downside of charismatic leadership.

How Transformations Take Place

The transformational leader attempts to overhaul the organizational culture or subculture. To bring about the overhaul, transformations take place in one or more of three ways.[33] First, the transformational leader raises people's awareness of the importance and value of certain rewards and how to achieve them. The leader might point out the pride workers would experience if the firm became number one in its field. He would also highlight the accompanying financial rewards.

Second, the transformational leader gets people to look beyond their self-interests for the sake of the work group and the firm. Such a leader might say, "I know you would like more support workers. But, if we don't cut expenses, we'll all be out of a job." Third, the transformational leader helps people go beyond a focus on minor satisfactions to a quest for self-fulfillment. He or she might explain, "I know that a long lunch break is nice. But, just think, if we get this project done on time, we'll be the envy of the company."

Johan Eliasch, the head of HTM, described at the beginning of this chapter, can be regarded as a transformational leader. C. Michael Armstrong, the CEO of AT&T (mentioned later also as charismatic), is a better-known transformational leader. Within three weeks after joining the company, he put AT&T on a different track by pulling the plug on the company's drive to resell local telephone service. Within one year Armstrong reversed profit declines by shedding thousands of jobs and accelerating sales growth. He expanded the company's wireless and Internet businesses and entered local telephone markets directly (not through reselling on borrowed lines). An investment portfolio manager commented on these accomplishments, "I'm pleasantly surprised and almost shocked that Armstrong in one year has turned the culture of AT&T around."[34]

The Link Between Charisma and Transformational Leadership

charisma
The ability to lead or influence others based on personal charm, magnetism, inspiration, and emotion.

Transformational leaders typically have **charisma**, the ability to lead or influence others based on personal charm, magnetism, inspiration, and emotion. To label a leader as charismatic does not mean that everybody perceives him or her in this manner. Even the most popular and inspiring leaders are perceived negatively by some members of their organization. Exhibit 11-9 presents glimpses of well-publicized managers who are perceived by many to have charisma.

Transformational and charismatic leaders have the characteristics and behaviors described at the start of the chapter. The list that follows presents transformational leaders' qualities that relate specifically to charisma.[35]

1. *Vision.* Charismatic leaders offer an exciting image of where the organization is headed and how to get there. A vision is more than a forecast, because it describes an ideal version of the future of an organization or organizational unit.

Leader and Organization	Sample of Charismatic Behavior or Reactions from Others
Kim Polese, CEO and cofounder of Marimba Inc., an Internet software company	Mobbed by autograph seekers at trade shows, she grabs the spotlight when possible. Takes risks by investing money in new personnel before business orders have been received. Her charm and wisdom attract investors.
C. Michael Armstrong, CEO of AT&T	Extraordinary confidence in what he is doing has energized thousands of employees who were worried about the future of AT&T before he arrived in 1997. Has converted the telecommunications giant into a growth company.
Steve Jobs, cofounder of Apple Computer Inc., and now interim CEO. Also CEO of Pixar Animation Studios	Projects great visions which inspire people to work 80 hours per week, and gets wealthy investors, including Bill Gates, to pour millions into his ventures. A folk hero among thousands of information technology fans.
Willy C. Shih, digital imaging executive at Eastman Kodak Co.	So excited about his products that he often snaps digital images of visitors and follows up by sending them e-mails of these images. Combines personal flair with excellent marketing strategy.
Martha R. Ingram, CEO of Ingram Industries, Inc., wholesale distributor of books and other information products	Uses her gracious southern charm to win the confidence of customers, as she cuts billion-dollar deals to strengthen the Ingram empire.
Herb Kelleher, CEO, Southwest Airlines	Engages in zany antics such as singing and dancing on the job, and kissing both male and female employees to encourage fun on the job. Projects personal belief that a positive attitude toward customer service leads to competitive advantage. His approach to leadership and the success of his company, along with his personality, have made him a favorite of management experts. He is cited and quoted in hundreds of articles and books about management.

EXHIBIT 11-9

Examples of Charismatic Leadership
The leaders mentioned here are perceived as charismatic by many work associates. To the right of each person mentioned is an example of their charismatic behavior, or its impact on others.

2. *Masterful communication style.* To inspire people, charismatic and transformational leaders use colorful language and exciting metaphors and analogies. The president of Coca-Cola tells people, "We give people around the world a moment of pleasure in their daily lives."

3. *Inspire trust.* People believe so strongly in the integrity of charismatic leaders that they will risk their careers to pursue the leader's vision.

4. *Help group members feel capable.* A technique that charismatic leaders often use to boost their followers' self-images is to let them achieve success on relatively easy projects. The group members are then praised and given more-demanding assignments.

5. *Energy and action orientation.* Similar to entrepreneurs, most charismatic leaders are energetic and serve as a model for getting things done on time.

6. *Intellectual stimulation to others.* Transformational leaders actively encourage group members to look at old problems or methods in new ways. They emphasize getting people to rethink problems and reexamine old assumptions.

7. *Provide inspirational leadership.* Partly as a result of the six characteristics listed above, transformational and charismatic leaders emotionally arouse people to the point that they want to achieve higher goals than they thought of previously. In short, the charismatic leader is an inspiration to many others.

Developing Charisma

Managers can improve their chances of being perceived as charismatic by engaging in favorable interactions with group members, using a variety of techniques.[36] A starting point is to *use visioning.* Develop a dream about the future of your unit and discuss it with others. *Make frequent use of metaphors.* Develop metaphors to inspire the people around you. A commonly used one after the group has experienced a substantial setback is to say, "Like the phoenix, we will rise from the ashes of defeat." It is important to *inspire trust and confidence.* Get people to believe in your competence by making your accomplishments known in a polite, tactful way.

Remember to *make others feel capable* by giving out assignments on which others can succeed, and lavishly praising their success. *Be highly energetic and goal oriented* so you can impress others with your energy and resourcefulness. To increase your energy supply, exercise frequently, eat well, and get ample rest. It is important to *express your emotions frequently.* Freely express warmth, joy, happiness, and enthusiasm. *Smile frequently, even if you are not in a happy mood.* A warm smile indicates a confident, caring person, which contributes to perceptions of charisma. *Make everybody you meet feel that he or she is quite important.* For example, at a company meeting shake the hand of every person you meet.

A relatively easy characteristic to develop is to *multiply the effectiveness of your handshake.* Shake firmly without creating pain, and make enough eye contact to notice the color of the other person's eyes. When you take that much trouble, you project care and concern. Finally, *stand up straight and also use other nonverbal signs of self-confidence.* Practice having good posture. Minimize fidgeting and speaking in a monotone.

The Downside of Charismatic Leadership

Charismatic business leaders are seen as corporate heroes when they can turn around a failing business or launch a new enterprise. Nevertheless, this type of leadership has a dark side. Some charismatic leaders manipulate and take advantage of people, such as by getting them to invest retirement savings in risky company stock. Some charismatic leaders are unethical and lead their organizations toward illegal and immoral ends. People are willing to follow the charismatic leader down a quasi-legal path because of his or her charisma. Frank Lorenzo, the former top executive at Eastern Airlines (now defunct) and Continental Airlines, had charismatic appeal to some people. He was able to attract enough followers to support his plan to crush the labor unions at both airlines and sell off valuable assets. Lorenzo ultimately walked away from a financially troubled Continental, manipulating a settlement of $30 million for himself.

Explain how to exercise SuperLeadership.

SUPERLEADERSHIP: LEADING OTHERS TO LEAD THEMSELVES

An important goal for a leader is to become a **SuperLeader**, one who leads others to lead themselves.[37] When people are self-directing, they require a minimum of external control. A SuperLeader leads others to lead themselves by acting as a teacher and a coach, not a director. The key aspect of SuperLeadership deals with learning the right thought patterns. The formulators of the SuperLeadership theory, Charles Manz and Henry Sims, contend that the leader must teach team members how to develop productive thinking. He or she should reward employees when they think constructively. The purpose of productive, or constructive, thinking is to enable workers to gain control over their own behavior. The SuperLeader serves as a model of constructive thought patterns. For example, the leader should minimize expressing pessimistic, self-critical thoughts to team members.

Charles Manz recommends several desirable ways of establishing and altering thought patterns in order to practice self-leadership.[38]

1. *Identify destructive beliefs and assumptions.* After identifying negative thoughts, replace them with more accurate and constructive ones. For example, an employee might regard the manager's criticism as an indicator of personal dislike. A more productive thought is that the manager is just trying to help him or her perform at a higher level.
2. *Make a habit of talking to yourself positively and constructively.* Convert negative thoughts into positive ones. Avoid a statement such as, "My math skills are too poor to prepare a budget." Instead say, "In order to prepare a budget, I will have to improve my math skills. I'll get started tonight."
3. *Visualize methods for effective performance.* Imagine yourself moving effortlessly through a challenging assignment, using methods that have worked in the past. For example, visualize yourself making a hard-hitting presentation to management, a presentation similar to one with lesser stakes that you made in the past.

In summary, the SuperLeader helps create conditions whereby team members require very little leadership. Achieving such a goal is important because organizations have reduced the number of managers. Also, work arrangements such as teams and horizontal structures require self-management.

THE LEADER'S ROLE AS A MENTOR

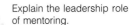

Another vital part of leadership is directly assisting less experienced workers to improve their job performance and advance their careers. A **mentor** is a more experienced person who develops a protégé's abilities through tutoring, coaching, guidance, and emotional support. The idea of mentoring traces back to ancient Greece when a warrior entrusted his son to the tutor Mentor. Although never out of style, mentoring is more important than ever as workers face complex and rapidly changing job demands.

The mentor, a trusted counselor and guide, is typically a person's manager or team leader. However, a mentor can also be a staff professional or coworker. A mentor is usually somebody who works for the same employer, yet many people are advised and coached by somebody outside their organization. Mentors are typically within the field of expertise of the protégé, but can also come from another specialty. For example, an accountant might be mentored by a manufacturing manager. A leader can be a mentor to several people at the same time, and successful individuals often have several mentors during their career.

Helping the protégé solve problems is an important part of mentoring. Mentors help their protégés solve problems by themselves and make their own discoveries. A comment frequently made to mentors is, "I'm glad you made me

SuperLeader
A person who leads others to lead themselves.

285

Explain the leadership role of mentoring.

mentor
A more experienced person who develops a protégé's abilities through tutoring, coaching, guidance, and emotional support.

think through the problem by myself. You put me on the right track." A mentor can also give specific assistance in technical problem solving. If the mentor knows more about the new technology than the protégé, he or she can shorten the person's learning time. Many developments in information technology are likely to be taught by a coworker serving as a mentor, because a manager often has less current technology knowledge than a group member.

Mentoring has traditionally been an informal relationship based on compatibility between two personalities. Since a mentor is a trusted friend, good chemistry should exist between the mentor and the protégé. Many mentoring programs assign a mentor to selected new employees. One study found that 31 out of 79 supervisor protégés were assigned a mentor.[39] Many formal mentoring programs began during the push for affirmative action in the 1970s. In the current era, formal mentors often supplement the work of managers by assisting a newcomer to acquire job skills and understand the organization culture.

Mentoring has been noted for its importance in helping minorities advance in their careers. A study was conducted of 280 minority senior managers making at least $100,000 in annual salary. The sample was composed of 161 African Americans, 63 Asian Americans, 43 Hispanic Americans, and 13 who identified themselves as "other." An important finding was that minorities with supportive superiors and coworkers (part of mentoring) have faster total compensation growth and progress more rapidly through the organization. The study also found that it was important for the mentor to be sufficiently highly placed in the organization to make an impact. The director of the study listed several actions that can help minority managers (as well as majority managers) advance:[40]

- Develop or build on good relationships with superiors and request feedback on performance at least once a year.
- Find and identify an informal mentor who is willing to be an advocate for your upward mobility within the organization, help you learn the informal rules of the workplace, and help you make valuable contacts.
- Identify the informal rules of the company that are helpful in navigating through the organization. (An example would be "Never turn down a request from upper management.")
- Build a set of self-management skills, including the ability to overcome potential roadblocks, remain focused on tasks, and assign priorities to tasks. (See Chapter 17.)

The link between the behaviors and competencies just mentioned and mentoring is that the leader/mentor can help the protégé achieve them. Being a good mentor therefore enables the leader to develop group members.

SUMMARY OF KEY POINTS

 Differentiate between leadership and management.
Management is a set of explicit tools and techniques, based on reasoning and testing, that can be used in a variety of situations. Leadership is more concerned with vision, change, motivation, persuasion, creativity, and influence.

 Describe how leaders are able to influence and empower team members.
Power is the ability to get other people to do things or the ability to control resources. Authority is the formal right to wield power. This chapter described six types of power: legitimate, reward, coercive, expert, referent

(stemming from charisma), and subordinate. Through subordinate power, team members limit the authority of leaders. To get others to act, leaders also use tactics such as leading by example, assertiveness, rationality, ingratiation, exchange, coalition formation, and joking and kidding.

Empowerment is the process of sharing power with team members to enhance their feelings of personal effectiveness. Empowerment increases employee motivation, because the employee is accepted as a partner in decision making.

 Identify important leadership characteristics and behaviors.
Certain personal characteristics are associated with successful managerial leadership in many situations, including the following: drive and achievement motive, and passion; power motive; self-confidence; trustworthiness and honesty; good intellectual ability, knowledge, and technical competence; sensitivity to people; sense of humor; and emotional intelligence.

Effective leaders need to demonstrate adaptability, stable performance, and high standards of performance, and provide emotional support to group members. They should give frequent feedback, have a strong customer orientation, recover quickly from setbacks, and perhaps be a servant leader.

 Describe the leadership continuum, Theory X and Theory Y, Leadership Grid, situational, and entrepreneurial styles of leadership.
Leadership style is the typical pattern of behavior that a leader uses to influence employees to achieve organizational goals. Autocratic leaders attempt to retain most of the authority. Participative leaders share decision making with the group. One subtype of participative leader is the consultative leader, who involves subordinates in decision making but retains final authority. A consensus leader also involves subordinates in decision making and bases the final decision on group consensus. A democratic leader confers final authority on the group. Free-rein leaders turn over virtually all authority and control to the group.

The distinctions between Theory X and Theory Y are made to help managers critically examine their assumptions about workers. According to Theory X assumptions, people basically dislike work and need to be controlled. According to Theory Y assumptions, people enjoy their work and want to be self-directing.

The Leadership Grid classifies leaders according to how much concern they have for both production and people. Team management, with its high emphasis on production and people, is considered the ideal.

The situational leadership model explains how to match leadership style to the readiness of group members. The model classifies leadership style according to the relative amount of task and relationship behavior the leader engages in. *Readiness* refers both to ability and willingness to accomplish a specific tasks. As group member readiness increases, a reader should rely more on relationship behavior and less on task behavior. When a group member becomes very ready, however, minimum task or relationship behavior is required.

Entrepreneurial leaders are generally task-oriented and charismatic. They have a strong achievement need, high enthusiasm and creativity, and a visionary perspective. They are uncomfortable with hierarchy and bureaucracy and are always in a hurry.

 Describe transformational and charismatic leadership.
The transformational leader helps organizations and people make positive changes. He or she combines charisma, inspirational leadership, and intellectual stimulation. Transformations take place through such means as pointing to relevant rewards, getting people to look beyond self-interest, and encouraging people to work toward self-fulfillment. Charismatic leaders provide vision and masterful communication. They can inspire trust and help people feel capable, and they are action-oriented. Some charismatic leaders are unethical and use their power to accomplish illegal and immoral ends.

 Explain how to exercise SuperLeadership.
An important goal for a leader is to become a SuperLeader, one who leads others to lead themselves. Teaching team members to develop productive thought patterns, such as encouraging them to talk to themselves positively and constructively, helps develop self-leadership.

Explain the leadership role of mentoring.
Mentoring is more important than ever as workers face complex and rapidly changing job demands. Mentors can be higher-ranking individuals, coworkers, or people outside the organization or from another specialty. Mentors help protégés solve problems by themselves and make their own discoveries. Mentoring can share an informal or formal relationship, and has been noted for its importance in helping minorities advance their careers.

KEY TERMS AND PHRASES

Leadership, *264*

Power, *266*

Authority, *266*

Zone of indifference, *267*

Coalition, *268*

Achievement motivation, *269*

Power motivation, *269*

Open-book company, *272*

Leadership style, *275*

Autocratic leader, *276*

Participative leader, *276*

Free-rein leader, *277*

Leadership grid, *277*

Situational leadership model, *279*

Task behavior, *279*

Relationship behavior, *279*

Readiness, *279*

Transformational leader, *282*

Charisma, *282*

SuperLeader, *285*

Mentor, *285*

QUESTIONS

1. Describe how a businessperson could be an effective leader yet an ineffective manager.
2. What steps can you take in the next several months to become a more powerful person?
3. Which influence tactic do you think would be particularly well suited to influencing an intelligent and well-educated person? Explain your reasoning.
4. Many career counselors believe that if a person spends too many years working for a large corporation, he or she becomes ill suited to exercising entrepreneurial leadership. For what reason might this observation be true?
5. For what type of leadership situation might a transformational leader be inappropriate?
6. Why might the practice of SuperLeadership make charisma less important?
7. New hires for technical and professional positions at many companies are assigned to a mentor, in addition to having a manager. In what way might this practice be less effective than finding a mentor by oneself?

SKILL-BUILDING EXERCISE 11-A: How Participative Is Your Leadership Style?

The purposes of this quiz are to: (1) specify what kind of behaviors are represented by an ideal participative leader, and (2) give you an opportunity to compare your behavior (or potential behavior) to that ideal. Be more concerned about giving yourself the gift of candid self-appraisal than attempting to give the "right" answer. Grade your leadership style by rating the frequency with which you use (or would use if placed in the situation) the behaviors listed: 3 = Almost Always; 2 = Sometimes; 1 = Never.

	AA	S	N
1. I believe that employee involvement is critical to my work group's success.	3	2	1
2. I hardly ever review our corporate mission statement with our group.	3	2	1
3. My work group develops its own measurable goals.	3	2	1
4. I communicate how my work group contributes to the success of the entire organization.	3	2	1
5. I allow my group to establish its own performance measures.	3	2	1
6. I provide informal performance feedback to my group.	3	2	1
7. My group plays an active role in determining its own recognition and rewards.	3	2	1
8. I appropriately delegate my responsibilities to my work group.	3	2	1
9. I support my work group by providing the resources it needs.	3	2	1
10. I emphasize the importance of work.	3	2	1

Scoring and interpretation: Subtract your answers to question 2, 3, 5, and 7 from the sum of your remaining answers.

11–14   You are already a participative leader (or already think and act like one).

7–10   You are well on your way to becoming a participative leader.

4–6   You have begun the shift to participative leadership (or are beginning to think in that direction).

0–3   You are still leading in a traditional manner (or are thinking like one who does).

Source: Adapted from a quiz from Suzanne W. Zoglio, *The Participative Leader* (Doylestown, PA: Tower Hill Press, 1994).

INTERNET SKILL-BUILDING EXERCISE: Analyzing a Business Leader's Knowledge or Expertise

An important part of being a successful leader is having valuable knowledge. Choose one of the leaders mentioned in this chapter, or another business leader of interest to you. Use one or more search engines to find additional information about the leader. After finding the information, prepare a brief description of what appears to be that leader's expertise or important knowledge. (For example, Johan Eliasch, described at the beginning of this chapter, is an expert at doing turnarounds, and has built a career on this expertise.) Also explain why this knowledge has contributed to the leader's success.

CASE PROBLEM 11-A: The Sensational Michael Dell of Dell Computer Corp.

Back in 1984, 19-year-old Michael Dell borrowed $1,000 to start a computer company from his University of Texas dormitory room. Today he is the fourth richest person in the United States, and the richest person in Texas. During a recent interview in a New York City hotel lobby, he calmly described how his computer company outperformed bigger rivals Compaq and IBM. "It makes you wonder whether we're doing well because we're doing a good job or because our competitors aren't doing a good job," Dell said in his monotone voice.

When photographed, Dell is usually wearing a business suit, and he lacks the eccentricities people often expect in an information-technology visionary. He is soft-spoken, and does not enjoy small talk. He works standing at a podium desk, absorbed in and invigorated by his work. Dell is married with four children.

Through 1998, company sales were growing at a 50-percent annual rate, and Dell Computer stock has had one of the most rapid climbs in the history of American business (up by 29,600 percent in the 1990s). For these reasons Dell has been labeled as one of the most successful entrepreneurs in American history. Recently, Dell returned to the University of Texas to speak to an entrepreneurship class. A student asked the young multibillionaire, "Why don't you just sell out, buy a boat, and sail off to the Caribbean?" Dell stared at him and replied, "Sailing's *boring*. Do you have any idea how much fun it is to run a billion-dollar company?"

At age 33, Dell is the youngest and longest-serving chief of a big computer company, and he is the most imitated technology manager. (Other companies have imitated his direct selling and mass customization of computers.) Dell Computer has just edged out Compaq as the number-one U.S. seller of desktop computers. One after another, his biggest competitors—IBM, Hewlett-Packard, and Compaq—have been pounded by price-cutting wars in the computer business. As a result, they have been forced into profound changes in how they make and sell computers. Dell's strategy of selling most of its computers directly to the customer and eliminating the middle person has become an industry standard.

Having started out as a mail-order company, Dell deploys a direct sales force to largely cut out the retailers, specialty stores, and distributors who can drive up prices. Annual sales are running at nearly $13 billion, making the company the world's biggest direct seller of computers. Dell Computer builds machines as customers order them. So instead of stockpiling products for distributors, the company can buy parts like disk drives and memory chips at the last minute. Inventory turnover at the company is seven days, compared with an industry average of about 80 days. The method saves money because component prices tend to fall many times throughout the year. Dell often shares the savings with its customers. Dell's army of sales representatives are intensely devoted to selling Dell machines, typically working 70 hours per week. The reps with the biggest accounts earn six-figure incomes.

The lowest-priced Dell Computer is $1,400, including the monitor. Commenting on lower-priced machines, Dell says, "If you look at a lot of these low-priced machines, they might appear as a brilliant strategy to expand the market. But many of these machines are stockpiled older models that don't run a lot of new software."

As a college freshman, Dell began buying surplus PCs from dealers and embellishing them with graphics cards and other parts that appealed to the computer-savvy buyer. He sold $180,000 in computers in his first month of business, essentially by spotting a market niche. Dell says, "I saw that you'd buy a PC for about $3,000, and inside that PC was about $600 worth of parts." Dell hired a small staff and began selling his machines over the phone and through the mail. Several years later he created the industry's first on-site service program, in which the repair technician visits your office or home. Dell says, chuckling, "That was a pretty important plus because we didn't have any stores." Consumed by his business, Dell decided to postpone completing his formal education. Shortly after his 23rd birthday, Dell took his company public.

Dell Computer encountered troubles in 1993 when the company attempted to sell computers through retail stores and unsuccessfully launched its first laptops. To rebound, the company quickly refocused on its roots, and hired top industry managers to help run what had become a multibillion-dollar direct-sales business. A management consultant said, "Michael realized he needed professionals to run the company, so that he could continue to be a visionary." In 1996, Dell began a highly successful initiative of selling more powerful business machines, called servers, that run networks of desktops.

The company has continued to expand its staff to fit its growth, and continues to prosper even when and where the computer industry runs into trouble. During the depths of the Asian economic crisis, Dell Computer was able to make money in the Far East, where sales were up by 77 percent in 1998. Dell explains that the cost and price advantages of the direct model allow for profit in any kind of market.

Dell's latest drive is boosting sales over the Internet. The company is already the biggest online seller of computers, with a remarkable $6 million per day in sales just two years after launching the Web store. The company is also trying to help its name catch up with its explosive sales. Recognizing that its image may not be as familiar as IBM or Compaq, Dell launched a major advertising campaign. Dell says in his laid-back manner, "We do see an opportunity to grow much faster in the market. Our focus is on the possibility, not just revenues."

Michael Dell believes that he built his successful enterprise by keeping his mind clearly focused on doing business instead of making money. He has concentrated on one major task: building high-quality computers and selling them at a lower price. He sees himself as a methodical person who squeezes the maximum out of an idea, and then tirelessly executes the idea. (Dell's foray into retail selling was an exception.) "I'm not a deal junkie," says Dell.

Discussion Questions

1. Identify three leadership behaviors or practices of Michael Dell by citing specific information from the case description just presented.
2. Identify three leadership traits or personal characteristics of Michael Dell by citing specific information from the case description just presented.
3. What suggestions can you offer Michael Dell for being an even more effective leader/manager? (The author of this book admits he would rather ask than answer this question.)

Sources: David E. Kalish, "For Whom the Dell Tolls," The Associated Press, August 24, 1998; "The Best Managers," *Business Week*, January 12, 1998, p. 64; Richard Murphy, "Michael Dell's Billion-Dollar Secret," *Success*, January 1999, pp. 50–53.

CASE PROBLEM 11-B: Big Changes at State Bank of India, California

State Bank of India (SBI) is the oldest and largest bank in India, and also has offices throughout the world. Brejein Kumar, a manager who had been with the bank for 31 years, had developed a reputation as a troubleshooter who could turn around problem situations. In 1992, he was sent on a four-year assignment as manager of SBI Washington. Two years later, however, he was appointed president and CEO of SBI California, located in Los Angeles. The change in assignment came about because the California division was experiencing numerous problems.

SBI California is composed of the downtown Los Angeles Branch, the Los Angeles Agency, and the Artesia Branch. When Kumar arrived in Los Angeles, he was shocked to discover the poor visibility and reputation of SBI California. The bank was virtually unknown to the large Indian community in California. Many new customers soon closed their accounts because of what they perceived as poor service and lack of caring for customer welfare. Regulatory agencies had given the bank a poor rating because of its sloppy policies and procedures.

Kumar said, "SBI California was the greatest challenge of my life. I needed to change the bank by improving its performance, and build good relations with customers and regulators. It was also necessary to make the Indian community aware of the bank."

Kumar focused first on improving relations with the regulators, with the hope of improving SBI California's ratings. He dug into paperwork, reviewing details of previous years' operations to understand why the bank was not performing well. After three weeks of analysis, Kumar devised a strategy for improving the bank's performance. He personally interviewed 25 employees to obtain their suggestions for improving the bank's reputation and performance. He added policies and procedures, all of which complied with government regulations. As a result, SBI California received an above-average rating by the regulators.

Next, Kumar focused on strengthening customer relations. He arranged for customer-contact workers to take training courses in management and customer relations. Employees deficient in computer skills were given appropriate training. Soon the entire work environment was computerized, allowing for faster customer service. Unlike previous bank managers, Kumar met personally with customers. He organized several meetings to which he invited prominent Indian businesspeople to see the improved SBI California.

Another Kumar initiative was to sponsor programs such as Youth Awards, events for India's Independence and Republic Days, and Indian classical music concerts. He redesigned many of SBI's brochures and promoted the bank through advertisements that were telecast on the International Channel during Indian programming. Another change Kumar implemented was to assemble an impressive board of directors comprised of corporate executives and industrialists, as well as the former ambassador to India.

SBI made front-page news in the Indian newspapers distributed in California. New business started pouring into the bank, and profits increased substantially. In the summer of 1996, SBI's chairman came from India to visit the California operation, and was greatly impressed by the bank's outstanding performance. The regulators, along with the board

of directors, persuaded the chairman to extend Kumar's stay in California one more year.

Company officers requested that Kumar open a branch in San Jose, based on both the booming Silicon Valley and the substantial Indian population in the area. Kumar played a major role in all aspects of launching the San Jose Branch to choosing the site, overseeing the setup, hiring employees, and developing an information-technology environment. He also developed a branch slogan that caught on quickly: "An American Bank with an Indian Heritage." The branch became an immediate success.

Kumar's U.S. assignment ended in September 1997. He received several awards for his enormous efforts and for his contribution to the Indian community as a whole. Upon his departure several bank employees said there would never be another leader as dynamic as Brejein Kumar.

Discussion Questions

1. How would you characterize Kumar's leadership style?
2. What suggestions would you make for improving Kumar's approach to leadership and management?
3. To what extent does Kumar qualify as a transformational leader?

Source: Cased researched by Kamini Kumar, Rochester Institute of Technology, 1998.

ENDNOTES

1. Excerpted and adapted from Lisa J. Adams, "CEO at Head Has Knack for Serving Up Aces," The Associated Press story, July 12, 1998.
2. W. Chan Kim and Renee A. Maubourgne, "Parables of Leadership," *Harvard Business Review*, July–August 1992, p. 123.
3. George B. Weathersby, "Leadership at Every Level," *Management Review*, June 1998, p. 5.
4. "Leadership—A Skill for Everyone!" *Keying In*, March 1997, p. 1.
5. John P. Kotter, *A Force for Change: How Leadership Differs from Management* (New York: Free Press, 1990); David Fagiano, "Managers vs. Leaders," *Management Review*, November 1997, p. 5.
6. John R. P. French, Jr., and Bertram Raven, "The Bases of Social Power," in Dorwin Cartwright and Alvin Zander (eds.), *Group Dynamics: Research and Theory* (New York: Harper & Row, 1960), pp. 607–623.
7. Jeffrey D. Kudisch, Mark L. Poteet, Gregory H. Dobbins, Michael C. Rush, and Joyce E. A. Russell, "Expert Power, Referent Power, and Charisma: Toward the Resolution of a Theoretical Debate," *Journal of Business and Psychology*, Winter 1995, p. 189.
8. Work of Jay Conger cited in Perry Pascarella, "Persuasion Skills Required for Success," *Management Review*, September 1998, p. 68.
9. Andrew J. DuBrin, "Sex and Gender Differences in Tactics of Influence," *Psychological Reports, 68*, 1991, pp. 645–646.
10. Mark Mulder, R. D. DeJong, L. Koppelaar, and J. Verlnage, "Power, Situation, and Leaders' Effectiveness: An Organizational Field Study," *Journal of Applied Psychology*, August 1986, pp. 556–570.
11. Frank J. Navran, "Empowering Employees to Excel," *Supervisory Management*, August 1992, p. 5.
12. Orlando Behling, "Employee Selection: Will Intelligence and Conscientiousness Do the Job?" *Academy of Management Executive*, February 1998, pp. 77–86; Shelly A. Kirkpatrick and Edwin A. Locke, "Leadership: Do Traits Matter?" *The Academy of Management Executive*, May 1991, pp. 48–60.
13. J. Leslie Sopko, "Investors Bet Bucks on Bagels," Rochester, New York, *Democrat and Chronicle*, September 5, 1997, p. 14D.
14. Genevieve Capowski, "Anatomy of a Leader: Where Are the Leaders of Tomorrow?" *Management Review*, March 1994, p. 15. Similar conclusions are reached in Robert F. Pearse and Gary Bonvillian, "Educating for Sustained High-Performance Leadership," *Compensation & Benefits Management*, Spring 1998, pp. 49–58.
15. John Case, "HR Learns How to Open the Books," *HRMagazine*, May 1998, p. 72.

16. Martin M. Chemers, *An Integrative Theory of Leadership* (Mahwah, NJ: Lawrence Erlbaum Associates, 1997), p. 39.
17. Dale Zand, *The Leadership Triad: Knowledge, Trust and Power* (New York: Oxford University Press, 1997), p. 23.
18. Herman Cain, "Leadership Is Common Sense," *Success*, January/February 1997, p. 47.
19. Sandra McElwaine, "A Different Kind of War," *USA Weekend*, October 3–5, 1997, p. 6.
20. Daniel Goleman, "What Makes a Leader?" *Harvard Business Review*, November–December 1998, pp. 91–102.
21. Nicola Godfrey, "Revamping a Vamp," *Working Woman*, September 1998, pp. 34–36.
22. Steve Hamm, "Bill's Co-pilot," *Business Week*, September 14, 1998, pp. 76–90.
23. "The Chief Salesman," *Success*, May 1991, p. 14.
24. Robert K. Greenleaf, "The Servant as Leader." www.stolaf.edu (accessed May 27, 1997).
25. Joel Stein, "Bosses from Hell," *Time*, December 7, 1998, p. 181.
26. Richard Pascale, "Change How You Define Leadership, and You Change How You Run a Company," *Fast Company*, April–May 1998, pp. 114–120.
27. Robert R. Blake and Anne Adams McCanse, *Leadership Dilemmas—Grid Solutions* (Houston: Gulf Publishing, 1991).
28. Paul Hersey, Kenneth H. Blanchard, and Dewey E. Johnson, *Management of Organizational Behavior: Utilizing Human Resources*, 7th ed. (Upper Saddle River, NJ: Prentice-Hall, 1996), pp. 188–227.
29. Quoted in "The Boom In Entrepreneurship," *Keying In*, March 1998, p. 1.
30. David C. McClelland, *The Achieving Society* (New York: Van Nostrand Reinhold, 1961).
31. Quoted in Gail Dutton, "Wanted: A Practical Visionary," *Management Review*, March 1998, p. 34.
32. Jane M. Howell and Bruce J. Avolio, "Transformational Leadership, Transactional Leadership, Locus of Control, and Support for Innovation: Key Predictions of Consolidated-Business-Unit Performance," *Journal of Applied Psychology*, December 1993, pp. 891–902.
33. John J. Hater and Bernard M. Bass, "Superiors' Evaluations and Subordinates' Perceptions of Transformation and Transactional Leadership," *Journal of Applied Psychology*, November 1988, p. 695.
34. "Earnings Jump 61% at AT&T," Bloomberg News story, October 27, 1998.
35. Alan J. Dubinsky, Francis J. Yammarino, and Marvin A. Jolson, "An Examination of Linkages Between Personal Characteristics and Dimensions of Transformational Leadership," *Journal of Business and Psychology*, Spring 1995, p. 315; Henry Mintzberg, "Covert Leadership: Notes on Managing Professionals," *Harvard Business Review*, November–December 1998, p. 140.
36. Andrew J. DuBrin, *Personal Magnetism: Discover Your Own Charisma and Learn How to Charm, Inspire, and Influence Others* (New York: AMACOM, 1997), pp. 93–111; Roger Dawson, *Secrets of Power Persuasion: Everything You'll Ever Need to Get Anything You'll Ever Want* (Upper Saddle River, NJ: Prentice Hall, 1992), pp. 18–183.
37. Charles C. Manz and Henry P. Sims, Jr., "SuperLeadership: Beyond the Myth of Heroic Leadership," *Organizational Dynamics*, Spring 1991, p. 18.
38. Charles C. Manz, "Helping Yourself and Others to Master Self-Leadership," *Supervisory Management*, November 1991, p. 9.
39. Bennett J. Tepper, "Upward Maintenance Tactics in Supervisory Mentoring and Nonmentoring Relationships," *Academy of Management Journal*, August 1995, p. 1195.
40. Survey conducted by Korn/Ferry International and Columbia University Business School reported in Jerry Langdon, "Minority Executives Benefit from Mentors," Gannett News Service story, December 7, 1998.

Twelve Chapter

Gilberto Heredia was standing outside an unemployment office in Texas when he first learned about McKay Nursery in Waterloo, Wisconsin. A migrant labor organizer told him about a place 1,000 miles to the north where worker housing was decent and free, and longevity was rewarded with something unheard of among migrant workers: employee stock ownership programs and retirement pensions. Intrigued, Heredia signed on for the next four years, journeying to Waterloo each fall. The fifth year, he stayed. "I got tired of going back and forth," he says. "Most of us do."

McKay is a 70-year-old, small-town horticulture nursery that year-round employs 60 people, mostly Mexican migrant workers. With annual sales estimated at $15 million, the company has offered an employee stock ownership plan (ESOP) to its full-time employees since 1984. McKay also offers profit sharing, and for employees who work a minimum of 1,000 hours yearly, a bonus in the form of cash or stock equaling 20 to 25 percent of their annual wages.

"The workers talk about them all the time—the ESOP and profit sharing," says Heredia, a general worker whom McKay can plug in whenever an experienced hand is needed. "It gives them a reason to talk about the future and plan for their kids and families." To keep employees informed, McKay president Griff Mason holds an annual meeting at the Waterloo town library. A Spanish interpreter explains the ESOP and profit sharing, and answers questions.

OBJECTIVES

After studying this chapter and doing the exercises, you should be able to:

 Explain the relationship between motivation and performance.

 Present an overview of major theories of need satisfaction in explaining motivation.

 Explain how goal setting is used to motivate people.

 Describe the application of behavior modification to worker motivation.

 Describe the role of financial incentives, including profit sharing and gainsharing, in worker motivation.

 Explain the conditions under which a person will be motivated according to expectancy theory.

293

Motivation

Upon retirement, employees must sell their stock back to McKay. Because the stock is not publicly traded, no one outside the company knows its per-share value. But for Heredia and his fellow employees, the prospect of retirement income, no matter how modest, makes a hard life much easier.

Heredia says the ESOP and profit sharing are not a drain on the company profits. "We are a very strong company. If the company has good sales, at the end of the year we get a bonus and dividend money." The program, he says, inspires hard work, and hard work makes the nursery competitive. Despite Waterloo's distance from Mexico (resulting in families separated by distance), word about McKay seems to be spreading. Says Heredia, "This is the first year I've seen so many Hispanic people looking for a job in Wisconsin."[1]

The employee stock ownership plan and financial bonuses offered at the Wisconsin nursery illustrate a fundamental truth about motivation: The right incentives can help build and retain a loyal and hard-working staff. A working knowledge of motivation theory and techniques (in this case stock ownership and financial bonuses) can help managers achieve good financial results. Understanding motivation is also important because how to motivate employees is a perennial challenge faced by managers. Low motivation contributes to low-quality work, superficial effort, indifference toward customers, and high absenteeism and tardiness.

The term *motivation* refers to two different but related ideas. From the standpoint of the individual, motivation is an internal state that leads to the pursuit of objectives. Personal motivation affects the initiation, direction, intensity, and persistence of effort. (A motivated worker gets going, focuses effort in the right direction, works with intensity, and sustains the effort.) From the standpoint of the manager, motivation is the process of getting people to pursue objectives. Both concepts have an important meaning in common. **Motivation** is the expenditure of effort to accomplish results. The effort results from a force that stems from within the person. However, the manager or team leader, or the group, can be helpful in igniting the force.

motivation
The expenditure of effort to accomplish results.

This chapter will present several theories or explanations of motivation in the workplace. In addition, it will provide descriptions of specific approaches to motivating employees. Exhibit 12-1 presents an overview of the various motivation theories and techniques this chapter will discuss. Referring back to this

12-1

Overview of Motivation Theories and Techniques In this chapter we present both theories and explanations of motivation, along with techniques based on them.

I. Theories and explanations of motivation
   1. Motivation through need satisfaction
      a. Maslow's need hierarchy
      b. Satisfaction of needs such as achievement, power, affiliation, and recognition
      c. Herzberg's two-factor theory
   2. Goal theory
   3. Behavior modification
   4. Expectancy theory
II. Specific motivational techniques stemming from theories
   1. Recognition programs
   2. Positive reinforcement programs
   3. Motivation through financial incentives
      a. Linking pay to performance
      b. Profit sharing and gainsharing
      c. Employee stock ownership programs and stock option plans
      d. Team incentives

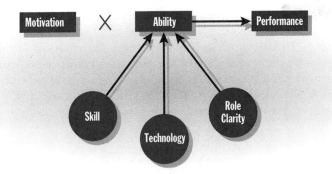

EXHIBIT
12-2

*Motivation and Ability as Factors in Performance
Motivation does contribute substantially to performance, but not as directly as many people think.*

figure will help you integrate the information in this chapter. All the ideas presented in this chapter can be applied to motivating oneself as well as others. For instance, when you read about the expectancy theory of motivation, ask yourself: "What rewards do I value strongly enough for me to work extra hard?"

THE RELATIONSHIP BETWEEN MOTIVATION AND PERFORMANCE

Many people believe the statements "You can accomplish anything you want" and "Think positively and you will achieve all your goals." In truth, motivation is but one important contributor to productivity and performance. Abilities, skills, and the right equipment are also indispensable. An office supervisor at a bank desperately wanted to become chairperson of the board within three years. Despite the intensity of his motivation, he did not reach his goal. The factors against him included his lack of formal business education, limited conceptual skills, underdeveloped political skills, and inadequate knowledge of high finance. Furthermore, the current chairperson had no intention of leaving the post.

Exhibit 12-2 shows the relationship between motivation and performance. It can also be expressed by the equation $P = M \times A$, where P refers to performance, M to motivation, and A to ability. Note that skill, technology, and role clarity contribute to ability.[2] For instance, if you are skilled at using a computer, if you have the right hardware and software, and if your assignment is clear, you can accomplish desktop publishing.

Group norms are another contributor to both motivation and performance. If group norms and organizational culture encourage high motivation and performance, the individual worker will feel compelled to work hard. To do otherwise is to feel isolated from the group. Group norms favoring low motivation and performance will often lower individual output.

A manager contributes to performance by motivating group members, improving their ability, increasing role clarity, and helping to create a positive work culture. Has a manager ever contributed to your performance?

Before studying specific explanations of motivation in the workplace, do Self-Assessment Exercise 12-A found on page 316. Taking the quiz will give you a preliminary idea of your current level of knowledge about motivation.

MOTIVATION THROUGH NEED SATISFACTION

The simplest explanation of motivation is one of the most powerful: people are willing to expend effort toward achieving a goal because it satisfies one of their important needs. A **need** is a deficit within an individual, such as a craving for

---

(1)

Explain the relationship between motivation and performance.

$P = M \times A$
An expression of the relationship between motivation and performance, where P refers to performance, M to motivation, and A to ability.

295

Present an overview of major theories of need satisfaction in explaining motivation.

need
A deficit within an individual, such as a craving for water or affection.

water or affection. Self-interest is thus a driving force. The principle is referred to as "What's in it for me?" or WIIFM (pronounced wiff'em). Reflect on your own experiences. Before working hard to accomplish a task, you probably want to know how you will benefit. If your manager asks you to work extra hours to take care of an emergency, you will most likely oblige. Yet underneath you might be thinking, "If I work these extra hours, my boss will think highly of me. As a result, I will probably receive a good performance evaluation and maybe a better-than-average salary increase."

People are motivated to fulfill needs that are not currently satisfied. An important implication of the need-satisfaction approach is that there are two key steps in motivating workers. First, you must know what people want—what needs they are trying to satisfy. To learn what the needs are, you can ask directly or observe the person. You can obtain knowledge indirectly by getting to know employees better. To gain insight into employee needs, find out something about the employee's personal life, education, work history, outside interests, and career goals.

Second, you must give each person a chance to satisfy needs on the job. To illustrate, one way to motivate a person with a strong need for autonomy is to allow that person to work independently.

This section examines needs and motivation from three related perspectives. First, we describe the best-known theory of motivation, Maslow's need hierarchy. Then we discuss several specific needs related to job motivation and move on to another cornerstone idea, Herzberg's two-factor theory.

Maslow's Need Hierarchy

Maslow's need hierarchy
The motivation theory that arranges human needs into a pyramid-shaped model with basic physiological needs at the bottom and self-actualizing needs at the top.

Based on his work as a clinical psychologist, Abraham M. Maslow developed a comprehensive view of individual motivation.[3] **Maslow's need hierarchy** arranges human needs into a pyramid-shaped model with basic physiological needs at the bottom and self-actualization needs at the top. (See Exhibit 12-3.) Lower-order needs, call **deficiency needs,** must be satisfied to ensure a person's existence, security, and requirements for human contact. Higher-order needs, or **growth needs,** are concerned with personal development and reaching one's potential. Before higher-level needs are activated, the lower-order needs must be satisfied. The five levels of needs are described next.

deficiency needs
Lower-order needs that must be satisfied to ensure a person's existence, security, and requirements for human contact.

growth needs
Higher-order needs that are concerned with personal development and reaching one's potential.

1. *Physiological needs* refers to basic bodily requirements such as nutrition, water, shelter, moderate temperatures, rest, and sleep. Most office jobs allow us to satisfy physiological needs. Fire fighting is an occupation with potential to frustrate some physiological needs. Smoke inhalation can block need satisfaction.

2. *Safety needs* include the desire to be safe from both physical and emotional injury. Many operatives who work at dangerous jobs would be motivated by the prospects of obtaining safety. For example, computer operators who are suffering from cumulative trauma disorder would prefer a job that requires less intense pressure on their wrists. Any highly stressful job can frustrate the need for emotional safety.

3. *Social needs* are the needs for love, belonging, and affiliation with people. Managers can contribute to the satisfaction of these needs by promoting teamwork and allowing people to discuss work problems with each other. Many employees see their jobs as a major source for satisfying social needs.

296

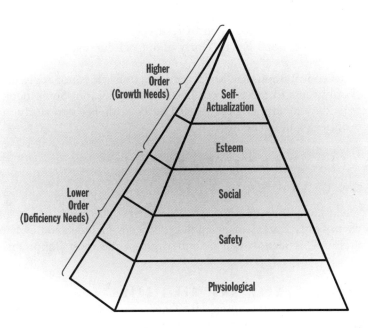

EXHIBIT 12·3

Maslow's Need Hierarchy As you move up the hierarchy, the needs become more difficult to achieve. Some physiological needs could be satisfied with pizza and a soft drink, whereas it might take becoming rich and famous to satisfy the self-actualization need.

4. *Esteem needs* reflect people's desire to be seen by themselves and others as a person of worth. Occupations with high status are a primary source for the satisfaction of esteem needs. Managers can help employees satisfy their esteem needs by praising the quality of their work.

5. *Self-actualization needs* relate to the desire to reach one's potential. They include needs for self-fulfillment and personal development. True self-actualization is an ideal to strive for, rather than something that automatically stems from occupying a challenging position. Self-actualized people are those who are becoming all they are capable of becoming. Managers can help group members move toward self-actualization by giving them challenging assignments and the chance for advancement and new learning.

THE NEED HIERARCHY IN PERSPECTIVE   Maslow's need hierarchy is a convenient way of classifying needs and has spurred thousands of managers to take the subject of human motivation more seriously. Its primary value has been that it dramatizes the importance of satisfying needs in order to motivate employees. Furthermore, Maslow has shown why people are difficult to satisfy. As one need is satisfied, people want to satisfy other needs or different forms of the same need. The need hierarchy has helped three generations of students understand that it is normal to be constantly searching for new satisfactions.

The need hierarchy is relevant in the current era because so many workers have to worry about satisfying lower-level needs. Despite the general prosperity, large business firms continue to downsize about 650,000 workers per year. Many of these downsizings come about because of consolidations and mergers designed to squeeze more profits out of the same sales volume. In the 1960s, Maslow reported that U.S. workers were 85-percent satisfied in their physiological needs, 70-percent satisfied in their safety needs, and 50-percent satisfied in their social needs. Florence Stone of the American Management Association observes that with downsizings announced almost daily, could we now say the same?[4] The point is that lower-level needs might be a source of motivation for many workers. Even if finding new employment is relatively easy, many workers feel more secure when they do not have to worry about conducting a job search to pay for necessities.

Despite its contribution, Maslow's need hierarchy does not apply universally. Not everybody wants to satisfy needs in a stepwise fashion. Some people try to achieve esteem before satisfying their social needs. Others try to satisfy more than one group of needs simultaneously.

Specific Needs People Attempt to Satisfy

Maslow's need hierarchy refers to classes of needs. The work setting offers the opportunity to satisfy dozens of psychological needs included somewhere in the need hierarchy. This section will describe four of the most important of these needs.

ACHIEVEMENT, POWER, AND AFFILIATION   According to David McClelland and his associates, much job behavior can be explained by the strength of people's needs for achievement, power, and affiliation.[5] The achievement and power needs (or motives) have already been described in relation to leadership. The **affiliation need** is a desire to have close relationships with others and to be a loyal employee or friend. Affiliation is a social need, while achievement and power are self-actualizing needs.

A person with a strong need for affiliation finds compatible working relationships more important than high-level accomplishment and the exercise of power. Successful executives, therefore, usually have stronger needs for achievement and power than for affiliation. Workers with strong affiliation needs, however, typically enjoy contributing to a team effort. Befriending others and working cooperatively with them satisfies the need for affiliation.

RECOGNITION   The workplace provides a natural opportunity to satisfy the **recognition need,** the desire to be acknowledged for one's contributions and efforts and to feel important. A manager can thus motivate many employees by making them feel important. Employee needs for recognition can be satisfied both through informal recognition and by giving formal recognition programs.

Praising workers for good performance is closely related to informal recognition. An effective form of praise describes the worker's performance rather than merely making an evaluation. Describing good performance might take this form: "You turned an angry customer into an ally who has referred new business to us." A straightforward evaluation would be "You did a great job with that angry customer." Even more effective would be to combine the two statements.

Although praise costs no money and only requires a few moments of time, many workers rarely receive praise. One researcher found that out of 1,500 workers surveyed, more than 50 percent said they seldom or never received spoken or written thanks for their efforts.[6] Managers therefore have a good opportunity to increase motivation by the simple act of praising good deeds. Other informal approaches to recognizing good performance include taking an employee to lunch, a handshake from the manager or team leader, and putting flowers on an employee's desk.

Formal recognition programs are more popular than ever as companies attempt to retain the right employees, and keep workers productive who worry

affiliation need
A desire to have close relationships with others and be a loyal employee or friend.

recognition need
The desire to be acknowledged for one's contributions and efforts and to feel important.

about losing their jobs or having no private work area. Company recognition programs include awarding watches and jewelry for good service, plaques for good performance, and on-the-spot cash awards (around $25 to $50) for good performance. For example, Federal Express managers are authorized to make awards on the spot by giving employees a set of flags symbolizing a job well done, and a check for $50 to $100.

The more sophisticated recognition programs attempt to link recognition awards with performance and behavior tied to corporate objectives. At the Prudential Insurance Company, the formal recognition program of the operations and technology function focuses on rewarding innovative, technology-based solutions for internal business clients.[7] For example, an information systems specialist who developed a way of minimizing sending repeated bills to deceased policyholders would be recognized.

Teams, as well as individuals, should receive recognition to enhance motivation. Motivation consultant Bob Nelson recommends that to build a high-performing team, the manager should acknowledge the success of all team members. As with individual recognition, a personal touch works best. Examples include a manager thanking group members for their involvement, suggestions, and initiatives. Holding a group luncheon for outstanding team performance is also a potential motivator.[8] We emphasize *potential* because team recognition does not take into account individual differences in preferences for rewards. For example, some employees object to group luncheons because it diverts time they might want to use for personal purposes.

Herzberg's Two-Factor Theory

The study of the need hierarchy led to the **two-factor theory of work motivation.** The key point to the theory is that there are two different sets of job factors. One set of factors can satisfy and motivate people. The other can only prevent dissatisfaction.

Psychologist Frederick Herzberg and his associates interviewed hundreds of professionals about their work.[9] They discovered that some factors of a job give people a chance to satisfy higher-level needs. Such elements are satisfiers or motivators. A *satisfier* is a job factor that, if present, leads to job satisfaction. Similarly, a *motivator* is a job factor that, if present, leads to motivation. When a motivator is not present, the effect on motivation is neutral rather than negative. Herzberg's theory originally dealt with job satisfaction, but now it is also considered a theory of job motivation.

Individuals vary somewhat in the particular job factors they find satisfying or motivating. However, satisfiers and motivators generally refer to the content (the heart or guts) of a job. These factors are achievement, recognition, challenging work, responsibility, and the opportunity for advancement. All the factors are self-rewarding. The important implication for managers is that, as managers, they can motivate most people by giving them the opportunity to do interesting work or to be promoted. The two-factor theory is thus the psychology that underlies the philosophy of job design through job enrichment and the job characteristics model, as described in Chapter 8.

Herzberg also discovered that some job elements are more relevant to lower-level needs than upper-level needs. Referred to as dissatisfiers, or hygiene factors, these elements are noticed primarily by their absence. A *dissatisfier* is a job element that, when present, prevents dissatisfaction; it does not, however, create

two-factor theory of work motivation
The theory contending that there are two different sets of job factors. One set can satisfy and motivate people, and the other set can only prevent dissatisfaction.

299

EXHIBIT
12-4

*The Two-Factor Theory of
Work Motivation*

Satisfiers or Motivators	Presence	Positive effect on motivation and satisfaction
	Absence	No negative effect on motivation or satisfaction

1. Achievement   4. Responsibility
2. Recognition   5. Advancement
3. Work itself   6. Growth

Dissatisfiers	Presence	No positive effect on motivation or satisfaction
	Absence	Negative effect on motivation and satisfaction

1. Company policy   6. Relationships with peers
2. Supervision   7. Personal life
3. Relationship with supervisor   8. Relationships with subordinates
4. Work conditions   9. Status
5. Salary   10. Job security

satisfaction. People will not be satisfied with their jobs just because hygiene factors are present. For example, not having a handy place to park your car would create dissatisfaction. But having a place to park would not make you happier about your job.

Dissatisfiers relate mostly to the context of a job (the job setting or external elements). These include relationships with coworkers, company policy and administration, job security, and money. All these factors deal with external rewards. Money, however, does work as a satisfier for many people. Some people want or need money so much that high pay contributes to their job satisfaction. (See the discussion of financial incentives later in this chapter.) One reason that money can be a motivator is that high pay is often associated with high status and high esteem.

Exhibit 12-4 summarizes the major aspects of the two-factor theory of job motivation. The exhibit illustrates an important point: The opposite of satisfaction is no satisfaction—not dissatisfaction. Similarly, the opposite of dissatisfaction is no dissatisfaction—not satisfaction.

EVALUATION OF THE TWO-FACTOR THEORY   Herzberg's theory has had considerable influence on the practice of management and job design. The two-factor theory has prompted managers to ask, "What really motivates our employees?" Nevertheless, Herzberg's assumption—that all workers seek more responsibility and challenge on the job—may have been incorrect. It is more likely that people in higher-level occupations strive for more responsibility and challenge. But even in a given occupational group, such as managers or production workers, not everybody has the same motivational pattern. One executive admitted to this author that she finds the status she receives as a company president to be highly motivational. Also, many workers are motivated by a secure job when they have heavy financial obligations.

Another problem with the two-factor theory is that it goes too far in concluding that hygiene factors cannot contribute to satisfaction and motivation. Many people do experience high job satisfaction and motivation because of more job elements such as job security and pleasant working conditions. Also, companies now emphasize benefits as a way of attracting and retaining employees. Joining a company and staying there involve some degree of work motivation, even if not aimed directly at producing more.

MOTIVATION THROUGH GOAL SETTING

Goal setting, including management by objectives (see Chapter 5), is a pervasive managerial activity. This section is concerned with the psychology behind goal setting; why and how it leads to improved performance. Case Problem 12-A at the end of this chapter provides additional information about how goals are used throughout an organization to boost performance.

(3)

Explain how goal setting is used to motivate people.

The Basics of Goal Theory

Goal setting is an important part of most formal motivational programs and managerial methods of motivating employees. The premise underlying goal theory is that behavior is regulated by values and goals. A *value* is a strongly held personal standard or conviction. It is a belief about something very important to the individual, such as dignity of work or honesty. Our values create within us a desire to behave consistently with them. If an executive values honesty, the executive will establish a goal of trying to hire only honest employees. He or she would therefore make extensive use of reference checks and honesty testing.

With respect to planning, a goal has been defined as an overall condition one is trying to achieve. Its psychological meaning is about the same. A *goal* is what the person is trying to accomplish, or a conscious intention to act.

Edwin A. Locke and Gary P. Latham have incorporated hundreds of studies about goals into a theory of goal setting and task performance.[10] Exhibit 12-5 summarizes some of the more consistent findings and the following list describes them.

1. *Specific goals lead to higher performance than do generalized goals.* Telling someone to "do your best" is a generalized goal. A specific goal would be "Decrease the turnaround time on customer inquiries to an average of two working days."
2. *Performance generally increases in direct proportion to goal difficulty.* The harder one's goal, the more one accomplishes. There is an important exception,

301

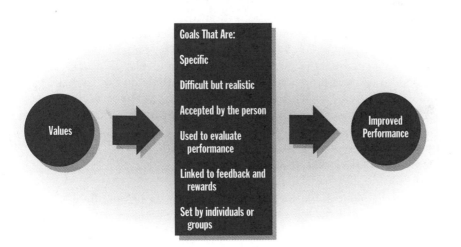

EXHIBIT
12-5

The Basics of Goal Theory
Goals that meet the illustrated conditions have a positive impact on motivation, as revealed by a wide variety of research studies.

Goals That Are:

Specific

Difficult but realistic

Accepted by the person

Used to evaluate performance

Linked to feedback and rewards

Set by individuals or groups

Values → Improved Performance

however. When goals are too difficult, they may lower performance. Difficulty in reaching the goal leads to frustration, which in turn leads to lowered performance.

3. *For goals to improve performance, the employee must accept them.* If you reject a goal, you will not incorporate it into your planning. This is why it is often helpful to discuss goals with employees, rather than just imposing the goals on them. Participating in setting goals has no major effect on the level of job performance, except when it improves goal acceptance. Yet participation is valuable because it can lead to higher satisfaction with the goal-setting process.

   A study of pizza deliverers compared the contribution of assigned versus participative goal setting. All the deliverers were college students, whose average age was 21. At one store the employees participated in setting goals about making complete stops at intersections. At the other store, the pizza-delivery specialists were assigned a goal. Both groups significantly increased their number of complete stops at intersections, as measured by trained observers hiding behind nearby windows. A surprising finding was that the participative groups also increased the use of turn signals and safety belts.[11] Perhaps participating in goal setting made the deliverers feel more responsible!

4. *Goals are more effective when they are used to evaluate performance.* When workers know that their performance will be evaluated in terms of how well they attained their goals, the impact of goals increases. Management by objectives is built around this important idea.

5. *Goals should be linked to feedback and rewards.* Workers should receive feedback on their progress toward goals and be rewarded for reaching them.[9] *Feedback* is information about how well someone is doing in achieving his or her goals. Rewarding people for reaching goals is perhaps the best-accepted principle of management. Feedback is also important because it is a motivational principle within itself. The process of receiving positive feedback encourages us to repeat the behavior; receiving negative feedback encourages us to discontinue the behavior. Assume a person is using a recent version of the software program Word, and uses the File menu to save changes to a document. A work associate says, "Click the Save button on the toolbar, it's faster." The person tries this several times, and the feedback is positive because saving is quicker using the Save button (this is referred to as built-in feedback). The feedback leads to learning, and it provides the motivation to continue. In contrast, if clicking the toolbar button deleted the file, the negative feedback would eliminate any further motivation to use this shortcut.

   A practical way of building more feedback into goal setting is to set achievable short-term goals. In this way, goal accomplishment will be measured more frequently, giving the goal setter regular feedback. Short-term goals also increase motivation because many people do not have the patience and self-discipline to work long and hard without seeing results.

6. *Group goal setting is as important as individual goal setting.* Having employees work as teams with a specific team goal, rather than as individuals with only individual goals, increases productivity. Furthermore, the combination of the compatible group and individual goals is more effective than either individual or group goals.

Despite the contribution of goals to performance, technically speaking, they are not motivational by themselves. Rather, the discrepancies created by what individuals do and what they aspire to do creates self-dissatisfaction. The dissatisfaction in turn creates a desire to reduce the discrepancy between the real and the ideal.[12] When a person desires to attain something, the person is in a state of mental arousal. The tension created by not having already achieved a goal spurs the person to reach the goal. Assume your goal is to prepare a 25-page report for your manager by 10 days from now. Your dissatisfaction with not having started would propel you into action.

You may have observed that in this chapter the emphasis is on specific motivational techniques. Keep in mind, also, that a dedicated, hard-driving, and charismatic leader often motivates others by his or her presence. The right type of leader, for example, might inspire you to set difficult goals outside of a specific program of goal setting. The accompanying Manager in Action describes such a leader.

BEHAVIOR MODIFICATION

The most systematic method of motivating people is **behavior modification.** It is a way of changing behavior by rewarding the right responses and punishing or ignoring the wrong responses. A reward is something of value received as a consequence of having attained a goal. This section will describe several key concepts and strategies of behavior modification (also referred to as OB Mod).

Key Concepts of Behavior Modification

The **law of effect** is the foundation principle of behavior modification. According to this principle, behavior that leads to positive consequences tends to be repeated. Similarly, behavior that leads to negative consequences tends not to be repeated. Perceptive managers rely on the law of effect virtually every day. Assume that a supervisor of a paint shop wants her employees to put on a face mask every time they use a spray gun. When she sees an employee using a mask properly, she might comment, "Good to see that you're wearing the safety mask today." If the supervisor noticed that an employee was not wearing a mask, she might say, "Please put down the spray gun, and go get your mask. If this happens again, I will be forced to suspend you for one day."

Behavior modification is generally associated with extrinsic rewards such as financial bonuses and prizes. However, intrinsic rewards are also used. A worker might receive a more challenging assignment as a reward for performing well on the previous assignment.

Behavior Modification Strategies

There are four behavior modification strategies used either individually or in combination: positive reinforcement, negative reinforcement, extinction, and punishment.

1. *Positive reinforcement* increases the probability that behavior will be repeated by rewarding people for making the right response. The phrase "increases the probability" is noteworthy. No behavior modification strategy guarantees that people will always make the right response in the future. However, it increases the chance that they will repeat the desired behavior. The term *reinforcement* means that the behavior (or response) is strengthened or en-

Describe the application of behavior modification to worker motivation.

behavior modification
A way of changing behavior by rewarding the right responses and punishing or ignoring the wrong responses.

law of effect
The underlying principle of behavior modification stating that behavior leading to positive consequences tends to be repeated and that behavior leading to negative consequences tends not to be repeated.

303

Manager *in Action*

The Motivational Ken Chenault of American Express

Back in his college days Ken Chenault argued that the advancement of African Americans was best ensured by rising to power within the establishment instead of attacking it from the outside. Today he is president and chief operating officer of American Express Co. (AmEx), the owner of one of the world's premier consumer brands. Recently his authority was enlarged to include the only two operating divisions not already reporting to him. He was also recently elected to the IBM board of directors.

After graduating from Bowdoin College, Chenault earned a degree from Harvard Law School. After being a member of a law firm for several years, he worked as a management consultant before joining AmEx. He rose rapidly at the consulting firm, and was regarded as a person with the potential to become a corporate CEO partly because of his ability to work with and motivate others, and also because of his strategic thinking.

Chenault has an impressive physical appearance, is quietly charismatic and even tempered, and has exceptional drive. His admirerers lavish him with praise. The chairman of the lead advertising agency for AmEx offers this description: "Ken radiates such a depth of belief that people would do anything for him." A former AmEx executive says, "He's a true leader. I can say unequivocally that I admire Ken more than anyone else I've ever worked with. I think he will be our generation's Jack Welch."

Still rising in the corporate world, Chenault is an established star in what the president of Time Warner calls "the circle of African American professionals who have achieved." Chenault worked his way up through the giant card and travel unit (TRS) that generates most of AmEx's revenue and profits. He was instrumental in reviving and reinventing TRS, which was suffering from widespread complacency. Chenault is considered the leading contender for promotion to the top position at AmEx, chairman and chief executive.

Top AmEx executive Harvey Golub says he promoted Chenault to president because the challenge of developing more market share and global reach was too overwhelming to deal with alone. Golub also identified Chenault as a successor and wanted him perceived as more a collaborator than a subordinate. "What I sought was a horizontal relationship with Ken that would enable him to do more and more of what I was doing." The two executives work smoothly together, and agree consistently on decisions.

Work associates regard Chenault as hard driving and pragmatic. Yet at the same time he is able to engage the emotions of his colleagues as well as their intellects. Another former AmEx executive said that "Ken has the hearts and minds of the people at the TRS company." A survey of work associates indicates that Chenault lacks the rough edges and impatience that usually accompany highly ambitious people. None of the people interviewed could recall him losing his temper or even raising his voice. He takes the time to make small talk with secretaries when he telephones their bosses. Chenault has taken the initiative to mentor dozens of high-potential AmEx managers. He has also contributed to making layoff decisions during difficult times for the company.

Chenault is a methodical decision maker who collects input from others and who leaves his door open to direct reports and encourages candor. A veteran AmEx employee said, "With Ken, there is no game playing, no politics whatsoever." Yet despite his even temper, Chenault has fired managers he thought lacked the skills he needed for his organization. During a time in which AmEx was going through substantial changes to stop the slide in American Express card use, he fired most of a group of managers who resisted the changes. During the same period of turmoil, Chenault often met with important customers to resolve problems about AmEx charging them a higher rate than did traditional credit card companies. At one time four restaurant owners in Boston were threatening to boycott AmEx in response to the high charges. Chenault met with them personally and was able to get the owners to back down.

An important part of Chenault's managerial approach is to interact directly with rank-and-file employees. He regularly conducts a monthly "meet the president" session over lunch. "I've gotten some of my best ideas this way," he says. An example is that Platinum card members can now purchase two international business-class tickets for the price of one. Chenault prefers to occupy the role of team leader, rather than boss. He says, "It's critical to share the credit."

Sources: Based on facts reported in Anthony Bianco, "The Rise of a Star," *Business Week*, December 21, 1998, pp. 60–68; Carrie Shook, "Leader, Not Boss," *Forbes*, December 1, 1997.

trenched. For example, your response of placing your left pinky on the *a* of your keyboard is probably reinforced through thousands of successful attempts.

Positive reinforcement is the most effective behavior modification strategy. Most people respond better to being rewarded for the right response than to being punished for the wrong response. The IBM decision to base sales representative's compensation in part on customer satisfaction illustrates rewarding the desired behavior to improve performance.

2. *Negative reinforcement* (or *avoidance motivation*) is rewarding people by taking away an uncomfortable consequence. It is a method of strengthening a desired response by making the removal of discomfort contingent on the right response. Assume that an employee is placed on probation because of excessive absenteeism. After 20 consecutive days of coming to work, the employer rewards the employee by removing the probation. Because the opportunity for removing punishments is limited, negative reinforcement is not a widely used behavior modification strategy.

Negative reinforcement or avoidance motivation is often confused with punishment. In reality, negative reinforcement is the opposite of punishment. It is rewarding someone by enabling him or her to avoid punishment.

3. *Extinction* is the weakening or decreasing of the frequency of undesirable behavior by removing the reward for such behavior. It is the absence of reinforcement. Extinction often takes the form of ignoring undesirable behavior. It works this way: Suppose an employee engages in undesirable behavior, such as creating a disturbance just to get a reaction from coworkers. If the coworkers ignore the disturbance, the perpetrator no longer receives the reward of getting attention and stops the disturbing behavior. The behavior is said to be extinguished.

Extinction must be used with great care because there are many times when it does not work. An employee may habitually come to work late. If the boss does not reprimand the employee, the employee's tardiness may strengthen. The employee may interpret the boss's attempt at extinction as condoning the behavior.

4. *Punishment* is the presentation of an undesirable consequence for a specific behavior. Yelling at an employee for making a mistake is a direct form of punishment. Another form of punishment is taking away a privilege, such as working on an interesting project, because of some undesirable behavior. In order to be effective, punishment not only tells people what not to do, it teaches them the right behavior. When used appropriately, punishment can be a motivator for those punished and those observing the punishment. This means delivering it in a manner that is clearly impersonal, corrective, focused on a specific act, and relatively intense and quick.

Seventy-seven managers, each from a different organization, were interviewed to obtain their views on a variety of issues related to punishment. A consistent finding was that punishment is an effective learning tool. The punished workers learned what they did wrong and coworkers learned what type of performance and behavior would not be tolerated. Managers themselves learned more about following organizational policies and procedures.[13]

A serious disadvantage of punishment is that it may cause adverse consequences for managers and the organization. Employees who are punished often become defensive, angry, and eager to seek revenge. Many incidents of workplace violence, such as killing a former supervisor, occur after a mentally unstable employee has been fired—even when the dismissal is justified.

Successful Application of Positive Reinforcement

Behavior modification may take the form of an overall company program, such as a highly structured behavior modification program, or a rewards and recognition program. Managers use positive reinforcement more frequently, on an informal, daily basis. The following list presents suggestions for making effective use of positive reinforcement, whether as part of a company program or more informally.

1. *State clearly what behavior will lead to a reward.* The nature of good performance, or the goals, must be agreed to by both manager and group member. Clarification could take this form: "What I need are inventory reports without missing data. When you achieve this, you'll be credited with good performance."

2. *Use appropriate rewards.* An appropriate reward is an effective one because it is valued by the person being motivated. Examine the list of rewards in Exhibit 12-6. Note that some have more appeal to you than do others. The best way to motivate people is to offer them their preferred rewards for good performance. Managers should ask employees what they are interested in attaining.

3. *Make rewards contingent on good performance.* Contingent reinforcement means that getting the reward depends on giving a certain performance. Unless a reward is linked to the desired behavior or performance it will have little effect on whether the behavior or performance is repeated. For example, saying "You're doing great" in response to anything an employee does will not lead to good performance. Yet if the manager reserves the "doing great" response for truly outstanding performance, he or she may reinforce the good performance.

4. *Administer rewards intermittently.* Positive reinforcement can be administered under different types of schedules. The most effective and sensible type is an intermittent schedule, in which rewards are administered often, but not always, when the appropriate behavior occurs. A reward loses its effect if given every time the employee makes the right response. (Would you become tired

EXHIBIT 12-6

Rewards Suitable for Use in Positive Reinforcement Rewards can be used to motivate individuals and teams, and many of them are low-cost or no-cost. An important condition for something being rewarding is that the person being motivated thinks it is valuable.

Monetary

Salary increases or bonuses
Company-paid vacation trip
Discount coupons
Company stock
Extra paid vacation days
Profit sharing
Paid personal holiday (such as a birthday)
Movie or athletic event passes
Free or discount airline tickets
Discounts on company products or services
Gift selection from catalog

Job and Career Related

Empowerment of employee
Challenging work assignments
Job security (relatively permanent job)
Favorable performance appraisal
Freedom to choose own work activity
Promotion
Build fun into work
More of preferred task
Role as boss's stand-in when he or she is away
Contribute to presentations to top management
Job rotation
Encourage learning and continuous improvement
Provide ample encouragement
Allow employees to set own goals

Food and Dining

Business luncheon paid by company
Company picnics
Department parties or special banquet
Holiday turkeys and fruit baskets

Social and Price Related

Compliments
Encouragement
Comradeship with loss
Access to confidential information
Pat on back or handshake
Public expression of appreciation
Meeting of appreciation with executive
Note of thanks
Employee-of-the-month award
Wall plaque indicating accomplishment
Special commendation
Compay recognition program
Team uniforms, hats, tee shirts, or mugs

Status Symbols

Bigger desk
Bigger office or cubicle
Exclusive use of fax machine or copier
Freedom to personalize work area
Private office
Cellular phone privileges
Online service privileges

Sources: A few of the rewards above are suggested from Dean R. Spitzer, "Power Rewards: Rewards that Really Motivate," *Management Review*, May 1996, p. 48; Bob Nelson, "Does One Reward Fit All?" *Workforce*, February 1997, p. 70.

of receiving praise every time you did something right?) Thus intermittent rewards sustain desired behavior for a long time by helping to prevent the behavior from fading away when it is not rewarded.

In addition to being more effective, intermittent rewards are generally more practical than continuous rewards. Few managers have enough time to dispense rewards every time team members attain performance goals.

5. *Vary the size of the reward with the size of accomplishment.* Big accomplishments deserve big rewards, and small accomplishments deserve small rewards. Rewards of the wrong magnitude erode their motivational power. An important corollary of this principle is that people become embarrassed when praise is overly lavish.

6. *Administer rewards promptly.* The proper timing of rewards may be difficult because the manager is not present at the time of good performance. In this case, a telephone call or a note of appreciation within several days of the good performance is appropriate.

7. *Change rewards periodically.* Rewards grow stale quickly; they must be changed periodically. A repetitive reward can even become an annoyance. How many times can one be motivated by the phrase "nice job"? Suppose the reward for making a sales quota is a CD player. How many CD players can one person use?

8. *Reward the team as well as the individual.* Janet Barnard conducted a study of rewards used by companies that were nominated for a national quality award. Many of the managers agreed that a reward process was needed that offers incentives to encourage teamwork, yet also lets star performers shine. A results-oriented system, such as management by objectives, was found to be a good basis for determining who gets rewarded. The evaluation should be done by the project or team leader who is closest to the team's activities and best able to make a valid evaluation of both the team and its members.[14]

9. *Make the rewards visible.* When other workers notice the reward, its impact multiplies because the other people observe what kind of behavior is rewarded. Assume that you were informed about a coworker's having received an exciting assignment because of high performance. You might strive to accomplish the same level of performance.

Evidence about the Effectiveness of Behavior Modification

Two researchers analyzed the results of behavior modification programs conducted with a total of 2,818 workers. In general, behavior modification programs increased various measures of task performance by 17 percent. Behavior modification programs were found to work better in manufacturing than in service settings such as banks and retail stores. For manufacturing groups, nonfinancial incentives, such as recognition and praise, were as effective as financial incentives. However, in service organizations financial incentives seemed to improve performance more than nonfinancial incentives. Yet for both manufacturing and service organizations, nonfinancial incentives were useful in boosting performance.[15]

Despite the many good results achieved with behavior modification, it remains controversial. The arguments against behavior modification center around the use of external rewards in general. Some researchers believe external rewards interfere with the joy of work. We will return to this perspective in the discussion of financial incentives.

Describe the role of financial incentives, including profit sharing and gainsharing, in worker motivation.

MOTIVATION THROUGH FINANCIAL INCENTIVES

A natural way to motivate workers at any level is to offer them financial incentives for good performance. Linking pay to performance improves the motivation value of money. Using financial incentives to motivate people fits behavior modification principles. Financial incentives, however, predate behavior modification. The paragraphs that follow will discuss linking pay to performance, profit sharing and gainsharing, and employee stock ownership (and option) plans; and problems associated with financial incentives.

Linking Pay to Performance

Financial incentives are more effective when they are linked to (or contingent upon) good performance. Linking pay to performance motivates people to work harder. Production workers and sales workers have long received contingent fi-

Performance Level of Staff Members	Merit Increase (Percentage of Pay)
Demonstrate exceptional performance and make outstanding contributions during the year	4.75–5.50
Give consistently productive performance that meets all standards and exceeds some	3.75–4.74
Give consistently productive performance that meets expectations	2.00–3.74
Demonstrate performance that is not wholly satisfactory, even though some expectations may be met or even exceeded	1.00–1.99
Generally fail to meet key expectations and standards; substantial improvement is necessary and essential	0.00

EXHIBIT 12-7

Guidelines for Performance-Based Merit Increases at a Hospital Merit pay is additional income earned for meeting performance standards.

nancial incentives. Many production workers receive, after meeting a quota, bonuses per unit of production. Most sales representatives receive salary plus commissions. Exhibit 12-7 presents a typical approach to linking employee pay to performance, a plan that is often referred to as *merit pay*. A cost-of-living adjustment is not considered merit pay because it is not related to performance.

Managers and others continue to fine-tune methods of linking pay to individual performance. A method now in use by many companies calculates base pay according to a variety of factors. Among them are ability to communicate, customer focus, dealing with change, interpersonal skills, and job knowledge. Managers are rated on employee development, team productivity, and leadership. Merit pay for both individual contributors and managers is based on actual results. Merit pay runs from 5 to over 15 percent of total compensation.

Although many employers believe they link pay to performance, research suggests that merit pay may not be so closely linked to performance. A team of researchers pulled together the results of 39 studies about the relationship between pay and performance. A striking conclusion was that pay had little relationship to quality of work, but did show a moderately positive relationship with quantity of work. However, managers are not completely to blame. It is often easier to measure how much work employees are performing than how well they are performing. The analysis in question also confirms the obvious: People will produce more work when money is at stake.[16] In defense of employers, it is easier to elevate quantity than quality.

Profit Sharing and Gainsharing

A substantial number of organizations attempt to increase motivation and productivity through a companywide plan linking incentive pay to increases in performance. Here we describe briefly profit sharing in general, and a specific form of sharing profits called gainsharing.

PROFIT SHARING   **Profit-sharing plans** give workers supplemental income based on the profitability of the entire firm or a selected unit. The motivational principle is that employees will work harder because they believe that by contributing to profitability they will eventually share some of the profits. Ideally, all employees should believe that they are working for a common good (all boats rise with the same tide). Employee contributions to profits may take a variety of forms such as product quantity, product quality, reducing costs, or improving work methods.

profit-sharing plan
A method of giving workers supplemental income based on the profitability of the entire firm or a selected unit.

A profit-sharing plan based on participative management was developed at Honeywell's Commercial Avionics Division in Phoenix. The division needed to align its compensation plan to reward for performance. Instead of implementing an established incentive system the company formed an employee team to create a compensation program. The new risk-sharing (a type of profit-sharing) plan links 3.5 percent of all employees' pay to company profit. Workers can also receive an additional 5 percent when the company exceeds certain goals. Both management and employees are pleased with the program, and worker participation in building the plan enhanced acceptance of the new compensation system. After two years of operation, goals for profit and economic value added were exceeded by 10 percent.[17]

gainsharing
A formal program allowing employees to participate financially in the productivity gains they have achieved.

GAINSHARING   Another approach to profit sharing is to focus on productivity increases more directly attributable to worker ideas and effort. **Gainsharing** is a formal program of allowing employees to participate financially in the productivity gains they have achieved. Rewards are distributed after performance improves. As in other forms of profit sharing, the participants can consist of the entire organization or a unit within the firm. Gainsharing is accomplished through establishing a payout formula and getting employees involved.

The formulas used in gainsharing vary widely, but there are common elements. Managers begin by comparing what employees are paid to what they sell or produce. Assume that labor costs make up 50 percent of production costs. Any reductions below 50 percent are placed in a bonus pool. Part of the money in the bonus pool is shared among workers. The company's share of the productivity savings in the pool can be distributed to shareholders as increased profits. The savings may allow managers to lower prices, a move that could make the company more competitive.

The second element of gainsharing is employee involvement. Managers establish a mechanism that actively solicits, reviews, and implements employee suggestions about productivity improvement. A committee of managers and employees reviews the ideas and then implements the most promising suggestions. The third key element is employee cooperation. To achieve the bonuses for productivity improvement, group members must work harmoniously with each other. Departments must also cooperate with each other, because some suggestions involve the work of more than one organizational unit.[18]

Gainsharing plans have a more than 65-year history of turning unproductive companies around and making successful companies even more productive. Lincoln Electric Co. of Cleveland, Ohio, is regularly cited as the ideal example of gainsharing. Lincoln manufactures and sells welding machines and motors. Its productivity rate is double to triple that of any other manufacturing operation that uses steel as its raw material and that has 1,000 or more employees. The company offers no paid holidays or sick days, but has a no-layoff policy.

The Lincoln gainsharing plan rewards workers for producing high-quality products efficiently while controlling costs. All employees receive a base salary, and production workers also receive piecework pay (money in relation to units produced). A year-end bonus supplements the piecework pay based on increases in profits. Bonus payments are determined by merit ratings based on output, quality, dependability, and personal characteristics (such as cooperativeness).

Production workers typically receive bonuses averaging around $20,000. Total yearly compensation for these workers, including wages, profit sharing, and bonuses averages $45,000. Lincoln Electric is consistently profitable and has paid out $500 million dollars in year-end bonuses to employees since it began its bonus program in 1934.[19]

Employee Stock Ownership and Stock Option Plans

An increasingly popular way of motivating workers with financial incentives is to make them part owners of the business through stock purchases. Two variations of the same idea of giving workers equity in the business are stock ownership and stock option plans. Stock ownership can be motivational because employees participate in the financial success of the firm as measured by its stock price. If employees work hard, the company may become more successful and the value of the stock increases.

Under an *employee stock ownership plan (ESOP)* employees at all levels in the organization are given stock. The employer either contributes shares of its stock or the money to purchase the stock on the open market. Stock shares are usually deposited in employee retirement accounts, as you may recall from the case about the Wisconsin tree nursery. Upon retirement, employees can choose to receive company stock instead of cash. ESOPs are also significant because they offer tax incentives to the employer. For example, a portion of the earnings paid to the retirement fund are tax deductible.

Employee stock options are more complicated than straightforward stock ownership. Stock options give employees the right to purchase company stock at a specified price at some point in the future. If the stock rises in value, you can purchase it at a discount. If the stock sinks below your designated purchase price, your option is worthless. Thousands of workers in the information technology field, particularly in Silicon Valley, have become millionaires and multimillionaires with their stock options. A specific example is Heather Beach, who at age 25 took a pay cut to join software maker Siebel Systems as its office manager. Within four years the value of her options exceeded $1 million.[20] Exhibit 12-8 shows you the arithmetic behind a stock option.

Problems Associated with Financial Incentives

Although financial incentives are widely used as motivators, they can create problems. A major problem is that workers may not agree with managers about the value of their contributions. Financial incentives can also pit individuals and groups against each other. The result may be unhealthy competition rather than cooperation and teamwork.

The most researched argument against financial rewards is that it focuses the attention of workers too much on the reward such as money or stocks. In the

Brokerage sells 400 shares of company stock at $35 each (400 shares × $35) =	$14,000
Brokerage deducts exercise price (400 shares × $10.57)	−4,228
	$ 9,772
Taxes withheld (28% for federal income tax + 7.56% for social security tax)	−3,475
	$ 6,297
Brokerage deducts fees/commissions/interest	−100
	$ 6,197
Brokerage pays profit to employee	$ 6,197

Source: Carrington Nelson, "Exercising Your Stock Options," Gannett News Service, July 26, 1998.

EXHIBIT 12-8

How a Stock Option Works
Employee decides to exercise option for 400 shares at $10.57 each when stock reaches $35 per share.

process, the workers lose out on intrinsic rewards such as joy in accomplishment. Instead of being passionate about the work they are doing, people become overly concerned with the size of their reward. One argument is that external rewards do not create a lasting commitment. Instead, they create temporary compliance, such as working hard in the short run to earn a bonus. A frequent problem with merit pay systems is that a person who does not receive a merit increase one pay period then feels that he or she has been punished. Another argument against financial incentives is that rewards manipulate people, as do bribes.[21]

Organizational theory specialist Jeffrey Pfeffer explains that people do work for money, but they work even more for meaning in their lives. Work brings people a meaningful type of fun. Pfeffer believes that people who ignore this truth are essentially bribing their employees and will pay the price in lack of loyalty and commitment. He illustrates his position with the SAS Institute, a successful software company that emphasizes excellent benefits and exciting work rather than financial incentives.[22]

In reality, workers at all levels want a combination of internal rewards and financial rewards along with other external rewards such as praise. The ideal combination is to offer exciting (internally rewarding) work to people, and simultaneously pay them enough money so they are not preoccupied with matters such as salary and bonuses. Money is the strongest motivator when people have financial problems. Furthermore, people who find extreme joy in their work will leave one organization for another to perform the same work at much higher pay. Another practical problem is that even if a firm offers exciting work, great benefits, and wonderful coworkers, they usually need to offer financial incentives to attract quality workers.

EXPECTANCY THEORY OF MOTIVATION

Explain the conditions under which a person will be motivated according to expectancy theory.

expectancy theory of motivation
An explanation of motivation that states that people will expend effort if they expect the effort to lead to performance and the performance to lead to a reward.

According to the **expectancy theory of motivation,** people will put forth the greatest effort if they expect the effort to lead to performance and the performance to lead to a reward. Expectancy theory has an advantage over need theories: It takes into account individual differences and perceptions. Expectancy theory is often preferred to behavior modification because it emphasizes the rational, or thinking, side of people.

A Basic Model of Expectancy Theory

Expectancy theory integrates important ideas found in the other generally accepted motivation theories. Exhibit 12-9 presents a basic version of expectancy theory. According to expectancy theory, four conditions must exist for motivated behavior to occur.[23]

Condition A refers to *expectancy*, which means that people will expend effort because they believe it will lead to performance. This is called the $E \rightarrow P$ expectancy, in which subjective probabilities range between 0.0 and 1.0. Rational people ask themselves, "If I work hard, will I really get the job done?" If they evaluate the probability as being high, they probably will invest the effort to achieve the goal. People have higher $E \rightarrow P$ expectancies when they have the appropriate skills, training, and self-confidence.

Condition B is based on the fact that people are more willing to expend effort if they think that good performance will lead to a reward. This is referred to as $P \rightarrow O$ instrumentality, and it too ranges between 0.0 and 1.0. (*Instrumentality*

EXHIBIT 12-9

Basic Version of
Expectancy Theory of
Motivation

An individual will be motivated when:

A. The individual believes effort (E) will lead to favorable performance (P)—that is, when $E \rightarrow P$ (also referred to as expectancy).

B. The individual believes performance will lead to favorable outcome (O)—that is, when $P \rightarrow O$ (also referred to as instrumentality).

C. Outcome or reward satisfies an important need (in other words, valence is strong).

D. Need satisfaction is intense enough to make effort seem worthwhile.

refers to the idea that the behavior is instrumental in achieving an important end.) The rational person says, "I'm much more willing to perform well if I'm assured that I'll receive the reward I deserve." A cautious employee might even ask other employees if they received their promised rewards for exceptional performance. To strengthen a subordinate's $P \rightarrow O$ instrumentality, the manager should give reassurance that the reward will be forthcoming.

Condition C refers to *valence*, the value a person attaches to certain outcomes. The greater the valence, the greater the effort. Valences can be either positive or negative. If a student believes that receiving an A is very important, he or she will work very hard. Also, if a student believes that avoiding a C or a lower grade is very important, he or she will work hard. Valences range from −1 to +1 in most versions of expectancy theory. A positive valence indicates a preference for a particular reward. A clearer picture of individual differences in human motivation spreads valences out over a range of −1,000 to +1,000.

Most work situations present the possibility of several outcomes, with a different valence attached to each. Assume that a purchasing manager is pondering whether becoming a certified purchasing manager (CPM) would be worth the effort. The list that follows cites possible outcomes or rewards from achieving certification, along with their valences (on a scale of −1,000 to +1,000).

- Status from being a CPM, 750
- Promotion to purchasing manager, 950
- Plaque to hang on office wall, 250
- Bigger salary increase next year, 900
- Letters of congratulations from friends and relatives, 500
- Expressions of envy from one or two coworkers, −250

Valences are useful in explaining why some people will put forth the effort to do things with very low expectancies. For example, most people know there is only one chance in a million of winning a lottery, becoming a rock star, or writing a best-selling novel. Nevertheless, a number of people vigorously pursue these goals. They do so because they attach an extraordinary positive valence to these outcomes (perhaps 1,000!).

Condition D indicates that the need satisfaction stemming from each outcome must be intense enough to make the effort worthwhile. Would you walk two miles on a very hot day for one glass of ice water? The water would undoubtedly satisfy your thirst need, but the magnitude of the satisfaction would probably not be worth the effort. Similarly, an operative employee turned down a promotion to the position of inspector because the raise offered was only 50 cents per hour. The worker told his supervisor, "I need more money. But I'm not willing to take on that much added responsibility for twenty dollars a week."

Implications for Management

Expectancy theory has several important implications for the effective management of people. The theory helps pinpoint what a manager must do to motivate group members and diagnose motivational problems.[24]

1. *Individual differences among employees must be taken into account.* Different people attach different valences to different rewards, so a manager should try to match rewards with individual preferences. Behavior modification also makes use of this principle.
2. *Rewards should be closely tied to those actions the organization sees as worthwhile.* For example, if the organization values quality, people should be rewarded for producing high-quality work.
3. *Employees should be given the appropriate training and encouragement.* This will strengthen their subjective hunches that effort will lead to good performance.
4. *Employees should be presented with credible evidence that good performance does lead to anticipated rewards.* Similarly, a manager should reassure employees that good work will be both noticed and rewarded. As part of this implication, managers must listen carefully to understand the perceived link employees have between hard work and rewards. If instrumentality is unjustifiably low, the manager must reassure the employee that hard work will be rewarded.
5. *The meaning and implications of outcomes should be explained.* It can be motivational for employees to know the values of certain outcomes. If an employee who is interested in working on a special task force knows that assignment to the task force is linked to successful completion of a project, the employee will give special attention to the project.

SUMMARY OF KEY POINTS

 Explain the relationship between motivation and performance.

From the standpoint of the individual, motivation is an internal state that leads to the pursuit of objectives. From the standpoint of the manager, motivation is an activity that gets subordinates to pursue objectives. The purpose of motivating employees is to get them to achieve results. Motivation is but one important contributor to productivity and performance. Other important contributors are abilities, skills, technology, and group norms.

 Present an overview of major theories of need satisfaction in explaining motivation.

Workers can be motivated through need satisfaction, particularly because most people want to know "What's in it for me?" First, needs must be identified. Second, the person must be given an opportunity to satisfy those needs.

Maslow's need hierarchy states that people strive to become self-actualized. However, before higher-level needs are activated, certain lower-level needs must be satisfied. When a person's needs are satisfied at one level, he or she looks toward satisfaction at a higher level. Specific needs playing an important role in work motivation include achievement, power, affiliation, and recognition.

The two-factor theory of work motivation contends that there are two different sets of job-motivation factors. One set gives people a chance to satisfy higher-level needs. These are satisfiers and motivators. When present, they increase satisfaction and motivation. When satisfiers and motivators are absent, the impact is neutral. Satisfiers and motivators generally relate to the content of a job. They include achievement, recognition, and opportunity for advancement. Dissatisfiers are job elements that appeal more to lower-level needs. When they are present, they prevent dissatisfaction, but they do not create satisfaction or motivation. Dissatisfiers relate mostly to the context of a job. They include company policy and administration, job security, and money.

Explain how goal setting is used to motivate people. Goal setting is an important part of most motivational programs, and it is a managerial method of motivating group members. It is based on these ideas: (a) specific goals are better than generalized goals; (b) the more difficult the goal, the better the performance; (c) only goals that are accepted improve performance; (d) goals are more effective when used to evaluate performance; (e) goals should be linked to feedback and rewards; and (f) group goal setting is important.

 Describe the application of behavior modification to worker motivation. Behavior modification is the most systematic method of motivating people. It changes behavior by rewarding the right responses and punishing or ignoring the wrong ones. Behavior modification is based on the law of effect: Behavior that leads to positive consequences tends to be repeated, and behavior that leads to negative consequences tends not to be repeated.

There are four behavior modification strategies. Positive reinforcement rewards people for making the right response. Negative reinforcement, or avoidance motivation, rewards people by taking away an uncomfortable consequence. Extinction is the process of weakening undesirable behavior by removing the reward for it. Punishment is the presentation of an undesirable consequence for a specific behavior. Punishment is often counterproductive. If used appropriately, however, it can be motivational.

Suggestions for the informal use of positive reinforcement in a work setting include: (a) state clearly what behavior leads to a reward, (b) use appropriate rewards, (c) make rewards contingent on good performance, (d) administer intermittent rewards, (e) vary the size of rewards, (f) administer rewards promptly, (g) change rewards periodically, and (h) reward the team as well as the individual.

 Describe the role of financial incentives, including profit sharing and gainsharing, in worker motivation. A natural way to motivate workers at any level is to offer financial incentives for good performance. Linking pay to performance improves the motivational value of financial incentives. Research has shown that pay is more often linked to quantity than quality of work.

Profit-sharing plans give out money related to company or large unit performance. Gainsharing is a formal program that allows employees to participate financially in productivity gains they have achieved. Bonuses are distributed to employees based on how much they decrease the labor cost involved in producing or selling goods. Employee involvement in increasing productivity is an important part of gainsharing.

Employee stock ownership plans set aside a block of company stock for employee purchase, often redeemable at retirement. Stock option plans give employees the right to purchase company stock at a specified price at some future time. Both plans attempt to motivate workers by making them part owners of the business.

 Explain the conditions under which a person will be motivated according to expectancy theory. Expectancy theory contends that people will expend effort if they expect the effort to lead to performance and the performance to lead to a reward. According to the expectancy model presented here, a person will be motivated if the person believes effort will lead to performance, the performance will lead to a reward, the reward satisfies an important need, and the need satisfaction is intense enough to make the effort seem worthwhile.

KEY TERMS AND PHRASES

Motivation, *294*
$P = M \times A$, *295*
Need, *296*
Maslow's need hierarchy, *296*
Deficiency needs, *296*

Growth needs, *296*
Affiliation need, *298*
Recognition need, *298*
Two-factor theory of work motivation, *299*
Behavior modification, *303*

Law of effect, *303*
Profit-sharing plan, *309*
Gainsharing, *310*
Expectancy theory of motivation, *312*

QUESTIONS

1. What information does this chapter have to offer the manager who is already working with a well-motivated team?
2. How could an employer motivate workers by appealing to lower-level needs in Maslow's need hierarchy?

3. Some managers object to systematic approaches to motivating employees by expressing the thought, "Why should you have to go out of your way to motivate people to do what they are paid to do?"

4. Identify two occupations in which you think intrinsic (internal) motivation would be particularly high.
5. For what reasons are stock ownership plans and stock option plans supposed to encourage employees to work harder?
6. Imagine getting in contact with one of the researchers who contend that internal motivators, such as enjoyable work, are much more important than external motivators such as money. You invite that person to visit your class and give a talk on his or her theories. You explain, however, that because he or she probably believes so strongly in the joy of teaching and research, you are offering no travel expenses or a speaking fee. Also, ask the same researcher if he or she should would consider switching to another university and performing similar work at double the salary. What do you think would be the reaction of the researcher? And what would the reaction tell you about the role of external motivators?
7. How might SuperLeadership (discussed in Chapter 11) relate to effort-to-performance expectancies?

SELF-ASSESSMENT EXERCISE 12-A: My Approach to Motivating Others

Describe how often you act or think in the way indicated by the statements below when you are attempting to motivate another person. Use the following scale: very infrequently (VI); infrequently (I); sometimes (S); frequently (F); very frequently (VF).

	VI	I	S	F	VF
1. I ask the other person what he or she is hoping to achieve in the situation.	1	2	3	4	5
2. I attempt to figure out if the person has the ability to do what I need done.	1	2	3	4	5
3. When another person is heel-dragging, it usually means he or she is lazy.	5	4	3	2	1
4. I tell the person I'm trying to motivate exactly what I want.	1	2	3	4	5
5. I like to give the other person a reward up front so he or she will be motivated.	5	4	3	2	1
6. I give lots of feedback when another person is performing a task for me.	1	2	3	4	5
7. I like to belittle another person enough so that he or she will be intimidated into doing what I need done.	5	4	3	2	1
8. I make sure that the other person feels treated fairly.	1	2	3	4	5
9. I figure that if I smile nicely enough I can get the other person to work as hard as I need.	5	4	3	2	1
10. I attempt to get what I need done by instilling fear in the other person.	5	4	3	2	1
11. I specify exactly what needs to be accomplished.	1	2	3	4	5
12. I generously praise people who help me get my work accomplished.	1	2	3	4	5
13. A job well done is its own reward. I therefore keep praise to a minimum.	5	4	3	2	1
14. I make sure to let people know how well they have done in meeting my expectations on a task.	1	2	3	4	5
15. To be fair, I attempt to reward people about the same no matter how well they have performed.	5	4	3	2	1
16. When somebody doing work for me performs well, I recognize his or her accomplishments promptly.	1	2	3	4	5
17. Before giving somebody a reward, I attempt to find out what would appeal to that person.	1	2	3	4	5
18. I make it a policy not to thank somebody for doing a job he or she is paid to do.	5	4	3	2	1
19. If people do not know how to perform a task, their motivation will suffer.	1	2	3	4	5
20. If properly designed, many jobs can be self-rewarding.	1	2	3	4	5

Total Score _____

Scoring and interpretation: Add the numbers circled to obtain your total score.

90–100 You have advanced knowledge and skill with respect to motivating others in a work environment. Continue to build on the solid base you have established.

50–89 You have average knowledge and skill with respect to motivating others. With additional study and experience, you will probably develop advanced motivational skills.

20–49 To effectively motivate others in a work environment, you will need to greatly expand your knowledge of motivation theory and techniques.

Source: The ideas for this quiz are from David A. Whetton and Kim S. Cameron, *Developing Management Skills*, 3rd ed. (New York: Harper Collins, 1995), pp. 358–359.

316

SKILL-BUILDING EXERCISE 12-A: Identifying the Most Powerful Motivators

The class divides itself into small groups. Working alone, group members first attach a valence to all the rewards in Exhibit 12-6. Use the expectancy theory scale of −1,000 to +1,000. Next, do an analysis of the top ten motivators identified by the group, perhaps by calculating the average valence attached to the rewards that at first glance were assigned high valences by most group members. After each group has identified its top ten motivators, the group leaders can post the results for the other class members to see. After comparing results, answer these questions:

1. What appear to be the top three motivators for the entire class?
2. Do the class members tend to favor internal or external rewards?
3. Did career experience or gender influence the results within the groups?
4. Of what value to managers would this exercise be in estimating valences?

INTERNET SKILL-BUILDING EXERCISE: What Motivates the Surfers?

Millions of people worldwide are strongly motivated to spend long hours surfing the Internet, usually visiting Web sites or participating in chat rooms. Some chat rooms entail visiting members with a common interest such as Civil War buffs. Your assignment is to analyze the reasons why people surf so much (their motivation). What needs are they satisfying? Use your intuition, and communicate with others on line.

For example, you might visit a few chat rooms and ask some of the participants why they spend so much time on line. You might obtain fruitful answers by asking informal questions such as, "What keeps you glued to your computer?" or "What keeps you hanging out on line?" Relate your answers to at least one explanation of motivation presented in this chapter.

CASE PROBLEM 12-A: LINK Performance Management at Sprint

Sprint, a global communications company best known for long-distance telephone service, is based in Westwood, Kansas. Karen Mailliard, vice-president of human resource development, helped develop a program to keep 48,000 worldwide employees focused on the bottom line in the rapidly changing, intensely competitive telecommunications industry. At the time, Sprint had realigned its business units following several mergers and consolidations. It appeared that the different business units, which were dependent on each other to accomplish their work, knew what they were accomplishing individually. But many groups within the units did not clearly understand their contribution to the company's overall business objectives.

Another concern of management was that the performance evaluation system used at Sprint based compensation exclusively on whether employees met their numbers (achieved their quantitative goals). As a result, many employees met their numbers but in the process damaged relationships with other groups that were critical to the company's overall success. For example, a worker who needed replacement telecommunications equipment in a hurry might be overly aggressive in demanding the equipment.

Mailliard and other managers began to assess other companies' performance management processes and looked at the importance of employee behavior in achieving objectives. The managers realized that a performance management process should measure and reward employees both on what they achieve and how they achieve it. The result was the "LINK Performance Management" process, a company-wide system that connects employee performance with bottom-line results. With LINK, Sprint's corporate objectives are aligned vertically and horizontally throughout the company. The alignments mean that people in the same chain of command, as well as across units, are working in the same direction. The corporate objectives serve as the basis for setting each employee's performance objectives (as in a system of management by objectives).

In addition to measuring performance by how well employees achieve these objectives, LINK also provides a set of behavior-based parameters that are used to measure performance improvement and professional development. These parameters are set out in "Sprint Dimensions," which establishes the skills and behaviors considered necessary for company success. (See the following box.)

SPRINT DIMENSIONS:
A COMMON LANGUAGE

Managers and employees need to speak the same language when they discuss behaviors that are essential to a company's success. Sprint developed this common language with the Sprint Dimensions component of the LINK Performance Management System. Sprint Dimensions includes seven categories of behaviors employees must practice to support the company's goals of growing profitable market share and appropriately reducing costs. The dimensions are:

- Leadership
- Communications
- Management
- Personal effectiveness
- Professional knowledge/global awareness
- Customer focus
- Team approach

The 7 dimensions include 29 subdimensions used as specific, observable performance criteria in employee reviews. Each year, an employee chooses one subdimension from each of the seven categories to work on developing. To create this type of development language, a company must define the behaviors that are important to its culture and strategic objectives.

In essence, Sprint Dimensions serves as a corporate development language that reflects the company's vision, business goals, and values. It allows managers and employees to use a common language in discussing critical behaviors

that previously were evaluated in a highly subjective manner. Employees work with their managers to choose the skills and behaviors they want to strengthen during the year and establish these objectives in their development. The plan is a living document in the sense that objectives can be modified, added, or removed in response to changes in the marketplace or workplace.

Each quarter, managers evaluate how well employees have met their bottom-line objectives and incorporated the Sprint Dimensions into their jobs. Their pay incentives are then based on both these elements. If an employee meets his objectives but does not demonstrate the expected behaviors, he may not receive a salary increase or incentive compensation. An example would be an employee who meets her sales-call volume but does not practice her customer-service behaviors.

To date, 70 percent of Sprint's exempt employees have made the transition to LINK and a continued inclusion of other employees is underway. A study of employees who had participated in the program for three years attributed nearly $118 million in increased sales and/or reduced costs to the system. The return on investment (ROI) for the program is more than 3,700 percent.

The LINK Performance Management System supports two fundamental goals: maximizing profitable market share and appropriately reducing unit costs. Top-level management wants employees at every level of the company to understand how their jobs tie into these goals.

Discussion Questions

1. Why does Sprint management place so much emphasis on employee behaviors as well as achieving objectives?
2. How does Link Performance Management relate to employee motivation?
3. What does it mean to say that the LINK program has an ROI of more than 3,700 percent?
4. How does the LINK program get around any potential problems with external rewards?

Source: Adapted from Karen Mailliard, "Case Study: Linking Performance to the Bottom Line," *HRfocus*, June 1997, pp. 17–18.

CASE PROBLEM 12-B: The Incentive Hassle

Pat Lancaster founded Lantech in 1972. The company manufactures machines for wrapping large bundles of products, such as breakfast cereal, in plastic film for shipment to retailers. Today the company has 325 employees and annual sales of about $65 million.

Lancaster was among the pioneers in companywide incentive pay. During the mid-1970s, Lantech employees were requested to evaluate one another's job performance. Bonuses were distributed according to workers' scores on these evaluations. The program created so much tension that it was disbanded. Faced with tough competition in the 1980s, Lancaster was determined to make incentive pay work. He also implemented other modern management practices such as just-in-time inventory.

At one time, each of Lantech's five manufacturing divisions was given a bonus based on how much profit it made. A worker could receive a bonus up to as much as 10 percent of base pay. The interdependence of the divisions, however, made it difficult to assess an equitable share for each division. "That led to so much secrecy, politicking, and sucking noise you wouldn't believe it," says CEO Jim Lancaster, the 29-year-old son of chairman Pat Lancaster.

An example of interdependency is between the division that manufactures standard machines and the one that adds custom design features to them. The two divisions depend on each other for parts, engineering expertise, and scheduling. The two groups entered into conflict, each one attempting to assign costs to the other and claim credit for revenues.

Pat Lancaster recalls, "By the early 1990s I was spending 95 percent of my time on conflict resolution instead of on how to serve our customers." The divisions argued so long over who would be charged for overhead cranes to haul heavy equipment that their installation was delayed two years. At the end of each month, the divisions would scurry to fill orders from other divisions in the company. As a result, the division that filled the order would earn a profit, but the recipient of the orders was left with piles of unnecessary and costly inventory.

Some employees even argued over who should have to pay for paper toweling in the common restrooms. One employee suggested that employees from another division had dirtier jobs so they should absorb more of the costs for hand soap.

Pat Lancaster concluded, "Incentive pay is toxic because it is open to favoritism and manipulation." As a consequence, Lantech has abandoned individual and division performance pay. Instead it relies on a profit-sharing system in which all employees receive bonuses based on salary. Much of the anger has subsided, and the company is prospering. However, bonuses are still paid to executives and sales representatives.

Discussion Questions

1. What mistakes did Lantech make in designing and implementing the company incentive system?
2. Has Lantech really abandoned incentive pay for all workers?
3. Should the company continue its incentive program for executives and sales personnel?

Source: Based on facts reported in Peter Nulty, "Incentive Pay Can Be Crippling," *Fortune* (November 13, 1995, p. 235.

ENDNOTES

1. Adapted from "Alternative Benefits: Financial Benefits," *Fast Forward*, September 1997, p. 2.
2. Ruth Kanfer and Philip L. Ackerman, "Motivation and Cognitive Abilities: An Integrative/Aptitude-Treatment Interaction Approach to Skill Acquisition," *Journal of Applied Psychology*, August 1989, p. 657.
3. Abraham M. Maslow, "A Theory of Human Motivation," *Psychological Review*, July 1943, pp. 370–396; Maslow, *Motivation and Personality* (New York: Harper & Row, 1954), Chapter 5.
4. Florence M. Stone, "Motivating Employees: The Danger of Applying '60s Theories to '90s Situations," *HR/OD*, June 1998, p.3.
5. Michael J. Stahl, "Achievement, Power, and Managerial Motivation: Selecting Managerial Talent with the Job Choice Exercise," *Personnel Psychology*, Winter 1983; David C. McClelland, *Power: The Inner Experience* (New York: Irvington, 1975).
6. Research by Gerald Graham reported in "Motivating Entry-Level Workers," *WorkingSMART*, October 1998, p. 2.
7. Gillian Flynn, "Is Your Recognition Program Understood?" *Workforce*, July 1998, pp. 31–32.
8. Bob Nelson, "Does One Reward Fit All?" *Workforce*, February 1997, pp. 67–70.
9. Frederick Herzberg, *Work and the Nature of Man* (Cleveland: World, 1966).
10. Edwin A. Locke and Gary P. Latham, *A Theory of Goal Setting & Task Performance* (Upper Saddle River, NJ: Prentice Hall, 1990).
11. Timothy D. Ludwig and E. Scott Geller, "Assigned Versus Participative Goal Setting and Response Generalization: Managing Injury Control Among Professional Pizza Deliverers," *Journal of Applied Psychology*, April 1997, pp. 253–261.
12. P. Christopher Earley and Terri R. Lituchy, "Delineating Goal and Efficacy Effects: A Test of Three Models," *Journal of Applied Psychology*, February 1991, p. 83.
13. Kenneth D. Butterfield, Linda Klebe Trevino, and Gail A. Ball, "Punishment from the Manager's Perspective: A Grounded Investigation and Inductive Model," *Academy of Management Journal*, December 1996, p. 1506.
14. Janet Barnard, "What Works in Rewarding Problem-Solving Teams?" *Compensation & Benefits Management*, Winter 1998, pp. 55–58.
15. Alexander D. Stajkovic and Fred Luthans, "A Meta-Analysis of the Effects of Organizational Behavior Modification on Task Performance, 1975–95," *Academy of Management Journal*, October 1997, pp. 1122–1149.
16. G. Douglas Jenkins, Jr., "Are Financial Incentives Related to Performance? A Meta-Analytic Review of Empirical Research," *Journal of Applied Psychology*, October 1998, pp. 777–787.

17. Shari Caudron, "How Pay Launched Performance," *Personnel Journal*, September 1996, pp. 70–76.

18. Susan C. Hanlon, David C. Meyer, and Robert K. Taylor, "Consequences of Gainsharing: A Filed Experiment Revisited," *Group and Organizational Management*, 19 (1), 1994, pp. 87–111.

19. Carolyn Wiley, "Incentive Plan Pushes Production," *Personnel Journal*, August 1993, pp. 86–91; www.lincolnelectric.com.

20. Justin Fox, "The Next Best Thing to Free Money," *Fortune*, July 7, 1997, p. 58.

21. Alfie Kohn, "Why Incentive Plans Cannot Work," *Harvard Business Review*, September–October 1993, pp. 54–63; Bob Nelson, "Does One Reward Fit All?" *Workforce*, February 1997, p. 70.

22. Jeffrey Pfeffer, "Six Dangerous Myths About Pay," *Harvard Business Review*, May–June 1998, p. 110.

23. The original explanation of expectancy theory as applied to work motivation is from Victor H. Vroom, *Work and Motivation* (New York: Wiley, 1964).

24. Walter B. Newsom, "Motivate Now!" *Personnel Journal*, February 1990, pp. 51–52.

Chapter Thirteen

Jack Applegate, the team leader for a corporate new ventures group, was looking for ways to improve the efficiency of the group in preparing for and conducting meetings. Jack was concerned that the group spent too much time scrambling for information prior to the meetings. He also thought team members were spending too much time preparing elaborate slides for their meetings that they looked at briefly then never used again. Toward the end of another hectic day, Jack sent the following e-mail to the team:

From: Jack F. Applegate ⟨jackapplegate@frontiernet.net⟩
To: Venture_Team@frontiernet.net
Subject: More Effective Meetings
Date: Monday, May 10, 1999 5:17 PM

Hey gang, I have an idea I want you to consider. We're spending too much professional time gathering basic information and putting together fancy slides to impress each other. I'm recommending that when feasible, you give Donna [the department administrative assistant] a list of the basic information you need. Donna has first-rate research skills. Donna can then fetch what she can. What she can't fetch, you dig up.

Also, you might send Donna a brief e-mail about what you want in a PowerPoint slide. She can then do the fancy graphics for you, saving you time that you can invest in working on new ventures. Let me know what you think.

OBJECTIVES

After studying this chapter and doing the exercises, you should be able to:

1. Describe the steps in the communication process.

2. Recognize the major types of nonverbal communication in the workplace.

3. Explain and illustrate the difference between formal and informal communication channels.

4. Identify major communication barriers in organizations.

5. Develop tactics for overcoming communication barriers.

6. Describe how to conduct more effective meetings.

7. Describe how organizational (or office) politics affects interpersonal communication.

Communication

The venture specialists on the team replied to Jack's e-mail quite positively. Donna, however, almost had an attack of office rage. She replied to the entire distribution list, "Jack, I am appalled at your insensitivity to me as a human being. Your sexism and disregard for the rights of women is obvious in your message. I am shocked because I thought you were a modern manager and a gentleman at the same time. What right do you have to consider me a dog? Who said I should be FETCHING information for the team? Do you want me to FETCH your slippers and newspaper also? I am seriously considering filing a sexual harassment charge against you."

After reading Donna's reply, Jack walked out of his office, with dictionary in hand, and said to Donna, "Hold on Donna, I think we have a little semantics problem right here. According to my dictionary [*Random House Webster's College Dictionary*], *fetch* means to go and bring back. There is not one mention of fetch referring to dogs. You get down to the 21st meaning before fetch means anything even a little negative. And there it says to 'perform menial tasks.' Sorry to have hurt your feelings, especially because I hold you in high regard."

"Okay," said Donna. "But still please never use the word fetch in relation to me."

The somewhat humorous, yet still hurtful, communication snafu just described illustrates the importance of avoiding communication barriers in the workplace. Anybody whose work involves interacting with people either orally or in writing must be on guard not to erect communication barriers. So vital is communication that it has been described as the glue that holds the organization together. Poor communication is the number one problem in virtually all organizations and the cause of most problems. Communication problems can be immensely expensive. John O. Whitney says, "I have, as a manager or consultant in business turnarounds, observed losses totalling more than $1 billion in organizations where people, early in the game, either knew absolutely or had strong premonitions about the problem, but were intimidated, squelched, or ignored."[1]

Communication is an integral part of all managerial functions. Unless managers communicate with others, they cannot plan, organize, control, or lead. For example, a manager cannot communicate a vision without superior communication skills. Person-to-person communication is as much a part of managerial, professional, technical, and sales work as running is a part of basketball and tennis. Furthermore, the ability to communicate effectively is closely related to career advancement. Employees who are poor communicators are often bypassed for promotion, particularly if the job includes people contact.

The information in this chapter is designed to improve communication among people in the workplace. Two approaches are used to achieve this end. First the chapter will describe key aspects of organizational communication, including communication channels and barriers. Second, the chapter presents many suggestions about how managers and others can overcome communication barriers and conduct effective meetings. We also study a subtle aspect of communications called office politics.

THE COMMUNICATION PROCESS

Describe the steps in the communication process.

Anytime people send information back and forth to each other they are communicating. **Communication** is the process of exchanging information by the use of words, letters, symbols, or nonverbal behavior. Sending messages to other people, and having the messages interpreted as intended, is both complex and difficult. A major part of the problem is that communication is dependent on perception. People may perceive words, symbols, actions, and even colors differently, depending on their background and interests.

A typical communication snafu took place at quality-improvement meeting. The supervisor said to a technician, "Quality is in the eye of the beholder." The technician responded, "Oh, how interesting." Later the technician told the rest of the team, "It's no use striving for high quality. The boss thinks quality is too subjective to achieve." The message the supervisor was trying to communicate is that the consumer is the final judge of quality.

communication
The process of exchanging information by the use of words, letters, symbols, or nonverbal behavior.

Steps in the Communication Process

Exhibit 13-1 illustrates the complexity of the communication process. This diagram is a simplification of the baffling process of sending and receiving messages. The theme of the model is that two-way communication involves major steps and that each step is subject to interference, or noise. The four steps are: encoding, transmission, decoding, and feedback.

ENCODING THE MESSAGE   **Encoding** is the process of organizing ideas into a series of symbols, such as words and gestures, designed to communicate with the receiver. Word choice has a strong influence on communication effectiveness. The better a person's grasp of language, the easier it is for him or her to encode. If the choice of words or any other symbol is appropriate, the better the chance that communication will proceed smoothly. The supervisor mentioned at the beginning of this section chose to use the somewhat vague phrase: "Quality is in the eye of the beholder." A more effective message would have been: "Quality is measured by customer acceptance."

encoding
The process of organizing ideas into a series of symbols designed to communicate with the receiver.

COMMUNICATION MEDIA   The message is sent via a communication medium, such as voice, telephone, paper, or electronic mail. It is important to select a medium that fits the message. It would be appropriate to use the spoken word to inform a coworker that his shirt was torn. It would be inappropriate to send the same message over an electronic bulletin board. Many messages in organizations are sent nonverbally, through the use of gestures and facial expressions. For example, a smile from a superior in a meeting is an effective way of communicating the message "I agree with your comment." Exhibit 13-2 presents additional ideas about choosing the best medium for your message.

323

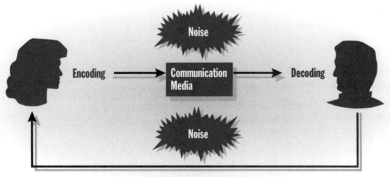

Feedback

The Communication Process
Exchanging messages as intended is complex because noise, or interference, so often gets in the way.

EXHIBIT 13-2

Choosing the Right Medium for Your Message

Several options exist for communicating an important message on the job. Before choosing an option, think of its major pros and cons.

Quick Telephone Call: On the positive side, a quick call is efficient. It is personal, informal, and allows for an exchange of ideas. A disadvantage is that phone calls are intrusive. You are asking the recipient to stop what he or she is doing, and the person may feel pressured into giving you an immediate response.

Face-to-Face Meeting: On the positive side, visiting a person at his or her work area can get a problem resolved quickly. On the negative side, you can annoy people by dropping by without an appointment. Making an appointment can also be disturbing because the person has to place you on his or her schedule. Dropping in on a high-ranking person may be unwelcome in a hierarchical organization.

E-mail: Sending a message by e-mail is excellent for wide distribution, and you will have a permanent record of your message. Your receiver also has control over when to receive the message. A negative is that the tone of an e-mail message can be misinterpreted. Remember too, that once you hit the send button it is too late to change your mind. Also, with so many people sending e-mail, your message might get overlooked.

Hard-Copy Memo: Paper memos appear quite official, and are a standard part of organizational communications. You are also more likely to carefully compose and edit a hard-copy memo than an electronic one. Written memos, however, may appear stiff, and some people will misplace a written memo before or after reading it. If your firm makes extensive use of e-mail, a paper memo will appear out of date.

Fax: A fax is generally used for the same purpose as any other hard-copy memo; however, it is now used primarily for transmitting factual information, and when a document with a personal signature is required. It can be an intrusive, interruptive form of communication if the fax machine is nearby the receiver.

Scheduled Meeting: If you schedule a meeting, you are in charge and you will be able to interact with several people about your issue. Holding a meeting dramatizes the importance of the topic. A disadvantage of a meeting is that some participants will be annoyed if the topic does not appear substantial enough to justify calling a meeting.

Source: Based on ideas from "The Right Medium for Your Message," *Working Smart*, January 1995, p. 5.

---

decoding

The communication stage in which the receiver interprets the message and translates it into meaningful information.

DECODING THE MESSAGE   In **decoding,** the receiver interprets the message and translates it into meaningful information. Barriers to communication are most likely to surface at the decoding step. People often interpret messages according to their psychological needs and motives. The technician mentioned earlier may have been looking for an out—a reason not to be so concerned about achieving high standards. So he interpreted the message in a way that minimized the need to strive for quality.

After understanding comes action—the receiver does something about the message. If the receiver acts in the manner the sender wants, the communication has been totally successful. From the manager's perspective, the success of a message is measured in terms of the action taken by a group member. Understanding alone is not sufficient. Many people understand messages but take no constructive action.

FEEDBACK   Messages sent back from the receiver to the sender are referred to as *feedback*. Without feedback it is difficult to know whether a message has been received and understood. The feedback step also includes the reactions of the receiver. If the receiver takes actions as intended by the sender, the message has been received satisfactorily.

Action is a form of feedback, because it results in a message being sent back to the original sender from the receiver. Suppose a small-business owner receives this message from a supplier: "Please send us $450 within 10 days to cover your overdue account. If we do not receive payment within 10 days, your account will be turned over to a collection agent." The owner understands the message but decides not to comply, because the parts for which the $450 is owed were defective. The owner's noncompliance is not due to a lack of understanding.

Many missteps can occur between encoding and decoding a message. **Noise,** or unwanted interference, can distort or block the message. Later in the chapter the discussion of communication barriers will examine the problem of noise and how it prevents the smooth flow of ideas between sender and receiver.

noise
In communication, unwanted interference that can distort or block a message.

NONVERBAL COMMUNICATION IN ORGANIZATIONS

Recognize the major types of nonverbal communication in the workplace.

The most obvious modes of communication are speaking, writing, and sign language. (Many large business meetings today include an interpreter who signs for deaf members of the audience.) A substantial amount of interpersonal communication also occurs through **nonverbal communication,** the transmission of messages by means other than words. Body language refers to those aspects of nonverbal communication directly related to movements of the body such as gestures and posture.

nonverbal communication
The transmission of messages by means other than words.

Nonverbal communication usually supplements rather than substitutes for writing, speaking, and sign language. The general purpose of nonverbal communication is to express the feeling behind a message, such as shaking one's head vigorously to indicate an emphatic "yes." Nonverbal communication incorporates a wide range of behavior. Nevertheless, it can be divided into the following nine categories.[2]

1. *Environment.* The physical setting in which the message takes place communicates meaning. Included here would be office decor, type of automobile, and the restaurant or hotel chosen for a business meeting. What kind of message would you send to people if you drove to work in a Chevy Tahoe or a Land Rover?

2. *Body placement.* The placement of one's body in relation to someone else is widely used to transmit messages. Facing a person in a casual, relaxed style indicates acceptance. Moving close to another person is also a general indicator of acceptance. Yet moving too close may be perceived as a violation of personal space, and the message sender will be rejected.

3. *Posture.* Another widely used clue to a person's attitude is his or her posture. Leaning toward another person suggests a favorable attitude toward the message that person is trying to communicate. Leaning backward communicates the opposite. Standing up straight is generally interpreted as an indicator of self-confidence, while slouching is usually a sign of low self-confidence.

4. *Hand and body gestures.* Your hand and body movements convey specific information to others. Positive attitudes toward another person are shown by frequent gesturing. In contrast, dislike or disinterest usually produces few gestures. An important exception here is that some people wave their hands while in an argument, sometimes to the point of making threatening gestures. The type of gesture displayed also communicates a specific message. For example, moving your hand toward your body in a waving motion communicates the message "Come here, I like you" or "Tell me more." Palms spread outward indicate perplexity.

5. *Facial expressions and movement.* The particular look on a person's face and movements of the person's head provide reliable cues as to approval, disapproval, or disbelief.

EXHIBIT
13-3 *How to Speak with an Authoritative Voice*

A good voice alone will not make a businessperson successful. Yet, like clothing, voice quality should always add to a person's image, not subtract from it. Here are several practical suggestions, developed by voice coaches, for improving voice quality:

- **Avoid having a nasal-sounding voice.** The only sounds that should come through the nose are the sounds of *m*, *n*, and *ng*. The rest of speech should be sounded in the mouth. There's an easy test to see if you talk through your nose: Say "that." Now, pinch your nose and say "that" again. There should be no difference. If you sound like a duck when you pinch your nose and say "that," then you have a nasal voice. To solve this problem, throw open your mouth and repeat "that" as you yawn. This will bring the vowel down into your mouth. With practice, you will sound the vowels in your mouth and lose the nasal tone.

- **Vary your tone.** If you speak in a monotone, your voice will sound mechanical. One way to overcome a monotone is to practice singing several of your typical presentations. This will help you develop skill in using vocal variety.

- **Decrease voice hesitations.** Vocal hesitations are a nonverbal clue to weakness and insecurity. When you hesitate between words, people may think you have not thought through your comments. This problem can be solved by slowing down your speech.

- **Avoid breathiness.** People who take a breath after almost every word appear anxious. To remedy breathiness, take the time to fill your lungs with air before speaking. Practice until you can speak two sentences without taking a breath.

- **Practice conveying commitment in the sound of your voice.** Tape yourself as you talk extemporaneously about a topic you care about, such as describing your fantasy goals in life. Replaying the tape, you will hear your voice move up and down the musical scale. The emotion shown reflects commitment.

Source: Based on information in Charles Livingston McCain, "Say It in the Voice of Authority," *Success*, May 1984, pp. 48, 51; and Roger Ailes and Jon Kraushar, "Are You a Communications Wimp?" *Business Week Careers*, June 1988, p. 76.

6. *Voice quality.* Aspects of the voice such as pitch, volume, tone, and speech rate may communicate confidence, nervousness, and enthusiasm. Intelligence is often judged by how people sound. Research suggests that the most annoying voice quality is a whining, complaining, or nagging tone.[3] Exhibit 13-3 provides some suggestions for developing impressive voice quality.

7. *Clothing, dress, and appearance.* The image a person conveys communicates such messages as "I feel powerful" and "I think this meeting is important." For example, wearing one's best business attire to a performance appraisal interview would communicate that the person thinks the meeting is important. Another important meaning of dress is that it communicates how willing the employee is to comply with organizational standards. By deviating too radically from standard, such as wearing a suit on "Dress Down" day, the person communicates indifference. As two researchers note, "Employees failing to maintain dress standards suffer consequences that range from insults and ridicule to termination."[4]

8. *Mirroring.* To mirror is to build rapport with another person by imitating his or her voice tone, breathing rate, body movement, and language. Mirroring relies 20 percent on verbal means, 60 percent on voice tone, and 20 percent on body physiology. A specific application of mirroring is to conform to the other person's posture, eye movements, and hand movements. The person feels more relaxed as a result of your imitation.

Adjusting your speech rate to the person with whom you are attempting to establish rapport is another mirroring technique. If the person speaks rapidly, so do you. If the other person speaks slowly, you decelerate your pace. This technique could get confusing if you attempt to establish rapport simultaneously with two people who speak at different rates.

9. *Use of time.* A subtle mode of nonverbal communication in organizations is the use of time. High-status individuals, such as executives, send messages about their power by keeping lower-ranking people waiting. Ambitious people attempting to get ahead are seldom late for appointments (in the American culture). However, a high-ranking official might be late for a meeting, and that same amount of lateness might be perceived as a symbol of importance or busyness. Looking at your watch is usually interpreted as a sign of boredom or restlessness. Yet when a high-status person looks at his or her watch in a two-person meeting, the action is likely to be interpreted as meaning, "Hurry up and make your point. You have used up almost all the time I can grant you."

Keep in mind that many nonverbal signals are ambiguous. For example, a smile usually indicates agreement and warmth, but at times it can indicate nervousness. Even if nonverbal signals are not highly reliable, they are used to judge your behavior as illustrated in the accompanying Manager in Action.

ORGANIZATIONAL CHANNELS AND DIRECTIONS OF COMMUNICATION

Messages in organizations travel over many different channels, or paths. Communication channels can be formal or informal and can be categorized as downward, upward, horizontal, or diagonal. As described in Chapter 2, the widespread use of e-mail and Intranets has greatly facilitated sending messages in all directions.

Explain and illustrate the difference between formal and informal communication channels.

Manager *in Action*

Interpreting Body Language

Sandra Johnson, an operations manager, was asked by the recruiting manager why she was leaving her current position. Without hesitation Johnson replied, "Growth opportunities are limited." Not satisfied with that response, the interviewer continued to probe until Johnson finally acknowledged that a disagreement with the operations vice-president over departmental procedures triggered her resignation.

After the interview, Johnson wondered what she had said that prompted the interviewer to pursue the issue. What Johnson didn't realize is that her body language was a tipoff that she was being less than forthright.

Up until that moment in the interview, Johnson was sitting with her right leg crossed over her left leg, hands resting in her lap, eyes focused directly at the interviewer's face. When the question about leaving her present position surfaced, without conscious awareness, Johnson shifted slightly in her seat, crossed her left leg over her right, leaned forward slightly, and placed her hands on the desk in front of her. Changes in her body language were enough to suggest to the savvy interviewer that she was not being completely honest.

Source: "The Importance of Body Language," *HRfocus*, June 1995, p. 22.

327

Formal Communication Channels

formal communication channels
The official pathways for sending information inside and outside an organiza-tion.

Formal communication channels are the official pathways for sending in-formation inside and outside an organization. The primary source of information about formal channels is the organization chart. It indicates the channels mes-sages are supposed to follow. By carefully following the organization chart, a maintenance technician would know how to transmit a message to the chairman of the board. In many large organizations, the worker may have to go through eight management or organizational levels. Modern organizations, however, make it easier for lower-ranking workers to communicate with high-level managers.

In addition to being pathways for communication, formal channels are also means of sending messages. These means include publications such as newslet-ters and newspapers, meetings, written memos, e-mail, traditional bulletin boards, and electronic bulletin boards.

One important communication channel can be classified as formal or infor-mal. *Management by walking around* involves managers intermingling freely with workers on the shop floor, in the office, with customers, and at company social events. By spending time in personal contact with employees, the manager en-hances open communication. Because management by walking around is sys-tematic, it could be considered formal. However, a manager who circulates throughout the company violates the chain of command. She or he, therefore, is not following a formal communication path.

Communication Directions

Messages in organizations travel in four directions: downward, upward, hori-zontally, and diagonally. Over time, an organization develops communication networks corresponding to these directions. A **communication network** is a pattern or flow of messages that traces the communication from start to finish.

communication network
A pattern or flow of mes-sages that traces the com-munication from start to finish.

Downward communication is the flow of messages from one level to a lower level. It is typified by a supervisor giving orders to a team member or by top-level managers sending an announcement to employees. Downward communi-cation is often overemphasized at the expense of receiving upward communica-tion. A survey of employees from different companies indicated that an area of concern is the quantity and quality of communications that they received from management. A representative employee complaint is as follows:

> I still feel like I don't know what's going on around this company. I feel like decisions are being made and I never hear about it and when I do it's often too late.[5]

Upward communication is the transmission of messages from lower to higher levels in an organization. Although it may not be as frequent as downward com-munication, it is equally important. Remember the $1 billion mistake mentioned at the outset of the chapter? Upward communication tells management how well messages have been received. The same communication path is also the most im-portant network for keeping management informed about problems. Management by walking around and simply speaking to employees facilitates upward com-munication. In addition, companies have developed many programs and policies to facilitate bottom-up communication. Three such approaches follow:

1. *Open-door policy.* An open-door policy allows any employee to bring a gripe to top management's attention—without first checking with his or her im-

mediate manager. The open-door policy can be considered a grievance procedure that helps employees resolve problems. However, the policy also enhances upward communication because it informs top management about problems employees are experiencing.

2. *Workout program at GE.* General Electric conducts three-day town meetings across the company, attended by a cross-section of about 50 company personnel—senior and junior managers, and salaried and hourly workers. Facilitators are present to encourage the audience to express their concerns freely. Participants evaluate various aspects of their business, such as reports and meetings. They discuss whether each one makes sense and attempt to "work out" problems. By using upward communication, GE attempts to achieve more speed and simplicity in its operations.

3. *Complaint program.* Many organizations have formal complaint programs. Complaints sent up through channels include those about supervisors, working conditions, personality conflicts, sexual harassment, and inefficient work methods.

Horizontal communication is sending messages among people at the same organizational level. Horizontal communication frequently takes the form of coworkers from the same department talking to each other. When coworkers are not sharing information with and responding to each other, they are likely to fall behind schedules and miss deadlines. Also, efforts are duplicated and quality suffers. Another type of horizontal communication takes place when managers communicate with other managers at the same level.

Horizontal communication is the basis for cooperation. People need to communicate with each other to work effectively in joint efforts. For example, they have to advise each other of work problems and ask each other for help when needed. Horizontal communication is especially important because it is the basis for the horizontal organization described in Chapter 9. Moreover, recent evidence confirms the belief that extensive lateral communication enhances creativity. Exchanging and "batting around" ideas with peers sharpens imagination.[6]

Diagonal communication is the transmission of messages to higher or lower organizational levels in different departments. A typical diagonal communication event occurs when the head of the marketing department needs some pricing information. She telephones or sends an e-mail to a supervisor in the finance department to get his input. The supervisor, in turn, telephones a specialist in the data processing department to get the necessary piece of information. The marketing person has thus started a chain of communication that goes down and across the organization.

329

Informal Communication Channels

Organizations could not function by formal communication channels alone. Another system of communication, called an **informal communication channel,** is also needed. Informal communication channels are the unofficial network that supplements the formal channels. Most of these informal channels arise out of necessity. For example, people will sometimes depart from the official communication channels to consult with a person with specialized knowledge. Suppose the manager of pension services in a bank was familiar with the methods of calculating exchange rates between the U.S. dollar and other currencies. Bank employees from other departments would regularly consult this manager when they faced an exchange-rate problem. Any time two or more employees

informal communication channel
An unofficial network that supplements the formal channels in an organization.

consult each other outside formal communication channels, an informal communication channel has been used. Two other major aspects of informal communication channels are the grapevine and the rumors it carries.

grapevine
The informal means by which information is transmitted in organizations.

THE GRAPEVINE AND RUMOR CONTROL   The **grapevine** is the informal means by which information is transmitted in organizations. As such, it is the major informal communication channel. The term *grapevine* refers to tangled pathways that can distort information. This perception is an oversimplification. The grapevine is sometimes used purposely to disseminate information along informal lines. For example, management might want to hint to employees that the plant will be closed unless the employees become more productive. Although the plans are still tentative, feeding them into the grapevine may result in improved motivation and productivity. Some important characteristics of the grapevine are:[7]

- A substantial number of employees consider the grapevine to be their primary source of information about company events. The grapevine often has a bigger effect on employees than do messages sent over formal channels. Messages sent over formal communication channels are often perceived to be stale news.
- Information is usually transmitted along the grapevine with considerable speed. The more important the information, the greater the speed. For example, information about the firing or sudden resignation of an executive can pass through the company in 30 minutes.
- Approximately three-fourths of messages transmitted along the grapevine are true. Because so many grapevine messages are essentially correct, employees believe most of them. They have received intermittent reinforcement for having believed them in the past. Nevertheless, messages frequently become distorted and misunderstood. By the time a rumor reaches the majority of employees, it is likely to contain false elements.

  An example of this is the case of a company president who gave a personal donation to a gay-rights group. The funds were to be used to promote local legislation in favor of equal employment opportunities for gay people. The last version of the story that traveled over the grapevine took this form: "The president has finally come out of the closet. He's hiring three gay managers and is giving some year-end bonus money to the Gay Alliance."
- Only about 10 percent of employees who receive rumors pass along the information to others. Those who do, however, usually communicate the information to several other employees, rather than to only one.

The grapevine is the primary medium for transmitting rumors and therefore can create some problems. Participating in or not controlling the company grapevine can result in legal liability, such as being sued for defamation of character. Defamation of character occurs when an individual communicates something that is not true to a third person without any kind of professional privilege to do so.[8] One company faced a lawsuit when a bookkeeper spread the rumor that the CFO was stopped for shoplifting by a store security guard. An out-of-court settlement was reached.

Another problem is that false rumors can be disruptive to morale and productivity. Some employees will take action that hurts the company and themselves in response to a rumor. Valuable employees might leave a firm in response to rumors about an impending layoff. The valuable workers often leave first because they have skills and contacts in demand at other firms. Severe negative rumors dealing with products or services, especially about product defects or poisonings, must be neutralized to prevent permanent damage to an organization. Several years ago, a major soft drink company had to deal with the false rumor that drug syringes had been placed in some beverage cans. The company had to recall thousands of cans of beverage and work actively with the media to dispel the rumor. A child-care center lost 90 percent of its clients when a competitor started the rumor that a worker at the center had a prior conviction for child molestation.

Based on developments in *rumor theory*, here are suggestions for neutralizing rumors.[9] First, if a rumor seems entirely ridiculous, *ignore it* because it will probably die on its own. (A case in point is the recent rumor that Kellogg's was going to drop its name-brand cereals and make only store-brand cereals.) Second, *make a comment* rather than saying "no comment," because refusing comment is generally taken as "yes." The manager might explain that the rumor is so absurd that it does not require a lengthy response. Third, if the rumor is to be denied, *base the denial on truth*. If the truth is denied, public reaction can be severe. Fourth, *hold town meetings and other forums* with employees and perhaps the public to discuss the rumor. Part of this approach can be setting up an e-mail address or Web page to deal with the rumor. Employees are encouraged to ask questions about the rumor and share comments they have heard in a chat room format. All inquires should be answered within 48 hours. Open discussion can help decrease suspicion about a catastrophic rumor such as that the company has squandered a pension fund.

CHANCE ENCOUNTERS   Unscheduled informal contact between managers and employees can be an efficient and effective informal communication channel. John P. Kotter found in his study of general managers that effective managers do not confine their communications to formal meetings. Instead, they collect valuable information during chance encounters.[10] Spontaneous communication events may occur in the cafeteria, near the water fountain, in the halls, and on the elevator. For example, during an elevator ride, a manager might spot a purchasing agent and ask, "Whatever happened to the just-in-time inventory purchasing proposal?" In 2 minutes the manager might obtain the information that would typically be solicited in a 30-minute meeting. A chance encounter differs from management by walking around in that the latter is a planned event; the former occurs unintentionally.

BARRIERS TO COMMUNICATION

Identify major communication barriers in organizations.

Messages sent from one person to another are rarely received exactly as intended. Barriers exist at every step in the communication process. Exhibit 13-4 shows how barriers to communication influence the receiving of messages. The input is the message sent by the sender. Ordinarily, the message is spoken or written, but it could be nonverbal. Barriers to communication, or noise, are shown as *throughput*, the processing of input. Noise is always a potential threat to effective communication because it can interfere with the accuracy of a message. Noise creates barriers to effective transmission and receiving of messages. The barriers may be related to the receiver, the sender, or the environment. The output in this model is the message as received.

Which messages are the most likely to encounter the most barriers? Interference is most likely to occur when a message is complex, arouses emo-

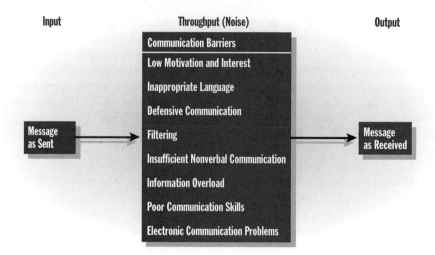

EXHIBIT
13.4

Barriers to Communication
*Many factors make it diffi-
cult to get messages across as
intended. A sampling of
these barriers to communication is listed here.*

tion, or clashes with a receiver's mental set. An emotionally arousing message
deals with such topics as money or personal inconvenience (e.g., being assigned
a less convenient work schedule). A message that clashes with a receiver's usual
way of viewing things requires the person to change his or her typical pattern of
receiving messages. To illustrate this problem, try this experiment. The next time
you order food at a restaurant, order the dessert first and the entrée second. The
server will probably not hear your dessert order.

Low Motivation and Interest

Many messages never get through because the intended receiver is not motivated
to hear the message or is not interested. The challenge to the sender is to frame
the message in such a way that it appeals to the needs and interests of the receiver. This principle can be applied to conducting a job campaign. When sending a message, the job seeker should emphasize the needs of the prospective employer. An example would be: "If I were hired, what problem would you like
me to tackle first?" Many job seekers send low-interest messages of this type:
"Would this job give me good experience?"

Sending a message at the right time is part of appealing to motives and interest. Messages should be sent at a time when they are the most likely to meet
with a good reception. Following this principle, a good time to ask for new
equipment is early in the fiscal year, when most of the money has not yet been
spent. Sending the message late in the fiscal year can also be effective. The manager might have some unspent money he or she does not want to return to the
general fund.

Inappropriate Language

The language used to frame a message must be suited to the intended receivers.
Language can be inappropriate for a host of reasons. Two factors of particular
significance in a work setting are semantics and difficulty level.

Semantics is the study of meaning in language forms. The message sender
should give careful thought to what certain terms will mean to receivers.
(Remember Donna's reaction to the word "fetch" at the beginning of the chapter?) A good example is the term *productive*. To prevent erecting communication

barriers, you may have to clarify this term. Assume a manager says to the group members, "Our department must become more productive." Most employees will correctly interpret the term as meaning something like "more efficient," but some employees will interpret it as "work harder and longer at the same rate of pay." Consequently, these latter employees may resist the message.

The *difficulty level of language* is its ease of comprehension. Communicators are typically urged to speak and write at a low difficulty level. There are times, however, when a low difficulty level is inappropriate. For instance, when a manager is communicating with technically sophisticated employees, using a low difficulty level can create barriers. The employees may perceive the manager as patronizing and may tune him or her out. The use of jargon, or insider language, is closely related to difficulty level. When dealing with outsiders, jargon may be inappropriate; with insiders (people who share a common technical language), it may be appropriate. Jargon can help the sender establish a good relationship with the receivers.

Defensive Communication

An important general communication barrier is **defensive communication**—the tendency to receive messages in a way that protects self-esteem. Defensive communication is also responsible for people sending messages to make themselves look good. People communicate defensively through the process of *denial*, the suppression of information one finds to be uncomfortable. It serves as a major barrier to communication because many messages sent in organizations are potentially uncomfortable. A middle manager was told that the company would be shifting entirely to a team structure, thereby eliminating most middle manager positions. He was advised that he was eligible to apply for a business analyst position on one of the new teams. When the manager was asked two months later what he had decided about applying for a new position, he responded, "I would like to have four teams reporting to me, and change my title to team manager."

defensive communication
The tendency to receive messages in a way that protects self-esteem.

Filtering

Filtering is coloring and altering information to make it more acceptable to the receiver. Telling the manager what he or she wants to hear is part of filtering. It is another variation of defensive communication. For example, suppose an employee becomes aware of information that should be communicated to management. The employee realizes, however, that managers would be upset if they knew the full story. The employee filters the truth, to avoid dealing with the wrath of management.

filtering
Coloring and altering information to make it more acceptable to the receiver.

333

Insufficient Nonverbal Communication

Effective communicators rely on both verbal and nonverbal communication. If verbal communication is not supplemented by nonverbal communication, messages may not be convincing, as the following situation illustrates.

A customer-service representative at a cable television station approached her manager with a preliminary proposal for increasing the number of subscribers. Her idea was to interview former customers who had dropped the service. With a blank expression on his face, the manager replied, "I see some merit in your idea. Work with it further." Two months later the manager asked the representative if she had completed the proposal. She replied that she had dropped the idea because "you seemed so unresponsive to my proposal."

Information Overload

Information overload, or **communication overload,** occurs when an individual receives so much information that he or she becomes overwhelmed. As a result, the person does a poor job of processing information and receiving new messages. Many managers suffer from information overload because of extensive e-mail in addition to the messages from office telephones, cellular telephones, voice mail, pagers, hard-copy correspondence, and trade magazines. Many managers receive about 150 e-mail messages daily. A study of workers in general found that they sent and received an average of 190 messages each day, most of them requiring at least some response.[11] Exhibit 13-5 presents the breakdown on messages sent and received by the workers.

Poor Communication Skills

A message may fail to register because the sender lacks effective communication skills. The sender might garble a written or spoken message so severely that the receiver cannot understand it, or the sender may deliver the message so poorly that the receiver does not take it seriously. Communication barriers can result from deficiencies within the receiver. A common barrier is a receiver who is a poor listener.

Electronic Communication Problems

Advanced technology has become a fundamental part of communication in the workplace, yet it has created several communication problems. The problems associated with e-mail are representative of these barriers, particularly the problem

EXHIBIT 13-5

Breakdown of 190 Daily Messages Received by a Variety of Workers
Message overload appears to be taking its toll because workers receive so many messages requiring some kind of response.

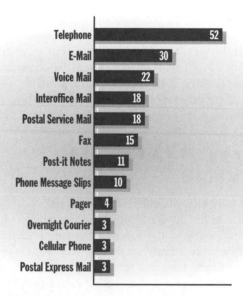

Telephone	52
E-Mail	30
Voice Mail	22
Interoffice Mail	18
Postal Service Mail	18
Fax	15
Post-it Notes	11
Phone Message Slips	10
Pager	4
Overnight Courier	3
Cellular Phone	3
Postal Express Mail	3

Source: Pitney Bowes Managing Communication in the 21st Century Workplace Study, as printed in Kristin Downey Grimsley, "Message Overload Is Taking a Toll," *The Washington Post* syndicated story, June 1, 1998.

of impersonality. Many people conduct business with each other exclusively by e-mail, thus missing out on the nuances of human interaction. A manager can smile and express sympathy through a nod of the head. When somebody asks or answers a question in person, it is easier to probe for more information than if the interaction took place through e-mail. Many people supplement their e-mail messages with *emoticoms* to add warmth and humor. For example, a half "smiley" face is ;-). Another impersonality problem with e-mail is that much like any printed document, an electronic message can seem much harsher than a spoken message.

E-mail, in general, is better suited to communicating routine rather than complex or sensitive messages. According to an analysis of new etiquette for evolving technologies, when dealing with sensitive information it is better to deliver the message face to face or at least in a telephone conversation. In this way both parties can have questions answered and misunderstandings are minimized.[12]

The Internet and private online services such as AOL are creating communication barriers of their own. Because of their comprehensiveness and 24-hour-per-day accessibility, they contribute to information overload. Another problem relates to the intrinsic satisfaction associated with "surfing" the information superhighway. Many workers become so preoccupied with searching for information and sending messages to other subscribers that interaction with officemates is perceived as an interference. Customer inquires can also get sidetracked while the online service user is perusing computerized information.

Telephone answering machines and voice mail create their own frustrations and communication barriers to both senders and receivers. Senders may dislike the impersonality of not being able to communicate with a live person. If so, they may be less receptive to conducting business with the other party. Receivers who get negative messages by machine may react more strongly than if a person delivered the messages.

Another advanced electronic communication device, videoconferencing, is gaining in acceptance. In a videoconference, people in different locations talk to each other while viewing each other's images on a television screen. With videoconferencing, a meeting can be held with workers in several different locations. One result is decreased travel expenses. The technique also increases productivity, because employees only have to travel to the videoconferencing center near their office. Videoconferencing creates some communication problems because it lacks the give-and-take of in-person interaction. Some nonverbal communication is lost because conference members tend to act more stiffly in front of cameras than in person.

A general principle is that electronic communication should be supplemented with face-to-face communication if relationship building is important. When geography permits, it is helpful to visit a customer or internal work associate from time to time to build a relationship not possible by electronic communication alone.

OVERCOMING BARRIERS TO COMMUNICATION

Develop tactics for overcoming communication barriers.

Most barriers to communication are surmountable. The general strategy for overcoming them has two parts. First, you must be aware that these potential barriers exist. Second, you should develop a tactic to deal with each one. For example, when you have an important message to deliver, make sure you answer the following question from the standpoint of the receiver: "What's in it for me?"

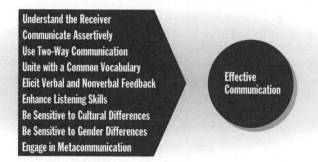

EXHIBIT
13-6

*Overcoming
Communication Barriers
The chances of getting
around the noise in the communication process increase
when the sender uses the
strategies and tactics shown
at the right.*

This section will describe nine strategies and tactics for overcoming communication barriers. Exhibit 13-6 lists the strategies.

Understand the Receiver

To be an effective communicator, you must understand the receiver. Understanding the receiver is a strategy that can assist in overcoming every communication barrier. For example, part of understanding the receiver is to be aware that
he or she may be overloaded with information or be poorly motivated. Achieving
understanding takes *empathy*, the ability to see things as another person does or
to "put yourself in the other person's shoes."

Empathy leads to improved communication, because people are more willing to engage in a dialogue when they feel understood. Managers especially need
empathy to communicate with employees who do not share their values. A typical situation involves an employee who does not identify with company goals
and is therefore poorly motivated. To motivate this employee, the manager might
talk about productivity leading to higher pay rather than to higher returns to
stockholders. Another reason empathy improves communication is that it helps
build rapport with the other person. Rapport, in turn, substantially improves
communication. You may have noticed that conversation flows smoothly when
you have rapport with a work associate or friend.

Empathy is not sympathy. A manager might understand why an employee
does not identify with company goals. The manager does not have to agree, however, that the company goals are not in the employee's best interests.

Communicate Assertively

Many people create their own communication barriers by expressing their ideas
in a passive, or indirect mode. If instead they explained their ideas explicitly and
directly—and with feeling—the message would be more likely to be received.
Being assertive also contributes to effective communication because assertiveness
enhances persuasiveness. When both sides are persuasive, they are more likely to
find a shared solution.[13] Notice the difference between a passive (indirect) phras-
ing of a request versus an assertive (direct) approach:

Passive

Team member: *By any chance would there be some money left over in the budget? If
there would happen to be, I would like to know.*

Manager: *I'll have to investigate. Try me again soon.*

Assertive

Team member: *We have an urgent need for a fax machine in our department. Running to the document center to use their fax is draining our productivity. I am therefore submitting a requisition for a fax machine.*

Manager: *Your request makes sense. I'll see what's left in the budget right now.*

Another use of assertiveness in overcoming communication barriers in the workplace is **informative confrontation,** a technique of inquiring about discrepancies, conflicts, and mixed messages.[14] Confronting people about the discrepancies in their message provides more accurate information. As a manager, here is how you might handle a discrepancy between verbal and nonverbal messages:

You're talking with a team member you suspect is experiencing problems. The person says, "Everything is going great" (verbal message). At the same time the team member is fidgeting and clenching his fist (nonverbal message). Your informative confrontation might be: "You say things are great, yet you're fidgeting and clenching your fist."

Another way of being assertive is to repeat your message and use multiple channels. Communication barriers may prevent messages from getting through the first time they are sent. These barriers include information overload and the receiver's desire not to hear or see the information. By being persistent, your message is more likely to be received. An important message should be repeated when it is first delivered and repeated again one or two days later. Experienced communicators often repeat a message during their next contact with the receiver.

Repetition of the message becomes even more effective when more than one communication channel is used. Effective communicators follow up spoken agreements with written documentation. The use of multiple channels helps accommodate the fact that some people respond better to one communication mode than another. For example, a supervisor asked an employee why she did not follow through with the supervisor's request that she wear safety shoes. The employee replied, "I didn't think you were serious. You didn't put it in writing."

Use Two-Way Communication

Many communication barriers can be overcome if senders engage receivers in conversation. A dialogue helps reduce misunderstanding by communicating feelings as well as facts. Both receiver and sender can ask questions of each other. Here is an example:

Manager: *I want you here early tomorrow. We have a big meeting planned with our regional manager.*

Employee: *I'll certainly be here early. But are you implying that I'm usually late?*

Manager: *Not at all. I know you come to work on time. It's just that we need you here tomorrow about 30 minutes earlier than usual.*

Employee: *I'm glad I asked. I'm proud of my punctuality.*

Two-way interaction also overcomes communication barriers because it helps build connections among people. According to management advisor Jim Harris, a challenge facing most companies is transforming traditional one-way, top-down communication into a flexible, two-way communication loop. A face-to-face communication style can be implemented by talking directly with employees instead of relying so heavily on e-mail and printed messages.[15] A manager who

informative confrontation
A technique of inquiring about discrepancies, conflicts, and mixed messages.

337

takes the initiative to communicate face to face with employees encourages two-way communication.

Unite with a Common Vocabulary

People from the various units within an organization may speak in terms so different that communication barriers are erected. For example, the information systems group and the marketing group may use some words and phrases not used by the other. Steve Patterson recommends that managers should first identify the core work of a business, and then describe it in a shared business vocabulary.[16] All key terms should be clearly defined, and people should agree on the meaning. Assume that a company aims to provide "high-quality long-distance telephone service." Workers should agree on the meaning of high quality in reference to long distance. The various departments might retain some jargon, and their unique perspectives, but they would also be united by a common language.

Elicit Verbal and Nonverbal Feedback

To be sure that the message has been understood, ask for verbal feedback. A recommended managerial practice is to conclude a meeting with a question such as: "To what have we agreed this morning?" The receiver of a message should also take the responsibility to offer feedback to the sender. The expression "This is what I heard you say" is an effective feedback device. Feedback can also be used to facilitate communication in a group meeting. After the meeting, provide everyone in attendance with written follow-up to make sure they all left with the same understanding.

It is also important to observe and send nonverbal feedback. Nonverbal indicators of comprehension or acceptance can be more important than verbal indicators. For example, the manner in which somebody says "Sure, sure" can indicate if that person is truly in agreement. If the "Sure, sure" is a brush-off, the message may need more selling. The expression on the receiver's face can also be due to acceptance or rejection.

Enhance Listening Skills

active listening
Listening for full meaning, without making premature judgments or interpretations.

Many communication problems stem from the intended receiver not listening carefully. Unless a person receives messages as intended, he or she cannot get work done properly. Managers need to be good listeners because so much of their work involves eliciting information from others in order to solve problems. Reducing communication barriers takes active listening. **Active listening** means listening for full meaning, without making premature judgments or interpretations. An active listener should follow these six suggestions:[17]

1. *The receiver listens for total meaning of the sender's message.* By carefully analyzing what is said, what is not said, and nonverbal signals, you will uncover a fuller meaning in the message.
2. *The receiver forms an initial opinion about the information.* Assume that the information is not what the receiver wants to hear. An active listener will nevertheless continue listening.

3. *The receiver reflects the message back to the sender.* Show the sender that you understand by providing summary reflections such as "You tell me you are behind schedule because our customers keep modifying their orders."

4. *The sender and receiver both understand the message and engage in a concluding discussion.* In the preceding situation, the manager and the employee would converse about the challenges of making on-time deliveries despite changes in customer requirements.

5. *The receiver asks questions instead of making statements.* For example, do not say, "Maurice, don't forget that the Zytex report needs to be completed on Friday morning." Rather, ask, "Maurice, How is the Zytex report coming along? Any problems with making the deadline?" By asking questions you will start the type of dialogue that facilitates active listening.

6. *The receiver does not blurt out questions as soon as the employee is finished speaking.* Being too quick to ask questions gives the impression that you were formulating your reply rather than listening. Before you ask a question, paraphrase the speaker's words. An example is, "So what you're saying is. . . ." Then, ask your question. Paraphrasing followed by asking a question will often decrease miscommunication.

Be Sensitive to Cultural Differences

As organizations have become more culturally diverse, the possibility of culturally based communication barriers has increased. The list that follows presents several strategies and specific tactics to help overcome cross-cultural communication barriers.

- *Be sensitive to the fact that cross-cultural communication barriers exist.* Awareness of these potential barriers will alert you to the importance of modifying your communication approach.

- *Show respect for all workers.* An effective strategy for overcoming cross-cultural communication barriers is to simply respect all others in the workplace.[18] A key component of respect is to perceive other cultures as being different than but not inferior to your own. Respecting other people's customs can translate into specific attitudes, such as respecting one coworker for wearing a yarmulke on Friday, or another for wearing native African dress to celebrate Kwanza. Another way of being respectful would be to listen carefully to the opinion of a senior worker who says the company should have converted to E-commerce a long time ago (even though you disagree).

- *Use straightforward language and speak clearly.* When working with people who do not speak your language fluently, speak in an easy-to-understand manner. Minimize the use of idioms and analogies specific to your language. A sales representative from Juarez, Mexico, was attending a company sales meeting in San Antonio, Texas. The sales manager said that the chief competitor was "over the hill." The sales representative was confused because he thought perhaps the competitor had relocated to a new town just "over the hill."

- *Observe cultural differences in etiquette.* Violating rules of etiquette without explanation can erect immediate communication barriers. A major rule of etiquette in many countries is that people address each other by the last name unless they have worked together for a long time. Etiquette expert Letitia Baldrige recommends that you explain the difference in custom to prevent misunderstanding. Particularly if on an overseas assignment, ask your work associate when using his or her first name would be appropriate.[19]

- *Be sensitive to differences in nonverbal communication.* Be alert to the possibility that your nonverbal signal may be misinterpreted by a person from another culture. Hand gestures are especially troublesome. An engineer for a New Jersey company was asked a question by a German coworker. He responded OK by making a circle with his thumb and forefinger. The German worker stormed away because, in Germany, the same gesture is a personal insult.[20]

- *Do not be diverted by style, accent, grammar, or personal appearance.* Although these superficial factors are all related to business success, they are difficult to interpret when judging a person from another culture. It is therefore better to judge the merits of the statement or behavior.[21] A brilliant individual from another culture may still be learning your language and may make basic mistakes in speaking your language.

Be Sensitive to Gender Differences

Despite the trend toward equality in organizations, much has been made recently of identifying differences in communication styles between men and women. Awareness of these differences helps lower potential communication barriers between men and women. Nevertheless, the differences described next are stereotypes that overlook the fact that men and women vary among themselves in communication style. Differences in gender-related communication style include the following:[22]

- Women prefer to use communication for rapport building. In contrast, men prefer to use talk primarily as a means to preserve independence and status by displaying knowledge and skill.
- Men prefer to work their problems out by themselves, whereas women prefer to talk out solutions with another person.
- Women are more likely to compliment the work of coworkers, while men are more likely to be critical.
- Men tend to be more directive in their conversation, while women emphasize politeness.
- Women tend to be more conciliatory when facing differences, while men become more intimidating.
- Men are more interested than women in calling attention to their accomplishments or hogging recognition. As a result, men are more likely to dominate discussion during meetings.

Understanding these differences can help you interpret the behavior of people, thus avoiding a communications block. For example, if a team member who is male is stingy with praise, remember that he is simply engaging in gender-typical behavior. Do not take it personally. If a team member who is female talks about a problem without looking for a quick solution, do not get frustrated. She is simply engaging in gender-typical behavior by looking for support.

A general suggestion for overcoming gender-related communication barriers is for men to improve communication by becoming more empathic (showing more empathy) listeners. Women can improve communication by becoming more direct.

Engage in Metacommunication

When confronted with a communication problem, one response is to attempt to work around the barrier, perhaps by using one of the methods already described. A more typical response is to ignore the barrier by making no special effort to deal with the problem—a "take it or leave it" approach to communicating. Another possibility is to **metacommunicate,** or communicate about your communication to help overcome barriers or resolve a problem.[23] If you as a manager were facing heavy deadline pressures, you might say to a group member, "I might appear brusque today and tomorrow. Please don't take it personally. It's just that I have to make heavy demands on you because the group is facing a gruesome deadline."

Metacommunicating is also helpful when you have reached a communication impasse with another person. You might say, for example, "I'm trying to get through to you, but you either don't react to me or you get angry. What can I do to improve our communication?"

metacommunicate
To communicate about your communication to help overcome barriers or resolve a problem.

HOW TO CONDUCT AN EFFECTIVE MEETING

Describe how to conduct more effective meetings.

Much of workplace communication, including group decision making, takes place in meetings. When conducted poorly, meetings can represent a substantial productivity drain. Most of the information presented in this chapter and in Chapter 6, which discussed decision making, applies to meetings. The suggestions that follow are for those who conduct meetings. However, many also apply to participants. By following these suggestions, you increase the chance that the meetings you attend will be effective communication vehicles.

1. *Meet only for valid reasons.* Many meetings lead to no decisions because there was no valid reason for calling them. Meetings are necessary only when there is a need for coordinated effort and group decision making. Memos can be substituted for meetings when factual information needs to be disseminated and discussion is unimportant.

2. *Have a specific agenda and adhere to it.* Meetings are more productive when an agenda is planned and followed carefully. People should see the agenda in advance so they can give some careful thought to the issues—preliminary thinking helps people arrive at more realistic decisions. In addition, assign maximum discussion times to the agenda items.

3. *Share decision-making authority.* A key attribute of an effective problem-solving meeting is authority sharing by the leader. Unless authority is shared, the members are likely to believe that the hidden agenda of the meeting is to seek approval for the meeting leader's tentative decision.

4. *Keep comments brief and to the point.* A major challenge facing the meeting leader is to keep conversation on track. Verbal rambling by participants creates communication barriers because other people lose interest. An effective way for the leader to keep comments on target is to ask the contributor of a non sequitur, "In what way does your comment relate to the agenda?"

5. *Encourage critical feedback and commentary.* Meetings are more likely to be fully productive when participants are encouraged to be candid with criticism and negative feedback. Openness helps prevent groupthink and also brings important problems to the attention of management.

6. *Strive for wide participation.* One justification for conducting a meeting is to obtain multiple input. Although not everybody is equally qualified to voice a sound opinion, everyone should be heard. A skillful leader may have to

341

limit the contribution of domineering members and coax reticent members to voice their ideas.

7. *Provide summaries for each major point.* Many ideas are expressed in the typical meeting, so some members may have trouble following what has been accomplished. Summarizing key points can help members follow what is happening and make better-informed decisions. Without summaries, participants sometimes do not know what, specifically, they are voting for or against.

8. *Strive for consensus, not total acceptance.* Few groups of assertive individuals will reach total agreement on most agenda items. Furthermore, disagreement is healthy because it can sharpen and refine decision making. It is more realistic to strive for *consensus*—a state of harmony, general agreement, or majority opinion. When consensus is achieved, each member should be willing to accept the plan because it is logical and feasible. Several approaches to achieving consensus were described in Chapter 6 in relation to group decision making. Also, strive for win-win solutions and plans instead of using such methods as majority rule and coin flipping. Another consensus-builder is to ask if the group is ready to reach a decision. The question should be asked when it is apparent to you that a consensus solution is about to emerge; otherwise the question will disrupt problem solving and discussion.

9. *Congratulate members when they reach a decision.* Complimenting group members when they reach a decision reinforces decision-making behavior and increases the probability that consensus will be reached the next time the group faces a problem.

10. *Ensure that all follow-up action is assigned and recorded.* All too often, even after a decision has been reached, a meeting lacks tangible output. Distribute a memo summarizing who is responsible for taking what action and by what date.

ORGANIZATIONAL POLITICS AND INTERPERSONAL COMMUNICATION

Describe how organizational (or office) politics affects interpersonal communication.

organizational (or office) politics
Informal approaches to gaining power or other advantage through means other than merit or luck.

At various places in our study of management we have mentioned political factors. For example, Chapter 1 described political skill being essential to success as a manager, and Chapter 6 described the role of political factors in decision making. Politics is related to communication because so much interpersonal communication in organization is politically motivated. Our communication is often shaped by a desire to gain personal advantage. As used here, **organizational politics** refers to informal approaches to gaining power or other advantage through means other than merit or luck. In this section we describe a sampling of political tactics, classified as relatively ethical versus relatively unethical. We also mention what managers can do to control negative politics. The Manager in Action box on page 344 will enhance your understanding of how managers are concerned about organizational (or office) politics.

Relatively Ethical Political Tactics

A political tactic might be considered relatively ethical when it is used to gain advantage or power that serves a constructive organizational purpose, such as getting a powerful executive on your side so you can implement a company wellness program. Four useful and relatively ethical political tactics are described next.

1. *Develop power contacts.* After you have identified who the powerful people are in your organization, alliances with them must be established. Cultivating

friendly, cooperative relationships with organizational members and outsiders can advance the cause of the manager or professional. These people can support your ideas or directly assist you with problem solving. A modern use of power contacts is to schmooze with the information technology experts in your office who can help you resolve an urgent computer problem (such as retrieving seemingly lost data).[24]

2. *Be courteous, pleasant, and positive.* Having good human relations skills creates many more friends than enemies and can help you be chosen for good team assignments and stay off the downsizing list. It is widely acknowledged by human resource specialists that courteous, pleasant, and positive people are the first to be hired and the last to be fired (assuming they are also technically qualified).

3. *Ask satisfied customers to contact your boss.* A favorable comment by a customer receives considerable weight because customer satisfaction is a top corporate priority. If a customer says something nice, the comment will carry more weight than one from a coworker or subordinate. The reason is that coworkers and subordinates might praise a person for political reasons. Customers' motivation is assumed to be pure because they have little concern about pleasing suppliers.

4. *Send thank-you notes to large numbers of people.* One of the most basic political tactics, sending thank-you notes profusely, is simply an application of sound human relations. Many successful people (including Jack Welch of GE) take the time to send handwritten notes to employees and customers. Handwritten notes are warmer than e-mail messages, but both help create bonds with their recipients. In the words of Tom Peters, "The power of a thank you (note or otherwise) is hard—make that impossible—to beat.[25]

Relatively Unethical Political Tactics

In the ideal organization, each employee works harmoniously with work associates, all focused on achieving organizational goals rather than pursuing self-interest. Furthermore, everyone trusts each other. In reality not all organizations are ideal, and many people use negative political tactics to fight for political advantage. Downsizing has been a major contributor to devious office politics because many people want to discredit others so that the other person is more likely to be "tapped" for termination. Here we describe three widely practiced unethical political tactics.

1. *Back Stabbing.* The despised yet widely practiced back stab requires that you pretend to be nice, but all the while plan someone's demise. A frequent form of back stabbing is to initiate a conversation with a rival, or someone you just dislike, about the weaknesses of a common boss. You encourage negative commentary and make careful mental notes of what the person says. When these comments are passed along to the manager, the other person appears disloyal and foolish.

   E-mail has become a medium for back stabbing. The sender of the message documents a mistake made by another individual and includes key people on the distribution list. A sample message sent by one manager to a rival began as follows: "Hi Ruth. Thanks for being so candid about why you think our corporate strategy is defective. I was wondering if you had any ad-

Manager *in Action*

Learning to Deal with Office Politics

a corporate professional wrote a letter to a career advisor at *Fortune* magazine, and his letter along with an answer were published. The correspondence is reproduced verbatim, as follows:

Dear Annie: My boss is obviously disliked and not respected by his boss. The trouble is, his boss is the top guy in our division. This has a tremendous impact on the work I produce, since the big boss likes to find fault with everything the little boss and his team touch. This has already affected my pay and career prospects. Can I get around this?

Goodbye Without Leaving

Dear GWL: I love this "big boss" and "little boss" stuff—it's so Laurel and Hardy. But that brand of slapstick was no doubt way before your time, so here's the new kind: There's only one boss here, and guess who it is? It's you.

You can take your talent elsewhere, of course: a different division, a new company. But let's say you run into the same situation again—and you know, if you keep viewing the world in terms of "big" and "little" bosses, you really aren't going anywhere anyway. Instead, try thinking about what you have accomplished in very specific terms: Whom did it please? (The client, the audience, the tax accountants . . .) Why was it great? (What did they like about it? If you

don't know, go find out.) How much money did it bring in? (If the answer is a negative number, stop right here.) And then: If I try to sell this someplace else, who will jump at it? Exclude "bosses" from your calculations. At this point, they don't count.

Nancy Friedberg, a career coach at the Five O'clock Club in Manhattan who has heard your story many times, says this: "There are people watching you all the time—people in your business, your peers, your boss's peers, his boss's peers, your opposite number at some competing company. You may know who some of these people are right now, or you may not. But figure it out—and once you do, make sure you meet these people. And then don't talk about the weather."

Instead, come up with an eight-word summary of your best stuff, your latest triumph, your real interest (okay the ideal is eight words, but 20 isn't bad), and get it out there— over lunch, in an elevator, at a conference, in a trade-association meeting. "Once you have built a reputation apart from your company, your company will see you as more valuable," says Friedberg. "And in fact, you are."

You won't need big and little bosses then, will you? One thing does lead to another. Life is so surprising.

Source: Anne Fisher, "Ask Annie: Am I a Victim of Office Politics?" Reprinted from the March 2, 1998 issue of *Fortune* by special permission; copyright 1998, Time Inc.

ditional suggestions that you think would help the company compete successfully. . . ."

A useful counterattack to the back stab is to ask an open-ended question to justify his or her actions, such as, "I'm not sure I understand why you sent that e-mail about my not supporting the corporate strategy. Can you explain why you did that, and what made you think I do not support corporate strategy?"[26]

2. *Setting Up Another Person to Fail.* A highly devious and deceptive practice is to give another person an assignment with the hopes that he or she will fail

and therefore be discredited. The person is usually told that he or she is being chosen to tackle this important assignment because of a proven capability to manage difficult tasks. (If the person does perform well, the "set up" will backfire on the manager.) A typical example of setting a person up to fail is to assign a supervisor to a low-performing unit, staffed mostly with problem employees who distrust management.

3. *Playing Territorial Games*. Also referred to as *turf wars*, territorial games involve protecting and hoarding resources that give one power, such as information, the authority to make decisions, and relationships with key people. A relationship is "hoarded" in such ways as not encouraging others to visit a key customer, or blocking a high performer from getting a promotion or transfer. For example, the manager might tell others that his star performer is mediocre to prevent the person from being considered a valuable transfer possibility. Other examples of territorial games include monopolizing time with clients, scheduling meetings so someone cannot attend, and shutting out coworkers from joining you on an important assignment.[27]

Exercising Control of Negative Organizational Politics

Carried to excess, organizational politics can damage productivity and morale and hurt the careers of innocent people. The productivity loss stems from managers and others devoting too much time to politics and not enough time to useful work. Just *being aware of the presence of organizational politics* can help a manager stay alert for its negative manifestations such as back stabbing. The politically aware manager carefully evaluates negative statements made by one group member about another.

Open communication can also constrain the impact of political behavior. For instance, open communication can let everyone know the basis for allocating resources, thus reducing the amount of politicking. If people know in advance how resources will be allocated, the effectiveness of kissing up to the boss will be reduced. *Avoiding favoritism* (giving the best rewards to group member you like the most) is a powerful way of minimizing politics within a work group. If trying to be the boss's pet is not effective, people are more likely to focus on good job performance to get ahead. Annette Simmons recommends that managers should *find a way to talk about territorial games*. Addressing the issues and bringing them out in the open might make group members aware that their territorial behavior is under close observation.[28]

SUMMARY OF KEY POINTS

 Describe the steps in the communication process.
The communication process involves four basic elements, all of which are subject to interference, or noise. The process begins with a sender *encoding* a message and then *transmitting* it over a channel to a receiver, who *decodes* it. *Feedback* from receiver to sender is also essential. In successful communication, the receiver decodes the message, understands it, and then acts on it.

 Recognize the major types of nonverbal communication in the workplace.
The major modes of transmitting nonverbal messages are through the environment (physical setting); body

placement; posture; hand and body gestures; facial expressions and movement; voice quality; and clothing, dress, and appearance. Mirroring—the use of nonverbal communication to establish rapport—is significant, as is the use of time.

Explain and illustrate the difference between formal and informal communication channels.

Formal channels are revealed by the organization chart. Management by walking around can also be considered a formal communication channel. Messages are transmitted in four directions: upward, downward, sideways, and diagonally. Informal channels are the unofficial network of communications that supplement the formal pathways. The grapevine is the major informal communication pathway, and it transmits rumors. Management can take steps to neutralize negative rumors, such as publicly discussing them.

Identify major communication barriers in organizations.

Barriers exist at every step in the communication process. Among them are (1) low motivation and interest, (2) inappropriate language, (3) defensive communication, (4) filtering, (5) insufficient nonverbal communication, (6) information overload, (7) poor communication skills, and (8) electronic communication problems.

Develop tactics for overcoming communication barriers.

To overcome communication barriers you must (1) understand the receiver, (2) communicate assertively, (3) use two-way communication, (4) unite with a common vocabulary, (5) elicit verbal and nonverbal feedback, (6) enhance listening skills, (7) be sensitive to cultural differences, (8) be sensitive to gender differences, and (9) engage in metacommunication (communicate about the communication).

Describe how to conduct more effective meetings.

To improve the communication effectiveness (and decision-making quality) of meetings, follow these suggestions: (1) meet only for valid reasons, (2) adhere to a specific agenda, (3) share decision-making authority, (4) keep comments brief and to the point, (5) encourage critical feedback and commentary, (6) strive for wide participation, (7) provide summaries for major points, (8) strive for consensus, (9) congratulate members when they reach a decision, and (10) assign follow-up action.

Describe how organizational (or office) politics affects interpersonal communication.

Politics is related to communication because so much interpersonal communication in organizations is politically motivated. Relatively ethical political tactics include (a) develop power contacts, (b) be courteous, pleasant, and positive, (c) ask satisfied customers to contact your boss, and (d) send thank-you notes to large numbers of people. Three relatively unethical political tactics include (a) back stabbing, (b) setting up another person to fail, and (c) playing territorial games. Managers can use various techniques to control negative organizational politics such as using open communication and avoiding favoritism.

KEY TERMS AND PHRASES

Communication, *323*
Encoding, *323*
Decoding, *324*
Noise, *325*
Nonverbal communication, *325*
Formal communication channels, *328*

Communication network, *328*
Informal communication channel, *329*
Grapevine, *330*
Defensive communication, *333*
Filtering, *333*

Information overload (or communication overload), *334*
Informative confrontation, *337*
Active listening, *338*
Metacommunicate, *341*
Organizational (or office) politics, *342*

QUESTIONS

1. Employers continue to emphasize good communication skills as one of the most important qualifications for screening career-school and business graduates. What are some of the reasons for this requirement?

2. How might understanding the steps in the communication process help managers and professionals do a better job?

3. Why has horizontal communication become so important in the modern organization?

4. Several newspaper cartoons have appeared about the subject of one worker sending an e-mail to another worker in an adjoining cubicle or office. What is the justification for sending an e-mail to somebody such a short distance away?

5. Assume that you are a supervisor, and one of your direct reports tends to mumble and look in another direction when the two of you talk. Explain how you might use meta-communication to deal with this problem.

6. What practical use can a manager make of the information about gender differences in communication?

7. Why are political skills so important that they are classified as one of the five basic skills of managers (refer back to Chapter 1)?

SKILL-BUILDING EXERCISE 13-A: Active Listening

Before conducting the following role plays, review the suggestions for active listening in this chapter. The suggestion about reflecting the message is particularly relevant because the role plays involve an emotional topic.

The Elated Coworker

One student plays the role of a coworker who has just been offered a promotion to supervisor of another department. She will be receiving 10 percent higher pay and be able to travel overseas twice a year for the company. She is eager to describe full details of her good fortune to a coworker. Another student plays the role of the coworker to whom the first worker wants to describe her good fortune. The second worker decides to listen intently to the first worker. Other class members will rate the second student on his or her listening ability.

The Discouraged Coworker

One student plays the role of a coworker who has just been placed on probation for poor performance. His boss thinks that his performance is below standard and that his attendance and punctuality are poor. He is afraid that if he tells his girlfriend, she will leave him. He is eager to tell his tale of woe to a coworker. Another student plays the role of a coworker he corners to discuss his problems. The second worker decides to listen intently to his problems but is pressed for time. Other class members will rate the second student on his or her listening ability.

INTERNET SKILL-BUILDING EXERCISE: Enhancing Your Nonverbal Communication E-mail Skills

Hi! readers. The purpose of this assignment is to search the Internet for emoticoms—such as the ;-) for a wink and the :-) for a smile—and acronymns to incorporate nonverbal signals into your e-mail messages. Find a combination of 10 emoticoms and acronymns using the Internet. Compare your list with that of a few classmates, and look for a rare one. •IM [H]O it would be good to do it •ASAP. ⟨G⟩

P.S. Your Internet search should help you decode the last two acronymns and the last emoticom.

CASE PROBLEM 13A: Just Call Me "Kat"

Katherine Matthews had worked for many years in a variety of retail positions, including a three-year assignment as an assistant manager at a women's clothing store. Matthews was then involved in an automobile accident as the passenger in a friend's car. Although she was wearing a seat belt, Matthews was severely injured. Her right leg and ankle were broken when the door on her side caved in upon impact with a tree.

After four months of rehabilitation, Matthews walked well with the assistance of a cane. Yet she could not walk for long without enduring pain. Katherine, and the team of medical specialists assisting her, agreed that an on-the-feet job was not appropriate for her in the foreseeable future. Katherine assessed her financial situation and decided she needed to return to work soon. Her disability payments were ending soon, and her savings were down to $350.

To make the transition back to full-time employment in another field, Katherine signed on with OfficeTemps, a well-established temporary placement agency. Katherine explained that she sought work that was mentally challenging but not physically demanding on her right leg and ankle. After carefully assessing Katherine's capabilities and experiences, the employment interviewer, Jack Radison, created a computer file for her. Radison said, "I'll call you as soon as I find a suitable assignment."

One week later Radison called Katherine with good news. He had located a nine-month assignment for her as a telephone interviewer for a market research firm. The market research firm was hiring several people to conduct telephone interviews with dealers and retailers about the acceptability of a relatively new product, a personal air cooler. The cooler is about the size of the central processing unit on a personal computer, and would easily fit on a desk or adjacent to a television set. The air cooler evaporates water, thereby lowering the temperature by 12 degrees F (6.7 C) in a 7-foot area. Using an air cooler, a person would have less need for air conditioning. With the cooler operating, a person could either eliminate air conditioning, or set it at a higher temperature. The manufacturer of the cooler was interested in estimating the potential market for the product, now being sold primarily by mail order.

Katherine's task was to telephone specific people (usually store managers or owners) from a long list of names. Completing an interview would require about 30 minutes, and involved obtaining answers to 20 separate questions. Each market research interviewer was given a quota of six completed interviews per day.

As the interviewers perceived the task, a major challenge was to keep the interviewee on the line long enough to answer all the detailed questions. Quite often the interviewer had to dig for additional information (such as sales of room air conditioners and fans), or request that the interviewee search his or her files for appropriate information. The several interviewers also agreed that an even bigger challenge was to get through to the people on the list and get them to cooperate. Among the problems were reaching a voice mail system instead of the actual person, excuses about being too busy to be interviewed, and outright rejection and rudeness.

Following the script provided by the market research firm, Katherine began her pitch in this manner: "Hello, this is Katherine from Garson Research Associates in Chicago. I'm asking for your cooperation to participate in an important study about an exciting new product, personal coolers. My interview should only take approximately 30 minutes. May we conduct the interview right now, or would you prefer another time in the next few days?"

Four weeks into the job, Katherine was behind quota by an average of two interviews per day. Feeling fatigued one day, she slipped into introducing herself as "Kat," the name used by family members and close friends. The interviewee prospect responded, "Oh sure, Kat, I can talk now." Two days later, Katherine made a personal call to a friend, thus prompted again to think of herself as "Kat." She inadvertently introduced herself as "Kat" to the next person on her list. Again, the prospective interviewee responded with enthusiasm: "Hey Kat, I'm ready to talk."

Prompted by the second cooperative response, Katherine then shifted to introducing herself as "Kat." The percentage of prospects willing to be interviewed jumped from 10 percent to 20 percent. Katherine explained this unusual result to her supervisor, who said that using a nickname and achieving good results was probably just a coincidence, that maybe she had simply become more confident. The increased confidence was therefore responsible for the higher success ratio in obtaining interviews.

Katherine responded, "I'm not so sure. There must be some other reasons that Kat gets more interviews than Katherine."

Discussion Questions

1. How can information about overcoming communication barriers help explain why "Kat" gets more interviews than "Katherine"?

2. How might the sex of the receiver be related to the different success ratios of "Kat" and "Katherine" in obtaining interviews?

3. Based on Kat's good results, what recommendations can you offer the research firm to help them increase the percentage of people who agree to be interviewed?

CASE PROBLEM 13-B: Memo Warfare

OFFICE MEMO

TO: Office Staff of Balta Construction
FROM: Sherm Balta, president
SUBJECT: Budget overrun on fax charges

It has been brought to my attention that we are now 34 percent over budget on fax expenses, with a full one-third of the year remaining. Somehow this abuse of fax privileges must stop. This is certainly no way to run a construction company. I see three alternatives facing us. Number one, we can close down the construction company for the year, thus avoiding any more fax expenses (an alternative *most* of you would not enjoy). Number two, we can stop using faxes for the rest of the year. Number three, we can all develop a responsible and mature approach to budget management by making more prudent use of the fax machine.

OFFICE MEMO

TO: Sherm Balta
FROM: Yukiko Inose
SUBJECT: Your memo about fax machine use

I read your recent memo with dismay, since it is my department that makes extensive use of the fax machine. We use faxes for very important purposes such as getting cost updates to clients in a hurry. Are we in the business of keeping our clients informed about their construction costs or in the business of pinching quarters on fax machine costs?

Discussion Questions

1. What communication problems are revealed by this incident?
2. Rewrite Balta's first memo in such a way that it will be less likely to make Inose defensive.

OFFICE MEMO

TO: Yukiko Inose
FROM: Sherm Balta, president
SUBJECT: Your response to my memo about fax costs

It is obvious to me, Yukiko, that you are resisting the philosophy of budgeting. In today's business world, both the Bechtels and the Balta Construction companies must learn to respect the limits imposed by budgets. Perhaps it is time that you and I had a serious discussion about this matter. Please make an appointment to see me at your earliest convenience.

3. Rewrite Inose's memo in such a way that it will be less likely to make Balta counterdefensive.

ENDNOTES

1. John O. Whitney, *The Trust Factor: Liberating Profits and Restoring Corporate Vitality* (New York: McGraw-Hill, 1994).
2. Some of this information is based on Michael Argyle, *Body Communication*, 2nd ed. (Madison, CT: International Universities Press, 1990).
3. Jeffrey Jacobi, *The Vocal Advantage* (Upper Saddle River, NJ: Prentice-Hall, 1996).
4. Anat Rafaeli and Michael G. Pratt, "Tailored Meetings: On the Meaning and Impact of Organizational Dress, *Academy of Management Review*, January 1993, p. 32.
5. "Mapping Employee Opinions," *The Surcon Report*, July 1995, p. 2.
6. John J. Bush, Jr., and Alan L. Frohman, "Communication in a 'Network' Organization," *Organizational Dynamics*, Autumn 1991, pp. 23–26.
7. Alan Zaremba, "Working with the Organizational Grapevine," *Personnel Journal*, March 1989, p. 34.
8. Mary-Kathryn Zachary, "The Office Grapevine: A Legal Noose?" *Getting Results*, August 1996, p. 6.
9. Nicholas DiFonzo, Prashant Bordia, and Ralph L. Rosnow, "Reining in Rumors," *Organizational Dynamics*, Summer 1994, pp. 57–60; "Control the Rumor Mill: Make Gossip Work for You," *Executive Strategies*, September 1996, p. 1.
10. John P. Kotter, *The General Managers* (New York: The Free Press, 1991).
11. Gallup Organization survey reported in Kirstin Downey Grimsley, "Message Overload is Taking a Toll," *The Washington Post* syndicated story, June 1, 1998.
12. "New Etiquette for Evolving Technologies: Using E-Mail and Voice Mail Effectively," *Business Education Forum*, October 1998, p. 8; Edward M. Hallowell, "The Human Moment at Work," *Harvard Business Review*, January/February 1999, pp. 58–66.
13. Jay A. Conger, "The Necessary Art of Persuasion," *Harvard Business Review*, May–June 1998, p. 86.
14. William Cormier and Sherilyn Cormier, *Interviewing Strategies for Helpers* (Monterey, CA: Brooks/Cole, 1990).
15. Jim Harris, "Listen and Respond: The Communication Two-Step," *Leadership* (American Management Association International), June 1998, p. 4.
16. Steve Patterson, "Returning to Babel," *Management Review*, June 1994, pp. 44–48.
17. Andrew E. Schwartz, "The Importance of Listening: It Can't Be Stressed Enough . . ." *Supervisory Management*, July 1991, p. 7; "Train Yourself in the Art of Listening," *Positive Leadership*, sample issue, 1999, p. 10.
18. Jack L. Mendelson and C. Dianne Mendelson, "An Action Plan to Improve Difficult Communication," *HRMagazine*, October 1996, p. 119.
19. Barbara Ettore (Interviewer), "Letitia Baldrige: Arbiter of Business Manners and Mores," *Management Review*, April 1992, p. 50.
20. Roger E. Axtell, *Gestures: The Dos and Taboos of Body Language Around the World* (New York: Wiley, 1991).
21. David P. Tulin, "Enhance Your Multi-Cultural Communication Skills," *Managing Diversity*, 1, 1992, p. 5.
22. Deborah Tannen, *Talking from 9 to 5* (New York: William Morrow, 1994); Tannen, *You Just Don't Understand* (New York: Ballantine, 1990); John Gray, *Men are from Mars, Women are from Venus* (New York: HarperCollins, 1992).
23. Deborah S. Roberts, "Communication + Stress = Breakdown," *Dartnell's Communication at Work*, sample issue, undated.
24. Mildred L. Culp, "Work Productivity: Buddy-Up with Tech 'Fixers'," *WorkWise®*, syndicated column, January 10, 1999.
25. Tom Peters, "Power," *Success*, November 1994, p. 34.
26. "Did *You* Leave This Knife Here?" *Working Smart*, March 1997, p. 1.
27. Annette Simmons, *Territorial Games: Understanding and Ending Turf Wars at Work* (New York: AMACOM, 1998).
28. Simmons, *Territorial Games*, p. 218.

Fourteen

Fluid teams are responsible for most of the work at SEI Investments, a firm that manages $121 billion in assets, mostly in mutual funds, and back-office operations for the trust departments at 85 of the leading 200 U.S. banks. Work is distributed among 140 self-managed teams composed of 2 to 30 members. Most employees are assigned to one base team and three or four ad hoc (special purpose) teams. A few longstanding teams serve major clients or important markets. However, the ad hoc teams give SEI its unique culture of fluid motion: Workers come together to solve a problem and disband when the work is accomplished. Several factors at company headquarters in Oaks, Pennsylvania, facilitate working in teams and moving from one project to another:

- There are no walls, clerical support is limited, and all the furniture is on wheels so people can work together whenever they wish.
- When workers moved to Oaks from their old headquarters, each employee brought only two boxes of possessions. There were no prearranged office or floor plans. Teams had the responsibility to arrange things as they saw fit.
- Colorful cables, referred to as "pythons," spiral down from 25-foot-high ceilings. Each cable carries electricity, a dial tone, and Internet access.
- Team leaders are not appointed by top management. Instead, different

OBJECTIVES

After studying this chapter and doing the exercises, you should be able to:

 Identify various types of teams and groups.

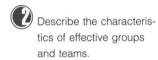 Describe the characteristics of effective groups and teams.

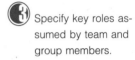 Specify key roles assumed by team and group members.

 Summarize managerial actions for building teamwork.

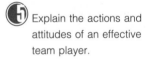 Explain the actions and attitudes of an effective team player.

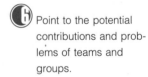 Point to the potential contributions and problems of teams and groups.

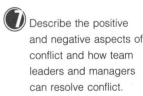 Describe the positive and negative aspects of conflict and how team leaders and managers can resolve conflict.

Teams, Groups, and Teamwork

people lead during different parts of the process, based on their skills and expertise.

- Leaders must use persuasion to accomplish their objectives because they lack the formal authority present in a hierarchy.
- Incentive compensation can range from 10 percent to more than 100 percent of base pay. Each team receives a pool of money for incentive compensation. Sometimes team members decide on dividing up the money, whereas other teams defer to the leader for making those decisions.

So far top management at SEI Investments is pleased with the team arrangement because company revenues and profits are rising rapidly.[1]

The modern work arrangements just described illustrate how self-managing work teams often enhance organizational effectiveness. The heavy emphasis on teams and group decision making in the workplace increases the importance of understanding teams and other types of groups. (You will recall the discussion of group decision making in Chapter 6, teams as part of job design in Chapter 8, and horizontal structures using teams in Chapter 9.)

We approach an additional understanding of teams, groups, and teamwork here by presenting several key topics: types of groups and teams, characteristics of effective teams and work groups, group member roles, building teamwork, and becoming a team player. We also describe the manager's role in resolving conflict, because so much conflict takes place within groups and between groups.

group
A collection of people who interact with each other, are working toward some common purpose, and perceive themselves to be a group.

Identify various types of teams and groups.

team
A special type of group in which members have complementary skills and are committed to a common purpose, a set of performance goals, and an approach to the task.

teamwork
The situation in which there is understanding and commitment to group goals on the part of all team members.

formal group
A group deliberately formed by the organization to accomplish specific tasks and achieve goals.

informal group
A group that emerges over time through the interaction of workers.

TYPES OF TEAMS AND GROUPS

A **group** is a collection of people who interact with each other, are working toward some common purpose, and perceive themselves to be a group. The head of a customer-service team and her staff would be a group. In contrast, 12 people in an office elevator would not be a group because they are not engaged in collective effort. A **team** is a special type of group. Team members have complementary skills and are committed to a common purpose, a set of performance goals, and an approach to the task. **Teamwork** means that there is understanding and commitment to group goals on the part of all team members.[2]

Groups and teams have been classified in many different ways. Here we describe the distinction between formal and informal groups, and among four different types of work teams.

Formal Versus Informal Groups

Some groups are formally sanctioned by management and the organization itself, while others are not. A **formal group** is one deliberately formed by the organization to accomplish specific tasks and achieve goals. Examples of work groups include departments, project groups, task forces, committees, and quality teams. In contrast, **informal groups** emerge over time through the interaction of workers. Although the goals of these groups are not explicitly stated, informal groups typically satisfy a social or recreational purpose. Members of a department who dine together occasionally would constitute an informal group. Yet the same group might also meet an important work purpose of discussing technical problems of mutual interest.

Types of Work Teams

All workplace teams have the common elements of people working together co-operatively and members possessing a mix of skills. We have already described self-managing work teams (often referred to as simply *work teams*) at three places in the text including the opener to this chapter. Four other representative work teams include cross-functional teams, top-management teams, affinity groups, and virtual teams. Projects, task forces, and committees are quite similar in design to cross-functional teams, so they do not receive separate mention here. No matter what label the team carries, its broad purpose is to contribute to a *collaborative workplace* in which people help each other achieve constructive goals. The idea is for workers to collaborate (a high level of cooperation) rather than compete with or prevent others from getting their work done.

As teams have become more common in the workplace, much effort has been directed toward specifying the skills and knowledge needed to function effectively on a team, particularly a self-managing work team. Exhibit 14-1 presents a representative listing of team skills as perceived by employers.

CROSS-FUNCTIONAL TEAMS   It is common practice for teams to be composed of workers from different specialties. A **cross-functional team** is a work group composed of workers from different specialties, but about the same organizational level, who come together to accomplish a task. The purpose of the

cross-functional team
A work group composed of workers from different specialties, but about the same organizational level, who come together to accomplish a task.

EXHIBIT 14-1

Team Skills

A variety of skills are required to be an effective member of various types of teams. Several different business firms use the skill inventory here to help guide team members toward the competencies they need to become high-performing team members. Review each team skill listed and rate your skill level for each one using the following classification:

S = strong (capable and comfortable with effectively implementing the skill)
M = moderate (demonstrated skill in the past)
B = basic (minimum ability in this area)
N = not applicable (not relevant to the type of work I do)

Communication Skills	**Skill Level (S, M, B, or N)**	**Thought Process Skills**	**Skill Level (S, M, B, or N)**
Speak effectively	___	Analyze issues	___
Foster open communications	___	Think "outside the box"	___
Listen to others	___	**Organizational Skills**	
Deliver presentations	___	Know the business	___
Prepare written communication	___	Use technical/functional expertise	___
Self-Management Skills		Use financial/quantitative data	___
Act with integrity	___	**Strategic Skills**	
Demonstrate adaptability	___	Recognize big picture impact	___
Engage in personal development	___	Promote corporate citizenship	___
Strive for results	___	Focus on customer needs	___
Commitment to work	___	Commit to quality	___
Thought Process Skills		Manage profitability	___
Innovate solutions to problems	___		
Use sound judgment	___		

cross-functional team is to get workers from different specialties to blend their talents toward a task that requires such a mix. A typical application of a cross-functional team would be to develop a new product like a Net TV. Among the specialties needed on such a team would be computer science, engineering, manufacturing, industrial design, marketing, and finance. (The finance person would help guide the team toward producing a Net TV that could be sold at a profit.) When members from different specialties work together, they take into account each other's perspectives when making their contribution. For example, if the manufacturing representative knows that a Net TV must sell for about one-half the price of a personal computer, then he or she will have to build the device inexpensively. A major advantage of a cross-functional team for product development is that they enhance communication across groups, thus saving time.

In addition to product development, cross-functional teams are used for such purposes as improving quality, reducing costs, and running a company (in the form of a top-management team). Northwestern Mutual Life has been using cross-functional teams for various purposes almost as long as the company has been in business. In recent years a cross-functional team created the company's Web site (www.northwesternmutual.com). Most Northwestern cross-functional teams now include an individual who has no responsibility for the problem—who is not a stakeholder. The outside perspective is thought to be effective in stimulating the thinking of other team members.

To perform well on a cross-functional team a person would have to think in terms of the good of the larger organization, rather than in terms of his or her own specialty. For example, a manufacturing technician might say, "If I propose using expensive components for the Net TV, would the product cost too much for its intended market?"

TOP-MANAGEMENT TEAMS   The group of managers at the top of most organizations are referred to as a team, the management team, or the top-management team. Yet as team expert Jon R. Katzenbach observes, few groups of top-level managers function as a team in the sense of the definition presented earlier in this chapter.[3] The CEO gets most of the publicity, along with credit and blame for what goes wrong. Nevertheless, groups of top-level managers are teams in the sense that most major decisions are made collaboratively with all members of the top-management group included. Michael Dell (Dell Computers) and Steve Jobs (Apple Computers) are examples of highly visible and brilliant CEOs who regularly consult with their trusted advisors before making major decisions.

The term *top-management team* has another less frequently used meaning. A handful of companies are actually run by a committee of two or more top executives who claim to share power equally. In this way they are like a husband-and-wife team running a household. An example of power sharing at the top to form a two-person team is the merger of Exxon and Mobil. Some observers are skeptical that a company can really be run well without one key executive having the final decision. Can you imagine your favorite athletic team having two head coaches, or your favorite band having two leaders?

AFFINITY GROUPS   Different types of work teams continue to emerge to meet organizational needs. A recent example of a new variation of a team is the **affinity group,** an employee-involvement group composed of professional-level (or knowledge) workers. The members are colleagues who meet regularly to share information, capture opportunities, and solve problems affecting the work

affinity group
An employee involvement group composed of professional-level workers who meet regularly to share information, capture opportunities, and solve problems affecting the work group and the larger organization.

group and the larger organization. The group is self-managing and has a formal charter.[4] An application of an affinity group took place at a large branch of Merrill Lynch. A group of investment counselors met regularly to discuss how they could better meet the needs of their many clients who were accepting early retirement. The group developed a package of investments that met the special needs of people who retired young and had a long life expectancy. The new program met with high acceptance from the clients it intended to serve.

VIRTUAL TEAMS   Some teams conduct most of their work by sending electronic messages to each other rather than conducting face-to-face meetings. A **virtual team** is a small group of people who conduct almost all of their collaborative work by electronic communication rather than face-to-face meetings. In the language of information technology, they engage in "cybercollaboration" by conducting "cybermeetings." E-mail is the usual medium for sharing information and conducting meetings. *Groupware* is another widely used approach to conducting a cybermeeting. Using groupware, several people can edit a document at the same time, or in sequence.[5] Desktop videoconferencing is another technological advance that facilitates the virtual team. Electronic brainstorming, as described in Chapter 6, is well suited for a virtual team.

Most high-tech companies make some use of virtual teams and cybermeetings. Strategic alliances in which geographically dispersed companies work with each other are a natural for virtual teams. It's less expensive for the field technician in Iceland to hold a cybermeeting with her counterparts in South Africa, Mexico, and California than to bring them all together in one physical location. IBM makes some use of virtual teams in selling information technology systems, partially because so many IBM field personnel work from their homes and vehicles.

Despite the efficiency of virtual teams, there are times when face-to-face interaction is necessary to deal with complex and emotional issues. Negotiating a new contract between management and a labor union, for example, is not well suited to a cybermeeting.

virtual team
A small group of people who conduct almost all of their collaborative work by electronic communication rather than face-to-face meetings.

CHARACTERISTICS OF EFFECTIVE WORK GROUPS

Groups, as do individuals, have characteristics that contribute to their uniqueness and effectiveness. *Effectiveness* includes such factors as objective measures of production (e.g., units produced), favorable evaluations by the manager, and worker satisfaction. As shown in Exhibit 14-2, and based on dozens of different studies, these characteristics can be grouped into seven factors or categories.[6]

Describe the characteristics of effective groups and teams.

1. *Enriched job design.* Effective work groups generally follow the type of job design associated with job enrichment (described in Chapter 8). For example, the task is perceived to be significant and the group members work on an entire task. A major theme is self-management, as practiced by self-managing work teams. A new Harley-Davidson plant has built job enrichment into the design of work teams. Working collaboratively with its two labor unions, Harley has created an environment in which workers are required to express their opinions and make decisions about how to build a better bike.[7]

2. *Interdependent tasks and rewards.* Effective work groups are characterized by several types of group member dependencies on one another. Such groups show task interdependence in that the members interact with and depend on one another to accomplish the work. Unless the task requires interdepen-

355

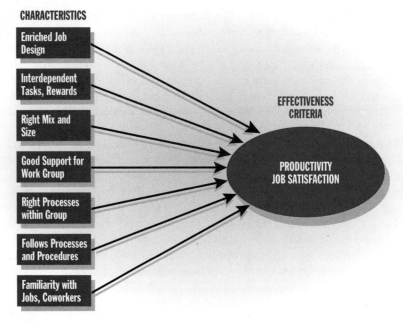

EXHIBIT 14-2

Work Group Characteristics Related to Effectiveness

CHARACTERISTICS

- Enriched Job Design
- Interdependent Tasks, Rewards
- Right Mix and Size
- Good Support for Work Group
- Right Processes within Group
- Follows Processes and Procedures
- Familiarity with Jobs, Coworkers

EFFECTIVENESS CRITERIA

PRODUCTIVITY
JOB SATISFACTION

Sources: Adapted and synthesized from Michael A. Campion, Ellen M. Papper, and Gina J. Medsker, "Relations between Work Team Characteristics and Effectiveness: A Replication and Extension," *Personnel Psychology*, Summer 1996, p. 431; David E. Hyatt and Thomas M. Ruddy, "An Examination of the Relationship between Work Group Characteristics and Performance: Once More into the Breech," *Personnel Psychology*, Autumn 1997, p. 579; Brian D. Janz, Jason A. Colquitt, and Raymond A. Noe, "Knowledge Worker Team Effectiveness: The Role of Autonomy, Interdependence, Team Development, and Contextual Support Variables," *Personnel Psychology*, Winter 1997, pp. 877–904.

dence, such as building a motorcycle, a team is not needed.[8] Interdependence of rewards refers to the fact that the group is working toward a common goal, and receives at least some of their rewards based on achieving group goals.

3. *Right mix and size.* A variety of factors relating to the mix of group members are associated with effective work groups. A diverse group of members with respect to factors such as experience, knowledge, and education generally improves problem solving. Cultural diversity tends to enhance creativity because various viewpoints are brought into play. Recent research cautions, however, that only when each member of the group enjoys high-quality interactions can the full benefits of diversity be realized. The interactions relate to both the task itself (such as talking about improving the motorcycle kick stand) and social interactions (such as chatting about children during a break).[9]

Groups should be large enough to accomplish the work, but when groups become too large, confusion and poor coordination may result. Also, larger groups tend to be less cohesive. Cross-functional teams, work teams, committees, and task forces tend to be most productive with 7 to 10 members. Another important composition factor is the quality of the group or team members. Bright people with constructive personality characteristics contribute the most to team effectiveness. A study involving 652 employees composing 51 work teams found that teams with members higher in mental ability, conscientiousness, extraversion, and emotional stability received higher supervisor ratings for team performance.[10] (Put winners on your team and you are more likely to have a winning team.)

4. *Good support for the work group.* One of the most important characteristics of an effective work group is the support it receives from the organization. Key support factors include giving the group the information it needs, coaching group members, providing the right technology, and granting recognition and other rewards. A contributing factor to the success of the Kansas City Harley plant mentioned earlier, is that workers say the higher-ups pay more than lip service to the concept of "partnership." They pay attention in such ways as granting worker requests for funding for new equipment and machinery.

5. *Right processes within the group.* Many processes (activities) take place within the group that influence effectiveness. One process characteristic is the belief that the group can do the job, reflecting high team spirit. Effectiveness is also enhanced when workers provide *social support* to each other through such means as helping each other have positive interactions. *Workload sharing* is another process characteristic related to effectiveness. *Communication and cooperation* within the work group also contributes to effectiveness. Collectively, the right amount of these process characteristics contributes to *cohesiveness*, or a group that pulls together. Without cohesiveness, a group will fail to achieve synergy.

6. *Follows processes and procedures.* Teams that can be trusted to follow work processes and procedures tend to perform better. Adhering to such processes and procedures is also associated with high-quality output.

7. *Familiarity with jobs and coworkers.* Another important set of factors related to work group effectiveness is familiarity. It refers to the specific knowledge group members have of their jobs, coworkers, and the work environment.

To help you pull together loads of information about the characteristics of effective work groups and teams, study the following summary of research conducted with professional-level workers in a financial services firm. The researchers concluded:

> The high-performing teams performed a variety of tasks that members perceived to be significant. They were allowed a high degree of self-management, were interdependent in terms of tasks, goals and feedback, and functioned as a single team. They tended to have members with complementary skills who were flexible in the tasks they performed. They were not too large for the tasks assigned them. They were well supported by the organization in terms of training, managerial support, and cooperation and communication from other teams. They had confidence in their teams' abilities, and members supported one another, communicated, cooperated, and fairly shared the workload.[11]

The characteristics of an effective work group or team should be supplemented by effective leadership. Team leaders must emphasize coaching more than controlling. Instead of being a supervisor, the leader becomes a team developer.

ROLES FOR TEAM AND GROUP MEMBERS

Another perspective on the group process is to identify team member roles.[12] Positive roles are described here to help you identify areas of possible contribution in group or team effort.

Specify key roles assumed by team and group members.

• *Knowledge Contributor.* Being technically proficient, the knowledge contributor provides the group with useful and valid information. He or she is intent upon helping with task accomplishment and values sharing technical ex-

357

pertise with team members. Referring again to the Harley-Davidson example, the knowledge contributor role is emphasized for production technicians because they are expected to make suggestions for improving quality and productivity. The plant general manager says, "What we're trying to do is get the work force to run the factory."[13]

- *Process Observer.* A person occupying this role forces the group to look at how it is functioning, with statements such as: "We've been at it for two and one-half hours, and we have only taken care of one agenda item. Shouldn't we be doing better?" The process observer might also point to excellent team progress.

- *People Supporter.* A person occupying this role assumes some of the leader's responsibility for providing emotional support to teammates and resolving conflict. He or she serves as a model of active listening while others are presenting. The people supporter helps others relax by smiling, making humorous comments, and appearing relaxed. He or she supports and encourages team members even when disagreeing with them.

- *Challenger.* To prevent complacency and noncritical thinking, a team needs one or more members who confront and challenge bad ideas. A challenger will criticize any decision or preliminary thinking that is deficient in any way, including being ethically unsound. Effective interpersonal skills are required to be a challenger. Antagonistic, attack-style people who attempt the challenger role lose their credibility quickly.

- *Listener.* Listening contributes so substantially to team success that it comprises a separate role, even though other roles involve listening. If other people are not heard, the full contribution of team effort cannot be realized. As a result of being a listener, a team member or team leader is able to summarize discussion and progress for the team.

- *Mediator.* Disputes within the group may become so intense and prolonged that two people no longer listen or respond to each other. The two antagonists develop such polarized viewpoints that they are unwilling to move toward each other's point of view. Furthermore, they have moved beyond the point that conciliation is possible. At this point the team leader or a team member must mediate the dispute.

- *Gatekeeper.* A recurring problem in group effort is that some members may fail to contribute because other team members dominate the discussion. Even when the viewpoints of the timid team members have been expressed, they may not be remembered because one or two other members contribute so frequently to discussion. When the opportunity gate is closed to several members, the gatekeeper pries it open. He or she requests that a specific team member be allowed to contribute, or that the member's past contribution be recognized.

A team member who plays several of the roles just described is likely to be perceived as an *informal leader*, or a person who exercises leadership without having the formal title. An example of informal leadership took place when Xerox Corp. turned a Habitat for Humanity project into a team-building event. (Habitat for Humanity is a nationwide organization that relies on volunteers to build homes for poor people.) The Xerox workers practiced teamwork skills and social responsibility simultaneously. One of the employees, Lori Padulo, had functional skills (the knowledge contributor role) in relation to leveling foundation blocks. At the same time her friendly demeanor and the encouragement she provided others gave her leadership status on the Habitat task.[14]

MANAGERIAL ACTIONS FOR BUILDING TEAMWORK

④

Summarize managerial actions for building teamwork.

The team player roles described previously point to actions the individual can take to become a team player. Here we highlight managerial actions and organizational practices that facilitate teamwork.[15] We use the term *managerial practices* to include team leader practices because many groups and teams do not use the title *team leader* for the person in charge. A department manager, for example, might be able to build teamwork. Good teamwork enhances, but does not guarantee, a successful team. For example, a group with excellent teamwork might be working on improving a service no longer valued by the company or customers. No matter what the output of the team, it probably will be ignored.

The manager can begin by helping team members believe they have an urgent, constructive purpose. A demanding performance challenge helps create and sustain the team. A major strategy for teamwork is to promote the attitude that working together effectively is an expected norm. Developing such a culture of teamwork will be difficult when a strong culture of individualism exists within the firm. The team leader can communicate the norm of teamwork by making frequent use of words and phrases that support teamwork. Emphasizing the words *team members* or *teammates*, and deemphasizing the words *subordinates* and *employees* helps communicate the teamwork norm. Exhibit 14-3 summarizes key culture changes necessary to achieve teamwork.

Using the consensus decision-making style is another way to reinforce teamwork. A sophisticated approach to enhancing teamwork is to feed team members valid facts and information that motivate them to work together. New information prompts the team to redefine and enrich its understanding of the challenge it is facing, thereby focusing on a common purpose. A subtle yet potent method of building teamwork is for the team to use language that fosters cohesion and commitment. In-group jargon bonds a team and sets the group apart from others. An example is a team of computer experts saying "Give me a core dump" to mean "Tell me your thoughts." The culture at Microsoft Corp. heavily emphasizes using hip jargon to build teamwork. Using the term *bandwith* as a synonym for intelligence appears to have been invented by CEO Bill Gates.

To foster teamwork, the manager should minimize **micromanagement,** or supervising group members too closely and second-guessing their decisions. Micromanagement can hamper a spirit of teamwork (potency) because team members do not feel in control of their own work.

micromanagement
Supervising group members too closely and second-guessing their decisions.

Creating physical structures suited for teams is an effective organizational intervention to support teamwork. SEI Investments, as described in the opening case, uses open space and furniture on wheels to facilitate collaboration among workers. Group cohesiveness, and therefore teamwork, is enhanced when teammates are

359

Individual Culture	Team Culture
Workers compete against each other for recognition, raises, and resources.	Workers learn to collaborate with each other.
Workers are paid for their individual efforts.	Workers are rewarded based on own efforts plus efforts of teammates.
Supervisors use authoritarian leadership or management style.	Supervisors become facilitative; they coach workers rather than only giving orders.

Source: Compiled from information in "The 'Facts of Life' for Teambuilding," *Human Resources Forum*, February 1995, p. 3.

EXHIBIT
14-3

Developing a Culture of Teamwork
Teamwork is more likely to persist when the organization establishes a culture of teamwork, as exemplified by the practices on the left.

located close together and can interact frequently and easily. Frequent interaction often leads to camaraderie and a feeling of belonging. A useful method for getting people to exchange ideas is to establish a shared physical facility, such as a conference room, research library, or beverage lounge. A key strategy for encouraging teamwork is to reward the team as well as individuals. The most convincing team incentive is to calculate compensation partially on the basis of team results.

A more general reward strategy is for managers to apply positive reinforcement whenever the group or individuals engage in behavior that supports teamwork. For example, if team members took the initiative to have an information-sharing session, this activity should be singled out and praised.

Many managerial actions to enhance teamwork focus exclusively on changing the structural aspects of how work is performed. Two such structural aspects are job definitions and reporting relationships. However, it is essential to also make process changes such as communication patterns and group norms. For example, people must be encouraged to communicate with coworkers, and a norm (or expectation) of teamwork should be established. Northwestern Mutual, as mentioned in regard to cross-functional teams, prides itself in having a culture of teamwork. In this way, workers adjust easily to working in teams.

Another option available to organizations for enhancing teamwork is to send members to outdoor training, a form of experiential learning. Participants acquire leadership and teamwork skills by confronting physical challenges and exceeding their self-imposed limitations. Rope activities are typical of outdoor training. Participants attached to a secure pulley with ropes will climb up a ladder and jump off to another spot. All of these challenges are faced in teams rather than individually, hence the development of teamwork. Outdoor training is likely to have the most favorable outcomes when the trainer helps the team members comprehend the link between such training and on-the-job behavior.

Managers must pick and choose from strategies and tactics to build teamwork. The Manager in Action illustrates the importance many business firms attach to a manager who can build a winning team.

BEING AN EFFECTIVE TEAM PLAYER

Explain the actions and attitudes of an effective team player.

Being an effective team player is important because without such capability, collaborative effort is not possible. Being an effective team player is also important because of managerial perceptions. A survey of 15 business organizations in 34 industries indicates that employers rate "team player" as the most highly ranked workplace behavior. Approximately 40 percent of the managers surveyed ranked team player as number one among seven desirable traits.[16] Here we describe a number of skills, actions, and attitudes contributing to effective team play. For convenience, five are classified as task-related, and five as people-related. In reviewing these attributes, remember that all team situations do not have identical requirements.

Task-Related Actions and Attitudes

Task-related actions and attitudes focus on the work the group or team is attempting to accomplish rather than on interpersonal relationships. An effective team player is likely to behave and think in the following ways:

1. *Possesses and shares technical expertise.* Most people are chosen to join a particular work team on the basis of their technical or functional expertise. Glenn

Manager *in Action*

Lloyd Ward of Maytag: Team Builder and Super Salesperson

Several years ago, traditional thinking in the appliance business was that the United States was a mature market leaving little room for growth. Fortunately for number-three appliance manufacturer Maytag Corp., Lloyd Ward is not bound by conventional wisdom. (You may recall the TV and print ads about the Maytag repairman who is lonely because Maytag washers and dryers hardly ever need repairs. Maytag quality is so high it retards replacement sales.) Since being appointed as head of Maytag's appliance division in 1996, Ward has amazed skeptics with his revival of the once declining unit.

Front-loading machines may not have the romantic appeal of E-commerce or the latest handheld computer that can access the Internet and send cellular telephone messages. However, the business results are impressive. When Ward took over the division—the company's biggest with 50 percent of revenues—the company was losing money steadily. But within two years, sales and profits were booming, and the Maytag stock price rose similarly.

Given the title of president of Maytag in 1998, Ward is considered a sure bet to succeed Leonard Hadley who plans to retire before 2000. This promotion would make Ward one of a handful of African-American executives who are now in reach of the top executive position in a major business corporation. An excellent salesperson, Ward scored a major victory in 1998 by positioning Maytag's top-of-the line Neptune model as the green (environmentally friendly) machine of washers and dryers. The Maytag cause was helped when Ward convinced both Best Buy and Sears, which sell one-third of all home appliances, to heavily promote the big front loaders as environmentally correct.

Ward's most effective leadership approach is that he gets people excited over whatever product he represents. Before joining Maytag, he had proved his marketing competence by building hefty profit margins as president of PepsiCo's large Frito-Lay midwestern operation. When Ward joined the company, he immediately began to work on a marketing plan. "I'm used to a very competitive environment. The appliance business is every bit as competitive as the snack wars and the cola wars," Ward said.

Within Maytag, Ward has developed a reputation as a team builder who excels at energizing the troops. Recent company progress at Maytag under Ward's leadership includes:

- 60 percent increase in the per share price of Maytag stock
- Anticipated 50 percent profit increase for current year to $271 million
- Expected revenue growth to $4 billion

A former Michigan State University basketball star, Ward is already preparing himself to play team captain at Maytag. He is overhauling marketing strategy at Maytag International, Hoover (best known for its vacuum cleaners), and other divisions. Company insiders and outside Maytag watchers are counting on Ward to keep driving the ball down court this year.

Sources: Based on facts in "Front-Load Lion," *Business Week*, January 11, 1999, p. 76; www.kentuckyconnect.com/heraldleader/news, accessed January 17, 1999.

361

Parker believes that to use your technical expertise to outstanding advantage you must be willing and able to share that expertise. It is also necessary for the technical expert to be able to communicate with team members in other disciplines who lack the same technical background.[17]

2. *Assumes responsibility for problems.* The outstanding team player assumes responsibility for problems. If a problem is free-floating (not yet assigned to a specific person), he or she says, "I'll do it." The task should be one suited for independent rather than coordinated activity, such as conducting research.

3. *Is willing to commit to team goals.* The exceptional team player will commit to team goals even if his or her personal goals cannot be achieved for now. For instance, the team member seeking visibility will be enthusiastic about pursuing team goals even if not much visibility will be gained.

4. *Is able to see the big picture.* As described in Chapter 1, a basic management skill is to think conceptually. Exceptionally good team players should have the same skill. In team efforts, discussion can get bogged down in small details. As a result, the team might temporarily lose sight of what it is trying to accomplish. The team player (or team leader) who can help the group focus on its broader purpose plays a vital role.

tough question
A question that helps the group achieve insight into the nature of a problem, what it might be doing better, and whether progress is sufficient.

5. *Is willing to ask tough questions.* A **tough question** helps the group achieve insight into the nature of the problem it is facing, what it might be doing wrong, and whether progress is sufficient. Tough questions can also be asked to help the group see the big picture. A major contribution of asking tough questions is that it helps the group avoid groupthink. Here is a representative tough question asked by a team member: "I've been to all our meetings so far. What in the world have we accomplished?"

6. *Is willing to try something new.* An effective team player is willing to experiment with new ideas even if the old method works relatively well. Trying something new leads to a spirit of inventiveness that helps keep the group vibrant. In one of the Harley-Davidson work teams, several of the workers designed a device to guide the brush in painting Harley's trademark striping. Although the more experienced manufacturing technicians had been successful with the hand-painting method, in the spirit of teamwork they were willing to try the new technique.

People-Related Actions and Attitudes

Outstanding team players are consciously aware of their interpersonal relations within the group. They recognize that effective interpersonal relationships are important for getting tasks accomplished. Outstanding team players are also aware that interpersonal relationships should contribute to task accomplishment. An outstanding team player is likely to do or think the following:

1. *Trust team members.* The cornerstone attitude of the outstanding team player is to trust team members. If you do not believe that the other team members have your best interests at heart, it will be difficult to share opinions and ideas. Trusting team members includes believing that their ideas are technically sound and rational until proven otherwise. Another manifestation of trust is taking a risk by trying out a team member's unproven ideas.

2. *Share credit.* A not-to-be-overlooked tactic for emphasizing teamwork is to share credit for your accomplishments with the team. Sharing credit is au-

thentic because other members of the team usually have contributed to the success of a project. Related to sharing credit, Steve Covey, best-selling author and consultant, says that teamwork is fostered when you don't worry about who gets the credit.[18] To the strong team player, getting the group task accomplished is more important than receiving individual recognition.

3. *Recognize the interests and achievements of others.* A fundamental tactic for establishing yourself as a solid team player is to recognize the interests and achievements of others. Let others know that you care about their interests by such means as asking, "How do my ideas fit into what you have planned?" Recognizing the achievements of others can be done by complimenting their tangible accomplishments.

4. *Listen actively and share information.* The skilled team player listens actively both inside and outside of meetings. As described previously, an active listener strives to grasp both the facts and feelings behind what is being said. Information sharing helps other team members do their job well and also communicates concern for their welfare. Information sharing can take many forms. These include bringing in news clips and magazine articles, informing teammates of useful Web sites, and recommending relevant books.

5. *Give and receive criticism.* The strong team player offers constructive criticism when needed, but does so diplomatically. A high-performance team demands sincere and tactful criticism among members. In addition to criticizing others in a helpful manner, the strong team player benefits from criticism directed toward him or her. A high-performing team involves much give and take, including criticism of each other's ideas. The willingness to accept constructive criticism is often referred to as *self-awareness*. The self-aware team player insightfully processes personal feedback to improve effectiveness.

6. *Don't rain on another team member's parade.* Pointing out the flaws in another person's accomplishments, or drawing attention to your own achievements when somebody else is receiving credit, creates disharmony within the group. When a teammate is the spotlight of attention, allow him or her to enjoy the moment without displaying petty jealousy.

POTENTIAL CONTRIBUTIONS AND PROBLEMS OF TEAMS AND GROUPS

Point to the potential problems of teams and groups.

Given that teams and groups are such an integral part of how organizations function, it is easy not to look critically at their contribution. However, researchers, writers, and managerial workers themselves have taken the time to assess the contributions of groups. Here we look at both the upside and downside of groups, including teams.

Potential Contributions of Teams and Groups

Teams and groups make a contribution to the extent that they produce results beyond what could be achieved without a high degree of collaboration among workers. Considerable case history evidence exists that supports the contribution of teams over independent effort. One such comparison of group and individual effort took place at the Ritz-Carlton Hotel in Dearborn, Michigan (near Detroit). The housekeeping managers at the hotel compared individual to team cleaning and restocking minibars. The team approach of having several people work on a room at the same time brought many tangible and intangible benefits, including the following:[19]

- Reduction of room cleaning cycle time by 65 percent
- Reduction in quality deficiencies per room by 42 percent
- Reduction in guest interruptions by 33 percent (by combining minibar replenishment with room cleaning)
- Increase in productivity from 13 to 15 rooms per person, with labor saving as a result
- Reduction in feelings of isolation from working alone and increase in job satisfaction from working as a team
- Job enrichment through coaching, feedback, and increased communication while performing housekeeping tasks

A study conducted over a 21-month period at an electromechanical plant provides another representative example of the potential contribution of work teams. The company produced a family of small motors used in industrial and residential applications. The teams were formed on four production lines. Quality was measured as the percentage of total units produced that were defective; productivity was measured as a ratio of the number of units produced to total production hours. Both quality and productivity increased over time after the formation of the teams.[20]

Potential Problems of Teams and Groups

Although the collaborative workplace has become quite popular, many concerns have been raised about teams and groups. In Chapter 6, discussing problem solving and decision making, we described two problems with groups: time wasting and groupthink. Here we look at other problems: limited productivity gains; group polarization; social loafing, legal risks, and career retardation.

LIMITED PRODUCTIVITY GAINS   A major concern about teams is not that they are harmful, but that their effectiveness is overrated. Teams lead to increases in productivity, quality, and job satisfaction only some of the time, not nearly all the time. The Saratoga Institute, a firm that studies performance measurement, surveyed 61 U.S. companies about their approaches to team design, performance measurement, and compensation. Only one-half of the companies said they are achieving positive results in meeting their operating objectives. One of the major problems cited was the difficulty in measuring the output of teams. Also, just because a team improves a group process (such as better cooperation among members) it does not necessarily lead to a competitive advantage. The survey results just presented also have a positive spin. Half the companies surveyed did think teams were producing good results. Also, although only half the operating managers thought teams were working out well, 80 percent of the companies said their team approach was meeting corporate expectations.[21]

A manager can often improve the productivity of teams by helping the team develop some of the characteristics of an effective work group discussed earlier. It is important to use teams primarily for interdependent tasks such as building a motorcycle or developing a new product.[22] Also, making a deliberate effort to develop teamwork can help a team realize its potential.

GROUP POLARIZATION   During group problem solving, or group discussion in general, members often shift their attitudes. Sometimes the group moves toward taking greater risks, called the risky shift. At other times the group moves toward a more conservative position. The general term for moving in either direction is **group polarization,** a situation in which post-discussion attitudes tend to be more extreme than pre-discussion attitudes.[23] For example, as a result of group discussion members of an executive team become more cautious about entering a new market.

Group discussion facilitates polarization for several reasons. Discovering that others share our opinions may reinforce and strengthen our position. Listening to persuasive arguments may also strengthen our convictions. The "devil-made-me-do-it" attitude is another contributor to polarization. If responsibility is diffused, a person will feel less responsible—and guilty—about taking an extreme position.

Group polarization has a practical implication for managers who rely on group decision making. Workers who enter into group decision making with a stand on an issue may develop more extreme post-decision positions. For example, a team of employees who were seeking more generous benefits may decide as a group that the company should become an industry leader in employee benefits.

SOCIAL LOAFING   An unfortunate byproduct of group and team effort is that an undermotivated person can often squeeze by without contributing a fair share. **Social loafing** is freeloading, or shirking individual responsibility, when a person is placed in a group setting and removed from individual accountability. Readers who have worked on group projects for courses may have encountered this widely observed dysfunction of collective effort.

Two motivational explanations of social loafing have been offered. First, some people believe that because they are part of a team, they can "hide in the crowd." Second, group members typically believe that others are likely to withhold effort when working in a group. As a consequence they withhold effort themselves to avoid being played for a sucker.

Tina L. Robbins conducted an experiment with college students in which they were given the opportunity to evaluate important proposals about student life. In the experimental group, a "confederate" told the group about his or her intention to put a lot of effort in the task or to hardly contribute. In the control (contrast) group, the students were not made aware of somebody working extra hard or contributing low effort. Students tended to work harder when they worked alone than when they had a partner contributing high effort. The results of the study demonstrated that social loafing can occur even when the task is thought-provoking, personally involving, and allows for unique contribution. Robbins concludes, "The performance of self-directed work teams or groups which are formed for the purpose of brainstorming, product idea generation, or for making proposal implementation decisions, may suffer the consequences of social loafing."[24]

One way a manager can minimize the effects of social loafing is to have group members contribute to the evaluation of each other. Concerns about being evaluated as a freeloader by peers would prompt some people to work harder.

LEGAL RISKS   Under certain circumstances managers may be in violation of labor law by forming work teams. According to the National Labor Relations Act (the NLRA or Wagner Act) a group is illegal if it can be proved to be

group polarization
A situation in which post-discussion attitudes tend to be more extreme than pre-discussion attitudes.

social loafing
Freeloading or shirking individual responsibility, when a person is placed in a group setting and removed from individual accountability.

365

employer-dominated and a labor organization under the law. An employee-involvement group, such as a work team or quality-improvement team, is usually employer-dominated. This is true because the employer establishes the group, provides a role for management, and funds the group. The key issue in many cases is whether the groups are classified as labor organizations within the meaning of the NLRA.

Concern about the legality of workplace teams led to a 1996 proposal called the TEAM Act. If passed, the bill would have amended the National Labor Relations Act to make clear that employers can convene groups of nonunion employees without violating federal labor law. Opponents of the bill were concerned that it would give employers too much power over employees, and enable the employers to essentially form *company unions* instead of labor unions. The issue about the legality of employer-dominated work teams is likely to surface again in the U.S. Congress in 2001, shortly after the new administration is in office.

Corporate lawyers have developed guidelines to help managers assess whether its work teams violate the Wagner Act. The major recommendation is to determine whether the issues addressed by an employee-involvement group constitute *conditions of employment*. Issues in possible violation include attendance policies, bonuses, grievances, labor disputes, wages, and hours of employment. To be legally safe, for now work teams of nonmanagerial personnel should bc limited to addressing production, quality, and safety matters.[25] Although the aforementioned legal precautions should be heeded, at present very few lawsuits have been filed over the use of various types of teams.

CAREER RETARDATION   A final concern about teams is that focusing too much on group or team effort, rather than individual effort, can retard a person's career. Some managers classify workers as team players versus leaders. (The perception is somewhat false because most effective leaders and managers are also good team players.) The element of truth in the perception is that a person who tries too hard to be a good team player might become a conformist and not seek individual recognition. People who do break away from the team and become higher-level managers are typically those known for independent thought and outstanding accomplishment.

For those who want to advance beyond being a team member, or team leader, it is important to be recognized for outstanding performance. As a team member, for example, volunteer to take on leadership roles such as chairing a team meeting or coordinating a special project. Bring a dossier of your individual accomplishments to your performance review. Every team has a most valuable player (MVP) who is still a good team player.[26]

RESOLVING CONFLICT WITHIN TEAMS AND GROUPS

Describe the positive and negative aspects of conflict and how team leaders and managers can resolve conflict.

conflict
The simultaneous arousal of two or more incompatible motives.

Although harmony and collaboration are an important goal of groups and teams, some disagreement and dispute is inevitable. **Conflict** is the simultaneous arousal of two or more incompatible motives. It is often accompanied by tension and frustration. Whenever two or more people in the group compete for the same resource, conflict occurs. Two team members, for example, might both want to take the team's one laptop computer on business trips they are taking on the same date. Conflict can also be considered a hostile or antagonistic relationship between two people. Here we look at three aspects of conflict particularly relevant to managers and team leaders of small groups: cognitive versus affective conflict, consequences of conflict, and methods of conflict resolution.

Cognitive Versus Affective Conflict

Some conflicts within the group deal mostly with disagreements over how work should be done. These are referred to as task-oriented or *cognitive conflicts*, because they deal mostly with the intellect rather than emotions. Two group members, for example, might argue over whether it is better to use their limited advertising budget to buy space on the outside of a bus versus on the radio. **Cognitive conflict** focuses on substantive, issue-related differences. These issues are tangible and concrete and can be dealt with more intellectually than emotionally.

Other conflicts within the group are more people-oriented. They occur because people have personality clashes, are rude to each other, or simply view many problems and situations from a different frame of reference. **Affective conflict** focuses on personalized, individually oriented issues. The conflict relates to subjective issues that are dealt with more emotionally than intellectually.[27] One symptom that affective conflict exists within the group is when, during a meeting, two people say to each other frequently, "Please let me finish. I'm still speaking."

Cognitive conflict is functional because it requires teams to engage in activities that foster team effectiveness. Team members engaged in cognitive conflict would critically examine alternative solutions and incorporate different points of view into their goals or mission statement. Because frank communication and different points of view are encouraged, cognitive conflict encourages innovative thinking. In contrast, affective conflict undermines group effectiveness by blocking constructive activities and processes. By such means as directing anger toward individuals and blaming each other for mistakes, affective conflict leads to cynicism and distrust.

The differences between cognitive and affective conflict are found in the executive suite as well as in lower-ranking organizational units. Allen C. Amason studied conflict as it relates to strategic decision making in top-management teams in the food-processing and furniture-making industries. Conflict was found to improve decision-making quality, and it was the cognitive dimension that accounted for the improvement. For example, the furniture company executives might argue over whether the company should sell nonassembled furniture to compete with its finished line of furniture. As a result of the strongly different opinions, they reach a decision that gains market share. Affective conflict, on the other hand, appeared to lower decision quality and affective acceptance (emotionally buying into a decision). The paradox uncovered is that conflict may improve decisions but it may hurt consensus and interpersonal relationships.[28]

Consequences of Conflict

Conflict has both positive and negative consequences. The right amount of conflict may enhance job performance, but too much or too little conflict lowers performance. If the manager observes that job performance is suffering because of too much conflict, he or she should reduce it. If performance is low because employees are too placid, the manager might profitably increase conflict. For example, the manager might establish a prize for top performance in the group.

cognitive conflict
Conflict that focuses on substantive, issue-related differences and is dealt with more intellectually than emotionally.

affective conflict
Conflict that focuses on more personal or subjective issues and is dealt with more emotionally than intellectually.

POSITIVE CONSEQUENCES OF CONFLICT   Many managers and scholars believe that job conflict can have positive consequences. When the right amount of conflict is present in the workplace, one or more of the following outcomes can be anticipated.

1. *Increased creativity.* Talents and abilities surface in response to conflict. People become inventive when they are placed in intense competition with others.
2. *Increased effort.* Constructive amounts of conflict spur people to new heights of performance. People become so motivated to win the conflict that they may surprise themselves and their superiors with their work output.
3. *Increased diagnostic information.* Conflict can provide valuable information about problem areas in the department or organization. When leaders learn of conflict, they may conduct investigations that will lead to the prevention of similar problems.
4. *Increased group cohesion.* When one group in a firm is in conflict with another, group members may become more cohesive. They perceive themselves to be facing a common enemy.

NEGATIVE CONSEQUENCES OF CONFLICT   When the wrong amount or type of conflict exists, job performance may suffer. Some types of conflict have worse consequences than others. A particularly bad form of conflict is one that forces a person to choose between two undesirable alternatives. Negative consequences of conflict include the following:

1. *Poor physical and mental health.* Intense conflict is a source of stress. A person under prolonged and intense conflict may suffer stress-related disorders.
2. *Wasted resources.* Employees and groups in conflict frequently waste time, money, and other resources while fighting their battles. One executive took a personal dislike to one of his managers and therefore ignored his cost-saving recommendations.
3. *Sidetracked goals.* In extreme forms of conflict, the parties involved may neglect the pursuit of important goals. Instead, they are intent on winning their conflicts. A goal displacement of this type took place within an information systems group. The rival factions spent so much time squabbling over which new hardware and software to purchase that they neglected some of their tasks.
4. *Heightened self-interest.* Conflict within the group often results in extreme demonstrations of self-interest at the expense of the group and the larger organization. Individuals or groups place their personal interests over those of the rest of the firm or customers. One common result of this type of self-interest is hogging resources. A team member might attempt to convince the team leader to place him on an important customer troubleshooting assignment even though he knows his rival on the team is better qualified.

Methods of Conflict Resolution

Managers spend as much as 20 percent of their work time dealing with conflict. A leader who learns to manage conflict effectively can increase his or her productivity. In addition, being able to resolve conflict enhances one's stature as a leader. Employees expect their boss to be able to resolve conflicts. Here we describe the five basic styles or methods of resolving conflict: forcing, accommodation, sharing, collaboration, and avoiding. An effective manager will choose the best approach for the situation.

FORCING   The forcing, or competitive, style is based on the desire to win one's own concerns at the expense of the other party, or to dominate. Autocratic leaders such as Al Dunlap, formerly of Scott Paper and Sunbeam Corp., chose to resolve conflict in this way. Dunlap's bullying style of resolving conflict, combined with his extensive job cutting, led many employees to cheer when he was fired as CEO of Sunbeam. A person with a forcing style is likely to engage in win-lose ("I win, you lose") power struggles, resulting in poor teamwork.

ACCOMMODATION   The accommodative style favors appeasement, or satisfying the other's concerns without taking care of one's own. People with this orientation may be generous or self-sacrificing just to maintain a relationship. An irate customer might be accommodated with a full refund "just to shut him (or her) up." The intent of such accommodation might also be to retain the customer's loyalty.

SHARING   The sharing style is midway between domination and appeasement. Sharers prefer moderate but incomplete satisfaction for both parties. The result is compromise. The term *splitting the difference* reflects this orientation. The sharing style of conflict resolution is commonly used in such activities as purchasing a house or car. Within the work group, sharing might take the form of each team member receiving the same percentage salary increase rather than haggle over dividing the pool of money available for increases.

COLLABORATION   In contrast to the sharing style, collaboration reflects an interest in fully satisfying the desire of both parties. It is based on an underlying win-win philosophy, the belief that after conflict has been resolved both sides should gain something of value. For example, a small-company president might offer the management team more stock options if they are willing to take a pay cut to help the firm through rough times. If the firm succeeds, both parties have scored a victory.

All parties benefit from collaboration, or a win-win approach to resolving conflict. In addition, compliance with the solution occurs readily, and the relationship between those in conflict improves.

A conflict-resolution technique built into the collaboration style is *confrontation and problem solving*. Its purpose is to identify the real problem and then arrive at a solution that genuinely solves it. First the parties are brought together and the real problem is confronted.

Another collaborative approach involves asking what action can break an impasse. When a conflict reaches a point where progress has reached a standstill, one of the parties asks, "What would you like me to do?" The other side often reacts with astonishment and then the first party asks, "If I could do anything to make this situation okay in your eyes, what would that be?"[29] Frequently the desired action—such as "Treat me with more respect"—can be implemented.

AVOIDING   The avoider combines uncooperativeness and unassertiveness. He or she is indifferent to the concerns of either party. The person may actually be withdrawing from conflict or relying upon fate. The avoiding style is sometimes used by a manager who stays out of a conflict between team members. The members are left to resolve their own differences.

SUMMARY OF KEY POINTS

Identify various types of teams and groups.
Formal groups are deliberately formed by the organization, whereas informal groups emerge over time through worker interaction. Several representative types of work teams are cross-functional teams, top-management teams, affinity groups, and virtual teams.

Describe the characteristics of effective groups and teams.
Effective work group characteristics are well documented. Jobs of members should be enriched and include a degree of self-management. Group members should be interdependent in terms of tasks and rewards. The group should reflect the right mix of experience, knowledge, education, and cultural diversity. Culturally diverse members should have task and social interaction. The group should be the right size. The intelligence and personality of group members are important factors in determining group effectiveness. The work group should have good support from management. The group process should include team spirit, workload sharing, and communication and cooperation. Following work processes and procedures is helpful, as is familiarity with jobs and co-workers.

Specify key roles assumed by team and group members.
Group member roles should include knowledge contributor (technical expert), process observer, people supporter, challenger, listener, mediator, and gatekeeper. A team member who plays several of the roles just described is likely to be perceived as an informal leader.

Summarize managerial actions for building teamwork.
Managers and leaders can enhance teamwork through many behaviors, attitudes, and organizational actions, including the following: give the team an urgent, constructive purpose; develop a norm of teamwork; use the consensus decision-making style; feed the team valid information; use in-group jargon; minimize micromanagement; create physical structures that foster teamwork; reward teamwork behavior; make process changes that enhance teamwork; and support outdoor training.

Explain the actions and attitudes of an effective team player.
Task-related actions and attitudes of effective team players include the following: sharing technical exper-

tise; assuming responsibility for problems; committing to team goals; seeing the big picture; asking tough questions; and trying something new. People-related actions and attitudes include the following: trusting team members; sharing credit; recognizing others; listening and information sharing; giving and receiving criticism; and not downplaying the success of others.

Point to the potential contributions and problems of teams and groups.
Teams and groups make a contribution when they lead to results that could not be achieved without collaboration. Evidence from both case histories and formal studies indicates that collective effort leads to enhanced productivity. Groups and teams also have potential problems. Sometimes they do not improve productivity; group polarization (taking extreme positions) may occur, and members may engage in social loafing (freeloading). Employee-involvement groups may be in violation of the NLRA, if they are employer-dominated and are classified as labor unions under the law. Also, focusing too much on group or team effort instead of attaining individual recognition can retard a person's career.

Describe the positive and negative aspects of conflict and how team leaders and managers can resolve conflict.
Although harmony and collaboration are an important goal of groups and teams, some conflict is inevitable. Cognitive conflict focuses on substantive, issue-related differences. Affective conflict focuses on personalized, individually oriented issues that are dealt with more emotionally than intellectually. Cognitive conflict leads to such positive outcomes as creative problem solving. Positive consequences of conflict also include increased effort, obtaining diagnostic information, and increased group cohesion. Negative consequences of conflict include wasting resources and heightened self-interest.

Five major modes of conflict management have been identified: forcing, accommodative, sharing, collaborative, and avoidant. Each style is based on a combination of satisfying one's own concerns (assertiveness) and satisfying the concerns of others (cooperativeness). Confrontation and problem solving is a widely applicable collaborative technique of resolving conflict.

KEY TERMS AND PHRASES

Group, *352*	Cross-functional team, *353*	Group polarization, *365*
Team, *352*	Affinity group, *354*	Social loafing, *365*
Teamwork, *352*	Virtual team, *355*	Conflict, *366*
Formal group, *352*	Micromanagement, *359*	Cognitive conflict, *367*
Informal group, *352*	Tough question, *362*	Affective conflict, *367*

QUESTIONS

1. In your own words, what is the difference between a group and a team?

2. Why is experience working on a cross-functional team particularly valuable for a person who aspires to a career in management?

3. Take any high-performing team familiar to you, and indicate which characteristics of an effective work group it appears to possess.

4. Give an example of a *tough question* a manager might ask a team.

5. Provide two examples of interdependent (or collaborative) tasks in the workplace for which teams are well suited.

6. The opening case to this chapter describes the practice of providing open work areas instead of cubicles or offices, to encourage teamwork. What might be the negative side effects to the individual and the organization from such arrangements?

7. Many communities object to having cellular telephone towers erected in certain locations. To overcome these objections some cellular telephone companies have erected, at their expense, silos and church steeples with cellular antennae hidden inside. Which method of conflict resolution does this represent?

SKILL-BUILDING EXERCISE 14-A: Team Member Roles

Small teams are formed to conduct a 45-minute meeting on a significant topic. Possibilities include (a) a management team deciding whether to lay off one-third of the work force in order to increase profits, or (b) a group of fans who have volunteered to find a new team mascot name to replace "Redskins."

While the team members are conducting their heated discussion, other class members make notes of which team members carry out which roles. Watching for the seven different roles can perhaps be divided among class members, such as people in the first row looking for examples of Knowledge Contributor. Use the role worksheet provided to help you make your observations. Summarize the comments indicative of the role.

Knowledge Contributor:

_____

_____

_____

Process Observer:

_____

_____

_____

People Supporter:

_____

_____

_____

371

Challenger:

_____

_____

_____

Listener:

_____

_____

_____

Mediator:

_____

_____

_____

Gatekeeper:

_____

_____

_____

INTERNET SKILL-BUILDING EXERCISE: The Dale Carnegie Approach to Building Teamwork

Hundreds of consulting firms and training organizations offer team-building exercises, including Dale Carnegie Training®, the organization that became famous by offering training in public speaking, the development of self-confidence, and sales skills. Visit www.dalecarnegie.com to investigate what type of teamwork training Dale Carnegie offers. Compare the ideas of Dale Carnegie Training with those presented in this chapter. What similarities and differences do you see? What is your impression of the Dale Carnegie approach to building teamwork?

CASE PROBLEM 14-A: Big Bashes in Silicon Valley

Inviting rock-and-roll bands to help high-tech firms celebrate milestones has become a regular industry practice. Applied Materials Inc., the world's largest maker of computer chip equipment, recently celebrated its 30th birthday by inviting rock legend Bob Dylan. The rock band, Chicago, helped Compaq Computer Corp. celebrate its merger with Tandem Computers Inc. Crosby Stills & Nash were present at a party to celebrate the merger of WorldCom Inc. and MCI Communications Corp.

Digital-age firms flush with Silicon Valley success increasingly are congratulating their employees by holding private rock concerts with some of the biggest names in the business. "These workers are in an exciting, trend-setting, important part of our culture: the world of computers and the Internet," said Richard Garwacki, vice-president of Bill Graham Special Events, which opened a new division in 1996 to handle the corporate demand. "How do you entertain, stimulate and reward your work force?" he said. "We like to use the word _magic_."

For Applied Materials, magic meant the party at San Jose Arena where Dylan and his son's band, the Wallflowers, played for an audience of 15,000. WorldCom rented out San Francisco's famed Fillmore. Sun Microsystems Inc. rented the Shoreline Amphitheater in Mountain View for a state-of-the-company address. At the gathering, CEO Scott McNealy rappelled down from the rafters dressed like Batman. Comedian Dana Carvey (of Saturday Night Live fame) also performed for the crowd. And Cisco Systems Inc. gambled at a roller rink transformed into a casino as acrobats on trapezes soared overhead.

Several Silicon Valley executives say that the intent of the lavish parties and perks is to make up for the 15-hour days typical in their industry and region. "It does make it fun, and builds team spirit," said Tracy Timpson, a former Silicon Graphics Inc. employee who saw Natalie Cole, Kenny G and Huey Lewis perform at company functions. Executives at several Silicon Valley firms regard the bashes as a tool to help hire and retain employees.

Software maker Adobe Systems Inc. throws holiday theme parties such as European masked balls or Cotton Club speakeasies. In contrast, its competitor, Macromedia Inc., hired the band Los Lobos to play for its staff of 20- and 30-somethings. "Being a hip employer is important for the young people," said Tom Hayes of Applied Materials.

It makes sense that high-tech is wooing the music industry. "They need music and video for the Internet and digital discs," Hayes said. "I don't think they would be doing that in Pittsburgh or other Industrial Age cities."

Asked her opinion about the impact of these parties on employees, a human resources professional said: "So long as this is anonymous, I'll give you my honest opinion. Five hundred employees screaming, shouting, and many of them over-drinking together is hardly a form of organization development. Some of the workers would prefer a quiet evening home with their families, but they feel pressured into showing up and acting like an out-of-control teenager. I'd say you would do more for teamwork if the company fed 2,000 starving children in Bangladesh for a year instead of throwing a wild party for employees."

Discussion Questions

1. Based on your knowledge of team building, what would be the impact of bashes on teamwork?
2. What else besides sponsoring bashes might Silicon Valley executives do to develop teamwork?
3. What is your evaluation of the statement that these bashes help attract and retain Silicon Valley employees?
4. In what way might the company's helping to relieve child starvation in an underdeveloped country help build teamwork?

Source: Most of the facts in this story are adapted from "Rock Is Rolling at High Tech Industry Parties," The Associated Press syndicated story, October 12, 1998.

CASE PROBLEM 14-B: The Unbalanced Team

Bluestone Security Systems is one of the largest security systems distributors in its city, with annual sales of $15 million. Two years ago, Bill Scovia, the vice-president of marketing and sales, reorganized the sales force. Previously the sales force consisted of inside sales representatives (who took care of phone-in orders) and outside sales representatives (who called on accounts). The reorganization divided the outside sales force into two groups: direct sales and major accounts. The direct sales representatives were made responsible for small commercial customers and individual homeowners. As before, they would service existing customers and prospect for new accounts. Servicing existing customers usually involves adding fire protection to burglary protection, and upgrading the burglary systems.

Three of the people who were direct sales representatives were promoted to major account executives. The account executives would service Bluestone's largest accounts, including prospecting for new business within those accounts. An example would be expanding the security system to other stores of a retailer. To promote teamwork and cooperation, Scovia assigned group sales quotas to the account representatives. Collectively, their goal was to bring in 21 new large accounts per month.

Given that the sales quota was a group quota, the account representatives were supposed to work together on strategy for acquiring new accounts. If a particular account exec did not have the expertise to handle his or her customer's problems, another account executive was supposed to offer help. Brian Marcos, for example, was the resident expert on the unique security problems of warehouses. If invited, Brian would join one of the two other account executives to call on a customer who owned a warehouse.

After the new sales organization had been in place 19 months, Elizabeth Kato, an account executive, was having lunch with Larry Starks, the manufacturing director at Bluestone. "I've about had it," said Elizabeth, "I'm tired of single-handedly carrying the team."

"What do you mean you are single-handedly carrying the team?" asked Larry.

"You're a trusted friend, Larry. So let me lay out the facts. Each month the group is supposed to bring in 21 new sales. If we don't average those 21 sales per month, we don't get our semiannual bonus. That represents about 25 percent of my income. So a big chunk of my money comes from group effort.

"My average number of new accounts brought in for the last 12 months has been 11. And we are averaging about 18 new sales per month. This translates into the other account execs averaging about seven sales among them. I'm carrying the group, but overall sales are still below quota. This means I didn't get my bonus last month.

"The other account execs are friendly and helpful in writing up proposals. But they just don't bring in their share of accounts."

Larry asked, "What does your boss say about this?"

"I've had several conversations with him about the problem. He tells me to be patient and to remember that the development of a fully balanced team requires time. He also tells me that I should develop a stronger team spirit. My problem is that I can't pay my bills with team spirit."

Discussion Questions
1. What does this case illustrate about teamwork?
2. What role or roles is Elizabeth occupying in the group?
3. To what extent are Elizabeth's complaints justifiable?

ENDNOTES

1. "Flexibility Creates Dynamic Teams," *The Pryor Report*, August 1998, p. 5.
2. Jon R. Katzenbach and Douglas K. Smith, "The Discipline of Teams," *Harvard Business Review*, March–April 1993, p. 113.
3. Jon R. Katzenbach, "The Myth of the Top Management Team," *Harvard Business Review*, November–December 1997, pp. 82–99.
4. Eileen M. Van Aaken, Dominic J. Monetta, and D. Scott Sink, "Affinity Groups: The Missing Link in Employee Involvement," *Organizational Dynamics*, Spring 1994, p. 38.
5. James L. Creighton and James W. R. Adams, "The Cybermeeting's About to Begin," *Management Review*, January 1998, pp. 29–31.
6. Michael A. Campion, Ellen M. Papper, and Gina J. Medsker, "Relations between Work Team Characteristics and Effectiveness: A Replication and Extension," *Personnel Psychology*, Summer 1996, p. 431; David E. Hyatt and Thomas M. Ruddy, "An Examination of the Relationship between Work Group Characteristics and Performance: Once More Into the Breech," *Personnel Psychology*, Autumn 1997, p. 579; Brian D. Janz, Jason A. Colquitt, and Raymond A. Noe, "Knowledge Worker Team Effectiveness: The Role of Autonomy, Interdependence, Team Development, and Contextual Support Variables," *Personnel Psychology*, Winter 1997, pp. 877–904.
7. Dan Fields, "Harley Plant Produces Teamwork," The Associated Press story, June 22, 1998.
8. Allan B. Drexler and Russ Forester, "Interdependence: The Crux of Teamwork," *HRMagazine*, September 1998, p. 52.
9. Priscilla M. Elsass and Laura M. Graves, "Demographic Diversity in Decision-Making Groups: The Experiences of Women and People of Color," *Academy of Management Review*, October 1997, p. 968.
10. Murray R. Barrick, Greg L. Stewart, Mitchell J. Neubert, and Michael K. Mount, "Relating Member Ability and Personality to Work-Team Processes and Team Effectiveness," *Journal of Applied Psychology*, June 1998, pp. 377–391.
11. Campion, Papper, and Medsker, "Relations between Work Team Characteristics and Effectiveness," p. 450.
12. Glenn M. Parker, *Team Players and Teamwork: The New Competitive Business Strategy* (San Francisco: Jossey-Bass, 1990), pp. 61–68; Thomas L. Quick, *Successful Team Building* (New York: AMACOM, 1992), pp. 40–52.
13. Fields, "Harley Plant Produces Teamwork."
14. Based in part on facts reported in "Habitat Project Cements Teamwork at Xerox," Rochester, New York, *Democrat and Chronicle*, July 10, 1998, p. 12D.
15. Katzenbach and Smith, "The Discipline of Teams," p. 112; Anthony R. Montebello, "How to Jump the 5 Barriers to Good Teamwork," A supplement to *The Pryor Report Management Newsletter*, 1995; John Syer and Christopher Connolly, *How Teamwork Works: The Dynamics of Effective Team Development* (London: McGraw-Hill, 1996).
16. "Team Player Gets Top Spot in Survey" (undated sample copy distributed by Dartnell Corporation, 1994), p. 3.
17. Glenn M. Parker, *Cross-Functional Teams: Working with Allies, Enemies & Other Strangers* (San Francisco: Jossey-Bass Publishers, 1994), p. 170.
18. Steven Covey, "Team Up For a Superstar Office," *USA Weekend*, September 4–6, 1998, p. 10.
19. "Work Alone or In Teams?" *The Pryor Report*, May 1998, p. 8.
20. Rajiv D. Banker, Joy M. Field, Roger C. Schroeder, and Kingshuk K. Sinha, "Impact of Work Teams on Manufacturing Performance: A Longitudinal Field Study," *Academy of Management Journal*, August 1996, pp. 867–890.
21. Jac Fitz-Enz, "Measuring Team Effectiveness," *HRfocus*, August 1997, p. 3.
22. Allan B. Drexler and Russ Forrester, "Interdependence: The Crux of Teamwork," *HRMagazine*, September 1998, pp. 52–62.
23. Gregory Moorhead and Ricky W. Griffin, *Organizational Behavior: Managing People and Organizations*, 4th ed. (Boston: Houghton Mifflin, 1995), pp. 278–279.
24. Tina L. Robbins, "Social Loafing on Cognitive Tasks: An Examination of the 'Sucker Effect,'" *Journal of Business and Psychology*, Spring 1995, p. 337.
25. "When Is a Team Not a Team? When the NLRB Says No," *Human Resources Forum*, February 1994, pp. 1–2.
26. "How To Be a 'Team Player' *and* an Individual Success," Preview Issue, *1998 Team Management Briefings*, p. 7; Andrew J. DuBrin, *The Breakthrough Team Player: Becoming the M .V. P. on Your Workplace Team* (New York: AMACOM, 1995), pp. 165–168.
27. Allen C. Amason, Wayne A. Hockwater, Kenneth R. Thompson, and Allison W. Harrison, "Conflict: An Important Dimension in Successful Management Teams," *Organizational Dynamics*, Autumn 1995, pp. 20–33.
28. Allen C. Amason, "Distinguishing the Effects of Functional and Dysfunctional Conflict on Strategic Decision Making: Resolving a Paradox for Top Management Teams," *Academy of Management Journal*, February 1996, pp. 123–148.
29. James A. Autry, *Love & Profit* (New York: Morrow, 1991).

Chapter Fifteen

The already battered stock of Detection System Inc. fell further recently in heavy trading. At one point it dipped to one-third of its all-time high. Profits had slipped to 2 cents a share versus 21 cents for the same quarter one year ago. Not long ago Detection Systems was a high flier. The security alarm maker changed itself from a one-location company to a global operator with a major factory in China and subsidiaries in England, France, Germany, Australia and other countries, serving customers from Russia to Texas.

Sales rose from $41.9 million in one year to $101.3 million the following year. But as the company grew it became too complicated to manage in Detection Systems' accustomed way, said security analysts. Dennis Linker, one of these analysts, observes that entrepreneurial companies typically stumble at two points in their history—when they reach about $40 million in sales and become too big for one individual to manage, and when they hit $100 million and become dependent on sophisticated information systems.

Information management was Detection Systems' stumbling block, Linker said. Only recently did its information management system become capable of tracking the location of its products in transit. Conversion of the Chinese computer system resulted in a $950,000 error, Detection Systems management said. Linker said the person responsible for that error has been let go. But during

OBJECTIVES

After studying this chapter and doing the exercises, you should be able to:

1 Explain how controlling relates to the other management functions.

2 Understand the different types and strategies of control.

3 Describe the steps in the control process.

4 Explain the use of non-budgetary control techniques.

5 Summarize the various types of budgets, and the use of budgets and financial ratios for control.

6 Explain how managers and business owners manage cash flow and control costs, and use nontraditional measures of financial performance.

7 Outline the basics of an information system.

8 Specify several characteristics of effective controls.

Essentials of Control

the next six months, a better system will come on line, improving the company's internal management. The company has now appointed a new accounting officer, a new information systems manager, and a new manager of worldwide operations.

Another analyst, Chris Quilty, said Detection Systems is in a growing industry and has a well-received product line. If the company can resolve internal problems, it's long-term outlook is good, he said.[1]

The case history just presented about a manufacturer of a well-received product illustrates the importance of good controls to maintain profitability. In particular, without a first-rate information system, a company's well being can be threatened. Keeping track of important information is part of a control system. The control function of management involves measuring performance and then taking corrective action if goals are not being achieved. When goals are being readily achieved, management will sometimes establish new, even more challenging goals.

As you will see in studying this chapter, controls make many positive contributions to the organization. An important purpose of controlling is to align the actions of workers with the interests of the firm. Without the controlling functions, managers have difficulty knowing if people are carrying out their jobs properly. Controls also enable managers to gauge whether the firm is attaining its goals.

Controls often make an important contribution to employee motivation. Achieving the performance standards set in a control system leads to recognition and other deserved rewards. Accurate control measurements give the well-motivated, competent worker an opportunity to be noticed for good work.

In this chapter we emphasize the types and strategies of controls, the control process, budgets and controls, how managers manage cash flow and cut costs, and the use of information systems in control. Finally, we describe characteristics of effective controls.

CONTROLLING AND THE OTHER MANAGEMENT FUNCTIONS

Explain how controlling relates to the other management functions.

Controlling has been referred to as the terminal management function because it takes place after the other functions have been completed. Controlling is most closely associated with planning, because planning establishes goals and the methods for achieving them. Controlling investigates the extent to which planning has been successful.

The links between controlling and other major management functions are illustrated in Exhibit 15-1. Controlling helps measure how well planning, organizing, and leading have been performed. The controlling function also measures the effectiveness of the control system. On occasion, the control measures are inappropriate. For example, suppose one measure of sales performance is the number of sales calls made. Such a measure might encourage a sales representative to call on a large number of poor prospects, just to meet the performance standard. Spending more time with better prospects would probably boost the sales representative's effectiveness. More will be said about effective control measures later.

The planning and decision-making tools and techniques described in Chapter 7 are also tools and techniques of control. For example, a Gantt chart is a tool that keeps track of how well target dates for a project are being met. Keeping track is a control activity. If an event is behind schedule, a project manager usually takes corrective action.

```
Planning    Organizing    Leading    Controlling
                    Control
```

EXHIBIT
15-1

The Links between Controlling and the Other Management Functions The control function is extremely important because it helps managers evaluate whether all four major management functions have been implemented.

TYPES AND STRATEGIES OF CONTROL

Controls can be classified according to the time at which the control is applied to the activity—before, during, or after. Another important way of describing controls relates to the source of the control—external versus internal.

② Understand the different types and strategies of control.

The Time Element in Controls

A **preventive control** (or precontrol) takes place prior to the performance of an activity. A precontrol prevents problems that result from deviation from performance standards. Preventive controls are generally the most cost-effective. A manufacturer that specifies quality standards for purchased parts has established a precontrol. By purchasing high-quality parts, the manufacturer prevents many instances of machine failure. The ISO 9000 standards described in Chapter 4 function as preventive controls for choosing suppliers. Precontrols are also used in human resource management. Standards for hiring employees are precontrols. For example, a company may require that all job candidates are nonsmokers. This preventive control helps decrease lost productivity due to smoking breaks and smoking-related illnesses.

preventive control
A control that takes place prior to the performance of an activity.

Concurrent controls monitor activities while they are being carried out. A typical concurrent control takes place when a supervisor observes performance, spots a deviation from standard, and immediately makes a constructive suggestion. For example, suppose a sales manager overhears a telemarketing specialist fail to ask a customer for an order. On the spot, the manager would coach the telemarketer about how to close an order.

concurrent control
A type of control that monitors activities while they are being carried out.

Feedback controls (or postcontrols) evaluate an activity after it has been performed. Feedback controls measure history by pointing out what went wrong in the past. The process of applying the control may provide guidelines for future corrective action. Financial statements are a form of feedback control. If a financial report indicates that one division of a company has lost money, top-level managers can then confer with division managers to see how to improve the situation. The earnings per share indicator used to detect the progress of Detection Systems illustrates a feedback control.

feedback control
A control that evaluates an activity after it has been performed.

Exhibit 15-2 summarizes the three types of time-based controls. Most firms use a combination of preventive, concurrent, and feedback controls. An important part of a manager's job is choosing controls appropriate to the situation.

External Versus Internal Controls

Controls can be classified according to their underlying strategy. **External control strategy** is based on the belief that employees are motivated primarily by external rewards and need to be controlled by their managers. Autocratic and

external control strategy
An approach to control based on the belief that employees are motivated primarily by external rewards and need to be controlled by their managers.

377

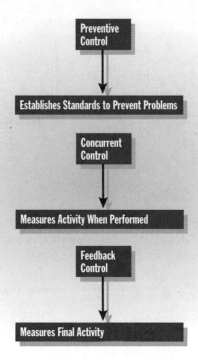

EXHIBIT 15-2

Three Types of Time-Based Controls
Controlling can take place before, during, or after an event or process. Preventive controls usually have the biggest payoff to the organization.

Theory X management use an external control strategy. An effective external control system involves three steps. First, the objectives and performance standards need to be relatively difficult in order to gain optimum effort of team members and leave little leeway in performance. Second, the objectives and measures must be set in such a way that people cannot manipulate or distort them. For instance, top-level management should make its own investigation of customer satisfaction rather than take the word of field personnel. Third, rewards must be directly and openly tied to performance.

An external control strategy has several different effects. On the positive side, employees may channel considerable energy into achieving objectives. Employees do so because they know that good performance leads to a reward. If the control system is tightly structured, the result will be a high degree of control over employee behavior.

External control can create problems, however. Employees may work toward achieving performance standards, but they may not develop a commitment to the firm. They may reach standards but not be truly productive. Reaching standards without being productive is sometimes referred to as "looking good on paper." Suppose the marketing and sales director of a telecommunications company establishes as a performance standard a very high number of customers processed. To achieve this standard, the customer-service manager instructs the customer-service representatives, "Take care of as many calls as you can. And minimize the time customers are kept on hold." As a result, the customer-service reps spend brief amounts of time on the phone attempting to resolve problems with most customers. Instead of customers being happy with customer service, many of them are dissatisfied with the abrupt treatment. The standard of taking care of more customers is met, yet at the same time customer service deteriorates.

Misdirected effort is another problem that can arise from an external control strategy. People may put too much effort into achieving performance standards and, as a result, neglect other important aspects of the job. High sales quotas may result in neglect of customer service. Externally imposed standards may also result in the filtering, or hiding, of poor performance.

Internal control strategy is based on the belief that employees can be motivated by building their commitment to organizational goals. Participative and Theory Y management use internal control strategy, as do self-managing work teams. Part of the success of the development of Windows NT was attributed to an internal control strategy. Two hundred and fifty programmers, testers, and program managers were involved in developing the software for personal computers. Control was directed from the bottom up, meaning that professionals established controls for their own work.[2]

Building an effective internal control system requires three steps. First, group members must participate in setting goals. These goals are later used as performance standards for control purposes. Second, the performance standards (control measures) must be used for problem solving rather than for punishment or blame. When deviations from performance are noted, superiors and subordinates should get together to solve the underlying problem. Third, although rewards should be tied to performance, they should not be tied to only one or two measures. An internal control strategy calls for evaluation of an employee's total contribution, not one or two quantitative aspects of performance.

A positive result of internal controls is that they usually lead to a higher commitment to attain goals. Thus, they may direct greater energy toward task performance. Another good result is that the system encourages the upward and horizontal flow of valid information about problems.

On the negative side, an internal control system may motivate employees to establish easy performance standards for themselves. Another problem is that the supervisor loses control over subordinates and may feel powerless as a result. Finally, an internal control system creates some problems in giving out equitable rewards. Because performance standards may be loose, it is difficult to measure good performance.

An internal control system is not necessarily good, and an external control system is not necessarily bad. Internal controls work satisfactorily when a high-caliber, well-motivated work force is available. External controls compensate for the fact that not everybody is capable of controlling their own performance. If applied with good judgment and sensitivity, external control systems work quite well. The effective use of controls thus follows a contingency, or "if . . . , then . . . ," approach to management.

internal control strategy
An approach to control based on the belief that employees can be motivated by building their commitment to organizational goals.

STEPS IN THE CONTROL PROCESS

Describe the steps in the control process.

The steps in the control process follow the logic of planning: (1) performance standards are set, (2) performance is measured, (3) performance is compared to standards, and (4) corrective action is taken if needed. The following discussion describes these steps and highlights the potential problems associated with each one. Exhibit 15-3 presents an overview of controlling.

Setting Appropriate Performance Standards

A control system begins with a set of performance standards that are realistic and acceptable to the people involved. A **standard** is a unit of measurement used to evaluate results. Standards can be quantitative, such as cost of sales, profits, or time to complete an activity. Standards can also be qualitative, such as a viewer's

standard
A unit of measurement used to evaluate results.

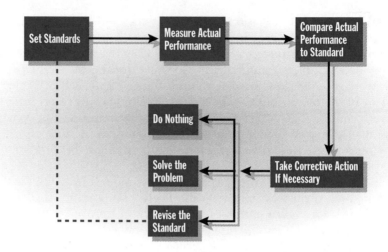

perception of the visual appeal of an advertisement. An effective standard has the same characteristics as an effective objective (see Chapter 5). Exhibit 15-4 presents two of the performance standards established for a customer-service representative unit within a telecommunications company.

Historical information about comparable situations is often used when standards are set for the first time. Assume a manufacturer wants to establish a standard for the percentage of machines returned to the dealer for repair. If the return rate for other machines with similar components is 3 percent, the new standard might be a return rate of no more than 3 percent.

At times performance standards are dictated by profit-and-loss considerations. A case in point is the occupancy-rate standard for a hotel. Assume break-even analysis reveals that the average occupancy rate must be 75 percent for the hotel to cover costs. Hotel management must then set an occupancy rate of at least 75 percent as a standard.

Measuring Actual Performance

To implement the control system, performance must be measured. Performance appraisals are one of the major ways of measuring performance. Supervisors often make direct observations of performance to implement a control system. A simple exam-

EXHIBIT
15-4

Two Performance Standards Established for a Customer-Service Operation
The performance standards shown here give customer-service representatives precise targets for meeting organizational objectives. Performance evaluation is based on how well customer-service representatives, individually and as a group, meet these standards.

CSR Objectives	Distinguished Performance (4 points)	Above-Standard Performance (3 Points)	Standard Performance (2 Points)	Below-Standard Performance (1 Point)
Customer Satisfaction	89% or higher overall customer satisfaction	86%–88% overall customer satisfaction	83%–85% overall customer satisfaction	<83% overall customer satisfaction
Calls Answered in 30 Seconds	Group consistently answers 80% or more of calls within 30 seconds.	Group consistently answers 75%–79% of calls within 30 seconds.	Group consistently answers 70%–74% of calls within 30 seconds.	Group consistently answers <70% of calls within 30 seconds.

ple would be observing to make sure a sales associate always asks a customer, "Is there anything else I could show you now?" A more elaborate performance measure would be a 10-page report on the status of a major project submitted to top-level management. The aspects of performance that accountants measure are manufacturing costs, profits, and cash flow (a statement of cash receipts and payments).

Measurement of performance is much more complex than it would seem on the surface. The list that follows presents three important conditions for effective performance measurement:[3]

1. *Agree on the specific aspects of performance to be measured.* Top-level managers in a hotel chain might think that occupancy rate is the best measure of performance. Middle-level managers might disagree by saying, "Don't place so much emphasis on occupancy rate. If we try to give good customer service, the occupancy rate will take care of itself. Therefore, let's try to measure customer service."

2. *Agree on the accuracy of measurement needed.* In some instances, precise measurement of performance is possible. Sales volume, for example, can be measured in terms of customer billing and accounts paid. The absolute number or percentage of customer returns is another precise measurement. In other instances, precise measurement of performance may not be possible. Assume top-level managers of the hotel chain buy the idea of measuring customer service. Quantitative measures of customer satisfaction—including the ratings that guests submit on questionnaires and the number of formal complaints—are available. However, many measurements would have to be subjective, such as the observation of the behavior of guests, including their spontaneous comments about service. These qualitative measures of performance might be more relevant than the quantitative measures.

3. *Agree on who will use the measurements.* In most firms, managers at higher levels have the authority to review performance measures of people below them in the chain of command. Few people at lower levels object to this practice. Another issue is how much access the staff has to control reports. Line managers sometimes believe that too many staff members make judgments about their performance.

Comparing Actual Performance to Standards

Once standards have been established and performance measurements taken, the next step is to compare actual performance to standards. Key aspects of comparing performance to standards include measuring the deviation and communicating information about it.

Deviation in a control system is the size of the discrepancy between performance standards and actual results. It is important to agree beforehand how much deviation from the standard is a basis for corrective action. When using quantitative measures, statistical analysis can determine how much of a deviation is significant. Recall the 75 percent occupancy-rate standard in the hotel example. A deviation of plus or minus 3 percent may not be considered meaningful but rather caused by random events. Deviations of 4 percent or more, however, would be considered significant. Taking corrective action on significant deviations only is applying the *exception principle.*

There are times when a deviation as small as 1 percent from standard can have a big influence on company welfare. If a division fails by 1 percent to reach

deviation
In a control system, the size of the discrepancy between performance standards and actual results.

381

$100 million in sales, the firm has $1 million less money than anticipated. At other times, deviations as high as 10 percent might not be significant. A claims department might be 10 percent behind schedule in processing insurance claims. However, the claims manager might not be upset, knowing that all the claims will eventually be processed.

When statistical limits are not available, it takes wisdom and experience to diagnose a random deviation. Sometimes factors beyond a person's influence lead to a one-time deviation from performance. If the manager believes this to be the case, the deviation can be ignored. For example, a person might turn in poor performance one month because he or she faced a family crisis.

For the control system to work, the results of the comparison between actual performance and standards must be communicated to the right people. These people include the employees themselves and their immediate managers. At times, the results should also be communicated to top-level managers and selected staff specialists. They need to know about events such as exceptional deviations from safety and health standards. For example, nuclear power plants are equipped with elaborate devices to measure radiation levels. When a specified radiation level is reached or exceeded, several key people are notified automatically.

Taking Corrective Action

After making an evaluation of the discrepancy between actual performance and a standard, a manager has three courses of action: do nothing, solve the problem, or revise the standard. Each of these alternatives may be appropriate, depending on the results of the evaluation.

DO NOTHING   The purpose of the control system is to determine if the plans are working. If the evaluation reveals that events are proceeding according to plan, no corrective action is required. Doing nothing, however, does not mean abdicating, or giving up, responsibility. A manager might take the opportunity to compliment employees for having achieved their objectives (thus increasing employee motivation), but do nothing about their approach to reaching objectives because performance measurements show it to be effective.

SOLVE THE PROBLEM   The big payoff from the controlling process concerns the correction of deviations from substandard performance. If a manager decides that a deviation is significant (nonrandom), he or she starts problem solving. Typically the manager meets with the team member to discuss the nature of the problem. Other knowledgeable parties might participate in the problem-solving process. At times, the deviation from a performance standard is so large that a drastic solution is required. A severe shortfall in cash, for example, might force a retailer to sell existing inventory at a loss.

Sometimes a manager can correct the deviation from a performance standard without overhauling current operations. An office manager in a group dental practice used a control model to measure the percentage of professional time allotted to patient care. The analysis revealed that nonbilled time had exceeded 10 percent—an unacceptable deviation. The corrective action involved two steps. First, workers scanned dental records to find patients who were overdue for cleaning and checkups. Second, the office manager telephoned these people and asked them if they would like to schedule an appointment for cleaning and a checkup. The telemarketing campaign was so successful that virtually all the slack time was filled within 10 days.

REVISE THE STANDARD   Deviations from standard are sometimes attributable to errors in planning rather than to performance problems. Corrective action is thus not warranted because the true problem is an unrealistic performance standard. Consider an analogy to the classroom: If 90 percent of the students fail a test, the real problem could be an unrealistically difficult test.

Standards often must be revised because of changes in the task environment. A sudden shift in consumers' preference—from large to small sports utility vehicles (SUVs) for example—could necessitate the revision of standards. Planning for a new task can also create a need for revised standards. Performance quotas may be based on "guesstimates" that prove to be unrealistically difficult or overly easy to reach. A performance standard is too difficult if no employee can meet it. A performance standard may be too easy if all employees can exceed it. As Exhibit 15-3 shows, revising standards means repeating the control cycle.

NONBUDGETARY CONTROL TECHNIQUES

One way of classifying control techniques is to divide them into those based on budgets versus those not based on budgets. In this section we describe nonbudgetary techniques, and classify them into two types. **Qualitative control techniques** are methods based on human judgments about performance that result in a verbal rather than a numerical evaluation. For example, customer service might be rated as "outstanding" rather than as 4.75 on a 1-to-5 scale. **Quantitative control techniques** are methods based on numerical measures of performance. Rating customer services as 4.75 on a 1-to-5 scale rather than as "outstanding" would indicate a quantitative control measure.

Exhibits 15-5 and 15-6 summarize qualitative and quantitative control techniques, respectively. The purpose in listing them is primarily to alert you to their existence. Chapter 7 provided details about four of the quantitative control techniques that Exhibit 15-6 describes. When interpreting the results of an audit, it

Explain the use of nonbudgetary control techniques.

qualitative control technique
A method of controlling based on human judgments about performance that result in a verbal rather than numerical evaluation.

quantitative control technique
A method of controlling based on numerical measures of performance.

Qualitative Control Techniques
The competence and ethics of people collecting information for qualitative controls influences the effectiveness of these controls.

Technique	Definition	Key Features
Audit	Examination of activities or records to verify their accuracy or effectiveness	Usually conducted by someone from outside the area audited
External audit	Verification of financial records by external agency or individual	Conducted by an outside agency, such as a CPA firm
Internal audit	Verification of financial records by an internal group of personnel	Wide in scope, including evaluation of control system
Management audit	Use of auditing techniques to evaluate the overall effectiveness of management	Examines wide range of management practices, policies, and procedures
Personal observation	Manager's first-hand observations of how well plans are carried out	Natural part of manager's job
Performance appraisal	Formal method or system of measuring, evaluating, and reviewing employee performance	Points out areas of deficiency and areas for corrective action; manager and group member jointly solve the problem
Policy	General guideline to follow in making decisions and taking action	Indicates if manager is following organizational intentions

EXHIBIT 15.6

Quantitative Control Techniques Used in Production and Operations Quantitative control techniques are widely accepted because they appear precise and objective.

Technique	Definition	Purpose
Gantt chart	Chart depicting planned and actual progress of work on a project	Describes progress on a project
CPM/PERT	Method of scheduling activities and events using time estimates	Measures how well project is meeting schedule
Break-even analysis	Ratio of fixed costs to price minus variable costs	Measures organization's performance and gives basis for corrective action
Economic-order quantity (EOQ)	Inventory level that minimizes ordering and carrying costs	Avoids having too much or too little inventory
ABC analysis	Method of assigning value to inventory; A items are worth more than B or C items	Indicates where emphasis should be placed to control money
Variance analysis	Major control device in manufacturing	Establishes standard costs for materials, labor, and overhead, and then measures deviations from these costs

is necessary to evaluate carefully the systems and procedures used to provide the information. A poorly developed performance appraisal system, for example, might not detect deviations from performance. Another factor to investigate is the political motivation of the people conducting the audit. Are the auditors going out of their way to please management? Are they out to make management look bad? Or are they motivated only to be objective and professional?

In recent years several incidents have been observed of audits that glossed over the truth in order to cover up unethical and or illegal actions by top management. An extreme case of questionable accounting and auditing procedures took place at Cendant Corp. Chairman Walter A. Forbes was reimbursed for $1 million in private jet and hotel expenses for approximately a three-year period. Forbes said the expenses were justified, but substantiation was lacking for most of the expenses. Several individuals close to the company said financial controls at Cendant were lax and insufficient for a company its size. Another problem was inadequate accounting software that required most revenues and expenses to be manually entered when preparing financial statements.[4]

Controls are widely used in firms to keep costs at acceptable levels. Feedback is often used when costs have risen too high. In response, managers begin to reduce as many variable costs as possible. Details about cost reduction are presented later in the discussion of managing cash flow. Some firms use preventive controls to guard against the need to trim costs. The use of temporary employees can be a preventive control. By hiring temporaries, a firm prevents a portion of payroll costs from reaching an unacceptable level. A firm pays a temporary worker only for the duration of the assignment. In contrast, permanent workers are often kept on the payroll when they are between assignments, because managers anticipate finding constructive work for them soon.

BUDGETS AND BUDGETARY CONTROL TECHNIQUES

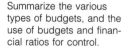

Summarize the various types of budgets, and the use of budgets and financial ratios for control.

When people hear the word *budget*, they typically think of tight restrictions placed on the use of money. The car-rental agency name Budget Rent-A-Car was chosen because of popular thinking that the adjective *budget* means conservative spending. In management, a budget does place restrictions on the use of money, but the allotted amounts can be quite generous. A **budget** is a plan, expressed in numerical terms, for allocating resources. The numerical terms typically refer to money, but they could also refer to such things as the amount of energy or the number of printer ribbons used. A budget typically involves cash outflow and inflow.

Virtually every manager has some budget responsibility, because a budget is a plan for allocating resources. Without budgets, there would be no way of keeping track of how much money is spent in comparison to how much money is available. Here we look at different types of budgets and how budgets are used for control. We also describe three other topics closely tied in with budgeting and control: managing cash flow and cost cutting, the balanced scorecard, and activity-based accounting. Readers who have studied accounting and finance will be familiar with much of this information.

Types of Budgets

Budgets can be classified in many ways. For example, budgets are sometimes described as either fixed or flexible. A *fixed budget* allocates expenditures based on a one-time allocation of resources. The organizational unit receives a fixed sum of money that must last for the budget period. A *flexible budget* allows for variation in the use of resources on the basis of activity. Under a flexible budget, a sales department would receive an increased telephone budget if the department increased its telemarketing program. Any type of budget can be classified as fixed or flexible.

Many different types of budgets help control costs in profit and nonprofit firms. Below are brief descriptions of seven commonly used budgets. Most other budgets are variations of these basic types.[5]

MASTER BUDGET   A **master budget** is a budget consolidated from the budgets of various units. Its purpose is to forecast financial statements for the entire company. Each of the separate budgets gives the projected costs and revenues for its own operations.

CASH BUDGET   A **cash budget** is a forecast of cash receipts and payments. The budget is compared against actual expenditures. The cash budget is an important control measure because it reflects a firm's ability to meet cash obligations. A firm that is working to capacity—such as a restaurant overflowing with customers—can still go bankrupt if its expenses are so high that even full production cannot generate enough revenue to meet expenses. (A typical problem is that the firm in this position has borrowed so much money that having a cash surplus becomes almost impossible. Principal and interest payments on the loans consume most of the cash receipts.)

Cash budgeting also serves the important function of showing the amount of cash available to invest in revenue-producing ventures. In the short range, businesses typically invest cash surpluses in stocks, bonds, and money market funds. In the long range, the cash is likely to be invested in real estate or in the acquisition of another company. Another long-range alternative is to use surplus cash to expand the business. Managers can also use cash surpluses to retire debt and consolidate ownership by buying up shares of the company owned by others.

REVENUE-AND-EXPENSE BUDGET   A **revenue-and-expense budget** describes in dollar amounts plans for revenues and operating expenses. It is the most widely used, and most readily understood, type of budget. The sales budget used

budget
A spending plan expressed in numerical terms for a future period of time.

master budget
A budget consolidated from the budgets of various units.

cash budget
A forecast of cash receipts and payments.

385

revenue-and-expense budget
A document that describes plans for revenues and operating expenses in dollar amounts.

by business firms is a revenue-and-expense budget. It forecasts sales and estimates expenses for a given period of time. Many firms use a monthly revenue-and-expense budget. The monthly budgets are later converted into quarterly, semi-annual, and annual budgets. Most revenue-and-expense budgets divide operating expenses into categories. Major operating expenses include salaries, benefits, rent, utilities, business travel, bulding maintenance, and equipment.

PRODUCTION BUDGET   After sales forecasts have been established, the units needed from the production area can be estimated. A **production budget** is a detailed plan that identifies the products or services that must be produced or provided to match the sales forecast and inventory requirements. A production budget can be considered a production schedule.

MATERIALS PURCHASE/USAGE BUDGET   After production demands have been forecast, it is necessary to estimate the cost of meeting this demand. A **materials purchase/usage budget** is a plan that identifies the raw materials and parts that must be purchased to meet production demands. In a retail business a comparable budget specifies the merchandise that must be purchased to meet the anticipated sales demand.

HUMAN RESOURCE BUDGET   To satisfy sales and production demands, money must be allocated for the labor to accomplish the work. A **human resource budget** is a schedule that identifies the human resource needs for a future period and the labor (or personnel) costs to meet those needs. Of particular interest to management is whether the number of employees will have to be substantially increased or decreased to meet sales and production forecasts.

CAPITAL-EXPENDITURE BUDGET   Organizations must invest in new equipment and buildings to stay in operation. A **capital-expenditure budget** is a plan for spending money on assets used to produce goods or services. Capital expenditures are usually regarded as major expenditures and are tied to long-range plans. Capital expenditures include money spent for buildings, machinery, equipment, and major inventories. In a typical budgeting system, the planned purchase of a computer network would be included in the capital budget. The monthly payment for postage and private delivery companies would be an operating expense.

Budgets and Financial Ratios as Control Devices

An important part of the control process is to use budgets and financial ratios as measures of performance. To the extent that managers stay within budget or meet their financial ratios they are performing according to standard.

BUDGETS AND THE CONTROL PROCESS   Budgets are a natural part of controlling. Planned expenditures are compared to actual expenditures, and corrective action is taken if the deviation is significant. Exhibit 15-7 shows a budget used as a control device. The nightclub and restaurant owner described in Chapter 7 operates with a monthly budget. The owner planned for revenues of $40,000 in March. Actual revenues were $42,500, a positive deviation. The discrepancy is not large enough, however, for the owner to change the anticipated revenues for April. Expenses

production budget
A detailed plan that identifies the products or services that must be produced to match the sales forecast and inventory requirements.

materials purchase/usage budget
A plan that identifies the raw materials and parts that must be purchased to meet production demands.

human resource budget
A schedule that identifies the human resource needs for a future period and the labor costs to meet those needs.

capital-expenditure budget
A plan for spending money on assets used to produce goods or services.

Item	Budget	Actual	Over	Under
Revenues	$40,000	$42,500	$2,500	
Beginning inventory	3,500	3,500		
Purchases	19,250	19,000		$250
End inventory	3,000	3,000		
Cost of goods sold	19,750	19,500		
Gross profit	20,250	23,000		
Salaries expense	10,500	10,500		
Rent and utilities expense	1,500	1,500		
Miscellaneous expense	100	250	150	
Maintenance expense	650	650		
Total operating expenses	12,750	12,900		
Net income before tax	7,500	10,100		
Taxes (40%)	3,000	4,040		
Net income	$4,500	$6,060		

EXHIBIT 15-7

March Revenue-and-Expense Budget for Nightclub and Restaurant

Budget summary: Revenues and Net Income exceed budget by $2,500 and $1,560, respectively.

Note: Data analyzed according to *Generally Accepted Accounting Principles* by Jose L. Cruzet of Florida National College.

were $150 over budget, a negative deviation the owner regards as insignificant. In short, the performance against budget looks good. The owner will take no corrective action on the basis of March performance.

FINANCIAL RATIOS AND THE CONTROL PROCESS
A more advanced method of using budgets for control is to use financial ratio guidelines for performance. Three such ratios are presented here. In addition, we look at economic value added (EVA), another measure of financial performance. One commonly used ratio is **gross profit margin**, expressed as the difference between sales and the cost of goods sold, divided by sales, or by

$$\text{Gross profit margin} = \frac{\text{Sales} - \text{Cost of goods sold}}{\text{Sales}}$$

gross profit margin
A financial ratio expressed as the difference between sales and the cost of goods sold, divided by sales.

The purpose of this ratio is to measure the total money available to cover operating expenses and to make a profit. If performance deviates significantly from a predetermined performance standard, corrective action must be taken.

Assume the nightclub owner needs to earn a 10 percent gross profit margin. For March, the figures are as follows:

$$\text{Gross profit margin} = \frac{\$42,500 - \$19,500}{\$42,500} = \frac{\$23,000}{\$42,500} = .54$$

Based on the gross-profit-margin financial ratio, the business is performing better than planned. One could argue that the gross profit margin presents an overly optimistic picture of how well the business is performing. Another widely used financial ratio is the **profit margin**, or return on sales. Profit margin measures profits earned per dollar of sales as well as the efficiency of the operation.

$$\text{Profit margin} = \frac{\text{Net income}}{\text{Sales}} = \frac{\$6,060}{\$42,500} = .14 \text{ or } 14\%$$

profit margin
A financial ratio measuring return on sales, or net income divided by sales.

A profit margin of 14 percent would be healthy for most businesses. It also appears to present a more realistic assessment of how well the nightclub in question is performing as a business.

return on equity

A financial ratio measuring how much a firm is earning on its investment, expressed as net income divided by owner's equity.

The last ratio described here is **return on equity,** an indicator of how much a firm is earning on its investment. It is the ratio between net income and the owner's equity, or

$$\text{Return on equity} = \frac{\text{Net Income}}{\text{Owner's Equity}}$$

Assume that the owner of the nightclub and restaurant invested $400,000 in the restaurant, and that the net income for the year is $72,500. The return on equity is $72,500/$400,000 = .181 or 18.1 percent. The owner should be satisfied, because few investments offer such a high return on equity.

Another measure of financial health that works much like a financial ratio is **economic value added (EVA).** EVA refers to how much more (or less) the company earns in profits than the minimum amount its investors expect it to earn. The minimum amount is called the *cost of capital* because this figure is what the company must pay the investors to use their capital. Cost of capital is also calculated as the overall percentage cost of the funds used to finance a firm's assets. If the sole source of financing were bonds that paid investors 10 percent, the cost of capital would be 10 percent. All earnings beyond the minimum are regarded as excess earnings.[6]

economic value added (EVA)

Measures how much more (or less) a company earns in profits than the minimum amount its investors expect it to earn.

For example, assume that investors give their company $2 million to invest and the investor's minimum desired return is 10 percent, or $200,000 per year. The company earns $300,000 per year. The EVA is $100,000 as follows:

Earnings:	$300,000
Cost of Capital:	$200,000 (10% x $2 million capital)
Excess earnings:	$100,000

Investors expect higher excess earnings when they invest in a risky venture, such as a company with unproven technology entering a new industry. An example might be manufacturing electronic communication systems for space stations. Investors are willing to settle for lower excess earnings when they invest in a company with proven technology in a stable industry, such as construction supplies. EVA is a frequently used control measure because it focuses on creating shareholder value. For example, the bonus plan at Eli Lilly requires managers to attain continuous, year-to-year improvements in EVA.[7]

Although EVA is considered a powerful tool for assessing the financial health of a company, managers still want to know how much cash the company has on hand, as measured by cash flow.

Managing Cash Flow and Cost Cutting

Explain how managers and business owners manage cash flow and control costs, and use nontraditional measures of financial performance.

cash flow

Amount of net cash generated by a business during a specific period.

Closely tied in with the cash budget is the special attention many managers pay to keeping enough cash on hand to prevent over-reliance on borrowing and being perceived by investors as a firm in financial trouble. Both cash flow and controlling, or cutting, costs, help meet these objectives. **Cash flow** is the amount of net cash generated by a business during a specific period. According to finance professor Ashok Robin, managers and accountants calculate cash flow differently,[8] as shown in Exhibit 15-8. A company that writes off many income deductions will have a better cash flow. The more depreciation charges a company has, the better its cash flow.

Cash Flow as Calculated by Accountants

Revenues	$15,000
Expenses	8,000
Depreciation	3,000
Taxable Income	4,000
Taxes at 40%	1,600
Net Income	2,400
Cash Flow	2,400 + 3,000 = $5,400 (Because you do not have to pay tax on the $3,000 depreciation, you can use it for other purposes.)

Cash Flow as Calculated by Managers

Revenue	$15,000
Expenses	8,000
Tax	1,600
Cash Flow	$ 5,400

EXHIBIT 15.8

Two Views of How Cash Flow Is Calculated
Although cash flow is a widely used term, accountants and managers tend to calculate it differently.

A firm that has a large cash flow is seen as a takeover target because the acquiring firm is likely to use the cash to pay off the cost of the acquisition. A company that does not want to be taken over might deliberately lower its cash flow by taking on a lot of debt. A large cash flow for a business owner contributes to peace of mind because the owner can keep operating without borrowing during a business downturn.

Cash flow analysis is well accepted because it gives a more accurate picture of financial health than does sales volume. A company will frequently make a sale but then not receive payment for a minimum of 30 days. Several years ago Sears, Roebuck & Co. was enjoying an impressive sales gain but its cash flow position was much less impressive. The problem was that delinquencies on Sears credit cards were quite high—customers were purchasing more but not all were paying their bills promptly. In some cases they were not even paying their bills. Sears had added 18 million cardholders, some of whom later declared bankruptcy. The company established $393 million in reserves for credit-card delinquencies, which also reduced cash flow.[9]

The ideal way to improve cash flow is to generate more revenue than expenses. However, generating more revenue can be an enormous challenge. Many companies therefore trim costs to improve cash flow. Even when revenues are increasing, some firms reduce costs to remain more competitive. As you may have noticed, the less cash you spend, the more you have on hand. Major cost-reduction activities include trimming payroll, selling off an unprofitable portion of the business, forcing discounts from suppliers, and reducing employee travel. Minor areas of cost cutting include restricting the use of photocopiers, canceling magazine subscriptions and online database services, and eliminating the purchase of fresh flowers for reception areas. The accompanying Organizations in Action presents a variety of measures companies use to reduce costs.

The Balanced Scorecard

Many researchers and managers have moved away from exclusive reliance on financial ratios and related indices to measure the health of a firm. Budgets reveal important, but incomplete, information. Substantial progress has been made in

389

Organization *in Action*

Cost-Cutting Maneuvers of Various Companies

many managers invest considerable mental effort and time into finding ways to cut costs. A sampling of these ideas follows. You are invited to judge which of these maneuvers create ethical problems.

- Robert Tienowitz, 33, is co-owner of The Spark Factory, an entertainment marketing company in Santa Monica, California. He says, "Some vendors accept credit cards. The trick is to know when your credit-card statement closes." Suppose your statement closes on March 25, and your vendor's bill is due on March 28. Transfer $1,000 from your credit card to your vendor between the closing date of the statement and the vendor's due date, perhaps March 27. Your credit-card bill, with the $1,000 charge, will show up sometime around April 23, with the payment due May 24. "Basically, you take a bill issued on February 28 and, without paying interest, have it due almost three months later," explains Tienowitz.
- Many companies ask suppliers if they give discounts for early payment. If discounts are not granted, it pays to pay bills, including taxes, utilities, and suppliers, as late as possible without incurring a fee. David L. Scott, a specialist in saving money, says, "The longer funds are under your control, the longer they're earning a return for you rather than someone else."
- Some business owners concentrate on being good neighbors. They split advertising and promotion costs with neighboring businesses. For example, they might jointly promote a sidewalk sale or take a marketing alliance further by sharing mailing lists, distribution channels, and suppliers. An example would be a plumbing company sharing a mailing list with a heating and cooling company.

- Many small-business owners and managers are setting up an e-mail box on the Internet, thereby virtually eliminating many courier, overnight delivery, and postage fees. The e-mail account is obtained either through an Internet service provider or a commercial online service.
- Some business owners and managers are saving on postage by sending fax messages. These managers have free local telephoning, so they send much of their local correspondence by fax. (However, the person who receives the fax must incur the cost of the fax paper.)
- Some small-business owners and managers have given up their car phones, and use a pager instead. These people save on costly cellular telephone bills, yet they can still be reached in an emergency.
- A few small companies are creating their own Web sites to save money. Often they visit the Web Marketing Info Center at www.wilsonweb.com/rfwilson/webmarket for links to Web marketing resources. The same site also provides information on creating a Web site for less than $1,000.
- To save on telephone bills while staying at hotels, some businesspersons are pressing the pound (#) key at the right moment. When using a charge card to connect from a hotel, these people are avoiding costly "connect" surcharges for each call by pressing the pound key. After hearing the dial tone, the next number can be dialed without redialing the account number.
- Kevin Williams, 26, is the owner of Oasis Newsfeatures Inc., which syndicates a cooking column to more than 70 newspapers, and has a food line based on its recipes. He offers the following desperate tactics for a firm in deep financial trouble:

overcoming the limited view of performance sometimes created by budgets. An accounting professor and a technology consultant have worked with over 100 companies to devise a **balanced scorecard**—a set of measures that provide a quick but comprehensive view of a business. The originators of this approach believe that managers using the balanced scorecard do not have to rely on short-term financial measures as the only indicators of a company's performance. The scorecard encourages managers to use four management processes that separately and in combination help link long-term strategic objectives with short-term actions. The four processes are as follows:[10]

balanced scorecard
A set of measures that provide a quick but comprehensive view of a business.

1. *Translating the vision* helps managers build a consensus around the organization's vision and strategy. Lofty statements do not always translate easily into operational terms that provide useful guides to action throughout the organization. Like management by objectives, the vision needs to be translated into day-by-day actions, such as every worker in a Harley plant working hard to make each cycle "breathtaking."
2. *Communicating and linking* lets managers communicate their strategy throughout the organization and link it to unit and individual objectives. The major intent of communicating and linking is to help units and individuals recognize that their efforts are not tied only to short-term financial goals. A production manager at the Harley plant might say to its group, "Sure we've got to ship 100 bikes this week, but that isn't the only reason we're here. We're helping bring pleasure and excitement to 100 different people and their families and friends."
3. *Business planning* enables management to integrate their business and financial plans. This involves combining long-term objectives, such as gaining market share, with various financial goals such as return on equity. The idea again is to focus on the long term without getting sidetracked by short-term targets. If the company objective is to become a world-class supplier, managers would hesitate to ship shoddy products just to make a quarterly financial target.
4. *Feedback and learning* enables companies to engage in strategic learning, much like a learning organization. With the balanced scorecard as the center of its management systems, the company can monitor or control short-term results from three additional perspectives: Are customers satisfied? How good are our internal business processes? Are we learning and growing as an organization?

Many companies are using a balanced scorecard in a more direct and less abstract manner than the version just described. Quite often the balanced scorecard

391

places importance on satisfying customers, yet other factors are also important. A balanced scorecard usually incorporates both financial yardsticks, such as return on equity, and operational yardsticks, such as customer satisfaction and the ability to innovate. Compensation is based on achieving all the factors included in the balanced scorecard. Exhibit 15-9 presents a composite balanced scorecard from 60 companies.

Activity-Based Costing

activity-based costing (ABC)
An accounting procedure that allocates the cost for producing a product or service to the activities performed and the resources used.

Concern that conventional methods of measuring financial performance may be misleading has led to another approach to understanding the true costs involved in conducting business. **Activity-based costing (ABC)** is an accounting procedure that allocates the costs for producing a product or service to the activities performed and the resources used. Activity-based cost systems help give managers a more strategic view of their business because it presents a comprehensive view of all the costs involved in making a product or service and getting it to market. In contrast, a more traditional cost system might focus most on costs such as labor, parts, and administrative overhead. By using activity-based costing managers can assess the productivity of products and business units by assigning costs based on the use of companywide resources. The profitability of customers can also be assessed: Some customers use up so many resources they are not profitable to keep.[11] Is it worth selling a $35 pair of shoes to a customer who tries on 20 pairs before making a decision? Similarly, an industrial customer might be unprofitable because he or she takes too much time to serve.

How does activity-based costing work in practice? Let's assume a company introduces two new cell phone models. One phone is for use in autos and other general purposes. The other phone is a waterproof model targeted at people who are so attached to technology, or are in such demand, that they want a cell phone that works in the shower. The manufacturing cost is $100 for the conventional model and $130 for the shower model. However, the activity-based cost is $125 for conventional model and $400 for the shower model. The reason for the difference is that many people have to be consulted in order to make the shower

EXHIBIT 15-9

The Balanced Scorecard for Measuring Business Unit Performance
Some companies use a balanced scorecard to evaluate the performance of their business units and to shape performance-based compensation. Here are the average weights assigned to the five types of performance measures in the balanced scorecard, as it is being used by 60 large firms surveyed by Towers Perrin, New York. Note that, on average, the companies assign "customer focus" a 19 percent weighting.

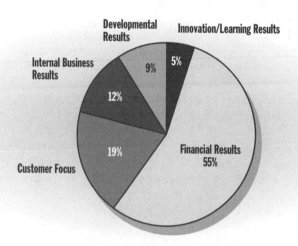

Developmental Results
Innovation/Learning Results
Internal Business Results
9%
5%
12%
19%
Customer Focus
Financial Results
55%

Source: Adapted with permission from "Compensation: The Link to Customer Satisfaction," *Human Resources Forum*, a supplement to *Management Review*, October 1996, p. 3.

model as safe as possible for shower use. The wet-look model also requires extensive consultation with the legal staff to iron out any possible product liability claims.

INFORMATION SYSTEMS AND CONTROL

An **information system (IS),** or **management information system (MIS),** is a formal system for providing management with information useful or necessary for making decisions. The IS is usually based on a mainframe computer, but recent advances allow some of these systems to be based on personal computers and servers. Many firms that decentralized their information systems have gone back to using a large centralized corporate mainframe. A centralized system reduces duplication and helps integrate the different functions. Several developments in recent years have contributed to the recentralization trend in information systems. The Internet explosion prompted businesses to connect their many networks. Companies put many essential applications on their intranets. Also, many companies have found that maintaining PCs on a network is too expensive to be cost effective.[12] Furthermore, mainframe computers crash less frequently than smaller computers.

The use of information systems has become widespread throughout all kinds of organizations, small businesses included. Advances in digital technology have helped make this possible—accessing computers from remote locations is easier than ever. With handheld information tools (or personal digital assistants), field personnel, including technicians, can get information from a central source. Sales representatives equipped with laptop computers or personal digital assistants can get needed information from the home office in seconds. Simultaneously, they can feed back to marketing vital information about customer orders and preferences.

Managerial control is based on valid information, so an IS is an indispensable part of any control system. The next sections describe the basic elements of an information system, how it can function as a control, data warehousing, and the electronic monitoring of work.

> Outline the basics of an information system.
>
> **information system (or management information system)** *A formal system for providing management with information useful or necessary for making decisions.*

Elements of an Information System

Establishing an information system usually involves four basic steps. As Exhibit 15-10 shows, these steps are: analyze the information requirements, develop an information base, design an information processing system, and build controls into the system.

ANALYZE INFORMATION REQUIREMENTS   The first step in designing an information system is to research the kinds of decisions managers and specialists need help in making. A related step is to decide what type of information is needed to provide that help. For example, research might show that managers need help in making decisions about which employees are qualified for overseas assignments. The IS designed to help them would include data about each employee's travel preferences, foreign-language skills, and ability to work without close supervision.

The people who are going to use the data from the information system should decide on the information requirements. This means managers must give the IS specialists a clear picture of their information requirements. This keeps users from getting stuck with an inadequate system; additionally, users are more committed to a system that they help select. Too often, when other people, such as systems analysts, decide on requirements, they make a wrong guess about what the users need. For example, the systems analyst may purchase software that is able to produce only limited information.

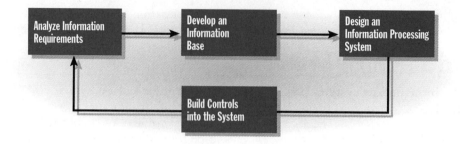

EXHIBIT 15-10

Basic Elements of an Information System Although information systems are complex and must be built with the assistance of information technology specialists, these systems all contain certain basic elements.

DEVELOP AN INFORMATION BASE   A base of valid information is the heart of any information system. Developing relevant information takes ingenuity. Sometimes, much of the information already exists in company records; it simply must be coded and stored in the IS. In other cases, information must be collected. In the overseas assignment example, managers and IS specialists might have to develop a questionnaire for job candidates. The questionnaire could be completed both by the candidate and by the manager during interviews. The results could be combined with the company information about work performance.

A recent Internet-based contribution to developing an information base is W*ebcasting*—software that brings information to your computer tailored to your individual needs. The information you want is delivered automatically to your desktop (and possibly to the company mainframe). The term *push technology* is used in relation to Webcasting because the information the manager needs is pushed through to him or her. Companies such as Amoco and Fruit of the Loom are using Webcasting to push industry news and other data to employees' desktops.[13] In Vancouver, British Columbia, a pig farmer uses Webcasting to be informed daily about the worldwide demand for pigs. (Selling pigs is more complicated today than in the predigital age.)

DESIGN AN INFORMATION PROCESSING SYSTEM   In this step, a system is designed for collecting, storing, transmitting, and retrieving information. Specialized knowledge about computer systems is required to complete this step successfully, so many firms use outside assistance. The total IS is a composite of a number of specific information systems. The same system that helps select candidates for overseas assignments cannot keep track of spare parts.

BUILD CONTROLS INTO THE SYSTEM   At the beginning of this chapter, we mentioned that one part of the controlling function is to evaluate the control system. Building controls into the IS is a special case of this general principle. Most information systems are impressive on the surface because they involve modern electronic equipment. However, despite outward sophistication, an IS can generate invalid or outdated information. The information system for foreign assignments might generate a list of employees at the press of a few buttons. If inaccurate performance-appraisal data had been entered, however, many of these people could be unqualified for overseas work. To use a tired cliché, "garbage in, garbage out."

Another type of control built into an information system is a control against misappropriation, or unauthorized use, of information. Controls against such computer theft include an elaborate system of passwords and other security devices. Programs to counter computer viruses are another aspect of computer security. A *computer virus* is an unauthorized program, placed secretly into a computer, that destroys stored data and other programs. A virus can also be introduced into a system accidentally by a contaminated disk from an outside source.

Effective controls enable managers to pinpoint the deficiencies in an IS. Effective controls are also useful in updating the system as information requirements change.

A constructive byproduct of IS specialists preparing for the Year 2000 (Y2K) problem is that it led to an upgrade of many information systems. While the potentially disastrous problem was being prevented, other faulty aspects of systems were discovered and repaired. For example, many companies achieved more efficient inventory management systems as a result of becoming Y2K compliant.

Control Information Supplied by an Information System

The field of information systems keeps expanding. This growth is partly attributable to the increasing need for useful control information. The control information that can be generated by an information system is virtually unlimited. Exhibit 15-11 shows a sampling of what an IS keeps track of. A company-specific example is that Southland Corp., which owns and franchises the 7-Eleven convenience stores, has a computerized information system to track inventory and forecast sales. The system can precisely track 2,300 items and helps individual stores stock the right number of items such as Slurpees and low-fat turkey breast on pita. Another advantage of the information system is that it can help analyze sales trends on such factors as time of day, weather, and socioeconomic level of the neighborhood. A computer information system of this type can help the individual store manager and owner cope with the major problems of overstocking perishable items and understocking hot items—such as beer, soft drinks, and snacks in response to a major sports event on television.

The Data Warehouse and Information Systems

An example of the productivity gains possible from the right information system is the *data warehouse*, used by many large retailing firms. The data warehouse is a centralized storehouse for data that flows in from diverse sources. The data are consolidated and stored for easy retrieval. According to Ernst & Young consultant Arthur Mason, "The data warehouse has matured from a luxury to a competitive necessity."[14]

Information systems can:

- Report on sales of products by territory, sales representative, and customer category
- Supply inventory-level information by region, plant, and department
- Describe magazine subscribers by age, income, occupational level, and ZIP code
- Report turnover rates by age, sex, job title, and salary level
- Supply information about budget deviations by location, department, and manager
- Automatically compile financial ratios and compare them to industry standards
- Automatically compile production and operation control indexes and compare them from plant to plant
- Print out a summary of overdue accounts according to customer, and goods or services purchased
- Report hospital-bed occupancy rates according to diagnosis, sex, and age of patient
- Calculate, by subsidiary, the return on investment of cash surpluses

EXHIBIT
15-11

Examples of Control Information Supplied by Information Systems

Data warehouses provide information used in such critical business functions as merchandising, operations, finance, and corporate systems. Data are typically updated daily because of the rapidly changing nature of retailing. For example, traditional retailers pore closely over trends in e-tailing to determine if they should investigate selling over the Internet.

Until recently, the emphasis has been on feeding information into the data warehouse. The new emphasis is to use these information systems for analyzing suppliers, promotions, and consumer behavior. Best-practice retailers have developed supplier scorecards that track gross margin and delivery records of vendors. In general, a supplier with lower markups and quicker delivery would be placed on a preferred list. However, these considerations are less important with a hot retail item such as a food supplement known to be used by a famous athlete. Some retailers are working on data warehousing systems capable of measuring customer spending patterns, including whether a specific promotion earned a profit.

Computer-Aided Monitoring of Work

Increasingly, information systems are being used for *computer-aided monitoring of work*. In this type of monitoring, a computer-based system gathers data about the work habits and productivity of employees. These systems capitalize upon the networking of computer terminals to monitor the work of employees who use computer terminals in their jobs or who operate complex machine tools. Once the monitoring software is installed, the central computer processes information from each terminal and records the employee's efficiency and effectiveness.

Office workers, including those who are in frequent telephone contact with the public, are the most likely to be monitored. Word processing specialists are measured by such factors as words keyed per minute, the number of breaks taken, and the duration of each break. The Internal Revenue Service uses an electronic monitoring system to evaluate workers who provide taxpayer assistance by telephone. AT&T uses electronic monitoring to evaluate operators, who must complete calls within a set time. Safeway Stores, Inc., equips its trucks with small, computerized boxes that record truck speed, gas mileage, gear shifting patterns, and whether the truck strays from its route.

The major advantage of an electronic monitoring system is the close supervision it allows managers. Some employees welcome computerized monitoring because it supplements arbitrary judgments by supervisors about their productivity. Computerized work-monitoring systems have substantial disadvantages, however. Many argue that these systems invade employee privacy and violate their dignity. Moreover, electronic monitoring often contributes to low levels of job satisfaction, absenteeism, high turnover, and job stress.

CHARACTERISTICS OF EFFECTIVE CONTROLS

Specify several characteristics of effective controls.

An effective control system improves job performance and productivity by helping workers correct problems. A system that achieves these outcomes has distinct characteristics. The greater the number of the following characteristics a given control system contains, the better the system will be at providing management with useful information and improved performance:

1. *The controls must be accepted.* For control systems to increase productivity, employees must cooperate with the system. If employees are more intent on beating the system than on improving performance, controls will not achieve

their ultimate purpose. For example, the true purpose of a time-recording system is to ensure that employees work a full day. If workers are intent on circumventing the system through such means as having friends punch in and out for them, the time-recording system will not increase productivity.

2. *The control measures must be appropriate and meaningful.* People tend to resist control measures that they believe do not relate to performance in a meaningful way. Customer-service telephone representatives, for example, may object to a control measure based primarily on the amount of inquiries processed. Experienced operators contend that giving the right assistance to fewer callers would be a better measure of performance. An classic example of the difference between a meaningful and a nonmeaningful control is as follows:

> At one point Continental Airlines was doing poorly. A contributing problem, according to Adam M. Pilarski, an aviation consultant and economist, was that the company was using a set of inappropriate incentives, such as rewarding pilots for saving fuel. In response to these standards, pilots were flying airplanes at slow speeds and rationing their use of air conditioning. As a result, many business passengers who were arriving late and sweaty decided to switch to other airlines, creating losses for Continental. A new incentive was introduced to pay every employee a monthly bonus if the airline was among the industry leaders in on-time performance. A dramatic turnaround took place. Business travelers returned to Continental and the airline is now profitable and no longer facing bankruptcy. The point of this story is that in terms of an airline becoming more profitable, on-time performance is a more effective control standard than saving fuel.[15]

3. *An effective control measure provides diagnostic information.* If controls are to improve performance, they must help people correct deviations from performance. A sales manager might be told that he or she was performing well in all categories except selling to small-business owners. This information might prompt the manager to determine what services the company sells that would have more appeal to small businesses.

4. *Effective controls allow for self-feedback and self-control.* A control system that is self-administering saves considerable time. Employees can do much of their own controlling if the system permits them access to their own feedback. An example is a system whereby clients complain directly to the employee instead of going to management.

5. *Effective control systems provide timely information.* Controls are more likely to lead to positive changes in behavior when the control information is available quickly. It is more helpful to give workers daily rather than monthly estimates of their performance against quota. Given day-by-day feedback, an employee can make quick adjustments. If feedback is withheld until the end of a month or a quarter, the employee may be too discouraged to make improvements.

6. *Control measures are more effective when employees have control over the results measured.* People rebel when they are held responsible for performance deviations beyond their control. For example, a resort hotel manager's profits might fall below expectations because of a factor beyond his or her control such as a sudden shift in weather that results in cancellations.

7. *Effective control measures do not contradict each other.* Employees are sometimes asked to achieve two contradictory sets of standards. As a result, they resist the control system. If employees are told to increase both quantity and qual-

ity, for example, the result can be confusion and chaos. A compromise approach would be to improve quality with the aim of increasing net quantity in the long run. If care is taken in doing something right the first time, less rework is required. With less time spent on error correction, eventually the quantity of goods produced increases.

8. *Effective controls allow for random variations from standard.* If a control allows for random variations that do not differ significantly from the standard, then it is more effective. An ineffective way of using a control system is to quickly take action at the first deviation from acceptable performance. A one-time deviation may not indicate a genuine problem. It could simply be a random or insignificant variation that may not be repeated for years. For example, would you take action if a team member exceeded a $3,000 travel-expense allowance by $2.78?

9. *Effective controls are cost-effective.* Control systems should result in satisfactory returns on investment. In many instances they don't because the costs of control are too high. Having recognized this fact, some fast-food restaurants allow employees to eat all the food they want during working hours. The cost of trying to control illicit eating is simply too high. (This policy has the added benefit of building worker morale.)

10. *A cross-functional team's measurement system must empower the team instead of top management retaining the power.* The ascendance of teams in organizations often requires that control measures for teams be given special consideration. Traditional performance measures may inhibit empowerment because team members do not have full control. One suggestion is for teams to create measures that track the process of delivering value. An example is that a product-development team might decide to measure the number or percentage of new parts to be used in a product. The rationale is that the more parts a product contains, the greater the possibility for malfunction.[16]

SUMMARY OF KEY POINTS

Explain how controlling relates to the other management functions.
Controlling is used to evaluate whether the manager has done a good job planning, organizing, and leading. Controls can also be used to evaluate control systems.

Understand the different types and strategies of control.
Controls can be classified according to the time when they are applied. Preventive controls are applied prior to the performance of an activity. Concurrent controls monitor activities while they are being carried out. Feedback controls evaluate and take corrective action after an activity has been performed.

Controls can also be classified according to their underlying strategy. An external control strategy is based on the assumption that employees are motivated primarily by external rewards and need to be controlled by their managers. An internal control strategy assumes that managers can motivate employees by building commitment to organizational goals.

Describe the steps in the control process.
The steps in the controlling process are to set standards, measure actual performance, compare actual performance to standards, and take corrective action if necessary. To measure performance, agreement must be reached on the aspects of performance to be measured, the degree of accuracy needed, and who will use the measurements.

The three courses of action open to a manager are to do nothing, to solve the problem, or to revise the standard. Taking corrective action on significant deviations only is called the exception principle.

Explain the use of nonbudgetary control techniques. Nonbudgetary control techniques can be qualitative or quantitative. Qualitative techniques include audits, personal observation, and performance appraisal. Quantitative techniques include Gantt charts, PERT, and economic-order quantity. Cost cutting is closely tied to the control function.

 Summarize the various types of budgets, and the use of budgets and financial ratios for control. A budget is a spending plan for a future period of time, and it is expressed in numerical terms. A fixed budget allocates expenditures based on a one-time allocation of resources. A flexible budget allows variation in the use of resources on the basis of activity. Seven widely used types of budgets are the (1) master budget, (2) cash budget, (3) revenue-and-expense budget, (4) production budget, (5) materials purchase/usage budget, (6) human resource budget, and (7) capital-expenditure budget.

Budgets are a natural part of controlling. Managers use budgets to compare planned expenditures to actual expenditures, and they take corrective action if the deviation is significant. Three key financial ratios are gross profit margin, profit margin, and return on equity. Economic value added (EVA) is another useful way of measuring the financial performance of a firm.

Explain how managers and business owners manage cash flow and control costs, and use nontraditional measures of financial performance. Closely tied in with the cash budget is the special attention many managers pay to cash flow. Cash flow is a measure of how much actual cash is available for conducting business. A firm that writes off many income deductions will have a bigger cash flow. Many companies trim costs to improve cash flow.

Many researchers and managers have moved away from exclusive reliance on financial ratios and related indices to measure the health of a firm. Instead, they use a balanced scorecard that measures various aspects of an organization's performance. The scorecard encourages managers to use various processes to link long-term objectives with short-range actions.

Activity-based costing is another approach to measuring financial performance that goes beyond traditional measures. The method focuses on the activities performed and the resources used to deliver a product or service.

 Outline the basics of an information system. An information system (IS), or management information system (MIS), is a formal system for providing management with information useful or necessary for making decisions. To develop an IS, you must analyze the information requirements, develop an information base, design an information processing system, and build controls into the system. An IS can keep track of a wide range of data that are used for control purposes. The data warehouse is a type of information system used in the retailing industry to collect important data from various sources.

Information systems are also used for the electronic monitoring of the work habits and productivity of employees. Although the method helps managers monitor employee performance, it has met with considerable criticism. Electronic monitoring works best when its results are used for constructive feedback.

 Specify several characteristics of effective controls. An effective control system results in improved job performance and productivity, because it helps people correct problems. An effective control measure is accepted by workers, apropriate, provides diagnostic information, allows for self-feedback and self-control, and provides timely information. It also allows employees some control over the behavior measured, does not embody contradictory measures, allows for random variation, and is cost-effective. Teams can sometimes select their own relevant control measures.

KEY TERMS AND PHRASES

QUESTIONS

1. Why don't managers who are great controllers generally receive as much publicity as managers who are great leaders?
2. What corrective action should a manager take when the department has spent all its budget for office supplies three months before the end of the fiscal year?
3. Identify one of the cost-cutting measures in the Organizations In Action that you regard as less than highly ethical. Explain the basis for your reasoning.
4. Why is EVA supposed to give a company an accurate picture of its profitability?
5. How can a family apply cash flow analysis to better control their finances?
6. Provide an example of how feedback from customers can be used as part of a control system.
7. What do you regard as the most important use a manager can make of an information system?

SKILL-BUILDING EXERCISE 15-A: Financial Ratios

Jessica Albanese invested a $50,000 inheritance as equity in a franchise print and copy shop. Similar to well-established national franchises, the shop also offers desktop publishing, fax, and computer graphics services. Listed below is Jessica's revenue-and-expense statement for her first year of operation.

Item	Financial Result
Revenues	$255,675
Beginning inventory	15,500
Purchases	88,000
End inventory	14,200
Cost of goods sold	89,300

Gross profit	166,375
Salaries expense	47,000
Rents and utilities expense	6,500
Miscellaneous expense	1,100
Maintenance expense	750
Total operating expenses	55,350
Net income before taxes	111,025
Taxes (40%)	44,410
Net income	66,615

Working individually or in small groups, compute the following ratios: gross profit margin, profit margin (return on sales), and return on equity. Groups might compare answers. Discuss whether you think that Jessica is operating a worthwhile business.

INTERNET SKILL-BUILDING EXERCISE: Cheap is Good

An important business tactic continues to be finding ways to cut costs without damaging quality or morale. The Organizations in Action in this chapter provided some ideas on this topic. Your assignment is to use the Internet to uncover some additional cost-cutting methods. A good starting point might be to visit CNNfn (www.cnnfn.com/index.html). Also visit standard business Web sites such as www.yahoo.com/business.

CASE PROBLEM 15-A: Shrinking Margins at Hewlett-Packard

The high-flying Hewlett-Packard Co. (H-P) has recently encountered some troubled waters. In anticipation of an inevitable downturn in business, for years CEO Lewis E. Platt has used the annual management-review meeting to warn company managers not to get careless. Hewlett-Packard had been increasing revenues at more than 20 percent a year, making it the most rapidly growing company of its size in the United States. So Platt thought it would have been easy for company execs to become less watchful about revenue and expenses. By January a year earlier, H-P had missed stock analyst's expectations for five consecutive quarters.

As a consequence, to kick off the weekend meeting at a resort hotel, Platt attempted a different tactic. The typically easygoing CEO openly criticized his 200-plus managers for shoddy execution, loose cost controls, and overdependence on slow-growth markets. Platt then told the managers to write down "two things you will do differently on Monday morning." Since all the managers were equipped with laptop computers

(H-P brand), Platt received their plans immediately. And he was disappointed with the plans he reviewed. The next day he told the management group, "You guys just don't get it, do you? I expect more coherent plans from you moving forward."

Since around June 1996, after years of exceeding the most bullish estimates, Hewlett-Packard sales have settled below the 20 percent growth rate analysts had come to expect. For fiscal year 1997, the company recorded a 12 percent revenue growth rate, down from 22 percent in 1996. The Asian crisis that began in 1998 and falling prices for personal computers and printers have also eaten into profit margins. Although sales growth recently surged to 16 percent, H-P showed an 18 percent increase in operating expenses and a 12 percent dip in earnings during a recent quarter. Platt conceded, "The competition has closed the gap. Our execution just isn't what it used to be."

H-P has suffered a number of embarrassing gaffes in recent years. In the summer of 1997, H-P ran short on supplies of its hot-selling LaserJet printer for several months. Shortly thereafter, the company experienced two painful delays in the delivery of high-end computer servers. For decades the company prospered on luscious gross profit margins exceeding 50 percent. Now, 60 percent of its revenues stem from lower-margin commodity products such as PCs and printers. The lower-margin products have dragged corporate gross margins down from 47.2 percent in 1990 to 34 percent in 1997. Also, operating costs rose in two recent quarters.

Despite the figures just cited, Hewlett-Packard remains a powerful company. Their sales growth still exceeds that of glamour companies like IBM, Sun Microsystems, and Compaq Computer. H-P still enjoys a 50 percent U.S. market share in printers, and the printers generate loads of ongoing revenue from paper, ink, and toner cartridges. However, H-P continues to search for a breakthrough innovation. Areas of promise include digital photography and printing off the Internet, yet a big payoff has not yet come through.

Without a new breakthrough product, H-P is forced to compete mostly on price. Richard E. Belluzzo, a former top H-P executive said, "H-P has got tremendous potential, people, technology, and a great brand, but there's something missing that would move the company to the next level." When Belluzzo was with H-P he urged the company to slash expensive overseas sales offices and divert investment from slower-growth traditional businesses to invest in high-growth areas such as PCs.

Platt now has a two-part fix-it plan to rejuvenate Hewlett-Packard. For the immediate term, he intends to cut costs and sharpen execution (implementation). For the intermediate term and long term he wants to ensure growth by extending current businesses and creating new ventures. To support these

plans he is giving business unit managers more freedom to define their own goals and policies. Platt also intends to link each manager's salary to the performance of their unit. Company PC chief Duane E. Zitzner will award stock options to his managers based on revenue growth, as well as shareholder value. By so doing he hopes that employees will not be tempted to offer unreasonable price breaks just to make quota. In one quarter, a sales group offered dealer discounts of up to 50 percent to keep business from rivals such as Compaq.

Platt is also attacking company costs, including a call for a 5 percent cut in operating expenses. The business units are responding. The personal computer division, which recently lost an estimated $50 million on a 70 percent increase in unit sales, is now pressuring suppliers for price breaks. Despite all the hand-to-hand combat in the computer industry, Platt will attempt to support the "H-P way" of showing respect for employees such as not laying off employees to protect profit margins. The company is also committed to the professional growth of people, which at times can mean payments for continuing education and participation in professional meetings.

Although Platt believes that cost cutting is essential, he places higher priority on sparking innovation. For example, he has created a special unit to nurture promising new technology ideas. The first project is an exciting new computer-display technology that Platt thinks could generate billions of dollars in sales.

To oversee the planned growth of H-P, Platt has formed an executive committee composed of himself as leader, and the chiefs of the company's six key business units (such as the ink jet printer business). Platt is not replacing Rick Belluzzo, the former number two executive who is now the top executive at Silicon Graphics Corp. Despite the need for expansion, Platt has made it clear the company is not going to chase market share at all costs, through such means as attempting to become the PC market share leader by 2001 (an earlier goal). Company insiders and outsiders are increasingly concerned that the computer business will be facing smaller growth profit margins in all product lines, not just PCs.

Discussion Questions

1. What other steps do you recommend to top management at HP to help them reduce costs while they are waiting for new product breakthroughs?

2. What should HP management do to improve gross profit margins?

3. Explain how the PC unit could possibly have experienced a 70 percent increase in sales yet lose $50 million.

Sources: Peter Burrows, "Lew Platt's Fix-It Plan for Hewlett-Packard," *Business Week*, July 13, 1998; Shelly Branch, "The 100 Best Companies to Work for in America," *Fortune*, January 11, 1999, p. 122.

CASE PROBLEM 15-B: How Well Is EFTEK Doing?

EFTEK is a package engineering and design company, whose primary product is called the Water Ballast/Rinser System. The system helps soft-drink bottling companies cope with the problem of top-heavy plastic bottles that tend to tip over before being filled at the plant. The result is that these bottles cannot be run through filling lines at anywhere near the speeds and efficiencies normally associated with glass or base-cup-equipped plastic bottles.

The heart of the patented system is injection of rinse water into the bottles in quantities sufficient to act as ballast. The bottles can then be moved on standard glass conveyor lines at speeds in excess of 1,000 per minute. The bottles are then emptied of rinse water, rinsed again, and then filled and capped.

The enhancement pays for itself financially in less than six months, making it appealing to cost-conscious managers at major bottlers like Coca-Cola, PepsiCo, and Perrier. According to the research of a group of financial analysts, the potential market for the ballaster in the United States and Canada is an estimated 4,000 packagers of beverage products. Added to this figure is another 6,000 units internationally. Following is a portion of projected financial information for EFTEK for 1998:

Units Sold	150
NET SALES	$21,235,500
Cost of Goods	8,167,500
GROSS PROFIT	13,068,000
Gross Margin	61.5%

Discussion Questions

1. Do you think the EFTEK Corp. has a product that meets customer requirements?
2. Apply financial ratio analysis to decide whether EFTEK is projected to have outstanding financial results.

Source: *Letter from the Publisher*, Berkshire Information Services, Inc., One Evertrust Plaza, Jersey City, N.J. 07032. E-mail: berkshire@growth.com

ENDNOTES

1. Phil Ebersole, "DSI Stock Pushed Lower," Rochester, New York, *Democrat and Chronicle*, February 25, 1998, pp. 9D, 10D.
2. C. Pascal Zachary, *Showstopper! The Breakthrough Race to Create Windows NT and the Next Generation of Microsoft* (New York: The Free Press, 1994).
3. Richard O. Mason and E. Burton Swanson, "Measurement for Management Decision: A Perspective," *California Management Review*, Spring 1979, pp. 70–81.
4. Amy Barrett, "Cendant: Who's to Blame?" *Business Week*, August 17, 1998, pp. 70–71.
5. Belverd E. Needles, Jr., Henry R. Anderson, and James C. Caldwell, *Principles of Accounting*, 4th ed. (Boston: Houghton Mifflin, 1990), pp. 1099–1113.
6. Don Delves, "EVA® for the Non-MBA," *HRfocus*, December 1998, p. 7.
7. "Eli Lilly Is Making Shareholders Rich. How? By Linking Pay to EVA." *Fortune*, September 9, 1996, p. 173.
8. Personal communication from Ashok J. Robin, Rochester Institute of Technology, 1999.
9. De'Ann Weimer, "Put the Comeback On My Card," *Business Week*, November 10, 1997, p. 120–121.
10. Robert S. Kaplan and David P. Norton, "Using the Balanced Scorecard as a Strategic Management System," *Harvard Business Review*, January–February 1996, pp. 75–77.
11. Robin Cooper and Robert S. Kaplan, "The Promise—and Peril—of Integrated Cost Systems," *Harvard Business Review*, July–August 1998, p. 111.
12. David Kirkpatrick, "Back to the Future with Centralized Computing," *Fortune*, November 10, 1997, p. 100.
13. Robert D. Hof, "A Way Out of the Web Maze," *Business Week*, February 24, 1997, p. 96.
14. "Data Warehouse Is the Latest Competitive Tool," *Business UpShot* (Ernst & Young LLP), November 1997, p. 3.
15. Adam Pilarski, "Computers—Headache or Panacea?" *Business Forum*, Spring–Fall 1997, p. 75.
16. Christopher Meyer, "How the Right Measures Help the Team Excel," *Harvard Business Review*, May–June 1994, p. 96.

Chapter Sixteen

Psychologist Gary Namie and his psychotherapist wife, Ruth Namie, are concerned that the American workplace is not just getting leaner, it's getting meaner. Attila-the-Hun bosses who yell or browbeat. Back-stabbing coworkers who spread malicious rumors or give you the silent treatment. This rude behavior has been called everything from workplace incivility to psychological aggression. Lawyers call it a hostile work environment. But the experts who study it have another term for the trend: workplace bullying.

The Namies have launched a national grassroots campaign on the World Wide Web (www.bullybusters.org). Their platform is simple: "Work shouldn't hurt." Their agenda is twofold: to help workers "bullyproof" themselves and to raise public awareness. Each month the Namies' Web site averages about 42,000 visitors—workers in a state of near despair over the abuse they say they suffer at the hands of a coworker or boss:

- A field-service technician for an equipment rental company complains that his manager's favorite put-down is: "Are you going to be stupid for the rest of your life?"
- An office worker from a large company says his boss works himself into fits of profanity and rage so violent that workers are reduced to tears.

OBJECTIVES

After studying this chapter and doing the exercises, you should be able to:

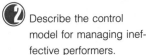

1 Identify factors contributing to poor performance.

2 Describe the control model for managing ineffective performers.

3 Know what is required to coach and constructively criticize employees.

4 Understand how to discipline employees.

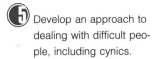

5 Develop an approach to dealing with difficult people, including cynics.

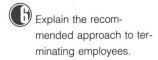

6 Explain the recommended approach to terminating employees.

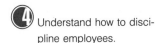

Managing Ineffective Performers

403

The bullied also complain of a range of psychological or even physical ailments: anxiety, sleeplessness, headache, irritable bowel syndrome, skin problems, panic attacks, and low self-esteem. The Namies' Web site and phone lines have been so flooded with mistreated workers and their stories, they are planning the first U.S. conference on workplace bullying and soon plan to publish a book on the subject. "We are employee advocates," Gary Namie said. "We are naïve enough to think we can do something about workplace bullying."[1]

The efforts of the two mental health specialists emphasize that managers must be alert to behavior (even of their own) that could contribute to ineffective performance. An important aspect of managerial control is dealing constructively with **ineffective job performance.** Job performance is considered ineffective when it lowers productivity below an acceptable standard. Ineffective performers are also referred to as problem employees because they create problems for management.

Ineffective performers lower organizational performance directly by not accomplishing their fair share of work. They also lower organizational productivity indirectly. Poor performers decrease the productivity of their superiors by consuming managerial time. Additionally, the productivity of coworkers is often decreased because coworkers must take over some of the ineffective performer's tasks. The relatively high turnover rate of poor performers also lowers productivity, because of the time and expense involved in recruiting and training replacements.

The consequences of ineffective performance are enormous. For example, one set of factors contributing to poor performance is employee deviancy. It includes behaviors such as stealing, cheating, and substance abuse. Alone these factors produce organizational losses estimated to range from $6 billion to $200 billion annually.[2] In this chapter, ineffective performance is regarded as a control problem for which the manager can take corrective actions. Poor performance, however, can also be viewed as a problem of motivation or staffing. Poor performers sometimes require effective motivation, and poor performance sometimes occurs because people are placed in the wrong job.

ineffective job performance
Job performance that lowers productivity below an acceptable standard.

FACTORS CONTRIBUTING TO INEFFECTIVE PERFORMANCE

Identify factors contributing to poor performance.

Employees are or become ineffective performers for many different reasons. The cause of poor job performance can be rooted in the person, the job, the manager, or the company. At times, the employee's personal traits and behaviors create so much disturbance that he or she is perceived as ineffective.

Exhibit 16-1 summarizes factors that can contribute to ineffective performance. Factors not listed here can also be contributors. These factors fall into one of four categories: personal, or related to the job, manager, or company. Usually, the true cause of ineffective performance is a combination of several factors. Assume that an employee is late for work so frequently that his or her performance becomes substandard. The contributing factors in this situation could be the worker's disrespect for work rules, an unchallenging job, and an unduly harsh supervisor. One factor may be more important than others, but they are all contributors.

A manager and a company can contribute significantly to ineffective performance through improper implementation of the various functions of management. For example, with poor planning and leadership, workers receive little guidance and may drift into poor work habits. Too much supervision can also

EXHIBIT 16-1

Factors Contributing to Ineffective Performance Dozens of factors can lower job performance. Many of the factors listed contribute to the majority of ineffective performance.

Factors Related to the Employee

Insufficient mental ability and education
Insufficient job knowledge
Job stress or burnout
Low motivation and loafing
Technological obsolescence
Excessive absenteeism and tardiness
Emotional problem or personality disorder
Alcoholism and drug addiction
Tobacco addiction or withdrawal symptoms
Conducting outside business on the job
Family and personal problems
Physical limitations
Preoccupying office romance

Factors Related to the Manager

Inadequate communication about job
  responsibilities
Inadequate feedback about job
  performance
Inappropriate leadership style
Bullying or intimidating manager

Factors Related to the Job

Ergonomics problems and cumulative trauma
  disorder
Repetitive, physically demanding job includ-
  ing heavy travel
Built-in conflict
Substandard industrial hygiene
A "sick" building

Factors Related to the Organization

Organizational culture that tolerates poor
  performance
Counterproductive work environment
Negative work group influences
Violence or threats of violence
Sexual harassment

cause problems. A system of tight controls can create enough stress to lower performance.

The following list expands on how the factors listed in Exhibit 16-1 are related to ineffective performance:

The Employee

- *Insufficient mental ability and education.* The employee lacks the problem-solving ability necessary to do the job. Poor communication skills are included here. A report by the Commission on the Skills of the American Workforce concluded that the knowledge and skill deficiency of the majority of American workers in lower-level positions reduces productivity.[3] Many employers today still agree strongly with this conclusion that was reached 10 years ago.
- *Insufficient job knowledge.* The employee is a substandard performer because he or she comes to the job with insufficient training or experience.
- *Job stress and burnout.* Severe short-term stress leads to errors in concentration and judgment. As a result of prolonged job stress, an employee may become apathetic, negative, and impatient. He or she can no longer generate the energy to perform effectively.
- *Low motivation and loafing.* An employee who is poorly motivated will often not sustain enough effort to accomplish the amount of work required to meet standards. Closely related to low motivation is goofing off and loafing. Sixty-three percent of human resource managers who responded to a survey said that employees are spending too much time surfing the Net or engaging in some other diversionary activity. These include making personal phone calls and running personal errands during working hours.[4]

- *Technological obsolescence.* The employee does not keep up with the state of the art in his or her field. He or she avoids using new ideas and techniques and becomes ineffective.
- *Excessive absenteeism and tardiness.* The employee is often not at work for a variety of personal or health reasons. Lost time leads to low productivity.
- *Emotional problem or personality disorder.* The employee may have emotional outbursts, periods of depression, or other abnormal behaviors that interfere with human relationships and work concentration. Cynical behavior may lower the performance of an entire work group if the negative attitude spreads to others.
- *Alcoholism and drug addiction.* The employee cannot think clearly because his or her mental or physical condition has been temporarily or permanently impaired by alcohol or other drugs. Attendance is also likely to suffer.
- *Tobacco addiction or withdrawal symptoms.* The employee who smokes is often fatigued and takes so many cigarette breaks that his or her work is disrupted. Sick leave may also increase. Even workers who stop smoking may suffer performance problems for awhile. Recent quitters report depression, anxiety, lower job satisfaction, more job tension, and increased short-term absence.[5]
- *Conducting outside business on the job.* The employee may be an "office entrepreneur" who sells merchandise to coworkers or spends time on the phone working on investments or other outside interests. Time spent on these activities lowers productivity.
- *Family and personal problems.* The employee is unable to work at full capacity because of preoccupation with an off-the-job problem such as a marital dispute, conflict with children, a broken romance, or indebtedness.
- *Physical limitations.* Job performance decreases as a result of injury or illness. For example, in the United States, lower-back problems account for approximately one-fourth of all workdays lost and cost between $15 and $20 billion per year.[6]
- *Preoccupying office romance.* For many people, a new romance is an energizing force that creates positive stress, resulting in a surge in energy directed toward work. For others, an office romance becomes a preoccupation that detracts from concentration. Time spent together in conversation and long lunch breaks can lower productivity. Office romances are increasing with around 50 percent of all romantic relationships beginning in the workplace.[7]

The Job

- *Ergonomics problems and repetitive motion disorder.* If equipment or furniture used on the job contributes to fatigue, discomfort, or injury, performance problems result. For example, if an employee develops neck pain and eyestrain from working at a poorly designed computer configuration, performance will suffer. As described in Chapter 8 about job design, repetitive motion disorder, including carpal tunnel syndrome, is a major problem stemming from poorly designed or poorly utilized computer equipment.
- *Repetitive, physically demanding job.* A repetitive, physically demanding job can cause the employee to become bored and fatigued, leading to lowered performance.
- *Built-in conflict.* The nature of the job involves so much conflict that job stress lowers performance. The position of collection agent for a consumer-loan company might fit this category.

- *Night-shift work assignments.* Employees assigned to all-night shifts suffer many more mental lapses and productivity losses than those assigned to daytime or evening shifts.
- *Substandard industrial hygiene.* Excessive noise, fumes, uncomfortable temperatures, inadequate lighting, high humidity, and fear of injury or contamination engender poor performance.
- *A "sick" building.* In some office buildings a diverse range of airborne particles, vapors, and gases pollute the indoor environment. The result can be headaches, nausea, and respiratory infections. Performance suffers and absenteeism increases.

The Manager

- *Inadequate communication about job responsibilities.* The employee performs poorly because he or she lacks a clear picture of what the manager expects.
- *Inadequate feedback about job performance.* The employee makes a large number of errors because he or she does not receive the feedback—early enough or at all—to prevent them.
- *Inappropriate leadership style.* The employee performs poorly because the manager's leadership style is inappropriate to the employee's needs. For example, an immature employee's manager gives him or her too much freedom and the result is poor performance. This employee needs closer supervision. Related to leadership style is the problem of some managers unwittingly setting up a group member to fail. The manager perceives a given group member as mediocre, and that person lives down to the manager's expectations, perhaps because the group member loses some self-confidence.[8]
- *Bullying or intimidating manager.* Many employees perceive that they are intimidated and bullied by their managers to the point that they cannot work effectively. Bullying and intimidation go far beyond being firm and setting high standards. They include such behaviors as publicly insulting group members, frequent yelling, and insensitivity toward personal requests, such as time off to handle a severe personal problem.[9]

The Company

- *Organizational culture that tolerates poor performance.* Suppose an organization has a history of not imposing sanctions on employees who perform poorly. When managers demand better performance, many employees may not respond to the new challenge.
- *Counterproductive work environment.* The employee lacks the proper tools, support, budget, or authority to accomplish the job. An example would be a sales representative who does not have an entertainment budget sufficient to meet customers' expectations.
- *Negative work group influences.* Group pressures restrain good performance or the work group penalizes a high-performance worker. Similarly, peer group social pressure may cause an employee to take overly long lunch breaks, neglecting job responsibilities. A recent study conducted in 20 organizations showed that antisocial behaviors such as lying, spreading rumors, loafing, and absenteeism were more frequent when coworkers exhibited the same behavior.[10]
- *Intentional threats to job security.* A company, for example, makes excessive work demands on an employee in the context of a veiled threat that the job

will be eliminated unless the extra work is done. Performance suffers as the worker becomes fearful and anxious.

- *Violence or the threat of violence.* Employees witness violent behavior in the workplace such as physical assaults, knifings, shootings, or threats of violence. Many employees not directly affected are nevertheless distracted and fearful, leading to lowered productivity.
- *Sexual harassment.* The employee who is sexually harassed usually experiences enough stress to decrease concentration and performance in general. The person who commits sexual harassment and is under investigation for or charged with the act is likely to experience stress and preoccupation about the charges.

behavior mismatch

A condition that occurs when one person's actions do not meet another's expectations.

Many performance problems just described can be viewed from the perspective of a **behavior mismatch.** Such a mismatch happens when one person's actions do not meet another's expectations.[11] In the present context, it is the group member's actions and the manager's expectations. A lack of understanding between the manager and the group member that stems from their different perspectives leads to different expectations. The perception of poor performance results from differing views and expectations.

Assume that a group member is experiencing the problem of a personal bankruptcy. His perception is that because he has personal problems, less should be expected of him. Perhaps he believes that 75 percent of his usual productivity is adequate performance. Yet his supervisor perceives him as not meeting job expectations.

You are invited to take the self-quiz in Exhibit 16-2 to ponder tendencies of your own that could ultimately contribute to substandard performance. Many sports figures, elected officials, and business executives experience the problems pinpointed in the questionnaire.

THE CONTROL MODEL FOR MANAGING INEFFECTIVE PERFORMERS

Describe the control model for managing ineffective performers.

The approach to improving ineffective performance presented here follows the logic of the control process shown in Exhibit 16-3. Problem identification and problem solving lie at the core of this approach. The control process for managing ineffective performers is divided into the eight steps illustrated in Exhibit 16-3, and should usually be followed in sequence. This section will describe each of these steps in detail. Another key method of improving ineffective performance—employee discipline—receives separate attention later in the chapter.

Two cautions are in order in using the control model for improving ineffective performance. First, the model may have to be modified slightly to follow company procedures. Company policy, for example, might establish certain procedures about documenting poor performance and reporting it immediately to higher levels of management. Second, the control process is not designed to deal with mental illness. An employee who suddenly begins to neglect the job because of a sudden change in personality should be referred immediately to a human resource specialist. (The personality change could be related to depression or a bipolar disorder that results in wide mood swings.) The specialist, in turn, will make an appropriate referral to a mental health professional.[12]

Define Performance Standards

Penalizing employees for not achieving performance standards that have not been carefully communicated is unfair. Therefore, the first step in the control model for managing ineffective performers is to clearly define what is expected of employees. (This step is identical to the step labeled "Set Standards" in the con-

Directions: Indicate how accurately each of the statements below describes or characterizes you, using a five-point scale: (0) very inaccurately, (1) inaccurately, (2) midway between inaccurately and accurately, (3) accurately, (4) very accurately. Consider discussing some of the questions with a family member, close friend, or work associate. Another person's feedback may prove helpful in providing accurate answers to some of the questions.

Answer

1. Other people have said that I am my worst enemy. _____
2. If I don't do a perfect job, I feel worthless. _____
3. I am my own harshest critic. _____
4. When engaged in a sport or other competitive activity, I find a way to blow a substantial lead right near the end. _____
5. When I make a mistake, I can usually identify another person to blame. _____
6. I have a sincere tendency to procrastinate. _____
7. I have trouble focusing on what is really important to me. _____
8. I have trouble taking criticism, even from friends. _____
9. My fear of seeming stupid often prevents me from asking questions or offering my opinion. _____
10. I tend to expect the worst in most situations. _____
11. Many times I have rejected people who treat me well. _____
12. When I have an important project to complete, I usually get sidetracked, and then miss the deadline. _____
13. I choose work assignments that lead to disappointments even when better options are clearly available. _____
14. I frequently misplace things such as my keys, then get very angry at myself. _____
15. I am concerned that if I take on much more responsibility people will expect too much from me. _____
16. I avoid situations, such as competitive sports, where people can find out how good or bad I really am. _____
17. People describe me as the "office clown." _____
18. I have an insatiable demand for money and power. _____
19. When negotiating with others, I hate to grant any concessions. _____
20. I seek revenge for even the smallest hurts. _____
21. I have a blinding ego. _____
22. When I receive a compliment or other form of recognition, I usually feel I don't deserve it. _____
23. To be honest, I choose to suffer. _____
24. I regularly enter into conflict with people who try to help me. _____
25. I'm a loser. _____

Total score _____

Scoring and interpretation: Add your answers to all the questions to obtain your total score. Your total score provides an approximate index of your tendencies toward being self-sabotaging or self-defeating. The higher your score, the more probable it is that you create conditions to bring about your own setbacks, disappointments, and failures. The lower your score, the less likely it is that you are a self-saboteur.

0–25: You appear to have very few tendencies toward self-sabotage. If this interpretation is supported by your own positive feelings toward your life and yourself, you are in good shape with respect to self-defeating behavior tendencies. However, stay alert to potential self-sabotaging tendencies that could develop at later stages in your career.

26–50: You may have some mild tendencies toward self-sabotage. It could be that you do things occasionally that defeat your own purposes. A person in this category, for example, might write an angry memo to an executive expressing disagreement with a decision that adversely affects his or her operation. Review actions you have taken during the past six months to decide if any of them have been self-sabotaging.

51–75: You show signs of engaging in self-sabotage. You probably have thoughts, and carry out actions, that could be blocking you from achieving important work and personal goals. People whose scores place in this category characteristically engage in negative self-talk that lowers their self-confidence and makes them appear weak and indecisive to others. For example, "I'm usually not good at learning new things." People in this range frequently experience another problem. They sometimes sabotage their chances of succeeding on a project just to prove that their negative self-assessment is correct.

76–100: You most likely have a strong tendency toward self-sabotage. (Sometimes it is possible to obtain a high score on a test like this because you are going through an unusually stressful period in your life.) You might discuss your tendencies toward undermining your own achievements with a mental health professional.

EXHIBIT 16-3

The Control Model for Managing Ineffective Performers
The most systematic and effective method for bringing ineffective performance up to standard is to follow the control process, referred to in this application as the control model.

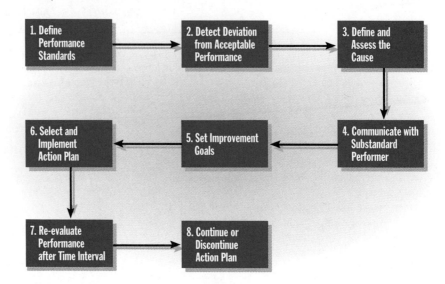

1. Define Performance Standards → 2. Detect Deviation from Acceptable Performance → 3. Define and Assess the Cause

6. Select and Implement Action Plan ← 5. Set Improvement Goals ← 4. Communicate with Substandard Performer

7. Re-evaluate Performance after Time Interval → 8. Continue or Discontinue Action Plan

trolling process shown in Exhibit 15-3.) Performance standards are commonly established by such means as job descriptions, work goals, production quotas, and formal discussions of what is to be accomplished in a position.

Detect Deviation from Acceptable Performance

Detection is the process of noting when an employee's performance deviates from an acceptable standard. Managers use the various control measures described in Chapter 15 to detect deviations from acceptable performance. For performance to be considered ineffective or poor, it must deviate significantly from the norm.

At times, quantitative measures can be used to define ineffective performance. For some jobs, ineffective performance might begin at 30 percent below standard. For other jobs, the cutoff point could be 20 or 50 percent, or any other percentage of deviation that fits the situation. What percentage of deviation from standard do you think would be acceptable for a quality inspector? For a loan specialist in a bank?

Personal observation plays a key role in detecting ineffective performance. One reason that observation is so important is that it is a concurrent control. By the time quantitative indicators of poor performance have been collected, substantial damage may have been done. Assume a bank manager observes that one of the loan officers is taking unduly long lunch hours on Fridays. Upon return, the officer appears to be under the influence of alcohol. Eventually, this unacceptable behavior will show up in quantitative indicators of performance. However, it might take a year to collect these data.

Define and Assess the Cause

At this stage the manager attempts to diagnose the real cause of the problem. Following the logic of Exhibit 16-1, the primary contributor to the problem could be a personal factor or a factor related to the job, the company, or the manager. A discussion with the employee (the next step in the control mode) may be necessary to reveal the major cause of the problem. For example, an office assistant was absent so frequently that her performance suffered. She claimed that extensive photocopying made her sick. The supervisor investigated further and called in the company health and safety expert. A medical examination confirmed that the office assistant was allergic to the trace fumes from the toner in the large-volume photocopier. After the office assistant was reassigned, her attendance became satisfactory.

Communicate with the Substandard Performer

After the unacceptable performance or behavior is detected, the manager must communicate concern to the worker. At times, a simple discussion will suffice. At other times, confrontation may be necessary. **Confrontation** means dealing with a controversial or emotional topic directly. Confrontation is necessary whenever the employee does not readily admit to experiencing a problem.

Managers often avoid confrontation for several reasons. They may have limited skill in criticizing employees. Or, they may prefer not to deal with the anger and resentment that confrontation is likely to trigger. A third reason is not wanting to make the employee feel uncomfortable.

A recommended confrontation technique is to communicate an attitude of concern about the confronted person's welfare. To do this, confront the person in a sincere and thoughtful manner. Using the words *care* and *concern* can be helpful. For instance, a manager might begin by saying: "The reason I'm bringing up this problem is that I care about your work. You have a good record with the company, and I'm concerned that your performance has slipped way below its former level."

confrontation
Dealing with a controversial or emotional topic directly.

Set Improvement Goals

The fifth step in the control model is to set improvement goals. An **improvement goal** is one that, if attained, will correct unacceptable deviation from a performance standard. The goals should be documented on paper or electronically. Improvement goals should have the same characteristics as other objectives (see Chapter 5). Above all, improvement goals should specify the behavior or result that is required. Vague improvement goals are not likely to cause changes in performance.

An example of a specific improvement goal is: "During this month, nine of your ten customer-service reports must be in on time." This specific goal is likely to be more effective than a general improvement goal, such as "Become more prompt in submitting customer-service reports."

If the ineffective performer expresses an interest in improvement, joint goal setting is advisable. By providing input into goal setting, the substandard performer stands a good chance of becoming committed to improvement. At times improvement goals have to be imposed on substandard performers, especially in cases involving a motivation problem. If substandard employees were interested in setting improvement goals, they would not have a motivation problem.

improvement goal
A goal that, if attained, will correct unacceptable deviation from a performance standard.

Select and Implement an Action Plan

The setting of improvement goals leads logically to the selection and implementation of action plans to attain those goals. Much of the art of remedying ineffective performance is contained in this step. Unless appropriate action plans are developed, no real improvement is likely to take place. Many attempts at improving substandard performance fail because the problem is discussed and then dropped. Thus the employee has no concrete method of making the necessary improvements.

TYPES OF ACTION PLANS   An action plan for improvement can include almost any sensible approach tailored to the specific problem. An action plan could be formulated to deal with every cause of ineffective performance listed in Exhibit 16-1.

Action plans for improving ineffective performance can be divided into two types. One type is within the power of the manager to develop and implement. Plans of this type include coaching, encouraging, and offering small incentives for improvement. The other type of action plan is offered by the organization or purchased on the outside. These include training programs, stress-management programs, and stays at alcoholism-treatment centers. Exhibit 16-4 lists a selection of feasible corrective actions.

Corrective Actions for Ineffective Performers
When attempting to bring ineffective performers up to standard or beyond, managers can either take action by themselves or refer employees to a company program designed to help them with performance problems.

Managerial Actions and Techniques

- **Coaching.** The manager points out specifically what the performer could be doing better or should stop doing. In daily interaction with the team members, the manager makes suggestions for improvement. One estimate is that coaching takes approximately 85 percent of the time a manager spends on performance improvement.[13]

- **Closer supervision.** The manager works more closely with the subordinate, offering frequent guidance and feedback.

- **Reassignment or transfer.** The manager reassigns the ineffective performer to a position that he or she can handle better.

- **Use of motivational techniques.** The manager attempts to improve employee motivation by using positive reinforcement or some other motivational technique.

- **Corrective discipline.** The manager informs the employee that his or her behavior is unacceptable and that corrections must be made if the worker is to remain employed by the firm. The employee is counseled as part of corrective discipline.

- **Temporary leave.** The manager offers the employee an opportunity to take a leave of absence for a specified time in order to resolve the problems causing the poor performance.

- **Lower performance standards.** If performance standards have been too high, the manager lowers expectations of the team member. Consultation with higher management would probably be necessary before implementing this step.

- **Job rotation.** If ineffective performance results from staleness or burnout, changing to a different job of comparable responsibility may prove helpful.

Organizational Programs

- **Employee assistance programs (EAPS).** The employee is referred to a counseling service specializing in rehabilitating employees whose personal problems interfere with work.

- **Wellness programs.** The organization encourages employees to participate in specialized programs that help them stay physically and mentally healthy. By doing so, employees may prevent or cope with health problems—such as heart disease or an eating disorder—that interfere with job performance or lead to absenteeism. The wellness program usually includes stress management.

- **Career counseling and outplacement.** The employee receives professional assistance in solving a career problem, including being counseled on finding a job outside the firm.

- **Job redesign.** Specialists in human resource management and industrial engineering redesign job elements that could be causing poor performance. For example, the job is changed so that the employee has less direct contact with others, leading to reduced conflict.

- **Training and development programs.** The employee is assigned to a training or development program linked directly to his or her performance deficiency. For example, a very reserved sales representative receives assertiveness training.

When attempting to improve ineffective performance that appears to stem from a variety of personal problems, the preferred action plan for many managers is to refer the troubled worker to an **employee assistance program (EAP).** The EAP is an organization-sponsored activity to help employees deal with personal and job-related problems that interfere with job performance. An employee assistance program is staffed by professionals who specialize in dealing with particular problems. Many companies that do not have an EAP of their own refer employees to such a program that serves many firms in the area.

Employees and their families use assistance programs to cope with a variety of personal and family problems and illnesses. Among them are alcoholism and other substance abuse, financial and legal difficulties, emotional problems, chronic illness such as AIDS or cancer, compulsive gambling, and weight control. Employees also use EAPs to deal with job-related concerns such as work stress, chronic job dissatisfaction, and sexual harassment.

employee assistance program (EAP)
An organization-sponsored activity to help employees deal with personal and job-related problems that hinder performance.

IMPLEMENTATION OF THE ACTION PLAN   After the action plan is chosen, it must be implemented. As shown in Exhibit 16-3, implementation begins in step 6 and continues through step 8. The manager has to utilize the approaches listed under "Managerial Actions and Techniques" in Exhibit 16-4. Human resources specialists outside the manager's department usually implement organizational programs.

An important part of effective implementation is continuation of the remedial program. Given the many pressures facing a manager, it is easy to forget the substandard performer who needs close supervision or a motivational boost. Often, a brief conversation is all that is needed.

Re-Evaluate Performance After a Time Interval

Step 7 in the controlling process helps ensure that the process is working. In this step the manager measures the employee's current performance. If the remedial process is working, the team member's performance will move up toward standard. The greater the performance problem, the more frequent the re-evaluations of performance should be. In instances of behavior problems, such as alcoholism, weekly performance checks are advisable.

FORMAL AND INFORMAL REVIEWS   A re-evaluation of performance can be formal or informal. A formal progress review takes the form of a performance-appraisal session. It might include written documentation of the employee's progress and samples of his or her work. Formal reviews are particularly important when the employee has been advised that dismissal is pending unless improvements are made. Reviews are critical to avoid lawsuits over a dismissal.

The first level of informal review consists of checking on whether the employee has started the action plan. For example, suppose a very reserved sales representative agreed to attend an assertiveness training program. One week later, the manager could ask the rep, "Have you signed up for or started the training program yet?"

The next level of informal review is a discussion of the employee's progress. The manager can ask casual questions such as, "How much progress have you made in accounting for the missing inventory?" Or the manager might ask, "Have you learned how to use the new diagnostic equipment yet?"

POSITIVE REINFORCEMENT AND PUNISHMENT   If the employee has made progress toward reaching the improvement goal, positive reinforcement is appropriate. Rewarding an employee for progress is the most effective way of sustaining that progress. The reward might be praise, encouragement, or longer intervals between review sessions. The longer time between reviews may be rewarding because the employee will feel that he or she is "back to normal."

Giving rewards for making improvement is generally more effective than giving punishments for not making improvement. Yet if the problem employee does not respond to positive motivators, some form of organizational punishment is necessary. More will be said about punishment in the discussion about employee discipline.

Continue or Discontinue the Action Plan for Improvement

Step 8 in the control model for managing ineffective performers is making the decision whether to continue or discontinue the action plan. This step can be considered the feedback component of the control process. If the performance review indicates that improvement goals have not been met, the action plan is continued. If the review indicates that goals have been met, the action plan is discontinued.

An important part of using the control model to manage ineffective performers is realizing that positive changes may not be permanent. Performance is most likely to revert to an unacceptable level when the employee is faced with heavy job pressures. For instance, suppose an employee and a manager formulated an action plan to improve the employee's work habits. The employee's performance improved as a result. When the employee is under pressure, however, his or her work may once again become badly disorganized. The manager should then repeat the last five steps of the process, beginning with confrontation.

COACHING AND CONSTRUCTIVE CRITICISM

Know what is required to coach and constructively criticize employees.

coaching
A method for helping employees perform better that usually occurs on the spot and involves informal discussion and suggestions.

constructive criticism
A form of criticism designed to help improve performance or behavior.

Most performance improvement takes place as a result of a manager dealing directly with the worker not meeting standards. The usual vehicle for bringing about this improvement is **coaching.** It is a method for helping employees perform better that usually occurs on the spot and involves informal discussion and suggestions. Workplace coaching is much like coaching on the athletic field or in the performing arts. Coaching involves considerable **constructive criticism,** a form of criticism designed to help people improve. The same technique is sometimes referred to as constructive *direction* because the intent is to help people and set them in the right direction. To be a good coach, and to criticize constructively, requires considerable skill.

Business psychologists James Waldroop and Timothy Butler point out that good coaching is simply good management. Coaching requires the same skills that contribute to effective management such as keen observation skills, sound judgment, and an ability to take appropriate action. Also, coaching shares one goal of effective management: to make the most of human resources.[14] The following suggestions will help you improve your coaching skill if practiced carefully:

1. *Focus on what is wrong with the work and behavior rather than the employee's attitudes and personality.* A major principle of employee coaching is to focus on

the substandard work behavior itself, not the person or his or her attitudes. When a person's self-image is attacked, he or she is likely to become hostile. Then the person will be focused on getting even, not getting better. Another way to upset the person being coached is to exaggerate the nature of the poor performance, such as saying, "You've committed the same mistake 100 times," when you have only observed the mistake four times.

2. *Listen actively.* An essential component of counseling employees is listening carefully to both their presentation of facts and their feelings. Your listening will encourage the employee to talk. As the employee talks about his or her problem, you may develop a better understanding of how to help improve performance.

3. *Ask good questions.* An effective workplace coach asks questions that help people understand their needs for improvement. Consultant Marilyn J. Darling says that effective coaching is based on asking good questions. She notes that the simpler the question the better:

   - What are you trying to accomplish?
   - How will you know if you've succeeded?
   - What obstacles do you believe are stopping you?
   - How can I help you succeed?[15]

   All the above questions are part of active listening because they are open ended. An open-ended question requests that the person provides details rather than a "yes" or "no" response. "What obstacles do you believe are stopping you?" is open ended because the worker must point to obstacles to answer the question. A closed question on the same topic would be "Are there any obstacles stopping you?" Such a question fails to promote dialogue.

4. *Engage in joint problem solving.* Work together to resolve the performance problem. One reason joint problem solving is effective is that it conveys a helpful and constructive attitude on the part of the manager. Another is that the employee often needs the superior's assistance in overcoming work problems. The manager is in a better position to get problems of this type resolved than is the employee.

5. *Offer constructive advice.* Constructive advice can be useful to the employee with performance problems. A recommended way of giving advice is first to ask an insightful question. You might ask the employee, "Could the real cause of your problem be poor work habits?" If the employee agrees, you can then offer some specific advice about improving work habits.

6. *Give the poor performer an opportunity to observe and model someone who exhibits acceptable performance.* A simple example of modeling would be for the manager to show the employee how to operate a piece of equipment properly. A more complex example of modeling would be to have the poor performer observe an effective employee making a sale or conducting a job interview. In each case the ineffective performer should be given opportunities to repeat the activity.

7. *Obtain a commitment to change.* Ineffective performers frequently agree to make improvements but are not really committed to change. At the end of a session, discuss the employee's true interest in changing. One clue that commitment may be lacking is when the employee too readily accepts everything you say about the need for change. Another clue is agreement about the need for change but with no display of emotion. In either case, further discussion is warranted.

8. *When feasible, conduct some coaching sessions outside of the performance review.* The coaching experience should focus on development and improvement, whereas the performance review is likely to be perceived by the ineffective performer as a time for judging his or her performance. Despite this perception, performance reviews should include an aspect of development.

Recently another form of coaching has become popular that supplements the manager's role as a coach. A *business coach* or an *executive coach* is an outside specialist who advises a person about performance improvement. Sometimes a company will hire the coach because a high-level worker is having performance problems. At other times, an executive or other worker will hire a coach to help develop skills that will lead to career advancement. Or the coach might be hired to present a fresh perspective on a problem the person faces, such as giving insight into whether or not to accept a job transfer.

According to career advisor Andrea Hecht, the goal of business coaching or executive coaching is to change behavior and enhance job performance rather than to impart knowledge. This type of coaching is an on-going process whereby an individual works with a coach to develop and fine tune behaviors. Sometimes the coach will work with the individual's manager and work team, and conduct 360-degree surveys.[16] In the past, this type of activity was conducted primarily by management psychologists. Today, however, people from a variety of educational backgrounds offer their services as business coaches. An example of what a coach might accomplish follows:

> Problem: An unorganized, unfocused employee who produces excellent results but often completes projects late. Solution: The coach slashed her e-mail time by 90 percent and helped her see the big picture. Her improved work approach improved so much that one client sponsoring a project sent the woman a $5,000 bonus.[17]

EMPLOYEE DISCIPLINE

Understand how to discipline employees.

discipline
Punishment used to correct or train.

summary discipline
The immediate discharge of an employee because of a serious offense.

corrective discipline
A type of discipline that allows employees to correct their behavior before punishment is applied.

Positive approaches to improving substandard performance have been emphasized so far in this chapter. There are times, however, when using the control model requires a manager to discipline employees in an attempt to keep performance at an acceptable level. It is also part of an effective manager's role to be willing to take harsh and unpopular action when the situation requires such behavior. **Discipline,** in a general sense, is punishment used to correct or train. In organizations, discipline can be divided into two types.

Summary discipline is the immediate discharge of an employee because of a serious offense. The employee is fired on the spot for rule violations such as stealing, fighting, or selling illegal drugs on company premises. In unionized firms, the company and the union have a written agreement specifying which offenses are subject to summary discipline.

Corrective discipline allows employees to correct their behavior before punishment is applied. Employees are told that their behavior is unacceptable and that they must make corrections if they want to remain with the firm. The manager and the employee share the responsibility for solving the performance problem. The controlling process for managing ineffective performers includes corrective discipline. Steps 4 through 7 in Exhibit 16-3 are based on corrective discipline.

Taking disciplinary action is often thought of in relation to lower-ranking employees. Managers, professionals, and other salaried employees, however, may also need to be disciplined. Textron, Inc., is an example of a company that has seen the need to state explicitly a discipline policy for salaried employees. The discipline procedure follows quite closely the approach to progressive discipline described here.

The paragraphs that follow will describe three other aspects of discipline. First, we describe the most widely used type of corrective discipline, progressive discipline. Second, we explain the rules for applying discipline. Third, we examine the positive consequences of discipline to the organization.

Progressive Discipline

Progressive discipline is the step-by-step application of corrective discipline, as shown in Exhibit 16-5. The manager confronts and then coaches the poor performer about the performance problem. If the employee's performance does not improve, the employee is informed in writing that improvements must be made. The written notice often includes a clear statement of what will happen if performance does not improve. The "or else" could be a disciplinary layoff or suspension. If the notice is ignored and the disciplinary action does not lead to improvement, the employee may be discharged.

Progressive discipline is an old concept but continues to be widely used for two key reasons. First, it provides the documentation necessary if a person is to be fired fairly. Second, many labor-management agreements require progressive discipline because of the inherent fairness of the step-by-step procedure.

Rules for Applying Discipline

This chapter has discussed discipline as it relates to the correction of ineffective performance. However, discipline is more frequently used to deal with infractions of policy and rules. The employee in these situations may not necessarily be a poor performer. The administration of discipline, whether for poor performance or infractions, should adhere to certain time-tested rules. Before applying

progressive discipline
The step-by-step application of corrective discipline.

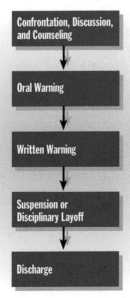

Steps in Progressive Discipline
Progressive discipline is a standard practice that remains important because it gives the worker a chance to improve, and it documents poor performance. Should discharge be necessary, it would be more difficult for the employee to claim unfair treatment and wrongful discharge.

417

these rules, a manager in a unionized firm must make sure they are compatible with the employee discipline clauses in the written union agreement.

The red-hot-stove rule is an old-fashioned but still valid principle in administering discipline. According to the *red-hot-stove rule*, employee discipline should be the immediate result of inappropriate behavior, just as a burn is the result of touching a very hot stove. The employee should receive a warning (the red metal), and the punishment should be immediate, consistent, and impersonal. A manager should keep this rule and those that follow in mind when disciplining employees. Several of these suggestions incorporate the red-hot-stove rule.

1. *All employees should be notified of what punishments will be applied for what infractions.* For example, paralegals might be told that discussing the details of client cases with outsiders, a violation of company policy, will result in discharge.
2. *Discipline should be applied immediately after the infraction is committed.* As soon as is practical after learning of a rule violation, the manager should confront the employee and apply discipline.
3. *The punishment should fit the undesirable behavior.* If the punishment is too light, the offender will not take it seriously. If, on the other hand, it is too severe, it may create anxiety and actually diminish performance.
4. *The manager should focus attention on the unsatisfactory behavior or performance, not on the person's attitudes or traits.* A core principle of discipline and punishment is for the person administering the discipline to point out what results are unacceptable rather than insulting or diagnosing the group member's personality. Thus the manager would say, "Your store received five consecutive below-average customer-service ratings." The same manager should not say, "You couldn't care less about customer service."
5. *Managers should be consistent in the application of discipline for each infraction.* Every employee who violates a certain rule should receive the same punishment. Furthermore, managers throughout the organization should impose the same punishment for the same rule violation.
6. *Disciplinary remedies should be applied impersonally to offenders.* "Impersonal," in this context, implies that everybody who is a known rule violator should be punished. Managers should not play favorites.
7. *There must be documentation of the performance or behavior that led to punishment.* Justification for the discipline must be documented in substantial detail. Documentation is essential for defending the company's action in the event of an appeal by the employee or the union or in the case of a lawsuit.
8. *When the discipline is over, return to usual work relations.* The manager should not hold a grudge or treat the rule violator as an outcast. How the person who violated the rule is treated could become a self-fulfilling prophecy. Treating the person who was disciplined as an outcast may make that person feel alienated, causing his or her performance to deteriorate. If the person is treated as someone who is expected not to commit mistakes, he or she will most likely try to live up to that expectation.

Positive Consequences of Punishment for the Organization

Conventional wisdom is that punishment should be avoided in the workplace or used only as a last resort because of its negative side effects. Workers who are punished may become anxious, fearful, revengeful, and even violent. More recent evidence, however, suggests that if punishment is perceived in certain ways, it can benefit the organization.[18]

A key factor in whether punishment is beneficial is the employee's *belief in a just world*, or that people get the rewards and punishments they deserve. Employees who believe in a just world are likely to accept punishment when they violate rules or perform poorly. The reason is that they believe they deserve to be punished. As a consequence, they do not complain about punishment, and might even spread the word that the organization is fair.

When employees observe that another employee has been punished justly (fairly), they will often rally on the side of management. The employees may think that the offending employee deserved the punishment. In some instances, other employees may desire that a rule violator be punished because it fits their sense of justice.

Another contribution of just punishment is that it informs employees that certain types of misconduct will not be tolerated, as documented in an interview study conducted with 77 managers from different organizations. Many managers therefore regard punishment as an opportunity to promote *vicarious learning* (in this sense, learning through others).[19] For example, if one employee receives a 10-day suspension for racial harassment, other employees learn that racial harassment is a serious rule violation.

DEALING WITH DIFFICULT PEOPLE, INCLUDING CYNICS

Develop an approach to dealing with difficult people, including cynics.

difficult person
An individual whose personal characteristics disturb other people.

The focus of this chapter has been on dealing with substandard performers. Another group of employees may perform adequately, yet they are annoying and they waste managers' time. At times their performance slips below standard because they divert their energy from getting work accomplished. A person in this category is often referred to as a **difficult person,** an individual whose personal characteristics disturb other people. Among such people are whiners and complainers, know-it-alls, dictators, pessimists, poor team players, and passive aggressives. A passive-aggressive person expresses anger and hostility by such means as neglecting to take care of an emergency or sitting silently in a meeting without making a contribution. Here we describe tactics for dealing with difficult people in general, and then highlight cynics because their numbers appear to be rising. (Or, are we being too cynical?)

Tactics for Dealing with Difficult People

Much of the advice about dealing with difficult people centers around certain tactics, as described next. It will often be necessary to use a combination of these tactics to help a difficult person become more cooperative. The more the difficult behavior is an ingrained personality pattern, the more difficult it will be to change. In contrast, it is easier to change difficult behavior that stems from the pressures of a given situation. For example, a worker might be sulking because he was not appointed as team leader rather than being a long-term passive-aggressive personality. The list that follows describes seven tactics for dealing with a variety of difficult people.

- *Stay focused on the issues at hand.* A general strategy for dealing with difficult people is to not react specifically to the problem-maker's antics and instead to stay focused on work issues. Describe the behavior you want changed, and explain why the behavior is disruptive. Pause for a moment, then wait for a response. Acknowledge what the person says, then state what needs to be changed, such as: "Please stop giving customers an exasperated look and a loud exhale when they make a special request." Ask how the difficult person will make the change, and then get a commitment to change.[20] (Notice the good coaching technique.)

- *Take the problem person professionally, not personally.* A key principle in dealing with difficult people is to not take what they do personally. Difficult people are not necessarily out to "get" the manager or coworker. You or somebody else might just represent an obstacle, or a stepping stone for them to get their way.[21] Remind yourself that you are paid to do your job, and dealing with difficult people is part of it. As you learn to take insults, slights, and back stabbing professionally rather than personally, you will experience less stress and harassment.

- *Use tact and diplomacy.* Team members who irritate you rarely do annoying things on purpose. Tactful actions on your part can sometimes take care of these problems without your having to go through the controlling process. For example, close your door if a team member is busily engaged in conversation outside your office. When subtlety does not work, you may have to confront the person. Incorporate tact and diplomacy into the confrontation. For example, as you confront a team member, point out one of his or her strengths.

- *Use humor.* Nonhostile humor can often be used to help a difficult person understand how his or her behavior annoys or blocks others. The humor should point to the person's unacceptable behavior but not belittle him or her. You might say to a subordinate who is overdue on a report: "I know we are striving for zero defects in our company. But if you wait until your report is perfect before submitting it, we may not need it anymore." Your humor may help the team member realize that timeliness is an important factor in the quality of a report.

- *Give recognition and attention.* Difficult people, like misbehaving children, are sometimes crying out for attention. Give them recognition and attention, and their difficult behavior will sometimes cease. For example, in a staff meeting, mention the person's recent contributions to the department. If the negative behavior is a product of a deeper-rooted problem, recognition and attention by themselves will not work. The employee may have to be referred for professional counseling.

- *Listen and then confront or respond.* When discussing the problem with the difficult person, allow the individual a full expression of feelings. Next, acknowledge your awareness of the situation, and confront the person about how you size up the situation. Finally, specify what you would like changed, such as: "Please stop complaining so much about factors beyond our control." Avoid judging the person ("You *shouldn't* be like that") or generalizing (You *always* act this way").[22]

- *Stand fast and do not make unwarranted concessions.* A variety of difficult people, but particularly bullies, expect you to sacrifice your position or standards such as breaking the rules just for them. If a person insults you, don't laugh it off or sidestep the remarks. Instead, say, "That's not called for. I cannot let your lack of professionalism pass unnoticed." If you are not intimidated, and do not appear insecure, the difficult person is less likely to keep pushing for the advantage.[23]

Dealing with Cynical Behavior

Many employees have extremely negative attitudes toward their employers, and these negative attitudes often take the form of cynicism. Much of the cynicism appears to be a reaction to top-level management actions such as boosting their own compensation substantially while laying off lower-ranking workers to save money. Hiring so many contract and temporary workers at the expense of offering full-time employment also leads to cynicism. Cynics are classified as difficult people because they express their cynicism more negatively and persistently than do others. Cynicism is usually expressed by finding something negative about even the best intentions of others. A recent investigation into the topic concludes that workplace cynicism is a negative attitude toward one's employer, comprising three dimensions:

- *A belief that the organization lacks integrity* (The cynic might say, "Our advertising is a pack of lies.")
- *A negative affect toward the organization* (Cynics frequently make such comments as, "This company is the pits," or "Who in his right mind would join this company today?")
- *Tendencies toward disparaging and critical behaviors toward the organization that are consistent with these beliefs and affect* (The cynic might use a competitor's consumer product and brag about it.)[24]

Managers may not want to suppress dissent, but too much cynicism in the workplace can lower the morale of others and interfering with recruiting positive people. Cynicism can also be distracting enough to harm productivity. One promising approach to dealing with cynics is to use the reinforcement strategy of extinction. Ignore cynical comments, and move on to another subject. If the cynic is seeking attention by being cynical, the lack of response will defeat the purpose of the sarcastic comments.

Cynical commentary can sometimes be reduced by demanding evidence to support harsh comments. Ask for the facts behind the opinion. A cynic might say, "I doubt there will be any money in the bonus pool this year. As usual, top management is taking care of themselves first and leaving little money for the rest of us." You might respond, "I seriously doubt top management is going to deny us raises. Where did you get your information?" As in dealing with most difficult people, changing the individual substantially is unlikely. However, you can work toward enough improvement to bring about a more positive working relationship.[25]

TERMINATION

When corrective actions fail to improve ineffective performance, an employee is likely to be terminated. The company may also assist the person in finding new employment. Termination is considered part of the control process because it is a corrective action. It can also be considered part of the organizing function because it involves placing people.

Termination is the process of firing an employee because of poor job performance, unacceptable behavior, or interpersonal problems. Termination is regarded as the last alternative. It represents a failure in staffing and in managing ineffective performers. Nevertheless, to maintain discipline and control costs, a firm is often forced to terminate nonproductive employees. When substandard performers are discharged, it communicates the message that adequate perfor-

Explain the recommended approach to terminating employees

421

termination
The process of firing an employee because of poor job performance, unacceptable behavior, or interpersonal problems.

EXHIBIT
16·6

Framework for Deciding
Whether to Terminate or
Provide Additional
Counseling to an
Employee
Managers must ponder care-
fully whether to terminate a
poorly performing employee
or provide him or her addi-
tional counseling.

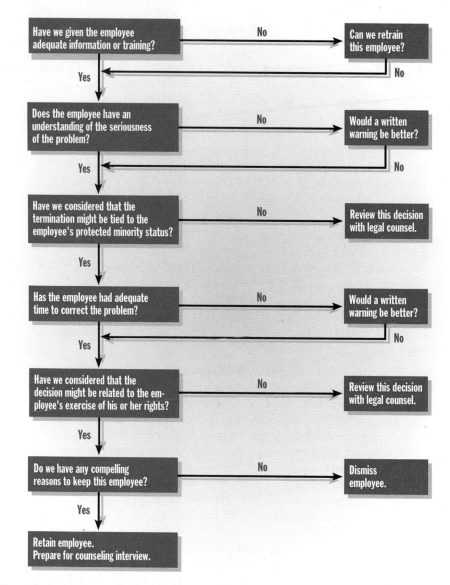

Source: Reprinted by permission of the publisher, from Steve Buckman, "To Fire or Not to Fire?" *Supervisory Management* February 1986, p. 31. Copyright © 1986 American Management Association, New York. All rights reserved.

mance must be maintained. Thus, a firing can also be valuable because it may increase the productivity of employees who are not fired.

Termination usually takes place only after the substandard performer has been offered the types of help described throughout this chapter. In general, every feasible alternative—such as retraining and counseling—should be attempted before termination. A manager must also accumulate substantial written documentation of substandard performance. Appropriate documentation includes performance appraisals, special memos to the file about performance problems, and statements describing the help offered the employee. Exhibit 16-6 summarizes the steps in making a termination decision.

If these steps are not documented, the employer can be accused of wrongful discharge. **Wrongful discharge** is the firing of an employee for arbitrary or

422

wrongful discharge
The firing of an employee
for arbitrary or unfair
reasons.

unfair reasons. Many employers have been sued for wrongfully discharging employees. Court rulings in the last decade have increasingly prohibited the termination of employees when good faith, fair dealing, and implied contracts have been at issue.

Another way of looking at wrongful discharge is to consider the idea that employees have certain rights in relation to preserving their jobs. According to **due process,** employees must be given a fair hearing before being dismissed. This includes the right to progressive discipline and the right to present one's side of the story to management.

In recognition of the delicate human relations and legal problems involved in firing poor performers, some firms turn to specialists to help them avoid lawsuits from dismissed workers. Others firms look to lower the risk of retaliation through employee violence. A consultant who specializes in firing people for other companies admits the work is difficult. In his words:

> It's not like, "Oh man, I get to fire someone today." It's the hardest thing because you're actually changing someone's life.[26]

After an employee is fired, the manager must deal with the questions and feelings of the group members within the unit. Often these people were close friends of the terminated employee. Be honest with the other employees, but do not bad-mouth the terminated worker. Avoid being too specific to avoid a lawsuit about defamation of character. Emphasize how performance factors led to the discharge. Allow coworkers to express their feelings and concerns in a group setting or one-on-one with you, the manager.[27]

The advice presented in the accompanying Management Advisor in Action should help managers avoid legal problems sometimes associated with firing substandard performers. Dismissing employees during a downsizing is different because positions are eliminated rather than firing people because of poor performance. However, managers must still guard against charges of including people on the downsizing list based on job discrimination.

due process
In relation to employee rights, giving a worker a fair hearing before he or she is dismissed.

Manager *in Action*
Labor Attorney
Elizabeth J. du Fresne

Labor attorney Elizabeth J. du Fresne, of Steel Hector & Davis, lectures regularly on the subject of terminating an incompetent employee. She offers blunt advice on how to get rid of ineffective employees while staying out of court. "Do it with a pure heart," she says. "Your reason for firing this individual is not because of their gender, race, national origin, religion, age, pregnancy, marital status, or disability." (These are categories covered by discrimination laws.)

"It's their competency, productivity, or attitude that was not as significant a problem in the past as it is now. It's because they have driven out one too many persons who were better than they were, and you can't afford to lose another valued employee," she said.

With one out of every five lawsuits in the

(continued)

423

United States being brought by a worker—and verdicts often reaching into the millions—managers need to arm themselves against the possibility of a multimillion-dollar jury verdict, she says. Du Fresne advises employers to be succinct and specific about why a worker is being asked to leave the company. Vague explanations are more likely to lead workers to believe they were discriminated against.

The core of du Fresne's advice: Before you fire, make sure you have a documented case of ongoing incompetence that will stand up before a tough jury should the employee decide to sue. If it looks like one person is being singled out and fired, they're more likely to be successful in a discrimination case.

"There's nothing that undercuts the defense of a termination case more than saying, 'This person did not do what I told them to do, so I fired them,'" du Fresne said. "They'll bring in five, or 10, or 15 other people who have had exactly the same scenario and have not been fired."

A common employer mistake is to fire someone on the spot. "It could be the most expensive staffing decision you make that year, or any other year," she said. But there's one exception to the rule of waiting to make a case: If an employee threatens violence, they need to be removed from the workplace immediately, du Fresne said. In that case, it's best to suspend them pending an investigation, then do the termination in a letter.

Another no-no is blabbing about an attempt to document poor performance. "Could anything be stupider that to tell anyone you're building a case?" du Frense asked. "Think about every aspect of how it will sound to working folk and retired folk on a jury. You'll sound like a mean, vindictive person who took this person's job away by nitpicking."

If a poorly performing employee has been getting nothing but excellent reviews from a soft-hearted boss, it's time to document what's been going on all those years. "We do a written warning which reflects all the things that we never got our act together to put in the file," she said. "The written warning that will stand up to a jury's scrutiny should offer one last chance. I want them to understand that their job's on the line. Your task is to truly give them every last chance."

It's important to give the appearance of fairness at every step. The person who investigates the case internally—and, if necessary, signs the termination letter—should be a person who's perceived as fair and equitable. It's essential that the person who signs the termination letter is willing to go to the witness stand if necessary to defend the company's actions.

Companies can avoid most of these problems by settling up with the employee at the time of termination, du Fresne said. Allow him or her to resign rather than be fired. Work out arrangements that won't cost money: a neutral or vaguely positioned letter of recommendation. If possible, ask them to sign a release saying they won't sue.

"As reluctant as we all are to give money to the employee who has driven us crazy, now is the time to bring closure, if you can. Settlements done in the course of a termination are notably cheaper than settlements done in the course of litigation."

Source: Adapted from Ellen Forman, "Faulty Firing Can Get You Burned," Knight Ridder news story, March 30, 1998.

SUMMARY OF KEY POINTS

 Identify factors contributing to poor performance.
Job performance is ineffective when productivity is below a standard considered acceptable at a given time.

Ineffective performers consume considerable managerial time. The causes of poor job performance can be rooted in the employee, the job, the manager, or the company. Usually, ineffective performance is caused by a combination of several factors.

Describe the control model for managing ineffective performers.

The approach to improving ineffective performance presented in this chapter is a controlling process. It consists of eight steps that should be followed in sequence: (1) define performance standards, (2) detect deviation from acceptable performance, (3) define and assess the cause, (4) confront the substandard performer, (5) set improvement goals, (6) select and implement an action plan for improvement, (7) re-evaluate performance after a time interval, and (8) continue or discontinue the action plan.

Corrective actions for ineffective performers are divided into managerial actions and techniques, and organizational programs. Managerial actions include close supervision and corrective discipline. Organizational programs include career counseling, outplacement, and job redesign.

Know what is required to coach and constructively criticize employees.

Coaching and constructive criticism are useful approaches to managing poor performers. Coaching consists of giving advice and encouragement. Most coaching includes constructive criticism. Skill is required to coach ineffective performers and criticize them constructively. Another approach to coaching is to hire a business (or executive) coach to assist in elevating performance, particularly with respect to interpersonal relationships.

Understand how to discipline employees.

The controlling process may also call for discipline. Summary discipline is the immediate discharge of an employee who commits a serious offense. Corrective discipline gives employees a chance to correct their behavior before punishment is applied. Both the manager and the employee share the responsibility for solving the performance problem. Corrective discipline involves counseling.

The major type of corrective discipline is called progressive discipline. It represents a step-by-step application of corrective discipline. The manager confronts the ineffective performer about the problem and then coaches him or her. If the employee's performance does not improve, the employee is given a written warning. If this fails, the employee is suspended or given a disciplinary layoff. The next step is discharge.

The red-hot-stove rule refers to administering discipline right away. The situation should include a warning; consistent, impersonal punishment should be administered immediately after the infraction is committed.

Punishment can help an organization because many employees believe that a rule violator should be punished. Also, punishment emphasizes that certain types of misconduct will not be tolerated.

Develop an approach to dealing with difficult people, including cynics.

When dealing with difficult people, stay focused on the issue at hand, and take the problem professionally, not personally. Also use humor, tact, and diplomacy, while giving recognition and attention. Listen to the difficult person and confront the person about how you size up the situation. Also, explain the importance of teamwork. One approach to dealing with cynics is to ignore cynical comments. However, the cynic might also be challenged to support the basis for his or her cynicism.

Explain the recommended approach to terminating employees.

Termination should take place only after the substandard performer has been offered the type of help built into the control model. Documentation of poor performance is required. Coworkers should be offered a performance-based explanation of why the substandard performer was terminated.

KEY TERMS AND PHRASES

QUESTIONS

1. What is the link between managing ineffective performers and organizational productivity?
2. Which levels (or types of) managers are the most likely to be involved with managing ineffective performers?
3. How can a person prevent himself or herself from becoming a substandard performer?
4. What negative consequences to the organization do cynics create?
5. In what way does having a highly competent mentor make it less important to hire a business coach?
6. The Management Advisor in Action suggested what employers should do to effectively terminate an employee. How might an employee use the same information to protect against being terminated unjustly?
7. Why should management be willing to rehabilitate employees through an employee assistance program when so many workers have been downsized in recent years?

SKILL-BUILDING EXERCISE 16-A: Data on Ineffective Performance

Each student asks an experienced manager what he or she thinks is the most frequent cause of ineffective performance. Relate the manager's answer to Exhibit 16-1. During class, students later make about a one-minute presentation of their findings. Look for trends, especially the most frequent cause of ineffective performance revealed by the research.

INTERNET SKILL-BUILDING EXERCISE: Can This Employee Be Salvaged?

To learn more about when employee termination is advisable or inadvisable, visit the Business Resource Center's Web site at www.morebusiness.com. Check out their free interactive questionnaire (Choose Templates, Business Checklists), which asks a manager 29 questions to determine if salvaging an ineffective performer is feasible. The site is also helpful to managers and future managers because it offers guidelines on wrongful discharge. You might ask the 29 questions about an ineffective performer you have observed in action, including a present or former coworker. Readers with supervisory experience might answer the questions about a former or present direct report.

CASE PROBLEM 16-A: Revenge Has Its Price

Caryn Andersen was the senior secretary to the regional vice-president of an insurance company, a position she had for six years. In Caryn's contacts with other regional offices she discovered that her counterparts had been promoted to executive assistants. Caryn wanted to be an executive assistant because the position would give her more status, salary, and vacation time. She approached Dana Leonard, her manager, and requested a promotion to executive assistant.

Dana liked the idea, and asked Caryn to draft a job description that would increase her level of responsibilities, including work on special assignments. Dana reviewed the description with Caryn, contacted the headquarters human resource department, and secured the reclassification. After the reclassification, Caryn could not understand why Dana was placing more demands on her time and requesting that she accomplish more things independently. Dana in turn could not understand why Caryn was blocking his requests because it was she who had asked for the promotion.

Caryn would openly complain, "What good is it to be an executive assistant and get more vacation time? Every time I turn around, Dana has some new project for me. I never get to take the vacation time I have." Caryn soon began bad-mouthing Dana. She would answer his calls and say such things as, "I don't know where Dana is. He never tells me anything anymore."

426

Caryn's disgruntlement continued, and she stopped providing Dana with the information she was supposed to. Twice when Dana asked her to set up a meeting at a designated time, she neglected to inform the people who were supposed to attend. When Dana returned after waiting futilely for the others, Caryn denied telling Dana that she had set up the meeting.

On one occasion, Caryn scheduled several people to meet with Dana but did not tell him about it until the last minute when a group suddenly appeared at his office. Caryn insisted to Dana, "I told you this meeting was scheduled. Don't you listen to me anymore?" Her rhetorical question was asked in front of the guests who had arrived for the meeting.

Caryn insisted that all the information sent to Dana had to be reviewed by her first, and that e-mail messages for Dana be sent to her for forwarding. Even hard-copy items were plucked from Dana's in-box and reviewed. Caryn would then openly pass judgment on the contents. Once she told a manager reporting to Dana that a promotion for one of her people would most certainly be approved by Dana. Yet Dana had not yet read the request.

One day the company president telephoned Dana, and Caryn took the opportunity to describe Dana's inability to run his operation. Upon speaking to Dana, the president said, "Muzzle her or fire her. I don't care which." Later that day,

Dana confronted Caryn: "Ever since your promotion, your performance and attitude have deteriorated. Worse yet, your loyalty to me and the organization have vanished. You wanted a promotion to executive assistant. You wanted all the advantages that went along with the position.

"Two things you didn't take into account. First, in order to attain that level, we expected a higher caliber of work. Not only did you not give us that, your performance deteriorated. Second, your constant harping about my work amounts to insubordination. I am recommending that you be demoted to an entry-level position in the staff support (central clerical pool) center. After one year of good performance, you may reapply for the position of senior secretary."

Caryn was stunned. She left for home for the day to decide on her options.

Discussion Questions

1. How might Dana have done a more effective job of managing Caryn as an ineffective performer?
2. What factors contributed most strongly to Caryn's ineffective performance?
3. Would Dana have been justified in firing Caryn when he found out that she told the president that Dana was having difficulty running his operation? Why or why not?

CASE PROBLEM 16-C: Purging the Old Guard

Hitech Corporation is a telecommunications company offering a variety of services and products throughout the United States. The company provides local and long-distance telephone service, cellular telephone service, wireless transmission of electronic data, and cable television. Hitech also sells hardware, including wired and cellular telephones, and personal digital assistants. The company has been a regulated, local telephone company for 75 years. Ten years ago Hitech made the transition to starting and acquiring nonregulated businesses such as cellular telephone services and teleconferencing.

Diane Preston, the Hitech CEO, was a key factor in moving Hitech from a traditional telephone company to a modern telecommunications corporation. Hitech has shown improved earnings for 20 consecutive quarters. Yet Preston and the executive vice-president, Rich Roncone, were not satisfied with the company's progress. As Preston explained during a meeting with her top-management team, "The stockholders are moderately satisfied with our earnings, and the media has been appreciative. But I'm not happy about our return on investment.

And I'm outright annoyed with our level of customer service.

"Too many company veterans still think we are a regulated monopoly that doesn't have to please the customer. They have the attitude that if the customers don't like the telephone service, let them create their own telephone system. Unfortunately, there are now four competitive telephone companies in our market from which the customer can choose."

Roncone then volunteered a comment: "Diane, I think the problem runs even deeper with some of the old guard. They are just not buying into our new vision of a world-class telecommunications company. They still think of us as 'the local telephone company.' Unfortunately, their perception is about 10 years behind the times."

Preston told the group, "I agree with Rich's analysis of employees who are not buying into our vision. The same employees are precisely those who don't get the point about competition. My job is to move the company forward. I'm losing my patience.

"Any manager, supervisor, or technician who keeps thinking like the old guard shouldn't have a job with us. I want all the people who are holding the company back to be out of here in three months. Put them at the top of the list in the next downsizing."

Another member at the meeting said, "Diane, you mean you want us to lay off people just because their thinking is behind the times?"

Preston responded, "The alternatives you have are to get people to update their attitudes or to get them out of the company."

Discussion Questions

1. Should the employees who still look upon Hitech as a regulated monopoly be considered ineffective performers? Explain.

2. What can the Hitech top-management team do to change the attitudes of those who still think of the company as a regulated monopoly?

3. Would dismissing people as Preston suggests be an act of wrongful discharge?

ENDNOTES

1. Adapted and excerpted from Jessica Guynn, "Bullying Behavior Affects Morale as Well as the Bottom Line," Knight Ridder story, November 2, 1998.
2. Sandra L. Robinson and Rebecca J. Bennett, "A Typology of Deviant Workplace Behaviors: A Multidimensional Scaling Study," *Academy of Management Journal*, April 1995, p. 555; Jane Easter Bahls, "Drugs in the Workplace," *HRMagazine*, February 1998, p. 82.
3. Phil Ebersole, "American System Abandons Workers, Needs Overhaul," Rochester, New York, *Democrat and Chronicle*, July 1, 1990, p. F1.
4. Brenda Paik Sunoo, "This Employee May Be Loafing. Can You Tell? Should You Care?" *Personnel Journal*, December 1996, pp. 54–62.
5. Michael R. Manning, Joyce S. Osland, and Asbjorn Osland, "Work-Related Consequences of Smoking Cessation," *Academy of Management Journal*, September 1989, p. 606.
6. John R. Hollenbeck, Daniel R. Iglen, and Suzanne M. Crampton, "Lower Back Disability in Occupational Settings: A Review of the Literature from a Human Resource Management Perspective," *Personnel Psychology*, Summer 1992, p. 247.
7. Charlene Marmer Solomon, "The Secret's Out: How to Handle the Truth of Workplace Romance," *Workforce*, July 1998, p. 43.
8. Jean-François Manzoni and Jean-Louis Barsoux, "The Set-Up-to-Fail Syndrome," *Harvard Business Review*, March–April 1998, pp. 101–113.
9. Harvey A. Hornstein, *Brutal Bosses and Their Prey* (New York: G.P. Putnam's Sons, 1996); www.myboss.com (accessed January 30, 1999).
10. Sandra L. Robinson and Anne M. O'Leary-Kelly, "Monkey See, Monkey Do: The Influence of Work Groups on the Antisocial Behavior of Employees," *Academy of Management Journal*, December 1998, pp. 658–672.
11. Rebecca Mann, *Behavior Mismatch: How to Manage "Problem" Employees Whose Actions Don't Match Your Expectations* (New York: AMACOM, 1993).
12. Dominic Bencivenga, "Dealing with the Dark Side," *HRMagazine*, January 1999, p. 50.
13. Kenneth H. Blanchard, "How to Turn Around Department Performance," *Supervisory Management*, March 1992, p. 3.
14. James Waldroop and Timothy Butler, "The Executive as Coach," *Harvard Business Review*, November–December 1996, p.111.
15. Marilyn J. Darling, "Coaching People through Difficult Times," *HRMagazine*, November 1994, p. 72.
16. "Executive Coaching in High Demand," *HR Fact Finder*, December 1998, p. 6.
17. Mildred L. Culp, "Business Coaches Teach Techniques for Success," *WorkWise®* syndicated column, October 25, 1998.
18. Gail A. Ball, Linda Klebe Trevino, and Henry P. Sims, Jr., "Just and Unjust Punishment: Influence on Subordinate Performance and Citizenship," *Academy of Management Journal*, April 1994, pp. 300–301.
19. Kenneth D. Butterfield, Linda Klebe Trevino, and Gail A. Ball, "Punishment form the Manager's Perspective: A Grounded Investigation and Inductive Model," *Academy of Management Journal*, December 1996, pp. 1493.
20. Marilyn Wheeler, *Problem People at Work* (New York: St. Martin's Griffin, 1995).
21. "Help! I'm Surrounded by Difficult People," *Working Smart*, March 25, 1991, p. 2.
22. Sam Deep and Lyle Sussman, *What to Say to Get What You Want* (Reading, MA: Addison-Wesley, 1991).
23. "Fighting off Bullies," *WorkingSMART*, October 1997, p. 1.
24. James W. Dean, Jr., Pamela Brandes, and Ravi Dharwadkar, "Organizational Cynicism," *Academy of Management Review*, April 1998, pp. 341–352.
25. "Shut Down a Cynic," *WorkingSmart*, September 1997, p. 1.
26. Martha Irvine, "Terminator Consultants Hired So They Can Fire," Associated Press story, November 2, 1998.
27. Robert McGarvey, "After the Fire," *Entrepreneur*, September 1995, p. 80.

Chapter Seventeen

Jennifer Johnson is now the principal strategist for Johnson & Co. in Santa Cruz, California. "I was a corporate warrior for about 15 years," says Johnson. "When I first left college, I immediately began working 80-hour weeks in my first job at Novell in Provo, Utah." As a 22-year-old editor, she turned the company's in-house newsletter into an international consumer magazine that Novell sold three years later to the McGraw-Hill Companies for $10 million.

Johnson recalls nights when she would stay at the office until 2 A.M., and was back in the office by 8 o'clock the next morning. "I realized it was the dues-paying time of my life and I actually thrived on the pace," Johnson admits. After she took a job in advertising at another firm, got married, and had children, the pace became dizzying. She vividly remembers her breaking point 19 months ago when life and work clashed in the extreme. "My husband, Scott, who headed the marketing function of one of 3Com's international business units, was returning from a trip to Japan. The plan was for me to hand off the kids to him at the airport, and then I was going to catch a plane for the East Coast." It turns out her husband's plane was 20 minutes late. The moment he arrived, she threw the children to him and sprinted to her own plane, luggage in tow.

In flight and exhausted, Johnson found herself writing a resignation letter. "I was laughing out loud as I wrote it

OBJECTIVES

After studying this chapter and doing the exercises, you should be able to:

 Identify techniques for improving work habits and time management.

 Identify techniques for reducing procrastination.

 Understand the nature of stress, including its consequences.

 Explain how stress can be managed effectively.

Enhancing Personal Productivity and Managing Stress

because it was so obviously what I needed to do," she says. Johnson then started her own company—a virtual marketing organization that teams 17 contractors, mostly women, from across the country. Many of them were as desperate to balance their lives as she was. "I saw a lot of women who were forced to make the choice of either working or taking care of their families because their companies wouldn't be flexible," says Johnson. "I'm now seeing a world in which employees, after being downsized and rightsized, are turning the tables and they're *my-sizing* their jobs."[1]

The former corporate warrior just described, who started her own firm, illustrates the relationship between work habits and stress. As her workload became overwhelming, her stress level became so elevated that she approached burnout. Only by taking the radical step of switching careers was she able to escape a stress-provoking job situation. The same woman might soon find self-employment overwhelming unless she develops the right work habits and time-management practices to get more work done in less time.

In this chapter we describe methods for both improving productivity and managing stress, because the two are as interlocked as nutrition and health. If you are well organized, you will avoid much of the negative stress that stems from feeling that your work and life are out of control. If your level of stress is about right, you will be able to concentrate better on your work and be more productive.

The emphasis in this final chapter of the book is about managing yourself rather than managing other people or managing a business. Unless you have your work under control, and effectively manage stress, it is unlikely you can be an effective manager or leader.

IMPROVING YOUR WORK HABITS AND TIME MANAGEMENT

Identify techniques for improving work habits and time management.

High personal productivity leads to positive outcomes such as higher income, more responsibility, and recognition. Furthermore, in an era of work streamlining and downsizings based on company consolidations, the demand for high productivity among managerial workers has never been higher. Productivity enhancers, such as daily planners, are selling at a record rate. High job productivity is also important because it allows you to devote more worry-free time to your personal life. In addition, high productivity helps reduce the stress experienced when a person's job is out of control.

Here we describe improving productivity by improving work habits and time management. In the next section productivity improvement is approached from the perspective of reducing procrastination.

DEVELOP A MISSION, GOALS, AND A STRONG WORK ETHIC   A major starting point in becoming a better organized and more productive person is to have a purpose and values that propel you toward being productive. Assume that a person says, "My mission in life is to become an outstanding office supervisor and a caring, constructive spouse and parent." The mission serves as a compass to direct that person's activities (such as getting done on time) to developing a reputation that will lead to promotion to supervisor. Goals are more specific than mission statements, and support the mission statement, but the effect is the same. For example, the person in question might set a goal one day to respond to 75 different customer inquiries that have accumulated on the

Internet by the end of the day. Accomplishing that amount of work today would be one more step toward being promoted to supervisor.

Closely related to establishing goals is to have a strong **work ethic**—a firm belief in the dignity and value of work. Developing a strong work ethic may lead to even higher productivity than goal setting alone. For example, one might set the goal of earning a high income. It would lead to some good work habits, but not necessarily to a high commitment to quality. A person with a strong work ethic believes in quality, is highly motivated, and minimizes time-wasting activities.

CLEAN UP YOUR WORK AREA AND SORT OUT YOUR TASKS   People sometimes become inefficient because their work area is messy. They waste time looking for things and neglect important papers. So to get started improving personal productivity, clean up your work area and sort out what tasks you need to accomplish. Cleaning up your work area includes your briefcase, your file of telephone numbers, your hard drive, and your e-mail files. Having loads of e-mail messages stacked in your Inbox, Sent, and Deleted files can easily lead to overlooking important new messages. Weeding out your mailing list is also important. Ask to be removed from the distribution of paper and e-mail that is of no value. Rebel against being *spammed*.

PREPARE A TO-DO LIST AND ASSIGN PRIORITIES   A to-do list lies at the heart of every time-management system. In addition to writing down tasks you need to do, assign priorities to them. A simple categorization, such as top priority versus low priority, works well for most people. In general, take care of top-priority tasks before low-priority ones. There are so many things to do on any job that some very low-priority items may never get done. Keep your to-do list on a desk calendar or a large tablet or in your computer. A word processing file may suffice, but more advanced software for work scheduling is also available. Small slips of paper in various locations are distracting and tend to get misplaced.

Many workers today use daily planners to serve as a to-do list. A planner typically divides the day into 15-minute chunks and also leaves room for the daily to-do list. Some planning systems are linked to a person's mission, thus giving an extra impetus to accomplishing tasks. No matter how elaborate the system that incorporates the humble to-do list, it will not boost productivity unless the items are referred to frequently. An exception is that some well-organized people plan their to-do list in their head. As they move through the day, they keep working the list.

Taking care of a small, easy-to-do task first—such as getting a refill for a ballpoint pen—has a hidden value. It tends to be relaxing because it gives you the emotional lift of having accomplished at least one item on your list. Also, accomplishing small tasks helps reduce stress.

STREAMLINE YOUR WORK   The most important new work habit and management principle is **work streamlining**—eliminating as much low-value work as possible and concentrating on activities that add value for customers or clients. To streamline work, justify whether every work procedure, memo, report, meeting, or ceremonial activity is contributing value to the firm. Group luncheon meetings away from the office might be cut in half, giving staff members more

work ethic
A firm belief in the dignity and value of work.

work streamlining
Eliminating as much low-value work as possible and concentrating on activities that add value for customers or clients.

431

EXHIBIT 17-1

Ways to Prevent and Overcome Time Wasting

Wasted time is a major productivity drain, so it pays to search for time wasters in your work activities. The following list suggests remedies for some of the major time wasters in the workplace.

1. Use a time log for two weeks to track time wasters.
2. Minimize daydreaming on the job by forcing yourself to concentrate.
3. Avoid the computer as a diversion from work, such as sending jokes back and forth to network members, playing video games, and checking out recreational Web sites during working hours.
4. Batch tasks together such as returning phone calls or responding to e-mail messages. For example, in most jobs it is possible to be productive by reserving two or three 15-minute periods per day for taking care of e-mail correspondence.
5. Socialize on the job just enough to build your network. Chatting with coworkers is a major productivity drain and one of the reasons so many managers work at home part of the time when they have analytical work to get done.
6. Be prepared for meetings, such as having a clear agenda and sorting through the documents you will be referring to. Make sure electronic equipment is in working order before attempting to use it during the meeting.

7. Keep track of important names, places, and things, to avoid wasting time searching for them.
8. Set a time limit for tasks after you have done them once or twice.
9. Prepare a computer template for letters and computer documents that you send frequently. (The template is essentially a form letter, especially with respect to the salutation and return address.)
10. When you only have to provide routine information, telephone people before and after normal working hours, leaving a message on their voice mail. (This saves conversation time.)
11. Avoid perfectionism, which leads you to keep redoing a project. Let go and move on to another project.
12. Make use of bits of time; for instance, 5 minutes between appointments. Invest those 5 minutes in sending a business e-mail, or revise your to-do list. (Note the exception to the batch principle.)
13. Minimize procrastination, the number-one time waster for most people.

Source: Suggestions 4, 5, and 6 are based on Stephen R. Covey with Hyrum Smith, "What if You Could Chop an Hour from Your Day for Things that Matter Most?" *USA Weekend*, January 22–24, 1999, pp. 4–5.

time during the day to conduct urgent work. Another example of work streamlining would be to decrease the number of holiday cards sent to work associates. What can you do to streamline schoolwork?

Work streamlining is a fruitful activity because almost every firm has some extremely low-value activity that could be eliminated. Sometimes these low-value activities are antiquated and useless. According to consultant Judith Bardwick, until a few years ago IBM employees were assigned an activity they labeled "phone-mail police." The task required calling work phone numbers to ensure that voice-mail messages conformed to "IBM-speak." To be fair, not all phone-mail policing is without value. Employee voice-mail greetings that are unprofessional in tone could detract from the image of a highly professional organization like IBM.

Wal–Mart is another example of a company looking to eliminate low-value work. Employees are told: "If you are required to do something that you think is garbage, you have permission not to do it. If no one asks you 'Why aren't you doing that?' for a week, you have permission to go up two levels higher than your manager to explain why you're not doing it."[2]

WORK AT A STEADY PACE Although a dramatic show of energy (as in "pulling an all-nighter") is impressive, the steady worker tends to be more productive in the long run. The spurt employee creates many problems for management; the spurt student is in turmoil at examination time or when papers are due. Managers who expend the same amount of effort day by day tend to stay in control of their jobs. When a sudden problem or a good opportunity comes to their attention, they can fit it into their schedule.

Working at a steady pace often means always working rapidly. To be competitive most organizations require that work be accomplished rapidly. Consultant Price Pritchett advises, "So you need to operate with a strong sense of urgency. Accelerate in all aspects of your work, even if it means living with a few more ragged edges. Emphasize *action*. Don't bog down in endless preparation trying to get things perfect before you make a move. Sure, high quality is crucial, but it must come quickly. You can't sacrifice speed."[3]

MINIMIZE TIME WASTERS   An important strategy for improving personal productivity is to minimize time wasters. Each minute diverted from unproductive activity can be invested in productive work and can save you from working extra long hours. For example, if you decrease lengthy social lunches on work days, you can leave the office on time. Exhibit 17-1 presents a list of significant ways to reduce wasted time. Many of the other suggestions in this chapter can also help you save time directly or indirectly.

CONCENTRATE ON ONE TASK AT A TIME   Productive managers have a well-developed capacity to concentrate on the problem facing them at the moment, however engulfed they are with other obligations. Intense concentration leads to sharpened judgment and analysis and also decreases the chances of making major errors. Another useful byproduct of concentration is reduced absentmindedness. The person who concentrates on the task at hand has less chance of forgetting what he or she intended.

An assist to concentrating on the task at hand is to use *performance cues*, or items you should be concentrating on when under pressure.[4] For example, when facing a difficult customer your performance cue might be a smile. Say to yourself, "I must smile now." Smiling is effective because it helps reduce the difficult customer's hostility. Another performance cue might be taking notes when major points come up in your conversation with a group member. Taking notes forces you to concentrate intently on the message sender. Your performance cue is, "When she says something of special importance, I will jot down the idea on paper."

CONCENTRATE ON HIGH-OUTPUT TASKS   To become more productive on the job or in school, concentrate on tasks in which superior performance could have a large payoff. For a manager, a high-output task would be to develop a strategic plan for the department. For a student, a high-output task would be to think of a creative idea for an independent study project. Expending your work effort on high-output items is analogous to looking for a good return on investment for your money. The high-output strategy also follows the Pareto Principle, described in Chapter 7.

DO CREATIVE AND ROUTINE TASKS AT DIFFERENT TIMES   To improve productivity, organize your work so you do not shift between creative and routine tasks. For many people it is best to work first on creative tasks because they require more mental energy than routine tasks. A minority of people prefer to get minor paperwork and e-mail chores out of the way so they can get to the pleasure of doing creative tasks. Whichever order you choose, it is impor-

433

tant not to interrupt creative (or high-output) tasks with routine activities such as sorting mail or rearranging the desk.

STAY IN CONTROL OF PAPERWORK, E-MAIL, AND VOICE MAIL

No organization today can accomplish its mission unless paperwork, including the electronic variety, receives appropriate attention. If you handle paperwork improperly, your job may get out of control. Once your job is out of control, the stress level will increase greatly. Invest a small amount of time in paperwork and electronic mail every day. The best time to take care of routine correspondence is when you are at less than peak efficiency but not overfatigued. Reserve your high-energy periods for high-output tasks.

Avoid becoming a paper shuffler or frequently re-reading e-mail messages. The ideal is to handle a piece of paper or an e-mail message only once. When you pick up a hard-copy memo or read an electronic one, take some action: throw it away or delete it, route it to someone else, write a short response to the sender, or flag it for action later. Loose ends of time can be used to take care of the flagged memos.

Staying in control of voice-mail and answering machine messages is also important to stay productive. Stacked up voice-mail messages will often detract from your ability to concentrate on other work. Not returning voice-mail messages promptly also creates the problem of perceived rudeness and poor customer service. Disciplining yourself to answer voice-mail messages in batches, as described in Exhibit 17-1, will help you manage these messages productively.

MAKE EFFECTIVE USE OF OFFICE TECHNOLOGY   Many managerial workers are able to boost their productivity by making effective use of office technology. Yet the productivity gains are not inevitable. For example, the U.S. Labor Department is having difficulty finding the productivity gains associated with using PCs in the office.[5] Just because a person can receive rapidly transmitted e-mail messages from all over the world, and can produce exquisite pie charts, increased sales and decreased costs do not always follow. Boosting your personal productivity is contingent upon choosing equipment that truly adds to productivity and does not drain too much time for purposes of learning and bringing it back and forth to the repair shop.

A major reason many workers do not achieve productivity gains with information technology is that they do not invest the time saved in other productive activity. If sending a batch of e-mail messages instead of postal mail saves you two hours, you will only experience a productivity gain if the two hours are then invested in a task with a tangible output, such as searching for a lower-cost supplier. Another problem is that some workers will duplicate their activities such as telephoning another person to find out if they were able to retrieve a file sent by e-mail.

Five suggestions are presented next for using technology devices to boost productivity in the office environment.

1. *Use personal information manager (PIM) software to organize your efforts.* The purpose of such software is to help you organize your work, following standard principles of time management. PIM software usually combines the functions of an address book, appointment book, alarm clock, to-do list, telephone dialer, and notepad. Among such software is *Lotus Organizer*, *Sharkware Pro*, *Sidekick*, and *Outlook 98*. Franklin Electronic Publishers offers a credit-card-

size organizer called the Rex PC Companion for those who adore miniaturization.

2. *Use a palm-size computer as your personal digital assistant (PDA).* Among the functions of the personal digital assistant are to store thousands of addresses, send e-mail, serve as a pocket calendar, record memos, and track expenses. You choose an application by tapping a pencil-like stylus on a touch screen. The keyboard is on screen and accessed by the stylus. Several palm-size computers are equipped with handwriting recognition systems. The palm-size computer can be synchronized with your desktop PC. Managerial and sales workers who spend a lot of time away from the office are those most likely to receive a productivity boost from the personal digital assistant. The Palm III produced by 3Com is the most popular PDA.

3. *Use a laptop computer when away from the office.* Large numbers of field workers carry laptops with them on business trips so they can access data, perform calculations, and make graphic presentations. A laptop can also boost productivity because you can word-process reports and memos in the field instead of writing them by hand then typing the report back at the office. However, many people experience difficulty typing with such small keyboards and a small screen. In contrast, some workers enjoy their laptops so much they run them by electricity back at the office.

4. *Use an interactive pager that enables you to transmit short text messages to other pagers, e-mail addresses, and faxes.* Transmitting computerized voices to telephones is also possible. The productivity gains from interactive pagers, regular pagers, and cell telephones stem from being able to receive and disseminate information rapidly. For example, a field technician in a remote location might be signaled to take care of an urgent customer need, thus saving an account. Two interactive pagers are the Motorola Pagewriter 2000 and the Research in Motion Inter@ctive Pager.

5. *Use groupware, or simply e-mail, for all members of a team to contribute to editing a team report.* Instead of calling one or two meetings to haggle over rewriting the report, team or group members insert their suggestions electronically, directly onto the document. The team leader synthesizes the comments and then resubmits the edited document for final approval. This method also saves an enormous amount of clerical support time in typing and retyping hardcopy versions of the document.

The above devices are attractive and intriguing. It is also important to know when simple mechanical or handwritten procedures are faster than office technology. For example, the simple 3×5 index card remains a powerful low-technology way of preparing and executing a to-do list. Managers and professionals who move from one location to another may find it a time waster to access a computer just to check their daily list. Even a palm-size computer can be more disruptive than simply glancing at an index card attached to a pocket calendar. A complaint some people have about large 8×11 planners is they are cumbersome to lug around unless you are carrying an attaché case. Also, they become dogeared rapidly.

Bill Marriott, the CEO of Marriott International, exemplifies a successful executive who knows when low technology is the method of choice. He keeps his schedule, usually drawn up three months ahead in collaboration with an administrative assistant, on a 3×5 index card that he carries in his left breast pocket. He glances at it several items a day and winces when he gets 15 minutes off track.[6]

peak performance
A mental state in which maximum results are achieved with minimum effort.

PRACTICE THE MENTAL STATE OF PEAK PERFORMANCE   To achieve maximum potential producivity one must transcend ordinary levels of concentration and devotion to duty. That occurs in **peak performance,** a mental state in which maximum results are achieved with mimum effort. Peak performers are mentally calm and physically at ease when challenged by difficult problems. They are intensely focused and involved, much like they would be in playing the best tennis games of their lives. You may have experienced the state of peak performance when totally involved with a problem or task. At that moment, nothing else seems to exist.

To achieve peak performance, you must continually work toward being mentally calm and physically at ease. Concentrate intensely, but not so much that you choke. In addition to frequent practice, peak performance can be achieved through visualization. In *visualization* you develop a mental image of how you would act and feel at the point of peak performance. For example, imagine yourself making a flawless presentation to top-level management about the contributions of your department. Psychologist Charles Garfield observed that people who achieve peak performance typically have an important mission in life—such as building a top-quality company.[7]

TAKE POWER NAPS   A fast-growing trend for increasing personal productivity is to take a *power nap*, a brief period of sleep of about 15 to 30 minutes designed to recharge the individual. Well-placed naps actually enhance rather than diminish productivity, and they are also an excellent stress reducer. You can combat procrastination by taking a brief nap before beginning an uncomfortable task.

According to one researcher, "The remarkable aspect of prophylactic napping, or napping in advance of an extended period of work, is that the benefits of the nap, even one of only 25 minutes duration, can be evident in performance hours afterward."[8] Naps can also prevent industrial disasters by overcoming grogginess before it leads to an accident such as the *Exxon Valdez* oil spill. Even better, with the proper amount of sleep, napping is much less necessary. According to the National Sleep Foundation, most adults need 8 hours of sleep to produce high-quality work. However, most adults average 6 hours and 57 minutes of sleep per night.[9] Again, individual differences are a major factor. Many successful people require less sleep, which allows them more time for work, life, and recreation.

In recognition of the importance of napping as a productivity booster and stress reducer, some firms offer napping areas for their employees.[10] Nevertheless, the organizational napper must use discretion in napping so as not to be perceived as sleeping on the job. Toward this end, some workers nap in their cars or in a storeroom during lunch break. In companies where the organization accepts such behavior, some employees nap with their heads resting on their desks or work tables during breaks.

PUT EXTRA EFFORT INTO MANAGING MULTIPLE PRIORITIES   A major time-management problem for employees is dealing with multiple demands placed on them from a variety of people. Clerical support personnel, for example, might support 10 workers, each of whom thinks he or she has a personal assistant. One approach to this problem is to let the people served know how you prioritize work. Among these priority systems are (a) first come first served, (b) giving top priority to work for major customers, and (c) giving top priority to work that goes to top-level management. The worker facing multiple demands can allocate certain times of the day or week to each assigned project. For example, Thursday morning is for budget preparation, and Monday afternoon is for processing expense account vouchers.

BUILD FLEXIBILITY INTO YOUR SYSTEM   A time-management system must allow some room for flexibility. How else could you handle unanticipated problems? If you work 50 hours per week, build in a few hours for taking care of emergencies. If your plan is too tight, delegate some tasks to others or work more hours. Perhaps you can find a quicker way to accomplish several of your tasks. Finally, to avoid staleness and stress, your schedule must allow sufficient time for rest and relaxation.

The Manager in Action presents an inside peek at the work habits of one of the best-known businesspersons of all time. As you will see, he would strongly endorse most of what you have read so far in this chapter.

UNDERSTANDING AND REDUCING PROCRASTINATION

The number-one time waster for most people is **procrastination,** the delaying of action for no good reason. Reducing procrastination pays substantial dividends in increased productivity, especially because speed can give a company a competitive advantage. Many people regard procrastination as a laughable weakness, particularly because procrastinators themselves joke about their problem. Yet procrastination has been evaluated as a profound, debilitating problem.[11] Exhibit 17-2 on page 439 gives you an opportunity to think about your own tendencies toward procrastination, so get to it without delay. Here we consider why people procrastinate, and what can be done about the problem.

Why People Procrastinate

People procrastinate for a many different reasons, with some of them being deep-rooted emotional problems, and others more superficial and related directly to the work. Here we look at six major reasons for procrastination.

First, some people fear failure or other negative consequences. As long as a person delays doing something of significance, he or she cannot be regarded as having performed poorly on the project. Other negative consequences include looking foolish in the eyes of others or developing a bad reputation. For instance, if a manager delays making an oral presentation, nobody will know whether he or she is an ineffective speaker.

Second, procrastination may stem from a desire to avoid uncomfortable, overwhelming, or tedious tasks.

Third, people frequently put off tasks that do not appear to offer a meaningful reward. Suppose you decide that your computer files need a thorough updating. Even though you know it should be done, having a completely updated directory might not be a particularly meaningful reward to you.

Fourth, some people dislike being controlled. When a procrastinator does not do things on time, he or she has successfully rebelled against being controlled by another person's time schedule.

Fifth, people sometimes are assigned tasks they perceive to be useless or needless, such as rechecking someone else's work. Rather than proceed with the trivial task, the individual procrastinates.

Identify techniques for reducing procrastination.

procrastination
The delaying of action for no good reason.

437

Manager *in Action*

Work Habits of the World's Richest Person

Many people have heard or read that the personal fortune of Microsoft Corp. Chairman Bill Gates (estimated at $100 billion for the year 2000) exceeds the gross domestic product of many nations, including Israel. Less well known about Gates is that his work habits contribute to his success as an executive. In addition to being the wealthiest person in the world, he is also considered to be one of the hardest-working businesspersons.

Bill Gates's work habits were scrutinized by a business magazine reporter who trailed him on a five-day business trip to India and South Africa. Sixteen-hour days were the norm for Gates, filled with customer meetings, audiences with heads of state, press interviews, photo sessions, speeches, and some autograph signing. Wedged in between were a few banquets at which Gates pushed his ideas, pep talks to local Microsoft workers, conferences with business partners, staged confabs with school children, and a few police-escorted motorcades.

Gates devotes about one-quarter of his work time each year to what he calls "evangelism"—trips to preach the Microsoft gospel. He measures his effectiveness by the number of events and meetings he can squeeze in. In reflecting on his 25,000-mile trip to India and South Africa, Gates said, "It was a great trip. The guys filled up my time really well."

A distinguishing characteristic about the Gates management style is how well he manages his time. Hardly a waking moment is squandered, whether he is roaming about as a high-tech ambassador, or back at headquarters plotting business strategy, or poring over tiny details of Microsoft's product-development efforts. In recent years Gates has also spent time helping build the argument that his company is not a monopoly. He has an almost macho attitude about his schedule, leaving only the tiniest cracks in the day for eating, chatting with people, or simply chilling out. What little spare time he did have on the trip in question he spent either catching up on his e-mail with a portable PC or hastily preparing for the next meeting.

During the trip he left no time for sightseeing other than what he could observe out the windows of the white Mercedes-Benzes that shuttled him between airports, hotels, and government offices. Nevertheless, Gates is intensely curious about the places he visits. He studies about each destination en route, reading books and magazine articles recommended by the heads of local subsidiaries. Once on the ground, he probes his escorts with endless questions, and concentrates intently on what they have to offer. These seemingly casual conversations often lead to direct action: Says Gates:

> I never realized that there are 14 distinct written and spoken languages in India. Now that I understand that, we're going to invest a whole lot more in localizing our products. And the raw software talent that you see there really grabs you. A billion people is a lot of people, and even though the country is really poor, there are a lot of talented people with world-class educations, and companies that are as forward-looking and capable as anywhere. I came back quite enthused about taking some of our software development overload here and moving it over there.

Recognizing that he is hero-worshipped at the company, Gates sets a vivid and pragmatic example of what he describes as a Microsoftian work ethic. His grueling schedule is just one not-so-subtle hint of what he expects from his employees. (A joke floats around Microsoft that the company has a flexible work schedule. You can work 16 hours a day, any days you choose.)

Gates always stays focused on the true purpose of his evangelical trips: to sell more software. Although he enjoyed meeting with the chiefs of state of South Africa and India, more important to Gates was conducting business. He held discussions with Indian government officials about the necessity of lowering taxes and import duties, enforcing stricter copyright laws, and modernizing the country's aging telecommunications infra-

structure. He also held business discussions with leading bankers in South Africa.

Commenting on the output of his trips, Gates said, "Believe me, I've got plenty to do already, so I wouldn't come on these trips if I didn't think I was getting something out of it that really helps Microsoft sell software."

Sources: Most of the facts presented are from Brent Schlender, "On the Road with *Chairman Bill*." Reprinted from the May 26,1997 issue of *Fortune* by special permission; copyright 1997, Time, Inc. Also included is information from Susan B. Garland, "A Tough Sell, But Not Impossible," *Business Week*, January 18, 1999, p. 44.

Sixth, a curious reason for procrastination is to achieve the stimulation and excitement that stems from rushing to meet a deadline. For example, some people enjoy fighting their way through traffic or running through an airline terminal so they can make an appointment or airplane flight barely on time. They appear to enjoy the rush of adrenaline, endorphins, and other hormones associated with hurrying.[12]

Circle yes or no for each item:

1. I usually do my best work under the pressure of deadlines.   Yes   No
2. Before starting a project, I go through such rituals as
   sharpening every pencil, straightening up my desk more
   than once, and discarding bent paper clips.   Yes   No
3. I crave the excitement of the "last minute rush."   Yes   No
4. I often think that if I delay something, it will go away, or
   the person who asked for it will forget about it.   Yes   No
5. I extensively research something before taking action,
   such as obtaining five different estimates before getting the
   brakes repaired on my car.   Yes   No
6. I have a great deal of difficulty getting started on most
   projects, even those I enjoy.   Yes   No
7. I keep waiting for the right time to do something, such
   as getting started on an important report.   Yes   No
8. I often underestimate the time needed to do a project,
   and say to myself, "I can do this quickly, so I'll wait until
   next week.   Yes   No
9. It is difficult for me to finish most projects or activities.   Yes   No
10. I have several favorite diversions or distractions that I
    use to keep me from doing something unpleasant.   Yes   No

                                                           Total yes responses ____

The greater the number of yes responses, the more likely it is that you have a serious procrastination problem. A score of 8, 9, or 10 strongly suggests that your procrastination is lowering your productivity.

EXHIBIT 17-2

Procrastination Tendencies

Approaches to Reducing and Controlling Procrastination

Procrastination often becomes a strong habit that is difficult to change. Nevertheless, the following strategies and tactics can be helpful in overcoming procrastination:

1. *Break the task down into smaller units.* By splitting a large task into smaller units, you can make a job appear less overwhelming. Subdividing the task is referred to as the "Swiss-cheese method" because you keep putting little holes into the overall task. This approach is useful, of course, only if the task can be done in small pieces.

2. *Make a commitment to others.* Your tendency to procrastinate on an important assignment may be reduced if you publicly state that you will get the job done by a certain time. You might feel embarrassed if you fail to meet your deadline.

3. *Reward yourself for achieving milestones.* A potent technique for overcoming any counterproductive behavior pattern is to give yourself a reward for progress toward overcoming the problem. Make your reward commensurate with the magnitude of the accomplishment.

4. *Calculate the cost of procrastination.* You can sometimes reduce procrastination by calculating its cost. Remind yourself, for example, that you might lose out on obtaining a high-paying job you really want if your résumé and cover letter are not ready on time. The cost of procrastination would include the difference in the salary between the job you do find and the one you really wanted. Another cost would be the loss of potential job satisfaction.

5. *Use subliminal messages about overcoming procrastination.* For example, software called *MindSet* flashes positive, reinforcing messages across your computer screen. The user can adjust the frequency and duration of the suggestions. The message can flash by subliminally (below the level of conscious awareness) or remain on screen for a few seconds. The antiprocrastination message reads: "My goals are obtainable. I am confident in my abilities. I make and keep deadlines." The same effect can be achieved by posting notes in your work and living areas, encouraging you to get something done by a particular time. For example, "The plan for recycling laser print cartridges is due September 15, and YOU CAN DO IT!!!!!"

6. *Counterattack.* Another way of combatting procrastination is to force yourself to do something uncomfortable or frightening. After you begin, you are likely to find that the task is not as onerous as you thought. Assume you have been delaying learning a foreign language even though you know it will help your career. You remember how burdensome it was studying another language in school. You grit your teeth and remove the cellophane from the audiocasette for the target language. After listening for five minutes, you discover that beginning to study a foreign language again is not nearly as bad as you imagined.

7. *Post a progress chart in your work area.* The time and activity charts presented in Chapter 7 can be applied to combating procrastination. As you chart your progress in achieving each step in a large project, each on-time accomplishment will serve as a reward, and each missed deadline will be self-punishing. The constant reminder of what needs to be accomplished by what date will sometimes prod you to minimize delays. Exhibit 17-3 presents a basic version of a chart for combating procrastination.

| Task to Be | Deadlines for Task Accomplishment | | | | | |
Accomplished	Jan 1	Jan 31	Feb 15	Feb 28	Mar 15	Mar 31
Expense reports	Did it					
Real estate estimates		Blew it				
Web site installed			One day late			
Replace broken furniture				Made it		
Plan office picnic					On time	
Collect delinquent account						Blew it

A Time and Activity Chart to Combat Procrastination
Charting key tasks and their deadlines, along with your performance in meeting the deadlines, can sometimes help overcome procrastination.

THE NATURE OF STRESS AND BURNOUT

Job stress, and its related condition, job burnout, have always been potential sources of discomfort and poor physical and mental health. In order to do an effective job of preventing and controlling stress, it is important to first understand the nature and causes of these conditions. A good starting point in understanding stress symptoms is to take the self-quiz presented in Exhibit 17-4. As used here, **stress** is the mental and physical condition that results from a perceived threat that cannot be dealt with readily. Stress is therefore an internal response to a state of activation. The stressed person is physically and mentally aroused. Stress will ordinarily occur in a threatening or negative situation, such as being fired. However, stress can also be caused by a positive situation, such as receiving a large cash bonus.

A person experiencing stress displays certain symptoms indicating that he or she is trying to cope with a stressor (any force creating the stress reaction). These symptoms can include a host of physiological, emotional, and behavioral reactions.

Physiological symptoms of stress include increased heart rate, blood pressure, breathing rate, pupil size, and perspiration. If these physiological symptoms are severe or persist over a prolonged period, the result can be a stress-related disorder, such as a heart attack, hypertension, migraine headache, ulcer, colitis, or allergy. Stress also leads to a chemical imbalance that adversely affects the body's immune system. Thus, the overly stressed person becomes more susceptible to disease and suffers more intensely from existing health problems.

When too much adaptive energy is required of a person in a given period of time, his or her immune systems breaks down.[13] People experiencing emotional stress may have difficulty shaking a common cold or recovering from sexually transmitted disease. In general, any disorder classified as psychosomatic is precipitated by emotional stress.

Emotional symptoms of stress include anxiety, tension, depression, discouragement, boredom, prolonged fatigue, feelings of hopelessness, and various kinds of defensive thinking. Behavioral symptoms include nervous habits such as facial twitching, and sudden decreases in job performance due to forgetfulness and errors in concentration or judgment. Increased use of alcohol and other drugs may also occur.

Not all stress is bad. People require the right amount of stress to keep them mentally and physically alert. If the stress is particularly uncomfortable or distasteful, however, it will lower job performance—particularly on complex, demanding jobs. An example of a stressor that will lower job performance for most

Understand the nature of stress, including its consequences.

stress
The mental and physical condition that results from a perceived threat that cannot be dealt with readily.

EXHIBIT 17-4

The Stress Questionnaire

Here is a brief questionnaire to give a rough estimate of whether you are facing too much stress. Apply each question to the last six months of your life. Check the appropriate column.

Mostly Yes	Mostly No	
☐	☐	1. Have you been feeling uncomfortably tense lately?
☐	☐	2. Do you frequently argue with people close to you?
☐	☐	3. Is your romantic life very unsatisfactory?
☐	☐	4. Do you have trouble sleeping?
☐	☐	5. Do you feel lethargic about life?
☐	☐	6. Do many people annoy or irritate you?
☐	☐	7. Do you have constant cravings for candy and other sweets?
☐	☐	8. Is your consumption of cigarettes or alcohol way up?
☐	☐	9. Are you becoming addicted to soft drinks, coffee, or tea?
☐	☐	10. Do you find it difficult to concentrate on your work?
☐	☐	11. Do you frequently grind your teeth?
☐	☐	12. Are you increasingly forgetful about little things, such as mailing a letter?
☐	☐	13. Are you increasingly forgetful about big things, such as appointments and major errands?
☐	☐	14. Are you making far too many trips to the lavatory?
☐	☐	15. Have people commented lately that you do not look well?
☐	☐	16. Do you get into verbal fights with others too frequently?
☐	☐	17. Have you been involved in more than one break-up with a friend lately?
☐	☐	18. Do you have more than your share of tension headaches?
☐	☐	19. Do you feel nauseated much too often?
☐	☐	20. Do you feel light-headed or dizzy almost every day?
☐	☐	21. Do you have churning sensations in your stomach far too often?
☐	☐	22. Are you in a big hurry all the time?
☐	☐	23. Are far too many things bothering you these days?
☐	☐	24. Do you hurry through activities even when you are not rushed for time?
☐	☐	25. Do you often feel that you are in the panic mode?

Scoring

0–6   Mostly Yes answers: You seem to be experiencing a normal amount of stress.

7–16   Mostly Yes answers: Your stress level seems high. Become involved in some kind of stress management activity, such as the activities described in this chapter.

17–25 Mostly Yes answers: Your stress level appears to be much too high. Seek the help of a mental health professional or visit your family doctor (or do both).

people is a bullying, abrasive manager who wants to see the employee fail. It is a person's perception of something (or somebody) that usually determines whether it will be a positive or negative stressor. For example, one person might perceive an inspection by top-level managers to be so frightening that he is irritable toward team members. Another manager might welcome the visit as a chance to proudly display her department's high-quality performance.

After prolonged exposure to job stress, a person runs the risk of feeling burned out—a drained, used-up feeling. **Job burnout** is a pattern of emotional, physical, and mental exhaustion in response to chronic job stressors. Cynicism, apa-

job burnout
A pattern of emotional, physical, and mental exhaustion in response to chronic job stressors.

thy, and indifference are the major behavioral symptoms of the burned-out worker. Hopelessness is another key symptom of burnout, with the worker often feeling that nothing he or she does can make a difference. Research evidence suggests that supervisors are more at risk for burnout than other workers because they deal so heavily with the demands of other people.[14]

Factors Contributing to Stress and Burnout

Factors within a person, as well as adverse organizational conditions, can cause or contribute to stress and burnout. Personal life stress and work stress also influence each other. Work stress can create problems—and therefore stress—at home. And stress stemming from personal problems can lead to problems—and therefore stress—at work.

FACTORS WITHIN THE INDIVIDUAL
Hostile, aggressive, and impatient people find ways of turning almost any job into a stressful experience. Such individuals are labeled Type A, in contrast to their more easygoing Type B counterparts. In addition to being angry, the outstanding trait of Type A people is their strong sense of time urgency, known as "hurry sickness." This sense of urgency compels them to achieve more and more in less and less time. Angry, aggressive (usually male) Type A people are more likely than Type Bs to experience cardiovascular disorders. In one study, Type A behavior was measured among 250 police workers and firefighters. A seven-year follow-up indicated that Type A people were more likely to have experienced cardiovascular disorders, including a fatal heart attack.[15]

Although type A behavior is associated with coronary heart disease, only some features of the Type A personality pattern may be related to cardiac disorders. The adverse health effects generally stem from hostility, anger, cynicism, and suspiciousness in contrast to impatience, ambition, and drive. Recognize also that not every hard-driving, impatient person is correctly classified as Type A. Managers who love their work and enjoy other people are not particularly prone to heart disease.

Another notable personality characteristic related to job stress is **locus of control,** the way in which people look at causation in their lives. People who believe that they have more control over their actions than do external events are less stress prone. For example, a 50-year-old person with an internal locus of control might lose his job and say, "I don't care if a lot of age discrimination in business exists. I have many needed skills and many employers will want me. Age will not be an issue for me in finding suitable employment." This man's internal locus of control will help him ward off stress related to job loss. A 50-year-old with an external locus of control will experience high stress because the person believes that he or she is helpless in the face of job discrimination. A study about job stress and locus of control among 288 managers concluded that managers who possess a high internal locus of control should be selected for stressful positions.[16]

People who have high expectations are likely to experience job burnout at some point in their careers, because there will be times when they do not receive as many rewards as they are seeking. People who need constant excitement are also at high risk of job burnout, because they bore easily and quickly.

locus of control
The way in which people look at causation in their lives.

ADVERSE ORGANIZATIONAL CONDITIONS   Under ideal conditions, workers experience just enough stress to prompt them to respond creatively and energetically to their jobs. Unfortunately, high stress levels created by adverse organizational conditions lead to many negative symptoms. A major contributor to job stress is work overload. Demands on white-collar workers appear to be at an all-time high, as companies attempt to increase work output and decrease staffing at the same time.

Entrepeneurs are particularly susceptible to work overload stress, as demonstrated in a recent study of 169 male and 56 female business owners from 12 small towns in Ontario. An entrepreneur was defined as a person who both owns and operates a service, retail, wholesale, or manufacturing business. Entrepreneurs scored higher on the workload scale of the Job Stress Questionnaire than did previously tested white collar, blue collar, and professional groups.[17]

Job frustrations caused by such factors as parts shortages, excessive politics, or insufficient funds can create job stress. Extreme conflict with other workers or with management is also a stressor. Having heavy responsibility without the right amount of formal authority upsets many employees. Another annoyance is short lead times—too little notice to get complex assignments accomplished. A powerful stressor today is job insecurity due to the many mergers and downsizings. Worrying about having one's job outsourced to another region, country, or a subcontractor is also a stressor.

job demand–job control model
A model demonstrating the relationship between high or low job demands and high or low job control. It shows that workers experience the most stress when the demands of the job are high yet they have little control over the activity.

According to the **job demand–job control model,** workers experience the most stress when the demands of the job are high, yet they have little control over the activity.[18] (See Exhibit 17-5.) A customer-service representative with limited authority who has to deal with a major error by the firm would fit this category. In contrast, when job demands are high and the worker has high control, the worker will be energized, motivated, and creative. A branch manager in a successful business might fit this scenario.

Absence of ample positive feedback and other rewards is strongly associated with job burnout. As a consequence of not knowing how well they are doing and not receiving recognition, employees often become discouraged and emotionally exhausted. The result is often—but certainly not always—job burnout.

Authors Christina Maslach and Michael P. Leiter believe that certain organizational practices contribute directly to burnout and stress. In general, burnout is caused by a mismatch between the nature of the job and the nature of the job holder in one or more of the following six areas:

- Work overload—longer hours and less free time
- Lack of control over one's work (such as explained in the job demand–job control model)
- Lack of reward for one's contribution (low pay and nonrecognition)
- The absence of a work community (lack of connections among people)
- Unfair treatment (lack of affirmation of self-worth or uneven application of rules) particularly during performance appraisal or consideration for promotion
- Value conflicts between work requirements and one's personal code of ethics (person-role conflict)[19]

EXHIBIT 17-5

The Job Demand–Job Control Model
A worker is likely to experience the most job stress when he or she exercises low control over a job with high demands.

	Low Job Demands	High Job Demands
Low Control	Passive Job	High-strain Job
High Control	Low-strain Job	Active Job

Such adverse conditions do not exist in all organizations. However, enough of these problems are present to make long-term stress and burnout a serious problem. Many employers recognize that workers often suffer from stressful conditions and therefore are taking constructive action to lessen the problem. At Merck & Co., employees were assigned to teams devoted to solving problems such as complaints about overwork, inadequate training, and poor new-hire screening. Work was analyzed and reorganized so that workers perceived they had more control over their workloads and schedules.

In one area of the company, payroll employees were dissatisfied with heavy amounts of overtime. Based on problem-solving discussions, team leaders discovered that most of the payroll work was more critical earlier in the week than toward the end. Among the solutions proposed were reducing commuting time by allowing employees to work at home more often, and implementing compressed work weeks. Merck provided the hardware and software needed to input data from home. After implementing the solutions to problems, turnover slowed from 45 percent to 32 percent, and overtime costs and absenteeism have decreased. Workload pressures were decreased by slashing overtime and commute time.[20]

STRESS MANAGEMENT TECHNIQUES

Explain how stress can be managed effectively.

As the Merck example illustrates, organizations can play a major role in preventing and remedying stress by correcting the kinds of conditions we have discussed and by offering wellness programs and work/life programs. This chapter, however, emphasizes what individuals can do to deal with stress and burnout. Techniques for managing job stress can be divided into three categories: control, symptom management, and escape.[21]

Methods for Control and Reduction of Stress

The five control techniques described next consist of both actions and mental evaluations that help people take charge in stressful situations.

1. *Get social support.* Few people can go it alone when experiencing prolonged stress. Receiving social support—encouragement, understanding, and friendship—from other people is an important strategy for coping successfully with job stress.
2. *Improve your work habits.* You can use the techniques described for improving your personal productivity to reduce stress. People typically experience stress when they feel they are losing or have lost control of their work assignments. Conscientious employees are especially prone to negative stress when they cannot get their work under control.
3. *Develop positive self-talk.* Stress-resistant people are basically optimistic and cheerful. This kind of positivism can be learned by switching to positive self-talk instead of thinking many negative thoughts. (Refer back to the discussion of SuperLeadership in Chapter 11.)
4. *Hug the right people.* Hugging is now being seriously regarded as vital for physical and mental well-being. People who do not receive enough quality touching may suffer from low self-esteem, ill health, depression, and loneliness. Conversely, quality touching may help people cope better with job stress. The hugging, however, has to represent loving and caring.

445

5. *Demand less than perfection from yourself.* By demanding less than 100-percent performance from yourself, you will fail less frequently in your own perceptions. Not measuring up to one's own unrealistically high standards creates a considerable amount of stress. Few humans can operate with zero defects or ever achieve six-sigma perfection!

Symptom Management

This category of stress management refers to tactics that address the symptoms related to job stress. Dozens of symptom management techniques have been developed, including the following:

relaxation response
A general-purpose method of learning to relax by yourself.

1. *Make frequent use of relaxation techniques.* Learning to relax reduces the adverse effects of stress. The **relaxation response** is a general-purpose method of learning to relax by yourself. The key ingredient of this technique is to make yourself quiet and comfortable. At the same time, think of the word *one* (or any simple chant or prayer) with every breath for about 10 minutes. The technique slows you down both physiologically and emotionally. An extremely easy relaxation method is to visualize yourself in an unusually pleasant situation, such as floating on a cloud, walking by a lake, or lying on a comfortable beach. Pick any fantasy that you find relaxing.

2. *Get appropriate physical exercise.* Physical exercise helps dissipate some of the tension created by job stress, and it also helps the body ward off future stress-related disorders. A physically fit, well-rested person can usually tolerate more frustration than can a physically run-down, tired person. One way in which exercise helps combat stress is that it releases endorphins. These are morphine-like chemicals produced in the brain that act as painkillers and antidepressants. More information about the benefits of physical exercise is presented in Exhibit 17-6.

3. *Try to cure hurry sickness.* People with hurry sickness should learn how to relax and enjoy the present for its own sake. Specific tactics include having at least one idle period every day; eating nutritious, not overly seasoned foods to help decrease nervousness; and finding enrichment in an area of life not related to work.

EXHIBIT 17-6

The Benefits of Physical Exercise

- Increases energy
- Reduces feelings of tension, anxiety, and depression
- Improves sleep
- Improves concentration
- Enhances self-esteem and self-confidence
- Helps you lose weight or maintain a healthy weight
- Reduces the risk of heart disease, or improves cardiac function if you have had a heart attack or bypass
- Reduces the risk of colon cancer
- Lowers high blood pressure and the risk of stroke
- Controls blood sugar levels if you have, or are at risk for, diabetes
- Improves bone density and lowers the risk of osteoporosis and fractures as you get older

Sources: The American Heart Association, the American College of Sports Medicine, Shape Up America!, The American Academy of Family Physicians, and National Cattlemen's Beef Association. As compiled by Shari Roan, "The Theory of Inactivity," *The Los Angeles Times*, syndicated story, March 9, 1998.

EXHIBIT
17-7

Stress Busters

- Take a nap when facing heavy pressures. "Power napping" is regarded as one of the most effective techniques for reducing and preventing stress.
- Give in to your emotions. If you are angry, disgusted, or confused, admit your feelings to yourself. Suppressing your emotions adds to stress.
- Take a brief break from the stressful situation and do something small and constructive like washing your car, emptying a wastebasket, or getting a haircut.
- Get a massage because it can loosen tight muscles, improve your blood circulation, and calm you down.
- Get help with a stressful task from a co-worker, boss, or friend.
- Concentrate on reading, surfing the Internet, a sport, or a hobby. Contrary to common sense, concentration is at the heart of stress reduction.

- Have a quiet place at home and have a brief idle period there every day.
- Take a leisurely day off from your routine.
- Finish something you have started, however small. Accomplishing almost anything reduces some stress.
- Stop to smell the flowers, make friends with a young child or elderly person, or play with a kitten or puppy.
- Strive to do a good job, but not a perfect job.
- Work with your hands, doing a pleasant task.
- Find somebody or something that makes you laugh, and have a good laugh.
- Minimize drinking caffeinated or alcoholic beverages. Drink fruit juice or water instead. Grab a piece of fruit, rather than a can of beer.

Escape Methods of Stress Management

Escape methods are actions and reappraisals of situations that provide the stressed individual some escape from the stressor. Eliminating the stressor is the most effective escape technique. For example, if a manager is experiencing stress because of serious understaffing in his or her department, that manager should negotiate to receive authorization to hire additional help. Mentally blocking out a stressful thought is another escape technique, but it may not work in the long run.

Given that you could probably locate 30,000 articles, books, and Internet comments on the subject of job stress, we have not mentioned every possible approach to managing stress. To prevent information overload, study Exhibit 17-7 to get a few more ideas on reducing stress, and reinforce a few suggestions made already.

SUMMARY OF KEY POINTS

 Identify techniques for improving work habits and time management.

One way of increasing your personal productivity is to improve your work habits and time management skills. To do this, develop a mission, goals, and a strong work ethic. Clean up your work area and sort out your tasks. Prepare a to-do list and assign priorities. Also, streamline your work; work at a steady pace; minimize times wasters; and concentrate on one task at a time. Concentrate on high-output tasks; do creative and routine work at different times; and stay in control of paperwork, e-mail, and voice mail. Making effective use of office technology is essential, including using a personal information manager and editing group reports by e-mail. Strive to achieve peak performance, take power naps, and put extra effort into managing multiple priorities.

447

Identify techniques for reducing procrastination.
Avoid procrastinating by understanding why you procrastinate and taking remedial action, including the following: break the task down into smaller units, make a commitment to others, reward yourself for achieving milestones, calculate the cost of procrastination, use subliminal messages, counterattack against an uncomfortable task, and post a progress chart.

 Understand the nature of stress, including its consequences.
Stress is the mental and physical condition that results from a perceived threat that cannot be dealt with readily. Job burnout is a pattern of emotional, physical, and mental exhaustion in response to chronic job stressors. Hopelessness is another key symptom of burnout. Key stress symptoms include tension, anxiety, and poor concentration and judgment. Job stress is caused by factors within the individual such as Type A behavior and an external locus of control. A variety of adverse organizational conditions, including work overload and low control over a demanding job, contribute to stress. People with high expectations are candidates for burnout. Limited rewards and lack of feedback from the organization contribute to burnout.

 Explain how stress can be managed effectively.
Methods of preventing and controlling stress and burnout can be divided into three categories: attempts to control stressful situations, symptom management, and escapes from the stressful situation. Specific tactics include eliminating stressors, getting sufficient physical exercise, using relaxation techniques, curing hurry sickness, getting emotional support from others, and improving work habits.

KEY TERMS AND PHRASES

Work ethic, *431*

Work streamlining, *431*

Peak performance, *436*

Procrastination, *437*

Stress, *441*

Job burnout, *442*

Locus of control, *443*

Job demand–job control model, *444*

Relaxation response, *446*

QUESTIONS

1. What is your mission in life? (If you do not have a mission, how might you be able to develop one?)
2. How can a person be well organized yet unproductive?
3. How can a person determine if answering e-mail is an important part of the job or a productivity drain?
4. How can a person use achieving a state of peak performance to reduce stress?
5. How can you apply the job demand–job control model to help you do a better job of managing stress?
6. What is the difference between literally sleeping on the job and taking a "power nap"?
7. Although this chapter is mostly about managing oneself, how might a manager use the information to help group members?

SKILL-BUILDING EXERCISE 17-A: Visualization for Stress Reduction

A standard, easy-to-use method for reducing stress symptoms is to visualize a pleasant and calm experience. If you are experiencing stress right now, try the technique. Otherwise, wait until the next time you perceive your body to be experiencing stress. In this context, visualization means to picture yourself doing something that you would like to do. Whatever fantasy suits your fancy will work, according to the advocates of this relaxation technique. Visualizations that work for some people include: smiling at a loved one, floating on a cloud, caressing a baby, petting a kitten or puppy, and walking in the woods. Notice that all of these scenes are relaxing rather than exciting. What visualization would work for you?

To implement the technique, close your eyes and bring the pleasant image into focus in your mind. Think of nothing else. Imagine that a videotape of the pleasant experience is playing on the television screen in your brain. Breathe softly and savor the experience. Slowly return to reality—refreshed, relaxed, and ready to tackle the challenges of the day.

INTERNET SKILL-BUILDING EXERCISE: Productivity Boosting on the Internet

The number of people on line in the United States and Canada and the rest of the world continues to grow rapidly, with thousands of people getting started everyday. Gather into small teams or work individually to identify 10 ways in which the Internet can increase personal productivity, either on the job or at home. To supplement your own thinking, you might search the Internet for ideas on how the Internet is supposed to boost productivity. I would look forward to being informed of your most creative ideas.

Happy surfing.

ajdubrin@frontiernet.net

CASE PROBLEM 17-A: The Busy Office Manager

Mike Powers looked at the kitchen clock and said to his wife, Ruth, "Oh no, it's 7:25. It's my turn to drop off Jason and Gloria at the child-care center. Jason hasn't finished breakfast, and Gloria is still in her pajamas. Can you get Gloria dressed for me?"

Ruth responded, "Ok, I'll help Gloria, but today is your turn to take care of the children. I have a client presentation at 8:30 this morning. I need to prepare for a few more minutes."

"Forget I asked," said Mike. "I'll take care of it. Once again I'll start my day in a frenzy, late for child care, and just barely making it to work on time."

"Why didn't you get up when the alarm rang the first time?" asked Ruth.

"Don't you remember, we talked until one this morning? It seems like we never get to talk to each other until midnight," Mike replied.

After getting Jason and Gloria settled at the child-care center, Mike dashed off to the public accounting firm where he worked as the office manager. After greeting several staff members, Mike turned on his computer to check his e-mail. Ann Gabrielli, one of the partners in the firm, left the following message: "See you today at 11:30 for the review of overhead expenses. Two other partners will be attending."

Mike quickly looked at his desk calendar. According to his calendar, the meeting was one week from today. Mike called Gabrielli immediately and said, "Ann, my apologies. My schedule says that the meeting is one week from today at 11:30, not today. I'm not ready with the figures for today's meeting."

"My calendar says the meeting is today," said Gabrielli harshly. "I'm ready for the meeting and so are Craig and Gunther (the other partners). This isn't the first time you've gotten your weeks mixed up. The meeting will go on, however poorly you have to perform."

"I'll be there," said Mike. "It's just a question of reviewing some figures that I've already collected."

After putting down the phone, Mike calculated that he had about 2 hours and 40 minutes in which to prepare a preliminary report on reducing overhead. He then glanced at his desk calendar to see what else he had scheduled this morning. The time looked clear except for one entry: "PA/LC."

"What is PA/LC?" thought Mike? "I can't imagine what these initials stand for. Wait a minute, now I know. The initials stand for performance appraisal with Lucy Cruthers, our head bookkeeper. I'm not ready for that session. And I can't do it this morning. Mike then sent Cruthers an e-mail message, suggesting that they meet the following week at the same time.

Cruthers answered back immediately. She wrote that she would not be able to meet the following week because that was the first day of her vacation. Mike sent her another note: "I'll get back to you later with another date. I don't have time now to make plans."

Next, Mike informed the department assistant, Lois Wang, that he had to hurriedly prepare for the 11:30 meeting. Mike asked for her cooperation in keeping visitors away the rest of the morning.

He then retrieved his computer directory to look for the file on overhead expenses that he began last week. As he scanned the directory, he found only three files that might be related to the topic: COST, EXPENSES, and TRIM. Mike reasoned that the file must be one of these three.

Mike retrieved the file, COST. It proved to be a summary of furniture expenses for the firm. Upon bringing EXPENSES up on the screen, Mike found that it was his expense account report for a business trip he took seven months ago. TRIM was found to be a list of cost estimates for lawn-care services.

Agitated, and beginning to sweat profusely, Mike asked Lois Wang to help him. "I'm stuck," he pleaded. "I need to find my file for the overhead expense analysis I was doing for the partners. Do you recall what I named the file? Did I give it to you on disk?"

"Let me seek if I can help," said Wang. "We''ll search your directory together." Wang scanned about 100 files. "What a clutter," she sighed. "You ought to clean out your files sometime soon. Here's a possibility, PTR."

"I doubt it," said Mike. " 'PTR' stands for partner. I'm looking for a file about overhead expenses."

"But you are preparing the file for the partners, aren't you?"

Lois proved to be right. The PTR file contained the information Mike sought. Within 30 minutes he completed the spreadsheet analysis he needed. He then prepared a brief memo explaining his findings. With 20 minutes left before the presentation, Mike asked Lucy if she could run off three copies in a hurry. Lucy explained that the photocopier was not operating and offered to print out three additional copies from Mike's computer files.

"Bring them into my meeting with the partners as soon as you can," said Mike. "I've run out of time."

On the way to the meeting, Mike exhaled a few times and consciously relaxed his muscles to overcome the tension accumulated from preparing the report under so much pressure. Mike performed reasonably well during the meeting. The partners accepted his analysis of overhead expenses and said they would study his findings further. As the meeting broke up at 12:30, the senior partner commented to Mike, "If you had gotten your weeks straight, I think you would have presented you analysis in more depth. Your report was useful, but I know you are capable of doing a more sophisticated analysis."

After returning from lunch, Mike revised his daily planner again. He noticed a Post-it™ note attached to the light on his desk. The entry on the slip of paper said, "Racquetball, Monday night with Ziggy."

"Not again," Mike said to himself in a groan of agony. "Tonight I've got to get Jason and Gloria to bed. Ruth has a class scheduled for her course in Japanese. I'll have to call Ziggy now. I hope he's in his office."

Mike left an URGENT message on Ziggy's e-mail, offering his apologies. He thought to himself, "I hope Ziggy won't

be too annoyed. This is the second time this year I've had to reschedule a match at the last moment."

Mike returned from lunch at 2:00 P.M. He decided to add more details to the overhead expense report he had prepared for the partners. By 4:00 P.M. Mike was ready to begin the tasks outlined on his daily planner. At that point Lois Wang walked into Mike's office and announced, "There's a representative here from AccountTemps. She said she was in the building so she decided to drop in to talk about their temporary employment services."

"Might as well let her in," said Mike. "We will be hiring some temporary bookkeepers soon. AccountTemps has a good reputation. It's getting too late to do much today anyway."

Mike made it to the child-care center by 5:45 and packed Jason and Gloria into the family minivan. Gloria, the eldest child, asked if the family could eat at Hardee's this evening. Mike said, "Ok, but I'll have to stop at an ATM first. I don't have enough cash on hand to eat out. We'll stop at the ATM then stop by the house and see if Mom wants to eat out tonight before class."

Mike and the children arrived home at 6:15 and asked Ruth if she would like to have a family dinner at Hardee's this evening.

"I have about one hour to spare before class," said Ruth. "Why not? By the way, how was your day?"

"My day?" asked Mike with a sigh. "I just fell one day farther behind schedule. I'll have to do some paperwork after the children are asleep. Maybe we can watch the late-night news together this evening. We should both be free by then."

Discussion Questions

1. What time-management mistakes does Mike appear to be making?
2. What does Mike appear to be doing right from the standpoint of managing time?
3. What suggestions can you offer Mike to help him get his schedule more under control?
4. What evidence do you find that Mike is experiencing negative stress?

CASE PROBLEM 17-B: The Distracted Claims Examiner

Rodney Perry works as a claims examiner at a drive-through claims office for a major insurance company. A drive-through claims office is an alternative to a claims examiner doing on-site inspections of damaged vehicles. If the vehicle (car, small truck, van, or motorcycle) is drivable, the person

with a claim against the company visits the drive-through office. The vehicles assessed for damages are either owned by company policyholders or were damaged by company policyholders. Each drive-through office is staffed by one claims examiner and one office assistant.

Rod has worked three years at the same drive-through location as a claims examiner. Based upon two years of excellent productivity and a positive attitude, he has been under consideration for promotion to claims manager. Based on his presumed promotability, Rod was asked to prepare a 30-page report analyzing the nature of claims at his branch. To prepare his report, Rod needs to regularly consult the computerized records available on the PC at his office.

Rod works on the company report whenever he can grab a few moments between claim inspections, telephone calls, preparing the computerized claim evaluations, and consulting with the office assistant. During extra-busy periods, he can find no time to work on the report. Rod's manager, Keith Piotrowski, telephoned him recently to discuss the report.

"Rod, I think we have a problem," said Piotrowski. "I asked you five months ago to prepare that claims analysis. You tell me you've made some progress, yet you still haven't delivered. When we considered you for promotion to claims manager, we didn't know you were a procrastinator."

"Keith, I don't consider myself to be a procrastinator. It's just that I'm in a very difficult position to write a report. Doing the claims work alone has me working about 50 hours a week. I thought claims examinations took priority over this report. I don't think you know how difficult it is to write a special report when I'm already overloaded with claims work.

"I would like to write the report at home, but all the records I need are at the office. Besides, I'm already putting in enough hours of unpaid overtime."

Piotrowski replied, "I hope I'm not hearing excuses from a man we thought had excellent potential for promotion. I want to see the report on my desk in two weeks, and I don't expect you to fall behind on claims work."

Discussion Questions

1. What responsibility should Rod take for not producing the report on time?
2. What responsibility should the company take for the report not being produced on time?
3. If you were Rod, how would you handle the ultimatum from Keith Piotrowski?

ENDNOTES

1. Excerpted from: "Overload" by Jennifer Laabs, copyright January 1999. Used with permission of ACC Communications Inc./Workforce, Costa Mesa, CA. All rights reserved.
2. The comment by Bardwick and the company examples are from "Remove the 'Garbage' from Their Jobs," Managers Edge, November 1998, p. 3. Based on Judith M. Bardwick, In Praise of Good Business: How Optimizing Risk Rewards Both Your Bottom Line and Your People (New York: Wiley, 1998).
3. Price Pritchett, The Employee Handbook of New Work Habits For A Radically Changing World (Dallas, TX: Pritchett & Associates, Inc., undated).
4. Shane Murphy, The Achievement Zone: Eight Skills for Winning All the Time from the Playing Field to the Boardroom (New York: G.P Putman's Sons, 1996).
5. "PC Productivity is Elusive," Kinght Ridder syndicated story, November 9, 1997.
6. Shelly Branch, "So Much Work, So Little Time," Fortune, February 3, 1997, p. 116.
7. Cited in Ingrid Lorch-Bacci, "Achieving Peak performance: The Hidden Dimension," Executive Management Forum, January 191, pp. 1–4.
8. Donald J. McNerney, "Napping at Work: You Snooze, You Win!" HRfocus, March 1995, p. 3.
9. Harriett Johnson Brackey, "Snoozing Studies Alarm Experts," Knight Ridder syndicated story, July 6, 1998.
10. Maggie Jackson, "New Skill for Today's Workplace: Sleeping on the Job," Associated Press syndicated story, May 19, 1997.
11. Robert Boice, Procrastination and Blocking: A Novel, Practical Approach (Westport, CT: Greenwood Publishing Group, 1996).
12. "When to Procrastinate and When to Get Going," Working Smart, March 1992, pp. 1–2.
13. Michael R. Manning, Conrad N. Jackson, and Marcelline R. Fusilier,

"Occupational Stress, Social Support, and the Costs of Health Care," Academy of Management Journal, June 1996, p. 745.
14. Cynthia L. Cordes and Thomas Doughtery, "A Review and an Integration of Research on Job Burnout," Academy of Management Review, October 1993, p. 644.
15. John Schaubroeck, Daniel C. Ganster, and Barbara E. Kemmer, "Job Complexity, 'Type A' Behavior, and Cardiovascular Disorder: A Prospective Study," Academy of Management Journal, April 1994, pp. 426–439.
16. M. Afzalur Rahim, "Relations of Stress, Locus of Control, and Social Support to Psychiatric Symptoms and Propensity to Leave a Job: A Field Study with Managers," Journal of Business and Psychology, Winter 1997, pp. 159–174.
17. Julie Aitken Harris, Robert Saltstone, and Maryann Fraboni, "An Evaluation of the Job Stress Questionnaire with a Sample of Entrepreneurs," Journal of Business and Psychology, Spring 1999, pp. 447–455.
18. Marilyn L. Fox, Deborah J. Dwyer, and Daniel C. Ganster, "Effects of Stressful Job Demands and Control on Physiological and Attitudinal Outcomes in a Hospital Setting," Academy of Management Journal, April 1993, pp. 290–292.
19. Christina Maslach and Michael P. Leiter, The Truth About Burnout: How Organizations Cause Personal Stress and What to do About It (San Francisco: Jossey-Bass, 1997).
20. Laabs, "Overload," pp. 34–35.
21. Janina C. Latack, "Coping with Job Stress: Measures and Future Directions for Scale Development," Journal of Applied Psychology, August 1986, pp. 522–526; David Antonioni, "Two Strategies for Responding to Stressors: Managing Conflict and Clarifying Work Expectations," Journal of Business and Psychology, Winter 1996, pp. 287–295; Gail Dutton, "Cutting-Edge Stressbusters," HRfocus, September 1998, pp. 11–12.

glossary

achievement motivation finding joy in accomplishment for its own sake.

action plans the specific steps necessary to achieve a goal or objective.

active listening listening for full meaning, without making premature judgments or interpretations.

activity in the PERT method, the physical and mental effort required to complete an event.

activity-based costing (ABC) an accounting procedure that allocates the cost for producing a product or service to the activities performed and the resources used.

affective conflict conflict that focuses on more personal or subjective issues and is dealt with more emotionally than intellectually.

affiliation need a desire to have close relationships with others and be a loyal employee or friend.

affinity group an employee involvement group composed of professional-level workers who meet regularly to share information, capture opportunities, and solve problems affecting the work group and the larger organization.

affirmative action an employment practice that complies with antidiscrimination law and correcting past discriminatory practices.

alternative work place a combination of nontraditional work practices, settings, and locations that supplements the traditional office.

anchoring in the decision-making process, placing too much value on the first information received and ignoring later information.

authority the formal right to get people to do things or the formal right to control resources.

autocratic leader a task-oriented leader who retains most of the authority for himself or herself and is not generally concerned with group members' attitudes toward decisions.

balance of trade a measure of the dollar volume of a country's exports relative to its imports over a specified time period.

balanced scorecard a set of measures that provide a quick but comprehensive view of a business.

behavior in performance appraisal, what people actually do on the job.

behavior mismatch a condition that occurs when one person's actions do not meet another's expectations.

behavior modification a way of changing behavior by rewarding the right responses and punishing or ignoring the wrong responses.

behavioral school of management the approach to studying management that emphasizes improving management through understanding the psychological makeup of people.

benchmarking the process of comparing a firm's quality performance to that achieved by a competing firm.

bounded rationality the observation that people's limited mental abilities, combined with external influences over which they have little or no control, prevent them from making entirely rational decisions.

brainstorming a group method of solving problems, gathering information, and stimulating creative thinking. The basic technique is to generate numerous ideas through unrestrained and spontaneous participation by group members.

break-even analysis a method of determining the relationship between total costs and total revenues at various levels of production or sales activity.

broadbanding in salary administration, basing pay more on the person than the position, thus reducing the number of pay grades.

budget a spending plan expressed in numerical terms for a future period of time.

bureaucracy a rational, systematic, and precise form of organization in which rules, regulations, and techniques of control are precisely defined.

capital-expenditure budget a plan for spending money on assets used to produce goods or services.

cash budget a forecast of cash receipts and payments.

cash flow amount of net cash generated by a business during a specific period.

cause-and-effect analysis a graphical technique for analyzing the factors that contribute to a problem. It relies on an Ishikawa, or fishbone, diagram.

centralization the extent to which authority is retained at the top of the organization.

charisma the ability to lead or influence others based on personal charm, magnetism, inspiration, and emotion.

classical school of management the original formal approach to studying management. This school of thought searches for solid principles and concepts that can be used to manage people and work productively.

coaching a method for helping employees perform better that usually occurs on the spot and involves informal discussion and suggestions.

coalition a specific arrangement of parties working together to combine their power, thus exerting influence on another individual or group.

cognitive conflict conflict that focuses on substantive, issue-related differences and is dealt with more intellectually than emotionally.

communication the process of exchanging information by the use of words, letters, symbols, or nonverbal behavior.

communication network a pattern or flow of messages that traces the communication from start to finish.

company intranet a Web site designed only for company employees, often containing proprietary information.

compressed work week a full-time work schedule that allows 40 hours of work in less than five days.

computer goof-offs people who spend so much time attempting new computer routines and accessing information of questionable value that they neglect key aspects of the job.

computer-based training a learning experience based on the interaction between the trainee and a computer.

concurrent control a type of control that monitors activities while they are being carried out.

conflict the simultaneous arousal of two or more incompatible motives.

conflict of interest a situation that occurs when one's judgment or objectivity is compromised.

confrontation dealing with a controversial or emotional topic directly.

constructive criticism a form of criticism designed to help improve performance or behavior.

contingency approach to management a perspective on management that emphasizes that there is no one best way to manage people or work. It encourages managers to study individual and situational differences before deciding on a course of action.

contingency plan an alternative plan to be used if the original plan cannot be implemented or a crisis develops.

contingent workers part-time or temporary employees who are not members of the employer's permanent workforce.

corporate social consciousness a set of consciously held shared values that guide decision making.

corporate social performance the extent to which a firm responds to the demands of its stakeholders for behaving in a socially responsible manner.

corrective discipline a type of discipline that allows employees to correct their behavior before punishment is applied.

creativity the process of developing novel ideas that can be put into action.

critical path the path through the PERT network that includes the most time-consuming sequence of events and activities.

cross-functional team a work group composed of workers from different specialties, but about the same organizational level, who come together to accomplish a task.

cultural diversity mix of cultures and subcultures in an organization's workforce, such as the Hispanic culture, deaf culture, or gay culture.

cultural sensitivity awareness of local and national customs and their importance in effective interpersonal relationships.

culture shock physical and psychological symptoms that can develop when a person is placed in a foreign culture.

cumulative trauma disorders injuries caused by repetitive motions over prolonged periods of time.

customer departmentalization an organization structure based on customer needs.

cycle time the interval between the ordering and delivery of a product or service.

decentralization the extent to which authority is passed down to lower levels in an organization.

decision a choice among alternatives.

decision tree a graphic illustration of the alternative solutions available to solve a problem.

decision-making software any computer program that helps a decision maker work through problem-solving and decision-making steps.

decisiveness the extent to which a person makes up his or her mind promptly and prudently.

decoding the communication stage in which the receiver interprets the message and translates it into meaningful information.

defensive communication the tendency to receive messages in a way that protects self-esteem.

deficiency needs lower-order needs that must be satisfied to ensure a person's existence, security, and requirements for human contact.

delegation assigning formal authority and responsibility for accomplishing a specific task to another person.

demographic diversity mix of group characteristics in an organization's workforce, including sex, race, and religion.

departmentalization the process of subdividing work into departments.

development a form of personal improvement that usually consists of enhancing knowledge and skills of a complex and unstructured nature.

deviation in a control system, the size of the discrepancy between performance standards and actual results.

difficult person an individual whose personal characteristics disturb other people.

disability a physical or mental condition that substantially limits an individual's major life activities.

discipline punishment used to correct or train.

downsizing the slimming down of operations to focus resources and boost profits or decrease expenses.

due process in relation to employee rights, giving a worker a fair hearing before he or she is dismissed.

economic value added (EVA) measures how much more (or less) a company earns in profits than the minimum amount its investors expect it to earn.

economic-order quantity (EOQ) the inventory level that minimizes both administrative costs and carrying costs.

emotional intelligence the ability to connect with people and understand their emotions.

employee assistance program (EAP) an organization-sponsored activity to help employees deal with personal and job-related problems that hinder performance.

employee benefit any noncash payment given to workers as a condition of their employment.

employee network groups employees within a company who affiliate on the basis of race, ethnicity, sex, sexual orientation, or physical ability to discuss ways to succeed in the organization.

employee orientation program a formal activity designed to acquaint new employees with the organization.

empowerment the process by which managers share power with group members, thereby enhancing employees' feelings of personal effectiveness.

encoding the process of organizing ideas into a series of symbols designed to communicate with the receiver.

entrepreneur a person who founds and operates an innovative business.

entropy a concept of the systems approach to management that states that an organization will die without continuous input from the outside environment.

ethically centered management an approach to management that emphasizes that the high quality of an end product takes precedence over its scheduled completion.

ethics the study of moral obligation, or separating right from wrong.

event in the PERT method, a point of decision or the accomplishment of a task.

expectancy theory of motivation an explanation of motivation that states that people will expend effort if they expect the effort to lead to performance and the performance to lead to a reward.

expected time the time that will be used on the PERT diagram as the needed period for the completion of an activity.

expected value the average return on a particular decision being made a large number of times.

external control strategy an approach to control based on the belief that employees are motivated primarily by external rewards and need to be controlled by their managers.

extranet a Web site that requires a password to enter.

feedback control a control that evaluates an activity after it has been performed.

filtering coloring and altering information to make it more acceptable to the receiver.

first-level managers managers who supervise operatives (also known as first-line managers or supervisors).

flat organization structure a form of organization with relatively few layers of management, making it less bureaucratic.

flexible benefit package a benefit plan that allows employees to select a group of benefits tailored to their preferences.

flexible working hours a system of working hours wherein employees must work certain core hours but can choose their arrival and departure times.

formal communication channels the official pathways for sending information inside and outside an organization.

formal group a group deliberately formed by the organization to accomplish specific tasks and achieve goals.

free-rein leader a leader who turns over virtually all authority and control to the group.

functional departmentalization an arrangement in which departments are defined by the function each one performs, such as accounting or purchasing.

gainsharing a formal program allowing employees to participate financially in the productivity gains they have achieved.

Gantt chart a chart that depicts the planned and actual progress of work during the life of a project.

global startup a small firm that comes into existence by serving an international market.

grapevine the informal means by which information is transmitted in organizations.

gross profit margin a financial ratio expressed as the difference between sales and the cost of goods sold, divided by sales.

group a collection of people who interact with each other, are working toward some common purpose, and perceive themselves to be a group.

group decision the process of several people contributing to a final decision.

group polarization a situation in which postdiscussion attitudes tend to be more extreme than prediscussion attitudes.

groupthink a psychological drive for consensus at any cost.

growth needs higher-order needs that are concerned with personal development and reaching one's potential.

human resource budget a schedule that identifies the human resource needs for a future period and the labor costs to meet those needs.

improvement goal a goal that, if attained, will correct unacceptable deviation from a performance standard.

ineffective job performance job performance that lowers productivity below an acceptable standard.

informal communication channel an unofficial network that supplements the formal channels in an organization.

informal group a group that emerges over time through the interaction of workers.

informal learning any learning that occurs in which the learning process is not determined or designed by the organization.

information overload (or communication overload) a condition in which an individual receives so much information that he or she becomes overwhelmed.

information superhighway the combination of computer, Internet, telecommunications, and video technologies for the purpose of disseminating and acquiring information.

information system (or management information system) a formal system for providing management with information useful or necessary for making decisions.

informative confrontation a technique of inquiring about discrepancies, conflicts, and mixed messages.

internal control strategy an approach to control based on the belief that employees can be motivated by building their commitment to organizational goals.

intuition an experience-based way of knowing or reasoning in which weighing and balancing evidence is done unconsciously and automatically.

ISO 9000 a series of management and quality-assurance standards developed for firms competing in international markets.

job analysis obtaining information about a job by describing its tasks and responsibilities and gathering basic facts about the job.

job burnout a pattern of emotional, physical, and mental exhaustion in response to chronic job stressors.

job characteristics model a method of job enrichment that focuses on the task and interpersonal dimensions of a job.

job demand–job control model a model demonstrating the relationship between high or low job demands and high or low job control. It shows that workers experience the most stress when the demands of the job are high yet they have little control over the activity.

job description a written statement of the key features of a job, along with the activities required to perform it effectively.

job design the process of laying out job responsibilities and duties and describing how they are to be performed.

job enlargement increasing the number and variety of tasks within a job.

job enrichment an approach to making jobs involve more challenge and responsibility, so they will be more appealing to most employees.

job involvement the degree to which individuals are identified psychologically with their work.

job rotation a temporary switching of job assignments.

job sharing a work arrangement in which two people who work part time share one job.

job specialization the degree to which a job holder performs only a limited number of tasks.

job specification a statement of the personal characteristics needed to perform the job.

judgmental forecast a qualitative forecasting method based on a collection of subjective opinions.

just-in-time (JIT) system a system to minimize inventory and move it into the plant exactly when needed.

lateral thinking a thinking process that spreads out to find many different alternative solutions to a problem.

law of effect the underlying principle of behavior modification stating that behavior leading to positive consequences tends to be repeated and that behavior leading to negative consequences tends not to be repeated.

leadership the ability to inspire confidence and support among the people who are needed to achieve organizational goals.

Leadership Grid® a visual representation of different combinations of a leader's degree of concern for task-related issues.

leadership style the typical pattern of behavior that a leader uses to influence his or her employees to achieve organizational goals.

learning organization an organization that is skilled at creating, acquiring, and transferring knowledge.

locus of control the way in which people look at causation in their lives.

management the process of using organizational resources to achieve organizational objectives through planning, organizing and staffing, leading, and controlling.

management by objectives (MBO) a systematic application of goal setting and planning to help individuals and firms be more productive.

management-science school the school of management thought that concentrates on providing management with a scientific basis for solving problems and making decisions.

manager a person responsible for the work performance of group members.

maquiladora a manufacturing plant close to the U.S. border that is established specifically to assemble American products.

Maslow's need hierarchy the motivation theory that arranges human needs into a pyramid-shaped model with basic physiological needs at the bottom and self-actualizing needs at the top.

mass customization a manufacturing system that allows hundreds of variations of a single product in order to respond to the unique preferences of individual customers.

master budget a budget consolidated from the budgets of various units.

materials purchase/usage budget a plan that identifies the raw materials and parts that must be purchased to meet production demands.

materials-requirement planning (MRP) a computerized manufacturing and inventory-control system designed to ensure that materials handling and inventory control are efficient.

matrix organization a project structure superimposed on top of a functional structure.

mentor a more experienced person who develops a protégé's abilities through tutoring, coaching, guidance, and emotional support.

metacommunicate to communicate about your communication to help overcome barriers or resolve a problem.

micromanagement supervising group members too closely and second-guessing their decisions.

middle-level managers managers who are neither executives nor first-level supervisors, but who serve as a link between the two groups.

milestone chart an extension of the Gantt chart that provides a listing of the subactivities that must be completed to accomplish the major activities listed on the vertical axis.

mission the firm's purpose and where it fits into the world.

modified work schedule any formal departure from the traditional hours of work, excluding shift work and staggered work hours.

moment of truth a situation in which a customer comes in contact with the company and forms an impression of its service.

moral intensity the magnitude of an unethical act.

moral laxity a slippage in moral behavior because other issues seem more important at the time.

motivation the expenditure of effort to accomplish results.

multicultural worker an individual who is aware of and values other cultures.

multiculturalism the ability to work effectively and conduct business with people from different cultures.

multinational corporation (MNC) a firm with units in two or more countries in addition to its own.

need a deficit within an individual, such as a craving for water or affection.

noise in communication, unwanted interference that can distort or block a message.

nominal-group technique (NGT) a group decision-making technique that follows a highly structured format.

nonprogrammed decision a decision that is difficult because of its complexity and the fact that the person faces it infrequently.

nonverbal communication the transmission of messages by means other than words.

open-book company a firm in which every employee is trained, empowered, and motivated to understand and pursue the company's business goals.

operating plans the means through which strategic plans alter the destiny of the firm.

operational planning planning that requires specific procedures and actions at lower levels in an organization.

organization structure the arrangement of people and tasks to accomplish organizational goals.

organizational (or office) politics informal approaches to gaining power or other advantage through means other than merit or luck.

organizational culture (or corporate culture) the system of shared values and beliefs that actively influence the behavior of organization members.

outsource the practice of hiring an individual or another company outside the organization to perform work.

P = M × A an expression of the relationship between motivation and performance, where P refers to performance, M to motivation, and A to ability.

paradigm the perspectives and ways of doing things that are typical of a given context.

Pareto diagram a bar graph that ranks types of output variations by frequency of occurrence.

participative leader a leader who shares decision making with group members.

peak performance a mental state in which maximum results are achieved with minimum effort.

performance appraisal a formal system for measuring, evaluating, and reviewing performance.

pet-peeve technique a creativity-training (or problem-solving) exercise in which the group thinks up as many complaints as possible about every facet of the department.

poka-yoke a quality control device initiated to prevent human errors in the manufacturing process and to assure proper use of the product on the part of the consumer.

policies general guidelines to follow in making decisions and taking action.

power the ability or potential to influence decisions and control resources.

power motivation a strong desire to control others or get them to do things on your behalf.

preventive control a control that takes place prior to the performance of an activity.

problem a discrepancy between ideal and actual conditions.

procedures a customary method for handling an activity. It guides action rather than thinking.

process a set of activities designed to achieve a goal.

procrastinate to delay in taking action without a valid reason.

procrastination the delaying of action for no good reason.

production budget a detailed plan that identifies the products or services that must be produced to match the sales forecast and inventory requirements.

product–service departmentalization the arrangement of departments according to the products or services they provide.

profit margin a financial ratio measuring return on sales, or net income divided by sales.

profit-sharing plan a method of giving workers supplemental income based on the profitability of the entire firm or a selected unit.

program evaluation and review technique (PERT) a network model used to track the planning activities required to complete a large-scale, non-repetitive project. It depicts all of the interrelated events that must take place.

programmed decision a decision that is repetitive, or routine, and made according to a specific procedure.

progressive discipline the step-by-step application of corrective discipline.

project organization a temporary group of specialists working under one manager to accomplish a fixed objective.

qualitative control technique a method of controlling based on human judgments about performance that result in a verbal rather than numerical evaluation.

quality the totality of features and characteristics of a product or service that bears on its ability to satisfy given needs.

quality control any method of determining the extent to which goods or services match some specified quality standard.

quantitative control technique a method of controlling based on numerical measures of performance.

readiness in situational leadership, the extent to which a group member has the ability and willingness or confidence to accomplish a specific task.

realistic job preview a complete disclosure of the potential negative features of a job to a job candidate.

recognition need the desire to be acknowledged for one's contributions and efforts and to feel important.

recruitment the process of attracting job candidates with the right characteristics and skills to fill job openings.

reengineering the radical redesign of work to achieve substantial improvements in performance.

reference check an inquiry to a second party about a job candidate's suitability for employment.

relationship behavior the extent to which the leader engages in two-way communication.

relaxation response a general-purpose method of learning to relax by yourself.

results in performance appraisal, what people accomplish, or the objectives they attain.

return on equity a financial ratio measuring how much a firm is earning on its investment, expressed as net income divided by owner's equity.

revenue-and-expense budget a document that describes plans for revenues and operating expenses in dollar amounts.

robust design the concept of designing a part or process so well that it can withstand fluctuations on the production line without a loss of quality.

role an expected set of activities or behaviors stemming from a job.

rule A specific course of action or conduct that must be followed. It is the simplest type of plan.

satisficing decision a decision that meets the minimum standards of satisfaction.

situational leadership model an explanation of leadership that explains how to match leadership style to the readiness of group members.

small-business owner an individual who owns and operates a small business.

social leave of absence an employee benefit that gives select employees time away from the job to perform a significant public service.

social loafing freeloading or shirking individual responsibility, when a person is placed in a group setting and removed from individual accountability.

social responsibility the idea that firms have obligations to society beyond their obligations to owners or stockholders and also beyond those prescribed by law or contract.

span of control the number of workers reporting directly to a manager.

stakeholder viewpoint the viewpoint on social responsibility contending that firms must hold themselves responsible for the quality of life of the many groups affected by the firm's actions.

standard a unit of measurement used to evaluate results.

statistical process control a technique for spotting defects during production that utilizes graphical displays for analyzing deviations.

stockholder viewpoint the traditional perspective on social responsibility that a business organization is responsible only to its owners and stockholders.

strategic human resource planning the process of anticipating and providing for the movement of people into, within, and out of an organization to support the firm's business strategy.

strategic planning a firm's overall master plan that shapes its destiny.

strategy the organization's plan, or comprehensive program for achieving its vision, mission, and goals.

stress the mental and physical condition that results from a perceived threat that cannot be dealt with readily.

suggestion program a formal method for collecting and analyzing employees' suggestions about processes, policies, products, and services.

summary discipline the immediate discharge of an employee because of a serious offense.

SuperLeader a person who leads others to lead themselves.

SWOT analysis a method of considering the strengths, weaknesses, opportunities, and threats in a given situation.

synergy a concept of the systems approach to management that states that the whole organization working together will produce more than the parts working independently.

systems approach a perspective on management problems based on the concept that the organization is a system, or an entity of interrelated parts.

tactical planning planning that translates a firm's strategic plans into specific goals by organizational unit.

task behavior the extent to which the leader spells out the duties and responsibilities of an individual or group.

team a special type of group in which members have complementary skills and are committed to a common purpose, a set of performance goals, and an approach to the task.

team leader a manager who coordinates the work of a small group of people, while acting as a facilitator and catalyst.

teamwork the situation in which there is understanding and commitment to group goals on the part of all team members.

techno-obsessives individuals obsessed with technological devices.

telecommuting an arrangement with one's employer to use a computer to perform work at home or in a satellite office.

termination the process of firing an employee because of poor job performance, unacceptable behavior, or interpersonal problems.

territorial departmentalization an arrangement of departments according to the geographic area served.

360-degree feedback a performance appraisal in which a person is evaluated by a sampling of all the people with whom he or she interacts.

time-series analysis an analysis of a sequence of observations that have taken place at regular intervals over a period of time (hourly, weekly, monthly, and so forth).

top-level managers managers at the top one or two levels in the organization.

total quality management (TQM) a management system for improving performance throughout a firm by maximizing customer satisfaction and making continuous improvements.

tough question a question that helps the group achieve insight into the nature of a problem, what it might be doing better, and whether progress is sufficient.

training any procedure intended to foster and enhance learning among employees, particularly directed at acquiring job skills.

traits stable aspects of people, closely related to personality.

transformational leader a leader who helps organizations and people make positive changes in the way they do things.

transnational teams a work group composed of multinational members whose activities span multiple countries.

two-factor theory of work motivation the theory contending that there are two different sets of job factors. One set can satisfy and motivate people, and the other set can only prevent dissatisfaction.

unity of command the classical management principle stating that each subordinate receives assigned duties from one superior only and is accountable to that superior.

valuing diversity programs company training programs designed to develop skills employees need in a diverse work environment.

vertical thinking an analytical, logical process that results in few answers.

virtual office an arrangement whereby employees work together as if they were part of a single office despite being physically separated.

virtual team a small group of people who conduct almost all of their collaborative work by electronic communication rather than face-to-face meetings.

vision an idealized picture of the future of an organization.

Web master an individual responsible for the creation and maintenance of a company's Web site.

whistle blower an employee who discloses organizational wrongdoing to parties who can take action.

work ethic a firm belief in the dignity and value of work.

work streamlining eliminating as much low-value work as possible and concentrating on activities that add value for customers or clients.

work team a group of employees responsible for an entire work process or segment that delivers a product or service to an internal or external customer.

wrongful discharge the firing of an employee for arbitrary or unfair reasons.

zero defections keeping every customer a company can profitably serve.

zero defects the absence of any detectable quality flaws in a product or service.

zone of indifference the psychological zone that encompasses acceptable behaviors toward which employees feel indifferent (do not mind following).

[Note: The letter *e* after a page number indicates an exhibit.]

100-percent inspection, 93–94
360-degree feedback, 253

ABC. *See* Activity-based costing
Acceptance inspection, 94
Achievement, 298
Achievement motivation, 269
Achievement tests, 245
Action plan, 109, 411–13, 412e
Active listening, 338
Activity, 169
Activity-based costing (ABC), 392–93
Activity-based reduction, 216
Administrator, 5
Advance Circuits, 81
Advantica, 40e
Affective conflict, 367
Affiliation, 298
Affinity group, 354–55
Affirmative action, 237
Age Discrimination in Employment Act (1967), 238e
Agreeableness, 246
Allied Signal, 82
Allison, Robert Elliott, 59
Alternative workplace, 198–201; and sharing office space and hoteling, 200–201; telecommuting and, 198–200
Amabile, Teresa M., 144
Amazon.com Inc., 119, 223e
American Express Co., 304–5
American Express Travel-Related Services, 66
Americans with Disabilities Act (1990), 238e
Amnesty International, 33
Analysis: break-even, 171–73, 172e; cause-and-effect, 96e, 96–97; job, 240; SWOT, 116, 118; time-series, 163, 165, 165e
Anchoring, 139
Antidiscrimination legislation, employment, 237, 238e, 239e
Apple Computer Co., 69
Appletree, Billy, 103–4
Aptitude test, 245
Asian American Association, 105
Asian economic crisis, 30–31
Assembly and packaging, local, 34
Assertiveness, 267; in communication, 336–37
Attitudes, dealing with, 79–82
Authority: definition of, 266; and leadership, 266–69
Autocratic leader, 276

Automation, and job specialization, 187
Avoidance motivation, 305

Back stabbing, 343–44
Background investigation, 248–49
Balance of trade, 32
Balanced scorecard, 389, 391–92, 392e
Baldrige quality award, 80
BankAmerica, 40e
Barad, Jill, 112–13
Barclays Global Investors (BGI), 35
Bardwick, Judith, 432
Barriers: to communications, 331–41, 332e, 336e; to goals and objectives, 109
Bausch & Lomb Inc., 55–56
Beeth, Gunnar, 51
Behavior, 254; relationship, 279; task, 279
Behavior mismatch, 408
Behavior modification, 303–8; definition of, 303; effectiveness of, 308; strategies, 303, 305–6
Behavioral school of management, 16–17
Belbin, Meredith, 102
Benchmarking, 82, 84
Bentley College, Center for Business Ethics at, 62
Bic Corp., 114
Bildman, Lars, 62
Bill of materials, 176
Blanchard, Kenneth H., 279
Bluestone Security Systems, 373–74
Blystone, John, 7
Body language, 327
Bounded rationality, 135
Brainstorming, 147e, 147–48
Break-even analysis, 171–73, 172e
Broadbanding, 256
BSR. *See* Business for Social Responsibility
Buddy system, 250
Budget, 109–10; and budgetary control techniques, 384–93; as control device, 386–87, 387e; definition of, 385; types of, 385–86
Budgetary control techniques, 384–93
Bureaucracy, 208–11, 209e, 210e, 214–19
Business coach, 416
Business ethics. *See* Ethics
Business for Social Responsibility (BSR), 71
Business strategies: development of, 114–18, 115e; nature of, 111–14, 113e; strategic planning and, 111–21; types of, 119–21
Butler, Timothy, 414